Mastering
Microsoft® Exchange
Server 2016

Mastering
Microsoft® Exchange
Server 2016

Clifton Leonard

Brian Svidergol

Byron Wright

Vladimir Meloski

SYBEX®

A Wiley Brand

Senior Acquisitions Editor: Kenyon Brown
Development Editor: Kelly Talbot
Technical Editor: Joseph Nguyen
Production Editor: Athiyappan Lalith Kumar
Copy Editor: Kathy Grider-Carlyle
Editorial Manager: Mary Beth Wakefield
Production Manager: Kathleen Wisor
Executive Editor: Jim Minatel
Proofreader: Nancy Bell
Indexer: Nancy Guenther
Project Coordinator, Cover: Brent Savage
Cover Designer: Wiley
Cover Image: ©i3d/Shutterstock

This book is dedicated to my loving, gorgeous wife, Marie, and to my incredible inspirations Pierce, Treyden, Gabrielle, Cheyenne, Taylor, Zoe, and Talon. Thank you for enduring all my late nights and continuously encouraging me through this journey. I love you all!
—Clifton Leonard

I'd like to thank my wife, Lindsay; my son, Jack; and my daughter, Leah, for the unending support and David Elfassy for reaching out to me to get involved with this project—thank you! Finally, I'd like to thank the original Exchange "super team"— Larry, Mike, Carl, George, Dennis, and the Chicago crew— you guys helped me elevate my game.
—Brian Svidergol

I dedicate this book to my parents who unwittingly put me on the path to working with technology by indulging me in my youth. Who knew buying a Commodore VIC-20 would get it all started? I am thankful for that and your support in many other ways over the years.
—Byron Wright

To my loving family who always supports me.
—Vladimir Meloski

Acknowledgments

Thank you once again, Microsoft, for a great release of Exchange Server. This is now the eighth major release of the well-known premier messaging system. In this release, we can see the effort and ingenuity come together in solving customer problems to create a truly superior product. Congratulations!

As the team that is working on this book completes the final steps required to send it to the printer, I continue to bring some real-world expertise into the content. I have deployed several Exchange Server 2016 infrastructures to date, but this product is so vast and so broad that I continue to find design options, best practices, and architecture recommendations on a daily basis. I'm pretty sure that I will be updating the content up to the last minute!

When I was approached to take on this book, several months before Exchange Server 2016 was about to release to manufacturing, my reaction was, "What about David and Jim?" David Elfassy authored the previous edition and has been an invaluable contributor to the Microsoft, and more specifically Exchange Server, community. Prior to David, Jim McBee authored three previous editions of this book and has been the pillar of the *Mastering Exchange Server* series. I consider it to be a true honor to take over for David Elfassy and Jim McBee as the lead author for this book, and I hope that this edition has adequately followed through on their traditions.

Throughout the book, we have tried to keep the tone and language similar to what was used in the previous editions of this book, so if you are familiar with both of these men's writing style, you should find comfort in these pages. In addition, we have removed some of the introductory technical information from previous editions, to reflect the depth of initial experience of the readers.

Taking on the responsibility of a 816-plus-page manual is no simple task and not one that can be undertaken by only one person. Along the way, I have invited several contributors to this effort. Their knowledge and expertise have added incredible value to this book. Having written anywhere from several paragraphs to complete chapters, Brian Svidergol, Byron Wright, and Vladimir Meloski are Exchange Server gurus who have provided key content for this book. These men are well respected within the Exchange Server community and are authors of Microsoft Official Curriculum, including Exchange Server 2016. They have been great contributions to this effort. Thank you!

There is also a man who has kept us all honest and has been the gatekeeper for technical accuracy in this book, and he has helped revise a couple of chapters more substantially. Joseph Nguyen agreed to take on the responsibility of technical reviewer for this book and has done a formidable job. I consider it an honor to have worked with him! Joseph, thank you!

The great folks at Wiley have been patient beyond belief when it comes to deadlines, content, and outline changes as well as our ever-changing list of contributors. They include acquisitions editor Ken Brown, developmental editor Kelly Talbot, and production editor Athiyappan Lalith Kumar.

And a special acknowledgment to those in my daily life, my father, DC Leonard; my mother, Lynette Leonard; my sister, Jaena Poppe; and my brothers, Jerry, Adam, and Jeff: thank you for always being supportive of all my endeavors.

—*Clifton Leonard*

About the Authors

Clifton Leonard, MCSE: Exchange Server, has more than 25 years' experience in the IT industry as an engineer, architect, consultant, trainer, and author. Clifton has extensive experience consulting on Active Directory, Exchange Server, Lync and Skype for Business Server, Identity Management, Office 365, and Azure cloud solutions. His clients include large energy corporations, K-12 schools, universities, technology manufacturers, financial institutions, the United States Air Force, and the Department of Defense. While Clifton cut his teeth on Microsoft Mail on Novell Netware and Exchange Server 5.0 on DEC Alpha, he has worked with every version of Exchange Server since then. He has also contributed as a subject matter expert to multiple Microsoft courses including Windows Desktop, Windows Server, Exchange Server, SharePoint Server, HyperV, Identity Management, Office 365, and Azure. Helping organizations migrate to the latest versions of Microsoft Exchange Server has always been a key focus of Clifton's consulting commitments.

Brian Svidergol builds Microsoft infrastructure and cloud solutions with Windows, Microsoft Exchange, Active Directory, Office 365, and related technologies. He holds the Microsoft Certified Trainer (MCT), Microsoft Certified Solutions Expert (MCSE) – Server Infrastructure, and several other Microsoft and industry certifications. Brian has authored books on Active Directory, Windows Server, Exchange Server, and related infrastructure technologies. He served as an MCT Ambassador at TechEd North America 2013 and at Microsoft Ignite 2015. Brian works as a subject matter expert (SME) on many Microsoft Official Curriculum courses, edX courses, and Microsoft certification exams. He has authored a variety of training content, blog posts, and practice test questions and has been a technical reviewer for a large number of books.

Byron Wright is the owner of BTW Technology Solutions where he provides, designs, and implements solutions using Exchange Server and Office 365. He has been a consultant, author, and instructor for 20 years, specializing in Exchange Server, Windows Server, Office 365, network design, network security, and related technologies. Byron has been a Microsoft MVP for Exchange Server since 2012.

Vladimir Meloski is a Microsoft Most Valuable Professional on Office Server and Services, Microsoft Certified Trainer, and consultant, providing unified communications and infrastructure solutions based on Microsoft Exchange Server, Skype for Business, Office 365, and Windows Server. With a bachelor's degree in computer sciences, Vladimir has devoted more than 20 years of professional experience to information technology. Vladimir has been involved in Microsoft conferences in Europe and in the United States as a speaker, moderator, proctor for hands-on labs, and technical expert. He also has been involved as an author and technical reviewer for Microsoft official courses, including Exchange Server 2016, 2013, 2010, and 2007; Office 365; and Windows Server 2012. As a skilled IT professional and trainer, Vladimir shares his best practices, real-world experiences, and knowledge with his students and colleagues and is devoted to IT community development by collaborating with IT Pro and developer user groups worldwide.

About the Technical Editor

Joseph Nguyen is a senior consultant for Microsoft. He has 20 years of experience as a system administrator, messaging engineer, IT analyst, systems engineer, consultant, and trainer providing messaging, communications, and collaboration expertise for a wide range of corporations and institutions. Joseph coauthored *Exchange Server 2010 Administration: Real World Skills for MCITP Certification and Beyond* and *MCITP Self-Paced Training Kit (Exam 70-238): Deploying Messaging Solutions with Microsoft Exchange Server 2007.*

Contents at a Glance

Contents

Introduction

Thank you for purchasing (or considering the purchase of) *Mastering Exchange Server 2016*; this is the latest in a series of Mastering Exchange Server books that have helped thousands of readers to better understand Microsoft's excellent messaging system. Along the way, we hope that this series of books has made you a better administrator and allowed you to support your organizations to the best of your abilities.

When we started planning the outline of this book more than a year before its release, Exchange Server 2016 appeared to be simply a minor series of improvements over Exchange Server 2013. Of course, the further we explored the product, the more we found that was not the case. Many of the improvements in Exchange Server 2016 were major improvements (such as Outlook on the web) and sometimes even complete rewrites (such as in the case of the Client Access services role) of how the product worked previously.

Another challenge then presented itself. The market penetration of Exchange Server 2013 was fairly dominant, but we found that many organizations still run Exchange Server 2010. Therefore, we needed to explain the differences for not only Exchange Server 2013 administrators but also for the Exchange Server 2010 administrators. On the other hand, Exchange Server 2003 reached end-of-life on April 8, 2014. As a result, Microsoft no longer provides security updates, offers free or paid support options, nor provides updated online content such as KB articles for Exchange Server 2003. Organizations with Exchange Server 2003 deployed after April 8, 2014, are responsible for their own support of the product and accept the risk associated with the deployment.

We took a step back and looked at the previous editions of the book to figure out how much of the previous material was still relevant. Some of the material from the Exchange Server 2013 book is still relevant but needed updating. Some required completely rewriting chapters to cover new technologies introduced in Exchange Server 2016 or technologies that have since taken on more importance in deployments and management. We faced the challenge of explaining two management interfaces, Exchange Management Shell and Exchange Admin Center, as well as describing the new roles and features.

We started working with the Exchange Server 2016 code more than a year before we expected to release the book. Much of the book was written using the RTM code that was first made available in October 2015, but as we continued writing the book, we made updates based on changes introduced in Cumulative Update 1 (March 2016). So, you can safely assume when reading this book that it is based on the latest bits of Exchange Server 2016 that released in late summer 2016. In writing this book, we had a few goals for the book and the knowledge we wanted to impart to the reader:

- We wanted to provide an appropriate context for the role of messaging services in an organization, outlining the primary skills required by an Exchange Server administrator.

- We wanted the reader to feel comfortable when approaching an Exchange Server environment of any size. The content in this book can assist administrators of small companies with only one server, as well as administrators who handle large Exchange Server farms.

- We wanted the skills and tasks covered in this book to be applicable to 80 percent of all organizations running Exchange Server.

- We wanted the book to educate not only "new to product" administrators but also those "new to version" administrators who are upgrading from a previous version.

- We wanted the book to familiarize administrators with Office 365 environments and the implementation of hybrid coexistence with on-premises Exchange Server deployments.

- We wanted to provide familiar references for administrators of previous versions, ensuring that Exchange Server 2010 and 2013 administrators can easily find equivalent solutions in Exchange Server 2016.

Microsoft listened to the advice of many of its customers, its internal consultants at Microsoft Consulting Services (MCS), Microsoft Certified Systems Engineers (MCSEs), Most Valuable Professionals (MVPs), Microsoft Certified Solutions Masters (MCSMs), and Microsoft Certified Trainers (MCTs) to find out what was missing from earlier versions of the product and what organizations' needs were. Much of this work started even before Exchange Server 2016 was released.

Major Changes in Exchange Server 2016

This book covers the many changes in Exchange Server 2016 in detail, but we thought we would give you a little sample of what is to come in the chapters. As you can imagine, the changes are once again significant, considering the tremendous effort that Microsoft sinks into the Exchange Server line of products. Exchange Server is a significant generator of revenue for Microsoft and is also a foundational service for Office 365. Microsoft has every reason to continue improving this most impressive market leader of email and collaboration services.

The primary changes in Exchange Server 2016 since the latest release (Exchange Server 2013) have come in the following areas:

- Client access services have been integrated into the Mailbox server role, and the Client Access server role has been removed.

- Outlook Web App is now known as Outlook on the web, is optimized for tablets, and provides platform-specific experiences for smart phones.

- MAPI over HTTP is now the default protocol that Outlook uses to communicate with Exchange, which allows a higher level of visibility of transport errors and enhanced recoverability.

- With SharePoint Server 2016, you can enable Outlook on the web users to link to and share documents stored in OneDrive for Business in an on-premises SharePoint server instead of attaching a file to the message.

- The Hybrid Configuration Wizard (HCW) is provided as a download to support changes in the Office 365 service and to provide a more stable deployment and consistent experience.

- Significant enhancements for Data Loss Prevention (DLP) have been added. With a DLP policy and mail flow rules, you can identify, monitor, and protect 80 different types of sensitive information.

- Public folder integration into the In-Place eDiscovery and Hold workflow enable you to search public folders in your organization and configure an In-Place Hold on public folders.

- A new eDiscovery search tool, called Compliance Search, provides improved scaling and performance capabilities so you can search very large numbers of mailboxes in a single search.

Of course, many more changes have been introduced in Exchange Server 2016, but the preceding list stands out to us as the most noteworthy improvements. Chapter 2, "Introducing the Changes in Exchange Server 2016," contains an exhaustive list of all significant changes, as well as changes since specific versions of Exchange Server (for example, Exchange Server 2010 and Exchange Server 2013).

How This Book Is Organized

This book consists of 25 chapters, divided into five broad parts. As you proceed through the book, you'll move from general concepts to increasingly detailed descriptions of hands-on implementation.

This book won't work well for practitioners of the time-worn ritual of chapter hopping. Although some readers may benefit from reading one or two chapters, we recommend that you read most of the book in order. Even if you have experience as an Exchange Server administrator, we recommend that you do not skip any chapter, because they all provide new information since the previous iterations of Exchange Server. Only if you already have considerable experience with these products should you jump to the chapter that discusses in detail the information for which you are looking.

If you are like most administrators, though, you like to get your hands on the software and actually see things working. Having a working system also helps many people as they read a book or learn about a new piece of software because this lets them test new skills as they learn them. If this sounds like you, then start with Chapter 7, "Exchange Server 2016 Quick

Start Guide." This chapter will take you briefly through some of the things you need to know to get Exchange Server running, but not in a lot of detail. As long as you're not planning to put your quickie server into production immediately, there should be no harm done. Before you put it into production, though, we strongly suggest that you explore other parts of this book. Following is a guide to what's in each chapter.

Part 1: Exchange Fundamentals

This part of the book focuses on concepts and features of Microsoft's Windows Server 2012 R2, Exchange Server 2016, and some of the fundamentals of operating a modern client/server email system.

Chapter 1, "Putting Exchange Server 2016 in Context," is for those administrators who have been handed an Exchange Server organization but who have never managed a previous version of Exchange Server or even another mail system. This will give you some of the basic information and background to help you get started managing Exchange Server and, hopefully, provide a little history and perspective.

Chapter 2, "Introducing the Changes in Exchange Server 2016," introduces the new features of Exchange Server 2016 as contrasted with previous versions.

Chapter 3, "Understanding Availability, Recovery, and Compliance," helps even experienced administrators navigate some of the new hurdles that Exchange Server administrators must overcome, including providing better system availability, site resiliency, backup and restoration plans, and legal compliance. This chapter does *not* cover database availability groups in detail; instead, that information is covered in Chapter 20, "Creating and Managing Database Availability Groups."

Chapter 4, "Virtualizing Exchange Server 2016," helps you decide whether you should virtualize some percentage of your servers, as many organizations are doing.

Chapter 5, "Introduction to PowerShell and the Exchange Management Shell," focuses on and uses examples of features that are enabled in PowerShell through the Exchange Server 2016 management extensions for PowerShell. All administrators should have at least a basic familiarity with the Exchange Management Shell extensions for PowerShell even if you rarely use them.

Chapter 6, "Understanding the Exchange Autodiscover Process," helps you to come up to speed on the inner workings of the magic voodoo that is Autodiscover, a feature that greatly simplifies the configuration of both internal and external clients.

Part 2: Getting Exchange Server Running

This section of the book is devoted to topics related to meeting the prerequisites for Exchange Server and getting Exchange Server installed correctly the first time. While installing Exchange Server correctly is not rocket science, getting everything right the first time will greatly simplify your deployment.

Chapter 7, "Exchange Server 2016 Quick Start Guide," is where everyone likes to jump right in and install the software. This chapter will help you quickly get a single server up and running for your test and lab environment. While you should not deploy an entire enterprise based on the content of this one chapter, it will help you get started quickly.

Chapter 8, "Understanding Server Roles and Configurations," covers the primary services that run on the Exchange Server: mailbox services, transport services, and client access services.

Chapter 9, "Exchange Server 2016 Requirements," guides you through the requirements (pertaining to Windows Server, Active Directory, and previous versions of Exchange Server) that you must meet in order to successfully deploy Exchange Server 2016.

Chapter 10, "Installing Exchange Server 2016," takes you through both the graphical user interface and the command-line setup for installing Exchange Server 2016.

Chapter 11, "Upgrades and Migrations to Exchange Server 2016 or Office 365," helps you decide on the right migration or transition approach for your organization. It recommends steps to take to upgrade your organization from Exchange Server 2010 or 2013 to Exchange Server 2016 or to Office 365. Also included in this chapter are recommendations for migration phases and hybrid coexistence with Office 365.

Part 3: Recipient Administration

Recipient administration generally ends up being the most time-consuming portion of Exchange Server administration. Recipient administration includes creating and managing mailboxes, managing mail groups, creating and managing contacts, and administering public folders.

Chapter 12, "Management Permissions and Role-Based Access Control," introduces one of the most powerful features of Exchange Server 2016, Role-Based Access Control, which enables extremely detailed delegation of permissions for all Exchange Server administrative tasks. This feature will be of great value to large organizations.

Chapter 13, "Basics of Recipient Management," introduces you to some concepts you should consider before you start creating users, including how email addresses are generated and how recipients should be configured.

Chapter 14, "Managing Mailboxes and Mailbox Content," is at the core of most Exchange Server administrators' jobs since the mailboxes represent the direct customer (the end user). This chapter introduces the concepts of managing mailboxes, mailbox data (such as personal archives), and mailbox data retention.

Chapter 15, "Managing Mail-Enabled Groups, Mail Users, and Mail Contacts," covers management of these objects, including creating them, assigning email addresses, securing groups, and allowing for self-service management of groups, and it offers guidelines for creating contacts.

Chapter 16, "Managing Resource Mailboxes," discusses a key task for most messaging administrators. A resource can be either a room (such as a conference room) or a piece of equipment (such as an overhead projector). Exchange Server 2016 makes it easy to allow users to view the availability of resources and request the use of these resources from within Outlook or Outlook on the web.

Chapter 17, "Managing Modern Public Folders," introduces you to the new public folder storage and management features in Exchange Server 2016. Although public folders are being deemphasized in many organizations, other organizations still have massive quantities of data stored in them. Microsoft has reinvented public folders in this latest release of Exchange Server.

Chapter 18, "Managing Archiving and Compliance," covers not only the overall concepts of archiving and how the rest of the industry handles archiving but also the exciting archival and retention features.

Part 4: Server Administration

Although recipient administration is important, administrators must not forget their responsibilities to properly set up the Exchange server and maintain it. This section helps introduce you to the configuration tasks and maintenance necessary for some of the Exchange Server 2016 services as well as safely connecting your organization to the Internet.

Chapter 19, "Creating and Managing Mailbox Databases," helps familiarize you with the changes in Exchange Server 2016 with respect to mailbox database, storage, and basic sizing requirements. Many exciting changes have been made to support large databases and to allow Exchange Server to scale to support more simultaneous users.

Chapter 20, "Creating and Managing Database Availability Groups," is a key chapter in this book that will affect all administrators from small to large organizations. Exchange Server 2016 relies heavily on Windows Failover Clustering for its site resilience and high availability functionalities. This chapter covers the implementation and management of high availability solutions.

Chapter 21, "Understanding the Client Access Services," introduces you to the critical client access services and the related components running on the Mailbox server.

Chapter 22, "Managing Connectivity with Transport Services," brings you up to speed on the Transport services that run with the mailbox and client access services. This chapter discusses mail flow and the transport pipeline in detail.

Chapter 23, "Managing Transport, Data Loss Prevention, and Journaling Rules," shows you how to implement a feature set that was first introduced in Exchange Server 2007 but has since been greatly improved: the transport rule feature. This chapter also discusses message journaling and Data Loss Prevention policies.

Part 5: Troubleshooting and Operating

Troubleshooting and keeping a proper eye on your Exchange servers' health are often neglected tasks. You may not look at your Exchange servers until there is an actual problem. In this part, we discuss some tips and tools that will help you proactively manage your Exchange Server environment, ensuring that you can track down problems as well as restore any potential lost data.

Chapter 24, "Troubleshooting Exchange Server 2016," introduces you not only to troubleshooting the various components of Exchange Server 2016 but also to good troubleshooting techniques. This chapter also includes a discussion of some of the Exchange Server 2016 built-in tools, such as the Exchange Management Shell test cmdlets and the Remote Connectivity Analyzer.

Chapter 25, "Backing Up and Restoring Exchange Server," includes discussions on developing a backup plan for your Exchange Server 2016 servers as well as how to implement appropriate backup solutions for Exchange Server configuration, databases, logs, and any other relevant information.

Conventions Used in This Book

We use the code-continuation character on PowerShell commands to indicate that the line of text is part of a previous command line.

Many of the screen captures in this book have been taken from lab and test environments. However, sometimes you will see screen captures that came from an actual working environment. We have obscured any information that would identify those environments.

Any examples that include IP addresses have had the IP addresses changed to private IP addresses even if we are referring to Internet addresses.

Remember, Exchange Server is designed to help your organization do what it does better, more efficiently, and with greater productivity. Have fun, be productive, and prosper!

The Mastering Series

The *Mastering* series from Sybex provides outstanding instruction for readers with intermediate and advanced skills, in the form of top-notch training and development for those already working in their field and clear, serious education for those aspiring to become pros. Every *Mastering* book includes the following:

◆ Real-World Scenarios, ranging from case studies to interviews, that show how the tool, technique, or knowledge presented is applied in actual practice

◆ Skill-based instruction, with chapters organized around real tasks rather than abstract concepts or subjects

◆ Self-review test questions, so you can be certain you're equipped to do the job right

Part 1

Exchange Fundamentals

Chapter 1

Putting Exchange Server 2016 in Context

Email is one of the most visible services that Information Technology (IT) professionals provide; most organizations have become dependent on "soft" information to run their business. As a result, users have developed an attachment to email that goes beyond the hard value of the information it contains. If there's a problem with email, it affects users' confidence in their ability to do their jobs—and their confidence in IT.

Microsoft's Exchange Server products play a key role in electronic messaging, including email. This chapter is a high-level primer on Exchange Server–based email administration and good administration practices, and it prepares you to put Exchange Server 2016 into the proper context. An experienced email administrator may want to proceed to more technical chapters. However, if you are new to the job or need a refresher, or maybe you just want to put email services back into perspective, this chapter is for you!

IN THIS CHAPTER, YOU WILL LEARN TO:

◆   Understand email fundamentals

◆   Identify email-administration duties

Email's Importance

If you're responsible for electronic messaging in your organization, no one has to tell you about its steadily expanding use—you see evidence every time you check the storage space on your disk drives or need an additional tape to complete the backup of your mail server. This section discusses some aspects of electronic mail and the ever-changing nature of email. Even experienced Exchange Server administrators may want to review this section to better understand how their users and requirements are evolving.

Billions of emails are sent every day (more than 200 billion worldwide, according to research firm The Radicati Group). That's a lot of email messages, on a lot of servers—many of them Exchange servers.

Sure, sending simple text email and file attachments is the most basic function, but email systems (the client and/or the server) may also perform the following important functions:

◆   Act as a personal information manager, providing storage for and access to personal calendars, personal contacts, to-do and task lists, personal journals, and chat histories.

◆   Provide the user with a single "point of entry" for multiple types of information, such as voicemail, faxes, and electronic forms.

◆ Provide shared calendars, departmental contacts, and other shared information.

◆ Provide notifications of workflow processes, such as finance/accounting activities, IT events (server status information), and more.

◆ Archive important attachments, text messages, and many other types of information.

◆ Allow users to access their "email data" through a variety of means, including clients running on Windows computers, Apple computers, Unix systems, web browsers, mobile phones, and even a regular telephone.

◆ Perform records management and enable long-term storage of important information or information that must be archived.

◆ Enable near-time communication of sales and support information with vendors and customers.

These are just a few of the types of things that an email system may provide to the end user either via the client interface or as a result of some function running on the server.

How Messaging Servers Work

At the core of any messaging system, you will find a common set of basic functions. These functions may be implemented in different ways depending on the vendor or even the version of the product. Exchange Server has evolved dramatically over the past 20 years, and its current architecture is almost nothing like Exchange Server 4.0 from 1996. Common components of most messaging systems include the following:

◆ A message transport system that moves messages from one place to another. Examples include the Simple Mail Transport Protocol (SMTP).

◆ A message storage system that stores messages until a user can read or retrieve them. Messages may be stored in a client/server database, a shared file database, or even in individual files.

◆ A directory service that allows a user to look up information about the mail system's users, such as a user's email address.

◆ A client access interface on the server that allows the clients to get to their stored messages. This might include a web interface, a client/server interface, or the Post Office Protocol (POP).

◆ The client program that allows users to read their mail, send mail, and access the directory. This may include Outlook, Outlook on the web, and a mobile device such as a Windows phone, an iPhone, or an Android device.

Working in tandem with real-time interactive technologies, electronic messaging systems have already produced a set of imaginative business, entertainment, and educational applications with high payoff potential. All of this action, of course, accelerates the demand for electronic messaging capabilities and services.

Most organizations that deploy an email system usually deploy additional components from their email software vendor or third parties that extend the capabilities of the email system or provide required services. These include the following:

◆ Integration with existing phone systems or enterprise voice deployments to pull voice messages into the mailbox

◆ Message-hygiene systems that help reduce the likelihood of a malicious or inappropriate message being delivered to a user

◆ Backup and recovery, disaster recovery, and business continuity solutions

◆ Message archival software to allow for the long-term retention and indexing of email data

◆ Electronic forms routing software that may integrate with accounting, order entry, or other line-of-business applications

◆ Mail gateways to allow differing mobile devices, such as BlackBerry devices, to access the mail server, along with native access through Exchange ActiveSync

◆ Email security systems that improve the security of email data either while being transferred or while sitting in the user's mailbox

◆ A link load balancer to balance the load between multiple Internet-facing servers or internal servers

What Is Exchange Server?

In its simplest form, Exchange Server provides the underlying infrastructure necessary to run a messaging system. Exchange Server provides the database to store email data, the transport infrastructure to move the email data from one place to another, and the access points to access email data via a number of different clients.

However, Exchange Server, when used with other clients such as Outlook or Outlook on the web, turns the "mailbox" into a point of storage for personal information management such as your calendar, contacts, task lists, and any file type. Users can share some or all of this information in their own mailbox with other users on the message system and start to collaborate.

The Outlook and Outlook on the web clients also provide access to public folders. Public folders look like regular mail folders in your mailbox, except that they are in an area where they can be shared by all users within the organization. A folder can have specialized forms associated with it to allow the sharing of contacts, calendar entries, or even other specialized forms. Further, each public folder can be secured so that only certain users can view or modify data in that folder.

The Unified Messaging features in Exchange Server 2016 further extend the functions of Exchange Server in your organization by allowing your Exchange Server infrastructure to also act as your voicemail system and direct voicemails and missed-call notifications automatically to the user's mailbox.

While integrated voicemail solutions are nothing new for Exchange Server customers, Microsoft is now providing these capabilities out of the box rather than relying on third-party products.

Exchange Server 2016 tightens the integration of collaborative tools in its integration with Skype for Business Server 2015, the Skype for Business client, and the Skype for Business mobile client. Skype for Business provides a core set of Session Initiation Protocol (SIP)–based enterprise voice capabilities that allows it to act as a PBX in many cases. With Exchange Server, Skype for Business, Outlook, and the Skype for Business client, users enjoy full Unified Messaging with software-based telephony from their computer, including the voicemail and missed-call notification provided by Exchange Server and Outlook. Furthermore, Skype for Business can log chat and instant-message conversation logs to a folder in the user's mailbox. Exchange Server 2016 further pushes this integration, embedding basic instant messaging (IM) and presence capabilities into the Outlook on the web premium experience.

The capabilities of the client can be extended with third-party tools and forms-routing software so that electronic forms can be routed through email to users' desktops.

About Messaging Services

Electronic messaging is far more than email. Together, Exchange Server 2016 and its clients perform a variety of messaging-based functions. These functions include email, unified messaging, message routing, scheduling, and support for several types of custom applications. Together these features are called messaging services.

Many Modes of Access

For years, the only way to access your email system was to use a Windows, Mac, or Unix-based client and access the email system directly. In the case of Outlook and Exchange Server, this access was originally in the form of a MAPI client directly against the Exchange server. As Exchange Server has evolved, it has included support for RPC over HTTP, MAPI over HTTP, Exchange Web Services (EWS), and finally mobile device access (via ActiveSync). Exchange Server 2016 doesn't offer any radically new modes of mailbox access as Exchange Server 2007 did, but it does provide ongoing support and refinement of existing Exchange Server 2007 technologies, such as Exchange Web Services, that can provide additional mechanisms for accessing data in mailboxes and a move away from RPC in client connectivity in favor of Outlook on the web and mobile devices.

Outlook on the web (formerly Outlook Web Access) has evolved quickly and, in Exchange Server 2016, bears almost no resemblance to the original version found in Exchange Server 5.0 in terms of features, functions, and the look of the interface. Exchange Server 2016 Outlook on the web is a step beyond Exchange Server 2013. It expands the previous option configuration experience of the Exchange Control Panel (ECP), which gives users a much greater degree of control over their mailboxes, contacts, and group memberships. ECP is built into the Outlook on the web interface. Using ECP, end users can create and join distribution groups (where permissions have been assigned), track their own messages throughout the organization, and perform other functions that in Exchange 2010 and earlier versions required help-desk or IT professional intervention. Another significant feature of Outlook on the web is the ability to use the web-based interface when working offline and completely disconnected from the network.

With Exchange Server 2016, Exchange ActiveSync (EAS) continues to offer significant partnerships with and control over mobile devices. Many vendors have licensed EAS to provide their mobile devices with a high-performance, full-featured push mobile synchronization experience that extends beyond mobile phones and into tablet devices.

With all of these mechanisms for retrieving and sending email, it is not unusual for users to access their mailboxes using more than one device. In some cases, we have seen a single user accessing her mailbox from her desktop computer, her tablet device using Outlook Anywhere, and her Windows Phone device.

In medium and large organizations, the fact that users are accessing their mailboxes from more than one device or mechanism will affect not only hardware sizing but also, potentially, your licensing costs.

How Messaging Services Are Used

Certainly, email is a key feature of any messaging system, and the Outlook Calendar is far better than previous versions of Microsoft's appointment and meeting-scheduling software. Outlook 2016 together with Exchange Server 2016 introduces even more synergy. Figure 1.1 and Figure 1.2 show the Outlook 2016 client Calendar and Inbox in action.

FIGURE 1.1
Outlook 2016 Appointment scheduling on an Exchange Server 2016 mailbox

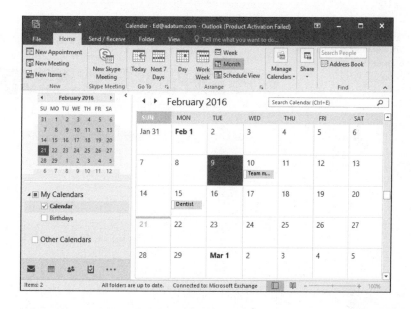

Figure 1.3 shows the new Outlook on the web 2016 web browser client. Outlook on the web provides the full, premium user experience for browsers other than Internet Explorer; it also supports Mac OS X Safari, Firefox, and Chrome. Those coming from older versions of Exchange Server will immediately notice a cleaner, less-cluttered interface and new functionalities such as Offline Usage.

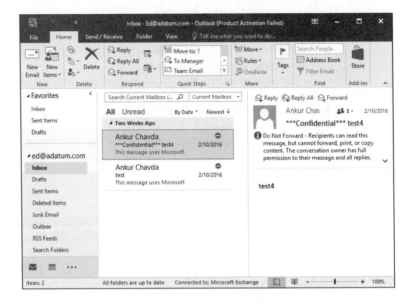

FIGURE 1.3
Outlook on the web
on an Exchange
Server 2016
mailbox

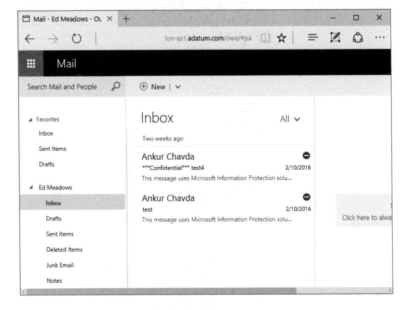

Email clients are exciting and sexy, but to get the most out of Exchange Server 2016 you need to throw away any preconceptions you have that messaging systems are only for email and scheduling. The really exciting applications are not those that use simple email or scheduling but those that are based on the routing capabilities of messaging systems. These applications bring people and computers together for improved collaboration.

The Universal Inbox

Email systems are converging with their voicemail and enterprise voice-solution cousins. The concept of unified messaging is nothing new to email users. For the past 20 years, third-party vendors have included email integration tools for voicemail, network faxing solutions, and third-party integration. However, for most organizations, integrated voicemail remains the exception rather than the rule. Exchange Server 2007 introduced integrated voice, which Exchange Server 2016 continues to improve.

Organizations with IP-based telephone systems or telephone systems with an IP gateway can easily integrate a user's voicemail with the Exchange Server user's mailbox. The Exchange Server 2016 Unified Messaging features handle the interaction between an organization's telephone system and Exchange Server mailboxes. Inbound voicemail is transferred into the user's mailbox as a cross-platform-friendly MP3 file attachment; this message includes an Outlook or Outlook on the web form that allows the user to play the message. As well, the voicemail text can be transcribed into the body of the email message for quick reading by the user during meetings or rapid glancing at the Inbox. Because the default format is MP3 in Exchange Server 2016 (it was a Windows Media file in Exchange Server 2007, using a custom codec), this file can be easily played on mobile devices from any manufacturer, allowing easy on-the-go access to voicemail. A short voicemail message may be anywhere from 40 KB to 75 KB in size, whereas longer voicemail messages may range from 200 KB to 500 KB in size. One estimate that is frequently used for the size of a voicemail message is around 5 KB per second of message.

Inbound voicemail increases the demands on your Exchange server from the perspective of required disk space and possible additional server hardware. As an administrator, you need to consider this.

JUST THE FAX, MA'AM

In Exchange Server 2007, the Unified Messaging features included the out-of-the-box capability to capture incoming facsimile (fax) messages. There were some limitations, but it provided good basic functionality. For outbound fax capability, organizations had to deploy some other solution, typically a third-party fax package.

Since Exchange Server 2010, Microsoft made the decision to cut this feature. When talking with the product group, it's not hard to figure out why; the inbound-only fax functionality wasn't enough for the customers who needed fax integration. Exchange Server needed to either add outgoing fax capability and beef up its feature set (and lose other desired functionality) or drop the existing functionality because the majority of Exchange Server 2007 customers needed a third-party product anyway. Although it's always disappointing to lose a feature, most of the organizations we've talked to didn't use it to begin with. We think that Microsoft definitely made the right call, if you'll pardon the pun.

Architecture and Core Functionality Overview

Understanding a bit about how Exchange Server works from an architectural perspective will help make you a better administrator. You don't have to be able to reproduce or write your own client/server messaging system, but it helps to know the basics.

THE EXTENSIBLE STORAGE ENGINE

The Exchange Server database uses a highly specialized database engine called the Extensible Storage Engine (ESE). Generically, you could say it is almost like SQL Server, but this is technically not true. It is a client/server database and is somewhat relational in nature, but it is designed to be a single-user database (the Exchange server itself is the only component that directly accesses the data). Further, the database has been highly tuned to store hierarchical data, such as mailboxes, folders, messages, and attachments.

Without going into a lot of techno-babble on the database architecture, it is important that you understand the basics of what the database is doing. Figure 1.4 shows conceptually what is happening with the ESE database as data is sent to the database. In step 1, an Outlook client sends data to the Exchange server (the Information Store service); the Information Store service places this data in memory and then immediately writes the data out to the transaction log files associated with that database.

FIGURE 1.4

Exchange data and transaction logs

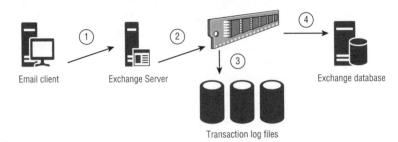

Email client   Exchange Server   Exchange database

Transaction log files

The transaction log that is always written to is the current transaction log for that particular database (e00.log, for example). Each transaction log file is exactly 1 MB in size, so when the transaction log is filled up, it is renamed to the next sequential number. For example, an old transaction log file might be named like this: e000004032.log. We often get questions about the logic of the transaction logs, and how they reserve space on the disk, whether they are empty or full. An easy way to look at it is to compare a log file to a carton of milk. When you have a carton of milk, it always takes up the same space in your fridge, empty or full. The same is true of the log files. Empty log files (current log file and *reserved* log files) are empty, or partially full; the renamed, *old*, log files are full. However, they take up the same amount of space on the disk.

The data, such as new email messages that enter the organization, is retained in RAM for some period of time (maybe as little as 5 seconds or maybe even 60 seconds or more) before it is flushed to the database file. The actual period that data is retained in memory will depend on how much cache memory is available, what types of operations are happening in the data, and how busy the server is. The important operation, though, is to make sure that as soon as the data is sent to the Exchange server, it is immediately flushed to the transaction log files. If the server crashes before the data is written to the database file, the database engine (the store process) will automatically read the transaction log files once the server is brought back up and compare them to the data that's stored in the corresponding mailbox databases. Any inconsistency is resolved by replaying the missing data operations from the transaction logs back into the database, assuming that the entire transaction is present; if it's not, the operations are not written (and you can be confident that the operation wasn't completed at the time the crash happened). This helps ensure that the integrity of the mailbox database is preserved and that half-completed data operations aren't written back into the database and allowed to corrupt good data.

The transaction log files are important for a number of reasons. They are used by Microsoft replication technologies (as you'll learn in Chapter 19, "Creating and Managing Mailbox Databases"), but they can also be used in disaster recovery. The transaction logs are not purged off the log disk until a full backup is run; therefore, every transaction that occurred to a database (new data, modifications, moves, deletes) is stored in the logs. If you restore the last good backup to the server, Exchange Server can replay and rebuild all the missing transactions back into the database—provided you have all the transactions since the last full backup.

In early versions of Exchange Server, you had two separate mail store objects: the *storage group*, which was a logical container that held an associated set of transaction logs, and the *mailbox database*, a set of files that held the actual permanent copies of user mailboxes. You often had multiple mailbox databases per storage group, meaning that one set of transaction logs contained interwoven transaction data for multiple databases (which could have detrimental effects on performance, space, and backups).

In Exchange Server 2016, you still have mailbox databases. However, storage groups were removed in Exchange Server 2010; each mailbox database now has its own integral set of transaction log files. In fact, mailbox databases—which were once tightly coupled with specific servers—can have copies on multiple servers in the organization, even spread across multiple sites. This functionality was introduced by moving the mailbox databases from the Server hierarchy to the Organization hierarchy, essentially rendering them a *shared* object that can become active on any server in the organization. The *database availability group* container is now available to contain servers that participate in the replication of mailbox databases with each other.

Exchange and Active Directory

We could easily write two or three chapters on how Exchange Server interacts with Active Directory, but the basics will have to do for now. Exchange Server relies on Active Directory for information about its own configuration, user authentication, and email-specific properties for mail-enabled objects such as users, contacts, groups, and public folders. Look at Figure 1.5 to see some of the different types of interactions that occur between Exchange Server and Active Directory.

Figure 1.5
Active Directory and Exchange Server

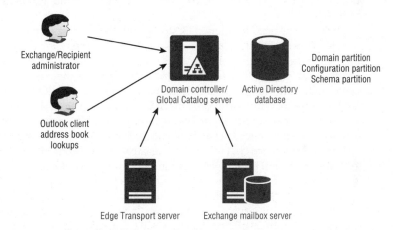

Because most of the Exchange Server configuration data for an Exchange server is stored in Active Directory, all Exchange Server roles must contact a domain controller to request its configuration data; this information is stored in a special partition of Active Directory database called the *configuration partition*. The configuration partition is replicated to all domain controllers in the entire Active Directory forest. Note that you can have only a single Exchange organization per Active Directory forest.

Each of the Exchange Server components uses Active Directory for different things. Some of those functions include:

Mailbox Components   For mailbox operations, Exchange Server must query Active Directory to authenticate users, enumerate permissions on mailboxes, look up individual mailbox limits, and determine which mailboxes are on a particular server. They also require access to global catalog servers to look up email addressing information, distribution list membership information, and other data related to message routing.

Client Access Components   For client access, Exchange Server requires access to Active Directory to look up information about users, Exchange ActiveSync, and Outlook on the web user restrictions.

Controlling Mailbox Growth

As users have become more savvy and competent at using Outlook and the features of Exchange Server, and email messages themselves have become more complex, the need for email storage has grown. Back in the days of Exchange Server 4.0, an organization that gave its users a 25 MB mailbox was considered generous. With Exchange Server 2003, a typical user's mailbox may have a storage limit of 300 to 500 MB, with power users and VIPs requiring even more. At TechEd 2006, Exchange Server gurus were tossing about the idea that in the future a default mailbox limit would be closer to 2 GB as users start incorporating Unified Messaging features. Current discussions now look forward to and assume unlimited-sized mailboxes within the next few years.

We all see users with mailbox sizes in the gigabyte range, but is your organization prepared for a typical user with an unlimited mailbox size? What sort of concerns will you face when your average user has 25 GB, 50 GB, 100 GB, or even unlimited content (not just email!) in their mailbox?

Certainly, the need for more disk storage will be the first factor that organizations need to consider. However, disk storage is reasonably cheap, and many larger organizations that are supporting thousands of mailbox users on a single Mailbox server already have more disk space than they can practically use. This is due to the fact that they require more disk spindles to accommodate the number of simultaneous I/Os per second (IOPS) that are required by a large number of users. While early versions of Exchange Server were primarily *performance-bound*— meaning that they would require more drive performance before they required more disk capacity—versions since Exchange Server 2007 have solidly pushed that to being *capacity-bound*. With the performance characteristics and capacities of modern drives, it becomes feasible to economically provision Exchange Server storage in support of large mailboxes.

For most administrators with large amounts of mail storage, the primary concern they face is the ability to quickly and efficiently restore data in the event of a failure. These administrators are often faced with service-level agreements that bind them to maximum restoration times. In even the most optimal circumstances, a 300 GB mailbox database will take some time to restore from backup media. However, these issues have largely been mitigated by the use of database availability groups (DAGs), which ensure constant *copies* of mailbox databases that reside on other servers, essentially providing a constant *live* backup of mailbox databases on other servers, and in other datacenters.

Microsoft recommends that you do not allow an Exchange Server mailbox database to grow larger than 200 GB unless you are implementing continuous-replication technologies in

Exchange Server 2016. If you use database availability groups to replicate databases to multiple servers, the maximum database size recommendation goes up (way up) to 2 TB. However, the maximum supported database size is actually 64 TB. If you require more than the maximum recommend database storage, Exchange Server 2016 Standard Edition allows you to have up to 5 mailbox databases and Exchange Server 2016 Enterprise Edition allows you to have up to 100.

The solution in the past was to restrain the user community by preventing them from keeping all of the mail data that they might require on the mail server. This was done by imposing low mailbox limits, implementing message-archival requirements, keeping deleted items for only a few days, and keeping deleted mailboxes for only a few days.

However, as Unified Messaging data arrives in a user's mailbox and users have additional mechanisms for accessing the data stored in their mailbox, keeping mail data around longer is a demand and a requirement for your user community. The Exchange Server 2016 archive mailbox feature also drives the need for more storage, as message archival moves away from the PST files and back into Exchange Server in the form of archive mailboxes. Those archive mailboxes can be *segregated* to a dedicated mailbox database and be set to a different backup schedule and their own set of management practices.

Personal Folders or PST Files

While we're on the subject of PST files, let's discuss this pesky feature of client management. The Outlook Personal Folder, or PST files, can be the very bane of your existence. Outlook allows users to create a local database, named Personal Folder, in which users can create folders and archive email. Although this seems like a good feature on the surface, there are a few downsides:

◆ Once data is in a user's PST file, you, as the server administrator, have lost control of it. If you ever had to find all copies of a certain message, perhaps for a lawsuit, you would be out of luck. PSTs can become a management and security nightmare as data is suddenly distributed all over your network.

◆ The data in PST files take up more space than the corresponding data on the server.

◆ The default location for a PST is the local portion of the user's profile; this means it is stored on the local hard disk of their computer and is not backed up.

◆ PST files can get corrupted, become misplaced, or even be lost entirely. PSTs are not designed for access over a network connection; they're meant to be on the local hard drive, which wastes space, as well as complicates the backup and management scenarios.

◆ Starting with Exchange Server 2010, Personal Archives stored on the server can be populated from PST files, therefore offering a true alternative to those pesky local files.

Email Archiving

Sometimes, managing a mail server seems like a constant race between IT and users to keep users from letting their mailbox run out of space. Users are pack rats and generally want to keep everything. If there is a business reason for them to do so, you should look at ways to expand your available storage to accommodate them.

However, as databases become larger and larger, the Exchange server will be more difficult to manage. You might start requiring hundreds and hundreds of gigabytes (or even terabytes) of storage for email databases. Worse still, performing backups and data recovery take longer.

Exchange Server 2016 provides some archiving features, such as the Personal Archive. Also, large mailboxes could be moved to an Office 365 subscription, in a hybrid coexistence model.

For those organizations that are *not* opting to head out to the cloud or do *not* choose Office 365 as their email solution, this is where email archiving becomes useful. The last time we counted, several dozen companies were in the business of supplying email archiving tools and services. Archiving products all have a lot of functions in common, including the ability to keep data long term in email archival, to allow the users to search for their own data, and to allow authorized users to search the entire archive.

If you look at how email is archived, archive systems generally come in one of three flavors:

- Systems that depend on journaling to automatically forward every email sent or received by specified users on to the archive system.

- Systems that perform a scheduled "crawl" of specified mailboxes, looking for messages that are eligible to be moved or copied to the archive.

- Systems that move data to the archive by copying the log files from the production Mailbox servers and then replaying the logs in to the archive. This is called log shipping.

Each of these methods has its advantages and disadvantages with respect to using storage, providing a complete archive, and dealing with performance overhead.

In the previous section, we discussed briefly the archive mailbox as an alternative to the management of PST files. However, its ability goes beyond the manual move of email messages to a dedicated location on the server. For any user who requires email archival, a Personal Archive can be created for that user. As email ages past a certain point, the mail is moved from the active mailbox to the archive mailbox by using Archive Policies. The user can still access and search the archive mailbox from Outlook on the web or Outlook, though. The email data remains on the Exchange server and, therefore, does not require an additional email archival infrastructure.

We often are asked if this information can be made available offline; keep in mind that it cannot. Personal Archives cannot be included in Offline Stores (OST) files. This is by design, and we're kind of glad that it works this way, because we are continuously trying to reduce the email footprint on the client computers. OST files get very large, very fast, and can cause plenty of headaches as well. Note that with Outlook 2013 and Outlook 2016, you can adjust how many days, weeks, months, or years to sync offline.

IF I USE A THIRD-PARTY SOLUTION, DOES IT MATTER HOW I ARCHIVE?

Every third-party archival vendor is going to tell you how their product is best and give you long technical reasons why their approach is so much better than the competition's. The dirty little secret is that all three approaches have their pros and cons:

Journaling is based on SMTP. If content doesn't run across SMTP, it won't get journaled and, therefore, won't get archived. Journaling is great for capturing messaging and calendaring traffic that involves multiple parties or external entities, but it won't capture what happens to messages and other mailbox data once they're in the mailbox. Journaling can also place an additional load on the Hub Transport servers, depending on the amount and type of messaging traffic your users generate.

Crawling can capture changes only at certain intervals; it can't capture every single change, even though it overcomes many of the limitations of journaling. For example, if one user sends a message to another in violation of policy and both hard-delete their copy of the message before the next crawl interval, that message won't be detected and archived. The more often you schedule the crawl, the more of a performance impact your Mailbox servers will suffer.

Log shipping is the best of all options; it captures every transaction and change, allowing you to capture the entire history of each object while offloading the performance hit from your Exchange servers. However, the Exchange Server product team does not like the concept of log shipping and tries to discourage its use—mainly because there are vendors who try to inject data back into Exchange Server by modifying logs. This, needless to say, results in mailbox data that won't be supported by Microsoft.

Public Folders

The end-user experience for public folders has not changed in Exchange Server 2016, though the architecture has changed in recent years—mainly the storage of the public folders, which is now in a mailbox database, instead of the public folder database. Public folders are for common access to messages and files. Files can be dragged from file-access interfaces, such as File Explorer, and dropped into public folders. The whole concept of public folders has many organizations in a quandary as they try to figure out the best place for these collaborative applications. Increasingly, applications that were once "best suited" for a public folder are now better suited for web pages or portals, such as SharePoint workspaces. Although the whole concept of public folders is perceived as being deemphasized since Exchange Server 2007, Microsoft continues to support public folders, and many organizations will continue to find useful applications for public folders for the foreseeable future.

A key change in public-folder storage occurs in Exchange Server 2016, one that finally breaks the paradigm of dedicated public folder databases and public folder replication. Although we discuss this change in Chapter 2, "Introducing the Changes in Exchange Server 2016," we just briefly note here that public folders are now stored in mailbox databases and can be replicated as mailbox database copies in a database availability group.

You can set up sorting rules for a public folder so that items in the folder are organized by a range of attributes, such as the name of the sender or creator of the item or the date that the item was placed in the folder. Items in a public folder can be sorted by conversation threads. Public folders can also contain applications built on existing products such as Word or Excel or built with Exchange Server or Outlook Forms Designer, client or server scripting, or the Exchange Server API set. You can use public folders to replace many of the maddening paper-based processes that abound in every organization.

For easy access to items in a public folder, you can use a *folder link*. You can send a link to a folder in a message. When someone navigates to the folder and double-clicks a file, the file opens. Everyone who receives the message works with the same linked attachment, so everyone reads and can modify the same file. As with document routing, applications such as Microsoft Word can keep track of each person's changes to and comments on file contents. Of course, your users will have to learn to live with the fact that only one person can edit an application file at a time. Most modern end-user applications warn the user when someone else is using the file and if so allow the user to open a read-only copy of the file, which of course can't be edited.

Things Every Email Administrator Should Know

The information in this section is something that we often find even our own email administrators and help-desk personnel unaware of. Sometimes the most important skill any technology administrator has is not a specific knowledge of something but generic knowledge that they can use to quickly find the right answer.

A Day in the Life of the Email Administrator

We know and work with a lot of email administrators, and we can honestly say that no two people have the same set of tasks required of them. Your CEO, director of information technology, or even your supervisor is going to ask you to pull rabbits out of your hat, so don't expect every day to be the same as the last one. (And invest in some rabbits.) Keep up with your technology and supporting products so that you can be ready with answers or at the very least intelligent responses to questions.

DAILY ADMINISTRATIVE TASKS

So, what are some typical tasks that you may perform as part of your duties as an email administrator? These tasks will depend on the size of your organization, the number of administrators you have running your Exchange Server organization, and how administrative tasks are divided up.

Recipient Management Tasks   These are certainly the biggest day-to-day tasks that most Exchange Server administrators in medium and large organizations will experience. Recipient management tasks may include:

- Assigning a mailbox to a user account
- Creating mail-enabled contacts
- Creating and managing mail groups
- Managing mail-enabled object properties such as users' phone numbers, assigning more email addresses to a user, or adding/removing group members

Basic Monitoring Tasks   These ensure that your Exchange servers are healthy and functioning properly:

- Checking queues for stalled messages
- Verifying that there is sufficient disk space for the databases and logs
- Making sure that the message-hygiene system is functioning and up-to-date
- Running and verifying daily backups
- Reviewing the event logs for unusual activity, errors, or warnings
- Checking Performance Monitor to gauge how the Exchange servers are performing

Daily Troubleshooting Tasks   These include the following:

- Reviewing nondelivery report messages and figuring out why some mail your users are sending might not have been delivered

- Looking up errors and warnings that show up in the event logs to determine if they are serious and warrant corrective action

- Looking at mail flow in the organization to identify why delivery to some recipients is taking a long time

Security-Related Tasks   Some of these are performed daily, while others are performed only weekly or monthly:

- Looking at server and service uptimes to ensure that servers are not rebooting unexpectedly

- Reviewing the event logs for warnings that may indicate users are inappropriately accessing other users' data

- Saving the IIS (Internet Information Services) and SMTP and connectivity logs or even reviewing their content

Email Client Administration Tasks   These include the following:

- Troubleshooting Autodiscover connectivity and client issues

- Diagnosing problems with mobile or tablet devices that use Exchange ActiveSync connectivity

Application Integration Tasks   These are performed on an as-needed basis and may include the following:

- Establishing and diagnosing SMTP connectivity with email-enabled third-party applications such as web servers

- Configuring, testing, and troubleshooting Unified Messaging interoperability with voice and Session Initiation Protocol (SIP) systems

- Configuring, testing, and troubleshooting connectivity with SharePoint Server site mailboxes

COMMUNICATING WITH YOUR USERS

Communicating with your users is probably one of the most important things you do. Keeping your users informed and delivering good customer service are almost as important as delivering the IT service itself. Keeping users informed of full or partial service outages such as mobile or iPhone support or web connectivity may not score any immediate points, but users appreciate honest, forthright information. Remember how you felt the last time you were waiting for an airplane to arrive that kept on being delayed and delayed, and all the airline could do was be evasive?

Also, remember to have multiple avenues of communication available to your users. For example, you may need to get out to your users the message that you will be having downtime on the weekend. Postings on your company intranet or even the bulletin board in the cafeteria or on the wall of the elevator are good ways to keep your users informed.

PREPARING REPORTS

Maybe we have just worked in large IT environments for too long now, but it seems to us that information technology is more and more about reports and metrics. We are frequently asked to provide reports, statistics, and information on usage—not necessarily information on performance (how well the system performed for the users) but other types of metrics. Depending on your management, you may be asked to provide the following:

◆ Total number of mailboxes and mailbox sizes

◆ Top system users and top source/destination domains

◆ Antispam and message-hygiene statistics

◆ Disk space usage and growth

◆ System availability reports indicating how much unscheduled downtime may have been experienced during a certain reporting period

◆ Total number of messages sent and received per day

◆ Average end-to-end email delivery time

Exchange does not provide you with a way to easily access most of this data. The mailbox statistics can be generated using the Exchange Management Shell, but many of these will actually require an additional reporting product, such as System Center 2012 R2.

Something that you can do to prepare for a reporting requirement is to ensure that you are keeping two to four weeks' worth of message-tracking and protocol logs.

SCHEDULED DOWNTIME, PATCHES, AND SERVICE PACKS

As the discussion over moving to "the cloud" becomes more prevalent in most industries, the common argument that keeps on coming back in favor for moving Exchange Server services to some version of Exchange Online or Office 365 is server availability. No one likes downtime, whether it is scheduled or not. Management may actually be holding you to a specific service-level agreement (SLA) that requires you to provide so many hours of uptime per month or to provide email services during certain hours. Unscheduled downtime is anything that happens during your stated hours of operation that keeps users from accessing their email.

Even a small organization can provide very good availability for its mail services, and without large investments in hardware. Good availability begins with the following:

◆ Server hardware should always be from a reputable vendor and listed in the Microsoft Server Catalog.

◆ Server hardware should be installed using the vendor recommended procedures and updated regularly. Problems with servers are frequently caused by outdated firmware and device drivers.

◆ Once the server is in production, it should not be used as a test bed for other software. Keep an identically configured server that uses the same hardware for testing updates.

Don't underestimate the importance of training and documentation. In general, the industry formula for providing better availability for any system is to spend more money to purchase redundant servers and build failover clusters. But often better training for IT personnel and a simple investment in system documentation, as well as system policies and procedures, can improve availability—and for less money.

 Real World Scenario

INTERNAL STAFF TRAINING IS JUST AS IMPORTANT AS YOUR INFRASTRUCTURE

Company LMNO P invested hundreds of thousands of dollars in their infrastructure to improve server uptime. Three months into the operation of the new system, an untrained operator accidentally brought down a 15,000-mailbox database availability group (DAG) simply because he had been asked to do a task he had never done before and the organization did not have documentation on how to proceed. So keep in mind that documentation, training, and procedures are very important in improving uptime.

Even the biggest mailbox servers in large database availability groups need some scheduled downtime. Even if it is scheduled in the wee hours of the morning, undoubtedly someone, somewhere, somehow will need access when you are working on the system. Thankfully, the DAG solution for high availability ensures that users may never notice the scheduled server downtime, since mailbox services can be switched over to another member server in the DAG. That being said, when you are driving your car with no spare tire in the trunk, you are more vulnerable to a flat tire. The same is true of the DAG, because when a member server is offline for maintenance, the DAG loses a potential mailbox server that is capable of taking over in the event of server failure.

When your scheduled downtime will affect components that can impact server availability for your users, that downtime should be well communicated. Also, you should document your scheduled downtime as part of your operational plans and let your user community know about these plans. The specific time window for maintenance should always be the same; for some organizations, this might be 6:30 PM to 10:30 PM on Thursday once per month, whereas other organizations might schedule downtime from 11:00 PM Saturday until 4:00 AM every Sunday.

The number-one reason for downtime is to apply updates and fixes to the operating system or to the applications running on the server. Microsoft releases monthly security updates for the operating system and applications if vulnerabilities are discovered. Every few months, Microsoft releases updates for Exchange Server 2016 that fix bugs or that may even add slight functionality. New for Exchange Server 2016, Microsoft uses a quarterly update release cycle. Each quarter, a cumulative update (CU) is released for Exchange Server 2016. You can install the CU in your environment to update it with the latest updates and fixes, and you do not need to install previous CUs before you install the latest CU.

Microsoft's updates are usually downloaded to your servers shortly after they are released. The server can download them directly from Microsoft, or they can be downloaded from Windows Software Update Service (WSUS), Microsoft System Center Configuration Manager 2012 R2, or another third-party server inside your network. Whichever you choose, it is important that you make sure that the machine is a server and not a workstation. For example, make sure the automatic updates component of Windows Server is configured correctly. Figure 1.6 shows the Change Settings options for Windows Update.

FIGURE 1.6
Configuring auto-
matic updates

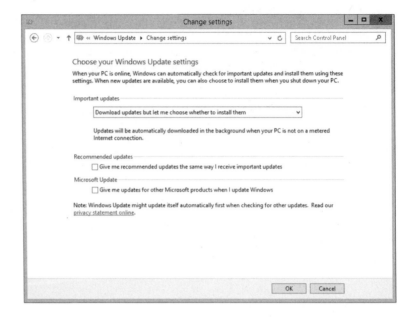

For production Exchange servers, you should configure the server with the option Download Updates But Let Me Choose Whether To Install Them. This is an important setting because if you choose the Install Updates Automatically (Recommended) option, the server will automatically apply any update within a day or so of downloading it. This is not a desirable action for a production mail server. Instead, you want the server to download the updates and notify you via the updates icon in the system tray. You can then investigate the updates and schedule appropriate downtime to apply them manually.

Finding Answers

This topic deserves special attention. One of our jobs is working in Tier 3 support for a large organization. The thing we respect the most about the administrators who actually run the system and handle the trouble tickets is that they do their homework prior to coming to us with a problem.

Too often techies make up an answer when they are not sure about something. Don't do that! When you are asked a question that you don't know the answer to, it is okay to say you don't know the answer—but make sure to follow that up by indicating that you will find the answer. Knowing the right resources (where to get answers) is just as important as the technical knowledge it takes to implement the answer. Key players in your organization will respect you much more when they know that you are willing to accept the limitations of your knowledge and have the appropriate resources to find the resolution to a problem or the answer to a question.

HELPFUL RESOURCES

Exchange Server has to be one of the most documented and discussed products (short of maybe Windows) that Microsoft produces. This means that most of the questions that we have about

Exchange Server can usually be answered via the right search or by looking in the right place. The most obvious place to start when you have a problem or a question is to perform an Internet search, but many other resources are available:

Exchange Server Documentation   There is a world of free information on the Internet, but let's start right on the local hard disk of your Exchange Server or any place you have installed the admin tools. Microsoft has done an excellent job of providing better and better documentation for Exchange Server over the past few years. The Exchange Server 2016 documentation is comprehensive and so readable you will wonder if it is really from Microsoft. A link to the documentation can be found in the installation directory of Exchange Server. Look for the following file:

```
C:\Program Files\Microsoft\Exchange Server\v15\Bin\ExchHelp.url
```

You can also run it from the Microsoft Exchange Server 2016 folder on the Start menu. Either option will open a web browser that navigates to the TechNet reference library for Exchange Server.

Exchange Server Release Notes   Another good resource for "I wish I had known that" types of things is the release notes. You should be able to find a link to the release notes here:

```
C:\Program Files\Microsoft\Exchange Server\v15\
```

Exchange Server Forums   If you have a question for which you have done your due diligence in searching and researching the problem but you don't have an answer, it is time to ask the world. A good place to start is the Microsoft forums, also known as social.technet .microsoft.com. You can find the Exchange Server section here:

```
http://social.technet.microsoft.com/forums/en-US/category/exchangeserver/
```

When you post your question, please take a moment to think about what information the other readers are going to need to answer your question. Although you can post a vague question such as "Exchange is giving me an error," doing so is only going to result in (at best) delays while other forum participants have to request specific information from you. Instead, post the exact error message and any error codes you are seeing. Also, indicate, at minimum, what version of the software you are using (including service pack), the role of the server, and what operating system you are using.

You Had Me at EHLO   This is the Microsoft Exchange Team's blog. This is the best site on the Internet for getting the inside scoop on how Exchange Server works, best practices, and the future of Exchange Server. You can read articles written by Exchange Server developers and Customer Support Services engineers. When changes to the product are announced, or customers request changes in the product, you will hear *first* from the product group engineers about the way they have chosen to deal with the issue.

```
http://blogs.technet.com/b/exchange/
```

MSExchange.Org Website   One of the best sites on the Internet for free, easy-to-access content about Exchange Server is www.msexchange.org. The articles are written by Exchange Server gurus from all over the world and are usually in the form of easy-to-read and easy-to-follow tutorials. There is also a forums section where you can post questions or read other people's questions.

CALLING FOR SUPPORT

If your system is down or your operations are seriously hindered and you don't have a clue what to do next, it is time to call in the big guns. Sure, you should do some Internet searches to try to resolve your problem, but Internet newsgroups and forums are not the place to get support for business-critical issues.

Microsoft Product Support Services (PSS) is Microsoft's technical support organization. Its home page is http://support.microsoft.com. Professional support options (ranging from peer-to-peer support to telephone support) can be found at the following URL, where a web browser–based wizard guides you through your support options:

https://gettechsupport.microsoft.com/default.aspx?locale=en-us&supportregion=en-us&pesid=14886

If you do not have a Microsoft Premier agreement, Microsoft telephone support may seem to be a bit expensive, but believe me, when an Exchange server is down and the users are burning you in effigy in the company parking lot, a few hundred dollars for business hours support is cheap.

When you call and get a support technician on the phone, don't be surprised or offended if they start at the beginning and ask you a lot of elementary questions. They have to double-check everything you have done before they can look into more advanced problems. Frequently, one of these basic questions will help you locate a problem that you were convinced was more complicated than it really was. Though the beginning of the call may be underwhelming, the technician will stay with you on the phone until the problem is resolved or some kind of an acceptable resolution is put in place.

We always encourage people to call PSS if they truly need assistance. But PSS engineers are not mind readers, nor do they know every bit of Exchange Server code. You will do both yourself and the PSS engineer a big favor if you have all of your ducks in a row before you call. Do the following before you call:

◆ Attempt a graceful shutdown and restart of the server in question, if applicable.

◆ Perform a complete backup if possible.

◆ Have a complete, documented history of everything you have done to solve the problem. At the first sign of trouble, you should start keeping a chronological log of the things you did to fix the problem.

◆ Find out if you are allowed to initiate support sessions with remote support personnel through a tool like Skype for Business 2015 or WebEx.

◆ Be at a telephone that is physically at the server's console, or be in a place where you can access the server remotely via the Remote Desktop client. Your support call will be very brief if you cannot immediately begin checking things for the PSS engineer.

◆ Have the usernames and passwords that will provide you with the right level of administrative access. If you don't have those, have someone nearby who can log you in.

◆ Save copies of the event logs. Be prepared to send these to PSS if requested.

◆ Know the location of your most recent backup and how to access it when needed.

◆ Keep copies of all error messages. Don't paraphrase the message. Screen captures work great in this case. Pressing Alt+Print Scrn (or using the Snipping tool) and saving the screen capture as a file works great, too. We usually create a document with screen captures along with notes of what we were doing when we saw each message.

Be patient; telephone support is a terribly difficult job. A little kindness, patience, and understanding on your part will most certainly be returned by the PSS engineer.

Tools You Should Know

Out of the box, Exchange Server is an excellent product, but sometimes the base software that you install can use some assistance. Some of these tools are actually installed with Exchange Server, whereas you may need to download other tools.

PowerShell and the Exchange Management Shell   Even here in the very first chapters, we are extolling the virtues of PowerShell. PowerShell enables some basic Windows management functions, such as managing event logs and services, to be performed via a command-line interface. This interface is simple to use and easy to learn, even for a GUI guy. The Exchange Server team pioneered the adoption of PowerShell when they built the entire Exchange Server 2007 management interface, known as the Exchange Management Shell (EMS), as an extension to PowerShell. Exchange Server 2013 and Exchange Server 2016 continue to follow this pattern.

Although almost every chapter in this book will include at least some information about using EMS to perform Exchange Server management tasks, we have dedicated all of Chapter 5, "Introduction to PowerShell and the Exchange Management Shell," to helping you learn your way around EMS.

Exchange Management Shell Test Cmdlets   The Exchange Management Shell has a series of command-line tools that are very good for testing and diagnosing problems. These include tools for testing Outlook on the web connectivity, Unified Messaging connectivity, Outlook connectivity, and even mail flow. They are installed when you install the Exchange Server 2016 Management Tools. For more information, at the EMS prompt, enter **Get-Excommand test***.

Microsoft Remote Connectivity Analyzer (Previously Exchange Remote Connectivity Analyzer)   Available at www.testexchangeconnectivity.com, the Remote Connectivity Analyzer is likely going to be the most useful tool in your troubleshooting arsenal. Initially started as a side project by two Microsoft employees, this website acts as the ultimate connectivity troubleshooting catch-all. The basic troubleshooting scenarios for Exchange Server 2016 (on-premises) are shown in Figure 1.7.

Those of you who have used "analyzers" from Microsoft in the past may remember the Exchange Best Practices Analyzer (ExBPA). The Remote Connectivity Analyzer should not be confused with the ExBPA. In fact, a new version of the ExBPA has not been released for Exchange Server since Exchange Server 2010.

FIGURE 1.7
Viewing the
Microsoft Remote
Connectivity
Analyzer

FIGURE 1.7
Viewing the Microsoft Remote Connectivity Analyzer

The Bottom Line

Understand email fundamentals. To gain the best advantage from Exchange Server 2016, you should have a good grounding in general email applications and principles.

Master It What two application models have email programs traditionally used? Which one does Exchange Server use? Can you name an example of the other model?

Identify email-administration duties. Installing an Exchange Server system is just the first part of the job. Once it's in place, it needs to be maintained. Be familiar with the various duties and concerns that will be involved with the care and feeding of Exchange Server.

Master It What are the various types of duties that a typical Exchange Server administrator will expect to perform?

Chapter 2

Introducing the Changes in Exchange Server 2016

Email clients used to be fairly simple and text based. Email servers had few connectivity options, no high-availability features, and no integrated directory. Then, beginning in the mid-1990s, we saw a big push toward providing email service to most of our user communities. We also saw email go from an occasionally used convenience to a business-critical tool. Business management and users demanded more features, better availability, and more connectivity options as the email client and server evolved.

Microsoft released Exchange Server 4.0 (the first version of Exchange Server) in 1996, and the product has been evolving ever since. Exchange Server 2016 is the eighth major release of the Exchange Server family and represents continued evolution of the product. The features and functions of this new release include not only features requested from many thousands of Microsoft's customers but also requirements shared internally at Microsoft by Microsoft Consulting Services and their own IT department, which supports more than 100,000 mailboxes.

We'll explore how some product features have evolved to this latest release, providing context for functionalities that were added, removed, modified, renamed, or reinvented. As of this writing, most Exchange Server customers are still using Exchange Server 2013 rather than Exchange Server 2016. Therefore, we'll focus on the changes that have been made to Exchange Server since Exchange Server 2013.

IN THIS CHAPTER, YOU WILL LEARN TO:

♦ Understand the changes in Exchange server architecture

♦ Understand the changes in the Exchange Server roles

Getting to Know Exchange Server 2016

It seems that we approach any new release of Exchange Server with a sense of both excitement and trepidation. We look forward to the new features and capabilities that are introduced with a newer version of the product. Certainly, the new site-resiliency features, compliance functionalities, resource management, management features, and security features will allow us to deliver better, more reliable messaging services to our end users.

On the other side of the coin is the feeling that we have to learn a whole new series of features inside and out so that we can better use them. Sure, we know Exchange Server 2013 pretty well, but there will be new details to learn with Exchange Server 2016. Sometimes we have to learn these implementation or management details the hard way.

However, this milestone in the evolution of Exchange Server is a good one. We can't help but be excited about learning about this new version and sharing what we have learned. We hope that you will feel the same sense of excitement. We have picked a top-ten list of new features that we like and hope that you will investigate further as you start to learn Exchange Server 2016. Some of these are summarized in this chapter and many of these you will find in more detail in later chapters.

◆ Simplicity of server roles: Mailbox and Edge Transport

◆ Proxy traffic from and to Exchange Server 2016

◆ Outlook on the web (formerly Outlook Web App)

◆ MAPI over HTTP as the default protocol

◆ Document collaboration with SharePoint 2016 and OneDrive for Business

◆ Wizard for hybrid Office 365 environments

◆ New conditions and actions for Data Loss Prevention (DLP) policies

◆ Public folder support for In-Place eDiscovery and In-Place Holds

◆ Compliance Search with eDiscovery

◆ Redesigned architecture for mailbox searches

LEARN THE EXCHANGE MANAGEMENT SHELL (AND WEAR SUNSCREEN!)

To those of you who have been around the Internet long enough to remember the "Wear Sunscreen" email, that was supposedly the 1997 commencement address to MIT given by Kurt Vonnegut but was in reality a column written by the *Chicago Tribune*'s Mary Schmich, we give you "Learn the Management Shell (and Wear Sunscreen)" to help you prepare for Exchange Server 2016, project management best practices, and the world in general:

◆ If we could offer you one important tip when learning Exchange Server 2016, it would be that you should get to know the Exchange Management Shell (EMS). Sure, it looks intimidating and nearly everything you will ever need to do is in the Exchange Admin Center. Many Exchange Server gurus will back us up on the value and usefulness of the EMS, whereas they might not agree with us on things such as using real-time block lists, making full backups daily, and keeping lots of free disk space available.

◆ Make regular Exchange Server data backups.

◆ Document.

◆ Don't believe everything you read from vendors; their job is to sell you things.

- ◆ Don't put off maintenance that might affect your uptime.

- ◆ If you get in trouble, call for help sooner rather than later. A few hundred dollars for a phone call to your vendor or Microsoft Product Support Services is better than a few days of downtime.

- ◆ Share your knowledge and configuration information with coworkers.

- ◆ Accept certain inalienable truths: disks will fail, servers will crash, users will complain, viruses will spread, and important messages will sometimes get caught in the spam filter.

- ◆ Get to know your users and communicate with them.

- ◆ Implement site resiliency and high availability for mailboxes *and* for public folder mailboxes.

- ◆ Make regular backups of your Active Directory.

- ◆ If a consultant is telling you something that you know in your gut is wrong, double-check their work or run their recommendation by another colleague. Second opinions and another set of eyes are almost always helpful.

- ◆ Think twice. Click once.

But trust me on the EMS.

In this chapter, we will cover the features of Exchange Server 2016 not only to give experienced Exchange Server administrators the proper perspective on Exchange Server 2016 but also to educate newly minted Exchange Server administrators on just how powerful Exchange Server has become. Some features we'll discuss in this chapter aren't brand new, but they are so key to the product and have been so greatly improved in this release that we are compelled to mention them at the outset.

Exchange Server Architecture

Over the last several releases, a number of significant changes have been made to the architecture of Exchange Server. These changes positively improve the performance and scalability of Exchange Server, but they also result in some pretty significant differences in the platform on which you support Exchange Server.

Windows Server 2012 R2 and Exchange Server 2016

Because of some of the underlying requirements of Exchange Server 2016, you must run Windows Server 2012 or Windows Server 2012 R2. The following editions of Windows Server will support Exchange Server 2016:

- ◆ Windows Server 2012 Standard Edition

- ◆ Windows Server 2012 Datacenter Edition

◆ Windows Server 2012 R2 Standard Edition

◆ Windows Server 2012 R2 Datacenter Edition

It may also be safe to assume that Exchange Server 2016 will also be supported on Windows Server 2016. However, at the time of this writing, Windows Server 2016 is still only available as a technical preview. Because of this, Exchange Server 2016 has not yet been qualified on Windows Server 2016.

Exchange Server 2016 also has several other requirements. These requirements include:

◆ Windows Management Framework 4.0

◆ Microsoft .NET Framework 4.5.2

◆ A forest function level of Windows Server 2008 or higher

◆ All domain controllers must be running Windows Server 2008 or later

The supported Outlook clients for Exchange 2016 include:

◆ Outlook 2016 with the latest service packs and updates

◆ Outlook 2013 with the latest service packs and updates

◆ Outlook 2010 with the latest service packs and updates

◆ Outlook for Mac for Office 365

The management tools for Exchange Server 2016 can be installed on a computer that has one of the following operating systems:

◆ Windows Server 2012 Standard or Datacenter

◆ Windows Server 2012 R2 Standard or Datacenter

◆ Windows 10 64-bit

◆ Windows 8.1 64-bit

Note that Exchange Server 2016 and Exchange Server 2007 cannot coexist in the same environment.

To install Exchange Server 2016 with Exchange Server 2010, the Exchange Server 2010 server must be running Update Rollup 11 for Exchange 2010 SP3 or later.

To install Exchange Server 2016 with Exchange Server 2013, Exchange 2013 Cumulative Update 10 or later must be installed on all Exchange Server 2013 servers in the organization.

Server Roles

Exchange Server 2013 had three server roles: the Client Access server role, the Edge Transport server role, and the Mailbox server role. In Exchange Server 2016, there are now just two server roles. The Client Access server role has been retired. Now, the two server roles are the Mailbox server role and the Edge Transport server role. The Mailbox server role includes all of the components that a Client Access server role provided with Exchange Server 2013. The Mailbox server role now provides these services:

- Client Access protocols
- Transport service
- Mailbox databases
- Unified messaging

The Edge Transport server role is designed to enable you to deploy a messaging server in a perimeter network, outside of an Active Directory Domain Services (AD DS) environment. This assists in minimizing the attack surface of your Exchange environment. It also assists by adding a point of security for messages that include viruses and spam, keeping them out of the internal network.

Exchange Server 2016 also gives you the ability to proxy traffic from an Exchange Server 2013 environment, as well as from Exchange Server 2016 to Exchange Server 2013. This flexibility enables you to control the process of migrating to Exchange Server 2016, such as with a phased mailbox approach. It is also beneficial for interoperability between Exchange Server 2013 and Exchange Server 2016 because any mailbox server can proxy clients to the correct server, regardless of whether the server is running Exchange Server 2013 or Exchange Server 2016. We talk more about migrations and interoperability in Chapter 11, "Upgrades and Migrations to Exchange Server 2016 or Office 365."

HIGH-AVAILABILITY DECISIONS

High-availability decisions do not need to be made at installation time. High availability for Exchange Server 2016 databases is added incrementally *after* the initial deployment of the Mailbox server. There is no clustered Mailbox server installation option; however, administrators create Database Availability Groups (DAGs) to implement high availability. High availability is discussed in detail in Chapter 20, "Creating and Managing Database Availability Groups." Mailbox databases can be added to database availability groups at any point in the game. The databases can be removed from database availability groups as well, as needed. Essentially, the high-availability decisions can be done incrementally after a deployment has occurred and reversed if they no longer serve the needs of the organization. It is important to note that a DAG can contain only servers that run the same version of Exchange Server. Adding an Exchange Server 2016 to a DAG that contains Exchange Server 2013 servers is not supported, and vice versa.

THE MAILBOX SERVER ROLE

The Mailbox server role is responsible for so much, yet changes in the architecture have ensured that it requires few resources to perform all its necessary tasks. We will discuss, in later chapters, the database benefits with regard to the database schema and memory utilization in Exchange Server 2016. Recent improvements are designed to enhance the ability of a Mailbox server to do so much more with so much less.

Another very significant change in the Mailbox server role is the number of Client Access features that are now handled by this role. In Exchange Server 2016, a Mailbox server handles the data rendering for client requests, runs all of the client access protocols, and still maintains all mailboxes.

The Mailbox server role is responsible for the following functionality (this list isn't exhaustive):

◆ Hosts mailbox databases

◆ Hosts public folder database

◆ Provides transport-related services, including proxying (note that transport was originally handled by a Hub Transport server role that went away in Exchange Server 2013)

◆ Provides client connectivity for all clients (note that client access was handled by the Client Access server role in Exchange Server 2013 but is now handled by the Mailbox server role in Exchange Server 2016)

THE EDGE TRANSPORT SERVER ROLE

The amount of spam, malicious email, and viruses that some organizations receive is staggering. Even small organizations are receiving tens of thousands of pieces of spam, dozens of viruses, and hundreds of thousands of dictionary spamming attacks each week. Some organizations estimate that more than 90 percent of all inbound email is spam or other unwanted content. Keeping this unwanted content away from your Exchange servers is important. A common practice for messaging administrators is to employ additional layers of message hygiene and security. The first layer is usually some type of appliance or third-party SMTP software package that is installed in the organization's perimeter network. The problem with these third-party utilities is that the administrator has to become an expert on an additional technology. An easier method that some organizations choose is to use a cloud-based solution. The Exchange Online Protection (EOP) service from Microsoft is a popular cloud-based message protection solution.

Exchange Server 2016 includes a server role named Edge Transport. The role remains similar to the role from Exchange Server 2010 and Exchange Server 2013. The Edge Transport server role is recommended for perimeter networks outside of an AD DS environment. Although it is possible to install the Edge Transport role on a domain server, none of the Exchange services used for Edge Transport require AD DS. The Edge Transport server role uses Active Directory Lightweight Directory Services (AD LDS) to store configuration and recipient information.

An Edge Transport server will handle all inbound and outbound messaging traffic for a Mailbox server. This includes mail relay and smart host services for the Exchange environment. You can deploy multiple Edge Transport servers to enable redundancy and failover capabilities in the perimeter network. You can also load balance incoming messages by distributing the SMTP traffic to multiple Edge Transport servers.

IS THE EDGE TRANSPORT SERVER ROLE REQUIRED?

A common misconception is that the Edge Transport role is required for an Exchange Server organization. This is not the case, especially for organizations that choose to use a cloud-based message protection solution. Inbound email can be sent directly to the Mailbox server, or you can continue to use your existing third-party antispam/message-hygiene system to act as an inbound message relay for Exchange Server.

The Edge Transport server is a stand-alone message transport server that is managed using the EMS and the same basic management console that is used to manage Exchange Server 2016. A server functioning in an Edge Transport role should not be a member of the organization's internal Active Directory domain, although it can be part of a separate management forest used in a perimeter network.

Content filtering and Microsoft Forefront Security for Exchange are implemented on the Edge Transport server through content filtering and other antispam features. You can also run the features on the mailbox server if you do not have Edge Transport servers.

An example of how an organization might deploy an Edge Transport server is shown in Figure 2.1. Inbound email is first delivered to the Edge Transport servers that are located in the organization's perimeter network, where the message is inspected by the content filter, Forefront Security for Exchange, and any message transport rules. The inbound message is then sent on to the internal servers. Additionally, the Exchange Server Mailbox servers are configured to deliver mail, leaving the organization to the Edge Transport servers rather than configuring the internal servers to deliver mail directly to the Internet.

FIGURE 2.1

Deploying an Edge
Transport server

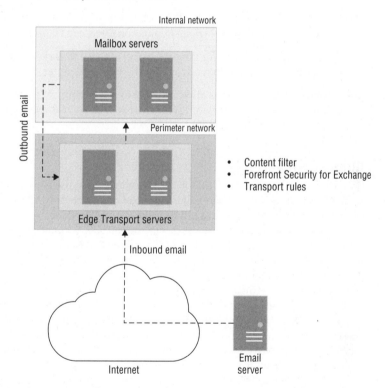

The Edge Transport server is a fully functional SMTP message-hygiene system with many of the same features that are found in expensive message-hygiene software packages and appliances. The following features are included:

◆ Per-user safe-sender, safe-recipient, and blocked-sender lists are automatically replicated from the user's mailbox to the Edge Transport server. Recipient filtering is enabled when valid recipients are synchronized to the Edge Transport server's local Active Directory Lightweight Directory Services (AD LDS) database.

- Sender and recipient filtering can be configured via administrator-controlled lists.

- Integrated Microsoft content filter is included for spam detection. Spam can be rejected, deleted, quarantined, or delivered to the user's Junk email.

- Multiple message-quarantines allow messages that are highly likely to be spam to be quarantined and sent to a quarantine mailbox on your Exchange server. A separate quarantine exists in the form of the user's Junk email folder for messages that are still tagged as spam but with a lower Spam Confidence Level.

- Microsoft Forefront Security for Exchange Server is available for the Edge Transport server when Enterprise client access licenses are used. However, this will be a short-lived solution, since Microsoft has announced that the entire suite of Forefront products is being decommissioned. Instead, many organizations use EOP or another third-party solution.

- Daily content filter and virus signature updates are available for organizations using Microsoft Forefront Security for Exchange Server.

- Real-time block lists and the IP Reputation Service allow an IP address to be checked to see if it is a known source of spam. Reputation filters can be updated on a daily basis.

- Sender ID filters allow for the verification of the mail server that sent a message and whether it is allowed to send mail for the message sender.

- Sender reputation filters allow a sender to be temporarily placed on a block list based on characteristics of mail coming from that sender, such as message content, sender ID verification, and sender behavior.

Client Connectivity

With Exchange Server 2013, Outlook clients connected to the Exchange Server by using RPC over HTTP (Outlook Anywhere). This enabled Outlook to connect to an Exchange server, regardless of its location, by using the Outlook Anywhere service.

Beginning with Exchange Server 2016, Outlook clients connect to the Exchange server by using MAPI over HTTP. RPC over HTTP is still available, but is official de-emphasized (meaning that it may not be included in future releases of Exchange Server). MAPI over HTTP is the default communication method between the client and the server.

MAPI over HTTP increases reliability and stability of the client connection. This protocol enables a higher level of visibility to errors that might occur between the client and server, as well as enhanced recoverability. MAPI over HTTP also includes support for a pause and resume function, which enables the clients to change networks while maintaining a connection to the Exchange Server. MAPI over HTTP can also reduce the total number of client connections, which can be helpful from a performance perspective.

While MAPI over HTTP is the default connection protocol for new Exchange Server 2016 environments, if you install Exchange Server 2016 in an environment with Exchange Server 2013, the protocol will not be used automatically. This is because MAPI over HTTP is not enabled by default in Exchange Server 2013 and was introduced with Exchange Server 2013 Service Pack 1.

Hybrid Improvements

Exchange Server 2016 can be implemented with Office 365 for a hybrid on-premises and cloud-based service. When configuring a hybrid organization with Exchange 2016, you will be prompted to download the Hybrid Configuration Wizard. This wizard is included to assist configuring the hybrid environment.

The wizard has been updated for Exchange Server 2016 to include the following features:

- ◆ Easy updates for changes in Office 365 services

- ◆ Assists in troubleshooting a hybrid environment configuration

- ◆ Improved diagnostic information to resolve problems

- ◆ Support for both Exchange Server 2013 and 2016 hybrid environments

Hybrid deployments should be performed by using Azure Active Directory Connect (AAD Connect). AAD Connect provides functionality to synchronize multiple on-premises AD DS forests with a single Office 365 account.

In a hybrid environment, Exchange ActiveSync clients will be automatically directed to Office 365 if the user's mailbox is moved to the cloud. To support this automatic redirection, the ActiveSync client must support HTTP 451 redirects. After the client has been redirected, the Exchange profile on the device will be updated to use the new URL of the Exchange Online service. At this point, the client will not contact the on-premises environment for mailbox information.

OneDrive for Business Integration

With Exchange Server 2016 and SharePoint 2016, Outlook on the web users can link to and share documents that are stored in OneDrive for Business or on an on-premises SharePoint server. Instead of attaching a file to an email message, users can link to documents directly from Outlook on the web. Users can collaborate in an on-premises deployment just as they can with Office 365.

If a user receives a Word, Excel, or PowerPoint file that is stored in OneDrive for Business or SharePoint 2016, the recipient can view and edit the file directly from Outlook on the web. For an on-premises environment, a server must be running Office Online Server, which is in preview at the time of this writing, in the on-premises organization.

After editing the file within Outlook on the web, the recipient can save or upload the file to OneDrive.

Performance

The new architecture of Exchange Server 2016 combines the core features into a single server role. As part of that architecture, the search functionality has also been redesigned. In previous versions of Exchange Server, the searching functions were not fault-tolerant and were performed synchronously. In Exchange Server 2016, searching is performed asynchronously and is decentralized. Search functions are distributed across all Exchange Servers in the organization, and retries are attempted if servers are too busy.

The search scalability has also been improved. Previously, up to 5,000 mailboxes could be searched simultaneously from the web app. With Exchange Server 2016, this has increased to 10,000 mailboxes. When using the EMS, there is no limit to the number of mailboxes that can be searched.

Improved Policy and Compliance Features

Exchange Server 2016 has made significant improvements to both Data Loss Prevention (DLP) and eDiscovery.

DATA LOSS PREVENTION (DLP)

In Exchange Server 2016, transport rules have been updated with several new predicates and actions. Also, the coolest new feature to hit transport rules is DLP policies. DLP policies are designed to prevent users from sharing sensitive information with unauthorized users.

Every transport rule has three components: conditions, actions, and exceptions. The conditions specify under which circumstances the rule applies, whereas the exceptions specify under which conditions it will not apply. Exchange Server 2016 has the ability to identify, monitor, and protect 80 different types of sensitive information based on conditions and actions.

A new condition, "Any attachment has these properties, including any of these words," will cause a trigger if an attached Office document contains the defined words. This condition enables you to integrate the transport rules with SharePoint, Windows Server 2012 R2 File Classification Infrastructure, or a third-party classification system.

A new action, "Notify the recipient with a message," will send a customizable message to the recipient. For example, you can notify the recipient if the email was rejected or quarantined based on the contents.

The existing action "Generate incident report and send it to" has been updated so that the report can be messaged to multiple distribution lists.

The actions are the interesting part of the transport rule. Figure 2.2 shows the conditions on the New Rule window of the Transport Rule Wizard; this screen has three parts. The first part is checking on which object to take action, the second is simply checking the actions to take, and the third part specifies more details about the action.

FIGURE 2.2
Examining a
transport rule

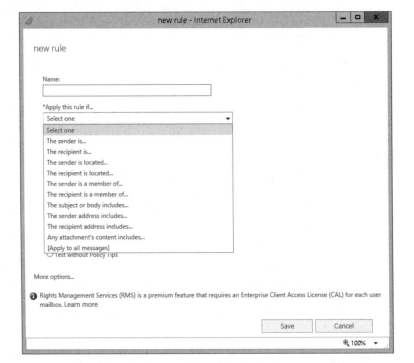

eDISCOVERY AND PUBLIC FOLDERS

The market for third-party tools to support Exchange Server has grown rapidly. At one point, there were more than 60 third parties providing email archive solutions for Exchange Server. The sheer volume of email that users receive and their demand to keep historical email have made these tools very attractive.

Exchange Server 2010 introduced, and Exchange Server 2016 continues, a premium feature that allows for the integration of email archiving. The email archiving feature is actually a series of features that interact directly with the user's mailbox:

Archive Mailbox   An archive mailbox is a secondary mailbox for a user that is used to store long-term email (archive email). An archive mailbox can be used in place of .pst files. Users can copy email messages from their primary mailbox to their archive mailbox. Archive mailboxes help users deal with large volumes of email while staying within mailbox size limits. The archive mailbox is defined on a user-by-user basis because not all users need an archive mailbox. The content in the archive mailbox can be accessed by users using the Outlook 2010 or later client or Outlook on the web.

Retention Policies   Retention policies define the types of mail and how long the mail can be retained within the user's primary mailbox. Retention policies take the place of messaging records management (MRM) in Exchange Server 2007 and Exchange Server 2010. Retention policies can be defined to control when items are permanently deleted or when they are moved into the archive mailbox. With Outlook 2010 or later, end users can participate in the retention process by applying retention tags to messages or an entire folder.

eDiscovery (aka Multi-Mailbox and Federated Search)   The eDiscovery features enables an authorized user to search for content across multiple data sources (both the user's "active" mailbox as well as their "personal archive mailbox") within an organization. You are able to search for information across Exchange, SharePoint, and Skype for Business archives, as well as use the eDiscovery Center in SharePoint 2013 to search for content in Exchange Server. Discovery managers can also export mailbox content to a .pst file from the SharePoint 2013 eDiscovery console. You can opt to use the Exchange Admin Center (EAC) to perform eDiscovery or opt to use SharePoint's eDiscovery Center. The eDiscovery Center offers some expanded capabilities, such as the ability to search and preserve content across multiple sources from a single console.

Exchange Server 2016 also introduces support for integrating public folders into eDiscovery. With In-Place eDiscovery, you can query public folders in the organization and put holds on public folders. Similar to placing a mailbox on hold, public folders support query-based and time-based holds. As of this writing, you can only search and hold all public folders. The ability to choose individual public folders to search and hold is expected in a later release.

In-Place Hold   In-Place Hold enables an administrator to place a hold on a user's mailbox so that deleted and edited items are held during the hold period. This would be necessary in the event of legal action or an investigation regarding the conduct of one or more of your users.

Ultimately, the Exchange Server 2016 archiving and retention policies are intended to replace the messaging records-management features that were introduced in Exchange Server 2007.

eDiscovery and Compliance Search

A new feature of eDiscovery in Exchange Server 2016 is Compliance Search. Compliance Search is performed from the EMS, so there is no limit to the number of mailboxes that can be searched. For In-Place eDiscovery, you can search up to 10,000 mailboxes with a single search. Each Exchange Server organization can run up to two In-Place eDiscovery searches simultaneously.

To perform a Compliance Search, you must be assigned the Mailbox Search management role or be a member of the Discovery Management role group. The new EMS cmdlets available with Compliance Search are

- `Get-ComplianceSearch`

- `New-ComplianceSearch`

- `Remove-ComplianceSearch`

- `Set-ComplianceSearch`

- `Start-ComplianceSearch`

- `Stop-ComplianceSearch`

Message Transport Rules

Message transport rules are quite similar to Outlook rules and can even be created using a wizard similar to the one used to create Outlook rules. However, these rules are quite a bit more powerful and are run on Mailbox servers. Because all messages are processed by a Mailbox server regardless of whether they are inbound, outbound, or for local delivery, you can build powerful policies to control the messages and data that flow within your organization. Transport rules can also be defined at your organization's perimeter by using the Edge Transport server role in Exchange Server 2016.

New and Improved Outlook on the Web

Those of us who gushed when we saw the Outlook Web Access (OWA) interface in Exchange 2003 thought a web interface could not get much better. For Outlook on the web in Exchange 2013, the Exchange team started over from scratch to build a much more functional interface than ever before. For Exchange 2016, it has been updated and enhanced further! First, the name has changed! The new name is Outlook on the web. Here are some of the features in Outlook on the web:

- Platform-specific experiences for iOS and Android

- Premium Android experience with Chrome on Android version 4.2 or later

- Email improvements to the Inbox view and reading pane

- Contact linking with LinkedIn

- Updated calendar, including email reminders

- Search suggestions

- Thirteen new themes

- Preview URL links within messages

◆ Inline video playback from URLs

◆ Document collaboration with SharePoint 2016 and OneDrive for Business

Overview of Changes Since Exchange Server 2013

Since Exchange Server 2013, the primary changes to Exchange Server 2016 are

◆ Combined services (HT, CAS, MBX) in the Mailbox server role

◆ Integration with OneDrive and SharePoint 2016

◆ Additional policy and compliance features

◆ Outlook Web App redesigned as Outlook on the web

These are the key feature differences since Exchange Server 2013 and have been discussed in this chapter. Knowing some of the changes and introduction of features can be half of the battle to upgrading your knowledge on a newly released product.

Now, Where Did That Go?

As new and better functions and APIs have been introduced, naturally some functions are no longer emphasized or supported. We've already mentioned a few features that have been removed, but there are many more. There has been a lot of confusion surrounding what will continue to be supported in Exchange Server 2016 and what will no longer work. The phrase "no longer supported" itself tends to generate a lot of confusion because an unsupported function may continue to work because it has not truly been removed. Your mileage may vary when it comes to features that are no longer supported.

What's been removed from Exchange Server really depends on your perspective. Are you an Exchange Server 2010 expert? Is Exchange Server 2013 your comfort zone? We've broken down the next section of removed features based on your perspective.

Features No Longer Included

As Exchange Server has evolved into its current form, the code has experienced significant changes. Some features and APIs have been completely removed. Although most of these features will not affect the majority of Exchange Server deployments, you should keep them in mind and thoroughly evaluate your existing messaging environment to make sure you are not dependent on a feature that has no equivalent in Exchange Server 2016. If you require any of the features or APIs that were not carried over from Exchange Server 2010 or 2013, you may need to keep an older version of Exchange Server in operation.

EXCHANGE SERVER 2016 ESCHEWS EXCHANGE SERVER 2007

Only Exchange Server 2010 and Exchange Server 2013 can coexist with Exchange Server 2016 in the same organization. If you still require features provided by the Exchange Server 2007 platform, you will not be able to transition to Exchange Server 2016 until you can replace that particular feature requirement with newer software.

EXCHANGE SERVER 2010 FEATURES REMOVED FROM EXCHANGE SERVER 2016

The following features were included with Exchange Server 2010 but are no longer available in Exchange Server 2016:

♦ Unified Messaging directory lookups using Automatic Speech Recognition.

♦ Managed Folders for messaging retention management, including the Port Managed Folder Wizard.

♦ Antispam agents from the GUI. With Exchange Server 2016, antispam can be managed only from the EMS.

♦ Connection and Attachment filtering on Mailbox server roles. The only way to enable Connection Filtering is to use an Edge Transport server in a perimeter network.

♦ The ability to link a send-and-receive connector has been removed.

♦ Outlook Web App has been renamed to Outlook on the web. Additionally, spell check, customizable filters, message flags, chat contact lists, and search folders have been removed from the web client.

♦ Outlook 2003 and 2007 are not supported. Outlook clients must use either Outlook Anywhere (RPC over HTTP) or MAPI over HTTP.

♦ The Exchange Management Console and Exchange Control Panel have been replaced by the Exchange Admin Center.

♦ The Hub Transport and Unified Messaging server roles have been removed. Both server roles are included as features in the Mailbox server role.

EXCHANGE SERVER 2013 FEATURES REMOVED FROM EXCHANGE SERVER 2016

The following features are being de-emphasized with Exchange Server 2016 and may not be included in future versions:

♦ Third-party replication APIs.

♦ RPC over HTTP for client connections.

♦ Database Availability Group support for failover cluster administrative access points.

♦ Client Access server role. The functions of this role have been included in the Mailbox server role.

♦ The MAPI/CDO library has been replaced by Exchange Web Services, ActiveSync, and REST APIs.

Clearing Up Some Confusion

We mentioned earlier that Exchange has certainly been hyped a lot during the design and beta-testing process. This has generated a lot of buzz in the information technology industry, but this buzz has also generated a lot of confusion and some misinformation. Here we'll clear up the confusion by answering a few of the common questions about Exchange 2016.

Do I have to have two servers to run each of the server roles?   In the days of Exchange Server 2010, many organizations deployed different roles to different servers in large organizations. Many administrators reserved the consolidated server approach for small environments. However, the performance capabilities of Exchange Server 2016 surpass the previous versions to such an extent that all services are run within the Mailbox server role.

Is there a 32-bit version of Exchange Server 2016?   No, a 32-bit version of Exchange Server 2016 is not available.

Is the Edge Transport server required?   No, Edge Transport servers are not required. You can use any third-party message-hygiene system in your perimeter network, you can direct inbound and outbound mail through your internal servers, or you can do both.

Is EMS knowledge required? Do I have to learn scripting?   Most common administrative tasks can be performed through the Exchange Admin Center web-based interface. Command-line management and scripting for Exchange Server 2016 have been greatly improved through the use of the EMS. Many tasks are simpler or more powerful through the EMS, but it is not necessary to learn scripting in order to start working with Exchange Server 2016. We strongly encourage you to get to know many of the powerful features of the EMS as you get comfortable with Exchange Server 2016. A number of advanced administration tasks do not have a graphical user interface option.

What is happening with public folders?   The use of public folders with Exchange Server 2016 is still available and supported. However, for years, there has been talk about moving away from public folders, potentially removing support for them at some point. At the time of this writing, there isn't any information to indicate that this is coming soon (or coming at all). But you may want to examine your public folder applications with an eye toward migrating them to systems such as Microsoft SharePoint Server 2016 to take advantage of the latest collaboration features. Also, remember that the traditional public folder databases are no longer available in Exchange Server 2016 and that you must now store all public folders in a public folder mailbox.

The Bottom Line

Understand the key changes in Exchange Server 2016.   Significant updates were made to the Exchange Server 2016 architecture to continue the improvement to the scalability, security, and stability. The Mailbox role handles mailboxes, public folders, transport, and client connectivity. Compliances features, such as compliance search and eDiscovery, are greatly enhanced and simplified. The disk I/O requirements continue to be reduced, enabling organizations to run their Exchange servers on lower-performing storage.

> **Master It**   You are planning your email data storage strategy, especially for long-term storage. You want to minimize or eliminate the use of .pst files. Which technology should you use to maintain email data indefinitely?

Understand the Mailbox role's expanded duties.   Over the last couple of versions of Exchange Server, the Exchange server roles have been updated. In each version, a server role was consolidated, enabling organizations to reduce their server footprint and simplify their environments.

> **Master It**   You are planning a training session for your junior administrators to prepare them in their SMTP connectivity troubleshooting tasks. Which server role should you recommend they inspect when attempting to troubleshoot email delivery problems?

Chapter 3

Understanding Availability, Recovery, and Compliance

The modern business world is getting more complex, not less; email in turn evolves to keep up. As an Exchange Server administrator or implementer, you need to know more about a wider variety of topics without losing your core competency in Exchange Server.

IN THIS CHAPTER, YOU WILL LEARN TO:

◆ Distinguish between availability, backup and recovery, and disaster recovery

◆ Determine the best option for disaster recovery

◆ Distinguish between the different types of availability meant by the term *high availability*

◆ Implement the four pillars of compliance and governance activities

Changing from a Technology to a Business Viewpoint

You've probably heard the old proverb that "every cloud has a silver lining." It can be a comfort to know that good can usually be found during even the worst occasions. When a mailbox database server's RAID controller goes bad and corrupts the drive array containing the executive mailboxes, you have the opportunity to validate your backup strategy and demonstrate that it works perfectly under pressure.

However, the unacknowledged corollary is Murphy's Law: "Anything that can go wrong will go wrong." Every feature, functionality, and component that is added to a messaging infrastructure increases complexity and the number of potential failures. If you think for a moment about the spread of email and how it has changed from a luxury to a utility, you can see that electronic messaging administrators have become victims of their own success.

Gone are the days where you simply had to worry about editing and publishing the correct DNS records for your domains, provisioning and configuring your T1 routers, and wrestling with server hardware. Today's challenges involve meeting more goals, supporting more complex environments, meeting business requirements, and analyzing risks. These are common scenarios:

◆ Ensuring that mailbox servers have the proper storage back-end design to allow backups to happen within a defined window

◆ Ensuring that your users continue to have access to their mailboxes even when a server fails, a flaky router takes a site offline, or power fails for an entire rack of servers

- Ensuring that a plan exists for quick recovery and restoration of your core messaging capabilities when the storage is offline or corrupt

- Ensuring that the messages users send to external clients are in compliance with all business policies and regulations

- Determining the risks associated with failing to provide disaster-recovery plans and the risks associated with a failure to meet service-level agreements

- Balancing business costs versus risks associated with providing recovery, ensuring compliance, and providing a specified level of service

What's in a Name?

Backup and recovery, high availability, disaster recovery, and *compliance and governance*—you have likely heard of these many times. Each plays a role in the overall protection strategy for your organization's data.

Each of these topics must be evaluated by every modern Exchange Server administrator and professional, along with appropriate business stakeholders, even if they are not actively addressed in every deployment of Exchange Server 2016. When you do need to address them in your planning, Exchange Server 2016 provides a variety of options to ensure that the deployment meets the particular needs of your business. One size and one set of capabilities do not fit all organizations. To make the best use of the tools that Exchange Server gives you, you must clearly understand the problems that each capability is designed to solve. It doesn't help to use a screwdriver when you need a hammer—and you can't solve a disaster-recovery problem by using an eDiscovery search.

In this section, a common vocabulary will be presented for discussing these topics. This will enable you to get the most from our discussions of the new features and functionality in Exchange Server 2016 that are covered in later chapters. You should clearly understand how Microsoft intended Exchange Server 2016's features to be deployed and used, so that you have confidence that they will meet your business goals.

Backup and Recovery

Let us begin with a topic that is one of the core tasks for any IT administrator, not just Exchange Server administrators: backup and recovery.

Backup is the process of preserving one or more point-in-time copies of a set of data, regardless of the number of copies, frequency and schedule, or media type used to store them.

As an administrator, you need to make sure your backups include all of the components you need to get Exchange Server services up and running again. That means more than just the databases. You should also consider the following components:

- **Active Directory Domain Services.** Exchange Server relies on Active Directory, so it is critical that Active Directory is highly available and backed up. Your Active Directory administrators probably handle this. But no matter who handles it, you should ensure that the backups are in place.

- **Operating system for the Exchange servers (System State as a minimum).** Prior to virtualization, backing up the Exchange server operating systems was quite important because building a new physical server (or rebuilding a physical server) from scratch was time-consuming. Today, with virtualization, building a new server is quite fast. Some organizations opt to deploy new servers and forgo the backup of the operating system for some servers. However, without a backup of the operating system or system state, you will lose customizations such as in IIS and the Registry.

◆ **File system.** The file system has log files, configuration files, and other data that can be helpful in a disaster-recovery situation.

◆ **Database and database log files.** The Exchange databases are a critical piece of your backups because all of the email data is stored in the databases!

As you can see, backing up all of the components can quickly become complicated. It is important to have the right backup tools at your disposal. As part of your disaster-recovery planning, you should look at the available tools, including third-party tools, to figure out which tools best meet your requirements and provide the best administrative experience.

With Exchange Server, there are four main types of database backups:

Full Backups (Normal)   Full backups capture an entire set of target data; in early versions of Exchange Server, this is a storage group with the transaction log files and all the associated mailbox databases and files. Beginning with Exchange Server 2010 and continuing in Exchange Server 2013 and Exchange Server 2016, each mailbox database is a separate backup target, since there is now an enforced 1:1 relationship between mailbox databases and transaction logs (it was "strongly recommended" in earlier versions). Full backups take the most time to perform and use the most space. If circular logging is disabled for a mailbox database, full backups must be executed on a regular basis. A successful full backup informs Exchange Server that the databases and transaction logs have been preserved and that saved transaction logs can be purged. Circular logging will be discussed in more depth later.

Copy Backups   Copy backups are exactly like full backups, except that saved transaction logs are not purged.

Incremental Backups   Incremental backups capture only a partial set of the target data—specifically, the data that has changed since either the last full backup or the last incremental backup. For Exchange Server, this means any new transaction logs. Incremental backups are designed to *minimize how often* full backups are performed, as well as *minimize the space used* by any particular backup set. As a result, a backup set that includes incremental backups can be more time-consuming and fragile to restore; successful recovery includes first recovering the latest full backup and then each successive incremental backup. Incremental backups also instruct Exchange Server to purge the saved transaction logs after the backup is complete. Incremental backups are not available when circular logging is enabled.

Differential Backups   Differential backups also capture only a partial set of the target data—specifically, the data that has changed since the last full backup. No other backups (incremental or differential) are considered. For Exchange Server, this means any transaction logs generated since the last full backup. Differential backups are designed to *minimize how many* recovery operations you have to perform in order to fully restore a set of data. In turn, differential backups use more space than incremental backups, but they can be recovered more quickly and with fewer opportunities for data corruption; successful recovery includes first recovering the latest full backup and then the latest differential backup. A differential backup does not purge saved transaction logs. Differential backups are not available when circular logging is enabled.

Also known as restoration, recovery is the process of taking one or more sets of the data preserved through backups and making it once again accessible to administrators, applications, and/or end users. Most recovery jobs require the restoration of multiple sets of backup data, especially when incremental and differential backups are in use. Two metrics are used to determine if the recovery time and the amount of data recovered are acceptable:

Recovery Time Objective   Recovery Time Objective (RTO) is a metric commonly used to help define successful backup and restore processes. The RTO defines the time window in which you must restore Exchange Server services and messaging data after an adverse event. You may have multiple tiers of data and service, in which case it could be appropriate to have a separate RTO for each tier. Often, the RTO is a component of (ideally, an input into, but that's not always the case) your service-level agreements. As a result, the RTO is a critical factor in the design of Exchange Server mailbox-database storage systems; it's a bad idea to design or provision mailbox databases that are larger than you can restore within your RTO.

Recovery Point Objective   Recovery Point Objective (RPO) is a metric that goes hand in hand with the RTO. While the RTO measures a time frame, the RPO sets a benchmark for the maximum amount of data (typically measured in hours) you can afford to lose. Again, multiple tiers of service and data often have separate RPOs. The RPO helps drive the backup frequency and schedule. It's worth noting that this metric makes an explicit assumption that all data within a given category is equally valuable; that's obviously not true, which is why it is important to properly establish your categories. Remember, though, if you have too many classes or categories, you'll just have confusion.

One thing to note about Exchange Server 2016 databases is that they support only online backups and restores created through the Windows Volume Shadow Copy Service (VSS). VSS provides several advantages compared to other backup methods, including the ability to integrate with third-party storage systems to speed up the backup and recovery processes. The most important benefit VSS gives, though, is that it ensures that the Exchange Server information store flushes all pending writes consistently, ensuring that a backup dataset can be cleanly recovered.

We will use the phrase "backup set" several times. A *backup set* is a copy of all of the various backups that are required to perform a particular recovery. This will almost always include at least the last full backup and may include one or more incremental or differential backups

---

HOW MUCH DATA GETS COPIED?

One thing that Volume Shadow Copy Service does not natively provide is the ability to reduce the amount of data that must be copied during a backup operation. VSS simply creates either a permanent or temporary replica (depending on how the invoking application requested the replica be created) of the disk volume; it's then up to the application to sort out the appropriate files and folders that make up the dataset. Usually, this is the entire disk volume, but depending on the selected *VSS writers* it may only be a portion of a disk volume or specific files on a disk volume. Many Exchange Server–aware backup applications simply copy the various transaction log files and mailbox database files to the backup server.

Some applications, however, are a bit more intelligent; they keep track of which blocks have changed in the target files since the last backup interval. These applications can copy just those changed blocks to the backup dataset—typically some percentage of the blocks in the mailbox database file as well as all the new transaction log files—thus reducing the amount of data that needs to travel over the network and be stored. Block-level backups help strike a good balance between storage, speed, and reliability. As you go forward with VSS-aware Exchange Server–compatible backup solutions, be sure to investigate whether they offer this feature. Microsoft's System Center Data Protection Manager does offer this feature.

Disaster Recovery

Regular backups are important; the ability to successfully restore them is even more important. This capability is a key part of your extended arsenal for problem situations. Restoring the occasional backup is fairly straightforward but assumes that you have a functional Exchange server and the dependent network infrastructures. What do you do if an entire site or datacenter goes down and your recovery operations extend beyond a single Exchange Server mailbox database? The answer to this question is a broad topic that can fill many books, blog postings, and websites of its own.

Disaster recovery (DR) is the practice of ensuring that critical services can be restored when some disaster or event causes large-scale or long-term outage. A successful DR plan requires the identification of critical services, dependencies, and data, creation of documentation that lists the necessary tasks to re-create and restore them, and modification of the relevant policies and processes within your organization to support the DR plan.

It's not enough to consider how to rebuild Exchange servers and restore Exchange Server mailbox databases. Exchange Server is a complex application with many dependencies, so your plans need to accommodate the following issues:

Network Dependencies   These include subnets, IP address assignments, DNS, load balancers, DHCP services, switch configurations, network/Internet access, and router configurations. Are you rebuilding your services to have the same IP addresses or new ones? Whatever you decide, you'll need to make sure that required services and clients can reach the Exchange servers.

Active Directory Services   These include associated DNS zones and records. Exchange Server cannot function without reliable access to global catalog servers and other domain controllers. Which forests and domains hold objects Exchange Server will need to reference? Does your existing replication configuration meet those needs during a DR scenario? What would happen if an Active Directory user account that was associated with a mailbox was accidentally deleted?

Third-Party Applications   These include monitoring, backup, archival, or other programs and services that require messaging services or interact with those services. Don't just blindly catalog everything in production; be sure these systems are also being addressed as part of the disaster-recovery plan.

There's a blurry line between disaster recovery and the associated concept of *business continuity* (also called *business continuance*). Business continuity (BC) is the ability of your organization to continue providing some minimum set of operations and services necessary to stay in business during a large-scale outage, such as during a regional event or natural disaster (for example, a hurricane or earthquake). In a business continuity plan, your organization will identify and prioritize the most critical services and capabilities that need to provide at least some level of operational capacity as soon as possible, even without full access to data or applications.

It's important to note that the business continuity plan is designed and implemented alongside your disaster-recovery efforts. In many organizations, they will be maintained by two separate groups of professionals. It is imperative that these groups should have good lines of communication in place.

 Real World Scenario

DRAWING THE LINE BETWEEN DISASTER RECOVERY AND BUSINESS CONTINUITY

There's a lot of confusion over exactly how disaster recovery and business continuity relate to each other. We have good news and bad news: The good news is that it's a simple relationship. The bad news is, "It depends."

Both types of plans are ultimately aimed at the goal of repairing the damage caused by extended outages. The biggest difference is the scope; many business-continuity plans focus very little on technology and look instead at overall business processes. In contrast, disaster-recovery plans of necessity have to be concerned with the finer details of IT administration. The reality is that both levels of focus are often needed—and must be handled in parallel, with coordination, and in support of any additional ongoing crisis management.

We'll try to clarify the difference by providing an example. Acme Inc. is a national manufacturer and supplier of various goods, mainly to wholesale distributors but with a small and thriving mail-order retail department for the occasional customer who needs quality Acme products but has no convenient retail outlet in their locale. Acme's main call center has a small number of permanent staff but a large number of contract call center operators.

Unfortunately, Acme's main order fulfillment center—for both bulk wholesale orders, as well as the relatively small amount of mail-order traffic—gets hit by a large fragment in a meteor shower, causing a fire that rapidly transforms the entire site into smoking rubble even as all personnel are safely evacuated. The call center and supporting datacenter are completely destroyed and, conservatively, will take several months to fully rebuild. Obviously, Acme is going to suffer some sort of setback, but with proper planning they can minimize the effects. What types of actions would Acme's BC and DR plans each be taking?

> **Acme's Business Continuity Plan**   Acme is concerned with getting the minimum level of operational function back online as quickly as possible. In this case, it's going to take a while before they can resume call center operations. Their immediate needs are to establish at least some level of messaging support for the temporary call center workers the BC plan brings in. Their BC plan does not assume that they will have in-house capability, so it makes provisions—if required—to use hosted Exchange Server services as a short-term stopgap so that communications with customers and wholesalers will proceed until Acme's IT staff can bring up sufficient Exchange servers to switch back to on-premises services.

Acme's Data Recovery Plan   Acme is concerned with rebuilding critical structures. In addition to restoring critical network infrastructure services, Acme's Exchange Server administrators are tasked with first rebuilding sufficient Exchange servers in their DR location to recover the mailbox databases for the call center's permanent staff. They also need to then create sufficient Exchange servers to allow the recovery of operator mailbox databases to extract message data pertaining to currently open cases that need investigation. Once the datacenter is rebuilt, they can build the rest of the Exchange servers and restore operations from the DR site.

Location, Location, Location

One factor tends to consistently blur the line between regular backups, disaster recovery, business continuity, and even high availability: where your solution is located. We have talked to many administrators who have the false assumption that once a recovery activity moves off-site, that automatically makes it disaster recovery (or business continuity, or high availability). This is an understandable misconception—but it's still not true.

In reality, the question of "where" is immaterial. If you're taking steps to protect your data, it's backup and recovery. If you're taking steps to rebuild services, it's disaster recovery. If you're taking steps to ensure you can still do business, it's business continuity. This is obviously an oversimplification, but it'll do for now unless we start looking at all the ways the lines can blur. However, we do want to touch on one of those complications now: where you deploy your recovery operations. There are three overall approaches: on-premises, off-premises, or a combination of the two.

ON-PREMISES RECOVERY SOLUTIONS

Most of what we do as Exchange Server administrators, especially in backup and restore work, is *on-premises*. In an on-premises solution, you have one or more sites where your Exchange servers are deployed, and those same sites host the backup and disaster-recovery operations. Note that this definition of "on-premises" differs somewhat from traditional disaster-recovery terminology, which talks about *dedicated disaster-recovery sites*. These sites are still part of your premises and so are still "on-premises" for our purpose.

Many organizations can handle all their operations in this fashion through the use of Exchange Server, storage and networking devices, and third-party applications. Some, however, can use additional help. When you need on-premises help in the Exchange Server world, there are two broad categories:

Appliances   Appliances are self-contained boxes or servers, usually a sealed combination of hardware and software, placed into the network. They are designed to interface with or become part of the Exchange Server organization and provide additional abilities. Appliances are useful for smaller organizations that want sophisticated options for disaster recovery but don't have the budget or skill level to provide their own. Appliances can be used to provide services such as cross-site data replication, site monitoring, or even additional services aimed at other types of functionality.

On the upside, appliances are typically easy to install. On the downside, they can quickly become a single point of failure. The temptation to place an appliance and treat it as a "fire-and-forget" solution is high. In reality, most appliances need to be tested, monitored, and upgraded on a regular basis.

Remote Managed Services   Remote managed services (or remote management) are service offerings. Instead of buying a sealed black box, the customer purchases a period of service from a vendor. The service provider provides design, deployment, and ongoing maintenance services as part of the offering for the customer—sometimes as a package, sometimes as a set of à la carte offerings. Like appliances, these offerings can extend beyond traditional disaster-recovery offerings.

These types of service providers are able to provide trained Exchange Server expertise on a scale that is typically available only to very large organizations. They can do this through economies of scale; by using these highly trained personnel to monitor, maintain, and troubleshoot many disparate customer organizations of all sizes and types, they can both afford this type of staff and offer them the kind of challenges necessary to retain them.

Some solutions exist that combine these two approaches; customers purchase both an appliance, as well as a managed service offering.

Off-Premises Recovery Solutions

Some problems are easier to solve—or more efficient to solve—if you let someone else deal with them. In the Exchange Server world, this translates to *hosted services*—services or offerings provided by a third party. Hosted services may provide a large variety of functionality to an Exchange Server organization, ranging from backup, disaster recovery, and business continuity to such services as message hygiene, archival, and compliance and governance.

There's a close similarity between hosted services and remote managed services. Both are provided by an external service model. They can both offer a combination of features, performance, and convenience that makes them attractive to small- and medium-sized organizations. The difference is that with hosted services, messaging traffic is targeted—whether externally or internally—to the hosting provider, which then performs specific actions. Depending on the specific service, traffic may then be rerouted back to the organization or it may continue to reside at the hosting provider.

Most hosted services charge on a per-user or per-mailbox basis. Because of this, they were often originally favored by smaller organizations or for specific portions of a larger enterprise. However, today's costs for hosted services are so low that even very large organizations have deployed hosted services. Hosted services can also require a large amount of bandwidth, depending on the overall amount of traffic between your organization and the service. This can drive the costs higher than just the up-front per-user price.

One of the main differences between hosted services and remote managed services is that a hosted service provider usually (but not always) has an internal Exchange Server deployment that is designed to host multiple tenants. For many years, the retail version of Exchange Server was designed around the assumption that each deployment would be used for a single organization or corporate entity.

Beginning with Exchange Server 2000, Microsoft began adding enhancements to Exchange Server to provide better support for multi-tenant deployments. However, it was not until after the release of Exchange Server 2007 and Microsoft's own initial multi-tenant offering (BPOS – Business Productivity Online Suite) that Microsoft began to invest significant resources into improving the Exchange Server story around multi-tenant support. These improvements continued with Exchange Server 2013 and have further continued with Exchange Server 2016.

With Office 365, Microsoft is hosting millions of mailboxes based on Exchange Server 2013 and Exchange Server 2016. Exchange Server 2016 can be run on-premises, in the cloud, or in a hybrid configuration of the two. In each case, the available functionality is almost identical irrespective of where the mailboxes are located (on-premises or in the cloud).

So now that we've talked quite a bit about backup and recovery, there is another concept to talk about. This new concept, called Exchange Native Data Protection, is new since Exchange 2013. Native Data Protection is an Exchange deployment that is configured to use all of the built-in Exchange Server features to minimize or eliminate traditional backups. The following features help deliver Native Data Protection:

◆ **Multiple datacenters to house Exchange servers.** You need to have a minimum of two datacenters to house Exchange servers, but more can be helpful, too. From a pure Native Data Protection standpoint, three datacenters is optimum.

◆ **Unbound namespace.** The namespace for your environment dictates which domains and fully qualified domains are used to connect to Exchange services. A bound namespace is a namespace that is designed to have specific users operate out of specific datacenters. An unbound namespace is a namespace that is designed to be site agnostic, enabling users to use any datacenter. The unbound namespace presents a simplified configuration, but it may not be feasible in every organization.

◆ **Multiple copies of each database.** You should opt for a minimum of three copies of each database. In doing so, you can potentially eliminate database backups. However, there are still risks to your databases, namely logical corruption, which can replicate to each copy of your database. Luckily, it doesn't happen often in most organizations, and Exchange has a mitigating feature, a lagged database copy, which we discuss next.

◆ **Lagged copy of each database.** A lagged database copy is a copy of a database that is a specific amount of time behind the source database. For example, you might have a primary database named DB01. It replicates to a lagged database. But the lagged database is eight hours behind. All of the changes in the past eight hours are in transaction logs and not played into the database yet. If logical corruption occurs and replicates, you have eight hours to catch it and stop it from playing into the lagged copy.

◆ **Email data recovery.** This concerns deleted item retention and single item recovery. This enables you and/or users to recover email data without the use of traditional backups.

The Native Data Protection route is enhanced by having highly available components in your infrastructure. This includes power, cooling, Internet connectivity, routers, switches, firewalls, load balancers, and storage. While Native Data Protection is a good thing, it often isn't realistic for most organizations for a variety of reasons such as cost and complexity. Some organizations choose to go with Native Data Protection and traditional backups, with the idea being that Native Data Protection provides everything that is needed and backups are there as a secondary approach (and, hopefully, they are never required).

Management Frameworks

There's a lot of great guidance out there (including fine books such as this one) on the technical aspects of designing, installing, configuring, and operating Exchange servers and organizations. There's a lot less material that provides a coherent look at the issues of the entire life cycle of IT management in general, let alone Windows or Exchange Server deployments in particular.

There may be, however, more than you think: every organization of every size struggles with common nontechnical issues and needs a good defined framework for managing IT resources. Having this type of framework in place makes it easier to properly plan for disaster recovery and business continuity concerns, as well as other common management tasks. Think of management frameworks as having all employees working in the same way, using the same processes. For example, every deployment of Exchange server would have a methodology behind it, facilitating the planning, preparation, design, deployment, and support. Documentation is a big part of most frameworks. As you can see, with a management framework in place, your company is better situated to deal with a disaster-recovery situation.

There are several frameworks you may want to examine, or with which you are already familiar in some fashion:

◆ The *Information Technology Infrastructure Library (ITIL)* is the 900-pound gorilla of the IT management framework world. ITIL provides a generic set of tools for IT professionals to use as template concepts and policies when developing their own management processes of their IT infrastructure and operations.

◆ Microsoft has developed the *Microsoft Operations Framework (MOF)*, a detailed framework based on the concepts and principles of ITIL. MOF takes the generic framework offered by ITIL and provides greater detail optimized for Windows and other Microsoft technologies.

◆ Like Microsoft, IBM offers its own ITIL-centric framework: the *IBM Tivoli Unified Process (ITUP)*. ITUP provides guidance on taking generic ITIL concepts and processes and linking them into real-world processes and tasks that map to real IT objectives.

◆ The *Control Objectives for Information and Related Technologies (COBIT)* best practices framework was initially created as a way to help organizations develop IT governance processes and models. While COBIT is typically thought of as optimized for IT audits, it offers supplemental practices suitable for IT management.

So how necessary are management frameworks in real deployments? Why are we wasting valuable space talking about ITIL and MOF when we could be cramming in a couple more nuggets of yummy Exchange Server 2016 technical goodness? The answer is simple: we can't include everything. No matter how thorough (and long) the book, there will always be more technical details that we can't include. Instead, we wanted to include at least an introduction to some of the nontechnical areas that can give you an advantage.

While a deep dive into any of these alternatives is out of scope for this book, we do want to take a short peek at two of them: first ITIL and then MOF. Although you don't have to know anything about these subjects to be a low-level Exchange Server administrator (but you should!), Microsoft has begun introducing exposure to these concepts into the training for their high-level Exchange Server certifications.

ITIL

The best way to learn about ITIL is to go through one of the training and certification events. Outside such classes, ITIL is in essence a collection of best practices in the discipline of IT service management. IT service management is just what it sounds like: effective and consistent management of IT services. IT management is in many respects nonintuitive and offers several specific challenges that are not common to many other management disciplines; most people need specific training to learn how to manage IT in the most effective way. ITIL represents the most accepted IT management approach in the world.

ITIL was developed by the UK Central Computer and Telecommunications Agency in an attempt to develop a centralized management standard for IT throughout the various British government agencies. This effort was not successful—in part due to the change from mainframe-based computing to personal computers and networks and the resulting lowering of barriers to server acquisition and deployment. However, it did allow the formation of existing best practices and thoughts on IT service management into a single collection of best practices and procedures, supported by tasks and checklists IT professionals can use as a starting point for developing their own IT governance structures. ITIL is supported and offered by a wide variety of entities, including many large enterprises and consulting firms, with training and certification available for IT professionals.

ITIL has been through several iterations. The most current version, ITIL 2011, became available in July 2011 and consists of five core texts:

Service Strategy   Demonstrates how to use the service management discipline and develop it as both a set of capabilities and a large-scale business asset

Service Design   Demonstrates how to take your objectives and develop them into services and assets through the creation of appropriate processes

Service Transition   Demonstrates how to take the services and assets previously created and transition them into production in your organization

Service Operation   Demonstrates the processes and techniques required to manage the various services and assets previously created and deployed

Continual Service Improvement   Demonstrates the ongoing process of improving on the services and assets

For more information on ITIL, see its official website at https://www.axelos.com/best-practice-solutions/itil. For a great improvement over the official ITIL texts, see *ITIL Foundation Exam Study Guide* (Sybex, 2012).

MOF

Microsoft has worked with ITIL for more than 10 years, beginning in 1999. As ITIL has developed and grown in popularity, Microsoft has seen that its customers needed more specific guidance for using the principles and concepts of ITIL in the context of Microsoft technologies and applications. As a result, they created the Microsoft Operations Framework, which they describe in the following manner:

> *The Microsoft strategy for IT service management is to provide guidance and software solutions that enable organizations to achieve mission-critical system reliability, availability, supportability, and manageability of the Microsoft platform. The strategy includes a model for organizations and IT pros to assess their current IT infrastructure maturity, prioritize processes of greatest concern, and apply proven principles and best practices to optimize performance on the Microsoft platform.*

MOF is not a replacement for ITIL; it is one specific implementation of ITIL, optimized for environments that use Microsoft products. It's specifically designed to help IT professionals align business goals with IT goals and develop cohesive, unified processes that allow the creation and management of IT services throughout all portions of the IT life cycle. It is currently on version 4.0, which aligns with ITIL v3.

MOF defines four stages of the IT service management life cycle:

Plan   Plan is the first stage of the cycle: new IT services are identified and created, or necessary changes are identified in existing IT services that are already in place.

Deliver   Deliver is the second stage: the new service is implemented for use in production.

Operate   Operate is the final stage of the cycle: the service is deployed and monitored. It feeds back into the Plan stage in order to affect incremental changes as necessary.

Manage   Manage is not a separate stage; instead, it is an ongoing set of processes that take place at all times throughout the cycle to measure and monitor the effectiveness of your efforts. This is illustrated in Figure 3.1.

FIGURE 3.1
The four stages of the Microsoft IT service management life cycle

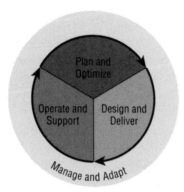

For more information on MOF, see the following web page:

`https://technet.microsoft.com/en-us/library/dd320379.aspx`

WHAT ARE YOU MEASURING?

Let's demonstrate the practical value of some of this "management framework" mumbo jumbo by tackling a hot topic: availability and uptime. We've heard a lot of executives talk about "five nines of availability"—but what, exactly, does that mean? You can't have a meaningful discussion about availability without knowing exactly what kind of availability you're talking about (which we'll get to later in this chapter), and without knowing that, you can't measure it, let alone to the ludicrous degree of detail that five nines represents.

Now let's discuss uptime. Uptime has a pretty well-defined meaning; you just need to know what scope it applies to. Are you talking server uptime, mailbox uptime, or service uptime? Once you have that defined, you can take measurements and apply numbers for quantitative comparisons.

ITIL and MOF give you not only the conceptual framework for agreeing on what you're measuring but also guidance on how to put the process of measurement into place. That kind of discipline can give you a lot of long-term advantages and help keep your Exchange Server deployment better managed than you could do on your own. The thing to remember is that these frameworks are starting points; they're not cast in stone, and they're not laws you must rigidly obey. If you find some aspect that doesn't work for your organization, you should first make sure you understand what the purpose of that feature is and how it's intended to work. Once you're sure that it doesn't apply as is, feel free to make documented changes to bring it into alignment with your needs.

A Closer Look at Availability

We've already talked about disaster recovery and how it can be confused with general data protection (backup and recovery) and business continuity. Perhaps an even more common confusion, though, is the distinction between high availability and disaster recovery. This is a common enough error that we felt it was worth devoting a separate section of this chapter.

High availability (HA) is a design strategy. The strategy is simple: try to ensure that users keep access to services, such as their Exchange Server mailboxes or Unified Messaging servers, during periods of outage or downtime. These outages could be the result of any sort of event:

◆ Hardware failure, such as the loss of a power supply, a memory module, or the server motherboard

◆ Storage failure, such as the loss of a disk, disk controller, or data-level corruption

◆ Network failure, such as the cutting of a network cable or a router or a switch losing configuration

◆ Some other service failure, such as the loss of an Active Directory domain controller or a DNS server

HA technologies and strategies are designed to allow a given service to continue to be available to users (or other services) in the event of these kind of failures. No matter which technology is involved, there are two main approaches, one or both of which are used by each HA technology and strategy:

Fault Tolerance and Redundancy   This involves placing resources into a pool so that one can take up the load when another member of the pool fails. This strategy removes the presence of a single point of failure. Fault tolerance needs to be accompanied by some mechanism for selecting which of the redundant resources is to be used. These mechanisms are either *round-robin* or *load balancing*. In the former, each resource in the pool is used in turn, regardless of the current state or load. In the latter, additional mechanisms are used to direct users to the least loaded member of the resource pool. Many higher-end hardware systems use redundant parts to make the overall server system more redundant to many common types of hardware failures.

Replication   This process involves making copies of critical data between multiple members of a resource pool. If replication happens quickly enough and with a small enough time interval, when one member of the resource pool becomes unavailable, another member can take over the load. Most replication strategies, including Exchange Server's database replication features, are based on a *single master* strategy, where all updates happen to the master (or active) copy and are replicated to the additional copies. Some technologies such as Active

Directory are designed to allow *multimaster replication*, where updates can be directed to the closest member. Exchange Server 2016 can use database availability groups (DAGs) to replicate copies of data from one Mailbox server to another and to provide failover in the event the database where the mailbox resides fails.

MEASURING AVAILABILITY

It is not uncommon to find that availability of a system is measured differently depending on the organization. Typically, to report the percentage of availability, you take the amount of time during a measurement period and then subtract the total downtime during that period. Finally, you divide that number by the total elapsed time.

So, let's say that during a 30-day period of time, there was no *scheduled* downtime, but there was a 4-hour period of time when patches were applied to the system. So, 30 days – .17 days = 29.8 days of total uptime, and 29.8/30 = 99.3 percent availability.

This is just a sample calculation, of course. In the real world, you may have a maintenance window during your operations that would not count against your availability numbers. You want to do your very best to minimize the amount of unplanned downtime, but you also have to take in to consideration scheduled maintenance and planned downtime.

In some organizations, no downtime, planned or unplanned, is acceptable. You must design your systems accordingly.

SERVICE AVAILABILITY

When we have discussions with people about high availability in Exchange Server organizations, we find that the level of high availability that most of them are actually thinking about is *service availability*. That is, they think of the Exchange Server deployment as an overall service and think of how to ensure that users can get access to everything (either that or they think solely of hardware clusters, storage replication, and the other low-end technologies). It is important to note that when discussing service availability, this term may mean different things to different people.

Service availability is an important consideration for the overall availability strategy. It doesn't make a lot of sense to plan for redundant server hardware if you forget to deploy sufficient numbers of those servers with the right Exchange Server roles in the appropriate locations. (We'll discuss the proper ratios and recommendations for role and server placement in Chapter 8, "Understanding Server Roles and Configurations.") To ensure true service availability, you need to consider all the other levels of availability.

The other aspect of service availability is to think about what other services Exchange Server is dependent on:

◆ The obvious dependency is Active Directory. Each Exchange server requires access to a domain controller, as well as global catalog servers. The more Exchange servers in the site, the more of each Active Directory role that the site requires. If your domain controllers are also DNS servers, you need enough DNS servers to survive the loss of one or two. If you lose all DNS servers or all domain controllers in an Active Directory site, Exchange Server will fail.

♦ What type of network services do you need? Do you assign static IP addresses and default gateways or do you use DHCP and dynamic routing? Do you have extra router or switching capacity? What about your firewall configurations—do you have only a single firewall between different network zones or are those redundant as well?

♦ What other applications do you deploy as part of your Exchange Server deployment? Do you rely on a monitoring system such as Microsoft System Center Operations Manager? What will occur if something happens to your monitoring server; is there a redundant or backup system that takes over, or will additional faults and failures go unnoticed and be allowed to impact the Exchange Server system? Do you have enough backup agents and servers to protect your Mailbox servers?

Service availability typically requires a combination of redundancy and replication strategies. For example, you deploy multiple Active Directory domain controllers in a site for redundancy, but they replicate the directory data between each other.

Network Availability

The next area we want to talk about is network availability. By this, we don't mean the types of network services we mentioned in the previous section. Instead, what we mean is the ability to ensure that you can receive new connection requests from clients and other servers, regardless of whether your organization uses Exchange servers, PBX systems and telephony gateways, or external mail servers. Network availability is a key part of Exchange Server infrastructure and must be considered as a part of your overall service availability.

The typical strategy for network availability is load balancing. This is network-level redundancy. Simple network load balancers use a round-robin mechanism to alternate and evenly (on the basis of numbers) distribute incoming connections to the members of the resource pool. Other solutions use more sophisticated mechanisms, such as monitoring each member of the pool for overall load and assigning incoming connections to the least-loaded member.

For larger organizations and complex Exchange Server deployments, it's common to use hardware load balancers. Hardware systems are typically more expensive and represent yet more systems to manage and maintain, so they add a degree of complexity that is often undesirable to smaller organizations. Smaller organizations often prefer to use software-based load-balancing solutions, such as Windows Network Load Balancing (WNLB).

Unfortunately, WNLB isn't generally suitable for Exchange Server 2016 deployments. This is the official recommendation of both the Exchange Server product group and the Windows product group, the folks who develop the WNLB component. WNLB has a few characteristics that render it unsuitable for use with Exchange Server in any but the smallest of deployments or test environments:

♦ WNLB simply performs round-robin balancing of incoming connections. It doesn't detect whether members of the load-balance cluster are down, so it will keep sending connections to the downed member. This could result in intermittent and confusing behavior for clients and loss or delay of messages from external systems. If you must deploy WNLB, also consider deploying scripts that can monitor application health and updated WNLB accordingly, as demonstrated here:

http://msdn.microsoft.com/en-us/library/windows/desktop/cc307934.aspx

◆   WNLB is incompatible with the Windows Failover Clustering. This means that small shops can't deploy a pair of servers with the Mailbox role and then use WNLB to load balance client access or use continuous replication to replicate the mailbox databases.

Even when using hardware network load balancing, there are several things to remember and best practices to follow. (For more information on load balancing, DNS, and WNLB, see Chapter 21, "Understanding the Client Access Server.")

DATA AVAILABILITY

We've seen many Exchange Server organization designs and deployment plans. Most of them spend a lot of time ensuring that the mailbox data will be available.

In all versions of Exchange Server prior to Exchange Server 2007, having high availability for mailbox databases meant using Windows Failover Clustering (WFC), which was a feature of Windows Enterprise Edition. One of the features provided by WFC is the ability to create groups of servers (clusters) that share storage resources. Within this cluster of servers, one or more instances of Exchange Server would be running and controlling the mailbox databases. If one hardware node were to fail, the active server instance would fail over to another hardware node, and the shared storage resources would move with it.

Failover clustering is a common HA strategy, and WFC is a proven technology. This turned out to be a good strategy for many Exchange Server organizations. However, failover clustering has some cons. For clusters that rely on a shared quorum, the biggest is the reliance on shared storage—typically, a storage area network. Shared storage increases the cost and complexity of the clustering solution, but it doesn't guard against the most common cause of Exchange Server outage: disk failure or corruption.

Exchange Server 2007 introduced a data-availability solution called *continuous replication* to help overcome some of the weaknesses associated with failover clustering and to allow more organizations to take advantage of highly available deployments. Continuous replication, also known as log shipping, copies the transaction logs corresponding to a mailbox database from one Mailbox server to another. The target then replays the logs into its own separate copy of the database, re-creating the latest changes.

Exchange Server 2010 added more features to continuous replication, including data encryption and compression. With Exchange Server 2016, a Mailbox server can have up to 15 replication partners. You can join servers into a *database availability group*; members of that group can replicate one or more of their mailbox databases with the other servers in the group. Each database can be replicated separately from others and have one or more replicas. A DAG can cross Active Directory site boundaries, thereby providing site resiliency, and activation of a passive copy can be automatic.

We'll go into more detail about DAGs and continuous replication in Exchange Server 2016 in Chapter 20, "Creating and Managing Database Availability Groups."

HA vs. DR: Not the Same

We'll provide a quick comparison between the typical Exchange Server HA deployment and DR deployment. If you think that by having disaster recovery you have availability, or vice versa, think again.

In an HA Exchange Server environment, the focus is usually on keeping mailboxes up and running for users, transferring mail with external systems, and keeping Exchange Server services up. In a DR environment, the focus is usually on restoring *a bare minimum* of services, often for a smaller portion of the overall user population. In short, the difference is that of *abundance* versus *triage*.

For Exchange Server, an HA design can provide several advantages beyond the obvious availability goals. A highly available Exchange Server environment often enables server consolidation; the same technologies that permit mailbox data to be replicated between servers or to keep multiple instances of key Exchange Server services also permit greater user mailbox density or force the upgrading of key infrastructure (like network bandwidth) so that a greater number of users can be handled. This increased density can make proper DR planning more difficult by increasing the requirements for a DR solution and making it harder to identify and target the appropriate user populations.

That's not to say that HA and DR are incompatible. Far from it; you can and should design your Exchange Server 2016 deployment for both. To do that effectively, though, you need to have a clear understanding of what each technology and feature actually provide you, so you can avoid design errors. For example, if you have separate groups of users who will need their mailboxes replicated to a DR site, set them aside in separate mailbox databases, rather than mingling them in with users whose mailboxes won't be replicated.

Storage Availability

Many administrators and IT professionals immediately think of storage designs when they hear the word *availability*. Although storage is a critical part of ensuring the overall service availability of an Exchange Server organization, the impact of storage design is far more than just availability; it directly affects performance, reliability, and scalability.

An Overview of Exchange Storage

In medium-sized and large organizations, the Exchange Server administrator is usually not responsible for storage. Many medium-sized and large organizations use specialized storage area networks that require additional training to master. Storage is a massive topic, but we feel it is important that you at least be able to speak the language of storage and be knowledgeable about storage concepts.

From the very beginning, messaging systems have had a give-and-take relationship with the underlying storage system. Even on systems that aren't designed to offer long-term storage for email (such as ISP systems that offer only POP3 access), email creates demands on storage:

◆   The transport components must have space to queue messages that cannot be immediately transmitted to the remote system.

◆   The delivery component must be able to store incoming messages that have been delivered to a mailbox until users can retrieve them.

◆   The message store, in systems like Exchange Server, permits users to keep a copy of their mailbox data on central servers.

◆   As the server accepts, transmits, and processes email, it keeps logs with varying levels of detail so administrators can troubleshoot and audit activities.

Although you'll have to wait for subsequent chapters to delve into the details of planning storage for Exchange Server, the following sections go over the two broad categories of storage solutions that are used in modern Exchange Server systems: direct attached storage (DAS) and storage area networks (SANs). The third type of storage, network-attached storage (NAS), is generally not supported with Exchange Server 2013 or Exchange Server 2016.

Direct attached storage is the most common type of storage in general. DAS disks are usually internal disks or directly attached via cable. Just about every server, except for some high-end varieties, such as blade systems using boot-over-SAN, uses DAS at some level; typically, at least the boot and operating system volumes are on some DAS configuration. However, in versions of Exchange Server prior to Exchange Server 2010, DAS has drawbacks: it doesn't necessarily scale as well for either capacity or performance. Further, organizations that have invested significant amounts of money in their SANs may still require that Exchange Server use the SAN instead of DAS.

To solve these problems, people looked at NAS devices as one of the potential solutions. These machines—giant file servers—sit on the network and share their disk storage. They range in price and configuration from small plug-in devices with fixed capacity to large installations with more configuration options than most luxury cars (and a price tag to match). Companies that bought these were using them to replace file servers, web server storage, SQL Server storage—why not Exchange Server?

However, the only version of Exchange Server that supported NAS was Exchange Server 2003. Instead of continuing to support NAS, the Exchange Server development team switched to reducing the overall I/O requirements so that DAS configurations become practical for organizations. Exchange Server 2007 moved to a 64-bit architecture to remove memory-management bottlenecks in the 32-bit Windows kernel, allowing the Exchange Information Store to use more memory for intelligent mailbox data caching and reduce disk I/O. Exchange Server 2010 in turn made aggressive changes to the on-disk mailbox database structures, such as moving to a new database schema that allows pages to be sequentially written to the end of the database file rather than randomly throughout the file. The schema updates improve indexing and client performance, allowing common tasks, such as updating folder views to happen more quickly while requiring fewer disk reads and writes. These changes help improve efficiency and continue to drive mailbox I/O down.

Every version of Exchange Server has reduced the I/O requirements for running Exchange Server. Exchange Server 2016 is no exception. Prior to Exchange Server 2016, Exchange Server 2013 made significant changes to the I/O profile presented by Exchange Server. Between Exchange Server 2010 and Exchange Server 2013, Microsoft reduced I/O requirements between 33 percent and 50 percent. From Exchange Server 2003 to Exchange Server 2013, I/O requirements have been reduced by over 90 percent! However, these reductions in I/O requirements now make it practical to reexamine DAS as a solution for Exchange Server storage (and, in fact,

DAS is recommended by Microsoft for Exchange Server 2010 and later versions). If you opt to use DAS for your implementation, consider using four database copies for each database to meet Microsoft's recommendation for maximizing availability and minimizing issues.

The premise behind a SAN is to move disks to dedicated storage units that can handle all the advanced features you need—high-end RAID configurations, hot-swap replacement, on-the-fly reconfiguration, rapid disk snapshots, tight integration with backup and restore solutions, and more. This helps consolidate the overhead of managing storage, often spread out on dozens of servers and applications (and their associated staff), into a single set of personnel. Then, dedicated network links connect these storage silos with the appropriate application servers. Yet this consolidation of storage can also be a serious pitfall because Exchange Server is usually not the only application placed on the SAN. Applications, such as SharePoint, SQL, archiving, and file services may all be sharing the same aggregated set of spindles and cause disk contention, which leads to poor performance.

Direct Attached Storage

As used for legacy Exchange Server storage, DAS historically displays two main problems: performance and capacity. As mailbox databases got larger and traffic levels rose, pretty soon people wanted to look for alternatives; DAS storage under Exchange Server 2000 and Exchange Server 2003 required many disks to meet I/O requirements, because Exchange Server's I/O profile was optimized for the 32-bit memory architecture that Windows provided at the time.

To get more scalability on logical disks that support Exchange Server databases, you can always try adding more disks to the server. This gives you a configuration known as Just a Bunch of Disks (JBOD).

Although JBOD can usually give you the raw disk storage capacity you need, it has three flaws that render it unsuitable for all but the smallest of legacy Exchange Server deployments:

JBOD Forces You to Partition Your Data   Because each disk has a finite capacity, you can't store data on that disk if it is larger than the capacity. For example, if you have four 250 GB drives, even though you have approximately 1 TB of storage in total, you have to break that up into separate 250 GB partitions. Historically, this has caused some interesting design decisions in messaging systems that rely on filesystem-based storage.

JBOD Offers No Performance Benefits   In many JBOD implementations, each disk is responsible for only one chunk of storage, so if that disk is already in use, subsequent I/O requests will have to wait for it to free up before they can go through. A single disk can thus become a bottleneck for the system, which can slow down mail for all your users (not just those whose mailboxes are stored on the affected disk).

JBOD Offers No Redundancy   If one of your disks dies, you're out of luck unless you can restore that data from backup. True, you haven't lost all your data, but the one-quarter of your users who have just lost their email are not likely to be comforted by that observation.

Several of the Exchange Server 2010 design goals focused on building in the necessary features to work around these issues and make a DAS JBOD deployment a realistic option for more organizations. Exchange Server 2016 design goals included continuing to reduce the total I/O requirement necessary for Exchange Server, making DAS even more realistic for many organizations. In fact, Office 365 runs off DAS!

However, legacy versions of Exchange Server contain no mechanisms to work around these issues. Luckily, some bright people came up with a great generic answer to JBOD that also works well for legacy Exchange Server: the Redundant Array of Inexpensive Disks (RAID).

The basic premise behind RAID is to group the JBOD disks together in various configurations with a dedicated disk controller to handle the specific disk operations, allowing the computer (and applications) to see the entire collection of drives and controller as one very large disk device. These collections of disks are known as arrays; the arrays are presented to the operating system, partitioned, and formatted as if they were just regular disks. The common types of RAID configurations are shown in Table 3.1.

TABLE 3.1: RAID Configurations

RAID LEVEL	NAME	DESCRIPTION
None	Concatenated drives	Two or more disks are joined together in a contiguous data space. As one disk in the array is filled up, the data is carried over to the next disk. Though this solves the capacity problem and is easy to implement, it offers no performance or redundancy whatsoever and makes it more likely that you're going to lose all your data, not less, through a single disk failure. These arrays are not suitable for use with legacy Exchange servers.
RAID 0	Striped drives	Two or more disks have data split among them evenly. If you write a 1 MB file to a two-disk RAID 0 array, half the data will be on one disk, half on the other. Each disk in the array can be written to (or read from) simultaneously, giving you a noticeable performance boost. However, if you lose one disk in the array, you lose all your data. These arrays are typically used for fast, large, temporary files, such as those in video editing. These arrays are not suitable for use with Exchange Server; while they give excellent performance, the risk of data loss is typically unacceptable.
RAID 1	Mirrored drives	Typically done with two disks (although some vendors allow more), each disk receives a copy of all the data in the array. If you lose one disk, you still have a copy of your data on the remaining disk; you can either move the data or plug in a replacement disk and rebuild the mirror. RAID 1 also gives a performance benefit; reads can be performed by either disk, because only writes need to be mirrored. However, RAID 1 can be one of the more costly configurations; to store 500 GB of data, you'd need to buy two 500 GB drives. These arrays are suitable for use with legacy Exchange Server volumes, depending on the type of data and the performance of the array. RAID 1 is fairly common for the operating system disk.

TABLE 3.1:   RAID Configurations *(CONTINUED)*

RAID LEVEL	NAME	DESCRIPTION
RAID 5	Parity drive	Three or more disks have data split among them. However, one disk's worth of capacity is reserved for parity checksum data; this is a special calculated value that allows the RAID system to rebuild the missing data if one drive in the array fails. The parity data is spread across all the disks in the array. If you had a four-disk 250 GB RAID 5 array, you'd have only 750 GB of usable space. RAID 5 arrays offer better performance than JBOD but worse performance than other RAID configurations, especially on the write requests; the checksum must be calculated and the data plus parity written to all the disks in the array. Also, if you lose one disk, the array goes into degraded mode, which means that even read operations will need to be recalculated and will be slower than normal. These arrays are suitable for use with legacy Exchange Server mailbox database volumes on smaller servers, depending on the type of data and the performance of the array. Due to their write performance characteristics, they are usually not well matched for transaction log volumes.
RAID 6	Double parity drive	This RAID variant is designed to provide RAID 5 arrays with the ability to survive the loss of two disks. Other than offering two-disk resiliency, base RAID 6 implementations offer mostly the same benefits and drawbacks as RAID 5. Some vendors have built custom implementations that attempt to solve the performance issues. These arrays are suitable for use with Exchange Server, depending on the type of data and the performance of the array.
RAID 10 RAID 0+1 RAID 1+0	Mirroring plus striping	A RAID 10 array is the most costly variant to implement because it uses mirroring. However, it also uses striping to aggregate spindles and deliver blistering performance, which makes it a great choice for high-end arrays that have to sustain a high level of I/O. As a side bonus, it also increases your chances of surviving the loss of multiple disks in the array. There are two basic variants. RAID 0+1 takes two big stripe arrays and mirrors them together; RAID 1+0 takes multiple mirror pairs and stripes them together. Both variants have essentially the same performance numbers, but 1+0 is preferred because it can be rebuilt more quickly (you only have to regenerate a single disk) and has far higher chances of surviving the loss of multiple disks (you can lose one disk in each mirror pair). These arrays have traditionally been used for high-end highly loaded legacy Exchange Server mailbox database volumes.

Note that several of these types of RAID arrays may be suitable for your Exchange server. Which one, if any, should you use? The answer to that question depends entirely on how many mailboxes your servers are holding, how they're used, and other types of business needs. Beware of anyone who tries to give hard-and-fast answers such as "Always use RAID 5 for Exchange Server database volumes." To determine the true answer, you need to go through a proper storage-sizing process, find out what your I/O and capacity requirements are really going to be, think about your data recovery needs and service-level agreements (SLAs), and then decide what storage configuration will meet those needs for you in a fashion you can afford. There are no magic bullets. Take a look at the Exchange Server Role Requirements Calculator, which provides good value for sizing for your Exchange environment, including storage. See `https://gallery.technet.microsoft.com/office/Exchange-2013-Server-Role-f8a61780` for more information.

In every case, the RAID controller you use—the piece of hardware, plus drivers, that aggregates the individual disk volumes for you into a single pseudo-device that is presented to Windows—plays a key role. You can't just take a collection of disks, toss them into slots in your server, and go to town with RAID. You need to install extra drivers and management software, you need to take extra steps to configure your arrays before you can even use them in Windows, and you may even need to update your disaster-recovery procedures to ensure that you can always recover data from drives in a RAID array. Generally, you'll need to test whether you can move drives in one array between two controllers, even those from the same manufacturer; not all controllers support all options. *After* your server has melted down and your SLA is fast approaching is not a good time to find out that you needed to have a spare controller on hand.

If you choose the DAS route (whether JBOD or RAID), you'll need to think about how you're going to house the physical disks. Modern server cases don't leave a lot of extra room for disks; this is especially true of rack-mounted systems. Usually, this means you'll need some sort of external enclosure that hooks back into a physical bus on your server, such as SAS or eSATA disks. Make sure to give these enclosures suitable power and cooling; hard drives pull a lot of power and return it all eventually as heat.

Also make sure that your drive backplanes (the physical connection points) and enclosures support hot-swap capability, where you can easily pull the drive and replace it without powering the system down. Keep a couple of spare drives and drive sleds on hand, too. Many enclosures support *hot spares,* which are disks that are installed in the enclosure but are not active until another drive fails. You don't want to have to schedule an outage of your Exchange server in order to replace a failed drive in a RAID 5 array, letting all your users enjoy the performance hit of a thrashing RAID volume because the array is in degraded mode until the replacement drives arrive.

RAID CONTROLLERS ARE NOT ALL CREATED EQUAL

Beware! Not all kinds of RAID are created equal. Before you spend a lot of time trying to figure out which configuration to choose, first think about your RAID controller. There are three kinds of them, and unlike RAID configurations, it's pretty easy to determine which kind you need for Exchange Server:

Software RAID   Software RAID avoids the whole problem of having a RAID controller by performing all the magic in the operating system software. If you convert your disk to dynamic volumes, you can do RAID 0, RAID 1, and RAID 5 (known as Simple, Mirror, or Parity storage layouts) natively in Windows Server 2012 R2 without any extra hardware. However, Microsoft strongly recommends that you not do this with Exchange Server, and the Exchange Server community echoes that recommendation. It takes extra memory and processing power, and it inevitably slows your disks down from what you could get with a simple investment in good hardware. You will also not be able to support higher levels of I/O load with this configuration, in our experience.

BIOS RAID   BIOS RAID attempts to provide "cheap" RAID by putting some code for RAID in the RAID chipset, which is then placed either directly on the motherboard (common in workstation-grade and low-end server configurations) or on an inexpensive add-in card. The dirty little secret is that the RAID chipset isn't really doing the RAID operations in hardware; again it's all happening in software, this time in the associated Windows driver (which is written by the vendor) rather than an official Windows subsystem. If you're about to purchase a RAID controller card for a price that seems too good to be true, it's probably one of these cards. These RAID controllers tend to have fewer ports, which limits their overall utility. Although you can get Exchange Server to work with them, you can do so only with a very low number of users. Otherwise, you'll quickly hit the limits these cards have and stress your storage system. Just avoid them; the time you save will more than make up for the up-front price savings.

Hardware RAID   This is the only kind of RAID you should even be thinking about for your Exchange servers. This means good-quality, high-end cards that come from reputable manufacturers that have taken the time to get the product on the Windows Hardware Compatibility List (HCL). These cards do a lot of the work for your system, removing the CPU overhead of parity calculations from the main processors, and they are worth every penny you pay for them. Better yet, they'll be able to handle the load your Exchange servers and users throw at them.

If you can't tell whether a given controller you're eyeing is BIOS or true hardware RAID, get help. Lots of forums and websites on the Internet will help you sort out which hardware to get and which to avoid. While you're at it, spring a few extra bucks for good, reliable disks. We cannot stress enough the importance of not cutting corners on your Exchange Server storage system; although Exchange Server 2016 gives you a lot more room for designing storage and brings back options you may not have had before, you still need to buy the best components that you can to make up the designed storage system. The time and long-term costs you save will be your own.

Storage Area Networks

Initial SAN solutions used fiber-optic connections to provide the necessary bandwidth for storage operations. As a result, these systems were incredibly expensive and were used only by organizations with deep pockets. The advent of Gigabit Ethernet over copper and new storage bus technologies, such as SATA and SAS, has moved the cost of SANs down into the realm where midsized companies can now afford both the sticker price and the resource training to become competent with these new technologies.

Over time, many vendors have begun to offer SAN solutions that are affordable even for small companies. The main reason they've been able to do so is the iSCSI protocol: block-based file access routed over TCP/IP connections. Add iSCSI with ubiquitous Gigabit Ethernet hardware, and SAN deployments have become a lot more common.

Clustering and high-availability concerns are the other factors in the growth of Exchange Server/SAN deployments. Exchange Server 2003 supported clustered configurations but required the cluster nodes to have a shared storage solution. As a result, any organization that wanted to deploy an Exchange Server cluster needed some sort of SAN solution (apart from the handful of people who stuck with shared SCSI configurations). A SAN has a certain elegance to it; you simply create a virtual slice of drive space for Exchange Server (called a LUN, or logical unit number), use Fibre Channel or iSCSI (and corresponding drivers) to present it to the Exchange server, and away you go. Even with Exchange Server 2007—which was reengineered with an eye toward making DAS a supportable choice for Exchange Server storage in specific CCR and SCR configurations—many organizations still found that using a SAN for Exchange Server storage was the best answer for their various business requirements. By this time, management had seen the benefits of centralized storage management and wanted to ensure that Exchange Server deployments were part of the big plan.

However, SAN solutions don't fix all problems, even with (usually because of) their price tag. Often, SANs make your environment even more complex and difficult to support. Because SANs cost so much, there is often a strong drive to use the SAN for all storage and make full use of every last free block of space. The cost per gigabyte of storage for a SAN can be between 3 and 10 times as expensive as DAS disks. Unfortunately, Exchange Server's I/O characteristics are very different than those of just about any other application, and few dedicated SAN administrators really know how to properly allocate disk space for Exchange Server:

◆ SAN administrators do not usually understand that total disk space is only one component of Exchange Server performance. For day-to-day operations, it is far more important to ensure enough performance. Traditionally, this is delivered by using lots of physical disks (commonly referred to as "spindles") to increase the amount of simultaneous read/write operations supported. It is important to make sure the SAN solution provides enough performance, not just free disk space, or Exchange Server will crawl.

◆ Even if you can convince them to configure LUNs spread across enough disks, SAN administrators immediately want to reclaim that wasted space. As a result, you end up sharing the same spindles between Exchange Server and some other application with its own performance curve, and then suddenly you have extremely noticeable but hard-to-diagnose performance issues with your Exchange servers. Shared spindles will crater Exchange Server performance.

◆ Although some SAN vendors have put a lot of time and effort into understanding Exchange Server and its I/O needs so that their salespeople and certified consultants can help you deploy Exchange Server on their products properly, not everyone does the same. Many vendors will shrug off performance concerns by telling you about their extensive write caching and how good write caching will smooth out any performance issues. Their argument is true—up to a point. A cache can help isolate Exchange Server from the effects of transient I/O events, but it won't help you come Monday morning when all your users are logging in and the SQL Server databases that share your spindles are churning through extra operations.

The moral of the story is simple: don't believe that you need to have a SAN. This is especially true with Exchange Server 2016; there have been a lot of under-the-hood changes to the mailbox database storage to ensure that more companies can deploy a 7200 RPM SATA JBOD configuration and be able to get good performance and reliability from that system, especially when you are using database availability groups and multiple copies of your data.

If you do find that a SAN provides the best value for your organization, get the best one you can afford. Make sure that your vendors know Exchange Server storage inside and out; if possible, get them to put you in contact with their on-staff Exchange Server specialists. Have them work with your SAN administrators to come up with a storage configuration that meets your real Exchange Server needs.

We'll go into more details about Exchange Server storage in Chapter 19, "Creating and Managing Mailbox Databases."

Compliance and Governance

Quite simply, today's legal system considers email to be an official form of business communication just like written memos. This means that any type of legal requirement or legal action against your organization (regarding business records) will undoubtedly include email. Unless you work in a specific vertical market, such as healthcare or finance, the emergence of compliance and governance as topics of import to the messaging administrator is a relatively recent event. The difference between compliance and governance can be summarized simply:

> *Governance is the process of defining and enforcing policies, while compliance is the process of ensuring that you meet external requirements.*

However, both of these goals share a lot of common ground:

◆ They require thorough planning to implement, based on a detailed understanding of what behaviors are allowed, required, or forbidden.

◆ Though they require technical controls to ensure implementation, they are at heart about people and processes.

◆ They require effective monitoring in order to audit the effectiveness of the compliance and governance measures.

In short, they require all the same things you need in order to effectively manage your messaging data. As a result, there's a useful framework you can use to evaluate your compliance and governance needs: Discovery, Compliance, Archival, and Retention, also known as the DCAR framework.

DCAR recognizes four key pillars of activity, each historically viewed as a separate task for messaging administrators. However, all four pillars involve the same mechanisms, people, and policies; all four in fact are overlapping facets of messaging data management. These four pillars are described in the following list:

Discovery   Finding messages in the system quickly and accurately, whether for litigation, auditing, or other needs. There are generally two silos of discovery: *personal discovery*, allowing users to find and monitor the messages they send and receive, and *organizational discovery*, which encompasses the traditional litigation or auditing activities most messaging administrators think about. It requires the following:

♦   Good storage design to handle the additional overhead of discovery actions

♦   The accurate and thorough indexing of all messaging data that enters the Exchange Server organization through any means

♦   Control over the ability of users to move data into and out of the messaging system through mechanisms such as personal folders (PSTs)

♦   Control of the user's ability to delete data that may be required by litigation

Compliance   Meeting all legal, regulatory, and governance requirements, whether derived from external or internal drivers. Although many of the technologies used for compliance also look similar to those used by individual users for *mailbox management*, compliance happens more at the organization level (even if not all populations within the organization are subject to the same regimes). It requires the following:

♦   Clear guidance on which behaviors are allowed, required, or prohibited, as well as a clear description of which will be enforced through technical means

♦   The means to enforce required behavior, prevent disallowed behavior, and audit for the success or failure of these means

♦   The ability to control and view all messaging data that enters the Exchange Server organization through any means

Archival   The ability to preserve the messaging data that will be required for future operations, including governance tasks. Like discovery, archival happens on two broad levels: the *user archive* is a personal solution that allows individual users to retain and reuse historical personal messaging data relevant to their job function, while the *business archive* is aimed at providing immutable organization-wide benefits such as storage reduction, eDiscovery, and knowledge retention. It requires the following:

♦   Clear guidance on which data must be preserved and a clear description of procedural and technical measures that will be used to enforce archival

♦   The accurate and thorough indexing of all messaging data that enters the Exchange Server organization through any means

♦   Control over the ability of users to move data into and out of the messaging system through mechanisms such as personal folders

Retention   The ability to identify data that can be safely removed without adverse impact (whether immediate or delayed) on the business. Although many retention mechanisms are defined and maintained centrally in the organization, it is not uncommon for many implementations to either depend on voluntary user activity for compliance or allow users to easily define stricter or looser retention policies for their own data. It requires the following:

♦ Clear guidance on which data is safe to remove and a clear description of the time frames and technical measures that will be used to enforce removal

♦ The accurate identification of all messaging data that enters the Exchange Server organization through any means

♦ Control over the ability of users to move data into and out of the messaging system through mechanisms, such as personal folders

If many of these requirements look the same, good; that emphasizes that these activities are all merely different parts of the same overall goal. You should be realizing that these activities are not things you do with your messaging system so much as they are activities that you perform while managing your messaging system. The distinction is subtle but important; knowing your requirements helps make the difference between designing and deploying a system that can be easily adapted to meet your needs and one that you will constantly have to fight. Some of these activities will require the addition of third-party solutions, even for Exchange Server 2016, which includes more DCAR functionality out of the box than any other previous version of Exchange Server.

What makes this space interesting is that many of these functions are being filled by a variety of solutions, including both on-premises and hosted solutions, often at a competitive price. Also interesting is the tension between Microsoft's view of how to manage messaging data in the Exchange Server organization versus the defined needs of many organizations to control information across multiple applications. More than ever, no solution will be one-size-fits-all; before accepting any vendor's assurance that their product will meet your needs, first make sure that you understand the precise problems you're trying to solve (instead of just the set of technology buzzwords that you may have been told will be your magic bullet) and know how their functionality will address the real needs.

WHERE JOURNALING FITS INTO DCAR

In our discussion of DCAR, we deliberately left out a common keyword that you inevitably hear about. *Journaling* is a common technology that gets mentioned whenever compliance, archival, and discovery are discussed. However, it often gets over-discussed. Journaling is not the end goal; it's simply a mechanism for getting data out of Exchange Server into some other system that provides the specific function that you really want or need.

Very simply, journaling allows Exchange Server administrators to designate a subset of messaging data that will automatically be duplicated into a *journal report* and sent to a third party—another mailbox in the Exchange Server organization, a stand-alone system in the organization, or even an external recipient, such as a hosted archival service. The journal report includes not only the exact, unaltered text of the original message but also additional details that the senders and recipients may not know, such as any BCC recipients, the specific SMTP envelope information used, or the full membership list and recipient distribution lists (as they existed at the time of message receipt). These reports are commonly used for one of two purposes: to capture data into some other system for archival or to provide a historical record for compliance purposes.

continues

continued

We don't know a single Exchange Server administrator who has ever come up to us and said, "I want to journal my data." Instead, they say, "I need to archive my data and I have to use journaling to get it to my archival solution." Journaling isn't the end goal; it's the means to the end. If journaling is a potential concern for you, you should stop and ask yourself why:

◆ What information am I trying to journal?

◆ What do I want the journaled information for?

◆ Perhaps most important, what am I going to do with the journaled information?

Understanding why you need journaling will give you the background you need to effectively design your Exchange Server organization, journaling requirements, and appropriate add-on applications and hosted solutions. It will also help you identify when journaling may not be the answer you need to solve the particular business problems you're facing.

You should also understand the impact that journaling will have on your system, as well as know what limitations journaling has. There are certain types of data that never get journaled, and if you need that data, you'll have to at a minimum supplement your solution with something that captures that data.

We will discuss Exchange Server 2016's journaling and archiving features in greater detail in Chapter 23, "Managing Transport, Data Loss Prevention, and Journaling Rules." For now, just be aware that they are merely tools that help you solve some other problem.

The Bottom Line

Distinguish between availability, backup and recovery, and disaster recovery. When it comes to keeping your Exchange Server 2016 deployment healthy, you have a lot of options provided out of the box. Knowing which problems they solve is critical to deploying them correctly.

> **Master It** You have been asked to select a backup type that will back up all data once per week but on a daily basis will ensure that the server does not run out of transaction log disk space.

Determine the best option for disaster recovery. When creating your disaster-recovery plans for Exchange Server 2016, you have a variety of options to choose from. Exchange Server 2016 further enhances the built-in capabilities to provide disaster recovery.

> **Master It** What are the different types of disaster recovery?

Distinguish between the different types of availability meant by the term high availability. The term *high availability* means different things to different people. When you design and deploy your Exchange Server 2016 solution, you need to be confident that everyone is designing for the same goals.

> **Master It** What four types of availability are there?

Implement the four pillars of compliance and governance activities. Ensuring that your Exchange Server 2016 organization meets your regular operational needs means thinking about the topics of compliance and governance within your organization.

Master It What are the four pillars of compliance and governance as applied to a messaging system?

Chapter 4

Virtualizing Exchange Server 2016

Virtualization started as a technique for making better use of mainframe computer resources, but in the mid-2000s, it made the jump to servers in the datacenter. While some organizations dabbled with virtualizing Exchange Server 2003 and 2007, Exchange Server virtualization matured with Exchange Server 2010 and Exchange Server 2013. In this chapter, we will discuss virtualizing Microsoft Exchange Server 2016.

IN THIS CHAPTER, YOU WILL LEARN TO:

- ◆ Evaluate the possible virtualization impacts
- ◆ Evaluate the existing Exchange environment
- ◆ Determine roles and scenarios to virtualize

Virtualization Overview

It is important to be clear about what kind of virtualization is under discussion. The modern datacenter offers a number of virtualization strategies and technologies: platform virtualization, storage virtualization, network virtualization, and desktop virtualization. Although all of these can affect an Exchange deployment, Exchange virtualization usually refers to *platform virtualization*, also known as *hardware or host virtualization*. Platform virtualization gives you the ability to create multiple independent instances of operating systems on a single physical server. These virtual instances are treated as separate servers by the operating system but are assigned physical resources from the host system. The administrator configures the required amount of physical resources for each virtual machine. Here are some of the resources you can manage and present to your virtual machines:

- ◆ CPU sockets and cores
- ◆ RAM
- ◆ Storage interfaces
- ◆ Number and type of hard drives
- ◆ Network interface cards

Platform virtualization is one of the key technologies in the current datacenter trends to reduce power and cooling costs, and deploy private cloud implementations. There are several types of platform virtualization, but the type used for Exchange is *hardware-assisted virtualization*, which uses a hypervisor to manage the physical host resources while minimizing the overhead of the virtualization solution. Depending on the solution used, the hypervisor can either be a full server operating system or a stripped-down minimalist kernel. Hypervisors do not provide emulation; the guest virtual machines provide the same processor architecture as the host server does. Modern hypervisors rely on specific instruction sets in the hardware processors designed to increase performance for virtual machines while decreasing hypervisor overhead.

There are compelling reasons to consider virtualization for your infrastructure, although not all situations or applications lend themselves equally to a positive virtualization experience. Some of these reasons will be covered a bit later in the chapter. You may even encounter both positive and negative experiences.

Technology continues to evolve, and we have seen great strides taken in the virtualization world over the past few years. Although there are multiple vendors in the virtualization game, VMware and Microsoft are at the top of the pile for virtualizing Exchange. These solutions provide the most rigorous and detailed guidance for successfully deploying Exchange on their virtualization solutions. Figure 4.1 gives a virtualization overview.

FIGURE 4.1
A look at virtualization

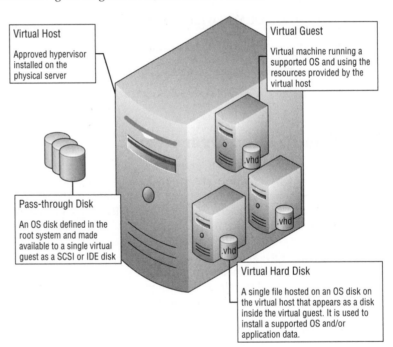

Virtual Host
Approved hypervisor installed on the physical server

Virtual Guest
Virtual machine running a supported OS and using the resources provided by the virtual host

Pass-through Disk
An OS disk defined in the root system and made available to a single virtual guest as a SCSI or IDE disk

Virtual Hard Disk
A single file hosted on an OS disk on the virtual host that appears as a disk inside the virtual guest. It is used to install a supported OS and/or application data.

Terminology

Table 4.1 contains terms you need to be familiar with as you move through this chapter and the virtualization world.

TABLE 4.1: Virtualization Terms

TERM	DEFINITION
Virtualization host, Host, Root, Parent	The physical server that is running the virtualization product. This is the computer that is sharing its physical resources to its virtual machines.
Guest, virtual machine	Virtual machine running a supported OS and using the resources provided by the virtualization host.
Database availability group (DAG)	A group of Mailbox servers that host a set of databases and provide automatic database-level recovery from failures.
Pass-through disk, Raw disk mapping (RDM)	Virtual hard disks that are directly linked to unformatted volumes on the host server, whether on local disks or some sort of storage array. These disks hold the operating system, applications, and other data for the virtual machine.
Virtual hard disk (VHD)	Virtual hard disks that are stored as files on a formatted volume on the host server, whether on local disks or some sort of storage array. These disks hold the operating system, applications, and other data for the virtual machine. Files can use the .vhd format or the newer .vhdx format.
Fixed VHD	A VHD whose underlying file on the host storage occupies its maximum size. For example, a 100 GB fixed disk with only 25 GB used in the guest will still use 100 GB on the host storage.
Dynamic VHD	A VHD whose underlying file on host storage occupies only the amount of space used in the guest. For example, a 100 GB dynamic VHD that is only 25 percent used in the guest will use only 25 GB on the host storage. There is a performance hit as the disk grows, and dynamic VHDs can be extremely fragmented even when the logical structure inside the disk seems to be defragmented.
Differencing VHD	A multiple-part VHD, with a read-only fixed or dynamic VHD as the baseline and a second VHD for all writes. New or updated disk blocks are written to the differencing VHD, not to the baseline VHD. Any changes can be rolled back to a previous state, and a baseline VHD can be used with many different differencing VHDs. These disks have significant performance penalties, for the increased level of I/O abstraction and CPU, as well as for the fragmentation in the differencing VHD file.

Understanding Virtualized Exchange

Exchange Server 2003 was the first version of Exchange that Microsoft officially supported under virtualization, although that support came late in the product's lifetime. Although customers had been virtualizing Exchange under VMware products for years, Microsoft's official support permitted Exchange Server 2003 to be run only under Microsoft's own Virtual Server product.

In 2008, Microsoft announced their new Server Virtualization Validation Program (SVVP). This program provides a central mechanism for on-premises and hosted virtualization providers to get their solutions validated in specific configurations. The SVVP allows Windows customers to get official Microsoft support for virtualized Windows servers and applications that are running on SVVP-certified virtualization configurations. Later the same year, Microsoft released their virtualization support statement for Exchange Server 2007 SP1 and later versions, building off of the baseline provided by the SVVP. This moved Exchange into the mainstream for applications that could take advantage of the benefits of virtualization.

Microsoft's support guidelines for virtualizing Exchange Server 2007 and Exchange Server 2010 have undergone many changes. Under the terms of the SVVP, Windows Server 2008 SP2 and Windows Server 2008 R2 were the only operating systems supported for virtual Exchange Server 2007 and 2010 deployments. Initially, the Unified Messaging role was not supported under virtualization, but an updated media component was introduced in Exchange Server 2010 SP1. At the same time, Microsoft relaxed some of their restrictions on the use of hypervisor availability features with Exchange. Now, with Exchange Server 2013 and Exchange Server 2016, a lot of the guidance for previous versions no longer applies because of the changes in service architecture. Now, besides using Hyper-V as the hypervisor for virtualizing Exchange Server, you can also use VMware's hypervisors or Citrix XenServer because they adhere to the SVVP. This expanded support of Exchange Server even extends to the cloud with Microsoft Azure. You can virtualize Exchange Server 2016 in Microsoft Azure.

The support for Exchange is a constantly evolving story, especially after Cumulative Update packs are released. When in doubt, visit http://technet.microsoft.com/en-us/library/jj619301.aspx to view the latest version of Microsoft's guidelines and recommendations for virtualizing Exchange Server 2016. The virtualized instances of Exchange must still meet the Exchange prerequisites.

MICROSOFT REQUIREMENTS AND RECOMMENDATIONS

Make sure you have read and are familiar with the "Exchange 2016 Virtualization" article at:

http://technet.microsoft.com/en-us/library/jj619301.aspx

The following hypervisor technologies are unsupported for use in your production Exchange Server 2016 servers:

♦ The use of hypervisors or hosting platforms that are not on the SVVP

♦ The use of file-level protocols (Network File System or Server Message Block—NFS or SMB) for storage pools used for Exchange VHDs or partitions

♦ Deploying on Azure virtual machines that use storage other than Azure Premium Storage

♦ Hypervisor snapshots of the Exchange virtual machines

♦ Differencing VHDs

♦ Host-based clustering and migration technologies that rely on saving Exchange virtual machine memory state to disk files

♦ Virtual-to-logical processor ratios greater than 2:1

◆ Dynamic memory or overcommitting of memory

◆ Any applications other than management software running on the hypervisor host

There is one exciting change in these requirements involving the SMB 3.0 protocol, which is new in Windows Server 2012 and other modern storage solutions that license this protocol. Under SMB 3.0 (and SMB 3.0 *only*), you can configure your hypervisor environment to mount SMB 3.0 file shares and store fixed-length virtual hard drive files on those mounts; these virtual hard drives can then be used to store Exchange data. In this configuration, the new features of SMB 3.0 help ensure that the specific type and order of Exchange data writes are preserved all the way to the physical disks, removing the typical risk of data loss or corruption that is present when using other file-based protocols.

This change helps simplify storage requirements for virtual Exchange Server deployments, but only if all of the following conditions are met:

◆ Both the client (the hypervisor) and the storage solution (SAN, Windows Server 2012 server, or other device) support the SMB 3.0 protocol and are configured to use it.

◆ Neither the client nor the storage solution is configured to fall back to an earlier version of SMB.

◆ The SMB 3.0 file share is mounted by the hypervisor systems and not directly by the Exchange server.

◆ The Exchange data is stored on fixed-length (full-size) virtual hard drive files on the SMB 3.0 mount.

Understanding Your Exchange Environment

Before virtualizing your Exchange environment, you must define your current environment. The better you understand your environment, the more prepared you will be to define the virtualized environment. Here is some of the information you need to gather:

◆ Number of users

◆ User profiles

◆ Number of messages sent/received per day, per user

◆ Server CPU utilization

◆ Server memory utilization

◆ Server network utilization

◆ Database sizes

◆ Storage patterns

◆ Storage type

◆ Current high-availability model

◆ Concurrently connected users

- Number and types of clients accessing the system

- Exchange connectors

- Administration model

As you gather this information, you will be painting a picture of your Exchange environment. This information will be placed into various calculations throughout the process to ensure that you have done a complete evaluation before moving forward with virtualization. This information will have a significant impact on the Exchange system moving forward.

Each bit of the information you gather will add another piece to the puzzle. As you put the puzzle together, you will have a good idea whether virtualization will meet your needs. You also will be able to validate whether you will get the performance from the virtualized environment that your users require. Later in the book, we look more closely at sizing and how the Exchange Role Requirements Calculator can be a tool to help.

Effects of Virtualization

The popularity of virtualization in the datacenter is due to the many benefits it brings, both tangible and intangible. However, not all applications are created equal. While virtualizing Exchange Server is technically possible, there are a number of additional impacts and issues that you should consider.

Environmental Impact

For most organizations, the environmental impact is one of the major driving factors behind virtualization initiatives. The concept is simple: reduce the number of servers and reduce the amount of power. Active servers consume electricity and convert it to heat, indirectly consuming more electricity in the form of cooling systems. Consolidating underutilized servers and replacing older servers with less-efficient hardware can result in a significant amount of saved power. This number is a completely fluid number and is dependent on the environment that you want to virtualize. An organization with 100 servers will see a much different impact than a company with only 15 servers. However, an organization with 100 lightly loaded servers will likewise see a much different impact than a company with 100 heavily loaded servers.

Space Impact

Environmental impact is important, but server consolidation has an impact that may not be as immediately obvious: reduced rack space in the server room or datacenter. Not all organizations will feel this impact, depending on their choice of host hardware.

Organizations that pay for server hosting in a separate facility may find that paying attention to this area of impact can result in additional cost savings. These savings may include the following basic costs associated with hosting:

- Rack mounting space for the physical servers

- Power

- Network connectivity

- Cooling

There may also be optional costs associated with your servers, such as the following:

◆   Monitoring of the hardware

◆   Additional firewall capabilities

◆   Out-of-band access to the servers

By deploying powerful physical hardware running a hypervisor environment, you can increase your physical hosting costs in a predictable, building-block fashion, build virtual application servers without having to visit the datacenter, and still provide cost efficiency. Depending on the workload of the servers before you virtualized them, you may need to deploy larger servers, which may increase the per-server cost for the space. Be sure to do the math before deciding that this approach will save you money.

Complexity Impact

Many savings estimates overlook the additional complexity that a virtualized environment can bring to the table. Depending on the level of availability required, the additional host servers and networking gear required to provide clustering and spare capacity—as well as the higher class of hardware to provide redundant components within the host servers—can whittle away the initial estimated savings.

Once the virtual servers are deployed, complexity almost always strikes in the operational processes and technical operational skills of your staff. Having the additional hypervisor layers in the networking, storage, and server stack can drive up the time involved in keeping virtual Exchange Server 2016 servers operating. The additional layers of dependency can also bring down the expected SLAs for the Exchange services in the event of an outage and lengthen the time it takes to troubleshoot problems.

Virtual Exchange deployments can also be bitten by the complexity bug when the designs do not adequately consider failure domains. Consider the impact of a failure of a host server and the corresponding virtual machines. Consider also the specific hypervisor features that cannot be used with Exchange, such as differencing disks, hypervisor snapshots, or file-level storage; determine the impact on the organization if those features are used with Exchange virtual machines and there is a problem. What features of Exchange, such as native data protection, are you going to be unable or less likely to use in a virtual deployment without offsetting the projected cost savings? Are these risks high enough to offset the value of virtualizing Exchange?

Additional Considerations

One of the ways companies are saving money is by virtualizing underused servers. By doing this, they reduce the power and cooling footprints that we have talked about. An underused server is thought to use less than 20 percent of its physical hardware. If your current Exchange environment has been sized properly, Exchange servers should not fall into the underused category.

This does not mean that you will not benefit from virtualizing Exchange; you need to do your research. For a good background on the impact virtualization can have, check out the white paper, "Comparing the Power Utilization of Native and Virtual Exchange Environments," available at http://technet.microsoft.com/en-us/library/dd901773.aspx. It was written for Exchange Server 2007, but the information is still applicable. The study shows a reduction of 50 percent in power utilization for the servers used in the study. The total power reduction for the servers and storage was between 34 and 37 percent, depending on the storage solution.

> ### 🌐 Real World Scenario
>
> #### ARE MY EXCHANGE SERVERS UNDERUTILIZED?
>
> With stand-alone Exchange Server 2016 servers, the process to determine utilization is relatively simple: first, establish a baseline performance set by running the Windows Performance Monitor (PerfMon) for at least a week using a combination of common counters for processor, memory, disk, and network resources. Once this baseline is established, you can use it to compare current performance levels when experiencing issues to identify notable areas of change.
>
> At the time of this writing, no specific performance guidance has been published for Exchange Server 2016, but at some point Microsoft will likely provide specific counter and threshold guidance. Until then, use a combination of the counters for an Exchange Server 2013 multirole server combined with some common sense and healthy skepticism to establish your current server baseline. If any specific counter (other than RAM) averages above 60 percent utilization or has frequent spikes above that threshold, the server may be undersized or misconfigured.
>
> One point to keep in mind is that DAG-member Mailbox servers in a load-balancing pool can't be directly measured. To ensure you accurately measure the load on these servers, take your measurements while they are running at the designed and expected maximum load. If your DAG is designed to lose two servers, then simulate the loss of two servers to perform your baseline measurement.
>
> Hypervisor and storage vendors usually give specific guidance for virtualizing Exchange. Make sure you obtain, read, and understand this guidance to ensure that your virtual Exchange deployment will be successful throughout its life.

Virtualization Requirements

Just as with any software you deploy, there are hardware and software requirements that you need to meet when you virtualize.

Hardware Requirements

For the modern virtualization technologies, make sure that your hardware supports the proper level of virtualization. Most of the current market-leading servers do have the proper BIOS, motherboard, and CPU support, but older models may not support the specific CPU extensions or technologies required by the hypervisors you will need to run Exchange Server 2016 on Windows Server 2012 or Windows Server 2012 R2. If you are building a server from scratch, review the hardware requirements for the hypervisor you will be using to make sure the server you are building will perform the way you intend it to perform. Also make sure that you follow the reference processor and memory recommendations and server ratios that are posted on TechNet. These guidelines should always be your first stop for planning, along with the Exchange Server Role Requirements Calculator.

Know which servers will be virtualized. You will find that there are different pitfalls for the virtualization host than what you normally see with physical servers. Because you will be sharing the virtualization host's physical resources, make sure that you have an idea what servers will be virtualized on the host, as well as what spare capacity the host will be expected to have and what virtual machines will be added to the workload during mainte-nance or outage. This will allow you to verify that you have enough RAM, processors, and network connections. Gather the physical requirements of each confirmed and provisional guest. Knowing what your guest virtual machines will need before you enter the planning stages for virtualization will put you in a better position for success.

Plan based on system resources.   No matter what workloads or how many servers you will be virtualizing, you need to plan. The virtualization host will require resources before the virtual machines are even started. Once you have started the virtual machines, your resources can deplete very quickly. Make sure that you have enough system resources to go around and that you have some breathing room.

Plan for your virtualization hosts to consume a CPU overhead of 9 to 12 percent. This will differ from installation to installation, but it is a good number to use when sizing your equip-ment and laying out your virtual machines. Try to validate your configuration in a lab (or by configuring your production hardware as a lab) before moving into production.

Plan based on storage requirements.   Knowing which workloads will be virtualized will also enable you to plan the proper storage for the virtual machines. Storage is a major design point for virtualizing Exchange. Exchange Server 2016 continues the trend of I/O improvements that favor disk capacity over disk performance. Virtual Exchange servers may have a significant amount of I/O overhead, depending on the specific storage options you have chosen; pass-through disks on local or iSCSI storage will have lower overhead than VHDs (.vhd or .vhdx). Begin your storage design with the Exchange storage calcula-tor and size your storage appropriately; then use that as input for the calculators for your virtualization and storage solutions to ensure that you're meeting all expectations.

Make sure that you have properly partitioned your storage. You don't want to have spindle contention between your virtualization host OS and the storage for your virtual machine OS or application data. For the majority of virtual workloads, you should have the underlying storage in a RAID configuration. The level of RAID that you choose is up to you and depends on the project requirements. However, if you are taking the option of using direct-attached storage on your virtualization host to provide storage for Exchange mailbox databases in a DAG and you plan to take advantage of Exchange-native data protection, you may not need RAID.

When you are creating your virtual machine OS VHDs, or logical unit numbers (LUNs), include enough space for operation of the virtual machine, including space for updates, addi-tional applications, and the page file. Use the following calculation to determine the mini-mum VHD size that will be needed for the virtual machine:

OS requirement + virtual machine RAM = minimum OS VHD size.   For normal virtual workloads, the disk requirements should include space for the memory state file (such as the .VSV and .BIN files used in Hyper-V during Quick Migration and VM pause operations). However, Microsoft's support guidelines are very emphatic: *the use of disk-based memory states is not supported with virtual Exchange servers.*

Plan based on networking configuration.   In addition to the storage-capacity requirements, make sure you have the appropriate bandwidth for all your virtual machines to access your storage subsystem. Exchange Server 2016 storage should be fixed VHDs, pass-through, or iSCSI LUNs. Microsoft recommends that you use pass-through disks or iSCSI LUNs to host the databases, transaction logs, and mail queues.

WHY CAN'T I USE NFS OR SMB?

One of the most commonly violated support guidelines for virtual Exchange deployments is the prohibition on file-level protocols in the storage stack. For some hypervisor deployments, such as VMware, it is very common to use network-attached storage or storage access networks (NAS or SAN storage) using NFS to provide the data stores used to hold virtual machine drives files. Often, the storage solution is entirely dedicated to the NFS partitions, and the entire virtual environment provisioning process is automated around building out the virtual machine disks (VMDKs). It's efficient, it's relatively inexpensive, and most importantly it's already working. Having to reclaim storage space only to carve it out as iSCSI LUNs or raw device mappings (RDMs) is a lot of work and will require a complete overhaul of the associated backup routines. You're already using VMDKs over NFS for all your other workloads. Why is it necessary to throw this big wrench in the works?

The answer is simple: you're putting your data at risk by lying to Exchange.

In order to maximize performance and keep your data safe, the Exchange storage engine has a very specific sequence of events for how it handles writes to disk. All writes to the database first must be written out to a transaction log file, and the updates to the various files and blocks have to happen in a very specific sequence or database corruption and data loss results. To make sure this happens, Exchange has to assume it's talking to the raw disk blocks; only by doing so can it ensure that all the data and metadata gets written to the disk in the correct order within the correct timeframe. Block-level protocols (iSCSI, FC, SATA/SAS, etc.) and pass-through disks can all make this guarantee. Even when write caching is in the mix (and it should be, using a proper battery backing), the caching controller is taking on the responsibility of ensuring the writes get committed to disk.

With file-level protocols, such as NFS and SMB (before SMB 3.0 when mounted by the hypervisor host), you don't have those same commitments. That's not to say that these protocols won't try to keep your data safe, because they do, but the ways they do it—and the features they provide, such as file locking and caching and disconnect time-outs—are very different than a block-level protocol would. As a result, Exchange is relying on one set of behaviors because it thinks it's talking to a physical disk, but by slipping NFS or SMB into the stack, you've silently changed those behaviors. The translations between the two work most of the time, but when they don't, the results can be amazingly destructive.

If you're going to deploy your Exchange VMs on file-level virtual hard disks, be smart. You can use these solutions for the base operating-system partition, but don't install Exchange on those drives. Instead, provision additional pass-through drives, RDMs, or block-level LUNs for your Exchange databases, logs, and binaries. Keep your Exchange data on volumes where it has a straight block-based path all the way back to the spindles. The data (and job) you save will be your own.

Make sure you have planned your network bandwidth. You are going to be sharing a limited number of physical network ports on your virtualization host with your virtual machines. Depending on your virtual machine layout and requirements, you will exhaust your physical network ports in short order.

You may end up needing to install multiple quad-port network interface cards (NICs) to get the port density required to support your Exchange design. Keep in mind that you may need several NICs per virtual machine. Depending on the role of the server, there may be replication traffic as well as client traffic. For virtualization hosts that will be hosting Exchange

Mailbox servers in a DAG, the replication NICs in the guests should not be bound to either of the following physical NIC types in the host:

- Any host NIC that connects to storage (such as iSCSI SANs)

- The host NICs bound to the primary guest client NICs

If you use NIC teaming on the host to increase bandwidth or provide availability, ensure that the teaming vendor supports the use of teamed NICs for virtualization in general and guest virtual networks that will be used with Exchange Server in particular.

Consider your physical server type.   You are not locked into one type of physical server for the virtualization host. You can use a standard server, or you may choose to use blade servers. Blade servers require a bit more planning than standard servers. Because you are sharing resources before you start your virtualization, be sure you have carved out your disks, network traffic, and storage traffic adequately.

Software Requirements

Your software requirements for the host OS will differ depending on which hypervisor you have decided to use. Check with your hypervisor provider to ensure that you have all the required software before you begin. There are differences in the base OSs that may preclude you from loading any hypervisor without a complete reload of the server. Although this is not a huge deal, it is time-consuming, and if you purchased an incorrect version, it is also expensive. Make sure that you know how many servers will be virtualized on the host servers as well. This may have an impact on what version of the OS you need to install to minimize the number of guest Windows licenses you need to purchase. Make certain that you have completed the virtual machine configuration before you start to load Exchange.

For the virtual machine, the software requirements and installation are straightforward. Once you have made the initial configurations for the virtual machine, load the appropriate Windows operating system for the designed Exchange roles. There are no requirements from a virtualization perspective as to which version of Windows you need to load as long as the version of hypervisor and Windows guest (virtual machine) are validated on the SVVP list. The guest OS will be driven by the business and technical requirements for the application and configuration you will be deploying. This is where your requirements-gathering will guide you to the correct OS and application versions.

In addition to the normal requirements for Exchange servers, ensure that the latest hypervisor integration drivers are loaded. For Microsoft Hyper-V guests, the Hyper-V integration components are part of the base Windows OS and service packs, although if the version of Windows the Hyper-V hosts are running is newer than the version in the guests, you may need to install the additional Hyper-V integration components. The other hypervisor vendors all have their own integration components or guest toolkits to load.

Regardless of which hypervisor you are using, it is critically important to keep your guests up-to-date on the latest integration drivers. As your hosts are updated to newer versions and patch levels, ensure that all of the guests on the host (or cluster) are running the latest drivers before hosts are upgraded to the new version, especially if not all of the virtualization hosts in the cluster will be upgraded at the same time. Exchange can be extremely sensitive to mismatches between the integration drivers and the host version, with catastrophic impacts to performance.

Operations

Operations include many factors, such as the patching and monitoring of the OS and application, daily maintenance, and troubleshooting. A popular misconception is that your operating costs will magically decrease when you start to virtualize, while your uptime and service availability will frolic with unicorns and rainbows. The reality is that without careful planning and the creation of mature processes, the chances are good that your costs will actually increase, as will your downtime. The reason for this mismatch between expectations and reality is that adding virtualization brings more to the table than just the technology. To have a successful virtual Exchange deployment, you need not only technology but also processes and personnel.

Virtualization technology is mature, but most virtualization guidance makes the assumption that all applications are the same in terms of ignorance about the underlying hardware. Over the years, Microsoft has gone to a lot of trouble to make Exchange as reliable as it can and to ensure that if there is unavoidable data loss, it is as small as possible. The friction between Exchange's assumptions about the hardware stack and the widespread scalability best practices for virtual environments can create a combination where Exchange is less reliable.

Balancing the virtual machines' needs against the host's resources and the users' requirements can be a daunting task. Doing so for Exchange guests typically increases the complexity by creating Exchange-specific technology challenges. These challenges can all be solved at the technology level, but doing so requires additional cross-training for your staff and specific exceptions in your virtualization processes and policies.

The size of your IT organization and the number and location of servers will affect the cost of operations. If you have enough staff to learn the virtualization technology, there may not be a huge impact to the bottom line. If you don't have adequate staff, you will most likely be looking for additional personnel to support your virtualization efforts. When you virtualize your Exchange servers, you still have to take care of the guest Windows installation and the Exchange application as well as the hypervisor hosts and environment.

Virtual Exchange servers have 100 percent of the daily operational requirements that physical Exchange servers do. You still have to test and patch your systems. You still have systems that will experience issues, and you need to spend time troubleshooting. On top of that, you now have added the hypervisor layer. This layer may or may not be familiar to your support and engineering staff. You can't just reboot a virtualization host because you feel that it is the best solution for a situation. You now have to expand your thought process to include the Exchange servers that are virtualized on that host and take these factors into consideration:

- What Exchange services will be affected by shutting down this host?

- Exchange virtual machines are on the virtualization host, but how will the users be affected when they are shut down?

- Do the affected services have a redundant nature?

- Are the redundant services located on the same virtualization host or on a different host? (If they are on the same virtualization host, are they really redundant?)

Deciding When to Virtualize

Deciding to virtualize is a big decision. It should not be taken lightly. Before you embark on the road to virtualizing Exchange Server, you need to make sure it is right for your organization.

While every organization has slightly different requirements and goals, the following list represents some of the common reasons that organizations choose to virtualize Exchange Server:

◆ **Save money.** While virtualization doesn't always save money (in fact, sometimes it can cost more money than having physical servers), it can save money in many environments, especially if an organization is virtualizing everything. Cost savings are associated with power, cooling, datacenter space, and sometimes operating system costs.

◆ **Adhere to your organization's common IT management platform.** Many organizations, especially large organizations, have a standardized set of IT management platforms and processes to support their environment. Much work has gone into developing the platforms and processes. Whenever a technology doesn't adhere to the common IT management platform, support can become inefficient, expensive, and prone to errors or downtime. If your organization has virtualized the vast majority of your servers, it might make sense to virtualize Exchange Server to take advantage of that investment in infrastructure and people.

◆ **Company mandate.** A while back, we were working with a company that had a mandate from the CIO. That mandate was to virtualize every server in the datacenters. If you wanted an exception, you had to present a strong case for it—and we mean really strong. Although such a mandate could come from costs or other factors, the reason often doesn't matter. In such a case, you need to prepare to virtualize!

These are just a few of the common reasons to virtualize. There are many others. As the administrator, you need to weigh the options, examine the pros and cons, and ultimately decide which route to take for your organization. If you decide to virtualize, your next step is to decide what to virtualize, which we talk about next.

Deciding What to Virtualize

No matter how many Exchange servers you plan to virtualize, you must do your research as you are planning the architecture for your environment. Plan your virtual machines just as though they were physical servers. Then include the additional overhead for the virtualization host. Make sure that you are thinking about the end product that you will deliver to your users. Consider the possible differences between the physical and virtualized environment. Will your user base be as happy with a virtualized environment if it means a decrease in performance? If you set the expectations, size the environment appropriately—and test appropriately. There should be no noticeable difference for your end users.

As with any architecture, things that you do can make positive or negative impacts. With Exchange Server 2007, Microsoft changed the Extensible Storage Engine (ESE) to allow Exchange Server 2007 to utilize as much RAM as needed to cache as much mailbox information as possible to drive down read I/O operations. In Exchange Server 2007 and Exchange Server 2010, the Exchange ESE—a monolithic Information Store process that handles all the databases on the server—uses all available physical memory in the system for this cache. If your server has 16 GB of memory, you can expect that ESE will consume roughly 14 GB of it until other processes need the resources. At that point, Exchange will not let go of that memory but will instead allow the operating system to place memory pages in the disk-based page file. With Exchange Server 2013 and Exchange Server 2016, the ESE spawns a separate process for each mailbox database on the server, completely changing how memory management works.

Understanding how these changes affect the behavior of the Exchange server allows you to properly plan and deploy virtual Exchange servers. You should know, for example, that using popular techniques like memory over-allocation or dynamic memory allocation would be a bad match for Exchange servers—and in fact, neither is supported by Microsoft for Exchange. However, over-allocation of CPU resources is supported up to a ratio of two virtual CPUs to every one physical CPU core (although it is recommended to have one virtual CPU for each CPU core). When looking at resource allocations, don't forget to plan for outages and ensure that having to move Exchange virtual machines in an emergency won't bump these allocations over the recommended numbers.

With Exchange Server 2013 and Exchange Server 2016, you can support mixing native Exchange and hypervisor high-availability technologies, as long as you stay within the Microsoft support boundaries. You can deploy Exchange DAGs on virtual clusters and move active DAG members around using hypervisor migration technologies, as long as you avoid using technologies that write the current memory state of the Exchange guest to a disk-based file. These technologies are commonly used to enhance availability and even disaster recovery at the hypervisor level without requiring the virtual machine operating system or application to explicitly support them. These technologies include the following:

◆ Hyper-V's Live Migration and VMware's vMotion both transfer memory pages of an active virtual machine from the source host to the target using a direct network connection. These methods, and others like them on other SVVP-validated hypervisors, are supported for use with virtual Exchange machines because they ensure that the memory of the transitioned machines won't grow overly stale compared with the other DAG members or cause the store caches to get out of sync with the on-disk data. Be aware that many organizations opt to use Exchange Server's native high availability features instead. This is because there can be occasional issues after a live migration or vMotion.

◆ Hyper-V's Quick Migration, and other technologies like it, is not supported. Quick Migration writes the memory state to a disk-based file. This slows down the transition and puts the virtual machine at risk of having a mismatch between the machine memory and the state of the other DAG members or the database cache and data on disk.

◆ Virtual snapshots create a file-based dump of memory. If the machine is ever rolled back to this snapshot, the on-disk database data will be severely out of date. Permanent data loss could result. Using virtual snapshots, and rolling back virtually, guarantees that you'll screw up your databases—and because Microsoft doesn't support virtual snapshots and rollbacks, you'll be on your own to clean up the mess.

◆ Technologies that bring up a failed virtual machine on another host, such as VMware's high availability, are supported as long as they bring up that new instance from a cold boot. But think carefully about whether you really want a failed Exchange server to come back up automatically without having a chance to analyze what's going on with it. In the worst-case scenario, you could have an Exchange server bouncing through the hosts in your virtual cluster, wreaking havoc on them.

◆ Technologies, such as VMware's Distributed Resources Scheduler and Hyper-V's integration with the System Center suite, have the capability to dynamically move virtual machines from one host to another to ensure resource utilization is balanced or stays within thresholds. This is a good capability in principle, but again, for Exchange servers this feature can create more problems than it solves. You should never allow multiple DAG members to be active on the same host; without careful management, these features can put your data at greater risk.

DAGs make it easier to plan for, configure, and maintain both high availability and site resilience in the Exchange application. Because DAGs are application-aware, your servers are always in control of any Exchange data. When in a DAG, the Exchange servers are in constant communication about the status of a database in the DAG; there should be minimal impact if a server or database goes down for any reason. Many administrators believe that native Exchange technologies provide a more effective, highly available Exchange environment compared to virtualization providing high availability and/or disaster recovery.

Exchange Roles

Previous versions (and service packs) of Exchange Server limited the roles you could virtualize. These limitations have been gone since Exchange Server 2013; you can virtualize both the Mailbox and Edge Transport roles. Make sure to follow common-sense best-practice guidelines:

- Don't place two of the same role on the same virtualization host, especially Mailbox servers in a DAG.

- In a virtual cluster, leave a host or two free of Exchange guests so you have the freedom to move Exchange virtual machines to respond to outages or emergencies.

- When planning capacity, don't forget to account for the impact of losing an Exchange guest. A Mailbox server that provides sufficient free headroom when the entire DAG is up and running may tip the host over to processor or memory overutilization when you take a DAG member down for patching.

Testing

As with any engineering effort, you need to make sure that you have a testing plan for the virtualized guests and host. Your plan needs to include testing all your virtual machines at the same time. One of the worst things you can do is to test only a single server at a time. Instead, test as close to real-world operating conditions as possible. Test the entire solution and not pieces of the solution. The solution should include any third-party applications that are in the environment, as well. Anything that you leave out of the testing cycle could come back to haunt you when you move to production.

Use the Microsoft Exchange–specific validation tools to test your configuration and ensure that you have all the settings properly dialed in. Jetstress was released for Exchange Server 2013 and is supported for Exchange Server 2016, and it is downloadable from the Microsoft download site. It is one of the key tools used to test the performance of the disk subsystem before Exchange is installed in the virtual machines. The information that Jetstress gives you should line up with the performance requirements you gathered early in the project. Load Generator for Exchange Server 2013, also available for free from Microsoft Downloads, will simulate the different client connections that will be in your environment. You will be able to define how many simulated clients will use each connection protocol and how much email traffic they will send and receive. When using the testing tools, try to emulate the user base that is currently in the environment. If none of your users use Outlook on the web, then don't put it in the test cases. If your organization includes heavy users of Exchange ActiveSync, make sure that you have included the correct information to heavily test for Exchange ActiveSync. At the time of this writing, Load Generator has not yet been updated for Exchange Server 2016.

Remember: in the virtualized environment, you should do everything you would normally do in a physical environment. Don't fall into the trap of thinking that because it is a virtualized environment, it is a different solution. You are the only one who should know that these servers are virtualized. The end users and the first line of the help desk should never be able to tell the difference.

Possible Virtualization Scenarios

In this section, we will look at several scenarios that could lead to a positive virtualization experience. These scenarios are not guarantees of success but examples of what *may* work. (Once you start testing your environment, you may find situations in which physical servers are the best solution.) We will discuss possible hardware for both the virtualization host and the virtual machine, but this is just an estimation of hardware that may be needed; we will not be looking at the physical specifications. These scenarios have not been tested in a lab for performance. They are merely examples of what could be virtualized.

Small Office/Remote or Branch Office

In this scenario, our office has a relatively small number of users, and we need to provide email services to them. We have determined that users would be better off using local Exchange servers than pulling email across the WAN. Because the users are in a remote office, we will be supplying directory services as well. We want to provide redundancy and high availability where possible. By using a small number of physical hosts as a virtual cluster, we can deploy the necessary servers, keep costs down, and meet our availability requirements.

We have determined through research, interviews with staff members, and data collection that we have light email users. We will be providing high availability via DAG. We also have a requirement for site resilience, so we will extend the DAG to the main datacenter.

As we start to build this solution, we must determine which virtual machines will be placed on which virtualization hosts. We see a need for the following:

◆ Two Exchange servers

◆ Two domain controllers

◆ A file server (which we can use as the file-share witness)

◆ A backup server

We can put this solution together with a minimum of two physical servers and storage, although for full redundancy—for patching, outages, and the like—we would need three. The exact specifications on the servers and storage are not being discussed. When we create the

DAG, we will specify the correct location for the file-share witness. We must not create an issue where the file-share witness ends up being on the same virtualization host as a Mailbox server in the DAG. If this were to happen and we created the file-share witness on Virtualization Host 1 or 3, then we'd have two voting members of the DAG on the same physical hardware. This is not a recommended solution. Following is a virtualization layout depicting a three-server solution.

Virtualization Host 1 will have the following virtual machines:

◆ Domain Controller 1

◆ Exchange 1

Virtualization Host 2 will have the following virtual machines:

◆ Domain Controller 2

◆ File server

Virtualization Host 3 will have the following virtual machines:

◆ Exchange 2

◆ Backup

With proper specifications, our physical servers will not be over-utilized by the planned workloads; there will be enough spare capacity to ensure that virtual machines can be moved for short periods of time. Instead of having six servers in use, we will have three servers—a 50 percent reduction in physical servers for this location.

Site Resilience

In this scenario, we'll set up a second location for site resilience. We assume that the primary datacenter is fully functional with Exchange Server 2016 physical servers. We have been handed a new requirement to provide site resilience for all users in our organization. We will also need to provide the same level of performance and reliability as the primary datacenter. Our primary datacenter has four Exchange servers in a DAG.

To meet the requirements, we will be deploying nine virtual machines: four domain controllers, one file server, and four Exchange servers. We are using four domain controllers to keep down the number of virtual processors and RAM on each domain controller.

We will need four physical servers for the solution. For ease of ordering, we will order all servers with the same hardware specifications.

Virtualization Host 1 will have the following virtual machines:

◆ Domain Controller 1

◆ Exchange Server 1

Virtualization Host 2 will have the following virtual machines:

◆ Domain Controller 2

◆ Exchange Server 2

Virtualization Host 3 will have the following virtual machines:

◆ Domain Controller 3

◆ Exchange Server 3

Virtualization Host 4 will have the following virtual machines:

◆ Domain Controller 4

◆ Exchange Server 4

In this scenario, we would manually place the file-share witness on an existing file server in the site. You may recall that the file-share witness is used when there is an even number of servers in the DAG. We have that here, but there are enough servers to separate the witness without putting the DAG in jeopardy.

By separating the virtual machines across four virtualization hosts, we have accomplished the task at hand. If we had chosen to mirror the production environment and use physical servers, we would have needed eight servers. At a minimum, we cut our servers by 50 percent with the inclusion of the domain controllers. The flip side of this is that we probably increased the number of processors and amount of RAM in the virtualization hosts. By doing this, we also increased the cost of the virtualization hosts. The cost increase may be minimal, but you should calculate it before implementing this solution. Depending on which hypervisor you choose, there may be costs associated with the hypervisor software. In addition, there are operational costs associated with each virtualization host.

Mobile Access

For the mobile solution, we have a customer that must react quickly to an emergency. They need to have their entire infrastructure physically with them. They do not need to tie back into a corporate environment, but they will be connecting to the Internet and must be able to send and receive email and surf the Internet. They also require a database server, file/print capabilities, and collaboration. There will be an external appliance to provide firewall protection. This is also considered a short-term solution. Once the disaster is over or a permanent datacenter has been established, the mobile solution will be decommissioned. This solution brings in several different technologies in addition to Exchange.

The customer has only 50 users, but they will be sending and receiving a large amount of email. With this number of users, there will not be a huge draw on any of the servers. Knowing this, we are able to minimize the server requirements. We can keep the file-share witness separated from the Exchange servers. We will place a node of the database cluster on the same virtualization host as one of the Exchange servers. This is not a recommended solution for environments with higher requirements, but because we have a small number of users and low demand, we should be fine with the layout.

Virtualization Host 1 will have the following virtual machines:

◆ Domain Controller 1

◆ Exchange Server 1

◆ Database Server Node 1

Virtualization Host 2 will have the following virtual machines:

◆   Domain Controller 2

◆   Exchange Server 2

◆   Collaboration Server 1

Virtualization Host 3 will have the following virtual machines:

◆   File and Print Node

◆   Database Server Node 2

◆   Collaboration Server 2

We are able to meet the requirements for the customer with only three physical servers. If during testing we decide that we need additional capacity, we can add another server or increase the specs on the existing servers. Looking at the numbers, you can see that we have decreased the number of physical servers from nine to three, which is a 66 percent reduction.

 Real World Scenario

VIRTUALIZE THE LAB

You will have plenty of opportunities to virtualize Exchange. One of those opportunities is in the lab. When you virtualize your lab, you can do a virtualization equal to what is going to be in production or you can have a different layout. There are benefits to both.

If you are able to duplicate the lab and production, you can include performance testing. Duplicating the lab to production means not only matching the number of servers and role designations but also determining whether they will be physical servers. If you are going to virtualize in production, this test will give you accurate results and a baseline for the production environment. You will also increase the hardware requirement for the virtualization hosts and the storage you will be using.

If you are not able to duplicate the lab, you must prepare yourself and inform management that the lab is for functional testing only. If you were to do any performance testing, the results would not be accurate. By using this method, you will save on hardware for the virtualization hosts and storage.

Both scenarios will give you a good base for testing your virtualized Exchange environment. One gives you the ability to test performance and functionality with an added hardware cost, while the other gives you the ability to do a functional test with minimal hardware costs.

The Bottom Line

Evaluate the possible virtualization impacts.   Knowing the impacts that virtualization can have will help you make the virtualization a success. Conversely, failure to realize how virtualization will impact your environment can end up making virtualization a poor choice.

Master It   What kind of impact would virtualizing Exchange have in your environment?

Evaluate the existing Exchange environment.   Before you can determine the feasibility of a virtualized Exchange environment, you must know how your current systems are performing.

Master It   Are your Exchange servers good candidates for virtualization?

Determine when physical servers are the right choice.   There will be times when virtualization of Exchange Server isn't appropriate for an organization.

Master It   What are some common reasons to stick with physical servers for Exchange Server?

## Chapter 5

Introduction to PowerShell and the Exchange Management Shell

Microsoft PowerShell is an extensible, object-oriented command-line interface for the Windows operating system. The Exchange Management Shell (EMS) is a set of Exchange Server–specific extensions to Microsoft's PowerShell. The EMS was first introduced with Exchange Server 2007 and has been enhanced with each subsequent release of Exchange Server. The latest release includes the ability to connect to remote sessions on other Exchange servers without the Exchange Management tools.

In this chapter, we introduce you to both PowerShell and the EMS. We hope to give you a basic idea of some of the capabilities and encourage you to learn more.

Is knowledge of the EMS required? Some administrators will manage their Exchange servers for years and rarely use the EMS, whereas others use it daily. However, we think it is safe to say that at least a limited knowledge of the EMS will be required by all administrators because some specialized configuration options can be set only from the EMS.

We hope that this chapter will provide you with enough of an introduction to PowerShell that you won't dread getting to know it.

IN THIS CHAPTER, YOU WILL LEARN TO:

- Use PowerShell command syntax

- Understand object-oriented use of PowerShell

- Employ tips and tricks to get more out of PowerShell

- Get help with using PowerShell

Why Use PowerShell?

Based on discussions in Internet newsgroups, web forums, and classrooms about the decision to put the management architecture of Exchange Server 2007 on top of PowerShell, you would think that this was one of the most controversial decisions Microsoft ever made. Originally, there was enthusiastic debate (and name-calling) on both sides of the fence. But some experienced Exchange Server administrators thought the Exchange Management Shell was the best improvement Microsoft had made since Exchange Server 2003. Now that Microsoft has extended PowerShell to virtually all of their core infrastructure products, more administrators are comfortable with PowerShell and are happy with it being a key management technology.

We have to admit to becoming big supporters of the EMS from the beginning. All it took was spending a bit of time with it and getting to know some of the basic functionality. The biggest fear that many administrators have is that they will have to learn not only some of the shell's commands (called cmdlets) but also a scripting language just to manage Exchange Server. That is not the case.

The intent of the EMS is to provide a consistent interface for performing management tasks for Exchange servers, whether performing automation tasks, writing scripts, or extending the management capabilities. Tasks or operations that once required multiple programming APIs and hundreds of lines of scripting can now be accomplished in a single command. Single commands can be joined together—the output of one command can be piped to another command as input—to perform extremely powerful functions.

The base PowerShell that ships with Windows Server 2012 and later versions provides thousands of built-in cmdlets, and there are several hundred additional Exchange Server–related cmdlets you can use in the EMS; the goal is to cover all Exchange Server–related administrative tasks. You will find cmdlets that manipulate other data in Active Directory (such as cmdlets for managing user accounts) and control Exchange Server–related data in the Registry or Internet Information Services, but the cmdlets will only manipulate or manage data related to Exchange Server. The Exchange team is expecting other internal Microsoft teams, such as the Active Directory or Internet Information Server team, to provide their own extensions to the management shell (which they have).

There are a lot of very good reasons for Microsoft to create this management layer across all its products. It provides a consistent management and scripting interface for all server products, develops a secure method for remote scripting, improves batching, and provides you with an easy way to automate and repeat anything you can do in the GUI. In fact, PowerShell, first integrated in Exchange Server 2007, is now the de facto management interface for all Microsoft enterprise products, such as System Center, SQL Server, and Skype for Business.

The Exchange Management Shell is built on top of Windows PowerShell. It has the built-in Exchange cmdlets that you'll use to perform all of your administrative work. You can use it to do everything you can do in the EAC and more. But, you can't import an Exchange PowerShell module at a standard PowerShell prompt. Well, while there are ways of doing so, it isn't supported and some functionality is missing. Thus, always plan on running the Exchange Management Shell when you want to use PowerShell for your Exchange-based administrative tasks.

Understanding the Command Syntax

The problem with a lot of scripting languages and command shells is that, as they get more complex and powerful, the command syntax gets more and more cryptic. PowerShell and the EMS seek to make using the command-line interface and scripting more intuitive. To this end, most PowerShell and EMS cmdlets consist of two components: a verb and a noun.

JUST IN CASE

PowerShell cmdlets and the EMS extensions for PowerShell are case insensitive. That means you can type everything in uppercase, type everything in lowercase, or mix and match the case of the letters in your commands.

For readability and per suggestions from folks on the Exchange Server team at Microsoft, we are using Pascal-casing in this book. When you use Pascal casing, the first character of each word is in uppercase; if the cmdlet has more than one word, the first letter in each word is in uppercase. All other letters in the cmdlet are lowercase; so for example, the cmdlet that is used to retrieve mailbox statistics is written as `Get-MailboxStatistics`.

Verbs and Nouns

The verb identifies the action that is being taken, and the noun indicates the object on which the action is being taken. The verb always comes first, and the verb and noun are separated by a hyphen (such as, `Get-Mailbox`). The following list shows some of the common verbs you'll use in the EMS; some of these are specific to the EMS, but most are generic to Windows PowerShell.

Get   Get is probably the most common verb you will use. `Get` retrieves information about the specified object and outputs information about the object.

Set   Set is probably the second most common verb you will use. `Set` allows you to update properties of the object specified in the noun.

New   New creates new instances of the object specified in the noun.

Enable   Enable activates or enables a configuration on the object specified, such as enabling an existing user account.

Add   Add can be used to add items to an object or to add properties of an object.

Remove   Remove deletes an instance of the object specified in the noun.

Disable   Disable disables or deactivates the object specified in the noun. An example of this is removing a mailbox from an existing user (but not deleting the user account).

Mount   Mount is used to mount an Exchange Server mailbox or public folder database.

Dismount   Dismount is used to dismount an Exchange Server mailbox or public folder database.

Move   Move can be used to activate a database copy on a mailbox server.

Test   Test performs diagnostic tests against the object specified by the noun and the identity option.

Update   Update is used to update specified objects.

The actual nouns that are used in conjunction with these verbs are too numerous to mention in even a few pages of text. The following is a list of common nouns; later in this chapter you'll learn how to use the online help to find more cmdlets that you need. The nouns in this list can be used in conjunction with verbs, such as the ones in the preceding list, to manipulate the properties of Exchange Server–related objects. However, not all verbs work with all nouns, and unfortunately it sometimes requires some trial and error to determine what works and what doesn't.

ActiveSyncMailboxPolicy   Properties of ActiveSync policies that can be assigned to a mailbox

CASMailbox   Properties of a mailbox relating to client features such as Outlook on the web and Exchange ActiveSync

ClientAccessServer   Properties specific to client access

DistributionGroup   Properties relating to mail-enabled distribution groups

DynamicDistributionGroup   Properties relating to a dynamic distribution group

EmailAddressPolicy   Properties relating to the policies that are used to define email addresses

ExchangeServer   Properties related to Exchange servers

Mailbox   Properties related to user mailboxes

MailboxDatabase   Properties related to mailbox databases

MailboxServer   Properties specific to an Exchange Server Mailbox server role

MailContact   Properties relating to mail-enabled contact objects

MailUser   Properties relating to a user that has an email address but not a mailbox

MoveRequest   Properties and actions related to move mailbox requests

ReceiveConnector   Properties relating to Receive connectors

SendConnector   Properties relating to Send connectors

TransportConfig   Properties specific to Exchange Server Transport services

UMMailbox   Properties relating to Unified Messaging

User   Properties relating to user objects

CMDLETS WORK ONLY WITH REMOTE POWERSHELL IN EXCHANGE SERVER 2010 AND LATER

One important thing to keep in mind with cmdlets is that they are not individual executables but rather .NET classes that are accessible only from within PowerShell and only if the Exchange Server extensions to PowerShell are loaded.

With Exchange Server 2010 and later, though, you can connect to a remote session on a remote Exchange Server computer to perform commands on that remote computer. This is often referred to as *remote PowerShell*, or the ability to connect remotely to a PowerShell session. *Whether you use the shell to administer a local server or administer a server across the country, remote PowerShell is used to perform the operation in Exchange Server.*

Unlike in Microsoft Exchange Server 2007, which uses a local Windows PowerShell, Windows PowerShell connects to the closest Exchange Server (version 2010 or later) server using Windows Remote Management. The PowerShell module then performs authentication checks and then creates a remote session. When the remote session is created, the user sees and has access only to the cmdlets and the parameters associated with the management role groups and management roles assigned to the user.

Help

There is a more detailed section near the end of this chapter titled "Getting Help"; however, as you start your journey into learning PowerShell and the EMS, you should know how to get quick and basic help. If you are using PowerShell version 3 or later, you first need to download all of the help content. You can run the `Update-Help` command to download the help content. Thereafter, you can use the `Get-Help` cmdlet to show what parameters any cmdlet takes. This is much like the man command on Linux systems:

```
Get-Help Get-Mailbox
```

The -*Identity* Parameter

For cmdlets that require input, usually the first parameter provided is the `-Identity` parameter. For example, if you want to retrieve information about a mailbox named Lawrence Cohen in the Corporate organizational unit (OU), you would run the following command:

```
Get-Mailbox -Identity 'contoso.com/Corporate/Lawrence Cohen'
```

However, you will quickly find that the `-Identity` parameter is not required. If your aliases or account names are unique, even the domain and organizational unit information is not required. For example, this command would yield the same result:

```
Get-Mailbox 'contoso.com/Corporate/Lawrence Cohen'
```

As long as there is only one Lawrence Cohen in Active Directory, you can even drop the domain and the OU name and this cmdlet will yield the same result:

```
Get-Mailbox 'Lawrence Cohen'
```

YOU CAN QUOTE ME ON THAT

Any time the identity you are using has a space in it, you must use quotes. Either single or double quotes will work.

The `-Identity` parameter is optional by design. As you will find shortly, the input for one cmdlet can even be piped in from the output of another cmdlet.

If you are not sure what input can be specified for the `-Identity` parameter, you can easily look up this information either in the Exchange Server online help or by using the EMS command-line help (more on this later in this chapter). For now, let's look at one small piece of the `Get-Mailbox` help screen that shows the different values that can be used to identify a mailbox:

```
-Identity <MailboxIdParameter>
```

The Identity parameter identifies the mailbox. You can use one of the following values:

```
* Name
* Display name
* Alias
* Distinguished name (DN)
* Canonical DN
* <domain name>\<account name>
* Email address
* GUID
* LegacyExchangeDN
* SamAccountName
* User ID or user principal name (UPN)
```

You can see that the -Identity parameter will take the mailbox GUID, the user's distinguished name, the domain name and account, the UPN name, the legacy Exchange Server distinguished name, the SMTP address, or the Exchange Server alias.

CMDLET VS. COMMAND

You will notice that sometimes we use "command" and sometimes we use "cmdlet" when talking about PowerShell. There is a subtle difference:

◆ A cmdlet is the verb-noun combination that performs a specific task; it is the base PowerShell object that takes input, does something to it, and produces some output.

◆ A complete command is the cmdlet along with any necessary options that the task might require. The command necessary to retrieve information about a specific mailbox looks like this:

```
Get-Mailbox "Gillian Katz"
```

Cmdlet Parameters

PowerShell and EMS cmdlets support a number of command-line parameters that are useful. Parameters can be categorized as mandatory or not and as positional or not. When a parameter is *mandatory*, PowerShell requires you to add the parameter with a given cmdlet and specify a value for it. If the use of a parameter is not mandatory, you are allowed to include it, but you don't have to do so. The cmdlet New-Mailbox illustrates this behavior nicely. When creating a new mailbox-enabled user, you have to include the parameter UserPrincipalName, but you are free to include the parameter OrganizationalUnit. The EMS will prompt you for the value of any mandatory parameter you forget to specify. Next to being mandatory or not, it is not always necessary to include the parameter name. When a parameter is *positional*, you can just add the value and leave out the parameter name. The cmdlet Get-Mailbox has no mandatory parameters but does have a positional parameter, namely -Identity. If we run the following EMS line, the shell will return the properties of a mailbox-enabled user whose Exchange alias is Oliver.Cohen:

```
Get-Mailbox Oliver.Cohen
Name              Alias           ServerName      ProhibitSendQuota
----              -----           ----------      ---------------
Oliver.Cohen      Oliver.Cohen    Ex1             unlimited
```

This is the same as running this:

```
Get-Mailbox -Identity Oliver.Cohen
Name                  Alias              ServerName       ProhibitSendQuota
----                  -----              ----------       ----------------
Oliver.Cohen          Oliver.Cohen       NYC-EX1             unlimited
```

However, if we run the following command, the shell will complain that it doesn't know any mailbox-enabled user by the name of Ex1, because the parameter `Server` is not positional:

```
Get-Mailbox Ex1
The operation couldn't be performed because object 'Ex1' couldn't be
found on 'dc01.contoso.com'.
    + CategoryInfo    : NotSpecified: (:) [Get-Mailbox],
ManagementObjectNotFoundException
    + FullyQualifiedErrorId : 3FEDEA30,Microsoft.Exchange.Management.
RecipientTasks.GetMailbox
```

However, if you apply the proper `-Server` parameter in your command, the server name becomes apparent to the Exchange server. Note that this command displays all of the mailboxes, not just those on EX1.

```
Get-Mailbox -Server Ex1
Name                         Alias                ServerName    ProhibitSendQuota
----                         -----                ----------    -----------------
Administrator                Administrator        NYC-EX1          unlimited
DiscoverySearchMailbox...    DiscoverySearchMa... NYC-EX1          unlimited
Bob Clements                 Bob Clements         NYC-EX1          unlimited
Jordan Chang                 JordanChang          NYC-EX1          unlimited
Tyler M. Swartz              Tyler M. Swartz      NYC-EX1          unlimited
Elias Mereb                  Elias Mereb          NYC-EX1          unlimited
John Rodriguez               JohnRodriguez        NYC-EX1          unlimited
Jonathan Long                JonathanLong         NYC-EX1          unlimited
Kevin Wile                   KevinWile            NYC-EX1          unlimited
John Park                    JohnPark             NYC-EX1          unlimited
Julie R. Samante             JulieR.Samante       NYC-EX1          unlimited
Jim McBee                    JimMcBee             NYC-EX1          unlimited
Chuck Swanson                ChuckSwanson         NYC-EX1          unlimited
Kelly Siu                    KellySiu             NYC-EX1          unlimited
Gerald Nakata                GeraldNakata         NYC-EX1          unlimited
```

The following are some of the parameters that cmdlets accept. Not all cmdlets will accept all of these parameters; these are usually optional, and, of course, some of them will not be relevant.

-Identity   `-Identity` specifies a unique object on which the cmdlet is going to act. The `-Identity` parameter is a positional parameter, which means that it does not necessarily have to be on the command line; PowerShell will prompt you for the identity if it is not specified. As noted previously, in most cases you do not need to specify the `-Identity` parameter but just the unique object name.

-WhatIf   `-WhatIf` tells the cmdlet to simulate the action that the cmdlet would actually perform but not actually make the change.

-Confirm -Confirm asks the cmdlet to prompt for confirmation prior to starting the action. This option type is Boolean, so you need to include either $True or $False. Some cmdlets (such as New-MoveRequest-) ask for confirmation by default, so you could specify -Confirm:$False if you did not want the confirmation request to occur.

-Validate -Validate will check the prerequisites of the cmdlet to verify that it will run correctly and let you know if the cmdlet will run successfully.

-Credential -Credential allows you to specify alternative credentials when running a PowerShell command.

-DomainController -DomainController allows you to specify the FQDN of a specific domain controller against which you want to perform a PowerShell task.

-ResultSize The -ResultSize option allows you to specify a maximum number of results when working with Get- cmdlets.

-SortBy The -SortBy option allows you to specify a sorting criteria when outputting data that is usually the result of a Get- cmdlet.

-Verbose -Verbose instructs Get- cmdlets to return more information about the execution of the cmdlet.

-Debug -Debug instructs the cmdlet to output more information and to proceed step-by-step through the process of performing a task. -Debug returns more information than a typical administrator needs to perform daily tasks.

If you are piping output of one cmdlet into another, the parameters must be within the cmdlet that you want the parameter to affect.

Tab Completion

In order to be descriptive and helpful, some of the cmdlets are pretty long. Consider if you had to type **Get-DistributionGroupMember** several times! However, PowerShell includes a feature called tab completion. If you type part of a command and then press the Tab key, PowerShell will complete the cmdlet with the first matching cmdlet it can find. For example, if you type **Get-Distri** and press Tab, PowerShell will automatically fill out Get-DistributionGroup. If you press Tab again, PowerShell will move on to the next matching cmdlet, or in this case Get-DistributionGroupMember.

The tab completion feature also works for cmdlet parameters. If you type a cmdlet followed by a space and a hyphen, such as **Get-Mailbox -**, and then press Tab, you will cycle through all the parameters for that particular cmdlet. When you include parameters with your cmdlet, it is not necessary to specify their full names. It is sufficient to enter enough letters to make sure the EMS can figure out which parameter you meant to define. For example, if you enter **Get-Mailbox -Se server1**, you will be given a list of all mailboxes housed on server1. But tab completion can be useful to help you keep an overview of your EMS lines.

Alias

PowerShell and the EMS also include aliases that allow you to invoke cmdlets using a familiar synonym. A typical example here is entering **Dir** to get a list of all files in the directory that you are in and all subdirectories after that directory, which is in fact an alias for the cmdlet Get-ChildItem. Table 5.1 shows some common aliases that are built into PowerShell.

TABLE 5.1:   PowerShell Common Aliases

ALIAS	DEFINITION
Dir	Get-ChildItem
Ls	Get-ChildItem
Type	Get-Content
Cat	Get-Content
Write	Write-Output
Echo	Write-Output
cd	Set-Location
sl	Set-Location
cls	Clear-Host

But it is important to remember that entering an alias in the end is like entering a cmdlet, thus imposing some constraints that do not apply when entering the aliases from Table 5.1 in a command prompt. If you would like to get a list of all files, and files located in subdirectories, you would be inclined to enter **dir /s**, but when doing so you will be faced with the following error message:

```
dir /s
Get-ChildItem : Cannot find path 'C:\s' because it does not exist.
At line:1 char:4
+ dir  <<<< /s
```

Of course, **dir /s** works at a command prompt. Using PowerShell, you know you need to include any parameter by adding a hyphen followed by the parameter name:

```
dir -Recurse:$True
or:
dir -r
```

Object-Oriented Use of PowerShell

One of the reasons PowerShell is so flexible is that the output of commands is not text based but rather object based. PowerShell uses an object model that is based on the Microsoft .NET Framework. PowerShell cmdlets accept and return structured data. Don't let the terms "object model" or "object-oriented" scare you, though. This is really quite simple. For example, Figure 5.1 shows the output of the Get-Mailbox cmdlet.

FIGURE 5.1
Output of the
Get-Mailbox
cmdlet

What you see on the screen is text to the user interface, but to PowerShell it is really a list of objects. You can manipulate the output to see the properties you want, filter the output, or pipe the output (the objects) to another cmdlet.

Filtering Output

In Figure 5.1, you can see that the cmdlet we used (Get-Mailbox) outputs every mailbox in the entire organization. There are a number of ways you can filter or narrow the scope of the output you are looking for from a specific cmdlet. In the case of Get-Mailbox and other cmdlets, you can specify just the identity of the mailbox for which you are looking.

PowerShell includes two options that can be used specifically for filtering the output. These are the Where-Object (or Where alias) and the Filter-Object (or Filter) objects. The Where clause can be used on most cmdlets, and the filter is applied at the client. The Filter clause is available only on a subset of the commands because this filter is applied by the server.

In the following command, the output of the Get-Mailbox cmdlet is piped to the Where clause, which filters the output:

```
Get-Mailbox | Where-Object {$_.MaxSendSize -gt 25000000}
```

In this case, the output is any mailbox whose -MaxSendSize parameter is greater than 25,000,000 bytes. Did you notice the portion of the Where statement $_.MaxSendSize? The $_ portion represents the current object that is being piped to the Where-Object cmdlet, and .MaxSendSize represents the MaxSendSize property of that object.

For nonprogrammers, this might seem a little difficult at first, but we promise it gets much easier as you go along. The operators are also simple to remember. Table 5.2 shows common operators that can be used in clauses such as Where-Object or just the Where alias. The Operator column defines how the value defined as an object property is treated.

TABLE 5.2:   Shell Values and Operators

SHELL VALUE	OPERATOR	FUNCTION
-eq	Equals	The object.property value must match exactly the specified value.
-ne	Not equals	The object.property value must not match the specified value.
-gt	Greater than	-gt works when the object.property value is an integer.
-ge	Greater than or equal to	-ge works when the object.property value is an integer.
-lt	Less than	-lt works when the object.property value is an integer.
-le	Less than or equal to	-le works when the object.property value is an integer.
-like	Contains	-like is used when the object.property value is a text string. The matching string can either match exactly or contain wildcards (*) at the beginning or end of the string.
-notlike	Does not contain	-notlike is used when the object.property value is a text string and you want to see if the values do not match the string. The matching string can contain wildcards (*) at the beginning or end of the string.

Sometimes, finding all of the properties that can be used with a particular cmdlet can be difficult. We would like to share a couple of tips that will help illustrate or discover these properties. Let's take the Set-Mailbox cmdlet as an example. First, you can simply use the available online help such as this:

```
set-mailbox -?
NAME
    Set-Mailbox
SYNOPSIS
    This cmdlet is available in on-premises Exchange Server 2016 and in the
    cloud-based service. Some parameters and
    settings may be exclusive to one environment or the other.
```

Use the Set-Mailbox cmdlet to modify the settings of existing mailboxes. For information about the parameter sets in the Syntax section below, see Syntax.

```
SYNTAX
    Set-Mailbox -Identity <MailboxIdParameter> [-AcceptMessagesOnlyFrom
<MultiValuedProperty>]
    [-AcceptMessagesOnlyFromDLMembers <MultiValuedProperty>] [-
AcceptMessagesOnlyFromSendersOrMembers
    <MultiValuedProperty>] [-AddressBookPolicy
<AddressBookMailboxPolicyIdParameter>] [-Alias <String>]
    [-AntispamBypassEnabled <$true | $false>] [-ApplyMandatoryProperties
<SwitchParameter>] [-Arbitration
    <SwitchParameter>] [-ArbitrationMailbox <MailboxIdParameter>] [-
ArchiveDatabase <DatabaseIdParameter>]
    [-ArchiveDomain <SmtpDomain>] [-ArchiveName <MultiValuedProperty>] [-
ArchiveQuota <Unlimited>] [-ArchiveStatus
    <None | Active>] [-ArchiveWarningQuota <Unlimited>] [-AuditAdmin
<MultiValuedProperty>] [-AuditDelegate
    <MultiValuedProperty>] [-AuditEnabled <$true | $false>] [-AuditLog
<SwitchParameter>] [-AuditLogAgeLimit
    <EnhancedTimeSpan>] [-AuditOwner <MultiValuedProperty>] [-
BypassModerationFromSendersOrMembers
    <MultiValuedProperty>] [-CalendarLoggingQuota <Unlimited>] [-
CalendarRepairDisabled <$true | $false>]
    [-CalendarVersionStoreDisabled <$true | $false>] [-ClientExtensions <$true
| $false>] [-Confirm
    [<SwitchParameter>]] [-CreateDTMFMap <$true | $false>] [-CustomAttribute1
<String>] [-CustomAttribute10 <String>]
    [-CustomAttribute11 <String>] [-CustomAttribute12 <String>] [-
CustomAttribute13 <String>] [-CustomAttribute14
    <String>] [-CustomAttribute15 <String>] [-CustomAttribute2 <String>] [-
CustomAttribute3 <String>]
    [-CustomAttribute4 <String>] [-CustomAttribute5 <String>] [-
CustomAttribute6 <String>] [-CustomAttribute7
    <String>] [-CustomAttribute8 <String>] [-CustomAttribute9 <String>] [-
Database <DatabaseIdParameter>]
    [-DefaultPublicFolderMailbox <RecipientIdParameter>] [-
DeliverToMailboxAndForward <$true | $false>] [-DisplayName
    <String>] [-DomainController <Fqdn>] [-DowngradeHighPriorityMessagesEnabled
<$true | $false>]
    [-DumpsterMessagesPerFolderCountReceiveQuota <Int32>] [-
DumpsterMessagesPerFolderCountWarningQuota <Int32>]
    [-EmailAddresses <ProxyAddressCollection>] [-EmailAddressPolicyEnabled
<$true | $false>]
    [-EnableRoomMailboxAccount <$true | $false>] [-EndDateForRetentionHold
<DateTime>] [-ExtendedPropertiesCountQuota
    <Int32>] [-ExtensionCustomAttribute1 <MultiValuedProperty>] [-
```

```
ExtensionCustomAttribute2 <MultiValuedProperty>]
    [-ExtensionCustomAttribute3 <MultiValuedProperty>] [-
ExtensionCustomAttribute4 <MultiValuedProperty>]
    [-ExtensionCustomAttribute5 <MultiValuedProperty>] [-ExternalOofOptions
<InternalOnly | External>]
    [-FederatedIdentity <String>] [-FolderHierarchyChildrenCountReceiveQuota
<Int32>]
    [-FolderHierarchyChildrenCountWarningQuota <Int32>] [-
FolderHierarchyDepthReceiveQuota <Int32>]
    [-FolderHierarchyDepthWarningQuota <Int32>] [-FoldersCountReceiveQuota
<Int32>] [-FoldersCountWarningQuota
    <Int32>] [-Force <SwitchParameter>] [-ForwardingAddress
<RecipientIdParameter>] [-ForwardingSmtpAddress
    <ProxyAddress>] [-GMGen <$true | $false>] [-GrantSendOnBehalfTo
<MultiValuedProperty>]
    [-HiddenFromAddressListsEnabled <$true | $false>] [-IgnoreDefaultScope
<SwitchParameter>]
    [-ImListMigrationCompleted <$true | $false>] [-ImmutableId <String>] [-
InactiveMailbox <SwitchParameter>]
    [-IsExcludedFromServingHierarchy <$true | $false>] [-IsHierarchyReady
<$true | $false>] [-IssueWarningQuota
    <Unlimited>] [-JournalArchiveAddress <SmtpAddress>] [-Languages
<MultiValuedProperty>] [-LinkedCredential
    <PSCredential>] [-LinkedDomainController <String>] [-LinkedMasterAccount
<UserIdParameter>] [-LitigationHoldDate
    <DateTime>] [-LitigationHoldDuration <Unlimited>] [-LitigationHoldEnabled
<$true | $false>] [-LitigationHoldOwner
    <String>] [-MailboxMessagesPerFolderCountReceiveQuota <Int32>] [-
MailboxMessagesPerFolderCountWarningQuota
    <Int32>] [-MailboxPlan <MailboxPlanIdParameter>] [-
MailboxProvisioningConstraint <MailboxProvisioningConstraint>]
    [-MailboxProvisioningPreferences <MultiValuedProperty>] [-MailRouting
<$true | $false>] [-MailTip <String>]
    [-MailTipTranslations <MultiValuedProperty>] [-Management <$true | $false>]
[-MaxBlockedSenders <Int32>]
    [-MaxReceiveSize <Unlimited>] [-MaxSafeSenders <Int32>] [-MaxSendSize
<Unlimited>]
    [-MessageCopyForSendOnBehalfEnabled <$true | $false>] [-
MessageCopyForSentAsEnabled <$true | $false>]
    [-MessageTracking <$true | $false>] [-MessageTrackingReadStatusEnabled
<$true | $false>]
    [-MicrosoftOnlineServicesID <SmtpAddress>] [-Migration <$true | $false>] [-
ModeratedBy <MultiValuedProperty>]
    [-ModerationEnabled <$true | $false>] [-Name <String>] [-NewPassword
<SecureString>] [-OABGen <$true | $false>]
    [-OABReplica <$true | $false>] [-Office <String>] [-OfflineAddressBook
<OfflineAddressBookIdParameter>]
    [-OldPassword <SecureString>] [-OMEncryption <$true | $false>] [-Password
<SecureString>] [-PrimarySmtpAddress
```

```
    <SmtpAddress>] [-ProhibitSendQuota <Unlimited>] [-ProhibitSendReceiveQuota
<Unlimited>] [-PstProvider <$true |
    $false>] [-PublicFolder <SwitchParameter>] [-QueryBaseDN
<OrganizationalUnitIdParameter>]
    [-QueryBaseDNRestrictionEnabled <$true | $false>] [-RecipientLimits
<Unlimited>] [-RecoverableItemsQuota
    <Unlimited>] [-RecoverableItemsWarningQuota <Unlimited>] [-
RejectMessagesFrom <MultiValuedProperty>]
    [-RejectMessagesFromDLMembers <MultiValuedProperty>] [-
RejectMessagesFromSendersOrMembers <MultiValuedProperty>]
    [-RemoteAccountPolicy <RemoteAccountPolicyIdParameter>] [-
RemoteRecipientType <None | ProvisionMailbox |
    ProvisionArchive | Migrated | DeprovisionMailbox | DeprovisionArchive |
RoomMailbox | EquipmentMailbox |
    SharedMailbox | TeamMailbox>] [-RemoveManagedFolderAndPolicy
<SwitchParameter>] [-RemovePicture <SwitchParameter>]
    [-RemoveSpokenName <SwitchParameter>] [-RequireSenderAuthenticationEnabled
<$true | $false>]
    [-ResetPasswordOnNextLogon <$true | $false>] [-ResourceCapacity <Int32>] [-
ResourceCustom <MultiValuedProperty>]
    [-RetainDeletedItemsFor <EnhancedTimeSpan>] [-RetainDeletedItemsUntilBackup
<$true | $false>] [-RetentionComment
    <String>] [-RetentionHoldEnabled <$true | $false>] [-RetentionPolicy
<MailboxPolicyIdParameter>] [-RetentionUrl
    <String>] [-RoleAssignmentPolicy <MailboxPolicyIdParameter>] [-
RoomMailboxPassword <SecureString>] [-RulesQuota
    <ByteQuantifiedSize>] [-SamAccountName <String>] [-SCLDeleteEnabled <$true
| $false>] [-SCLDeleteThreshold
    <Int32>] [-SCLJunkEnabled <$true | $false>] [-SCLJunkThreshold <Int32>] [-
SCLQuarantineEnabled <$true | $false>]
    [-SCLQuarantineThreshold <Int32>] [-SCLRejectEnabled <$true | $false>] [-
SCLRejectThreshold <Int32>]
    [-SecondaryAddress <String>] [-SecondaryDialPlan <UMDialPlanIdParameter>]
[-SendModerationNotifications <Never |
    Internal | Always>] [-SharingPolicy <SharingPolicyIdParameter>] [-
SimpleDisplayName <String>]
    [-SingleItemRecoveryEnabled <$true | $false>] [-
SkipMailboxProvisioningConstraintValidation <SwitchParameter>]
    [-StartDateForRetentionHold <DateTime>] [-TenantUpgrade <$true | $false>]
[-ThrottlingPolicy
    <ThrottlingPolicyIdParameter>] [-Type <Regular | Room | Equipment |
Shared>] [-UMDataStorage <$true | $false>]
    [-UMDtmfMap <MultiValuedProperty>] [-UMGrammar <$true | $false>] [-
UseDatabaseQuotaDefaults <$true | $false>]
    [-UseDatabaseRetentionDefaults <$true | $false>] [-UserCertificate
<MultiValuedProperty>] [-UserPrincipalName
    <String>] [-UserSMimeCertificate <MultiValuedProperty>] [-WhatIf
[<SwitchParameter>]] [-WindowsEmailAddress
```

```
    <SmtpAddress>] [-WindowsLiveID <SmtpAddress>] [<CommonParameters>]


    Set-Mailbox -Identity <MailboxIdParameter> [-AcceptMessagesOnlyFrom
<MultiValuedProperty>]
    [-AcceptMessagesOnlyFromDLMembers <MultiValuedProperty>] [-
AcceptMessagesOnlyFromSendersOrMembers
    <MultiValuedProperty>] [-AddressBookPolicy
<AddressBookMailboxPolicyIdParameter>] [-Alias <String>]
    [-AntispamBypassEnabled <$true | $false>] [-ApplyMandatoryProperties
<SwitchParameter>] [-Arbitration
    <SwitchParameter>] [-ArbitrationMailbox <MailboxIdParameter>] [-
ArchiveDatabase <DatabaseIdParameter>]
    [-ArchiveDomain <SmtpDomain>] [-ArchiveName <MultiValuedProperty>] [-
ArchiveQuota <Unlimited>] [-ArchiveStatus
    <None | Active>] [-ArchiveWarningQuota <Unlimited>] [-AuditAdmin
<MultiValuedProperty>] [-AuditDelegate
    <MultiValuedProperty>] [-AuditEnabled <$true | $false>] [-AuditLog
<SwitchParameter>] [-AuditLogAgeLimit
    <EnhancedTimeSpan>] [-AuditOwner <MultiValuedProperty>] [-
BypassModerationFromSendersOrMembers
    <MultiValuedProperty>] [-CalendarLoggingQuota <Unlimited>] [-
CalendarRepairDisabled <$true | $false>]
    [-CalendarVersionStoreDisabled <$true | $false>] [-ClientExtensions <$true
| $false>] [-Confirm
    [<SwitchParameter>]] [-CreateDTMFMap <$true | $false>] [-CustomAttribute1
<String>] [-CustomAttribute10 <String>]
    [-CustomAttribute11 <String>] [-CustomAttribute12 <String>] [-
CustomAttribute13 <String>] [-CustomAttribute14
    <String>] [-CustomAttribute15 <String>] [-CustomAttribute2 <String>] [-
CustomAttribute3 <String>]
    [-CustomAttribute4 <String>] [-CustomAttribute5 <String>] [-
CustomAttribute6 <String>] [-CustomAttribute7
    <String>] [-CustomAttribute8 <String>] [-CustomAttribute9 <String>] [-
Database <DatabaseIdParameter>]
    [-DefaultPublicFolderMailbox <RecipientIdParameter>] [-
DeliverToMailboxAndForward <$true | $false>] [-DisplayName
    <String>] [-DomainController <Fqdn>] [-DowngradeHighPriorityMessagesEnabled
<$true | $false>]
    [-DumpsterMessagesPerFolderCountReceiveQuota <Int32>] [-
DumpsterMessagesPerFolderCountWarningQuota <Int32>]
    [-EmailAddresses <ProxyAddressCollection>] [-EmailAddressPolicyEnabled
<$true | $false>]
    [-EnableRoomMailboxAccount <$true | $false>] [-EndDateForRetentionHold
<DateTime>] [-ExtendedPropertiesCountQuota
    <Int32>] [-ExtensionCustomAttribute1 <MultiValuedProperty>] [-
ExtensionCustomAttribute2 <MultiValuedProperty>]
    [-ExtensionCustomAttribute3 <MultiValuedProperty>] [-
ExtensionCustomAttribute4 <MultiValuedProperty>]
```

```
    [-ExtensionCustomAttribute5 <MultiValuedProperty>] [-ExternalOofOptions
<InternalOnly | External>]
    [-FederatedIdentity <String>] [-FolderHierarchyChildrenCountReceiveQuota
<Int32>]
    [-FolderHierarchyChildrenCountWarningQuota <Int32>] [-
FolderHierarchyDepthReceiveQuota <Int32>]
    [-FolderHierarchyDepthWarningQuota <Int32>] [-FoldersCountReceiveQuota
<Int32>] [-FoldersCountWarningQuota
    <Int32>] [-Force <SwitchParameter>] [-ForwardingAddress
<RecipientIdParameter>] [-ForwardingSmtpAddress
    <ProxyAddress>] [-GMGen <$true | $false>] [-GrantSendOnBehalfTo
<MultiValuedProperty>]
    [-HiddenFromAddressListsEnabled <$true | $false>] [-IgnoreDefaultScope
<SwitchParameter>]
    [-ImListMigrationCompleted <$true | $false>] [-ImmutableId <String>] [-
InactiveMailbox <SwitchParameter>]
    [-IsExcludedFromServingHierarchy <$true | $false>] [-IsHierarchyReady
<$true | $false>] [-IssueWarningQuota
    <Unlimited>] [-JournalArchiveAddress <SmtpAddress>] [-Languages
<MultiValuedProperty>] [-LinkedCredential
    <PSCredential>] [-LinkedDomainController <String>] [-LinkedMasterAccount
<UserIdParameter>] [-LitigationHoldDate
    <DateTime>] [-LitigationHoldDuration <Unlimited>] [-LitigationHoldEnabled
<$true | $false>] [-LitigationHoldOwner
    <String>] [-MailboxMessagesPerFolderCountReceiveQuota <Int32>] [-
MailboxMessagesPerFolderCountWarningQuota
    <Int32>] [-MailboxPlan <MailboxPlanIdParameter>] [-
MailboxProvisioningConstraint <MailboxProvisioningConstraint>]
    [-MailboxProvisioningPreferences <MultiValuedProperty>] [-MailRouting
<$true | $false>] [-MailTip <String>]
    [-MailTipTranslations <MultiValuedProperty>] [-Management <$true | $false>]
[-MaxBlockedSenders <Int32>]
    [-MaxReceiveSize <Unlimited>] [-MaxSafeSenders <Int32>] [-MaxSendSize
<Unlimited>]
    [-MessageCopyForSendOnBehalfEnabled <$true | $false>] [-
MessageCopyForSentAsEnabled <$true | $false>]
    [-MessageTracking <$true | $false>] [-MessageTrackingReadStatusEnabled
<$true | $false>]
    [-MicrosoftOnlineServicesID <SmtpAddress>] [-Migration <$true | $false>] [-
ModeratedBy <MultiValuedProperty>]
    [-ModerationEnabled <$true | $false>] [-Name <String>] [-NewPassword
<SecureString>] [-OABGen <$true | $false>]
    [-OABReplica <$true | $false>] [-Office <String>] [-OfflineAddressBook
<OfflineAddressBookIdParameter>]
    [-OldPassword <SecureString>] [-OMEncryption <$true | $false>] [-Password
<SecureString>] [-PrimarySmtpAddress
```

```
    <SmtpAddress>] [-ProhibitSendQuota <Unlimited>] [-ProhibitSendReceiveQuota
<Unlimited>] [-PstProvider <$true |
    $false>] [-PublicFolder <SwitchParameter>] [-QueryBaseDN
<OrganizationalUnitIdParameter>]
    [-QueryBaseDNRestrictionEnabled <$true | $false>] [-RecipientLimits
<Unlimited>] [-RecoverableItemsQuota
    <Unlimited>] [-RecoverableItemsWarningQuota <Unlimited>] [-
RejectMessagesFrom <MultiValuedProperty>]
    [-RejectMessagesFromDLMembers <MultiValuedProperty>] [-
RejectMessagesFromSendersOrMembers <MultiValuedProperty>]
    [-RemoteAccountPolicy <RemoteAccountPolicyIdParameter>] [-
RemoteRecipientType <None | ProvisionMailbox |
    ProvisionArchive | Migrated | DeprovisionMailbox | DeprovisionArchive |
RoomMailbox | EquipmentMailbox |
    SharedMailbox | TeamMailbox>] [-RemoveManagedFolderAndPolicy
<SwitchParameter>] [-RemovePicture <SwitchParameter>]
    [-RemoveSpokenName <SwitchParameter>] [-RequireSenderAuthenticationEnabled
<$true | $false>]
    [-ResetPasswordOnNextLogon <$true | $false>] [-ResourceCapacity <Int32>] [-
ResourceCustom <MultiValuedProperty>]
    [-RetainDeletedItemsFor <EnhancedTimeSpan>] [-RetainDeletedItemsUntilBackup
<$true | $false>] [-RetentionComment
    <String>] [-RetentionHoldEnabled <$true | $false>] [-RetentionPolicy
<MailboxPolicyIdParameter>] [-RetentionUrl
    <String>] [-RoleAssignmentPolicy <MailboxPolicyIdParameter>] [-
RoomMailboxPassword <SecureString>] [-RulesQuota
    <ByteQuantifiedSize>] [-SamAccountName <String>] [-SCLDeleteEnabled <$true
| $false>] [-SCLDeleteThreshold
    <Int32>] [-SCLJunkEnabled <$true | $false>] [-SCLJunkThreshold <Int32>] [-
SCLQuarantineEnabled <$true | $false>]
    [-SCLQuarantineThreshold <Int32>] [-SCLRejectEnabled <$true | $false>] [-
SCLRejectThreshold <Int32>]
    [-SecondaryAddress <String>] [-SecondaryDialPlan <UMDialPlanIdParameter>]
[-SendModerationNotifications <Never |
    Internal | Always>] [-SharingPolicy <SharingPolicyIdParameter>] [-
SimpleDisplayName <String>]
    [-SingleItemRecoveryEnabled <$true | $false>] [-
SkipMailboxProvisioningConstraintValidation <SwitchParameter>]
    [-StartDateForRetentionHold <DateTime>] [-TenantUpgrade <$true | $false>]
[-ThrottlingPolicy
    <ThrottlingPolicyIdParameter>] [-Type <Regular | Room | Equipment |
Shared>] [-UMDataStorage <$true | $false>]
    [-UMDtmfMap <MultiValuedProperty>] [-UMGrammar <$true | $false>] [-
UseDatabaseQuotaDefaults <$true | $false>]
    [-UseDatabaseRetentionDefaults <$true | $false>] [-UserCertificate
<MultiValuedProperty>] [-UserPrincipalName
```

```
    <String>] [-UserSMimeCertificate <MultiValuedProperty>] [-WhatIf
[<SwitchParameter>]] [-WindowsEmailAddress
    <SmtpAddress>] [-WindowsLiveID <SmtpAddress>] [<CommonParameters>]

    Set-Mailbox -Identity <MailboxIdParameter> [-AcceptMessagesOnlyFrom
<MultiValuedProperty>]
    [-AcceptMessagesOnlyFromDLMembers <MultiValuedProperty>] [-
AcceptMessagesOnlyFromSendersOrMembers
    <MultiValuedProperty>] [-AddressBookPolicy
<AddressBookMailboxPolicyIdParameter>] [-Alias <String>]
    [-AntispamBypassEnabled <$true | $false>] [-ApplyMandatoryProperties
<SwitchParameter>] [-Arbitration
    <SwitchParameter>] [-ArbitrationMailbox <MailboxIdParameter>] [-
ArchiveDatabase <DatabaseIdParameter>]
    [-ArchiveDomain <SmtpDomain>] [-ArchiveName <MultiValuedProperty>] [-
ArchiveQuota <Unlimited>] [-ArchiveStatus
    <None | Active>] [-ArchiveWarningQuota <Unlimited>] [-AuditAdmin
<MultiValuedProperty>] [-AuditDelegate
    <MultiValuedProperty>] [-AuditEnabled <$true | $false>] [-AuditLog
<SwitchParameter>] [-AuditLogAgeLimit
    <EnhancedTimeSpan>] [-AuditOwner <MultiValuedProperty>] [-
BypassModerationFromSendersOrMembers
    <MultiValuedProperty>] [-CalendarLoggingQuota <Unlimited>] [-
CalendarRepairDisabled <$true | $false>]
    [-CalendarVersionStoreDisabled <$true | $false>] [-ClientExtensions <$true
| $false>] [-Confirm
    [<SwitchParameter>]] [-CreateDTMFMap <$true | $false>] [-CustomAttribute1
<String>] [-CustomAttribute10 <String>]
    [-CustomAttribute11 <String>] [-CustomAttribute12 <String>] [-
CustomAttribute13 <String>] [-CustomAttribute14
    <String>] [-CustomAttribute15 <String>] [-CustomAttribute2 <String>] [-
CustomAttribute3 <String>]
    [-CustomAttribute4 <String>] [-CustomAttribute5 <String>] [-
CustomAttribute6 <String>] [-CustomAttribute7
    <String>] [-CustomAttribute8 <String>] [-CustomAttribute9 <String>] [-
Database <DatabaseIdParameter>]
    [-DefaultPublicFolderMailbox <RecipientIdParameter>] [-
DeliverToMailboxAndForward <$true | $false>] [-DisplayName
    <String>] [-DomainController <Fqdn>] [-DowngradeHighPriorityMessagesEnabled
<$true | $false>]
    [-DumpsterMessagesPerFolderCountReceiveQuota <Int32>] [-
DumpsterMessagesPerFolderCountWarningQuota <Int32>]
    [-EmailAddresses <ProxyAddressCollection>] [-EmailAddressPolicyEnabled
<$true | $false>]
    [-EnableRoomMailboxAccount <$true | $false>] [-EndDateForRetentionHold
<DateTime>] [-ExtendedPropertiesCountQuota
    <Int32>] [-ExtensionCustomAttribute1 <MultiValuedProperty>] [-
```

```
ExtensionCustomAttribute2 <MultiValuedProperty>]
    [-ExtensionCustomAttribute3 <MultiValuedProperty>] [-
ExtensionCustomAttribute4 <MultiValuedProperty>]
    [-ExtensionCustomAttribute5 <MultiValuedProperty>] [-ExternalOofOptions
<InternalOnly | External>]
    [-FederatedIdentity <String>] [-FolderHierarchyChildrenCountReceiveQuota
<Int32>]
    [-FolderHierarchyChildrenCountWarningQuota <Int32>] [-
FolderHierarchyDepthReceiveQuota <Int32>]
    [-FolderHierarchyDepthWarningQuota <Int32>] [-FoldersCountReceiveQuota
<Int32>] [-FoldersCountWarningQuota
    <Int32>] [-Force <SwitchParameter>] [-ForwardingAddress
<RecipientIdParameter>] [-ForwardingSmtpAddress
    <ProxyAddress>] [-GMGen <$true | $false>] [-GrantSendOnBehalfTo
<MultiValuedProperty>]
    [-HiddenFromAddressListsEnabled <$true | $false>] [-IgnoreDefaultScope
<SwitchParameter>]
    [-ImListMigrationCompleted <$true | $false>] [-ImmutableId <String>] [-
InactiveMailbox <SwitchParameter>]
    [-IsExcludedFromServingHierarchy <$true | $false>] [-IsHierarchyReady
<$true | $false>] [-IssueWarningQuota
    <Unlimited>] [-JournalArchiveAddress <SmtpAddress>] [-Languages
<MultiValuedProperty>] [-LinkedCredential
    <PSCredential>] [-LinkedDomainController <String>] [-LinkedMasterAccount
<UserIdParameter>] [-LitigationHoldDate
    <DateTime>] [-LitigationHoldDuration <Unlimited>] [-LitigationHoldEnabled
<$true | $false>] [-LitigationHoldOwner
    <String>] [-MailboxMessagesPerFolderCountReceiveQuota <Int32>] [-
MailboxMessagesPerFolderCountWarningQuota
    <Int32>] [-MailboxPlan <MailboxPlanIdParameter>] [-
MailboxProvisioningConstraint <MailboxProvisioningConstraint>]
    [-MailboxProvisioningPreferences <MultiValuedProperty>] [-MailRouting
<$true | $false>] [-MailTip <String>]
    [-MailTipTranslations <MultiValuedProperty>] [-Management <$true | $false>]
[-MaxBlockedSenders <Int32>]
    [-MaxReceiveSize <Unlimited>] [-MaxSafeSenders <Int32>] [-MaxSendSize
<Unlimited>]
    [-MessageCopyForSendOnBehalfEnabled <$true | $false>] [-
MessageCopyForSentAsEnabled <$true | $false>]
    [-MessageTracking <$true | $false>] [-MessageTrackingReadStatusEnabled
<$true | $false>]
    [-MicrosoftOnlineServicesID <SmtpAddress>] [-Migration <$true | $false>] [-
ModeratedBy <MultiValuedProperty>]
    [-ModerationEnabled <$true | $false>] [-Name <String>] [-NewPassword
<SecureString>] [-OABGen <$true | $false>]
    [-OABReplica <$true | $false>] [-Office <String>] [-OfflineAddressBook
<OfflineAddressBookIdParameter>]
```

```
    [-OldPassword <SecureString>] [-OMEncryption <$true | $false>] [-Password
<SecureString>] [-PrimarySmtpAddress
    <SmtpAddress>] [-ProhibitSendQuota <Unlimited>] [-ProhibitSendReceiveQuota
<Unlimited>] [-PstProvider <$true |
    $false>] [-PublicFolder <SwitchParameter>] [-QueryBaseDN
<OrganizationalUnitIdParameter>]
    [-QueryBaseDNRestrictionEnabled <$true | $false>] [-RecipientLimits
<Unlimited>] [-RecoverableItemsQuota
    <Unlimited>] [-RecoverableItemsWarningQuota <Unlimited>] [-
RejectMessagesFrom <MultiValuedProperty>]
    [-RejectMessagesFromDLMembers <MultiValuedProperty>] [-
RejectMessagesFromSendersOrMembers <MultiValuedProperty>]
    [-RemoteAccountPolicy <RemoteAccountPolicyIdParameter>] [-
RemoteRecipientType <None | ProvisionMailbox |
    ProvisionArchive | Migrated | DeprovisionMailbox | DeprovisionArchive |
RoomMailbox | EquipmentMailbox |
    SharedMailbox | TeamMailbox>] [-RemoveManagedFolderAndPolicy
<SwitchParameter>] [-RemovePicture <SwitchParameter>]
    [-RemoveSpokenName <SwitchParameter>] [-RequireSenderAuthenticationEnabled
<$true | $false>]
    [-ResetPasswordOnNextLogon <$true | $false>] [-ResourceCapacity <Int32>] [-
ResourceCustom <MultiValuedProperty>]
    [-RetainDeletedItemsFor <EnhancedTimeSpan>] [-RetainDeletedItemsUntilBackup
<$true | $false>] [-RetentionComment
    <String>] [-RetentionHoldEnabled <$true | $false>] [-RetentionPolicy
<MailboxPolicyIdParameter>] [-RetentionUrl
    <String>] [-RoleAssignmentPolicy <MailboxPolicyIdParameter>] [-
RoomMailboxPassword <SecureString>] [-RulesQuota
    <ByteQuantifiedSize>] [-SamAccountName <String>] [-SCLDeleteEnabled <$true
| $false>] [-SCLDeleteThreshold
    <Int32>] [-SCLJunkEnabled <$true | $false>] [-SCLJunkThreshold <Int32>] [-
SCLQuarantineEnabled <$true | $false>]
    [-SCLQuarantineThreshold <Int32>] [-SCLRejectEnabled <$true | $false>] [-
SCLRejectThreshold <Int32>]
    [-SecondaryAddress <String>] [-SecondaryDialPlan <UMDialPlanIdParameter>]
[-SendModerationNotifications <Never |
    Internal | Always>] [-SharingPolicy <SharingPolicyIdParameter>] [-
SimpleDisplayName <String>]
    [-SingleItemRecoveryEnabled <$true | $false>] [-
SkipMailboxProvisioningConstraintValidation <SwitchParameter>]
    [-StartDateForRetentionHold <DateTime>] [-TenantUpgrade <$true | $false>]
[-ThrottlingPolicy
    <ThrottlingPolicyIdParameter>] [-Type <Regular | Room | Equipment |
Shared>] [-UMDataStorage <$true | $false>]
    [-UMDtmfMap <MultiValuedProperty>] [-UMGrammar <$true | $false>] [-
UseDatabaseQuotaDefaults <$true | $false>]
```

```
    [-UseDatabaseRetentionDefaults <$true | $false>] [-UserCertificate
<MultiValuedProperty>] [-UserPrincipalName
    <String>] [-UserSMimeCertificate <MultiValuedProperty>] [-WhatIf
[<SwitchParameter>]] [-WindowsEmailAddress
    <SmtpAddress>] [-WindowsLiveID <SmtpAddress>] [<CommonParameters>]
```

```
DESCRIPTION
    You can use this cmdlet for one mailbox at a time. To perform bulk
    management, you can pipeline the output of
    various Get- cmdlets (for example, the Get-Mailbox or Get-User cmdlets) and
    configure several mailboxes in a
    single-line command. You can also use the Set-Mailbox cmdlet in scripts.

    You need to be assigned permissions before you can run this cmdlet.
    Although all parameters for this cmdlet are
    listed in this topic, you may not have access to some parameters if they're
    not included in the permissions
    assigned to you. To see what permissions you need, see the "Recipient
    Provisioning Permissions" section in the
    Recipients Permissions topic.

RELATED LINKS
    Online Version http://technet.microsoft.com/EN-US/library/a0d413b9-d949-
    4df6-ba96-ac0906dedae2(EXCHG.160).aspx

REMARKS
    To see the examples, type: "get-help Set-Mailbox -examples".
    For more information, type: "get-help Set-Mailbox -detailed".
    For technical information, type: "get-help Set-Mailbox -full".
    For online help, type: "get-help Set-Mailbox -online"
```

The Set-Mailbox -? command generates a lot of output to the screen, and it is compressed into a hard-to-read format. Because the Set-Mailbox cmdlet is manipulating the same object as the Get-Mailbox cmdlet, you could also use the following command to view all the properties that have been set on a particular mailbox (Oliver in this example):

```
Get-Mailbox Oliver | Format-List
RunspaceId                          : 0ba072d8-b808-472c-a1c0-ddbc58118450
Database                            : Mailbox Database 1
MailboxProvisioningConstraint       :
MessageCopyForSentAsEnabled         : False
MessageCopyForSendOnBehalfEnabled   : False
MailboxProvisioningPreferences      : {}
UseDatabaseRetentionDefaults        : True
RetainDeletedItemsUntilBackup       : False
DeliverToMailboxAndForward          : False
```

```
IsExcludedFromServingHierarchy      : False
IsHierarchyReady                    : True
HasSnackyAppData                    : False
LitigationHoldEnabled               : False
SingleItemRecoveryEnabled           : False
RetentionHoldEnabled                : False
EndDateForRetentionHold             :
StartDateForRetentionHold           :
RetentionComment                    :
RetentionUrl                        :
LitigationHoldDate                  :
LitigationHoldOwner                 :
LitigationHoldDuration              : Unlimited
ManagedFolderMailboxPolicy          :
RetentionPolicy                     :
AddressBookPolicy                   :
CalendarRepairDisabled              : False
ExchangeGuid                        : 4e417359-f557-4213-bc98-9e6982168d0c
MailboxContainerGuid                :
UnifiedMailbox                      :
MailboxLocations                    : {1;4e417359-f557-4213-bc98-
9e6982168d0c;Primary;Contoso.com;c421c171-bc76-4543-
                                      8b2f-43b2e92cc4a3}
AggregatedMailboxGuids              : {}
ExchangeSecurityDescriptor          :
System.Security.AccessControl.RawSecurityDescriptor
ExchangeUserAccountControl          : None
AdminDisplayVersion                 : Version 15.1 (Build 225.42)
MessageTrackingReadStatusEnabled    : True
ExternalOofOptions                  : External
ForwardingAddress                   :
ForwardingSmtpAddress               :
RetainDeletedItemsFor               : 14.00:00:00
IsMailboxEnabled                    : True
Languages                           : {}
OfflineAddressBook                  :
ProhibitSendQuota                   : Unlimited
ProhibitSendReceiveQuota            : Unlimited
RecoverableItemsQuota               : 30 GB (32,212,254,720 bytes)
RecoverableItemsWarningQuota        : 20 GB (21,474,836,480 bytes)
CalendarLoggingQuota                : 6 GB (6,442,450,944 bytes)
DowngradeHighPriorityMessagesEnabled : False
ProtocolSettings                    : {}
RecipientLimits                     : Unlimited
ImListMigrationCompleted            : False
IsResource                          : False
IsLinked                            : False
```

```
IsShared                        : False
IsRootPublicFolderMailbox       : False
LinkedMasterAccount             :
ResetPasswordOnNextLogon        : False
ResourceCapacity                :
ResourceCustom                  : {}
ResourceType                    :
RoomMailboxAccountEnabled       :
SamAccountName                  : Oliver
SCLDeleteThreshold              :
SCLDeleteEnabled                :
SCLRejectThreshold              :
SCLRejectEnabled                :
SCLQuarantineThreshold          :
SCLQuarantineEnabled            :
SCLJunkThreshold                :
SCLJunkEnabled                  :
AntispamBypassEnabled           : False
ServerLegacyDN                  : /o=ContosoOrg/ou=Exchange
Administrative Group

(FYDIBOHF23SPDLT)/cn=Configuration/cn=Servers/cn=NYC-EX1
ServerName                      : ex1
UseDatabaseQuotaDefaults        : True
IssueWarningQuota               : Unlimited
RulesQuota                      : 256 KB (262,144 bytes)
Office                          :
UserPrincipalName               : Oliver@contoso.com
UMEnabled                       : False
MaxSafeSenders                  :
MaxBlockedSenders               :
NetID                           :
ReconciliationId                :
WindowsLiveID                   :
MicrosoftOnlineServicesID       :
ThrottlingPolicy                :
RoleAssignmentPolicy            : Default Role Assignment Policy
DefaultPublicFolderMailbox      :
EffectivePublicFolderMailbox    :
SharingPolicy                   : Default Sharing Policy
RemoteAccountPolicy             :
MailboxPlan                     :
ArchiveDatabase                 :
ArchiveGuid                     : 00000000-0000-0000-0000-000000000000
ArchiveName                     : {}
JournalArchiveAddress           :
ArchiveQuota                    : 100 GB (107,374,182,400 bytes)
```

```
ArchiveWarningQuota                    : 90 GB (96,636,764,160 bytes)
ArchiveDomain                          :
ArchiveStatus                          : None
ArchiveState                           : None
DisabledMailboxLocations               : False
RemoteRecipientType                    : None
DisabledArchiveDatabase                :
DisabledArchiveGuid                    : 00000000-0000-0000-0000-000000000000
QueryBaseDN                            :
QueryBaseDNRestrictionEnabled          : False
MailboxMoveTargetMDB                   :
MailboxMoveSourceMDB                   :
MailboxMoveFlags                       : None
MailboxMoveRemoteHostName              :
MailboxMoveBatchName                   :
MailboxMoveStatus                      : None
MailboxRelease                         :
ArchiveRelease                         :
IsPersonToPersonTextMessagingEnabled   : False
IsMachineToPersonTextMessagingEnabled  : False
UserSMimeCertificate                   : {}
UserCertificate                        : {}
CalendarVersionStoreDisabled           : False
ImmutableId                            :
PersistedCapabilities                  : {}
SKUAssigned                            :
AuditEnabled                           : False
AuditLogAgeLimit                       : 90.00:00:00
AuditAdmin                             : {Update, Move, MoveToDeletedItems,
SoftDelete, HardDelete, FolderBind,

                                         SendAs, SendOnBehalf, Create}
AuditDelegate                          : {Update, SoftDelete, HardDelete,
SendAs, Create}
AuditOwner                             : {}
WhenMailboxCreated                     : 3/20/2016 11:49:39 PM
SourceAnchor                           :
UsageLocation                          :
IsSoftDeletedByRemove                  : False
IsSoftDeletedByDisable                 : False
IsInactiveMailbox                      : False
IncludeInGarbageCollection             : False
WhenSoftDeleted                        :
InPlaceHolds                           : {}
GeneratedOfflineAddressBooks           : {}
AccountDisabled                        : False
StsRefreshTokensValidFrom              :
Extensions                             : {}
```

```
HasPicture                              : False
HasSpokenName                           : False
AcceptMessagesOnlyFrom                  : {}
AcceptMessagesOnlyFromDLMembers         : {}
AcceptMessagesOnlyFromSendersOrMembers  : {}
AddressListMembership                   : {\Mailboxes(VLV), \All Mailboxes(VLV),
\All Recipients(VLV), \Default Global
                                          Address List, \All Users}
Alias                                   : Oliver
ArbitrationMailbox                      :
BypassModerationFromSendersOrMembers    : {}
OrganizationalUnit                      : contoso.com/Sales
CustomAttribute1                        :
CustomAttribute10                       :
CustomAttribute11                       :
CustomAttribute12                       :
CustomAttribute13                       :
CustomAttribute14                       :
CustomAttribute15                       :
CustomAttribute2                        :
CustomAttribute3                        :
CustomAttribute4                        :
CustomAttribute5                        :
CustomAttribute6                        :
CustomAttribute7                        :
CustomAttribute8                        :
CustomAttribute9                        :
ExtensionCustomAttribute1               : {}
ExtensionCustomAttribute2               : {}
ExtensionCustomAttribute3               : {}
ExtensionCustomAttribute4               : {}
ExtensionCustomAttribute5               : {}
DisplayName                             : Oliver Lee
EmailAddresses                          : {SMTP:Oliver@contoso.com}
GrantSendOnBehalfTo                     : {}
ExternalDirectoryObjectId               :
HiddenFromAddressListsEnabled           : False
LastExchangeChangedTime                 :
LegacyExchangeDN                        : /o=ContosoOrg/ou=Exchange
Administrative Group

(FYDIBOHF23SPDLT)/cn=Recipients/cn=4ae68cb0a00d48769bd97945e13b3f43-Oliver Lee
MaxSendSize                             : Unlimited
MaxReceiveSize                          : Unlimited
ModeratedBy                             : {}
ModerationEnabled                       : False
PoliciesIncluded                        : {98dda7b4-7ba7-4bf3-8de3-1cd7e78066aa,
```

```
{26491cfc-9e50-4857-861b-0cb8df22b5d7}}
PoliciesExcluded                        : {}
EmailAddressPolicyEnabled               : True
PrimarySmtpAddress                      : Oliver@contoso.com
RecipientType                           : UserMailbox
RecipientTypeDetails                    : UserMailbox
RejectMessagesFrom                      : {}
RejectMessagesFromDLMembers             : {}
RejectMessagesFromSendersOrMembers      : {}
RequireSenderAuthenticationEnabled      : False
SimpleDisplayName                       :
SendModerationNotifications             : Always
UMDtmfMap                               : {emailAddress:654837,
lastNameFirstName:533654837,

                                          firstNameLastName:654837533}
WindowsEmailAddress                     : Oliver@contoso.com
MailTip                                 :
MailTipTranslations                     : {}
Identity                                : Contoso.com/Sales/Oliver Lee
IsValid                                 : True
ExchangeVersion                         : 0.20 (15.0.0.0)
Name                                    : Oliver Lee
DistinguishedName                       : CN=Oliver Lee,OU=Sales,DC=Contoso,DC=com
Guid                                    : b3578263-b81c-40be-91b8-721f21b99da2
ObjectCategory                          : Contoso.com/Configuration/Schema/Person
ObjectClass                             : {top, person, organizationalPerson,
user}
WhenChanged                             : 3/20/2016 11:49:39 PM
WhenCreated                             : 10/21/2013 11:31:35 PM
WhenChangedUTC                          : 3/21/2016 6:49:39 AM
WhenCreatedUTC                          : 10/22/2013 6:31:35 AM
OrganizationId                          :
Id                                      : Contoso.com/Sales/Oliver Lee
OriginatingServer                       : DC1.Contoso.com
ObjectState                             : Unchanged
```

Note that some of the properties you see as a result of a Get- cmdlet cannot be set because they are system-controlled properties or they are manipulated using other cmdlets, such as ExchangeGuid or Database.

The third way to view all of the properties associated with an object is simply to use the Get-Member cmdlet. Here is an example where the Get-Mailbox cmdlet pipes its output to the Get-Member cmdlet and filters only the members that are properties. Because a full listing would include a few pages of information you can easily look up yourself and will provide little value to this discussion, the output is only a partial listing:

```
TypeName: Microsoft.Exchange.Data.Directory.Management.Mailbox

Name                                 MemberType Definition
----                                 ---------- ----------
AcceptMessagesOnlyFrom                          Property
Microsoft.Exchange.Data.MultiValuedProperty[Microsoft.Exchange.Dat...
AcceptMessagesOnlyFromDLMembers                 Property
Microsoft.Exchange.Data.MultiValuedProperty[Microsoft.Exchange.Dat...
AcceptMessagesOnlyFromSendersOrMembers Property
Microsoft.Exchange.Data.MultiValuedProperty[Microsoft.Exchange.Dat...
AccountDisabled                                 Property    bool AccountDisabled {get;set;}
AddressBookPolicy                               Property
Microsoft.Exchange.Data.Directory.ADObjectId AddressBookPolicy {ge...
AddressListMembership                           Property
Microsoft.Exchange.Data.MultiValuedProperty[Microsoft.Exchange.Dat...
AdminDisplayVersion                             Property
Microsoft.Exchange.Data.ServerVersion AdminDisplayVersion {get;}
AggregatedMailboxGuids                          Property
Microsoft.Exchange.Data.MultiValuedProperty[guid] AggregatedMailbo...
Alias                                           Property    string Alias {get;set;}
AntispamBypassEnabled                           Property    bool AntispamBypassEnabled
{get;set;}
ArbitrationMailbox                              Property
Microsoft.Exchange.Data.Directory.ADObjectId ArbitrationMailbox {g...
ArchiveDatabase                                 Property
Microsoft.Exchange.Data.Directory.ADObjectId ArchiveDatabase {get;}
ArchiveDomain                                   Property
Microsoft.Exchange.Data.SmtpDomain ArchiveDomain {get;set;}
ArchiveGuid                                     Property    guid ArchiveGuid {get;}
ArchiveName                                     Property
Microsoft.Exchange.Data.MultiValuedProperty[string] ArchiveName {g...
ArchiveQuota                                    Property
Microsoft.Exchange.Data.Unlimited[Microsoft.Exchange.Data.ByteQuan...
ArchiveRelease                                  Property    string ArchiveRelease {get;}
ArchiveState                                    Property
Microsoft.Exchange.Data.Directory.Recipient.ArchiveState ArchiveSt...
```

Formatting Output

If you look at the output of the Get-Mailbox cmdlet shown in Figure 5.1, you might be tempted to think that the output capabilities of PowerShell are limited, but this is far from the truth.

The default output of the Get-Mailbox cmdlet is a formatted table with the Name, Alias, ServerName, and ProhibitSendQuota properties as columns. However, you can select the properties you want by merely piping the output of the Get-Mailbox cmdlet to either the Format-Table (FT for short), Format-List (FL for short), or Select cmdlet:

```
Get-Mailbox | FT Name,ProhibitSendQuota,ProhibitSendReceiveQuota
```

Figure 5.2 shows the output of the preceding command.

FIGURE 5.2

Formatting output into a formatted table

The output of the Get-Mailbox cmdlet was directed to the Format-Table or FT cmdlet; the result was columns for the Name, ProhibitSendQuota, and ProhibitSendReceiveQuota limits.

You may be wondering how you can learn all the properties of an object. The default output of the Get-Mailbox cmdlet, for example, is probably not the most useful for your organization. We discuss getting help in PowerShell and the Exchange Management Shell later in this chapter, but here is a simple trick to see all the properties of an object: just direct the output of a Get-cmdlet to the Format-List (FL for short) cmdlet instead of the default Format-Table cmdlet.

When you direct the output of a cmdlet, such as Get-Mailbox to the Format-List cmdlet, you will see *all* the properties for that object. Figure 5.3 shows an example where we have directed the output of a Get-Mailbox cmdlet to the FL (Format-List) cmdlet. You will notice in Figure 5.3 that the properties filled up more than one screen. However, you will find that outputting all the properties of an object using the Format-List cmdlet is very useful if you need to know specific property names.

FIGURE 5.3

Formatting output to a formatted list

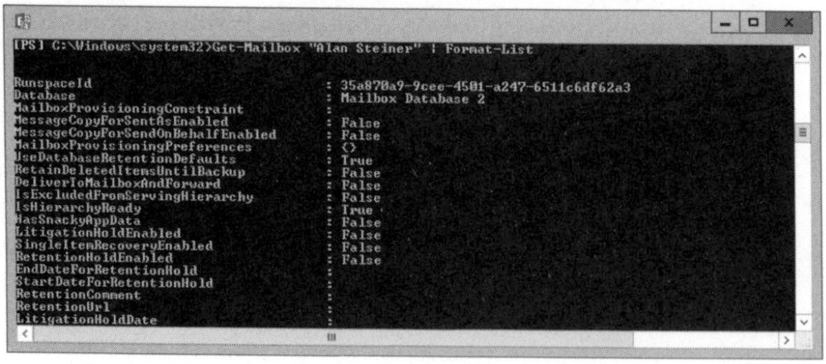

The command we used is as follows:

```
Get-Mailbox "Alan Steiner" | Format-List
```

Directing Output to Other Cmdlets

You have already seen a couple of examples where we used the pipe symbol (|) to direct the output of one command to be used as input for the next command, such as Get-Mailbox | Format-Table. You can do this because PowerShell commands act on objects, not just text. Unlike with other shells or scripting languages, you don't have to use string commands or variables to pass data from one command to another. The result is that you can use a single line to perform a query and complex task—something that might have required hundreds of lines of programming in the past.

One of our favorite examples is making specific changes to a group of people's mailboxes. Let's say you need to ensure that all executives in your organization can send and receive a message that is up to 50 MB in size rather than the default 10 MB to which the system limits the user. Earlier we showed you how you could get the properties of the mailbox that you were interested in, such as the MaxSendSize and MaxReceiveSize properties.

First, let's use the Get-DistributionGroupMember cmdlet to retrieve the members of the Executives distribution group:

```
Get-DistributionGroupMember "Executives"
Name                                            RecipientType
----                                            -------------
Zainal Arifin                                   UserMailbox
Sameer Athalye                                  UserMailbox
Adam Barr                                       UserMailbox
Anna Bedecs                                     UserMailbox
Dana Birkby                                     UserMailbox
Tomasz Bochenek                                 UserMailbox
Bryan Bredehoeft                                UserMailbox
Derek Brown                                     UserMailbox
Randy Byrne                                     UserMailbox
```

Remember that although you see the text listing of the group members, what is actually output are objects representing each of the members.

It is important to note that while piping the output of one cmdlet as input for another cmdlet works frequently, it does not work all the time. Piping input to a cmdlet will always work when the noun used by the two cmdlets is the same, such as this:

```
Get-Mailbox -Server Ex1 | Set-Mailbox -CustomAttribute1 "I am on a
great server! "
```

For cmdlets that do not support piping between them, you can usually use a trick, such as using the foreach cmdlet to process the data.

So, now let's pipe the output of that cmdlet to the Set-Mailbox cmdlet and do some real work! To change the maximum incoming and outgoing message size for the members of the Executives group, you would type the following command:

```
Get-DistributionGroupMember "Executives" | Set-Mailbox
-MaxSendSize:50MB -MaxReceiveSize:50MB
-UseDatabaseRetentionDefaults:$False
```

Notice that the Set-Mailbox cmdlet did not require any input because it will take as input the objects that are output from Get-DistributionGroupMember. When you run these two commands, there will be no output unless you have specified other options. But you can easily check the results by requesting the membership of the Executives group, piping that to the Get-Mailbox cmdlet, and then piping that output to the Format-Table cmdlet, as shown here:

```
Name                MaxSendSize                    MaxReceiveSize
----                -----------                    --------------
Zainal Arifin       50 MB (52,428,800 bytes)   50 MB (52,428,800 bytes)
Sameer Athalye      50 MB (52,428,800 bytes)   50 MB (52,428,800 bytes)
Adam Barr           50 MB (52,428,800 bytes)   50 MB (52,428,800 bytes)
Anna Bedecs         50 MB (52,428,800 bytes)   50 MB (52,428,800 bytes)
Dana Birkby         50 MB (52,428,800 bytes)   50 MB (52,428,800 bytes)
Tomasz Bochenek     50 MB (52,428,800 bytes)   50 MB (52,428,800 bytes)
Bryan Bredehoeft 50 MB (52,428,800 bytes)   50 MB (52,428,800 bytes)
Derek Brown         50 MB (52,428,800 bytes)   50 MB (52,428,800 bytes)
Randy Byrne         50 MB (52,428,800 bytes)   50 MB (52,428,800 bytes)
```

Pretty cool, eh? After just a few minutes working with PowerShell and the EMS extensions, we hope that you will be as pleased with the ease-of-use as we are.

PowerShell v3, v4, and v5

Exchange Server 2016 uses PowerShell version 4 (v4). Exchange Server 2013 uses PowerShell v3, whereas Exchange Server 2010 used PowerShell v2 and Exchange Server 2007 used the power of PowerShell v1 (or v2 with Exchange Server 2007 SP2). PowerShell v3 includes some amazing features, like remoting and eventing, which enable it to manage any IT environment even better than before. PowerShell v4, standard on Windows Server 2012 R2, added Desired State Configuration (DSC) and a few minor enhancements, but not as many as v3. PowerShell v5, standard on Windows Server 2016, adds more programming-like power to PowerShell, including the ability to develop by using classes like object-oriented programming languages.

Remote PowerShell

Exchange Server 2010 and later doesn't use local PowerShell anymore but relies on remote PowerShell to manage its roles.

You won't see any difference between using remote or local shell to manage Exchange Server. When you click the EMS shortcut, Windows PowerShell connects to the closest Exchange server using Windows Remote Management, performs an authentication check, and then creates a remote session for you to use. It's thanks to Remote PowerShell that Role-Based Access Control (RBAC) can be fully implemented. (For more information about RBAC, refer to Chapter 12, "Management Permissions and Role-Based Access Control.")

Another advantage of introducing Remote PowerShell is the ability to launch the shell and manage your Exchange servers by connecting to an Exchange server without requiring you to install the management tools locally on that machine; this was a requirement back in Exchange Server 2007.

Tips and Tricks

In this section, we discuss handling data output, sending output to a file, sending email from the PowerShell, and debugging.

Managing Output

Let's start by exploring how to massage or manipulate the output of PowerShell and EMS cmdlets. In this section, we are going to focus on the `Get-MailboxStatistics` cmdlet; we are using this cmdlet in our example because in our opinion its default output format is the least desirable of *all* the EMS cmdlets. Whoever set the defaults for this cmdlet's output clearly expected the user to be proficient at manipulating the output.

If you are coming from an Exchange Server 2007 environment, you may be used to running the `Get-MailboxStatistics` cmdlet with no parameters. Exchange Server 2013 and later expects you to specify either a mailbox name, server name (`-Server`), or mailbox database (`-Database`) in the command line. Here is an example of the `Get-MailboxStatistics` cmdlet's output specifying a mailbox server:

```
Get-MailboxStatistics -Server Ex1
DisplayName                ItemCount  StorageLimitStatus    LastLogonTime
-----------                ---------  ------------------    -------------
John Park                  7          BelowLimit
SystemMailbox{21db5e47...  1          BelowLimit
Chuck Swanson              6          BelowLimit
Online Archive - Tyler...  0          NoChecking
Microsoft Exchange         1          BelowLimit
Microsoft Exchange App...  1          BelowLimit
Gillian Katz               7          BelowLimit
Administrator              2          BelowLimit            8/9/2016 1:24:44 AM
Jim McBee                  6          BelowLimit
Discovery Search Mailbox   1          BelowLimit
Clayton K. Kamiya          27         NoChecking            7/24/2016 12:17:44 AM
Microsoft Exchange App...  1          BelowLimit
Tyler M. Swartz            6          BelowLimit
Julie R. Samante           6          BelowLimit
Michael G. Brown           9          BelowLimit
Jonathan Long              6          BelowLimit
SystemMailbox{94c22976...  1          BelowLimit
Kevin Wile                 8          BelowLimit
John Rodriguez             6          BelowLimit
Anita Velez                6          BelowLimit
```

Obviously, this output is not very useful for most of us.

OUTPUT TO LISTS OR TABLES

Keep in mind that internally, when PowerShell is retrieving data, everything is treated as an object. However, when you are displaying something to the screen, you see just the textual information. Most cmdlets output data to a formatted table, but you can also output the data to a formatted list using the Format-List cmdlet or FL alias. Here is an example of piping a single mailbox's statistics to the Format-List cmdlet:

```
[PS] C:\>Get-MailboxStatistics "Clayton K. Kamiya" | Format-List
RunspaceId                  : 3a8e6797-44a5-4c71-8a21-3022b379cb57
AssociatedItemCount         : 16
DeletedItemCount            : 0
DisconnectDate              :
DisplayName                 : Clayton K. Kamiya
ItemCount                   : 27
LastLoggedOnUserAccount     : contoso\Clayton.Kamiya
LastLogoffTime              : 7/24/2016 9:54:13 AM
LastLogonTime               : 7/24/2016 12:17:44 AM
LegacyDN                    : /O=Contoso/
OU=EXCHANGE ADMINISTRATIVE GROUP (FYDIBOHF23SPDLT)/
CN=RECIPIENTS/CN=CLAYTON K. KAMIYA
MailboxGuid                 : a9e676e9-f67b-4206-817e-ad07eca52659
ObjectClass                 : Mailbox
StorageLimitStatus          : NoChecking
TotalDeletedItemSize        : 0 B (0 bytes)
TotalItemSize               : 949.5 KB (972,245 bytes)
Database                    : MBX1
ServerName                  : NYC-EX1
DatabaseName                : MBX1
MoveHistory                 :
IsQuarantined               : False
IsArchiveMailbox            : False
Identity                    : a9e676e9-f67b-4206-817e-ad07eca52659
MapiIdentity                : a9e676e9-f67b-4206-817e-ad07eca52659
OriginatingServer           : NYC-EX1.contoso.com
IsValid                     : True
```

This example shows you all the properties that can be displayed via the Get-MailboxStatistics cmdlet.

The following are the default results of filtering the command through the Format-Table or FT alias:

```
Get-MailboxStatistics "Clayton K. Kamiya" | FT
DisplayName      ItemCount  StorageLimitStatus  LastLogonTime
-----------      ---------  ------------------  -------------

Clayton Kamiya   1063       BelowLimit          8/9/2016 1:33:31 PM
```

However, the Format-Table and Format-List cmdlets allow you to specify which properties you want to see in the output list. Let's say that you want to see the user's name, item count, and total item size. Here's the command you would use:

```
Get-MailboxStatistics "Clayton Kamiya" | FT DisplayName,
ItemCount,TotalItemSize
DisplayName              ItemCount TotalItemSize
-----------              --------- -------------
Clayton K. Kamiya             1063 4.00 MB (4,190,207 bytes)
```

There we go—that is a bit more useful.

SORTING AND GROUPING OUTPUT

Any output can also be sorted based on any of the properties that you are going to display. If you are using the Format-Table command, you can also group the output by properties. First, let's go back and look at the original example where we are outputting all the mailbox statistics for the local mailbox server. Let's say we are interested in sorting by the maximum mailbox size. To do so, we can pipe the output of Get-MailboxStatistics to the Sort-Object cmdlet. Here is an example:

```
Get-Mailbox | Get-MailboxStatistics -Server Ex1 | Sort-Object
TotalItemSize -Descending | Format-Table DisplayName,
ItemCountTotalItemsize
DisplayName          ItemCount      TotalItemSize
-----------          ---------      -------------------
Mike Brown                 306      22.92 MB (24,030,192 bytes)
Clayton Kamiya            1063      21.34 MB (22,376,612 bytes
Lawrence Cohen               2      221.3 KB(226,596 bytes)
Oliver Cohen                 2      71.75 KB (73,469 bytes)
Brian Tirch                  2      50.00 KB(51,200 bytes)
Elias Mereb                  6      50.00 KB(51,200 bytes)
```

This example used the command Sort-Object TotalItemSize -Descending, but we could also have used the -Ascending option. There are several far more sophisticated examples in PowerShell help.

We can take this a step further when using the Format-Table cmdlet by adding a -GroupBy option. Here is an example where we are exporting this data and grouping it using the StorageLimitStatus property:

```
Get-Mailbox | Get-MailboxStatistics | Sort-Object TotalItemSize
-Descending | Format-Table DisplayName, ItemCount, TotalItemSize
-GroupBy StorageLimitStatus
   StorageLimitStatus: MailboxDisabled
DisplayName          ItemCount      Total Item Size
-----------          ---------      ---------------
Mike Brown                 314      21.25 MB (21,763 bytes)
   StorageLimitStatus: ProhibitSend
```

```
DisplayName              ItemCount        Total Item Size
-----------              ---------        ---------------

Clayton Kamiya               1066        5.02 MB (5,145 bytes)
      StorageLimitStatus: BelowLimit
DisplayName              ItemCount        Total Item Size
-----------              ---------        ---------------

Lawrence Cohen                  8        1.09 MB (1,119 bytes)
Oliver Cohen                    6        286 B (286 bytes)
Oren Pinto                      6        286 B (286 bytes)
```

OUTPUT TO FILE

Outputting data to the screen is great, but it does not help you with reports. You can also output data to CSV and XML files. Two cmdlets make this easy to do:

- `Export-Csv` exports the data to a CSV file.
- `Export-Clixml` exports the data to an XML file.

Simply direct the output you want sent to a file, and these cmdlets will take care of converting the data to the proper format. Let's take our earlier example where we want a report of all mailboxes and their `ProhibitSend` and `ProhibitSendAndReceive` limits. We can't use the `Format-Table` cmdlet in this instance; we have to use the `Select-Object` or `Select` cmdlet to specify the output because we will be directing this output to another cmdlet. Here is an example of the `Get-Mailbox` cmdlet when using the `Select` command:

```
Get-Mailbox | Select Name, ProhibitSendQuota, ProhibitSendReceiveQuota
```

The output of this cmdlet is shown here:

```
Name                ProhibitSendQuota        ProhibitSendReceiveQuota
----                -----------------        ------------------------

Oren Pinto              unlimited                       unlimited
Zachary Elfassy         unlimited                       unlimited
Zoe Elfassy             unlimited                       unlimited
Savannah Elfassy        unlimited                       unlimited
Mike Brown              unlimited                       unlimited
Dan Holme               unlimited                       unlimited
Russ Zimmer             unlimited                       unlimited
Tyler Swartz            unlimited                       unlimited
Chris Pfennig           unlimited                       unlimited
```

To direct this output to the `C:\report.csv` file, we simply pipe it to the `Export-Csv` cmdlet as shown here:

```
Get-Mailbox | Select Name, ProhibitSendQuota, ProhibitSendReceiveQuota |
Export-Csv c:\report.csv
```

If you want to export the report to an XML file, simply use the `Export-Clixml` cmdlet instead of `Export-Csv`.

Finally, just as when working with the DOS prompt, you can redirect output of a command to a text file. To send the output of the Get-Mailbox to the file c:\mailboxes.txt, you would type this:

```
Get-Mailbox > c:\mailboxes.txt
```

Putting It All Together

Let's consider one more example of Get-MailboxStatistics piping. Hopefully, this will be an example you can use in the future. We will create a report of the mailbox statistics using the Get-MailboxStatistics cmdlet. Then we will export the mailbox statistics for a specific server. We will limit the output by using the Where-Object command, choose the properties to output using the Select command, and finally pipe that output to the Export-Csv cmdlet:

```
Get-MailboxStatistics -Server Ex1 | Sort-Object TotalItemSize
-Descending | Select-Object DisplayName,ItemCount,TotalItemSize
| Export-CSV c:\StorStats.csv
```

If you are thinking that this looks a bit sticky to implement, you are probably right. Getting this syntax together took the better part of an afternoon, and arguably, you should be able to perform common tasks like exporting mailbox storage statistics from the GUI. However, on the bright side, now we have the command we need to run each time we want to generate this report; further, the knowledge to do this particular type of report within PowerShell carries over into many other tasks.

Running Scripts

PowerShell scripts are easy to build and to run, but there are a few things you need to know to write your own scripts and/or to read others' scripts. Though this is certainly not a comprehensive briefing on PowerShell scripting or variables, we hope it will give you a quick introduction to a few things that we found interesting and helpful when we got started.

◆ The file extension for a PowerShell script is .PS1.

◆ You can't run the script from the source directory. You actually have to preface the script name with the path.

Say we have a script named c:\scripts\Report.ps1. We can't just change it to the c:\reports directory and run report.ps1, so we would have to type **.\report.ps1**.

◆ PowerShell (and scripts) use variables preceded with a $ symbol. You can set a variable within a script or just by typing it at the command line. The PowerShell variable is an object, so you can associate an object or an entire list of objects with a single variable.

For example, the following command associates the variable $Zach with the entire object for the user Zachary Elfassy:

```
$Zach = Get-User "Zachary Elfassy"
```

We could then use just specific properties of that object. For example, if we want to just output Zachary's display name, we could type this:

```
$Zach.DisplayName
```

Even better, we could then set Zachary's display name to a variable called $ZachDisplayName by doing this:

```
$ZachDisplayName = $Zach.DisplayName
```

We can set a single variable to a lot of objects and then manipulate them all at once via a script. Here is an example where we set the $AllUsers variable to all the users in the domain:

```
$AllUsers = Get-Users
```

Now here are some interesting things we can do with that variable. We can obtain a count of how many objects it contains:

```
$AllUsers.Count
944
```

Further, each of the 944 objects contained in the $AllUsers variable is treated as an item in an array, so we can retrieve individual ones, such as object number 939:

```
AllUsers[939] | FL SamAccountName,DisplayName,WindowsEmailAddress,Phone,
Office

SamAccountName       : Andrew.Roberts
DisplayName          : Andrew Roberts (Operations)
WindowsEmailAddress  : andrew.roberts@Contoso.com
Phone                : 011-77-8484-4844
Office               : Tokyo
```

SENDING EMAIL FROM THE EXCHANGE MANAGEMENT SHELL

Sometimes the smallest features are among the best features. In this particular case, we are talking about a PowerShell cmdlet called Send-MailMessage that allows you to easily send an email from within PowerShell.

For example, if you want to send an email message from the alias SystemMessages@Contoso.com to HelpDesk@Contoso.com, it would look something like this:

```
Send-MailMessage -To HelpDesk@contoso.com -Subject "This is a test
message" -From SystemMessages@contoso.com -BodyAsHtml -Body "This
is the body of the message" -SmtpServer Ex1
```

Note that you must specify an SMTP server that will either accept this connection or relay the message for you by using the -SmtpServer parameter, as shown in the preceding example.

Running Scheduled PowerShell Scripts

Frequently, PowerShell advocates will extol the virtues of creating simple PowerShell scripts (PS1 files) that you can schedule to perform routine tasks. There are quite a few articles and newsgroup postings about how easy this is to do. However, running the PS1 script using a scheduled task is a bit trickier. You can't just run a PS1 script from the DOS command prompt or the Task Scheduler. Before a PS1 script can be run, PowerShell has to be run, the Exchange Management Extensions have to be loaded, and then the script or command can be called.

The PowerShell executable (powershell.exe) is found in the C:\Windows\System32\ WindowsPowerShell\v1.0\ folder. PowerShell needs to be told from which Exchange server it will need to import the Exchange Server session (using the Import-PSSession cmdlet).

Finally, we need the name and the location of the script we are going to run, so let's say we are going to execute this command:

```
Get-Mailbox | Select Name, ProhibitSendQuota, ProhibitSendReceiveQuota
 | Export-Csv c:\report2.csv
```

Rather than pasting all this into the job scheduler, we can create a simple batch file that looks like this:

```
@echo off
cls
C:\Windows\System32\WindowsPowerShell\v1.0\PowerShell.exe
-command "& { c:\scripts\Report1.ps1 }"
```

Now we need to create the Report1.ps1 script that will run once PowerShell is opened:

```
$Session = New-PSSession -ConfigurationName Microsoft.Exchange
-ConnectionUri http://NYC-EX1/PowerShell/
Import-PSSession $session
Get-Mailbox | Select Name, ProhibitSendQuota, ProhibitSendReceiveQuota
 | Export-Csv c:\report2.csv
```

Debugging and Troubleshooting from PowerShell

PowerShell has a lot of features that will help you test your scripts and one-line commands.

Set-PSDebug   The cmdlet Set-PSDebug is designed to allow you to debug PowerShell scripts. To use this, add this command to your script: Set-PSDebug -Trace 1. This will allow you to examine each step of the script. You can enable more detailed trace logging by setting the trace level to 2: Set-PSDebug -Trace 2. If you add the -Step option to the command line, you will be prompted for each step. To turn off trace logging, use this command: Set-PSDebug -Off.

-WhatIf   Most cmdlets support the -WhatIf option. If you add the -WhatIf option to the command line, the cmdlet will run and tell you what will happen without actually performing the task. This is useful for checking to make sure the command you are about to run will really do what you want.

-Confirm   Most cmdlets support the -Confirm option and many cmdlets that perform more destructive types of options, such as those that begin with Remove-, Move-, Dismount-, Disable-, and Clear-, have the -Confirm option turned on by default. If this is turned on, the cmdlet will not proceed until you have confirmed it is OK to proceed. For cmdlets that confirm by default, you can include the -Confirm:$False option if you do not want to be prompted.

-ValidateOnly   The -ValidateOnly option is a bit more powerful than -WhatIf. The -ValidateOnly option will perform all the steps the cmdlet is specifying without actually making any changes and then will summarize what would have been done and if this would have caused any problems.

Getting Help

We have shown you a few simple yet powerful examples of how to use PowerShell and the EMS. Once you dig in and start using the EMS, you will need some references to help you figure out all the syntax and properties of each of the cmdlets.

Information is available on the cmdlets from within PowerShell. For a good starting point, you can just type the help command and this will give you a good overview of using PowerShell and how to get more help. The following list summarizes common methods of getting help on PowerShell and Exchange Management Shell cmdlets:

help   Provides generic PowerShell help information.

help *Keyword*   Lists all cmdlets that contain the keyword. For example, if you want to find all PowerShell v2 cmdlets that work with the Windows event log, you can type **help *EventLog***. To find all Exchange Server cmdlets that work with mailboxes, type **Get-ExCommand *mailbox***. You cannot use the help alias to locate all available Exchange Server cmdlets.

Get-Command *Keyword*   Lists all PowerShell cmdlets and files (such as help files) that contain the keyword.

Get-Command   Lists all cmdlets (including all PowerShell extensions currently loaded, such as the EMS cmdlets).

Get-ExCommand   Lists all Exchange Server cmdlets.

Get-PSCommand   Lists all PowerShell cmdlets.

Help *Cmdlet* or Get-Help *Cmdlet*   Lists online help for the specified cmdlet and pauses between each screen. Provides multiple views of the online help (such as detailed, full, examples, and default). In Figure 5.4, the help information for pipelining in PowerShell is displayed.

Cmdlet -?   Lists online help for the specified cmdlet.

When working with help within PowerShell, help topics are displayed based on the view of help that you request. In other words, you can't just type Get-Help and see everything about that cmdlet. The Get-Help cmdlet includes four possible views of help for each cmdlet. The following list explains the four primary views along with the parameters view:

Default View Lists the minimal information to describe the function of the cmdlet and shows the syntax of the cmdlet

Example View Includes a synopsis of the cmdlet and some examples of its usage

Detailed View Shows more details on a cmdlet, including parameters and parameter descriptions

Full View Shows all the details available on a cmdlet, including a synopsis of the cmdlet, a detailed description of the cmdlet, parameter descriptions, parameter metadata, and examples

Parameters View Allows you to specify a parameter and get help on the usage of just that particular parameter

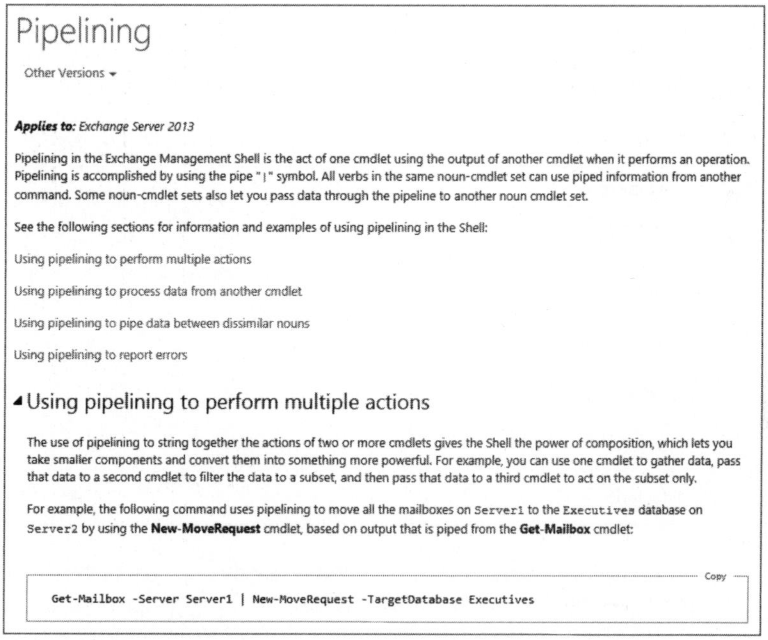

Pipelining

Other Versions

Applies to: *Exchange Server 2013*

Pipelining in the Exchange Management Shell is the act of one cmdlet using the output of another cmdlet when it performs an operation. Pipelining is accomplished by using the pipe "|" symbol. All verbs in the same noun-cmdlet set can use piped information from another command. Some noun-cmdlet sets also let you pass data through the pipeline to another noun cmdlet set.

See the following sections for information and examples of using pipelining in the Shell:

Using pipelining to perform multiple actions

Using pipelining to process data from another cmdlet

Using pipelining to pipe data between dissimilar nouns

Using pipelining to report errors

Using pipelining to perform multiple actions

The use of pipelining to string together the actions of two or more cmdlets gives the Shell the power of composition, which lets you take smaller components and convert them into something more powerful. For example, you can use one cmdlet to gather data, pass that data to a second cmdlet to filter the data to a subset, and then pass that data to a third cmdlet to act on the subset only.

For example, the following command uses pipelining to move all the mailboxes on `Server1` to the `Executives` database on `Server2` by using the **New-MoveRequest** cmdlet, based on output that is piped from the **Get-Mailbox** cmdlet:

Copy

```
Get-Mailbox -Server Server1 | New-MoveRequest -TargetDatabase Executives
```

FIGURE 5.4 Online help for pipelining using the Exchange Management Shell

The `Full` option for `Get-Help` includes in its output each parameter's metadata. The metadata is shown in the following list:

`Required?` Is the parameter required? This value is either `true` or `false`.

`Position?` Specifies the position of the parameter. If the position is `named`, the parameter name has to be included in the parameter list. Most parameters are named. However, the `-Identity` parameter is 1, which means that it is always the first parameter and the `-Identity` tag is not required.

`Default value` Specifies what a value will be for a parameter if nothing else is specified. For most parameters this is blank.

Accept pipeline input? Specifies if the parameter will accept input that is piped in from another cmdlet. The value is either true or false.

Accept wildcard characters? Specifies if the parameter accepts wildcard characters, such as the asterisk or question mark character. This value is either true or false.

Still not clear about what each view gives you? Perhaps Table 5.3 can shed some more light on the issue. This table shows you the various sections that are output when using each view option.

TABLE 5.3:   Information Output for Each Get-Help View

	DEFAULT VIEW	**EXAMPLE VIEW**	**DETAILED VIEW**	**FULL VIEW**
Synopsis	✓	✓	✓	✓
Detailed description	✓		✓	✓
Syntax	✓		✓	✓
Parameters			✓	✓
Parameter metadata				✓
Input type				✓
Return type				✓
Errors				✓
Notes				✓
Example		✓	✓	✓

To use these parameters, you would use the Get-Help cmdlet and the view option. For example, to see the example view for the Get-Mailbox, you would type the following:

```
Get-Help Get-Mailbox -Example
```

We feel it is important for administrators to understand the available online help options, so let's look at a couple more detailed examples for the Get-MailboxStatistics cmdlet. We are picking a cmdlet (Get-MailboxStatistics) that we feel is pretty representative of the EMS cmdlets but that also does not have a huge amount of help information. First, let's look at the default view:

```
Get-Help Get-MailboxStatistics
NAME
    Get-MailboxStatistics
SYNOPSIS
    This cmdlet is available in on-premises Exchange Server 2016 and in the
```

cloud-based service. Some parameters and
settings may be exclusive to one environment or the other.
Use the Get-MailboxStatistics cmdlet to obtain information about a mailbox,
such as the size of the mailbox, the
number of messages it contains, and the last time it was accessed. In
addition, you can get the move history or a
move report of a completed move request.
For information about the parameter sets in the Syntax section below, see
Syntax.

SYNTAX
```
    Get-MailboxStatistics -Identity <GeneralMailboxOrMailUserIdParameter> [-
Archive <SwitchParameter>] [-CopyOnServer
    <ServerIdParameter>] [-DomainController <Fqdn>] [-IncludeMoveHistory
<SwitchParameter>] [-IncludeMoveReport
    <SwitchParameter>] [-IncludeQuarantineDetails <SwitchParameter>] [-
NoADLookup <SwitchParameter>]
    [<CommonParameters>]

    Get-MailboxStatistics [-AuditLog <SwitchParameter>] [-Identity
<GeneralMailboxOrMailUserIdParameter>]
    [-DomainController <Fqdn>] [-IncludeMoveHistory <SwitchParameter>] [-
IncludeMoveReport <SwitchParameter>]
    [-IncludeQuarantineDetails <SwitchParameter>] [-NoADLookup
<SwitchParameter>] [<CommonParameters>]

    Get-MailboxStatistics -Database <DatabaseIdParameter> [-CopyOnServer
<ServerIdParameter>] [-Filter <String>]
    [-StoreMailboxIdentity <StoreMailboxIdParameter>] [-DomainController
<Fqdn>] [-IncludeMoveHistory
    <SwitchParameter>] [-IncludeMoveReport <SwitchParameter>] [-
IncludeQuarantineDetails <SwitchParameter>]
    [-NoADLookup <SwitchParameter>] [<CommonParameters>]

    Get-MailboxStatistics -Server <ServerIdParameter> [-Filter <String>] [-
IncludePassive <SwitchParameter>]
    [-DomainController <Fqdn>] [-IncludeMoveHistory <SwitchParameter>] [-
IncludeMoveReport <SwitchParameter>]
    [-IncludeQuarantineDetails <SwitchParameter>] [-NoADLookup
<SwitchParameter>] [<CommonParameters>]
```

DESCRIPTION
On Mailbox servers only, you can use the Get-MailboxStatistics cmdlet
without parameters. In this case, the cmdlet
returns the statistics for all mailboxes on all databases on the local
server.

```
The Get-MailboxStatistics cmdlet requires at least one of the following
parameters to complete successfully:
Server, Database, or Identity.

You can use the Get-MailboxStatistics cmdlet to return detailed move
history and a move report for completed move
requests to troubleshoot a move request. To view the move history, you must
pass this cmdlet as an object. Move
histories are retained in the mailbox database and are numbered
incrementally, and the last executed move request
is always numbered 0. For more information, see "Example 7," "Example 8,"
and "Example 9" in this topic.

You can only see move reports and move history for completed move requests.

You need to be assigned permissions before you can run this cmdlet.
Although all parameters for this cmdlet are
listed in this topic, you may not have access to some parameters if they're
not included in the permissions
assigned to you. To see what permissions you need, see the "Recipient
Provisioning Permissions" section in the
Recipients Permissions topic.
```

```
RELATED LINKS
    Online Version http://technet.microsoft.com/EN-US/library/cec76f70-941f-
4bc9-b949-35dcc7671146(EXCHG.160).aspx

REMARKS
    To see the examples, type: "get-help Get-MailboxStatistics -examples".
    For more information, type: "get-help Get-MailboxStatistics -detailed".
    For technical information, type: "get-help Get-MailboxStatistics -full".
    For online help, type: "get-help Get-MailboxStatistics -online"
```

The default view (as you could have predicted from Table 5.3) includes the synopsis, syntax, and detailed description sections. Let's change our approach and look at the example view:

```
[PS] C:\>Get-Help Get-MailboxStatistics -Examples
```

```
NAME
    Get-MailboxStatistics
SYNOPSIS
    This cmdlet is available in on-premises Exchange Server 2016 and in the
    cloud-based service. Some parameters and
    settings may be exclusive to one environment or the other.

    Use the Get-MailboxStatistics cmdlet to obtain information about a mailbox,
    such as the size of the mailbox, the
```

number of messages it contains, and the last time it was accessed. In
addition, you can get the move history or a
move report of a completed move request.

For information about the parameter sets in the Syntax section below, see
Syntax.
```
------------------------- Example 1 -------------------------
```
This example retrieves the mailbox statistics for the mailbox of the user
Ayla Kol by using its associated alias
AylaKol.
```
Get-MailboxStatistics -Identity AylaKol
------------------------- Example 2 -------------------------
```
This example retrieves the mailbox statistics for all mailboxes on the
server MailboxServer01.
```
Get-MailboxStatistics -Server MailboxServer01
------------------------- Example 3 -------------------------
```
This example retrieves the mailbox statistics for the specified mailbox.
```
Get-MailboxStatistics -Identity contoso\chris
------------------------- Example 4 -------------------------
```
This example retrieves the mailbox statistics for all mailboxes in the
specified mailbox database.
```
Get-MailboxStatistics -Database "Mailbox Database"
------------------------- Example 5 -------------------------
```
This example retrieves the mailbox statistics for the disconnected
mailboxes for all mailbox databases in the
organization. The -ne operator means not equal.
```
Get-MailboxDatabase | Get-MailboxStatistics -Filter 'DisconnectDate -ne $null'
------------------------- Example 6 -------------------------
```
This example retrieves the mailbox statistics for a single disconnected
mailbox. The value for the
StoreMailboxIdentity parameter is the mailbox GUID of the disconnected
mailbox. You can also use the LegacyDN.
```
Get-MailboxStatistics -Database "Mailbox Database" -StoreMailboxIdentity
3b475034-303d-49b2-9403-ae022b43742d
------------------------- Example 7 -------------------------
```
This example returns the summary move history for the completed move
request for Ayla Kol's mailbox. If you don't
pipeline the output to the Format-List cmdlet, the move history doesn't
display.
```
Get-MailboxStatistics -Identity AylaKol -IncludeMoveHistory | Format-List
------------------------- Example 8 -------------------------
```
This example returns the detailed move history for the completed move
request for Ayla Kol's mailbox. This example
uses a temporary variable to store the mailbox statistics object. If the
mailbox has been moved multiple times,
there are multiple move reports. The last move report is always
MoveReport[0].

```
$temp=Get-MailboxStatistics -Identity AylaKol -IncludeMoveHistory
$temp.MoveHistory[0]
------------------------- Example 9 -------------------------
This example returns the detailed move history and a verbose detailed move
report for Ayla Kol's mailbox. This
example uses a temporary variable to store the move request statistics
object and outputs the move report to a CSV
file.

$temp=Get-MailboxStatistics -Identity AylaKol -IncludeMoveReport
$temp.MoveHistory[0] | Export-CSV C:\MoveReport_AylaKol.csv
```

The example view does not have as much data, but a lot of techies learn by looking at examples, so we find this view particularly useful. Next, let's look at the detailed view; because this view includes the parameters, it will have quite a bit more information:

```
[PS] C:\>Get-Help Get-MailboxStatistics -Detailed
```

```
NAME
    Get-MailboxStatistics
SYNOPSIS
    This cmdlet is available in on-premises Exchange Server 2016 and in the
    cloud-based service. Some parameters and
    settings may be exclusive to one environment or the other.
    Use the Get-MailboxStatistics cmdlet to obtain information about a mailbox,
    such as the size of the mailbox, the
    number of messages it contains, and the last time it was accessed. In
    addition, you can get the move history or a
    move report of a completed move request.
    For information about the parameter sets in the Syntax section below, see
    Syntax.
SYNTAX
    Get-MailboxStatistics -Identity <GeneralMailboxOrMailUserIdParameter> [-
Archive <SwitchParameter>] [-CopyOnServer
    <ServerIdParameter>] [-DomainController <Fqdn>] [-IncludeMoveHistory
<SwitchParameter>] [-IncludeMoveReport
    <SwitchParameter>] [-IncludeQuarantineDetails <SwitchParameter>] [-
NoADLookup <SwitchParameter>]
    [<CommonParameters>]


    Get-MailboxStatistics [-AuditLog <SwitchParameter>] [-Identity
<GeneralMailboxOrMailUserIdParameter>]
    [-DomainController <Fqdn>] [-IncludeMoveHistory <SwitchParameter>] [-
IncludeMoveReport <SwitchParameter>]
    [-IncludeQuarantineDetails <SwitchParameter>] [-NoADLookup
<SwitchParameter>] [<CommonParameters>]
```

```
    Get-MailboxStatistics -Database <DatabaseIdParameter> [-CopyOnServer
<ServerIdParameter>] [-Filter <String>]
    [-StoreMailboxIdentity <StoreMailboxIdParameter>] [-DomainController
<Fqdn>] [-IncludeMoveHistory
    <SwitchParameter>] [-IncludeMoveReport <SwitchParameter>] [-
IncludeQuarantineDetails <SwitchParameter>]
    [-NoADLookup <SwitchParameter>] [<CommonParameters>]

    Get-MailboxStatistics -Server <ServerIdParameter> [-Filter <String>] [-
IncludePassive <SwitchParameter>]
    [-DomainController <Fqdn>] [-IncludeMoveHistory <SwitchParameter>] [-
IncludeMoveReport <SwitchParameter>]
    [-IncludeQuarantineDetails <SwitchParameter>] [-NoADLookup
<SwitchParameter>] [<CommonParameters>]
```

DESCRIPTION
    On Mailbox servers only, you can use the Get-MailboxStatistics cmdlet
without parameters. In this case, the cmdlet
    returns the statistics for all mailboxes on all databases on the local
server.

    The Get-MailboxStatistics cmdlet requires at least one of the following
parameters to complete successfully:
    Server, Database, or Identity.

    You can use the Get-MailboxStatistics cmdlet to return detailed move
history and a move report for completed move
    requests to troubleshoot a move request. To view the move history, you must
pass this cmdlet as an object. Move
    histories are retained in the mailbox database and are numbered
incrementally, and the last executed move request
    is always numbered 0. For more information, see "Example 7," "Example 8,"
and "Example 9" in this topic.

    You can only see move reports and move history for completed move requests.

    You need to be assigned permissions before you can run this cmdlet.
Although all parameters for this cmdlet are
    listed in this topic, you may not have access to some parameters if they're
not included in the permissions
    assigned to you. To see what permissions you need, see the "Recipient
Provisioning Permissions" section in the
    Recipients Permissions topic.
PARAMETERS
    -Database <DatabaseIdParameter>
        This parameter is available only in on-premises Exchange 2016.
        The Database parameter specifies the name of the mailbox database. When
you specify a value for the Database

parameter, the Exchange Management Shell returns statistics for all the mailboxes on the database specified.

You can use the following values:

* GUID

* Database

This parameter accepts pipeline input from the Get-MailboxDatabase cmdlet.

-Identity <GeneralMailboxOrMailUserIdParameter>

The Identity parameter specifies a mailbox. When you specify a value for the Identity parameter, the command

looks up the mailbox specified in the Identity parameter, connects to the server where the mailbox resides,

and returns the statistics for the mailbox.

This parameter accepts the following values:

* Example: JPhillips

* Example: Atlanta.Corp.Contoso.Com/Users/JPhillips

* Example: Jeff Phillips

* Example: CN=JPhillips,CN=Users,DC=Atlanta,DC=Corp,DC=contoso,DC=com

* Example: Atlanta\JPhillips

* Example: fb456636-fe7d-4d58-9d15-5af57d0354c2

* Example: fb456636-fe7d-4d58-9d15-5af57d0354c2@contoso.com

* Example: /o=Contoso/ou=AdministrativeGroup/cn=Recipients/cn=JPhillips

* Example: Jeff.Phillips@contoso.com

* Example: JPhillips@contoso.com

-Server <ServerIdParameter>

This parameter is available only in on-premises Exchange 2016.

The Server parameter specifies the server from which you want to obtain mailbox statistics. You can use one of

the following values:

* Fully qualified domain name (FQDN)

* NetBIOS name

When you specify a value for the Server parameter, the command returns statistics for all the mailboxes on all

the databases, including recovery databases, on the specified server. If you don't specify this parameter, the

command returns logon statistics for the local server.

-Archive <SwitchParameter>

The Archive switch parameter specifies whether to return mailbox statistics for the archive mailbox associated

with the specified mailbox.

You don't have to specify a value with this parameter.

-AuditLog <SwitchParameter>

This parameter is reserved for internal Microsoft use.

-CopyOnServer <ServerIdParameter>

This parameter is available only in on-premises Exchange 2016.

The CopyOnServer parameter is used to retrieve statistics from a specific database copy on the server

specified with the Server parameter.
-DomainController <Fqdn>
This parameter is available only in on-premises Exchange 2016.
The DomainController parameter specifies the domain controller that's used by this cmdlet to read data from or
write data to Active Directory. You identify the domain controller by its fully qualified domain name (FQDN).
For example, dc01.contoso.com.
-Filter <String>
This parameter is available only in on-premises Exchange 2016.
The Filter parameter specifies a filter to filter the results of the Get-MailboxStatistics cmdlet. For
example, to display all disconnected mailboxes on a specific mailbox database, use the following syntax for
this parameter: -Filter 'DisconnectDate -ne $null'
-IncludeMoveHistory <SwitchParameter>
The IncludeMoveHistory switch specifies whether to return additional information about the mailbox that
includes the history of a completed move request, such as status, flags, target database, bad items, start
times, end times, duration that the move request was in various stages, and failure codes.
-IncludeMoveReport <SwitchParameter>
The IncludeMoveReport switch specifies whether to return a verbose detailed move report for a completed move
request, such as server connections and move stages.
Because the output of this command is verbose, you should send the output to a .CSV file for easier analysis.
-IncludePassive <SwitchParameter>
This parameter is available only in on-premises Exchange 2016.
Without the IncludePassive parameter, the cmdlet retrieves statistics from active database copies only. Using
the IncludePassive parameter, you can have the cmdlet return statistics from all active and passive database
copies.
-IncludeQuarantineDetails <SwitchParameter>
This parameter is available only in on-premises Exchange 2016.
The IncludeQuarantineDetails switch specifies whether to return additional quarantine details about the
mailbox that aren't otherwise included in the results. You can use these details to determine when and why the
mailbox was quarantined.
Specifically, this switch returns the values of the QuarantineDescription, QuarantineLastCrash and
QuarantineEnd properties on the mailbox. To see these values, you need use a formatting cmdlet. For example,
Get-MailboxStatistics <MailboxIdentity> -IncludeQuarantineDetails |

```
Format-List Quarantine*.
    -NoADLookup <SwitchParameter>
        This parameter is available only in on-premises Exchange 2016.
        The NoADLookup switch specifies that information is retrieved from the
mailbox database, and not from Active
        Directory. This helps improve cmdlet performance when querying a
mailbox database that contains a large number
        of mailboxes.

    -StoreMailboxIdentity <StoreMailboxIdParameter>
        This parameter is available only in on-premises Exchange 2016.

        The StoreMailboxIdentity parameter specifies the mailbox identity when
used with the Database parameter to
        return statistics for a single mailbox on the specified database. You
can use one of the following values:

        * MailboxGuid
        * LegacyDN
        Use this syntax to retrieve information about disconnected mailboxes,
which don't have a corresponding Active
        Directory object or that has a corresponding Active Directory object
that doesn't point to the disconnected
        mailbox in the mailbox database.

    <CommonParameters>
        This cmdlet supports the common parameters: Verbose, Debug,
        ErrorAction, ErrorVariable, WarningAction, WarningVariable,
        OutBuffer, PipelineVariable, and OutVariable. For more information, see
        about_CommonParameters (http://go.microsoft.com/fwlink/?LinkID=113216).
-------------------------- Example 1 --------------------------
This example retrieves the mailbox statistics for the mailbox of the user
Ayla Kol by using its associated alias
AylaKol.
Get-MailboxStatistics -Identity AylaKol
```

Notice in the preceding output that we left out most of the examples because we had already shown them to you earlier. We did this with the full view as well because it contains even more information than the detailed view. The full view includes the metadata for each parameter, as well as examples:

```
 Get-Help Get-MailboxStatistics -Full
NAME
    Get-MailboxStatistics
SYNOPSIS
    This cmdlet is available in on-premises Exchange Server 2016 and in the
    cloud-based service. Some parameters and
    settings may be exclusive to one environment or the other.
```

Use the Get-MailboxStatistics cmdlet to obtain information about a mailbox, such as the size of the mailbox, the
number of messages it contains, and the last time it was accessed. In addition, you can get the move history or a
move report of a completed move request.
For information about the parameter sets in the Syntax section below, see Syntax.

SYNTAX

Get-MailboxStatistics -Identity <GeneralMailboxOrMailUserIdParameter> [-Archive <SwitchParameter>] [-CopyOnServer
<ServerIdParameter>] [-DomainController <Fqdn>] [-IncludeMoveHistory <SwitchParameter>] [-IncludeMoveReport
<SwitchParameter>] [-IncludeQuarantineDetails <SwitchParameter>] [-NoADLookup <SwitchParameter>]
[<CommonParameters>]

Get-MailboxStatistics [-AuditLog <SwitchParameter>] [-Identity <GeneralMailboxOrMailUserIdParameter>]
[-DomainController <Fqdn>] [-IncludeMoveHistory <SwitchParameter>] [-IncludeMoveReport <SwitchParameter>]
[-IncludeQuarantineDetails <SwitchParameter>] [-NoADLookup <SwitchParameter>] [<CommonParameters>]

Get-MailboxStatistics -Database <DatabaseIdParameter> [-CopyOnServer <ServerIdParameter>] [-Filter <String>]
[-StoreMailboxIdentity <StoreMailboxIdParameter>] [-DomainController <Fqdn>] [-IncludeMoveHistory
<SwitchParameter>] [-IncludeMoveReport <SwitchParameter>] [-IncludeQuarantineDetails <SwitchParameter>]
[-NoADLookup <SwitchParameter>] [<CommonParameters>]

Get-MailboxStatistics -Server <ServerIdParameter> [-Filter <String>] [-IncludePassive <SwitchParameter>]
[-DomainController <Fqdn>] [-IncludeMoveHistory <SwitchParameter>] [-IncludeMoveReport <SwitchParameter>]
[-IncludeQuarantineDetails <SwitchParameter>] [-NoADLookup <SwitchParameter>] [<CommonParameters>]

DESCRIPTION

On Mailbox servers only, you can use the Get-MailboxStatistics cmdlet without parameters. In this case, the cmdlet
returns the statistics for all mailboxes on all databases on the local server.
The Get-MailboxStatistics cmdlet requires at least one of the following parameters to complete successfully:
Server, Database, or Identity.
You can use the Get-MailboxStatistics cmdlet to return detailed move history and a move report for completed move

requests to troubleshoot a move request. To view the move history, you must pass this cmdlet as an object. Move
histories are retained in the mailbox database and are numbered incrementally, and the last executed move request
is always numbered 0. For more information, see "Example 7," "Example 8," and "Example 9" in this topic.
You can only see move reports and move history for completed move requests. You need to be assigned permissions before you can run this cmdlet.
Although all parameters for this cmdlet are
listed in this topic, you may not have access to some parameters if they're not included in the permissions
assigned to you. To see what permissions you need, see the "Recipient Provisioning Permissions" section in the
Recipients Permissions topic.
PARAMETERS
    -Database <DatabaseIdParameter>
        This parameter is available only in on-premises Exchange 2016.
        The Database parameter specifies the name of the mailbox database. When you specify a value for the Database
        parameter, the Exchange Management Shell returns statistics for all the mailboxes on the database specified.
        You can use the following values:
        * GUID
        * Database
        This parameter accepts pipeline input from the Get-MailboxDatabase cmdlet.

        Required?   true
        Position?   Named
        Default value
        Accept pipeline input?   True
        Accept wildcard characters?   false

    -Identity <GeneralMailboxOrMailUserIdParameter>
        The Identity parameter specifies a mailbox. When you specify a value for the Identity parameter, the command
        looks up the mailbox specified in the Identity parameter, connects to the server where the mailbox resides,
        and returns the statistics for the mailbox.
        This parameter accepts the following values:
        * Example: JPhillips
        * Example: Atlanta.Corp.Contoso.Com/Users/JPhillips
        * Example: Jeff Phillips
        * Example: CN=JPhillips,CN=Users,DC=Atlanta,DC=Corp,DC=contoso,DC=com
        * Example: Atlanta\JPhillips
        * Example: fb456636-fe7d-4d58-9d15-5af57d0354c2
        * Example: fb456636-fe7d-4d58-9d15-5af57d0354c2@contoso.com

```
            * Example: /o=Contoso/ou=AdministrativeGroup/cn=Recipients/cn=JPhillips
            * Example: Jeff.Phillips@contoso.com
            * Example: JPhillips@contoso.com
            Required?                    true
            Position?                    1
            Default value
            Accept pipeline input?       True
            Accept wildcard characters?  false
        -Server <ServerIdParameter>
            This parameter is available only in on-premises Exchange 2016.
            The Server parameter specifies the server from which you want to obtain
            mailbox statistics. You can use one of
            the following values:
            * Fully qualified domain name (FQDN)
            * NetBIOS name
            When you specify a value for the Server parameter, the command returns
            statistics for all the mailboxes on all
            the databases, including recovery databases, on the specified server.
            If you don't specify this parameter, the
            command returns logon statistics for the local server.
            Required?                    true
            Position?                    Named
            Default value
            Accept pipeline input?       True
            Accept wildcard characters?  false
        -Archive <SwitchParameter>
            The Archive switch parameter specifies whether to return mailbox
            statistics for the archive mailbox associated
            with the specified mailbox.
            You don't have to specify a value with this parameter.
            Required?                    false
            Position?                    Named
            Default value
            Accept pipeline input?       False
            Accept wildcard characters?  false
```

Yes, that's a lot of text for examples of one cmdlet, but we hope that these examples will make it easier for you to quickly learn the capabilities of all cmdlets and how you can use them.

The PowerShell help system also gives you some options with respect to getting help on parameters. For example, here is an example if you want help on just the -Database parameter of the Get-MailboxStatistics cmdlet:

```
Get-Help Get-MailboxStatistics -Parameter Database
-Database <DatabaseIdParameter>
    The Database parameter specifies the name of the mailbox database.
When you specify a value for the Database parameter, the Exchange
Management Shell returns statistics for all the mailboxes on the
database specified.
```

```
You can use the following values:
* GUID
* Server\Database
* Database
This parameter accepts pipeline input from the
Get-MailboxDatabase cmdlet.
Required?                       true
Position?                       Named
Default value
Accept pipeline input?          True
Accept wildcard characters?     false
```

The -Parameter option also accepts the asterisk (*) wildcard. Here is an example if you want to see help on all the parameters that contain SCLQuarantine for the Set-Mailbox cmdlet:

```
[PS] C:\>Get-Help Set-Mailbox -Parameter *SCLQuarantine*
-SCLQuarantineEnabled <Nullable>
    The SCLQuarantineEnabled parameter specifies whether messages
that meet the SCL threshold specified by the SCLQuarantineThreshold
parameter are quarantined. If a message is quarantined, it's sent
to the quarantine mailbox where the messaging administrator can
review it. You can use the following values:
    * $true
    * $false
    * $null
    Required?                       false
    Position?                       Named
    Default value
    Accept pipeline input?          False
    Accept wildcard characters?     false
-SCLQuarantineThreshold <Nullable>
    The SCLQuarantineThreshold parameter specifies the SCL
at which a message is quarantined, if the SCLQuarantineEnabled
parameter is set to $true. You must specify an integer from 0 through 9
inclusive.
    Required?                       false
    Position?                       Named
    Default value
    Accept pipeline input?          False
    Accept wildcard characters?     false
```

Getting Tips

You may have noticed a useful tip each time you launched the Exchange Management Shell (EMS). Figure 5.5 shows the Tip of the Day text that you see each time you launch the EMS. There are more than 100 of these tips.

FIGURE 5.5
Viewing the Tip of
the Day

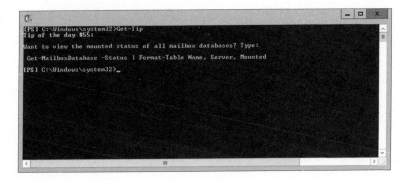

If you want to view additional tips, just type **Get-Tip** at the Exchange Management Shell prompt.

You can even add your own tips if you don't mind editing an XML file; the tips for English are found in C:\Program Files\Microsoft\Exchange Server\V15\Bin\ExTips.xml.

The Bottom Line

Use PowerShell command syntax.   The PowerShell is an easy-to-use command-line interface that allows you to manipulate many aspects of the Windows operating system, Registry, and filesystem. The Exchange Management Shell extensions allow you to manage all aspects of an Exchange Server organization and many Active Directory objects.

PowerShell cmdlets consist of a verb (such as Get, Set, New, or Mount) that indicates what is being done and a noun (such as Mailbox, Group, ExchangeServer) that indicates on which object the cmdlet is acting. Cmdlet options such as -Debug, -Whatif, and -ValidateOnly are common to most cmdlets and can be used to test or debug problems with a cmdlet.

> **Master It**   You need to use the Exchange Management Shell cmdlet Set-User to change the city to Irvine for all members of the IT distribution list. But you want to first confirm that the command will do what you want to do without actually making the change. Which command should you use?

Understand object-oriented use of PowerShell.   Output of a cmdlet is not simple text but rather objects. These objects have properties that can be examined and manipulated.

> **Master It**   You are using the Set-User cmdlet to set properties of a user's Active Directory account. You need to determine the properties that are available to use with the Set-User cmdlet. What can you do to view the available properties?

Get help with using PowerShell.   Many options are available when you are trying to figure out how to use a PowerShell cmdlet, including online help and the Exchange Server documentation. PowerShell and the EMS make it easy to "discover" the cmdlets that you need to do your job.

> **Master It**   How would you locate all the cmdlets available to manipulate a mailbox? You are trying to figure out how to use the Set-User cmdlet and would like to see an example. How can you view examples for this cmdlet?

Chapter 6

Understanding the Exchange Autodiscover Process

Being an Exchange Server administrator is rewarding and, at times, frustrating. One of the most common sources of frustration we've encountered is managing the interactions between our Exchange servers and the Outlook desktop client. In large organizations, two separate groups maintain these pieces of the common puzzle. In smaller organizations, though, the same people can handle both the server and the clients. It's in organizations like these that you learn the truth of the matter that Exchange Server and Outlook were developed by two separate product groups (although the groups are now joined).

Historically, many Outlook client issues were the result of mismatches between the Outlook profile settings and the actual server configurations. In Exchange Server 2007, Microsoft introduced the Autodiscover service, a component of the Client Access role, which was intended to allow both clients (such as Outlook, Windows Mobile, and Entourage) and other Exchange servers to automatically discover how your Exchange Server organization is configured and determine the appropriate settings without direct administrator involvement.

Many Exchange Server 2007 organizations ran into two main problems getting Autodiscover properly configured and deployed: understanding the concepts and getting the certificates properly deployed. By deploying Exchange Server 2010, administrators increased their knowledge of the Autodiscover processes. In this latest release of Exchange Server, the update is a much simpler, much more evolved, and a more *administrator-friendly* feature.

IN THIS CHAPTER, YOU WILL LEARN TO:

- Work with Autodiscover
- Troubleshoot Autodiscover
- Manage Exchange Server certificates

Autodiscover Concepts

Let's share an unpleasant truth that a lot of administrators have not yet learned: the Autodiscover service is *not an optional component* of an Exchange Server organization. It may seem as if it's optional, especially if you haven't yet deployed a version of Outlook, Windows Phone, or Office for Mac that takes advantage of it. More than that, you can't get rid of it—Autodiscover is on from the moment you install the first server in the organization. You can't shut it off, you can't disable it, and you can't keep clients and Exchange servers from trying to contact it (although you can cause problems by not properly configuring Autodiscover, breaking features, and forcing fallback to older, more error-prone methods of configuration).

We know several Exchange Server 2007 organizations that limped along seemingly just fine with Autodiscover improperly configured or just plain ignored. However, when Autodiscover has been neglected, this inevitably signals an Exchange Server organization with other problems— and this is even truer in Exchange Server 2016 than in previous versions. Autodiscover is more than just a way to ease the administration of Outlook client profiles. Other Exchange Server components, servers, and services also use Autodiscover to find the servers and settings with which they need to communicate. In order for the Outlook client to leverage many of the advanced features of Exchange Server, including the high-availability features, the client depends on a functional Autodiscover service. If you want to use the external calendar sharing or Skype for Business integration, you'd better get Autodiscover squared away.

In order to properly plan and deploy Autodiscover, you have to work through some of the most potentially confusing aspects of an Exchange Server deployment. The good news, though, is that once you have these issues solved, you will have headed off some confusing and annoying errors that might otherwise cause problems down the road. These issues include namespace planning and certificate management. Trust me that getting these issues sorted will make your client access deployment and your overall management tasks a lot easier.

What Autodiscover Provides

Autodiscover is necessary for far more reasons than that it makes configuring your Outlook clients easier. In Exchange Server 2007, the clients did benefit a great deal, which is part of the reason many people did not see the point of learning about the service. Either that, or it worked subtly behind the scenes, and some administrators lived in ignorant bliss, once some configuration was done. Beginning with Exchange Server 2013, both the client and the server benefits get better.

The information provided by Autodiscover includes the following:

◆ Outlook client connection configuration

◆ Configuration URLs for the Offline Address Book (OAB)

◆ Configuration URLs for free and busy information

◆ Outlook profile configuration information

CLIENT BENEFITS

Exactly what benefits you get from Autodiscover depends on which client you're using:

◆ Outlook 2010, Outlook 2013, and Outlook 2016 fully support Autodiscover. Outlook 2007 supports Autodiscover but isn't a supported client for Exchange Server 2016. Outlook versions prior to 2007 do not use Autodiscover, but they are not supported as clients of Exchange Server 2016 either. When we say "not supported," we mean that Microsoft won't provide support. In some cases, you may have basic functionality, but some other functionality may not work. Note that extended support for Office 2007 ends in October of 2017.

◆ iPhones, iPads, Android, Windows Mobile 6.1, Windows Phone 7.x/8.x, and Windows Phone 10 and later support Autodiscover, and many mobile users today rely on Autodiscover for easy configuration of a new device.

◆ The Windows Mail app that is built into the Windows 8 Pro and later also uses Autodiscover to configure client settings (incidentally, those clients are then configured as Exchange Server ActiveSync clients).

◆ If you're a Mac user, you may prefer using Outlook for Mac 2016. This version of Outlook works in a similar way to the PC version, except it does not support service connection point (SCP) lookup. SCP lookup is a method used for locating services, or more specifically the servers that run the services, and is explained later on in this chapter.

Even though you get all these great benefits from Autodiscover, likely the only time you will see Autodiscover working is when configuring a client, such as Outlook, for the first time. When running through an initial configuration wizard, a user is prompted to configure Outlook to connect to an email server. The only information they need to know is the email address and password. Then, their computer will look up the correct details using Autodiscover and configure the Outlook profile automatically as shown in Figure 6.1.

FIGURE 6.1
Completing the initial Outlook configuration using Autodiscover

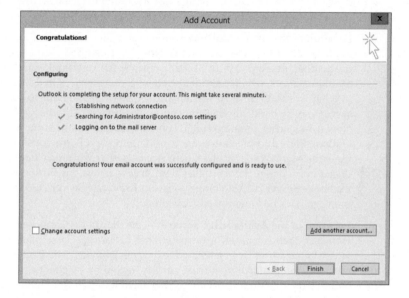

Although these are the main Autodiscover-aware clients, they're not the only ones. For example, the Microsoft Skype for Business client and devices use Autodiscover and Exchange Web Services. The behavior of Autodiscover has been clearly documented by Microsoft, so other third-party clients and mobile devices also utilize it. Features that Outlook and Windows Phone will leverage include the following:

Support for DNS A Records   By default, external clients attempt to find the Autodiscover service through DNS lookups based on the email address of the user.

Support for DNS SRV Records   Due to popular demand, starting in Exchange Server 2010, the Exchange Server and Outlook teams provided support for the use of Service Locator (SRV) records for organizations that couldn't use Address (A) records and didn't want to use CNAMEs. SRV records are also useful when Exchange is hosted in a separate forest.

Support for Active Directory Service Connection Point Objects   Domain-joined clients that can contact Active Directory—effectively any Windows client running Outlook 2010 or later—can utilize an Active Directory feature called service connection points. SCPs provide a number of benefits that aren't available with plain DNS lookups. SCPs allow clients to locate resources via SCP objects within the Active Directory. The SCP object contains the list of Autodiscover URLs for the Active Directory forest. You can use the `Set-ClientAccessService` cmdlet to modify the SCP object. (And of course, you can use `Get-ClientAccessService` to view the object.)

Internal Organization Settings   Services on Exchange Server 2016 servers have both internal URLs for clients within the firewall (such as Outlook and Skype for Business on domain-joined Windows devices) and external URLs for pretty much everything else. Internal settings use the appropriate Exchange Server FQDNs by default, unless you modify them (such as when using load balancers).

External Organization Settings   External settings allow services to be reached through Internet-available FQDNs. For some reason, many organizations don't like publishing the internal FQDNs of their Exchange servers. Using external settings may also ensure that connections are load balanced or sent through firewalls.

Location of the User's Mailbox Server   In earlier versions of Exchange Server, the user's Mailbox server was stored in Active Directory, stamped on the user object. However, with the architectural changes to Exchange Server 2013, Outlook can connect to one of several Mailbox servers, which provide the client access services in a site. The connection is stateless; in other words, there is no session affinity, so from one hour to the next a different Mailbox server may be handling the connection. This makes Autodiscover all the more important. Now using a user's mailbox GUID plus the domain name from the SMTP address of the user, Outlook finds a connection point to a Mailbox server. Previously, Outlook had a direct affinity to the Mailbox server or a Client Access server with the Client Access array feature introduced in Exchange Server 2010. Client Access arrays, the virtual RPC endpoint available in Exchange Server 2010, no longer exists in Exchange Server 2013 or Exchange Server 2016; but then again it's no longer necessary either.

Location of the Availability Service   Calendar items are stored in each user's mailbox. However, their free/busy information has historically been placed in a system public folder, which could suffer from latency due to replication lag. The Exchange Availability Service allows current information to be quickly looked up by clients (both in the organization and in federated organizations) as they need it, rather than having them dependent on stale data in public folders as was the case in previous versions.

Location of the Offline Address Book Service   OABs in Exchange Server 2016 are generated by an arbitration mailbox, known as an Organization mailbox. This creates the files that a Client Access service will deliver to Outlook clients via HTTPS. In Exchange Server 2010 and previous, clients could retrieve this from a public folder. Locating the OAB URL is essential, because Outlook runs in cached mode by default and relies on the OAB for address book lookups. Autodiscover directs Outlook to the OAB URL that can fetch the changes a client requires. If this or any other Exchange Web Services URL might change on the Exchange server, the client periodically checks the Autodiscover service to receive those updates and changes. Autodiscover is contacted not only during the startup process of Outlook but other times as well.

Outlook Anywhere Settings   With Exchange Server 2016, all Outlook connections use RPC over HTTPS, aka Outlook Anywhere, or MAPI over HTTP. Outlook Anywhere is now the connection method for internal, as well as external connections, and this latest version of Exchange Server no longer accepts MAPI over RPC connections from Outlook clients. Now, having the external URL information is a requirement for clients outside your corporate firewall, but more settings, such as the certificate validation name, are necessary for a successful Outlook Anywhere session to be established.

Later in this chapter, we'll walk through a typical Outlook 2016 Autodiscover session and show how all this information is used. For now, just be aware that the value of many of these options can be user dependent (such as the mailbox location) or site dependent. As a result, the Autodiscover service is a vital part of spreading load throughout the entire organization, minimizing traffic over WAN links between sites and branches, and ensuring that your users are connecting to the best servers they can reach at the time.

SERVER BENEFITS

Autodiscover isn't just useful for clients connecting to the Exchange Server infrastructure; it's also useful for other servers, both within the organization and without:

◆   Servers within the same organization and Active Directory forest use Autodiscover to locate various services on a user's behalf. For example, when a user performs a logon to Outlook on the web, the Mailbox server handling the Outlook on the web session needs several of the pieces of information provided by Autodiscover. Using Autodiscover reduces the load on Active Directory domain controllers and global catalog servers and removes reliance on cached information. This is true whether you're in a mixed Exchange Server 2016/2013 organization or are deploying Exchange Server 2016 for the first time.

◆   Servers within the same organization but in a different Active Directory forest depend on cross-forest service connection points and internal Autodiscover to cross the forest boundaries and discover the appropriate servers to use. In this situation, one Exchange server in the source forest will often act as a proxy for the appropriate services in the target forest, or it may simply redirect the client. In multiple-forest deployments, the use of Autodiscover is pretty much mandatory to ensure that Exchange servers in separate forests can interoperate properly.

◆   Servers within separate federated organizations require the use of the external Autodiscover information to reach federated availability services. This, plus the relevant authentication information, allows users to securely share calendar and free/busy information with their counterparts in federated Exchange Server organizations. With other Exchange Server organizations, federation greatly simplifies the configuration and management of these types of operations.

So, let's take a look at the nitty-gritty of how Autodiscover works.

How Autodiscover Works

Don't be fooled by the seeming complexity you're about to see. Autodiscover is pretty simple to understand. The biggest complications come from certificates and namespace planning, which we'll get to in a bit and which have gotten significantly simpler, with fewer namespaces required.

THE SERVICE CONNECTION POINT OBJECT

The first piece of the Autodiscover puzzle lies with the service connection point (SCP) object. As each Mailbox server instance is installed into your organization, it creates an SCP object in the Configuration-naming partition of the Active Directory domain to which it is joined, at the following location:

```
CN=<Mailbox Server NetBIOS Name>,CN=Autodiscover, CN=Protocols,CN=<CAS Server
NetBIOS Name>,CN=Servers,CN= Exchange Administrative Group
(FYDIBOHF23SPDLT),CN=Administrative Groups,CN=<Organization Name>,
CN=Microsoft Exchange,CN=Services,CN=Configuration,DC=<domain name>,DC=<domain
suffix>
```

Here's what a typical SCP object looks like when dumped from the LDP (LDP.EXE) tool:

```
ExpaNYC-nding base
'CN=EX1,CN=Autodiscover,CN=Protocols,CN=NYC-EX1,CN=Servers,CN=Exchange
Administrative Group (FYDIBOHF23SPDLT),CN=Administrative Groups,CN=First
Organization,CN=Microsoft
Exchange,CN=Services,CN=Configuration,DC=contoso,DC=com'...
Getting 1 entries:
Dn: CN=NYC-EX1,CN=Autodiscover,CN=Protocols,CN=NYC-EX1,CN=Servers,CN=Exchange
Administrative Group (FYDIBOHF23SPDLT),CN=Administrative Groups,CN=First
Organization,CN=Microsoft
Exchange,CN=Services,CN=Configuration,DC=contoso,DC=com
cn: EX1;
distinguishedName:
CN=NYC-EX1,CN=Autodiscover,CN=Protocols,CN=EX1,CN=Servers,CN=Exchange
Administrative Group (FYDIBOHF23SPDLT),CN=Administrative Groups,CN=First
Organization,CN=Microsoft
Exchange,CN=Services,CN=Configuration,DC=contoso,DC=com;
dSCorePropagationData: 0x0 = (  );
instanceType: 0x4 = ( WRITE );
keywords (2): Site=Default-First-Site-Name; 77378F46-2C66-4aa9-A6A6-3E7A48B19596;
name: NYC-EX1;
objectCategory: CN=Service-Connection-
Point,CN=Schema,CN=Configuration,DC=contoso,DC=com;
objectClass (4): top; leaf; connectionPoint; serviceConnectionPoint;
objectGUID: 44f44e8c-164a-446a-9eb8-f21a59b11b65;
serviceBindingInformation:
https://nyc-ex1.contoso.com/Autodiscover/Autodiscover.xml;
serviceClassName: ms-Exchange-AutoDiscover-Service;
serviceDNSName: NYC-EX1;
showInAdvancedViewOnly: TRUE;
systemFlags: 0x40000000 = ( CONFIG_ALLOW_RENAME );
```

```
uSNChanged: 184521;
uSNCreated: 184521;
whenChanged: 8/1/2016 6:05:05 PM Pacific Daylight Time;
whenCreated: 8/1/2016 6:05:05 PM Pacific Daylight Time;
```

There are a few key properties of these entries you should note:

◆ The objectClass property includes the serviceConnectionPoint type. This identifies the entry as an SCP, allowing it to be searched easily using LDAP.

◆ The serviceClassName property identifies this particular SCP as an ms-Exchange-AutoDiscover-Service entry. The computers searching for Autodiscover records can thereby determine that this is an entry pertaining to Autodiscover and that they should pay attention to it. The client searches the configuration-naming context for any objects that have a serviceClassName= ms-Exchange-Autodiscover-Service. Using the combination of objectClass and serviceClassName allows computers to efficiently find all relevant SCP entries (through an indexed search from a domain controller) without knowing any computer names ahead of time.

◆ The serviceBindingInformation points to the actual Autodiscover XML file that the client should access in order to retrieve the current Autodiscover information. More on this later.

◆ The keywords property holds additional information that the clients use. Specifically, take note of the Site= value. This value helps you control site affinity, ensuring that clients use nearby servers that aren't in far-off sites to provide their Exchange Server services (unless that is desirable).

The rest of the properties on an SCP object are fairly standard for Active Directory objects, so we won't discuss them further.

Now that you know what a service connection point is and where they're located, you're mostly set. The distinguished name of each SCP object uniquely identifies the host associated without that object. If the client search returns multiple SCP objects that the client will use, it will select among them according to alphabetical order. This can be useful to know.

Note also that an Exchange server instance publishes its corresponding SCP object to Active Directory only when it is installed (which is done automatically for you). If you change something about the Exchange server—such as which site it's located in—it will not update its SCP object. You have to do that manually. The best way is to use Exchange Management Shell. Here is a sample command that configures a server named NYC-EX1 to have an internal URL for the XML file location and also sets it to be authoritative for two sites:

```
Set-ClientAccessService -Identity NYC-EX1 -AutodiscoverServiceInternalURI
"https://mail.contoso.com/autodiscover/autodiscover.xml"
-AutoDiscoverSiteScope "Site1", "Site2"
```

THE DNS OPTION

The SCP is used when the client or server is joined to an Active Directory domain and can perform the search against the domain controllers. When the discovering computer is external or not domain joined, another mechanism is used: DNS lookups.

The following list describes the DNS lookups that are performed for the Autodiscover service in a given domain. For this example, let's use the user UserA@contoso.com. The client (or server) takes the domain portion (contoso.com) of this address and performs the following lookups in order until it finds a match:

1. A DNS A record (or CNAME record) for contoso.com that points to a web server that responds to the HTTPS URL https://contoso.com/Autodiscover/Autodiscover.xml.

2. A DNS A record (or CNAME record) for autodiscover.contoso.com that points to a web server that responds to the HTTPS URL https://autodiscover.contoso.com/Autodiscover/Autodiscover.xml.

3. A DNS A record (or CNAME record) for contoso.com that points to a web server that responds to the HTTP URL http://autodiscover.contoso.com/Autodiscover/Autodiscover.xml. (Note that this URL should be configured to redirect to the actual HTTPS location of the Autodiscover service.)

4. A DNS SRV record for autodiscover._tcp.contoso.com. (This record should contain the port number 443 and a hostname, such as mail.contoso.com, allowing the client to try the HTTPS URL https://mail.contoso.com/Autodiscover/Autodiscover.xml.)

If the requested hostname is returned through either a CNAME record or an SRV record, be aware that your clients (Outlook in particular) may display a warning dialog with the following text:

```
Allow this website to configure UserA@contoso.com server settings?
https://mail.contoso.com/autodiscover/autodiscover.xml
Your account was redirected to this website for settings.
You should only allow settings from sources you know and trust.
```

This warning will appear every time the client performs Autodiscover unless you check the Don't Ask Me About This Website Again check box. You can also prepopulate the Registry key to prevent this warning. See the Knowledge Base article at http://support.microsoft.com/kb/2480582.

Note that Autodiscover expects the use of HTTPS. Don't publish it over nonsecure HTTP and expect clients to be happy about it. You have a lot of sensitive information going through Autodiscover, including user credentials. As a result, certificate considerations will play a large part in your Autodiscover configuration.

 Real World Scenario

WHICH OPTION SHOULD I CHOOSE?

You can use several different methods to publish Autodiscover services through DNS. In the end, the option you choose is up to you and your business needs. However, you should consider these points to see how they align with your business objectives. Again, let's consider the case of contoso.com.

◆ Publishing Autodiscover under `https://contoso.com` doesn't require you to have an extra DNS name for internal clients. If you have HTTPS published on this hostname already, you don't need to use an extra certificate or hostname as long as you can ensure that the Autodiscover virtual directory can be published under the existing website. Most organizations will probably already have this namespace published in their DNS, but it could result in name-resolution collisions if the URL that it points to does not have the Autodiscover information.

◆ Publishing Autodiscover under `https://autodiscover.contoso.com` requires you to have an extra DNS name, but it's a hostname that isn't likely to be used by any other servers. However, you'll need to have a Subject Alternative Name (SAN) certificate or a wildcard certificate (not recommended—see the section "Planning Certificate Names") or use multiple certificates and a second virtual website. Publishing a second website is quite a bit more complicated than simply using the defaults, so keep that in mind.

◆ Publishing Autodiscover under the HTTP redirect not only requires you to have an extra DNS name but also invokes the security warning for each user. You'll need to configure the appropriate redirect, and you'll need to have a SAN certificate or a wildcard certificate or use multiple certificates and a second virtual website. This option may make sense for organizations that are hosting multiple servers or SMTP namespaces within a single Exchange Server organization.

◆ Publishing Autodiscover under an SRV redirect requires you to have external DNS servers that handle the SRV type. Most modern DNS servers can handle this, but some DNS hosting services do not. Additionally, this redirect invokes the security warning for each user. Finally, you'll need to have a SAN certificate or a wildcard certificate or use multiple certificates and a second virtual website.

In my experience, the second option (`https://autodiscover.contoso.com`) is the best combination of simplicity and control. It's the one that most organizations we've worked with have used. When Exchange Server 2007 was first introduced, certificate authorities that could provide SAN certificates were rare and the certificates themselves were expensive, making the alternative more palatable. Now, however, that is no longer the case. If you hesitate to deploy SAN certificates, there is a lot of good guidance out there to help you—including the section "Deploying Exchange Certificates," later in this chapter—and Exchange Server gives you better tools to manage them.

TWO STEP-BY-STEP EXAMPLES

Enough theory. Let's dive into our example with a company that has the `contoso.com` domain and show you a walk-through of a common scenario: a domain-joined Outlook 2016 client performing Autodiscover behind the organization firewall. To illustrate this scenario, we'll use a tool every Exchange Server administrator should know well: the Outlook Test E-Mail AutoConfiguration tool, shown in Figure 6.2. When using this tool, be sure to uncheck the Use Guessmart and Secure Guessmart Authentication options in order to get only the results of an Autodiscover query. The great thing about this tool is that it exposes all the URLs that are returned to the Outlook client. This allows the administrator to quickly identify misconfigured URLs and rule out several potential problems when troubleshooting connectivity.

FIGURE 6.2
Using the
Test E-mail
AutoConfiguration
tool

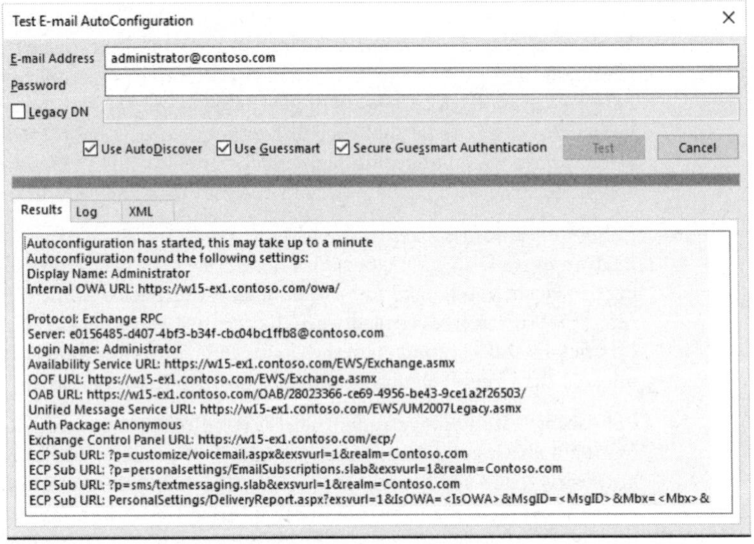

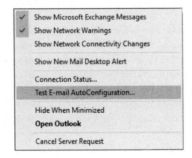

You can access this tool from Outlook by holding down the Ctrl key while right-clicking (or left-clicking) the Outlook icon in the notification area on the taskbar. This opens the menu shown in Figure 6.3. From this menu, select the Test E-mail AutoConfiguration option.

FIGURE 6.3
Accessing the
Test E-mail
AutoConfiguration
tool

When a domain-joined machine performs Autodiscover, it steps through the following process:

1. It performs an LDAP search for all SCP objects in the forest. Outlook enumerates the returned results based on the client's Active Directory site by sorting the returned SCP records using the keywords attribute; if there are no SCP records that contain a matching site value, all nonmatching SCP records are returned. If there are multiple matching SCP objects, Outlook simply chooses the oldest SCP record since the list is not sorted in any particular order.

2. Outlook attempts to connect to the configured URL specified in the SCP record's ServiceBindingInformation attribute: `https:// mail.contoso.com/Autodiscover/ Autodiscover.xml`.

3. When Outlook attempts to connect to the URL, the XML file is generated from the client request, and then the client successfully receives the XML file shown in Listing 6.1. (This output can be seen on the XML tab in the Test-Email AutoConfiguration screen.)

LISTING 6.1: An Autodiscover XML Response

```xml
<?xml version="1.0" encoding="utf-8"?>
<Autodiscover xmlns="http://schemas.microsoft.com/exchange/autodiscover/
responseschema/2006">
  <Response xmlns="http://schemas.microsoft.com/exchange/autodiscover/outlook/
responseschema/2006a">
    <User>
      <DisplayName>User One</DisplayName>
      <LegacyDN>/o=Contoso/ou=Exchange Administrative Group (FYDIBOHF23SPDLT)/
cn=Recipients/cn=3c180eec39b04806a3516ed579c88e7a-User One</LegacyDN>
      <AutoDiscoverSMTPAddress>User1@contoso.com</AutoDiscoverSMTPAddress>
      <DeploymentId>af1a8434-68f6-4a93-84c9-bd6129e1a10b</DeploymentId>
    </User>
    <Account>
      <AccountType>email</AccountType>
      <Action>settings</Action>
      <MicrosoftOnline>False</MicrosoftOnline>
      <ConsumerMailbox>False</ConsumerMailbox>
      <Protocol Type="mapiHttp" Version="1">
        <MailStore>
          <InternalUrl>https://nyc-ex1.contoso.com/mapi/emsmdb/
?MailboxId=b3f98068-b1a1-4ed9-a698-a53730b8845c@contoso.com</InternalUrl>
        </MailStore>
        <AddressBook>
          <InternalUrl>https://nyc-ex1.contoso.com/mapi/nspi/
?MailboxId=b3f98068-b1a1-4ed9-a698-a53730b8845c@contoso.com</InternalUrl>
        </AddressBook>
      </Protocol>
      <Protocol>
        <Type>WEB</Type>
        <Internal>
          <OWAUrl AuthenticationMethod="Basic, Fba">https://nyc-ex1.contoso.com/
owa/</OWAUrl>
          <Protocol>
            <Type>EXCH</Type>
            <ASUrl>https://nyc-ex1.contoso.com/EWS/Exchange.asmx</ASUrl>
          </Protocol>
        </Internal>
      </Protocol>
      <Protocol>
        <Type>EXHTTP</Type>
        <Server>nyc-ex1.contoso.com</Server>
```

```
        <SSL>Off</SSL>
        <AuthPackage>Ntlm</AuthPackage>
        <ASUrl>https://nyc-ex1.contoso.com/EWS/Exchange.asmx</ASUrl>
        <EwsUrl>https://nyc-ex1.contoso.com/EWS/Exchange.asmx</EwsUrl>
        <EmwsUrl>https://nyc-ex1.contoso.com/EWS/Exchange.asmx</EmwsUrl>
        <EcpUrl>https://nyc-ex1.contoso.com/owa/</EcpUrl>
        <EcpUrl-um>?path=/options/callanswering</EcpUrl-um>
        <EcpUrl-aggr>?path=/options/connectedaccounts</EcpUrl-aggr>
        <EcpUrl-mt>options/ecp/PersonalSettings/DeliveryReport.aspx?rfr=olk&amp;
exsvurl=1&amp;IsOWA=&lt;IsOWA&gt;&amp;MsgID=&lt;MsgID&gt;&amp;Mbx=&lt;
Mbx&gt;&amp;realm=contoso.com</EcpUrl-mt>
        <EcpUrl-ret>?path=/options/retentionpolicies</EcpUrl-ret>
        <EcpUrl-sms>?path=/options/textmessaging</EcpUrl-sms>
        <EcpUrl-photo>?path=/options/myaccount/action/photo</EcpUrl-photo>
        <EcpUrl-tm>options/ecp/?rfr=olk&amp;ftr=TeamMailbox&amp;exsvurl=1&amp;
realm=contoso.com</EcpUrl-tm>
        <EcpUrl-tmCreating>options/ecp/?rfr=olk&amp;ftr=TeamMailboxCreating&amp;
SPUrl=&lt;SPUrl&gt;&amp;Title=&lt;Title&gt;&amp;SPTMAppUrl=&lt;SPTMAppUrl&gt;
&amp;exsvurl=1&amp;realm=contoso.com</EcpUrl-tmCreating>
        <EcpUrl-tmEditing>options/ecp/?rfr=olk&amp;ftr=TeamMailboxEditing&amp;
Id=&lt;Id&gt;
&amp;exsvurl=1&amp;realm=contoso.com</EcpUrl-tmEditing>
        <EcpUrl-extinstall>?path=/options/manageapps</EcpUrl-extinstall>
        <OOFUrl>https://nyc-ex1.contoso.com/EWS/Exchange.asmx</OOFUrl>
        <UMUrl>https://nyc-ex1.contoso.com/EWS/UM2007Legacy.asmx</UMUrl>
        <OABUrl>https://nyc-ex1.contoso.com/OAB/
8e45a957-b581-4044-9014-628b1cb31aef/</OABUrl>
        <ServerExclusiveConnect>On</ServerExclusiveConnect>
        <CertPrincipalName>None</CertPrincipalName>
      </Protocol>
    </Account>
  </Response>
</Autodiscover>
```

There are six key sections to note in Listing 6.1:

- The User and Account sections list the user information for the authenticated user.

- The EXCH protocol section (identified by the EXCH tag) is for connections inside the firewall. Remember, all Outlook connections are now over HTTPS. The URLs provided in this section are based on the InternalURL values.

- The EXPR protocol section (identified by the EXPR tag) is Outlook Anywhere—RPC over HTTPS. The URLs provided in this section are based on the ExternalURL values.

- The WEB protocol section (identified by the WEB tag) is used for Outlook on the web and other types of clients. The URLs provided in this section are for clients and are based on the best URL for the users to use.

◆ You will notice what looks like a new provider, ExHTTP, in the list of returned providers to the Outlook client. However, ExHTTP isn't a provider; it just looks like one in the Autodiscover log. It is a calculated set of values from the EXCH and EXPR settings that are processed only by Outlook 2013 and later clients.

If the client had been outside the firewall, it would have followed a similar process, but instead it steps through the hostnames and URLs as described in the previous section on DNS names. An external client (for the domain contoso.com) using Autodiscover goes through these steps:

1. The client tries to connect to the Active Directory SCP but is unable to do so.

2. The client performs a DNS query for contoso.com and then autodiscover.contoso.com and tries to connect to the Autodiscover URL.

3. The client authenticates and retrieves autodiscover.xml from the Autodiscover HTTPS host.

4. The client parses through the WEB sections of the autodiscover.xml file in order to determine the correct URL to which it should connect.

5. The client initiates a connection to the appropriate external URL.

To help step through and troubleshoot external connectivity, you should be aware of the Microsoft Remote Connectivity Analyzer tool, available online from https://testconnectivity .microsoft.com/. This web-based tool from Microsoft provides a secure, reliable suite of tests to help diagnose problems with not only Autodiscover but all of the web-based Exchange Server remote client access protocols and also server-to-server tests like SMTP connectivity and connectivity from other clients such as Skype for Business.

We can't say enough about this great troubleshooting weapon, initially developed as a pet project by a couple of Microsoft engineers. Especially in the early days of Exchange Server 2010, this tool saved us in many situations. Today, we use it more as a validation tool than a troubleshooting tool, but regardless of your level of expertise with Autodiscover, you'll find happiness somewhere in the Remote Connectivity Analyzer.

Site Affinity (aka Site Scope)

You've gotten through the basics of Autodiscover, so you're ready for some advanced concepts, such as how site affinity works.

To understand the point of site affinity, consider an organization that has multiple locations—we'll say in Seattle, Washington (code SEA); Toledo, Ohio (code TOL); and New Orleans, Louisiana (code MSY). There are Exchange servers and users in each of these locations. The links between these locations run over WAN links from Seattle to Toledo and Toledo to New Orleans; it is neither optimal nor desired to allow users in Seattle to use Client Access services in New Orleans (or vice versa). Using site affinity, we can use the following commands to help ensure this does not happen:

```
Set-ClientAccessService -Identity "sea-ex01"
-AutodiscoverServiceInternalURI "https://sea-ex01.contoso.com/
autodiscover/autodiscover.xml" -AutodiscoverServiceSiteScope
"Site-SEA","Site-TOL"
```

```
Set-ClientAccessService -Identity "sea-ex02"
-AutodiscoverServiceInternalURI "https://sea-ex02.contoso.com/
autodiscover/autodiscover.xml" -AutodiscoverServiceSiteScope
"Site-SEA","Site-TOL"
Set-ClientAccessService -Identity "tol-ex01"
-AutodiscoverServiceInternalURI "https://tol-ex01.contoso.com/
autodiscover/autodiscover.xml" -AutodiscoverServiceSiteScope
"Site-SEA","Site-TOL","Site-MSY"
Set-ClientAccessService -Identity "tol-ex02"
-AutodiscoverServiceInternalURI "https://tol-ex02.contoso.com/
autodiscover/autodiscover.xml" -AutodiscoverServiceSiteScope
"Site-SEA","Site-TOL","Site-MSY"
Set-ClientAccessService -Identity "msy-ex01"
-AutodiscoverServiceInternalURI "https://msy-ex01.contoso.com/
autodiscover/autodiscover.xml" -AutodiscoverServiceSiteScope
"Site-TOL","Site-MSY"
Set-ClientAccessService -Identity "msy-ex02"
-AutodiscoverServiceInternalURI "https://msy-ex02.contoso.com/
autodiscover/autodiscover.xml" -AutodiscoverServiceSiteScope
"Site-TOL","Site-MSY"
```

Note that the `Set-ClientAccessService` cmdlet replaces the `Set-ClientAccessServer` cmdlet (although it still exists). When clients perform Autodiscover, they will match only the records for those Mailbox servers that match the site they are currently in.

Clients in Seattle will match only the SEA-EX01, SEA-EX02, TOL-EX01, and TOL-EX02 SCP objects. Because there are multiple objects, they will perform their initial discovery to TOL-EX01 (this was the last server configured), which will then return URLs for the servers in the Seattle site.

Likewise, clients in New Orleans will match only the MSY-EX01, MSY-EX02, TOL-EX01, and TOL-EX02 SCP objects. Because there are multiple objects, they will perform their initial discovery to MSY-EX01, which will then return URLs for the servers in the New Orleans site.

Clients in Toledo will match all six SCP objects. Because there are multiple objects, they will perform their initial discovery to MSY-EX01, which will then return URLs for the servers in the Toledo site.

If these are not the required behaviors, you should take a close look at the Exchange Server 2007 Autodiscover white paper at http://technet.microsoft.com/en-us/library/bb332063.aspx. Although this paper is for Exchange Server 2007, the concepts transfer to Exchange Server 2016 without much damage.

Planning Certificates for Autodiscover

The other hard part for Autodiscover is managing the required certificates. After working with a number of Exchange Server 2007 deployments, we began to realize that the biggest difficulty with Autodiscover certificates was inevitably the need to use a storage area network (SAN) certificate. While other scenarios are possible (such as creating a separate Autodiscover website on a separate IP address and using a second single-name certificate) as outlined in the Exchange Server 2007 Autodiscover white paper, these options ended up being far more complicated to run.

So what's so difficult about SAN certificates? We think that most people don't understand what certificates really are or how they work. Certificates and Public Key Infrastructures (PKI) are black magic—stark-naked voodoo—mainly because they've traditionally been complicated to deploy and play with. Getting even an internal PKI like the Windows Server 2012 R2 Active Directory Certificates Services in place and running can be hard to manage unless you already know what to do and what the results should look like. Add to that the difficulty of managing certificates with the built-in Windows tools, and most Exchange Server administrators we know want to stay far away from Transport Layer Security (TLS) and Secure Sockets Layer (SSL).

Although Exchange Server 2016 follows the lead of prior Exchange Server versions and installs self-signed certificates on each new server, these certificates are not meant to take you into production for all scenarios. It's technically possible to leave the self-signed certificate on some services, but the client access service absolutely requires that the self-signed certificate be replaced before entering a production environment. Internal Outlook clients *can* use the self-signed certificates, but Outlook does not ignore improperly matched names or expired certificates. Internal Outlook clients will notify the user that the certificate is from an untrusted certificate authority.

External or web-based clients won't accept a self-signed certificate without you manually importing the root certificate—which is a huge administrative burden for mobile clients. For externally facing deployments, you either need to have a well-managed PKI deployment or use a third-party commercial certificate authority. Make sure that you use one whose root and intermediate CA certificates are well supported by the operating systems and devices that will be connecting to your network.

The X.509 Certificate Standard

The digital certificates that Exchange Server and other SSL/TLS-aware systems use are defined by the X.509 v3 certificate standard. This standard is documented in RFC 2459 (and other related RFCs). The X.509 certificates were developed as part of the X.500 family of standards from the Open Source Initiative but proved to be useful enough that they were adopted by other standards organizations.

The X.509 certificates are based on the concept of *private key cryptography*. In this system, you have an algorithm that generates a pair of cryptographic keys for each entity that will be exchanging encrypted message traffic: a *private key* that only that entity knows and a corresponding *public key* that can be freely transmitted. As long as the private keys are kept safe, the system can be used not only to securely encrypt network communications and email messages but also to prove that messages were sent from the claimed sender. The exclusivity of the private key provides authentication as well as security.

For example, If UserA and UserB want to exchange encrypted messages using a private key system (S/MIME), here's how it works:

1. Both UserA and UserB ensure that they each have secure private keys. They have exchanged their corresponding public keys—maybe through email, by sending a digitally signed email, by publishing them on their websites, or by locating them in Active Directory.

2. UserA, when sending a message to UserB, will use UserA's private key to sign the message and UserB's public key to encrypt the message. All of this ensures that only

UserB will be able to decrypt the message and provides authenticity that the message came from UserA.

3. UserB receives the encrypted messages, validates the digital signature, and uses his private key to decrypt the message. This ensures that the message actually came from UserA.

When UserB receives the message, he uses his own private key to decrypt the message. If UserB wants to send a message to UserA in return, he simply reverses the process. If UserB later needs to open the message in his Sent Items folder, he would use his private key to decrypt it.

Digital certificates help streamline this process and expand it for more uses than just message encryption by providing a convenient wrapper format for the public keys plus some associated metadata. For our purposes, though, we're concerned about using certificates for server authentication and establishing the symmetric shared-session key for the TLS session.

In Windows, you can view digital certificates, examine their properties, and validate the certificate chain through the MMC. Although Windows doesn't include a preconfigured Certificate console, it does include the Certificates snap-in. Open an instance of MMC.exe and add the Certificates snap-in, configured for the local machine, as shown in Figure 6.4. You can now view and manage the server certificates that will be used by Exchange Server.

FIGURE 6.4
The Certificates
MMC snap-in

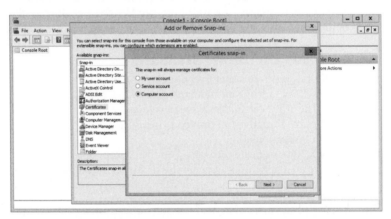

While you can view the properties of a certificate using the Certificate console, all certificates that are used by Exchange Server (for HTTPS, SMTP, UM Call Router, IMAP, or POP) should be managed using either the Exchange Admin Center or the Exchange Management Shell.

Let's take a look at the typical properties of an X.509v3 digital certificate as provisioned for Exchange Server:

Subject Name   This property provides the identity of the entity to which the certificate applies. This can be in X.500 format, which looks like LDAP, or in DNS format if intended for a server.

Subject Alternative Name   This is an optional property that lists one or more additional identities that will match the certificate. If the hostname in the URL that the client attempts to connect to doesn't match the subject name or subject alternative name properties, the certificate will not validate. Without this property, a certificate can match only a single hostname.

Common Name   Also known as the friendly name, this property provides a useful text tag for handling and managing the certificate once you have a collection of them.

Issuer   This property lists the identity of the issuing certificate authority (CA). This can be a root CA or an intermediate CA. Combined with the digital signature from the CA's own digital signature, this property allows establishment of the certificate chain of trust back to the root CA. What distinguishes a root CA? The fact that this property (plus signature) is self-signed.

Serial Number   This property allows the certificate to be easily published on a certificate revocation list (CRL) by the certificate authority if the certificate has been revoked. The location(s) of the CRL is usually included on the issuer's certificate. This is typically a URL. Many applications, including Outlook, attempt to check (directly or indirectly using Windows CAPI2) the CRL to verify that the certificate has been revoked.

Thumbprint   This property (and the corresponding thumbprint algorithm) is a cryptographic hash of the certificate information. This thumbprint is commonly used by Exchange Server as an easy identifier for certificates.

Valid From and Valid To   These properties define the effective duration of the certificate. They are evaluated as part of the certificate validation.

Public Key   This property contains the entity's associated cryptographic public key. The corresponding private key is never viewed with the certificate.

The Certificate Path tab of the properties dialog box displays the certificate trust chain and verifies that the proper CA certificates are installed. When installing a third-party or an internally generated certificate, it is essential that the Exchange server trusts all certificates in the certificate chain, similarly to the certificate validation that occurs on a client computer. The trust chain uses a simple transitive logic for trusting certificates. Certificates are issued by certification authorities that are already trusted by the Exchange servers. Or, as it was described to me in college, if you trust your father, and your father trusts his father, then you automatically trust your grandfather.

Deploying Exchange Certificates

Now that we've talked about certificates in general, let's dive into the issues of getting them deployed on your Exchange Server 2016 servers.

PLANNING CERTIFICATE NAMES

The first part of creating digital certificates for your Exchange Server 2016 servers is deciding which names you need. For the client access service, it's highly recommended that you accept the need for a SAN certificate. Although SAN certificates are more expensive than single-name certificates, you can often configure them so that you can reuse them on multiple servers. Otherwise, you need to use a lot of single-name certificates—potentially with multiple websites and virtual directories on your Exchange server instances. This can become an overwhelming amount of operational overhead.

Sure, you can use wildcard certificates for some scenarios, such as Outlook and Windows Phones. The wildcard certificate is issued for an entire domain, such as `*.contoso.com`. This certificate could then be used by multiple servers and sites. Naturally, wildcard certificates are usually more expensive than certificates issued for a single host. Be aware, also, that not all clients (such as earlier Windows Mobile phones) will recognize wildcard certificates. The Exchange Server product group does not recommend wildcard certificates, and neither do we. They present a bigger risk than SAN certificates, which point to specific named resources. That being said, for small organizations that do not have significant security concerns, a wildcard certificate can sometimes be a simpler overall deployment option.

Let's take the three-site `contoso.com` example from earlier in this chapter and some of the factors to consider when requesting certificates:

◆ For Internet connectivity, a single site will act as the gateway for all inbound Internet connectivity. That site will host the initial Autodiscover service and, therefore, the domain name `autodiscover.contoso.com`.

◆ We'll use the FQDN `mail.contoso.com` as our generic external access name. We don't need to use a separate domain name for this—we could easily use `autodiscover.contoso.com`, but users are accustomed to an easier-to-understand name.

◆ Having two names could mean either multiple IP addresses and websites or a SAN certificate. We don't want to incur the overhead of multiple certificates and websites, so we will use a SAN certificate. We can issue a single certificate for all the Client Access servers at each site. We'll include the FQDNs of each of the servers in the SAN. Most commercial CAs have a price increase after five names on a SAN certificate, so you need to keep that in consideration. But always consider all the places you may want to use a certificate, such as on multiple Client Access servers for load balancing.

So, if we have multiple sites, the certificate will require the distinctive names of the locations (such as `canada.contoso.com` and `europe.contoso.com`), as well as `mail.contoso.com` and `autodiscover.contoso.com`. We don't need to include the NetBIOS names of our servers—Exchange Server and its clients don't use them unless we choose to configure them otherwise.

As you start requesting certificates, it is important to note that poor namespace planning or separate internal namespaces (such as `contoso.com` for external clients but `contoso.local` for internal clients) will result in more complex certificate requirements. Ensure that you have carefully thought out the internal and external URL requirements as you are planning your Exchange Server 2016 deployment. Something to watch for is that you set the common name to be the preferred name that users will access the most and the one that is seen on the first properties page, so in our example we would most probably select `mail.contoso.com` as the common name in the certificate.

ISSUING AND ENABLING CERTIFICATES WITH EXCHANGE ADMIN CENTER

In Exchange Server 2007 and Exchange Server 2010, you had to do all your certificate requests and imports either through the Certificate MMC snap-in (which was a pain) or through the EMS. In Exchange Server 2013 and Exchange Server 2016, if you click the Servers node in the EAC, you can view, manage, and even request new certificates for your Exchange servers.

When you go through the Exchange Certificate Wizard to request a new certificate, it will prompt you for a variety of information. For example, on one page of the wizard, you need to specify the domain(s) for which each access type is available. For example, you may select

Outlook Web App (this represents Outlook on the web although the wording has not been updated in the EAC yet) and Exchange ActiveSync for contoso.com.

On the next page of the wizard, you will see the different types of names that you can include in your certificate request. For example, we could add mail.contoso.com and nyc-ex1 .contoso.com to populate the SAN names.

Note in Figure 6.5 that this server's internal Outlook on the web (shown as Outlook Web App in the Exchange Certificate screen) name is nyc-ex1.contoso.com and the external name is mail.contoso.com. For some of these fields, the New Exchange Certificate Wizard is making a "best guess" at the correct names, but you will need to fill in some of the others manually, depending on your naming preferences and what you have configured in DNS.

FIGURE 6.5
Viewing the domains to be included in the certificate request

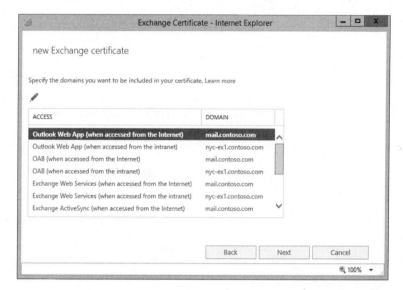

In Figure 6.6, you can see the Certificate Domains page; this page allows you to specify additional fully qualified domain names that will show up in the certificate request. The wizard is making another "best guess" for this certificate request by adding all of the accepted domains as well. You may want to check that the hostname Autodiscover is present for each of these domain names.

The Organization and Location page of the wizard requests information that most administrators who have already configured a certificate request will recognize. This includes the organization information, department, city, state, and country.

On the last page in the wizard you must provide a name and path where the certificate request file will be created. The completion of this wizard will execute the relevant cmdlet for you. In this case, the cmdlet New-ExchangeCertificate is being run, such as is shown here:

```
New-ExchangeCertificate
    {PrivateKeyExportable=True, FriendlyName=mail,
SubjectName=System.Security.Cryptography.X509Certificates.X500DistinguishedName,
DomainName={ex1.contoso.com, mail.contoso.com, EX1},
RequestFile=\\nyc-ex1\c$\cert.req, GenerateRequest=True, Server=NYC-EX1,
KeySize=2048}
```

FIGURE 6.6
The Certificate
Domains Wizard
page

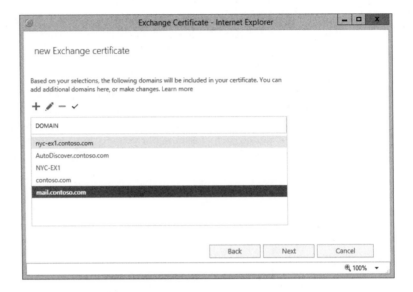

(This cmdlet comes, of course, with `Get-` and `Set-` partners as well, to view and configure the certificate.)

You can now submit to a certificate authority the contents of the file that was created. Once you have received back a signed certificate, you use the Complete Pending Request Wizard to complete the process. Start this by clicking Complete next to the certificate showing a pending state. This wizard will load the signed certificate into the certificate store on the appropriate server.

The final process after the certificate is fully loaded is to assign the certificate to be used by the appropriate services (such as SMTP or IIS). Select the certificate in the work pane, click the Edit button on the toolbar, and select the Services node on the left. On the Services node of the wizard (shown in Figure 6.7), select the appropriate services. When you select Internet Information Services (IIS), they include Outlook on the web, the Exchange Admin Center (EAC), the Exchange Control Panel (ECP), Exchange Web Services (EWS), and ActiveSync. Note that a service can be assigned to only one certificate at a time.

A WORD OF WARNING

Whichever tool you use to request certificates should be the tool you use to import them. Although you should be able to mix and match them in theory, we've seen odd results in practice. Also, don't use the Certificate Wizard in IIS to request Exchange Server certificates, especially if you need SAN certificates. Stick to the Exchange Server tools for certificate management and also for renewals; the non–Exchange Server tools will not install certificates or manage certificates in the appropriate locations or in the appropriate manner.

FIGURE 6.7
Selecting services
that will use the
certificate

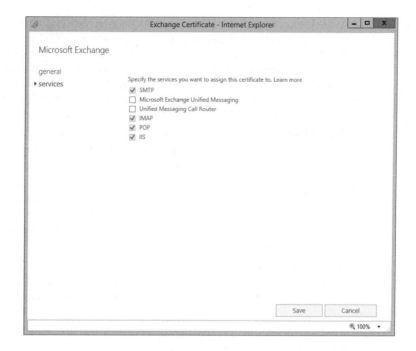

ISSUING AND ENABLING CERTIFICATES WITH EMS

Although Exchange Server 2016 provides an Exchange Admin Center interface for managing certificates, you can still manage certificates through the EMS. If you have done this in the past with older versions of Exhange Server, you might have to learn a few new tricks in order to work with certificates from the EMS. Because of the way PowerShell works via remoting now, you can no longer specify a path for a certificate request file. Instead, the certificate request is output to the shell, so you must capture that to a variable. Here's the command you would issue to generate a certificate request for the URL mail.contoso.com and capture it to the $Data variable:

```
$Data = New-ExchangeCertificate -GenerateRequest -SubjectName "c=US,
o=Contoso, cn=mail.contoso.com" -DomainName contoso.com
-PrivateKeyExportable $true
```

Next, we need to take output the value stored in the $Data variable to the file c:\CertRequest.req using this command:

```
Set-Content -path "C:\Docs\MyCertRequest.req" -Value $Data
```

Here are the details of the New-ExchangeCertificate cmdlet (discussed earlier, in the section "Issuing and Enabling Certificates with Exchange Admin Center"):

GenerateRequest This parameter tells Exchange Server to generate a certificate request. Had we left it off, the command would have generated a new self-signed certificate. That's usually not what you want. This request is suitable for either an internal PKI or a commercial CA.

PrivateKeyExportable This parameter is extremely important and is the cause of most certificate headaches we've seen. When a certificate request is generated, it includes the public key, but the private key stays in the secure Windows certificate store. If the CA is configured to allow export of the private key, the request must explicitly ask for the private key to be exportable in the first place. If this parameter wasn't included or was set to $false, we wouldn't be able to export the certificate's private key to import to the other CAS instance or on to the external firewall, which is often done.

FriendlyName This parameter is set for administrative convenience. If we have multiple certificates issued to the machine, it allows us to identify the certificate with which we're dealing.

DomainName This parameter allows us to set one or more domain names. If we specify more than one, Exchange Server will automatically create and populate the SAN property with all the requested hostnames and set the subject name of the certificate to the first hostname in the list. Although the cmdlet provides additional parameters to explicitly set the subject and alternate names, *you don't need them.*

A successful run of the cmdlet will generate the request output and a thumbprint of the request. Submit the request to your CA, download the corresponding certificate, and then import the certificate back on the same machine, as in the following example:

```
Import-ExchangeCertificate -FileData $(Get-Content
-Path c:\CertImport.pfx -Encoding byte)
-Password:(Get-Credential).password
```

This cmdlet will import the saved certificate if it matches a pending request and print out the thumbprint of the newly imported certificate. Ensure that you look after the PFX file that is used here. We've seen administrators leaving this on the desktop or the C: drive of Exchange servers. Best practice is *not* to store a copy of this on the server itself. By all means keep a copy in a safe place if it will not be possible or convenient to download a copy in the future.

You can now view the certificate in the Certificates snap-in in MMC or from the certificate management functionality in the Exchange Admin Center. From here you can view the details about the certificate, such as the thumbprint, SAN names, and which services the certificate is assigned to, as shown in Figure 6.8.

The final step is to enable Exchange Server services against the certificate:

```
Enable-ExchangeCertificate -Thumbprint <certificate thumbprint>
-Services <services>
```

<services> is a comma-separated list of one or more of the following values, depending on the protocols you have enabled and the roles you have installed:

SMTP For use with SMTP + TLS for front-end/back-end transport services.

UM Call Router For use with the Unified Messaging services' call router and connecting to the Client Access server.

UM   For use with general Unified Messaging services.

Federation   For use when configuring federated services with the Microsoft Federation Gateway. (You cannot assign this service with this cmdlet; it is configured when configuring a federated trust.)

IIS   For use with client access, including Autodiscover.

IMAP   For use with client access using the IMAP client protocol.

POP   For use with client access using the POP3 client protocol.

FIGURE 6.8
Viewing certificate properties

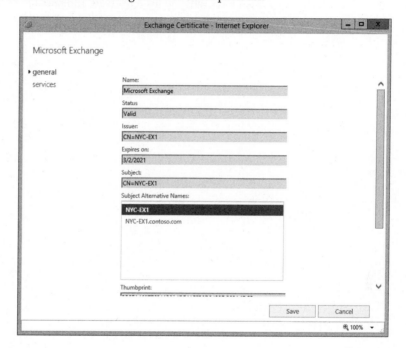

The Bottom Line

Work with Autodiscover.   Autodiscover is a key service in Exchange Server 2016, both for ensuring hassle-free client configuration and for keeping the Exchange servers in your organization working together smoothly. Autodiscover can be used by Outlook 2010, Outlook 2013, Outlook 2016, Entourage, Outlook for Mac 2016, Windows Mobile/Windows Phone, and other mobile devices like Android, iOS, and even Windows RT devices.

Master It   You are configuring Outlook 2016 to connect to Exchange Server and you want to diagnose a problem that you are having when connecting. Which tool can you use?

Troubleshoot Autodiscover. In a large organization with multiple Active Directory sites or multiple namespaces, it is essential to track the Autodiscover traffic and understand where client queries will be directed.

Master It If you have multiple Active Directory sites, what should you do to control the client flow of requests for Autodiscover information?

Manage Exchange Server certificates. Exchange Server 2016 servers rely on functional X.509v3 digital certificates to ensure proper TLS security.

Master It Which tools will you need to create and manage Exchange Server certificates?

Part 2

Getting Exchange Server Running

Chapter 7

Exchange Server 2016 Quick Start Guide

Reading through a *Mastering* book just to figure out how to get a quick installation of Exchange Server 2016 up and running may seem like a daunting task—especially if all you want to do is get a look at Exchange and play around with it. With that in mind, we'll present the steps for getting a lab or test server up and running quickly.

The purpose of building a test server is to learn and optimize the installation and configuration experience. Exchange is a feature-rich application and, as such, has many different ways to configure settings for optimization, performance, and stability. Using a test server to try various scenarios provides for a better production deployment—and a better-prepared administrator.

We won't cover every little detail on every setting or extensive design and best practices in this chapter—that's what the rest of this book is for—but we will discuss the requirements for getting a typical Exchange Server 2016 server up and running. A typical Exchange Server 2016 is one that holds the Mailbox role. The Mailbox role in Exchange Server 2016 contains all the functionalities that were previously located in the Exchange Server 2013 Client Access role and Mailbox role and all the functionalities that were previously located in the Exchange Server 2010 Client Access role, Hub Transport role, Mailbox role, and Unified Messaging role. Exchange Server 2016 Setup also includes the Edge Transport role; if you intend to use it, you'll need to install it on a separate computer because it is not possible to install the Mailbox role and the Edge Transport role on the same computer. Furthermore, the Edge Transport role should be installed on a computer configured as a workgroup computer located in a perimeter network.

IN THIS CHAPTER, YOU WILL LEARN TO:

- ◆ Quickly size a typical server
- ◆ Install the necessary Windows Server 2012 R2 or Windows Server 2012 prerequisites
- ◆ Install an Exchange Server 2016 Mailbox and Edge Transport server roles
- ◆ Configure Exchange to send and receive email
- ◆ Configure recipients, contacts, and distribution groups

Server Sizing Quick Reference

Although properly sizing a server for production is extremely important, sizing for a lab or test server is somewhat less involved if you're only interested in pushing some buttons and "kicking the tires" of Exchange Server 2016. For instance, a lab server might have enough storage for a few users, but a production server might be configured for many hundreds or thousands.

However, in order to have a responsive lab or evaluation environment, you still should pay attention to some basics when you're building a test server.

Hardware

In this section, we'll look at the hardware required to quickly set up a lab environment. We'll focus on memory, processors, storage, operating system, and virtualization considerations.

MEMORY

Exchange Server 2016 is the fourth generation to use 64-bit architecture. Although this gives overall better memory management, including the ability to handle higher amounts of physical memory, it also means that the baseline memory requirements have increased when compared to earlier versions of Exchange. The Exchange Server 2016 architecture, while reducing the number of roles required, necessarily increases the number of processes running on the typical server.

The baseline requirement for the Mailbox role is 8 GB of RAM. Although these minimums aren't enforced by the Setup program, Exchange will run very slowly without enough RAM. The ESE database component and Exchange services require more RAM even on a lightly loaded server. This overhead adds up on low-end servers such as test servers but scales for better caching and efficiency in servers with many users.

The final piece for memory utilization is to properly configure your Windows Server page file. By default, Windows will manage the page file on its own, but you need to change this to keep even lightly loaded lab Exchange servers from excessive paging. As shown in Figure 7.1, if your Exchange Server has 8 GB of RAM, set the page file to a static fixed size: physical RAM (8 GB = 8192 MB) plus 10 MB (8202 MB).

PROCESSORS

Server hardware that will host Exchange Server 2016 requires 64-bit processors. This includes either x64 Intel or AMD64 CPUs. Itanium IA64 processors are not supported for Exchange Server 2016. The minimum recommended number of processor cores for a lightweight test Exchange server is two. Even in a lab, two processor cores may not provide enough performance, so consider using four to eight processor cores. With a single core, expect installation to take an inordinately long time during normal operations.

DISK SPACE

Basic Exchange Server 2016 storage requirements include space for the Exchange binary files, message-tracking logs, mailbox databases and transaction logs, and transport-queue databases and transaction logs.

FIGURE 7.1
Setting a static page
file for 8 GB of RAM

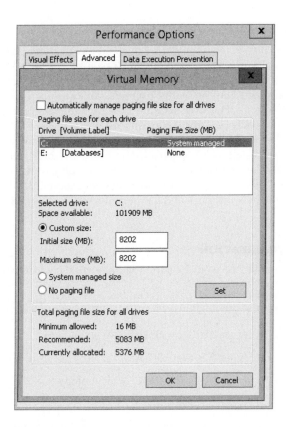

A typical installation requires at least the following:

- ◆ 30 GB available on the installation drive for binaries. Don't forget to keep free space available for utilities and cumulative updates.

- ◆ 200 MB available on the system drive (typically, C:), aside from the space used by the page file and any spare space you keep for system updates and normal operations (such as IIS logs).

- ◆ 500 MB available for the transport queue, by default on the installation drive.

- ◆ Space for mailbox databases and transaction logs.

When you're installing on Windows Server 2012, the system drive must, of course, be formatted with NTFS, as must all volumes used for Exchange Server 2016 binaries. The Resilient File System (ReFS) feature in Windows Server 2012 is supported and recommended by Exchange for volumes that host mailbox databases and transaction logs, where the integrity feature in ReFS should be disabled.

NETWORK

Exchange Server 2016 servers should have one 1 Gbps Ethernet network interface card that is not teamed. Additional cards can be used but aren't required, as the Microsoft preferred architecture for Exchange Server 2016 advises that only one network adapter is used.

If you're deploying a DAG on mailbox servers, you can't use Windows network load balancing on the Mailbox roles. However, with the new Exchange Server architecture, simple DNS round-robin records may be sufficient to test load balancing in a lab environment.

Finally, whether you're using IPv6 or not, there's no real advantage to disabling it. Windows (and Exchange) are tested with IPv6 enabled. If you do disable it, follow the Windows IPv6 FAQ guidelines on completely disabling IPv6, including keeping IPv4 enabled. Don't simply unbind it from your network adapters. This practice does not ensure that IPv6 components are no longer active in the network stack and has been the source of past Exchange network and stability issues.

SERVER VIRTUALIZATION

Both Exchange Server 2016 roles are supported in virtual environments when all the following conditions are true:

◆ The hardware virtualization software is running one of the following:

  ◆ Windows Server 2012 R2 with Hyper-V technology

  ◆ Microsoft Hyper-V Server 2012 R2

  ◆ Windows Server 2012 with Hyper-V technology

  ◆ Microsoft Hyper-V Server 2012

  ◆ Any third-party hypervisor that has been validated under the Windows Server Virtualization Validation Program

NOTE Theoretically, Microsoft supports any Hyper-V edition for Exchange Server virtualization. However, installing an older virtualization platform is not recommended due to the shorter support timeframe.

You can also use Microsoft Azure virtual machines for your test lab. However, for a production environment, Exchange Server 2016 running on Microsoft Azure is supported only if volumes used for Exchange mailbox databases, database transaction logs, and transport databases are configured for Azure Premium Storage. For a nonproduction environment, such as testing and development, Azure Premium Storage is not a requirement.

◆ The Exchange Server guest virtual machine meets all of the following requirements:

  ◆ Running Microsoft Exchange Server 2016.

  ◆ Deployed on Windows Server 2012 R2 or Windows Server 2012.

♦ Not backed up and restored using virtual machine snapshots; only Exchange-supported backup mechanisms are supported.

♦ Not protected by virtualization HA mechanisms that use disk-based state save files such as Hyper-V's Quick Migration.

♦ The virtual machine configurations meet the following conditions:

♦ No memory oversubscription or dynamic memory allocation is used.

♦ Processor oversubscription is at a ratio of no more than 2:1.

♦ The virtual storage meets the following conditions:

♦ If virtual hard drives are used, they should be a fixed size for performance and data stability, not dynamically expanding.

♦ It doesn't use differencing drives.

♦ It doesn't use any file-based storage, such as SMB or NFS at any layer in the stack, with the exception of SMB 3.0 when used to host fixed-size virtual drives; under no circumstances can you use file-based storage to direct-mount and host Exchange data files (see the "Microsoft Requirements and Recommendations" sidebar in Chapter 4, "Virtualizing Exchange Server 2016," for more information).

♦ The operating system drive should be at least 15 GB plus the size of the virtual memory, although realistically in many lab scenarios you will want this drive to be large enough for the boot partition, the operating system, the page file, the Exchange binaries, the default Exchange databases, and any patches.

Operating Systems

Exchange Server 2016 supports the following operating systems:

♦ Windows Server 2012 R2 (Standard or Datacenter Edition)

♦ Windows Server 2012 (Standard or Datacenter Edition)

Trial versions of each of these operating systems are available for download from Microsoft's website. They will provide months of use and can be installed over and over for testing. You cannot use the Server Core installation of either version of Windows for Exchange Server 2016 machines, however.

Windows Server 2012 R2 includes many stability-, performance-, and security-related updates from its predecessors. Exchange Server 2016 supports both Windows Server 2012 R2 and Windows Server 2012 Standard and Datacenter Editions. However, we recommend that you install Exchange Server 2016 on Windows Server 2012 R2 or Windows Server 2012 Standard Edition. Standard Edition is quite a bit cheaper, and it provides the same operating system functionality as Datacenter Edition. When looking at a new mail platform, it makes sense to use the latest operating system because of all the enhancements available. Building a test server is a perfect opportunity to get some experience with the new operating system. Additionally, it makes sense to deploy an operating system that will still be in mainstream support during the typical life cycle of a newly deployed server. Windows Server 2012 R2 and Windows Server 2012 include many of the prerequisites required for Exchange, making deployment quick and easy compared to previous Exchange Server and operating system versions.

Because we are focusing on getting an Exchange server up and running quickly in this chapter, we assume the following:

- The server is joined to an Active Directory domain, and the Active Directory domain is isolated from any production domains.

- The Active Directory forest and domain are at a minimum functional level of Windows Server 2008.

- The server has a static IP address assigned.

- Test Active Directory user accounts have been created.

- You have an administrative account that is a member of the Schema Admins, Domain Admins, and Enterprise Admins security groups.

- The server is not a domain controller.

- There are no other Exchange servers in the domain.

- There is a domain controller in the same Active Directory site in which the Exchange server will reside.

- If you have multiple domains in the forest, the first site in which you will install an Exchange server contains a writeable global catalog server from each domain.

Based on these assumptions, you should be able to go through this chapter and build a functioning Exchange Server 2016 server quickly.

 Real World Scenario

CONSIDER SETTING UP A LAB ENVIRONMENT

In many environments, space is at a premium. Administrators may see no need for a lab environment, or they may feel that they don't have the time, energy, or budget to get one approved by management. If you enjoy managing your Exchange organization in a reactive fashion—always fixing problems after the fact, always finding out the hard way about software incompatibilities, always realizing two hours after your maintenance window was supposed to end that you're actually not sure how a particular feature works—then you absolutely don't need a lab—or this chapter. Everyone else, read on.

Labs are one of the big factors that make the difference between on-time, on-budget Exchange deployments and cost/time overruns. If management ever feels the need for a lab, give them the following list:

- Labs allow you to test new patches and updates before risking production systems. Although it's not the norm, occasionally Windows and Exchange updates have problems that take down Exchange services. By updating your lab first, you have a better chance of finding these problems before they take you down.

◆ Labs allow you to be better trained and enable you to work out bugs and omissions in your procedures. If you've never applied updates to a DAG cluster before (or it's been a while since the last time), a lab is invaluable for clearing out the cobwebs. If you have a special work sequence that has to be performed, you can fine-tune that process in the safety of your lab. Want to make sure your disaster recovery (DR) staff knows how to perform a site-level failover? Do it in your lab.

◆ Labs can end up saving you time and money on support incidents. By replicating a problem in the lab before calling support, you can often narrow down the precise factors that are contributing to the problem. Whether you have a concise set of repro steps or end up finding the answer, you're likely to waste less time playing phone or email tag with support providers.

◆ Many administrative tasks can be efficiently performed in Exchange Management Shell. The lab environment allows you to test your Exchange Management Shell cmdlets and scripts before you run them in a production environment.

To meet these goals, however, your lab needs to meet a few essential criteria:

IT HAS TO BE A SEPARATE FOREST.

Remember, you can have only a single Exchange organization in an Active Directory forest. Keep that forest roughly in sync, though. If you have mixed levels of domain controllers in production, have one of each in the lab. Consider a forest trust and cross-forest group memberships so that your Exchange administrators can use their regular administrative credentials in the lab rather than juggle yet another username and password. Keep the DNS, AD, and Exchange infrastructure similar to the production environment so that tests performed in the lab environment will closely match to the production environment. However, configure test namespaces differently than the production namespaces to avoid confusing the lab environment with the production environment and mistakenly performing tests in the production environment. Consider a regular Active Directory dump of users from production to the lab.

SIMPLICITY IS KEY.

Introduce only as much complexity as you need—only your key third-party apps, client types, and systems need to be in the lab. You don't have to have a lab copy of each Exchange server in production, and you don't have to replicate all the sites. If you have multiple DAGs, note that your lab needs only one—and it needs only two or three members, not the full number in production. Your lab DR site doesn't typically need a fully redundant number of DAG members.

You don't need a full load balancer when a Windows box with Internet Information Server (IIS) and the Application Request Routing extension may give you the functionality you actually need in the lab. However, if you need your operators to be comfortable using these additional components as part of their normal processes, they should be in the lab.

DON'T FORGET CLIENTS.

Labs are fantastic for troubleshooting client issues if you include clients in the lab. Keep them up-to-date with the production clients. Don't waste time synching plug-ins and additional add-ons unless you are troubleshooting a problem that includes those components.

(continues)

(continued)

KNOW WHEN TO BREAK THE RULES.

Labs are a perfect place to use virtualization technologies and to ruthlessly exploit the benefits of virtualization, such as VM snapshots. While these features aren't supported in production environments, they're time-savers for a lab. However, when you're taking snapshots, capture *all* of the virtual machines (domain controllers, Exchange servers, clients, and everything else) at the same time so rollbacks all come back to a consistent known spot.

MAKE LAB MAINTENANCE A REGULAR ACTIVITY.

Keep time on the schedule to patch and update your lab. Spread the load for various maintenance tasks among your staff so that no one person gets stuck maintaining the entire lab while everyone else trashes it. Ensure that everyone knows the appropriate policies and procedures for resetting the lab and that there's an override in place for situations (such as support calls) when changes to the lab should not take place.

Having a badly implemented lab can require a lot of work. However, done smartly, a lab can increase your productivity and help you become more proactive about managing your Exchange organization.

Configuring Windows

In this section, we'll look at prerequisites. This includes those for Active Directory as well as the server and its operating system. We'll start with Active Directory.

Active Directory Requirements

It's important to keep your test environment isolated from your production environment. Exchange Server 2016 requires many changes to Active Directory through schema updates, and it introduces new objects and adds many parameters to existing objects. Exchange Server 2016 has the following Active Directory requirements:

◆ At least one domain controller that is at the same global catalog server in the same site must be Windows Server 2008 or higher.

◆ Read-only domain controllers and read-only global catalogs in the same Active Directory site are ignored by Exchange Server 2016. Because of this, a conventional writable domain controller and global catalog must exist in the AD site.

Active Directory forest and domain functional modes must be at least Windows Server 2008 to install Exchange Server 2016. To verify that they are, follow these steps:

1. Sign in to a domain controller as a domain administrator.

2. In Server Manager, select Tools ➤ Active Directory Domains And Trusts.

3. Right-click the domain in the left pane and choose Properties.

4. On the General tab of the properties dialog box, look for Domain functional level and Forest functional level; both appear in the lower half of the screen, as shown in Figure 7.2.

FIGURE 7.2

Checking the
domain and forest
functional levels

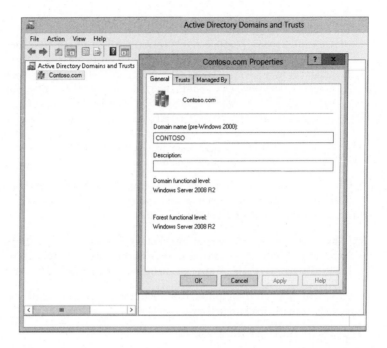

If the forest or domain functional level is not Windows Server 2008 or higher, it must be raised before Exchange is installed.

Although installing Exchange Server 2016 on a domain controller is a supported scenario, Microsoft strongly recommends not doing so for a number of reasons. Performance and security are enhanced when Exchange Server 2016 is installed on a member server. Once Exchange is installed, that server cannot be promoted to a domain controller or demoted to a member server. When Exchange is installed on a domain controller, that server must be configured as a global catalog because Exchange will not use any other domain controller. However, in this configuration, Name Service Provider Interface (NSPI) services are provided by the global catalog functionality and not by the Exchange Server NSPI component, which causes loss of functionality for features, such as address book policies. Finally, this combined server cannot be a member of a supported DAG configuration.

Operating System Prerequisites

The prerequisites are the same for Windows Server 2012 R2 and Windows Server 2012. This quick start guide assumes you will be preparing Active Directory for Exchange Server 2016 from the first server you install Exchange Server 2016 on.

To install the Exchange Server 2016 prerequisites for Windows Server 2012 R2 or Windows Server 2012, follow these steps:

1. Open an administrative instance of PowerShell by right-clicking its icon and selecting Run As Administrator.

2. Run the following command:

```
Install-WindowsFeature AS-HTTP-Activation, Desktop-Experience, NET-Framework-
45-Features, RPC-over-HTTP-proxy, RSAT-Clustering, RSAT-Clustering-
CmdInterface, RSAT-Clustering-Mgmt, RSAT-Clustering-PowerShell, Web-Mgmt-
Console, WAS-Process-Model, Web-Asp-Net45, Web-Basic-Auth, Web-Client-Auth,
Web-Digest-Auth, Web-Dir-Browsing, Web-Dyn-Compression, Web-Http-Errors,
Web-Http-Logging, Web-Http-Redirect, Web-Http-Tracing, Web-ISAPI-Ext, Web-
ISAPI-Filter, Web-Lgcy-Mgmt-Console, Web-Metabase, Web-Mgmt-Console, Web-Mgmt-
Service, Web-Net-Ext45, Web-Request-Monitor, Web-Server, Web-Stat-Compression,
Web-Static-Content, Web-Windows-Auth, Web-WMI, Windows-Identity-Foundation
```

Once you press Enter, the server will install the required roles and features and then automatically restart. Note that it is normal to see yellow warning text scroll by while this code is running, showing that a reboot is required.

NOTE Operating system components that are Exchange Server 2016 prerequisites can be also installed during the command line setup with the /InstallWindowsComponents switch. Only the .NET framework and UCMA need to be installed separately.

After you reboot the computer, run the following command to enable preparing Active Directory from the Exchange Server computer:

```
Install-WindowsFeature RSAT-ADDS
```

Next, locate the following add-in components from the Microsoft Download website and install them in the following order:

1. Microsoft .NET Framework 4.5.2.

2. Microsoft Unified Communications Managed API 4.0, Core Runtime 64-bit

Installing Exchange Server 2016

The installation of Exchange Server 2016 Mailbox Role requires an account with specific permissions. Installation must be performed with an account that has membership in the following groups:

◆ Domain Admins

◆ Schema Administrators (first server)

◆ Enterprise Administrators (first server)

During the installation, the Active Directory schema will be extended with attributes necessary for Exchange Server 2016, which is why the Schema Administrators group membership is required. A more detailed explanation of the Exchange Server 2016 installation, including the command-line procedure, is presented in Chapter 10, "Installing Exchange Server 2016."

At this point, you're ready to install Exchange Server 2016. You can use the GUI to install Exchange, or you can use the command line. Each approach has its advantages. First, let's look at the GUI-based installation.

GUI-Based Installation for Mailbox Server Role

Download or mount the Exchange Server 2016 installation media (you can right-click an `.iso` file and select Mount to have Windows treat it as a virtual CD or DVD), navigate to the root of the folder, and run `setup.exe`.

Once the Exchange Setup process starts, the first thing you will see is the option to go online and check for updates for the installer, as shown in Figure 7.3. Once updates are downloaded (if any are found), Setup will copy files and prepare other tasks necessary for the installation. Once these tasks are done, you'll see the introduction screen. This screen contains links to the TechNet documentation, supported languages, and the Exchange Server 2016 Deployment Assistant. Click Next to move on to the license agreement. Accept it and click Next to move on.

FIGURE 7.3
Checking for
updates

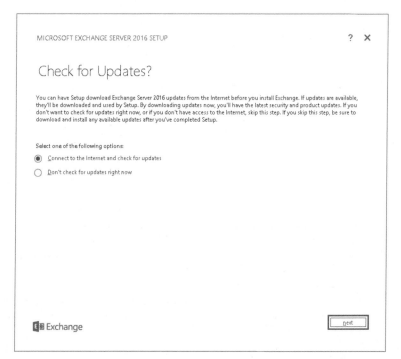

On the next screen, choose whether to send usage feedback to Microsoft and (more importantly) check for additional data online when errors occur. Choose an option and click Next to move on to the meat of the installation: the Server Role Selection screen, shown in Figure 7.4. Because this is the first Exchange Server 2016 server in the organization, you don't have the option to select only the Management tools; you must select one of the two server roles.

If you have not already manually installed the prerequisites, you can check the option to install them. This also serves as a confirmation that you've gotten the prerequisites installed properly. Even though you can install them here, it's recommended that you install them ahead of time to make sure you can run Windows Update to fix any bugs or problems. Click Next to move on.

FIGURE 7.4
Select the server
role

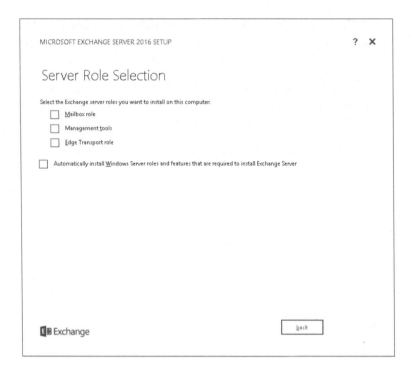

MICROSOFT EXCHANGE SERVER 2016 SETUP   ? ✕

Server Role Selection

Select the Exchange server roles you want to install on this computer:

☐ Mailbox role

☐ Management tools

☐ Edge Transport role

☐ Automatically install Windows Server roles and features that are required to install Exchange Server

E Exchange   [back]

Your next chore is to accept the default installation location or select a new location. For a test environment, this may not matter much. This screen also allows you to confirm that you have sufficient free space in your chosen folder. Once you make a selection, click Next to move on, as shown in Figure 7.5. If you want to change the path for the installation, click Browse, specify the appropriate folder, and then click OK. Click Next.

Because this is the first Exchange Server 2016 server in your organization, you are presented with the Exchange Organization screen (Figure 7.6). Type a name for your Exchange organization. This can be any name, such as your company name. The Exchange organization name can contain only the following characters:

◆ Letters *A* through *Z*, uppercase or lowercase

◆ Numbers 0 through 9

◆ Space (not leading or trailing)

◆ Hyphen or dash

The organization name can't be more than 64 characters long and can't be blank. Note that once you enter the Exchange organization name, you will not be able to modify it. When you've finished typing the name, click Next.

FIGURE 7.5
Choosing the installation location

FIGURE 7.6
Organization name

Exchange Server 2016 includes built-in malware screening that is by default enabled. If for some reason you feel the need to turn this off, choose that option on the next screen. Click Next to move on.

On the Readiness Checks screen, the setup routine will take some time to inspect the system to verify that Exchange can be successfully installed. This is based on the settings you've chosen, the rights of the user account, and the operating system prerequisites.

If Exchange finds everything in order, this is your last chance to stop before making modifications to your Active Directory forest. Exchange even warns you that this is the point of no return:

> Setup is going to prepare the organization for Exchange Server 2016 by using 'Setup / PrepareAD.' No Exchange Server 2010 and Exchange Server 2013 server roles have been detected in this topology. After this operation, you will not be able to install any Exchange Server 2010 or Exchange Server 2013 server roles.

This is expected; it's simply a notice that legacy versions of Exchange can't be installed after Exchange Server 2016 is installed into an organization. If you need to test Exchange Server 2016 coexistence with Exchange Server 2010 or Exchange Server 2013, install the earlier versions first.

View the status of the remaining items to determine whether the organization and server-role prerequisite checks completed successfully. If they have not completed successfully, you must resolve any reported errors before you can install Exchange Server 2016. After resolving an error, click Retry to rerun the prerequisite checks. However, some conditions may require you to quit Setup and run it again at a later time.

If all the other readiness checks have completed successfully, click Install to install Exchange Server 2016. The Setup program will display the Progress screen, which will show you each step of the process, as well as the outcome. Once the installation process is finished, the Setup Completed screen will display.

At this point, you can click the link shown in Figure 7.7 to pull up the current list of post-installation tasks, select the check box to launch Exchange Administration Center, or do neither. Whatever you choose, click Finish to exit the installer.

At some point, be sure to run Windows Update to install any critical updates that may now be required. Even if you are not prompted, reboot the server to complete the installation of Exchange Server 2016.

Command-Line Installation for Mailbox Server Role

As mentioned earlier, you can also install Exchange Server 2016 from the command line. The setup routine allows you to specify all necessary parameters in one line, thereby avoid having to click on things through a GUI. You do, however, need to manually prepare the Active Directory forest and domain in a separate step.

To install your first Exchange Server 2016 server from the command line, open a command prompt with administrative privileges and navigate to the DVD drive or the directory where installation files are located. From there, use the following commands:

```
Setup.exe /PrepareSchema /IAcceptExchangeServerLicenseTerms

Setup.exe /PrepareAD /IAcceptExchangeServerLicenseTerms /OrganizaionName:
"<Organization Name>"

Setup.exe /mode:install /role:Mailbox /IAcceptExchangeServerLicenseTerms
```

To find out more of the options available, run the following command:

```
Setup.exe /h:install
```

FIGURE 7.7
The Setup
Completed screen

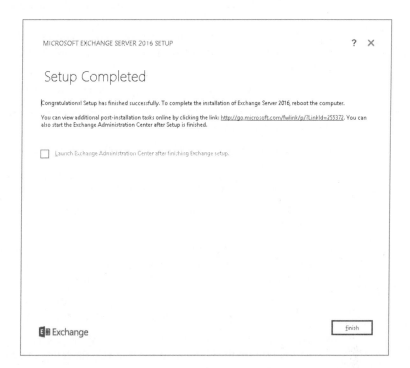

When the setup routine finishes, reboot the server as prompted. Once these steps are completed, continue with the rest of the configuration, as explained in the next section.

Command-Line Installation for Edge Transport Server Role

The Exchange Server 2016 Edge Transport server role can be installed from a GUI and from the command line. The installation steps in a GUI are similar to those for a Mailbox server role, where you choose the Edge Transport server role instead of the Mailbox server role.

To install the Exchange Server 2016 Edge Transport server role from the command line, you should log on to the server as a local administrator because the Edge Transport server role should be installed on a computer that is workgroup member. The steps needed to install the Edge Transport server role are as follows:

1. Open a PowerShell session with the appropriate administrative rights.

2. Run the Install-WindowsFeature cmdlet to install Active Directory Lightweight Directory Services (ADLDS):

```
Install-WindowsFeature ADLDS
```

3. From the Microsoft Download Center, download and install the .NET Framework 4.5.2 supplemental component:

```
https://www.microsoft.com/en-us/download/details.aspx?id=42642
```

4. Open a command prompt with administrative privileges and navigate to the DVD drive or the directory where the installation files are located. From there, use the following command:

```
Setup.exe /mode:install /role:EdgeTransport /IAcceptExchangeServerLicenseTerms
```

5. Finally, in order to synchronize Edge Transport server role to the Mailbox server role, perform the following steps:

- ◆ To create the Edge subscription file, on the Edge Transport server role, run the following command:

```
New-EdgeSubscription -FileName C:\Edge1.xml
```

- ◆ Copy the subscription file to a folder on the Mailbox server role—for example, C:\ Edge\.

- ◆ To import the Edge Subscription file Edge1.xml and to subscribe the Edge Transport server to the Active Directory site named Default-First-Site-Name, on the Mailbox server role, run the following command:

```
New-EdgeSubscription -FileData ([byte[]]$(Get-Content -Path "C:\Edge\Edge1.
xml" -Encoding Byte -ReadCount 0)) -Site "Default-First-Site-Name"
```

- ◆ To start the synchronization between the Mailbox server role and the Edge Transport server role, on the Mailbox server role, run the following command:

```
Start-EdgeSynchronization
```

Post-installation Configuration Steps

Once the server has rebooted, take a few minutes to verify that things are working the way they should. If you didn't look at the setup log at the end of the installation, review it now. It's located at `<system drive>\ExchangeSetupLogs\ExchangeSetup.log`. Look for errors and warnings.

Next, open the Exchange Management Shell and use the `Get-ExchangeServer` cmdlet to obtain information about installed roles. Here is an example:

```
Get-ExchangeServer | FT Name,ServerRole -auto
```

The output of this command will list installed roles for the Exchange server. You should see `Mailbox` listed under `ServerRole`.

Next, let's take a look using Event Viewer for any signs of problems. In Server Manager, select Tools ➤ Event Viewer. Navigate to Windows Logs ➤ Application. Look for errors and warnings that may indicate a problem. It's common to see warnings about various processes that haven't yet had a chance to complete.

When you're sure that the installation has been successful, you can move on to post-installation configuration. We'll start with the Exchange Admin Center. To open that, open Internet Explorer (IE) and enter the following URL:

```
https://servername/ecp
```

Accept any certificate warnings from the default self-signed certificate (you shouldn't see any if you're running IE from the same server you are connecting to), enter your credentials, and wait for the EAC to come up.

Final Configuration

Now that you're logged into the EAC, finish the steps necessary for the final basic configuration.

CONFIGURING THE OFFLINE ADDRESS BOOK

First, configure an Offline Address Book (OAB) on the default mailbox database. The OAB, which Outlook uses when running in Cached mode, contains a copy of the global address list. Use the following steps to associate the default OAB with the mailbox databases:

1. In the left pane, click Servers.

2. In the middle pane, click Databases.

3. Select the default mailbox database.

4. Click the pencil icon to edit the database properties.

5. On the left side of the property window, click Client Settings.

6. Click Browse next to Offline Address Book.

7. Click OK, and then click Save.

You can do the same in the Exchange Management Shell using both the `Get-MailboxDatabase` and `Set-MailboxDatabase` cmdlets together:

```
Get-MailboxDatabase | Set-MailboxDatabase -OfflineAddressBook
"\Default Offline Address Book"
```

SETTING SMTP DOMAINS

By default, Exchange Server 2016 configures a default accepted domain and email address policy using the fully qualified domain name of the Active Directory domain into which you installed. If you need to add a new SMTP domain, you can do so from the EAC:

1. In the left pane, click Servers.

2. In the middle pane, click Accepted Domains.

3. Click the + (Add) icon to create a new accepted domain.

4. Give the accepted domain a display name and an SMTP domain name for which Exchange will receive email.

5. Click Authoritative Domain to indicate that Exchange is responsible for delivering email for that domain in the Exchange organization.

6. Click Save.

7. Select the newly created accepted domain.

8. Click the pencil icon to edit the properties of the accepted domain.

9. Select the Set As Default check box.

10. Click Save.

You can accomplish the same thing in the Exchange Management Shell using the New-AcceptedDomain cmdlet and the Set-AcceptedDomain cmdlet together:

```
New-AcceptedDomain -Name yourdomain
-DomainName *.yourdomain
-DomainType authoritative |
Set-AcceptedDomain -MakeDefault $true
```

Email address policies define how email addresses are assigned to recipients within the organization. Configure one for your new domain using these steps in the EAC:

1. In the left pane, click Servers.

2. In the middle pane, click Email Address Policies.

3. Click the + (Add) icon to create a new email address policy.

4. Give the policy a name and an SMTP domain name for which Exchange will receive email.

5. Enter a name for the policy.

6. Under Email Address Format, click the + (Add) icon to create the email format.

7. Choose the new accepted domain from the pull-down list.

8. Select your chosen email address format.

9. Click Save to close the Email Address Format window.

10. Click Save to close the Email Address Policy window. Accept the warning.

11. Select the new address policy.

12. In the right pane, click Apply.

13. At the warning, click Yes.

14. Click Close once the policy has been applied.

As with all the previous configuration settings, you can use the Exchange Management Shell to make these changes using the New-EmailAddressPolicy and Update-EmailAddressPolicy cmdlets together:

```
New-EmailAddressPolicy -Name Contoso
-EnabledPrimarySMTPAddressTemplate "SMTP:%g.%s@contoso.com"
-IncludedRecipients AllRecipients -Priority 1 |
Update-EmailAddressPolicy
```

ENABLING EXTERNAL MAIL FLOW

In order for mail to flow into and out of the new Exchange organization, you need to modify the default connectors. The Send connector is an object that holds configuration information on how Exchange servers can send email from the organization. By default, there are no Send connectors.

Create a new Send connector to handle all outbound traffic from the EAC:

1. In the left pane, click Servers.

2. In the middle pane, click Send Connectors.

3. Click the + (Add) icon to create a new Send connector.

4. Give the connector a name, such as Default Internet.

5. Under Type, select Internet.

6. Click Next.

7. Accept the default network settings to allow your Exchange server to perform its own DNS lookups, and click Next.

8. Under Address Space, click the + (Add) icon to create the default address space.

9. Under Fully Qualified Domain Name, enter * (an asterisk). Click Save.

10. Click Next.

11. Under Source Server, click the + (Add) icon. Ensure the new Exchange server is selected, click Add, and then click OK.

12. Click Finish.

To accomplish this in the Exchange Management Shell, use the `New-SendConnector` cmdlet:

```
New-SendConnector -name "Default Internet"
-AddressSpaces "*" -DNSRoutingEnabled $true
-SourceTransportServers "MBX1" -Usage Internet
```

In a lab environment, it is common to pass all outgoing messages to a designated smart host rather than rely on looking up MX records for the target domains through DNS resolution. If this is the case in your lab, change the Send connector settings to use a smart host instead of DNS resolution.

A Receive connector is just the opposite of a Send connector. Receive connectors hold the configuration information for how Exchange will receive mail. This can include mail from client machines as well as from the Internet and other Exchange servers.

When Exchange Server 2016 is installed, multiple Receive connectors are created. Those associated with the client access services are proxy connectors. The Default Frontend Receive connector on each Exchange server is configured to receive email from the Internet from anonymous senders. Again, you must either configure external servers to forward messages sent to your test Exchange domains on to your Exchange mail servers or establish the appropriate MX records in DNS for your lab domains.

TESTING THE CONFIGURATION

You now have a significant portion of the configuration finished in Exchange. You can test Exchange using some built-in PowerShell cmdlets. To begin, start the Exchange Management Shell and type Test-mailflow. Check the results in the **TestMailflowResult** column. It should say Success.

Next, test MAPI client connectivity using Test-MAPIConnectivity. You should see Success under Result for each database.

You can verify that all necessary Exchange-related services are running by using Test-ServiceHealth. The output of this cmdlet breaks down the services needed for each of the installed server roles. If everything is running correctly, you should see True for each of the RequiredServicesRunning results.

CREATING AN SSL CERTIFICATE

In a production environment, using a third-party trusted secure sockets layer (SSL) certificate to secure client and server communications is highly recommended. When Exchange Server 2016 is installed, Exchange installs a self-signed certificate that is valid for five years. This is perfectly fine for testing in a lab environment. When testing Exchange using Outlook on the web, for example, you will be presented with a screen indicating that the security certificate was not issued by a trusted certificate authority if you connect from another machine. You can ignore these warnings during testing.

Creating a certificate request and installing a new certificate are outside the scope of this chapter. See Chapter 21, "Understanding the Client Access Services," for more details.

ENTERING THE PRODUCT KEY

You don't have to enter a product key in order to test Exchange Server 2016. However, if you do have a product key and would like to enter it into the server, it's very simple to do using these steps:

1. In the left pane, click Servers.

2. In the middle pane, click Servers.

3. In the right pane, click Enter Product Key.

4. Enter the digits for the product key.

5. When finished, click Save.

As with any other configuration, you can set the product key using the Exchange Management Shell with the Set-ExchangeServer cmdlet and the -ProductKey parameter:

```
Set-ExchangeServer -identity '<server>' -ProductKey <product key>
```

TESTING OUTLOOK ON THE WEB

You can also test Outlook on the web, the web-based email client for Exchange Server 2016:

1. Open a web browser and type **https://<servername>/owa**.

2. If you receive a server warning, click Continue To This Website (Not Recommended) at the certificate prompt.

3. Enter the domain and username for an Administrator that is mailbox-enabled during the setup automatically, and enter a password. Click OK.

4. Set your language and time zone, and click OK.

You will be logged into Outlook on the web, and you can test mailbox and ECP functionality. As mentioned earlier, because you're using an internal certificate, features that require a certificate will yield a certificate prompt first if you are using a machine other than the server. In all cases, you can click Continue To This Website (Not Recommended) to continue testing.

Configuring Recipients

Exchange Server 2016 has various types of recipients, including mailboxes, distribution groups, and contacts. Mailboxes can be further broken down, and that is explained elsewhere in this book. We'll focus on creating mailbox-enabled users and mail contacts.

Mailbox-enabled users are Active Directory accounts that have a mailbox located in Exchange. Take these steps to create a mailbox-enabled user from the EAC:

1. In the left pane, click Recipients.

2. In the middle pane, click Mailboxes.

3. Click the + (Add) icon to create a new mailbox.

4. Give the new mailbox an alias.

5. Select New User and fill in the account name details.

6. Provide the User Logon Name (typically, the same as the alias) and select the appropriate UPN suffix (typically, the same as the primary SMTP domain).

7. Type in the password and password confirmation.

8. Click Save.

Creating mailbox-enabled users for the existing Active Directory accounts in the Exchange Management Shell is quite simple; you'll use the `Enable-Mailbox` cmdlet to enable an existing user account:

```
Enable-Mailbox -Identity TestUser
```

Mail-enabled users are Active Directory accounts that do not have a mailbox located in Exchange but do have an external email address. They are usually assigned to users who work in your company for the short term, such as consultants, part-time workers, and interns. Take these steps to create a mail-enabled user from the EAC:

1. In the left pane, click Recipients.

2. In the middle pane, click Contacts.

3. Click the + (Add) icon and then choose Mail User.

4. Give the new user an alias.

5. Select New User and fill in the account name details.

6. Provide the User Logon Name (typically, the same as the alias) and select the appropriate UPN suffix (typically, the same as the primary SMTP domain).

7. Type in the password and password confirmation.

8. Click Save.

Mail-enabled contacts are objects in the global address list that represent external recipients, such as vendors or clients. Take these steps to create a new mail-enabled contact:

1. In the left pane, click Recipients.

2. In the middle pane, click Contacts.

3. Click the + (Add) icon to create a new contact.

4. Fill in the contact name details.

5. Give the new contact an alias.

6. Provide the external email address associated with the contact.

7. Click Save.

Creating a mail contact in the Exchange Management Shell is quite simple using the New-MailContact cmdlet:

```
New-MailContact -Name "Test Contact" -ExternalEmailAddress "user@domain.local"
```

To create a distribution group in the EAC, follow these steps:

1. In the left pane, click Recipients.

2. In the middle pane, click Groups.

3. Click the + (Add) icon to create a new distribution group.

4. Fill in the group display name and alias.

5. Under Members, click the + (Add) sign, select the mail-enabled recipients to be members of the new group, click Add, and click Save.

6. Click Save.

You can accomplish both creating a distribution group and adding members in one line of code in the Exchange Management Shell using something like this:

```
New-DistributionGroup -name "Group Name" |
Add-DistributionGroupMember -member "User"
```

Configuring a Postmaster Address

A postmaster address is needed to send nondelivery reports (NDRs) and other related messages to recipients outside the Exchange organization, and it is required by RFC 2821. Configuring your environment takes two steps. First, either create a new mailbox for the postmaster or assign the address to an existing mailbox, such as Administrator. Second, use the Exchange Management Shell to set the external postmaster address in Exchange. To do so, open the Exchange Management Shell and execute the Set-TransportConfig cmdlet and the -ExternalPostmasterAddress parameter, using the following format:

```
Set-TransportConfig -ExternalPostmasterAddress
<ExternalPostmasterSMTPAddress>
```

Here's an example:

```
Set-TransportConfig -ExternalPostmasterAddress
postmaster@contoso.com
```

The Bottom Line

Quickly size a typical server. Using a properly equipped server for testing can yield a much more positive experience than using a poorly equipped one. Taking the time to obtain the right hardware will avoid problems later.

Master It What parameters must be kept in mind when sizing a lab/test server?

Install the necessary Windows Server 2012 or Windows Server 2012 R2 prerequisites. Certain settings must be configured before Exchange Server 2016 is installed.

Master It What is involved in installing and configuring the prerequisites?

Install an Exchange Server 2016 server. You should provide a basic, bare-bones server for testing and evaluation.

Master It What installation methods can be used to install Exchange Server 2016?

Configure Exchange to send and receive email. Your new Exchange server should interact with other email systems.

Master It What are the configuration requirements for sending and receiving email?

Configure recipients, contacts, and distribution groups. Add mailbox-enabled users, mail-enabled contacts, and distribution groups to Exchange.

Master It How are recipients created, and what's the difference between them?

Chapter 8

Understanding Server Roles and Configurations

Exchange Server 2016, similarly to Exchange Server 2013, 2010, and 2007, provides a role-based installation procedure. This procedure provides only two server-role choices: the Mailbox server role and the Edge Transport server role. As discussed in previous chapters, the former Client Access, Hub Transport, and Unified Messaging server role functionalities from Exchange Server 2007 and 2010 and the Client Access role functionalities from Exchange Server 2013 have been now rolled into the Mailbox server role, providing a simplified installation process and deployment architecture. This chapter will discuss the server roles, their preferred deployment options, and the components installed with each role.

IN THIS CHAPTER, YOU WILL LEARN TO:

- ◆ Understand the importance of server roles

- ◆ Understand the Exchange Server 2016 server roles

- ◆ Explore server role configurations

The *Roles* of Server Roles

Although the concept of roles is not new, the number of roles available in Exchange Server 2016 has changed from previous versions. In Exchange Server 2007 and Exchange Server 2010, you had five roles to select from during installation: Mailbox, Hub Transport, Client Access, Unified Messaging, and Edge Transport. In Exchange Server 2013, the number of roles was reduced to three: Mailbox, Client Access, and Edge Transport; in Exchange 2016, it has been reduced to only two, Mailbox and Edge Transport. All of the components of the Client Access role, Hub Transport role, and Unified Messaging role in Exchange 2010 and all the components in the Client Access server in Exchange 2013 have been stripped down and placed into the Mailbox server role.

A key benefit of having role-based installation has always been the ability to segregate or separate Exchange Server functionalities onto separate servers. Maximizing the usage of server resources has traditionally been a driver for architects designing Exchange Server messaging solutions, and role-based installation has been used as a solution to achieve a more optimal design. Virtualization solutions have provided an alternative solution to use these hardware resources appropriately. In time, the need to segregate Exchange Server roles has become less relevant and beneficial, which has resulted in the new Exchange Server architecture.

Furthermore, the Microsoft preferred architecture for Exchange Server 2013 deployment had suggested that both the Client Access and Mailbox roles be collocated on each server in Exchange organization. This preferred architecture resulted in the integration of those two roles in a single Mailbox server role in Exchange Server 2016.

The Edge Transport role retained similar functionality as in previous editions, acting as an SMTP gateway between the Internet and the internal network, located in the perimeter network, and providing SMTP routing, transport rules, anti-malware, and antispam functionality.

THE SEEDS OF SERVER ROLES

The concept of an Exchange Server role is not new. Microsoft officially introduced the concept in Exchange Server 2007, and it's been carried over to Exchange Server 2016.

During installation, you are prompted to choose which server roles a particular Exchange server will provide. Figure 8.1 shows the screen that you will see if you choose a custom setup of Exchange Server 2016. You are prompted for which server roles you need to install.

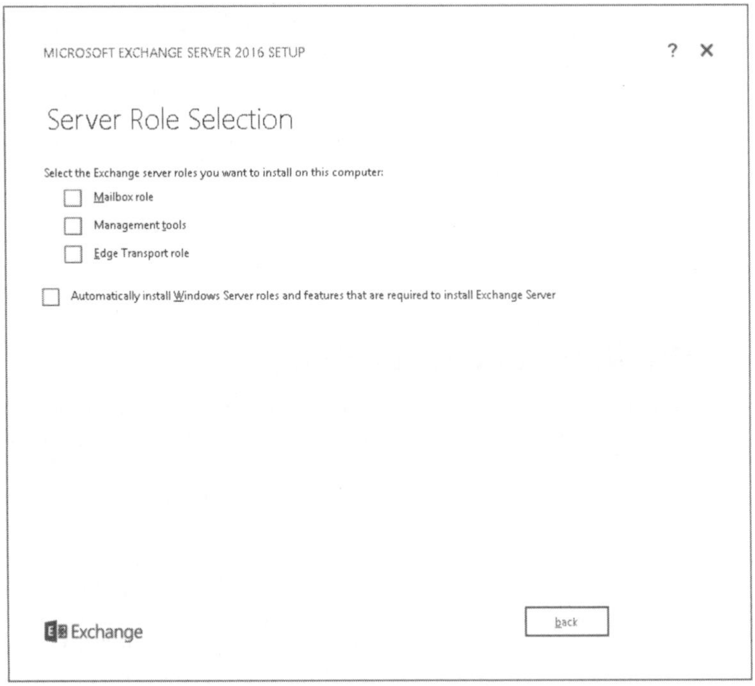

FIGURE 8.1
Selecting the Exchange Server 2016 roles

MICROSOFT EXCHANGE SERVER 2016 SETUP   ?   ✕

Server Role Selection

Select the Exchange server roles you want to install on this computer:

☐ Mailbox role

☐ Management tools

☐ Edge Transport role

☐ Automatically install Windows Server roles and features that are required to install Exchange Server

E☐ Exchange   [back]

There are some clear and important advantages to this approach, such as the following:

◆ It has a simplified architecture, also known as a *single building block architecture*.

◆ Server configuration complexity is reduced.

- It is a cost-effective solution because there are fewer servers, which means fewer licenses.

- Because there are fewer servers, it has a lower management cost.

- The load is distributed between multiple servers with the same role, which increases scalability and high availability.

Exchange Server 2016 Server Roles

Now, let's take a look at the specific Exchange Server 2016 roles you may find in your organization.

Mailbox Server

The Mailbox server role is at the center of the Exchange Server 2016 universe. The functionalities of the deprecated Client Access, Hub Transport, and Unified Messaging roles in Exchange Server 2010 have been moved to the Mailbox server role. The Mailbox server hosts all the services that process and store the data. The Mailbox server also hosts the logic that routes a specific protocol request to the protocol destination point. Moreover, users are always connected to client access services running on the Mailbox server. Client access services on the Mailbox server proxy the user request to the active mailbox database copy that hosts the user's mailbox. The client request is always processed by the protocol instance that is local to the active mailbox database copy that hosts the user's mailbox.

This section will cover the common Mailbox role functionality that is similar to legacy versions of Exchange, as well as the substantial changes that have been introduced in Exchange Server 2016 to the Mailbox role.

WHERE ARE ACTIVE AND PASSIVE CLUSTERED MAILBOXES?

If you have worked with Exchange Server 2007, you may be wondering where the Active Clustered Mailbox and Passive Clustered Mailbox server roles are. They are no longer necessary: clustering can be achieved after installation because the concept of a clustered mailbox server no longer exists as it did in previous versions. This concept is achieved through the implementation of database availability groups (DAGs) and relies on the Failover Clustering feature built into Windows Server 2012 and Windows Server 2012 R2.

MAILBOX DATABASES

Just as in previous versions of Exchange Server, the Mailbox server role hosts mailbox databases. The mailbox database can be replicated to other Mailbox servers when the Mailbox server is a member of a DAG, just as in Exchange Server 2010 and Exchange Server 2013.

If you have worked with Exchange Server 2007 or 2010, you will notice that unlike in those versions, you can no longer create public folder databases. Beginning from Exchange Server 2013 and continuing in Exchange Server 2016, public folders are stored within a public folder mailbox. End users now connect to a public folder mailbox to retrieve public folder content.

This means that public folder high availability is based on mailbox database replication and not on the all-too-troublesome public folder replication.

TRANSPORT SERVICES

Mail delivery (even mail going from one mailbox on a local database to another mailbox on the same database) is routed through Transport services on the Mailbox server. This is a major change from Exchange Server versions 2007 and 2010, which used the services on the Hub Transport server to deliver email messages. Three Transport services are created when the Mailbox role is installed: Transport service, Front End Transport service, and Mailbox Transport service. Mailbox Transport service consists of Mailbox Transport Submission service and Mailbox Transport Delivery service, which will be discussed later in this chapter.

Let's quickly see how these services handle email messages. When an email message is sent to a recipient on a different Mailbox server in a different delivery group, the message is picked up by the Mailbox Transport Submission service on the source server and passed to the Transport service on the destination server that is located on the least-cost route. Then, the Transport service submits the message to the Mailbox Transport Delivery service on the destination server, and then finally, the email message is written to the mailbox database.

MAIL ROUTING

Mail routing is now a responsibility of servers running the Mailbox role. The client access services on a Mailbox server provide proxy services for inbound and outbound email messages. During the installation of the Mailbox server role, three default receive connectors that are associated to the Microsoft Exchange Front End Transport service are created. One of the receive connectors that is created during installation listens over port 25 and is configured with proper permissions to accept email messages from the Internet.

On the Mailbox server, the Microsoft Exchange Front End Transport service still listens on port 25 and the Microsoft Exchange Transport service listens on port 2525.

UNIFIED MESSAGING

Another major change starting in Exchange Server 2013 and continuing in Exchange Server 2016 in the Mailbox role is that it is now responsible for all of the Unified Messaging features. In fact, the services that were installed on the Unified Messaging role for an Exchange Server 2007 or 2010 server are now installed on the Mailbox role for Exchange Server 2016. It should be noted that the client access service is the first service in the communication path for all inbound calls or Session Initiation Protocol (SIP) requests for Unified Messaging. However, once the traffic passes through the client access service, the Mailbox server receives unified communication and establishes the RTP and SRTP channels with the IP PBX or VOIP gateway.

On the Mailbox role, the client access services also play an integral part of Unified Messaging. The Microsoft Exchange Unified Messaging Call Router service now runs on the Mailbox servers and is responsible for redirecting SIP traffic from an incoming call to a Mailbox server.

MEMORY ALLOCATION

Memory allocation for database cache has been tweaked in Exchange Server 2016. When looking at memory consumption in Exchange Server 2007 and Exchange Server 2010, the Information

Store would consume, by far, the largest portion of the available memory. Memory consumption in Exchange Server 2016 servers running the Mailbox role comparing to Exchange Server 2010 is very different. The Mailbox server reserves 25 percent of the total RAM for database cache. Memory allocation in Exchange Server 2016 is based on the following:

◆ Total amount of memory

◆ Total number of active databases

◆ Total number of passive databases

◆ The max number of active databases

Essentially, the Exchange server looks at its memory requirements and then ensures that the most important process running on the server has enough resources available to function effectively.

When the Information Store service is started, a worker process and database cache is allocated per database. Based on the state of a database being active or passive, the amount of RAM allocated to the database cache will vary. An active copy of a mailbox database will use all of the allotted database cache. A passive database copy will use only 20 percent of the allocated database cache. Let's use this example:

◆ The mailbox server has 100 GB of RAM.

◆ Ten mailbox database copies exist on this server.

◆ Five mailbox database copies are active and five mailbox database copies are passive.

Because 25 percent of the available memory is allocated to the database cache, the total amount of memory allocated for the database cache is 25 GB. This means that each database is allocated 2.5 GB of the database cache. Each passive copy uses only 20 percent of the allocated database cache; therefore, the passive databases have a database cache of 512 MB.

If at any point a passive copy becomes activated, the database cache for that database copy will change from 512 MB to 2.5 GB.

Because the database cache is determined when the Information Store service is started, you must restart the Information Store service when a new database is added to an Exchange server. (The requirement for a service restart after a new database is created was introduced in Exchange Server 2013, and it is a direct result of the new database cache-allocation scheme.) This includes the creation of a new database or the addition of a passive copy of a mailbox database. You'll see the warning message shown in Figure 8.2 when a new database is added to a Mailbox server.

FIGURE 8.2
The warning message when a new database is added to a Mailbox server

warning

Please restart the Microsoft Exchange Information Store service on server LON-EX1 after adding new mailbox databases.

OK

Note that this is only a warning message and does not indicate an immediate problem. Performance issues may arise in the future if the Information Store service is not restarted and a new mailbox database becomes populated with a large number of mailboxes.

The formula used to determine memory sizing is as follows:

Active database cache allocated = (total server memory) × 25% ÷ (number of maximum allowed active databases + [(total number of databases on a server) – (number of maximum allowed active databases)] × 20%)

If the number of maximum allowed active databases is not set, then the maximum allowed active databases will equal the total number of databases on a server.

SERVICES

On an Exchange Server 2016 server that is dedicated to providing Mailbox server functionality, you will find quite a few Exchange services running. The Exchange Server 2016 Mailbox server services are as follows:

Microsoft Exchange Active Directory Topology/MSExchangeADTopology/ ADTopologyService.exe Locates Active Directory domain controllers and global catalog servers, and provides Active Directory topology information to Exchange Server services. Most Exchange Server services depend on this service; if it does not start, the Exchange server will probably not function.

Microsoft Exchange Anti-spam Update/MSExchangeAntispamUpdate/Microsoft .Exchange.AntispamUpdateSvc.exe This service is responsible for updating antispam signatures.

Microsoft Exchange Compliance Audit /MSComplianceAudit/ComplianceAuditService .exe This service is responsible for Microsoft Exchange Compliance Auditing.

Microsoft Exchange Compliance Service /MSExchangeCompliance/ MSExchangeCompliance.exe This service acts as a host for the compliance service.

Microsoft Exchange DAG Management /MSExchangeDAGMgmt/MSExchangeDAGMgmt .exe This service provides storage management and database layout management functionality for mailbox servers in a database availability group.

Microsoft Exchange Diagnostics/MSExchangeDiagnostics/Microsoft.Exchange .Diagnostics.Service.exe Uses an agent to monitor the health of the Exchange server.

Microsoft Exchange EdgeSync\MSExchangeEdgeSync\Microsoft.Exchange .EdgeSyncSvc.exe Keeps recipient and configuration data up-to-date when an Edge server is subscribed to the same AD site of which the Mailbox server is a member.

Microsoft Exchange Frontend Transport/MSExchangeFrontEndTransport/ MSExchangeFrontendTransport.exe Provides SMTP proxy for inbound and outbound email messages from/to the Internet.

Microsoft Exchange Health Manager/MSExchangeHM/MSExchangeHMHost.exe Monitors the health and performance of key services on the Exchange server.

Microsoft Exchange IMAP4/MSExchangeImap4/Microsoft.Exchange.Imap4Service .exe Authenticates the connection and passes the request to the appropriate Mailbox server. This service is set to manual by default.

Microsoft Exchange IMAP4 Backend/MSExchangeIMAP4BE/Microsoft.Exchange .Imap4Service.exe Provides IMAP4 clients with access to Exchange Server mailboxes. This service retrieves IMAP4 requests from the client access services. This service is set to manual by default.

Microsoft Exchange Information Store/MSExchangeIS/store.exe The Information Store is the actual Exchange database engine (also known as ESE). This service manages the mailbox databases. If the store.exe service does not start, databases will not be mounted.

Microsoft Exchange Mailbox Assistants/MSExchangeMailboxAssistants/ MSExchangeMailboxAssistants.exe Handles background processing functions for Exchange Server mailboxes.

Microsoft Exchange Mailbox Replication\MSExchangeMailboxReplication\ MSExchangeMailboxReplication.exe This service is responsible for mailbox moves.

Microsoft Exchange Mailbox Transport Delivery\MSExchangeDelivery\ MSExchangeDelivery.exe Accepts email messages from the Transport service and delivers the email messages to the mailbox.

Microsoft Exchange Mailbox Transport Submission\MSExchangeSubmission\ MSExchangeSubmission.exe Pulls the email messages from a mailbox and finds the best Transport service to which to send the message.

Microsoft Exchange Notifications Broker\MSExchangeNotificationsBroker\ Microsoft.Exchange.Notification.Broker.exe Generates and routes Exchange notifications to local and remote Exchange processes.

Microsoft Exchange POP3/MSExchangePop3/Microsoft.Exchange.Pop3Service .exe Authenticates the client connection and passes the request to the appropriate Mailbox server. This service is set to manual by default.

Microsoft Exchange POP3 Backend\MSExchangePOP3BE\Microsoft.Exchange .Pop3Service.exe Receives POP3 requests from the client access services. Once the request is processed, the Mailbox server provides access to the mailbox over POP3. The service startup type is manual by default.

Microsoft Exchange Replication/MSExchangeRepl/msexchangerepl.exe Provides the Continuous Replication service to copy log files from an active database to a server that hosts a passive copy of the database.

Microsoft Exchange RPC Client Access/MSExchangeRPC/Microsoft.Exchange .RpcClientAccess.Service.exe Handles the RPC connections for the Exchange server.

Microsoft Exchange Search/MSExchangeFastSearch/Microsoft.Exchange.Search .Service.exe Handles content indexing and queuing of Exchange Server data.

Microsoft Exchange Search Host Controller\HostControllerService\ hostcontrollerservice.exe Provides service management and deployment for applications on the local host.

Microsoft Exchange Server Extension for Windows Server Backup/wsbexchange/ wsbexchange.exe Allows the Windows Server Backup utility to back up and restore Exchange Server data.

Microsoft Exchange Service Host/MSExchangeServiceHost/Microsoft.Exchange .ServiceHost.exe Provides a service host for Exchange Server components that do not have their own service. These include components such as configuring Registry and virtual directory information.

Microsoft Exchange Throttling/MSExchangeThrottling/MSExchangeThrottling .exe Handles the limits on the rate of user operations to prevent any single user from consuming too many server resources.

Microsoft Exchange Transport\MSExchangeTransport\MSExchangeTransport .exe Handles SMTP connections from Edge, client access services, Submission and Delivery services, and other SMTP connection points.

Microsoft Exchange Transport Log Search/MSExchangeTransportLogSearch/ MSExchangeTransportLogSearch.exe Handles the remote search capabilities for the Exchange Server transport log files.

Microsoft Exchange Unified Messaging\MSExchangeUM\umservice.exe Handles UM requests from client access services. This service is responsible for unified communication to the Exchange server.

Microsoft Exchange Unified Messaging Call Router/MSExchangeUMCR/Microsoft .Exchange.UM.CallRouter.exe Provides call-routing features.

Client Access Services

Since Exchange Server 2007, the responsibilities of the Client Access role have changed dramatically from version to version. The common thread between the Exchange Server 2010 Client Access role and the Exchange Server 2013 Client Access role was that it provided most of the interface for accessing email data. In Exchange Server 2016, when a user connects to their mailbox, the connection from the client is established to client access services on a Mailbox server. The client access services on the Mailbox server role will authenticate the request, locate the mailbox, and proxy or redirect the client request to the appropriate Mailbox server. Client access services are also responsible for parts of mail routing and Unified Messaging. Microsoft made this change to simplify the deployment and management of Exchange Server 2016. Instead of having multiple server roles acting as an entry point for a variety of services, the client access services on Mailbox server handle client requests, mail flow, and phone calls.

The client access services coordinate all communication between clients. The functions of the client access services include:

◆ Supporting connections from Outlook MAPI over HTTP, which is the default protocol in Exchange Server 2016.

◆ Supporting connections from Outlook Anywhere clients (RPC over HTTP).

◆ Supporting connections from web clients by using Outlook on the web (named as Outlook Web App in Exchange Server 2013 and Outlook Web Access in Exchange Server 2010 and older versions).

- Supporting connections from mobile devices using Microsoft ActiveSync technology.

- Supporting connections from POP3 and IMAP4 clients.

- Proxying SMTP message for inbound and outbound email messages to/from the Internet.

- Supporting connections from other Exchange Web Services (EWS) applications.

- Proxying connections from various email clients to the relevant Exchange Server Mailbox server.

- Serving as an initial communication point for inbound calls and faxes.

- Proxying or redirecting connections from external Outlook MAPI over HTTP, Outlook Anywhere, Offline Address Book, Exchange Web Services, Outlook on the web, or Exchange ActiveSync clients to Client Access servers in other Active Directory sites. During the upgrade, different Exchange Server versions exist in the same organization, which is called a coexistence scenario. During the coexistence, DNS should be configured to connect all types of clients (except MAPI-RPC in Exchange Server 2010) to Exchange Server 2016. The actual mechanics of the connection depend on the client that is being used and the location of the mailbox:

  - If an Outlook on the web user's mailbox is on an Exchange Server 2010 server, DNS should be configured to connect a user to Exchange Server 2016. Once the user connects to Exchange 2016, the client access services on Exchange Server 2016 *proxy* or redirect the user to the Exchange Server 2010 CAS or 2013 Mailbox server role, based on the external URL set on the OWA virtual directory.

  - If an OWA user's mailbox is on an Exchange Server 2013 or Exchange Server 2010 server and the external URL on that server matches the external URL on the Exchange Server 2016 server, the Exchange Server 2016 client access services proxy the request to an Exchange Server 2013 or Exchange Server 2010 server running the CAS role in the same AD site the mailbox is in.

  - If an OWA user's mailbox is on an Exchange Server 2013 or Exchange Server 2010 server and the external URL on that server *does not* match the external URL on the Exchange Server 2016 server, the Exchange Server 2016 client access services redirect the request to the external URL set on the Exchange Server 2013 or Exchange Server 2010 server.

  - If an ActiveSync user's mailbox is on an Exchange Server 2013 or 2010 server and the external URL on that server matches the external URL on the Exchange Server 2016 server, the Exchange Server 2016 client access services proxy the request to an Exchange Server 2013 or 2010 server running the CAS role in the same AD site that the mailbox is in.

  - If an Outlook Anywhere user's mailbox is on an Exchange Server 2013 or 2010 server and the external URL on that server matches the external URL on the Exchange Server 2016 server, the Exchange Server 2016 client access services *proxy* the request to an Exchange Server 2013 or 2010 server running the CAS role in the same AD site that the mailbox is in.

REVERSE PROXY IN THE PERIMETER NETWORK

If your organization is going to allow external clients (Outlook on the web, mobile phones, Outlook MAPI over HTTP, Outlook Anywhere) to connect to your Exchange servers from the Internet, a common question is whether the reverse proxy server or a reverse proxy device should be deployed in the perimeter or DMZ (demilitarized zone) network. Some organizations use third-party proxy servers since Microsoft TMG Server 2010 has been discontinued, but Microsoft also instructs customers that reverse proxy is not necessarily needed.

While it can sometimes be tempting to place reverse proxy in the DMZ, especially since Microsoft has discontinued the Forefront Threat Management Gateway, there are better approaches to this problem. One solution that is picking up steam is to not place pre-authentication or reverse proxy to accept inbound connections from the Internet. Although a firewall appliance would still be placed in front of the Exchange servers, once the traffic goes through the firewall appliance, the packets would be sent directly to the Exchange servers. Before your chin hits the table, Microsoft has been diligent over the years in securing Exchange Server services out of the box. This might not be the right approach for all organizations, but it is worth considering.

HOW MANY MAILBOX SERVERS DO I NEED?

Organizations now have a simpler way to plan their Exchange Server 2016 deployments. Because only one Exchange Server role is located in the internal network (the Mailbox server role), organizations should estimate how many Mailbox server roles are needed in their organization and in which sites servers should be deployed. You can estimate the number of Mailbox server roles by using the Exchange Server Role Requirements Calculator (`https://gallery.technet.microsoft.com/Exchange-2013-Server-Role-f8a61780`). Note that the calculator supports Exchange Server 2016, even though the URL contains name Exchange 2013.

The location of Mailbox server roles depends on multiple factors such as:

◆ Dispersed user population in different regions and number of the users located in different regions

◆ Organization's need for distributed administration and security permissions

◆ Organization's need for site resilience

◆ Organization's need for addressing different disaster recovery scenarios

You should keep up with Microsoft's current recommendations for sizing because they change over time.

Edge Transport Server

The Edge Transport server role, as in previous Exchange Server versions, is located in the perimeter network and is responsible for managing all inbound and outbound Internet mail flow for your Exchange organization. Furthermore, the Edge Transport server role provides anti-malware and antispam protection and transport rules that manage the mail flow.

The Edge Transport server is not a domain member. The Edge server hosts ADLDS (Active Directory Lightweight Directory Services), which synchronizes information with Active Directory that is relevant for message transport, such as send connectors and recipient information. This data is synchronized to the Edge Transport server by the Microsoft Exchange EdgeSync service (EdgeSync).

Organizations might choose to install multiple Edge Transport servers for high availability and scalability.

SERVICES

On an Exchange Server 2016 server that is dedicated to providing Edge Transport functionality, you will find some different Exchange services compared to the Mailbox server role. The Exchange Server 2016 Edge Transport server services are as follows:

`Microsoft Exchange ADAM /ADAM_MSExchange/dsamain.exe -sn MSExchange` ADAM (Active Directory Application Mode) provides ADLDS (Active Directory Lightweight Directory Services) for the Edge Transport server role.

`Microsoft Exchange Anti-spam Update/MSExchangeAntispamUpdate/Microsoft .Exchange.AntispamUpdateSvc.exe` This service is responsible for updating antispam signatures.

`Microsoft Exchange Credential Service /MSExchangeEdgeCredential/Microsoft .Exchange.EdgeCredentialSvc.exe` This service is the Microsoft Exchange Credential service.

`Microsoft Exchange Diagnostics/MSExchangeDiagnostics/Microsoft.Exchange .Diagnostics.Service.exe` Uses an agent to monitor the health of the Exchange server.

`Microsoft Exchange Health Manager/MSExchangeHM/MSExchangeHMHost.exe` Monitors the health and performance of key services on the Exchange server.

`Microsoft Exchange Service Host/MSExchangeServiceHost/Microsoft.Exchange .ServiceHost.exe` Provides a service host for Exchange Server components that do not have their own service. These include components such as configuring Registry and virtual directory information.

`Microsoft Exchange Transport\MSExchangeTransport\MSExchangeTransport .exe` Handles SMTP connections from Edge, Client Access server, Submission and Delivery services, and other SMTP connection points.

`Microsoft Exchange Transport Log Search/MSExchangeTransportLogSearch/ MSExchangeTransportLogSearch.exe` Handles the remote search capabilities for the Exchange Server transport log files.

Possible Role Configurations

There are many possible configurations for Exchange Server 2016; unfortunately, there is no magic formula that will help you determine the exact number of servers you will need and the roles those servers should host—well, at least not a simple formula. Knowing exactly when to scale Exchange Server 2016 from a single server to multiple mailbox servers depends on a lot of factors:

◆ Server roles that your organization requires. Note that all Exchange Server organizations require at least one Mailbox server.

◆ The number of simultaneous users who will be using the system and their usage profile (light, average, heavy).

◆ The number of messages sent and received per hour and the average size of those messages.

◆ An organization's high-availability requirements.

◆ The distribution of your users (across various offices) as well as the WAN link speeds and latency between the offices.

◆ The number of transport rules, journaling rules, daily messaging records management events, daily archiving, and other Exchange Server features that are required.

◆ Any third-party products that place additional transport, mailbox, or I/O load on the server, such as discovery, compliance, antivirus, antispam, archiving, or mobile devices.

You might need to add server roles in a situation where you need to scale server configuration by ensuring that only specific server roles reside on a single Windows server.

Number of Mailbox Servers Deployed

For many companies, a single Windows Server 2012 R2 running Exchange Server 2016 with the Mailbox server role will be just fine depending on their usage patterns and number of simultaneous users. A company with only a few hundred users will fit perfectly well on a single server. However, this scenario is valid only for companies that do not have business requirements for high availability. These companies accept the possibility that in the event of a failure, they would work without email while Exchange Server is recovered from backup. Companies that need high availability would deploy at least two servers configured in a DAG.

When properly configured with sufficient memory, disk capacity, and CPU resources, the Mailbox server can easily support your user base, provided you don't overload the server and you have good disaster-recovery documentation. The disaster-recovery documentation is important because if the server ever has to be rebuilt, all server components have to be recovered at the same time.

 Real World Scenario

EXCHANGE SERVER 2016 AND DOMAIN CONTROLLERS COEXISTING

In almost no circumstances do we recommend installing Exchange Server 2016 on the same machine as a domain controller. Too many problems have arisen in every previous version of Exchange Server. Troubleshooting one or the other becomes more difficult when both Exchange Server and Active Directory are hosted on the same Windows server. We certainly see the logic that can be applied when buying server hardware, though.

For a company that supports only 50 mailboxes (and does not want to use a legacy Small Business server), it seems foolish to purchase two separate physical machines that will both be very lightly loaded. (Keep in mind that in those scenarios, Microsoft recommends a deployment of Office 365 to meet the needs of the company.)

For example, a company had 50 users and no business requirement for high availability; at any given time only about 30 of those users were using the email server. With the help of their consultant, they decided to use a host Windows Server 2012 R2 x64 operating system while running a domain controller on one Hyper-V virtual machine and the Exchange Server 2016 server on a different Hyper-V virtual machine. This kept the applications separated on different operating systems but did not require them to purchase two physical servers. A third Hyper-V machine was configured to run SharePoint and an additional web application and to act as their file/print server. The actual physical machine running these three guest operating systems had a dual quad-core processor and 128 GB of physical memory.

Scaling Exchange Server 2016 Roles

If you have determined that you can't address your organization's performance requirements with the initial number of Exchange Server Mailbox roles in a DAG, you will need to continue adding Mailbox server roles to multiple Windows servers. This will usually be because you need to scale to support a larger user load than the current number of servers can provide or you're using a virtualization solution that can't meet current sizing requirements.

One of the biggest design decisions organizations will face with Exchange Server 2016 deployments is the placement of roles. Each organization is different, but the process to determine the best approach for Exchange Server 2016 deployments is simple. Planning for each Exchange Server 2016 component is covered in its respective chapter, but proper planning based on the user types, technical requirements, and business requirements will drive the way Exchange Server 2016 is deployed within your organization. In most organizations, you must evaluate the impact on a server's resources, as well as the overall impact of where servers are deployed and whether roles must coexist.

For example, take an organization that needs to support 4,000 mailboxes and requires high availability for the Mailbox server role. In this example, the organization has purchased four servers, where each server has been sized to support up to 2,000 active mailboxes. By installing the Mailbox role on the four servers, the organization can place 1,000 mailboxes on each server and add all the Mailbox servers to the same DAG. This approach allows the organization to withstand the failure of two servers before reaching the 2,000-mailbox limit per server.

The preceding is a straightforward example of role placement. In more complex environments, the options aren't always as cut and dried. As organizations look to streamline server deployments by using the same hardware or by requiring all servers to be virtualized, many Exchange Server administrators find themselves between a rock and a hard place when it comes to role placement. Should you scale out and segregate the servers? Should you tell the customer not to virtualize and buy physical servers that can support the Mailbox server role? Frequently, a company's IT strategy doesn't align with the best deployment option. In these situations, you should provide the customer with two project plans. Each project plan should contain the pros, cons, and the overall costs of each design.

The Bottom Line

Understand the Exchange Server 2016 server roles. Exchange Server 2016 supports two unique server roles. The features of all the roles (except Edge Transport role) in Exchange Server 2007, 2010, and 2013 have been moved to the Mailbox server role in Exchange Server 2016. The Mailbox server handles much more in Exchange Server 2016 than just the Exchange Server database engine. The Mailbox role now handles Unified Messaging, Client Access, and Transport services.

The Client Access server role functionalities in Exchange Server 2013 are now part of the Mailbox server role. Client access services in Exchange 2016 hold a lot of key responsibilities. Client access services in Exchange 2016 are still the end point for most of the protocols in the organization, such as SMTP, HTTP, and RTP. The main functions of the client access services are to authenticate an incoming request, locate the next hop for the request, and proxy or redirect the request to the next hop.

> **Master It** Which Exchange server role provides access to the mailbox database for Outlook on the web and Outlook clients?

Explore possible server role configurations. Server role number and placement can be designed to meet most organizational and configuration requirements.

For small organizations that do not need high availability, one server that hosts the Mailbox role will suffice, provided it has sufficient hardware even if it needs to support 500 or more mailboxes. Companies that need high availability will deploy at least two mailbox server roles in DAG. Companies that need high availability but for some reason (such as budget constraints) are not able to provide high availability might choose to migrate to Office 365.

We do not recommend installing Exchange Server 2016 on a domain controller.

All server roles can be virtualized. Depending on the client load, Mailbox servers may also be virtualized as long as you remain within Microsoft's support boundaries. It is important to size out your Exchange Server 2016 deployment before committing to a virtual or physical server deployment.

> **Master It** Your company has approximately 400 mailboxes. Your users require only basic email services (email, shared calendars, Outlook, and Outlook on the web). You already have two servers that function as domain controllers/global catalog servers. What would you recommend to support the 400 mailboxes?

Chapter 9

Exchange Server 2016 Requirements

When you're planning for your Exchange Server 2016 installation, you need to make sure you have all the necessary prerequisites. As part of your preparation, you need to make sure you have the operating system and Active Directory prerequisites (software versions, patches, updates) and any required permissions. If you are upgrading from a previous version of Exchange Server, you must make sure you are at the right version and service pack for all your existing servers.

In this chapter, we will make sure you are aware of all these requirements so that when you are ready to install Exchange Server 2016, you will breeze through the installation quickly and without interruption.

IN THIS CHAPTER, YOU WILL LEARN TO:

- ◆ Use the right hardware for your organization

- ◆ Configure Windows Server 2012 R2 and Windows Server 2012 to support Exchange Server 2016

- ◆ Confirm that Active Directory is ready

- ◆ Verify that previous versions of Exchange Server can interoperate with Exchange Server 2016

Getting the Right Server Hardware

When you're looking at any manufacturer's hardware specifications, one of the things you can depend on is that the specs will provide the minimum recommendations necessary to run the product. However, Microsoft has learned that recommending a minimum configuration often yields unhappy customers; this is why when Microsoft suggests hardware configurations, you will typically see two: minimum and recommended.

The minimum hardware configuration works just fine if you are building a test lab or a classroom environment. But for production environments, you'll want to make sure your hardware can support a typical everyday workload. If running in a high-availability scenario, you have to ensure that in the event of a server failure, servers that are up and running can continue to work with the increased utilization. In this section, we will make some recommendations that are partially based on our own experiences and partially based on Microsoft's best practices.

Note that hardware configuration can vary quite a bit depending on the server's role and its workload. You may be supporting a single server with 100 mailboxes or a multiple-server infrastructure with 100,000 mailboxes. You should plan to comfortably support your maximum expected load and allow some room for growth. Your planning process will require making decisions according to your company's business requirements.

Real World Scenario

HARDWARE FOUNDATIONS: STABILITY, CONFIGURATION, AND MANAGEMENT

Ensuring that your Exchange servers function reliably and efficiently entails several key factors: correctly configured software, proper management, and properly planned and sized hardware, networks, and storage. If you fail to get any one of these right, the result will be poor performance, downtime, data loss, and unhappy users.

Windows hardware stability and compatibility are probably the most important factors in your choice for a server platform. These include not only the server model itself but also the components you will be using, such as network adapters and any third-party software. Selecting a stable hardware platform and vendor can be critical to a successful implementation.

Many vendors may be available to you. You should consider local support, service-level agreements, quality, and performance when you select a vendor.

Choose a server model that will provide you with the card slots and available disk drives. When evaluating server models, make sure the server model is near the beginning of its model life rather than near the end. It is not uncommon to purchase a server through a discount outlet that is near or at the end of its model life.

As you build your Windows servers, make sure you are running reasonably recent versions of all supporting software, such as device drivers, and that the operating system is patched. Plan accordingly for physical deployments or virtual deployments (discussed in Chapter 4, "Virtualizing Exchange Server 2016").

You will also want to implement a comprehensive management strategy. You can monitor some of your Exchange Server deployments by using built-in tools, such as Performance Monitor, Resource Monitor, and Event Viewer. After you have deployed Exchange Server in your environment, a number of different Exchange Server–specific objects and counters will be available in Performance Monitor. These counters can provide an abundance of data you can use to tune your deployment.

Other tools from Microsoft that you may be able to access include: System Center Operations Manager and System Center Configuration Manager. It is worth noting that Exchange Server and the System Center tools are designed to work together, and one dovetails into the other as part of a comprehensive management solution.

You may have researched and chosen to implement one of the many third-party network and application-monitoring tools. Some of these tools may be supplied by your systems vendor, while others are stand-alone applications. Prior to making any purchases, you will want to research those applications, including talking with your peers in Exchange Server user groups and various web forums.

Regardless of the management tools you choose to implement, a solution is only as good as the information you can draw from the data. Bad or incomplete data can lead to poor decisions about your configuration—and that leads to dissatisfied users. Monitor your systems over time, and tune them for optimum performance.

The Typical User

If you have worked with more than one organization, you have probably reached the same conclusion we have: no two Exchange Server organizations are exactly alike. Even businesses within the same industry can have dramatically different usage patterns based on slightly different business practices.

Where does this put the poor hapless person in charge of figuring out how much hardware to buy and how much capacity that hardware should have? If you are currently running an earlier version of Exchange Server, at least you have a leg up over other people.

You can use tools, such as Performance Monitor, to measure the number of messages sent and received per day and disk IOPS (Input/Output Operations Per Second).

Microsoft has done a lot of research in this area and has published some statistics on what they consider to be light, average, heavy, very heavy, and extra heavy Outlook users. They have also calculated that the average email message is 50 KB in size. Table 9.1 shows how Microsoft has defined each type of user.

TABLE 9.1:   Microsoft Outlook User Types

USER TYPE	MESSAGES SENT PER DAY	MESSAGES RECEIVED PER DAY
Light	5	20
Average	10	40
Heavy	20	80
Very heavy	30	120
Extra heavy	40	160

Just relying on emails sent and received may not give you the best estimate of the hardware capacity required. We will talk about other factors throughout the book, but here we'll just list some factors that can adversely affect performance:

- Email archiving
- Mobile device users (a BlackBerry can place a load four times higher on a server than that of a typical Outlook user)
- Antivirus scanning
- Messaging records management
- Transport rules
- Database replication

CPU Recommendations

Exchange Server 2016 runs only on Windows Server 2012 R2 and Windows Server 2012 and, therefore, only on hardware (physical or virtualized hardware) that is capable of supporting the x64 processor extensions. The primary benefit of 64-bit processing is the ability to take advantage of larger amounts of both virtual and physical memory. The processor should be at least 1.6 GHz, although you will certainly benefit from processors faster than 2 GHz as well as multicore processors. The processor must be one of the following:

◆ Intel Xeon or Intel Pentium x64 that supports the Intel 64 architecture (formerly known as EM64T)

◆ AMD Opteron 64-bit processor that supports the AMD64 platform

The Intel Itanium IA64 processor family is not supported.

For the Mailbox server role, similar to Exchange Server 2013, Microsoft recommends a server with a minimum of 2 processor cores and maximum of 24 processor cores. However, compared to Exchange Server 2013, processor requirements are increased based on the number of messages sent and received per mailbox per day, which is shown in Table 9.2.

TABLE 9.2: Processor Recommendations Based on Number of Messages Sent or Received per Mailbox per Day

MESSAGES SENT AND RECEIVED PER MAILBOX PER DAY	MCYCLES PER USER, ACTIVE DB COPY OR STAND-ALONE	MCYCLES PER USER, PASSIVE DB COPY
50	2.99	0.70
100	5.97	1.40
150	8.96	2.10
200	11.94	2.80
250	14.93	3.50
300	17.91	4.20
350	20.90	4.90
400	23.88	5.60
450	26.87	6.30
500	29.85	7.00

This may seem like a lot of processor power—and in some ways, it is—but remember that an Exchange Server 2016 server does a lot more than servers did in previous versions of Exchange Server. For example, on a mailbox server role, Exchange runs not only the database engine, web components, and message transport running, but components, such as transport rules, messaging records management, mailbox archival, and client access functions are also running.

If you have worked with Exchange Server in the past, you may also note that the CPU recommendations for the Exchange Server 2016 are similar to the Exchange Server 2013 Mailbox role and are higher than in Exchange Server 2010. If you are planning to use existing server hardware, consult your manufacturer's documentation for specific information on the processors and cores.

If you are not sure whether your existing hardware supports the x64 extensions, you can check this in a number of ways, including confirming it with the hardware vendor. If the computer is already running Windows, you can get use third-party software that will check your processor.

Notice in the CPU report information that this particular chip supports a variety of instruction sets, the most important being EM64T, Intel's 64-bit extension to the Intel 32-bit instruction set.

THE DISAPPEARANCE OF THE CLIENT ACCESS ROLE

One of the significant changes to Exchange Server 2016 is the removal of the Client Access role as a separate role. If you are still running Exchange Server 2010, you will notice that the Client Access, Hub Transport, and Unified Messaging roles are not available as separate roles anymore. The functionality of the Client Access role from Exchange Server 2013 and Client Access, Hub Transport, and Unified Messaging roles in Exchange Server 2010 have been retained, but they are now located in the Mailbox server role.

All access to mailbox content is now handled through the Client Access services running on the Mailbox server role (see the sidebar "The Disappearance of the Client Access Role"). Mobile devices, web clients, Outlook clients, POP3, and IMAP4 clients go through the client access services. One significant change to the client environment is that in Exchange Server 2010, the Outlook client connected to Exchange Server using MAPI, while Outlook Anywhere connected to the Client Access server role via RPC over HTTPS. In Exchange Server 2016, both internal and external Outlook users will use MAPI over HTTPS protocol as the default, while Outlook Anywhere is still supported.

The number of processors required on a Mailbox server mostly depends on the total number of simultaneous users, the protocol they use, and the messages sent and received per day. According to Microsoft, a dedicated Mailbox server with sufficient memory and a four-processor-core server should be able to support 2,000+ mailboxes. Microsoft estimates a factor for calculating CPU requirements is one CPU core for each 1,000 mailboxes; this guideline is based on some assumptions about the usage profiles of those 1,000 users. In this case, Microsoft assumes that 750 of those are active and heavy-usage mailboxes. Sizing your mailbox servers for 10 to 20 percent more capacity than you think you are going to need is a good practice.

A number of factors affect CPU requirements, including the usage profile of the typical user and the concurrency rate (the percentage of your users who are accessing the server at any given time). If you are planning to support 2,000 very heavy users who use Outlook 90 percent of the day, you may need more CPU capacity. Factors that affect mailbox server CPU requirements include the following:

♦ Number of simultaneous users and usage profile

♦ Email archiving processes

♦ Mobile device usage

Memory Recommendations

As mentioned previously, the advantage Exchange Server gets out of the x64 architecture is the ability to access more physical memory. Additional physical memory improves caching, reduces the disk I/O profile, and allows for the addition of more features.

Microsoft recommends a minimum of 8 GB of RAM in each Exchange Mailbox server role and a minimum of 4 GB of RAM in each Exchange Edge Transport server role. The amount of memory needed in production depends on the roles the server is supporting; for the Mailbox server role, it is recommended that it not be higher than 96 GB. Although Microsoft's minimum RAM recommendation for any server hosting the Mailbox role is 8 GB, we strongly recommend a minimum of 12 GB based on calculated requirements (12 GB should be adequate based on an 8-GB base, a message volume of 100 messages per day for 600 users, and rounded up). Once you have calculated the minimum amount of RAM that you require for the server, if you are configuring a Mailbox server, you will need to add some additional RAM for each mailbox. This amount will depend on either your user community's estimated message profile or the mailbox size. In other words, you should calculate the memory requirement based on not only the usage profile of your users but also the mailbox size; then use the larger of these two calculations. Let's start with the amount of memory required based on usage profiles. Table 9.3 shows the additional memory required based on the number of mailboxes supported. The user profiles were defined previously in Table 9.1. The general rule from Microsoft is 3 MB of RAM for every 50 messages sent or received daily.

TABLE 9.3: Additional Memory Factor for Mailbox Servers

USER PROFILE	PER-MAILBOX MEMORY RECOMMENDATION
Light	Add 1.5 MB per mailbox
Average	Add 3 MB per mailbox
Heavy	Add 6 MB per mailbox
Very heavy	Add 9 MB per mailbox
Extra heavy	Add 12 MB per mailbox

Next, let's look at the recommendations based on the mailbox size. Table 9.4 shows Microsoft's per-mailbox memory recommendations for mailboxes of different sizes.

TABLE 9.4: Memory Required Based on Mailbox Size

MAILBOX SIZE	PER-MAILBOX MEMORY RECOMMENDATION
Small (0 to 1 GB)	Add 2 MB per mailbox
Medium (1 to 3 GB)	Add 4 MB per mailbox

TABLE 9.4:   Memory Required Based on Mailbox Size   *(CONTINUED)*

MAILBOX SIZE	PER-MAILBOX MEMORY RECOMMENDATION
Large (3 to 5 GB)	Add 6 MB per mailbox
Very large (5 to 10 GB)	Add 8 MB per mailbox
Extra large (10 GB+)	Add 10 MB per mailbox

So, for example, a server handling a Mailbox server role should have 8 GB of memory plus the additional RAM per mailbox shown in Table 9.3 or the memory shown in Table 9.4 (whichever is larger). Let's do the calculations for a simple organization. If the Mailbox server is supporting 1,000 mailboxes and it is estimated that 500 of the users are average (1.75 GB of RAM if assuming 4 MB per mailbox) and 500 are heavy users (2.5 GB of RAM if assuming 6 MB per mailbox), the server should have about 12 GB of RAM. For good measure, we would recommend going with 16 GB of RAM so that there is additional RAM just in case it is needed.

However, when we perform an additional calculation based on mailbox size, we may arrive at a different amount of RAM. Of the 1,000 mailboxes that this server supports, 400 of these users have an average mailbox size that is in excess of 10 GB, whereas the remainder of the mailboxes average around 6 GB. This will require 4 GB of RAM (400 times 10 MB per mailbox) for the extra-large mailboxes and about 5 GB of RAM (600 times 8 MB per mailbox) for the very large mailboxes. That is a total of about 12 GB of RAM.

So in this case, going with at least 12 GB to 16 GB of RAM for mailbox caching would definitely be a good design decision. Remember that these RAM estimates are just that—estimates. Additional factors (message hygiene software, continuous replication, email archiving, and so on) may require more or less RAM (usually more) than the calculations and recommendations here. For example, antivirus and antispam software on Mailbox servers can place a significant burden on RAM. Microsoft has released the Exchange Server Role Requirements Calculator, which supports both Exchange Server 2016 and Exchange Server 2013 and can be useful when estimating RAM requirements; see this article on the Exchange Team Blog for more information:

```
http://blogs.technet.com/b/exchange/archive/2015/10/15/exchange-server-role-
requirements-calculator-update.aspx
```

Network Requirements

With earlier versions of Exchange Server, recommending network connectivity speeds was often a gray area because of the variety of networking hardware that most organizations were using. Essentially, not everyone had a Gigabit Ethernet backbone for their servers. Today, however, Gigabit Ethernet is present in most datacenters at least for the datacenter backbone.

So, a recommendation is pretty simple. All Exchange Server 2016 servers should be on a Gigabit Ethernet backbone. Will Exchange Server 2016 work on a 100 Mbps network? Sure, it will, but you will get the best results in even a medium-sized network if you are using Gigabit Ethernet.

All of the "client-to-server" communication traffic now takes place between the client (usually Outlook) and the Mailbox server.

If you are planning to implement database availability groups (DAGs) between two or more Exchange Server 2016 Mailbox servers, Microsoft recommends that each server should have only one network adapter installed. The network adapter will be used for both production LAN communications and for replication of the Information Stores. Even in large environments with multiple servers and dozens of databases in a DAG, consider using one network adapter per server that will be used for both replication and for client and server network connections.

If you are planning to put DAG members on a separate physical network to facilitate site resiliency, the maximum network latency between members should not exceed 500 milliseconds (ms), and there must be sufficient bandwidth to keep up with the volume of replication traffic.

Disk Requirements

When you're calculating disk requirements for some applications, deciding that a single 500 GB hard disk will solve your storage needs is easy. You might be tempted to think the same thing about Exchange Server.

With earlier versions of Exchange Server, getting the disk requirements sized correctly could be a bit tricky. That is not to say that doing so cannot still be tricky with Exchange Server 2016. This is because sizing a disk is not just a matter of figuring out how much storage capacity you need. Physical storage requirements are a big part of the sizing, of course, because if you don't get large enough disks to support your users, you will be going back to the boss for more money to buy more disks.

However, asking the boss to buy more physical disk drives because the users' mailboxes are full is at least asking for something tangible. The other side of the sizing requirement is ensuring that the disk IOPS will keep up with the database engine. The more users using Exchange Server, the greater the disk I/O capacity required by the disk subsystem will be. Try explaining to your boss that the disks have plenty of storage available but they can't keep up with the database load.

The disk subsystem that you choose has to be able to support not only the *amount* of storage required but also the IOPS *load* that the users will place on the disk subsystem. Therefore, understanding the IOPS profile as well as the amount of storage required is important. Helpfully, Microsoft has improved the IOPS profile with every iteration of Exchange Server, and Exchange Server 2016 is no exception, most notably improving the Input/Output Operations Per Second (IOPS) performance when replicating Information Store data between DAG nodes.

Microsoft's recommended system requirements for the disk include:

- The drive on which you install Exchange should be at least 30 GB.

- An additional 500 MB of disk space should be available for each Unified Messaging (UM) language pack you plan to install.

- The system drive should have 200 MB of available disk space.

- The hard disk that stores the message queue database should have at least 500 MB of free space.

- The page file size minimum and maximum must be set to physical RAM plus 10 MB, to a maximum size of 32,778 MB if you're using more than 32GB of RAM.

- Disk partitions should be formatted as NTFS file systems, which applies to the system partition, partitions that store Exchange binary files or files generated by Exchange diagnostic logging, and partitions containing database files and transaction log files.

NOTE   Partitions containing database files and transaction log files may also be formatted as ReFS with the data integrity features disabled.

Microsoft highly recommends using the Exchange Server Role Requirements Calculator to help plan the Exchange Server storage that will fit your organization requirements. The Exchange Server Role Requirements Calculator will recommend high availability strategies for your storage solution, as well as simulate different failover scenarios for planning purposes. Something else that you may find of benefit relative to Exchange Server 2013 that also applies to Exchange Server 2016 is the following web page, which addresses a number of factors associated with various storage architectures, physical disk types, and best practices:

http://technet.microsoft.com/en-us/library/ee832792%28v=exchg.150%29.aspx

Improved Caching and Reduced I/O Profiles

The IOPS profiles have changed significantly comparing to Exchange Server 2010 because of the incorporation of all message-routing functionality into the Mailbox server roles. The information in this section applies to servers that are hosting the Mailbox server role.

Hundreds of pages of material have been written on the concept of optimizing Exchange Server for maximum performance by improving IOPS performance with Exchange Server—and we certainly can't do the concept justice in just a few paragraphs—but understanding the basic IOPS profile of users is helpful. Microsoft has done a lot of research on reducing IOPS requirements based on the mailbox size and the average load that each user places on the server. In this vein, understanding the differences between Exchange Server 2010 I/O and Exchange Server 2013 and Exchange Server 2016 I/O is something you may find helpful.

One area Microsoft has continuously improved is IOPS. Since Exchange Server 2003, we've witnessed a number of changes to the structure of Exchange Server and its databases to improve performance. The most obvious improvement moving from Exchange Server 2003 to Exchange Server 2007 was the removal of the .STM database, a database for streamed Internet content. The .EDB database was modified to support that same content. Microsoft wasn't finished there. From Exchange Server 2007 and newer editions, Exchange Server is a 64-bit-only application, which increased the RAM memory that can be addressed to theoretically 2^{64} bytes.

The Exchange Server database team worked at further reducing the IOPS of Exchange Server 2010 Mailbox Server Role. One of the key factors that the database team focused on with Exchange Server 2010 was to further improve the I/O performance so that most types of affordable disk drives could be used (such as SATA, SAS, or SCSI). They did this by further optimizing the use of cache memory, increasing database page sizes, increasing I/O size, and performing sequential reads to reduce the frequency of reads and writes, changing the database schema, and optimizing how the database arranges data to be written to the disk.

The resulting improvements to the Exchange Server 2010 database engine further reduced the I/O requirements for the standard usage profiles. I/O requirements, of course, are just estimates, but they generally provide a pretty good guideline for the IOPS requirements for the disks that will host Exchange Server databases. The disks that will host the Exchange Server transaction logs will require approximately 10 to 20 percent of the IOPS requirements for their corresponding database.

There have been significant changes to the way Exchange Server 2013 and 2016 interact with Information Stores, but some numbers from Microsoft, as shown in Table 9.5, reflect the continuous improvement in I/O performance.

TABLE 9.5: User Type, Database Volume IOPS, and Messages Sent and Received per Day for Exchange Server 2016

USER TYPE	DATABASE VOLUME IOPS	MESSAGES SENT/RECEIVED PER DAY*
Light	0.017	5 sent/20 received
Average	0.034	10 sent/40 received
Heavy	0.067	20 sent/80 received
Large	0.101	30 sent/120 received

*Assumes average message size is approximately 50 KB.

It is reasonable to assume that there has been some variation in the testing methodology used to generate the data over the years. A lot of things have changed since Exchange Server 2003, but the fact is that Microsoft has worked to improve the overall performance of I/O operations as they relate to Mailbox servers. For an in-depth breakdown on performance improvements to Exchange Server 2016, check out this blog entry from the Microsoft Exchange Team:

```
http://blogs.technet.com/b/exchange/archive/2015/10/15/ask-the-perf-guy-sizing-
exchange-2016-deployments.aspx
```

MAILBOX STORAGE

Exchange servers holding the Mailbox server role consume the most disk space. Exchange Server system designers often fall short in their designs by not allowing sufficient disk space for database storage, transaction logs, and extra disk space. Often the disk space is not partitioned correctly, either. Here are some important points to keep in mind when planning your disk space requirements:

◆ Transaction log files should be on a separate set of physical disks (spindles) from their corresponding Exchange Server database files if you are deploying only a single database copy. RAID 1 or RAID 1+0 arrays provide better performance for transaction logs. However, if you are implementing a DAG, you don't need to separate the database copy and the transaction log files, because recovery takes place via a replicated copy hosted on another machine rather than a backup.

◆ Allow for 7 to 10 days' worth of transaction logs to be stored for each database. The estimated amount of transaction logs will vary dramatically from one organization to another, but a good starting point is about 4 GB of transaction logs per day per 1,000 mailboxes. This is just one estimate of a specific usage profile, though, and your actual mileage may vary. Tools like the Exchange Storage Calculator can be used to help determine disk space requirements.

◆ Allow for whitespace estimates in the maximum size of each of your database files. (The *whitespace* is the empty space that is found in the database at any given time.) The size of the whitespace in the database can be approximated by the amount of mail sent and received by the users with mailboxes in that database. For example, if you have one hundred 2 GB mailboxes (a total of 200 GB) in a database where users send and receive an average of 10 MB of mail per day, the whitespace is approximately 1 GB (100 mailboxes × 10 MB per mailbox). Factor in 5 to 10 percent additional disk space for the content index databases. You will have one content index database for each production database.

◆ Allocate enough free space on the disk or spare disks so that you can always make a backup copy of your largest database and still have some free disk space. A good way to calculate this is to take 110 percent of the largest database you will support; that will also allow you to perform maintenance on the database using Eseutil if necessary.

◆ Consider additional disk space for message tracking, message transport, and client access, as well as HTTP, POP3, and IMAP4 log files.

◆ Always have recovery in mind, and make sure you have enough disk space to be able to restore a database to a recovery database.

Let's move on to an example of a server that will support 1,000 mailboxes. We are estimating that we will provide the typical user with a Prohibit Send size warning of 500 MB and a Prohibit Send And Receive limit of 600 MB. In any organization of 1,000 users, you have to take into account that 10 percent will qualify as VIPs who will be allowed more mail storage than a typical user; in this case, let's allow 100 VIP users to have a Prohibit Send And Receive limit of 2 GB.

These calculations result in 540 GB of mail storage requirements (600 MB × 900 mailboxes) for the first 900 users plus another 200 GB (2 GB × 100 mailboxes) for the VIP users. This results in a maximum amount of mail storage of 740 GB. However, this estimate does not include estimates for deleted items in a user's mailbox and deleted mailboxes, so we want to add an additional overhead factor of about 15 percent, or about 111 MB, plus an additional overhead factor of another 15 percent (another 111 MB) for database whitespace.

Therefore, at any given time for these 1,000 mailboxes, we can expect mail database storage (valid email content, deleted data, and empty database space) to consume approximately 962 GB, but because we like round numbers, we'll round that up to 1,000 GB, or 1 TB.

In this example, let's say that we have decided the maximum database size we want to be able to back up or restore is 100 GB. This means that we need to split the users' mailboxes across 10 mailbox databases.

For the transaction logs, we estimate that we will generate approximately 5 GB of transaction logs per day. We should plan for enough disk space on the transaction log disk for at least 50 GB of available disk space.

Next, because full-text indexing is enabled by default, we should allow enough disk space for the full-text index files. In this case, we will estimate that the full-text index files will consume a maximum of about 10 percent of the total size of the mail data, or approximately 100 GB. If we combine the full-text index files on the same disk drive as the database files, we will need about 1.3 TB of disk space.

Any time you are not sure how much disk space you should include, it is a good idea to plan for more rather than less. Although disk space is reasonably inexpensive, unless you have sophisticated storage systems, adding additional disk space can be time consuming and costly from the perspective of effort and downtime.

PLANNING FOR MAIL GROWTH

Growth? You may be saying to yourself, "I just gave the typical user a maximum mailbox size of 600 MB and the VIPs a maximum size of 2 GB! How can my users possibly need more mailbox space?" Predicting the amount of growth you may need in the future is a difficult task. You may not be able to foresee new organizational requirements, or you might be influenced by future laws that require specific data-retention periods.

In our experience, though, mailbox limits, regardless of how rigid we plan to be, are managed by exception and by need. In the preceding example, we calculated that we would need 1.3 TB of disk space for our 1,000 mailboxes. Would we partition or create a disk of exactly that size? Possibly. One of the facts that Microsoft has taken into consideration is the increasing size factor as hard drives as large as 8 TB are becoming available on the market at an increasingly attractive price point.

Instead of carving out exactly the amount of disk space you anticipate needing, add a "fluff factor" to your calculations. As a baseline, we recommend adding approximately 20 to 25 percent additional capacity to the anticipated amount of storage you think you will require. In this example, we might anticipate using 1.3 TB of disk space if we added 25 percent to our expected requirements. Here are some factors that you may want to consider when deciding how much growth you should expect for your mailbox servers:

◆ Average annual growth in the number of employees

◆ Acquisitions, mergers, or consolidations that are planned for the foreseeable future

◆ Addition of new mail-enabled applications, such as Unified Messaging features or electronic forms routing

◆ Government regulations that require some types of corporate records (including email) to be retained for a number of years

Conversely, potential events in your future could reduce the amount of mailbox storage you require. Many organizations are now including message archival and long-term retention systems in their messaging systems. These systems archive older content from a user's mailbox and move it to some type of external storage such as disk, storage area network, network-attached storage, optical, or tape storage.

EMAIL ARCHIVING AND MAIL STORAGE

Email has emerged as the predominant form of business communications. Sales, marketing, ordering, human resources, legal, financial, and all other types of information are now disseminated via email.

Myriad companies provide archiving solutions for email systems. Some of these companies provide in-house solutions, whereas some are hosted solutions. There are just about as many reasons to implement an email archive system as there are archive vendors. The following are some of the reasons to implement email archiving:

◆ Reduces the size of mailbox databases and mailboxes (smaller databases and smaller mailboxes improve disaster-recovery response times and improve performance)

◆ Provides long-term retention of email data

◆ Provides users with a searchable index of their historical email data

◆ Allows for eDiscovery of email (message content, attachments, as well as email metadata) that often must be indexed for legal proceedings

◆ Eliminates the use of Outlook personal folder (PST) files

Third-party archive systems are great for organizations that must retain much of the information in their mailboxes but want to move it to external storage. However, depending on the system, you don't want to archive everything older than five days, for example, because that may prevent the user from accessing it via Outlook on the web or mobile devices. Further, once the content is archived and no longer residing in the user's mailbox, it will no longer be accessible from a user's desktop search engine, such as the the Windows Desktop search engine. Therefore, keeping a certain amount of content in the user's mailbox always makes sense.

Exchange Server 2016 has retained the email archive system created in Exchange Server 2010. Microsoft's approach is to establish an extra archive mailbox for each user who requires archiving. The email archive mailbox can reside on the same mailbox database as the user's mailbox or a different mailbox database hosted on a different server. This approach does serve the goal of reducing the size of the user's primary mailbox, but it does not reduce the size of the aggregate database volume. Furthermore, it allows users who may have been using PST files as an archival storage mechanism to return that email back into an Exchange Server archive mailbox for the purposes of eDiscovery and long-term archival.

If you are planning to use the Exchange Server 2016 mailbox archive feature, you will need to take this into account and plan for additional storage as needed.

Software Requirements

After you have chosen the right hardware to support Exchange Server 2016, you need to make sure that the software is ready. This includes getting the right version and edition of the operating system, software updates, and any prerequisite Windows roles or functions.

Operating System Requirements

The operating system requirements for Exchange Server 2016 are pretty cut and dried. Windows Server 2102 R2 and Windows Server 2012 are the only operating systems supported in the following configurations:

◆ Windows Server 2012 R2 Standard Edition

◆ Windows Server 2012 R2 Datacenter Edition

◆ Windows Server 2012 Standard Edition

◆ Windows Server 2012 Datacenter Edition

Additionally, you may be a fan of the Server Core installation, but Exchange Server 2016 does not run on Server Core.

If you are unsure as to whether you have the correct Service Pack installed on your system, you can acquire this information by opening `Control Panel\Programs\Programs and Features\ Installed Updates`. There you will see a comprehensive list of all Service Packs, Cumulative Rollups, and Hot Fixes that have been applied to your system.

Real World Scenario

NAME THE SERVER QUICKLY!

Once you have installed Windows Server 2012 R2 or Windows Server 2012, make sure that the server is assigned the correct name before you proceed. During installation, the Windows Server setup assigns a random name to the server. More than likely, this name will not be the one you want to use. Once Exchange Server 2016 is installed, you cannot change this name without uninstalling Exchange. Therefore, once you install Windows Server operating system on a server, be sure you change the server name in Server Manager console in Windows Server 2012 R2 or Windows Server 2012.

WINDOWS SERVER 2012 R2 AND WINDOWS SERVER 2012 ROLES AND FEATURES

You must add a number of roles and features to the default installation of Windows Server 2012 R2 and Windows Server 2012 to support the functionality of Exchange Server 2016. The roles and features are required for all versions of the host operating system.

Mailbox Server Role

You will want to use PowerShell once again to install the prerequisite features on Windows Server 2012 R2 and Windows Server 2012. There are some differences between the Mailbox server role and the Edge Transport server role.

1. Open a PowerShell session with the appropriate administrative rights to modify the installation.

2. Run the `Install-WindowsFeature` cmdlet to be able to prepare Active the directory from the Exchange Server computer:

```
Install-WindowsFeature RSAT
```

3. After that command is complete, you will need to run the following cmdlet to install the Windows Server prerequisites for the Exchange Server 2016 Mailbox server role:

```
Install-WindowsFeature AS-HTTP-Activation, Desktop-Experience, NET-
Framework-45-Features, RPC-over-HTTP-proxy, RSAT-Clustering, RSAT-
Clustering-CmdInterface, RSAT-Clustering-Mgmt, RSAT-Clustering-
PowerShell, Web-Mgmt-Console, WAS-Process-Model, Web-Asp-Net45, Web-
Basic-Auth, Web-Client-Auth, Web-Digest-Auth, Web-Dir-Browsing, Web-Dyn-
Compression, Web-Http-Errors, Web-Http-Logging, Web-Http-Redirect, Web-
Http-Tracing, Web-ISAPI-Ext, Web-ISAPI-Filter, Web-Lgcy-Mgmt-Console,
Web-Metabase, Web-Mgmt-Console, Web-Mgmt-Service, Web-Net-Ext45, Web-
Request-Monitor, Web-Server, Web-Stat-Compression, Web-Static-Content,
Web-Windows-Auth, Web-WMI, Windows-Identity-Foundation
```

4. The next step is to download from Microsoft Download Center and install the following supplemental components in the order listed:

    a. .Net Framework 4.5.2.

```
https://www.microsoft.com/en-us/download/details.aspx?id=42642
```

    b. Microsoft Unified Communications Managed API 4.0, Core Runtime 64-bit.

```
http://www.microsoft.com/en-us/download/details.aspx?id=34992
```

Edge Transport Server Role

The required components and packages are different when you install the Edge Transport server role by itself compared to a Mailbox server role system. To install the prerequisite features to support an Edge Transport server, take the following steps:

1. Open a PowerShell session with the appropriate administrative rights to modify the installation.

2. Run the `Install-WindowsFeature` cmdlet to install Active Directory Lightweight Directory Services (ADLDS)

```
Install-WindowsFeature ADLDS
```

3. The next step is to download from Microsoft Download Center and install the .Net Framework 4.5.2 supplemental component:

```
https://www.microsoft.com/en-us/download/details.aspx?id=42642
```

Windows 10 and Windows 8.1 Management Consoles

You can create a management console for your Exchange Server 2016 deployment on a domain-joined Windows 10 (64-bit) system with no additional configuration. The default installation is supported. You can also use Windows PowerShell to remotely connect to and manage Exchange Server with Exchange Management Shell, without installing the Exchange Management tools.

You can also configure a domain-joined Windows 8.1 (64-bit only) to function as a management console for your Exchange Server 2016 deployment, but you have to download and install .NET Framework 4.5.2 from the following URL:

```
https://www.microsoft.com/en-us/download/details.aspx?id=42642
```

Additional Requirements

In addition to making sure that the hardware and server software can support Exchange Server 2016, you need to consider a few infrastructure requirements. These include making sure that your Active Directory infrastructure can support Exchange Server 2016 and that you have the necessary permissions to prepare the forest and domain.

Active Directory Requirements

The Active Directory domain controller requirements to install Exchange Server 2016 into your forest can be a bit confusing. We've created a summary of the required settings for you. Here are some AD settings you must use to ensure that your Active Directory infrastructure will properly support Exchange Server 2016:

◆ All domain controllers in each Active Directory site where you plan to deploy Exchange Server 2016 must be running Windows Server 2008 at a minimum.

◆ The Active Directory forest must be in Windows Server 2008 forest functional level. Each Active Directory site in which you will install Exchange Server 2016 servers should contain at least two global catalog servers to ensure local global catalog access and fault tolerance.

◆ For organizations using domain controllers running x64 Windows and having enough RAM installed for the entire NTDS.DIT to be loaded into memory, each Active Directory site that contains Exchange servers should have one domain controller processor core for each of the eight Exchange Server Mailbox server processor cores.

◆ Always take into account that domain controllers may not be dedicated to just Exchange Server. They may be handling authentication for users logging into the domain and for other applications.

◆ Exchange Server 2016 doesn't use read-only domain controllers and global catalog servers, so do not include them when planning your domain controller.

Installation and Preparation Permissions

It might seem that the easiest possible way to install Exchange Server 2016 is to log on to a Windows Server 2012 R2 or Windows Server 2012 computer as a member of Domain Admins, Schema Admins, and Enterprise Admins. Indeed, using a user account that is a member of all three of those groups will give you all the rights you need.

In some larger organizations, though, getting a user account that is a member of all three of these groups is impossible. In some cases, the Exchange Server administrator may have to make a request from the Active Directory forest owner to perform some of the preparation tasks on behalf of the Exchange Server team. For this reason, it is important to know the permissions that are required to perform the different setup tasks, as shown in Table 9.6.

TABLE 9.6:   Task Permissions

TASK	GROUP MEMBERSHIP
Setup /PrepareSchema or setup /ps	Schema Admins and Enterprise Admins
Setup /PrepareAD or setup /p	Enterprise Admins
Setup /PrepareDomain or setup /pd	Domain Admins
Install Exchange Server 2016	Administrators group on the Windows server and Exchange Organization Management

Coexisting with Previous Versions of Exchange Server

Exchange Server is fairly widely deployed in most organizations, so it is likely that you will be transitioning or migrating your existing Exchange Server organization over to Exchange Server 2016. For some period of time (hopefully, short), your Exchange Server 2016 servers will be inter-operating with either Exchange Server 2013 and/or Exchange Server 2010 servers. For this rea-son, you must know the factors necessary to ensure successful coexistence.

The recommended order for installing Exchange Server 2016 servers and transitioning mes-saging services over to those new servers is as follows:

1. Install Mailbox servers and, depending on the clients you need to support, you will want to configure MAPI over HTTP, Outlook Anywhere, Outlook on the web, Exchange Active Sync, POP3, and IMAP4 clients on the new Mailbox servers.

2. Begin to transition mailboxes and public folders from the legacy servers to the new servers.

3. If your organization will use Edge Transport servers, install and configure Edge Transport servers.

COEXISTENCE WITH EXCHANGE SERVER 2013

If you are currently using Exchange Server 2013, prior to installing the first Exchange Server 2016 server, make sure that you meet the following prerequisites:

◆ All Exchange Server 2013 servers within the Active Directory where you are planning to introduce Exchange Server 2016 must be running a minimum of Exchange Server 2013 CU 11.

◆ The Active Directory forest must be at the Windows Server 2008 forest functional level.

◆ Each Active Directory site must have at least one global catalog server running Windows Server 2008 or later.

COEXISTENCE WITH EXCHANGE SERVER 2010

If you are currently using Exchange Server 2010, prior to installing the first Exchange Server 2016 server, make sure that you meet the following prerequisite: All Exchange Server 2010 servers, including the Edge Transport server, must be at Exchange Server 2010 Service Pack 3 RU 11.

The Bottom Line

Use the right hardware for your organization.   There are several tools provided online to help you properly size the amount of RAM, as well as the hard disk configuration, for your deployment. One other resource that you should not overlook is your hardware vendor. Very often vendors have created custom tools to help you properly size your environment relative to your organizational needs.

If you want to get a fair idea as to what you should plan, use the tables in this chapter, based on both mailbox size and message volume. Remember, you should try both sizing methods and select the option that projects the most RAM and the largest storage volume. You can never have enough RAM or storage space.

Ensure that the processor core number of Mailbox servers is adequate to keep up with the load clients will place on these servers.

Start with the Exchange Server 2016 Server Role Requirements Calculator and try different combinations of options. It can serve as a solid guideline for deployments, from small- to medium-size companies, as well as large multinational organizations.

If you are missing a component, you will receive feedback from Exchange Server 2016 when you attempt to install the application. The components are going to differ from server operating system to server operating system and from role combination to role combination.

If you find it necessary to integrate Exchange Server 2016 with either Exchange Server 2010 or Exchange Server 2013, you will want to make sure that you have installed the latest Service Packs and updates for the host operating systems and the server applications.

> **Master It**   What is the primary tool you can use to ascertain the appropriate configuration of an Exchange Server 2016 deployment based on the number of users and message volume?

Configure Windows Server 2012 R2 and Windows Server 2012 to support Exchange Server 2016.   Make sure you have all of the prerequisite features and modules. Using PowerShell is the most efficient method for quickly and completely installing all of the necessary components.

> **Master It**   You need to verify that all of prerequisites are met. How can you accomplish this from PowerShell?

Confirm that Active Directory is ready.   Make sure that you have set your Active Directory domain and forest functional levels to Windows Server 2008 at a minimum. You should not encounter any problems if you set your domain and forest functional levels to Windows Server 2012 or Windows Server 2012 R2.

Avoid frustration during installation or potential problems in the future that may result from domain controllers or global catalog servers running older versions of the software.

> **Master It**   You must verify that your Active Directory meets the minimum requirements to support Exchange Server 2016. What should you check?

Verify that previous versions of Exchange Server can interoperate with Exchange Server 2016.   Exchange Server 2016 will interoperate only with specific previous versions of Exchange Server.

> **Master It**   You must verify that the existing legacy Exchange servers in your organization are running the minimum versions of Exchange Server required to interoperate with Exchange Server 2016. What should you check?

Chapter 10

Installing Exchange Server 2016

People who install Exchange Server 2016 fall into two camps. The first camp—and most people probably fall into this one—contains people who simply run the Setup program with no command-line options and choose the default settings. The second camp consists of those who want to make custom configurations to the default settings at the time of installation and who may need the command-line options to successfully install those servers.

Regardless of which camp you fall into, getting the prerequisites out of the way first will ensure a smooth installation. Further, knowing your setup options will help to make sure you get everything right the first time.

IN THIS CHAPTER, YOU WILL LEARN TO:

◆ Implement important steps before installing Exchange Server 2016

◆ Prepare the Active Directory forest for Exchange Server 2016 without actually installing Exchange Server

◆ Employ the graphical user interface to install Exchange Server 2016

◆ Determine the command-line options available when installing Exchange

Before You Begin

Before you start installing Exchange Server, you need to have a plan. There are considerations for what level of high availability you need: disk throughput analysis, memory requirements planning, and client namespace planning. All of these topics are covered in later chapters on configuring mailbox databases and client access services. This chapter focuses on the mechanics of installation.

When you run the Exchange Server 2016 Setup program, it checks a number of things to ensure that not only Windows Server but also Active Directory and your specific permissions all meet the necessary prerequisites. Some missing prerequisites are easy to resolve, whereas others may take hours or even days.

You don't want these missing pieces and prerequisites to slow you down. If you have not already read Chapter 9, "Exchange Server 2016 Requirements," you should do so. Here we'll review only the prerequisites and best practices:

◆ If you have existing Exchange servers in your environment, run the Office 365 Best Practices Analyzer (ExBPA) for Exchange Server. Make sure you correct any serious problems the ExBPA finds.

◆ The Active Directory forest should be at least Windows Server 2008 Forest Functional mode.

◆ The Active Directory Schema Master role must be on a Windows Server 2008 domain controller or later.

◆ Every Exchange 2010 server in the organization, including Edge Transport servers, must be running at least Exchange Server 2010 SP3 Update Rollup 11 in order for you to install the first Exchange 2016 server into the organization.

◆ All existing Exchange 2013 servers, including Edge Transport servers, must be running at least Cumulative Update 10 for Exchange 2013.

◆ All Active Directory sites in which you plan to install Exchange 2016 servers should have at least one global catalog server, but preferably at least two for redundancy.

◆ Mailbox servers must have at least 8 GB of RAM and 30 GB of hard disk space free. However, ensure that you have performed the proper disk space and memory requirement calculations and that you are providing the right amount of disk space and physical memory. Microsoft provides the Exchange Server Role Requirements Calculator for this purpose. This calculator identifies the correct server specifications for your scenario. The minimum specifications are seldom sufficient for adequate performance.

◆ Windows Server 2012 or Windows Server 2012 R2 must be the operating system used on any server that will run Exchange Server 2016.

◆ If you have *storage area networks* (SANs), get your device drivers configured and your storage and *logical units* (LUNs) connected ahead of time. Don't mix Exchange troubleshooting with SAN troubleshooting.

◆ Install the required Windows Server roles and features.

◆ Confirm that you have the Exchange installation files (including any additional language packs above and beyond English) that you require. We recommend that you copy them onto a network share so that they are easily accessible.

Preparing for Exchange 2016

In some large organizations, you may find it necessary to prepare your Active Directory prior to installing Exchange Server 2016. You may need to do this for a number of reasons. Remember that the various steps to prepare the forest require membership in the Schema Admins and Enterprise Admins groups as well as Domain Admins membership in each of the forests' domains.

In a small- or medium-size business, you may be where the proverbial buck stops. You may have a user account that has all of these permissions, and you can run everything easily by yourself. In that case, simply log on as a user with the necessary permissions and run Setup.

However, large organizations are a bit different. Here are a few points you should consider:

◆ Large organizations may have configuration control and change management in place. Those are best practices. You may need to document the steps you will take, identify risks and rollback plans, request permission to proceed, and schedule the forest preparation.

◆ Large Active Directory implementations may have many Active Directory sites and domain controllers. Organizations that are distributed across large geographic areas may have replication delays on their domain controllers of anywhere from 15 minutes to seven days. Replication of schema and domain changes should be completed prior to proceeding with Exchange Server installations.

◆ Permissions to update the schema, configuration partition, and child domains are sometimes spread across a number of different individuals or departments. You may need to have another administrator log in for you to run various preparation steps.

If you have to prepare the Active Directory forest, you'll need to take a few steps. The number of steps will vary depending on the following factors:

◆ Whether you have a previous version of Exchange Server running

◆ The number of domains in your forest

◆ The permissions within the forest root domain and the child domains

---

IMPORTANT STEPS PRIOR TO PREPARING ANY DOMAIN

Before running any of the Active Directory preparation steps, make sure the machine from which you are running the setup.exe program is in the same Active Directory site as the Schema Master and has good connectivity to the Schema Master. It is also preferable to have a domain controller from each domain within the forest in the same site.

Existing Exchange Organizations

Exchange 2016 supports coexistence with only Exchange 2010 or later. If you have Exchange 2003 or Exchange 2007 in your organization, you must upgrade to Exchange 2010 or 2013 before introducing Exchange 2016 or else install Exchange 2016 into a new forest.

If you have Exchange 2010 or 2013 servers in your organization, you must prepare each server so that Exchange Server 2016 can properly communicate with it. To do this, install Exchange 2010 SP3 Update Rollup 11 or later on every Exchange 2010 server in the forest, and install Exchange 2013 Cumulative Update 10 or later on every Exchange 2013 server in the forest, including Edge Transport servers. If you have more than one site, the preferred sequence is to upgrade any Internet-facing sites first and then upgrade the internal sites. The first Internet-facing site that you should upgrade, if there are multiples, is the one where Autodiscover requests from the Internet are received. More information on upgrading from previous versions of Exchange can be found in Chapter 11, "Upgrades and Migrations to Exchange Server 2016 or Office 365."

Preparing the Schema

Next is the step that usually scares Active Directory administrators the most: extending the Active Directory schema. Essentially, the schema is the set of rules that define the structure (the objects and the attributes of those objects) for Active Directory. This operation requires the user account running this operation to have both Enterprise Admins and Schema Admins group memberships.

This scares Active Directory administrators for a couple of reasons. First, schema changes cannot be undone—ever. Second, once the schema changes are made, they replicate to every domain controller in the entire forest.

Even though many administrators get nervous about schema extensions, it is very rare for there to be problems. Conflicts only occur if your organization has made custom schema extensions that happen to be the same attributes as those in Exchange Server. Most organizations never make custom schema extensions. The most common problem is a schema extension not completing. If the schema extension doesn't complete, you just do it again. There is no corruption from a partially completed schema extension.

Naturally, schema changes are not made to an Active Directory forest very often. When schema changes are performed, often the Active Directory administrators want to know exactly what is being changed. This is a bit difficult to document for Exchange because of the sheer number of changes. An Active Directory that has never been prepped for Exchange will have more than 3,000 changes made to the schema, including new classes (object types), new attributes, new attributes being flagged for the global catalog replication, and existing attributes being flagged to replicate to the global catalog. If you want to point your Active Directory administrators to a specific list of changes, this URL is helpful:

> http://technet.microsoft.com/en-us/library/bb738144.aspx

If you, or your Active Directory administrators, are curious about what is being changed, take a look at the LDF files in the \Setup\Data folder within the Exchange 2016 setup files. For the most part, you probably don't have to worry about this unless you have done something nonstandard with your Active Directory, such as defining your own classes or attributes without giving them unique names and unique object identifiers.

To extend the schema effectively, the server from which you are running the schema preparation must be in the same Active Directory site as the Schema Master domain controller. You can locate the Schema Master by using the Schema Management console; the console is not available by default, so you first must register it. At the command prompt, type regsvr32.exe schmmgmt.dll; you will see a message indicating the schmmgmt.dll registration succeeded.

Then you can run the Microsoft Management Console program (mmc.exe) and add the Active Directory Schema snap-in. This snap-in will not appear unless the schmmgmt.dll registered properly. Once you have the Active Directory Schema console open, right-click Active Directory Schema and choose Operations Master. The Change Schema Master dialog (Figure 10.1) will show you which server currently holds the Schema Master role.

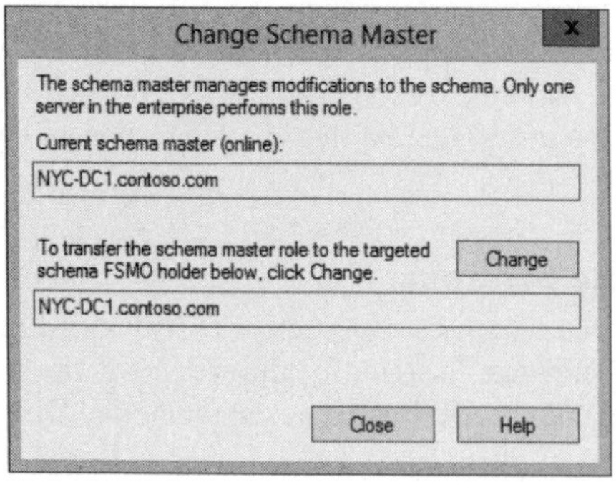

FIGURE 10.1
Determining which domain controller holds the Schema Master role

Change Schema Master

The schema master manages modifications to the schema. Only one server in the enterprise performs this role.

Current schema master (online):

NYC-DC1.contoso.com

To transfer the schema master role to the targeted schema FSMO holder below, click Change.

NYC-DC1.contoso.com

Change

Close   Help

An Easier Way to Determine the Schema Master

The preceding steps allow you to both determine which domain controller currently holds the Schema Master *flexible single master operations* (FSMO) role and relocate the Schema Master role to another domain controller. However, if you only want to find out which domain controller holds the Schema Master role without having to register the schmmgmt.dll file, you can simply run NetDOM /query FSMO. You can also find the Schema Master in Windows PowerShell by running Get-ADForest | Format-List *master.

To extend the schema, run the following command from within the Exchange 2016 Setup folder:

```
Setup.exe /PrepareSchema /IAcceptExchangeServerLicenseTerms
```

Note that this can take between 15 and 30 minutes depending on the speed of the computer on which you are running Setup, the speed of the Schema Master domain controller, and the network connection between the computers.

Important Aspects of Setup in Exchange 2016

Two aspects of Exchange 2016 Setup and Exchange 2013 Setup that are different from Exchange Server 2010 and earlier editions are important for administrators to be aware of. Both of them involve running Setup commands from the command line. First, Setup.com has been deprecated. There is now only one Setup program, which is setup.exe.

Second, whenever running Setup from the command line, you must specify that you agree to the Exchange Server licensing terms by including the /IAcceptExchangeServerLicenseTerms switch.

You will see setup.exe and /IAcceptExchangeServerLicenseTerms included repeatedly throughout this chapter—whenever command-line operations are referenced.

Preparing the Active Directory Forest

The next step is to prepare the Active Directory forest to support an Exchange organization. Although this process does not make as many changes to the forest, it does make quite a few more noticeable changes, such as creating the various Exchange configuration containers and creating Exchange security groups. Figure 10.2 shows an example of the configuration containers that are created.

Here are some of the tasks the Active Directory preparation process includes:

- Defining the Exchange organization name if it does not exist already in the Microsoft Exchange container under the Services container of the Active Directory configuration partition

- Creating configuration objects and containers under the Exchange organization container (see Figure 10.2)

FIGURE 10.2
Exchange configuration containers that are found in the Active Directory configuration partition

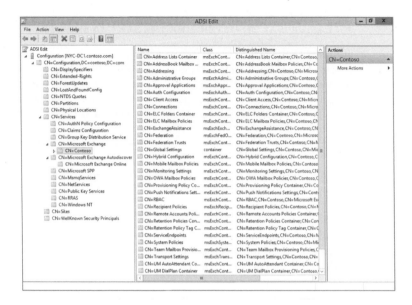

◆ Creating the Microsoft Exchange Security Groups organizational unit in the forest root domain and then creating the Exchange universal security groups:

   ◆ Compliance Management

   ◆ Delegated Setup

   ◆ Discovery Management

   ◆ Exchange Servers

   ◆ Exchange Trusted Subsystem

   ◆ Exchange Windows Permissions

   ◆ ExchangeLegacyInterop

   ◆ Help Desk

   ◆ Hygiene Management

   ◆ Organization Management

   ◆ Public Folder Management

   ◆ Recipient Management

   ◆ Records Management

   ◆ Server Management

   ◆ UM Management

   ◆ View-only Organization Management

◆ Importing Exchange-specific extended Active Directory rights and assigning the necessary permissions in Active Directory

◆ Creating the Microsoft Exchange System Objects container in the forest root domain

◆ Preparing the forest root domain for Exchange Server 2016

To run the forest preparation, you must be logged on as a member of the Enterprise Admins group. Further, you should run the forest-preparation process from a server that is in the same Active Directory site and domain that holds the Schema Master FSMO role.

You must use the Setup /PrepareAD option to prepare the Active Directory. You have two options when running /PrepareAD; the option you choose will depend on whether you have an existing Exchange organization. For example, to prepare a forest that has never supported any version of Exchange Server and to use the organization name Contoso, you would run the following command from the Exchange 2016 Setup folder:

```
Setup /PrepareAD /OrganizationName:Contoso /IAcceptExchangeServerLicenseTerms
```

CHOOSING AN EXCHANGE ORGANIZATION NAME

In early versions of Exchange Server, choosing the right organization name was often a source of great anxiety. With Exchange 5.5 and earlier, when you built an Exchange site, if you did not pick the right organization name, you could not replicate that site's global address list to the rest of the organization.

Even with Exchange 2000/2003, the organization name was visible at the top of the global address list and within the Exchange System Manager administrative console. Once the organization name is set, it cannot be changed. Fears of acquisitions, mergers, and company name changes still drive people to be concerned about this name.

Although we still recommend naming your organization something descriptive, the actual name is not as important because in Exchange 2016 the organization name is not going to be seen by the end users and is rarely (if ever) seen by the administrators. You can always set the organization name to something generic like ExchangeOrganization if you want something that would not be affected by reorganization.

When you pick an organization name, use a name that is 64 characters or less and uses only valid Active Directory characters for a container name. We recommend you stick to the basics:

◆ A–Z

◆ a–z

◆ 0–9

◆ Spaces and hyphens

However, if the forest already supports a previous version of Exchange Server, the /OrganizationName option is not necessary. You can simply run this command:

```
Setup /PrepareAD /IAcceptExchangeServerLicenseTerms
```

When the /PrepareAD process runs, it will check to see if the /PrepareSchema step needs to be run. If so, Setup will check to see if you have the necessary permissions and then run it if so. However, if running /PrepareSchema is necessary and you do not have the required permissions, you will see an error and Setup will fail.

Preparing Additional Domains

If you have only a single domain in your Active Directory forest, the Setup option /PrepareAD will prepare that domain and you will be ready to proceed with your first Exchange Server installation.

However, if you have additional domains in your Active Directory forest and they contain mail-enabled recipients or Exchange servers, you need to prepare these additional domains. To do so, use the /PrepareDomain or /PrepareAllDomains Setup option. This process includes the following:

◆ Assigning to the domain container various permissions to the Authenticated Users and Exchange universal security groups that are necessary for viewing recipient information and performing recipient-management tasks.

◆ Creating a Microsoft Exchange System Objects container in the root of the domain; this container holds mail-enabled recipient information for organization objects such as Exchange databases.

To prepare a single domain, you must be logged on as a member of that domain's Domain Admins group, and there should be a domain controller for that domain in the same site as the server from which you are running Setup. The domain controller should be running a minimum of Windows Server 2008. To prepare a domain called contoso.com, type this command:

```
Setup /PrepareDomain:contoso.com /IAcceptExchangeServerLicenseTerms
```

If you have a user account that is a member of the Enterprise Admins group, you can run this command and prepare all domains in the entire forest:

```
Setup /PrepareAllDomains /IAcceptExchangeServerLicenseTerms
```

Verifying Successful Preparation

Generally speaking, if the preparation steps for Exchange Server 2016 complete without generating an error, then preparation was successful. However, you can use ADSI Edit to verify that the necessary changes have been completed for the schema and domain.

◆ The rangeUpper property of the ms-Exch-Schema-Verision-Pt attribute in the schema defines the schema version for Exchange Server. This value is updated with every Exchange cumulative update. Verify that the version matches the cumulative update you are installing.

◆ The objectVersion property of the container for your Exchange organization in the Configuration partition of Active Directory is updated for some cumulative updates. The full path for the organization object is CN=Organization,CN=Microsoft Exchange, CN=Services,CN=Configuration,DC=Domain.

◆ The objectVersion property of the Microsoft Exchange System Objects in the forest root domain is also updated by many cumulative updates.

Microsoft provides a list of values for these properties that correspond with Exchange Server 2016 cumulative updates at https://technet.microsoft.com/en-us/library/bb125224(v=exchg.160).aspx#ADversions.

Graphical User Interface Setup

The simplest way to install Exchange Server 2016 is to use *the graphical user interface* (GUI). The GUI will be sufficient for most Exchange Server installations. We recommend first copying the Exchange Server 2016 installation files to the local hard disk or using a locally attached DVD from which to run the Exchange installation. Copying the Exchange binaries to the local hard disk will speed up the installation time.

As a best practice, you should download the latest cumulative update for Exchange 2016 and perform the installation from those files. Cumulative updates contain all of the files necessary to install Exchange 2016. This ensures that you have the latest files for setup and avoids the need to perform an update after installation. The publicly available cumulative updates can be used with volume licensing.

From the Exchange Server installation folder, run Setup.exe to see the initial setup screen, which will ask you if you want to check for updates. If you say yes, Setup will check the Microsoft website to see if a more recent Cumulative Update is available.

After the Check for Updates page, Setup will copy files, prepare resources, and then display the Microsoft Exchange Server 2016 Setup Wizard's introduction page. Click Next to proceed. On the next page, you will see the License Agreement screen. Select the I Accept The Terms In The License Agreement radio button and then click Next.

The fourth page of the Setup Wizard is titled Recommended Settings. Here you can specify whether you want to enable error reporting and participate in the Customer Experience Improvement Program (CEIP).

Enabling *error reporting* will allow Exchange to check online for solutions to errors and send reports of problems automatically to Microsoft. The server will send information back to Microsoft via HTTPS; this information may prove valuable for Microsoft in identifying errors in their software. Passing along this information also provides you (the customer) with good value because it means that Microsoft can more quickly identify bugs and software issues. The report sent back to Microsoft usually does not contain any information specific to your organization or to your server, but some organizations' Information Security departments will want you to block this anyway. If you are concerned about this, select Don't Use Recommended Settings. You can read more about the Microsoft Online Crash Analysis program, as well as Microsoft's privacy statement and what information might be collected, at http://oca.microsoft.com/en/dcp20.asp.

If you participate in the *Microsoft Customer Experience Improvement Program*, the server will periodically upload usage and configuration data that helps Microsoft when designing future versions of Exchange Server. The program is completely anonymous and will not be used to gather information about your organization. We recommend participating in the program, but this is a decision that each person installing Exchange must make. For more information on the CEIP, visit:

www.microsoft.com/products/ceip/en-us/default.mspx

Selecting Use Recommended Settings will enable both error reporting and participation in the CEIP. Selecting Don't Use Recommended Settings will disable both error reporting and participation in the CEIP. These settings can be changed later and managed individually after the installation has completed. When you have made your choice, click Next.

The next page on the wizard is the Server Role Selection screen (Figure 10.3). Here, you specify whether you want to install the Mailbox role, Management tools, or Edge Transport role. You can select only the Management tools if you want to configure the tools on a management workstation. When you select either Mailbox role or Edge Transport role, the Management tools are automatically selected also.

On this page, there is also an option to allow Windows to automatically install Windows Server roles and features that are required to install Exchange Server. Keep in mind, this will not guarantee that all software prerequisites are installed—just the ones that are a part of the native operating system. If you do choose to use this option, it is possible that you will need to reboot the server to complete the installation of some of the Windows features before Setup can proceed with the installation of Exchange.

FIGURE 10.3
The Server Role
Selection screen

MICROSOFT EXCHANGE SERVER 2016 SETUP   ? ✕

Server Role Selection

Select the Exchange server roles you want to install on this computer:

☐ Mailbox role

☐ Management tools

☐ Edge Transport role

☐ Automatically install Windows Server roles and features that are required to install Exchange Server

▣▣ Exchange   [back]

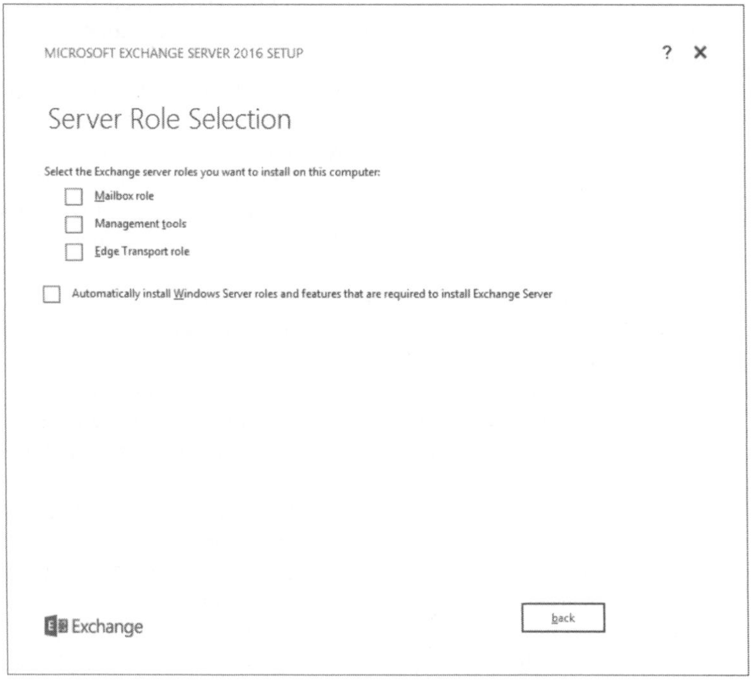

🌐 Real World Scenario

ENSURE SUCCESS BY INSTALLING COMPONENTS MANUALLY

The option Automatically Install Windows Server Roles And Features That Are Required To Install Exchange Server might require several restarts to finish the setup process. In order to save yourself some time and ensure a successful installation on the first try, a better option might be to install the required components manually beforehand using PowerShell. This is also useful when creating a standard operating system image for deploying Exchange Server 2016. Microsoft has made things easy by publishing the PowerShell syntax to install the required components on the following URL:

```
http://technet.microsoft.com/en-us/library/bb691354(v=exchg.160).aspx
```

For example, to install the operating system prerequisites for a Windows Server 2012 or Windows Server 2012 R2 computer that will have the Mailbox role installed, you would run the following command:

```
Install-WindowsFeature AS-HTTP-Activation, Desktop-Experience, NET-Framework-45-
Features, RPC-over-HTTP-proxy, RSAT-Clustering, RSAT-Clustering-CmdInterface, RSAT-
Clustering-Mgmt, RSAT-Clustering-PowerShell, Web-Mgmt-Console, WAS-Process-Model,
Web-Asp-Net45, Web-Basic-Auth, Web-Client-Auth, Web-Digest-Auth, Web-Dir-Browsing,
Web-Dyn-Compression, Web-Http-Errors, Web-Http-Logging, Web-Http-Redirect, Web-Http-
Tracing, Web-ISAPI-Ext, Web-ISAPI-Filter, Web-Lgcy-Mgmt-Console, Web-Metabase, Web-
Mgmt-Console, Web-Mgmt-Service, Web-Net-Ext45, Web-Request-Monitor, Web-Server, Web-
Stat-Compression, Web-Static-Content, Web-Windows-Auth, Web-WMI, Windows-Identity-
Foundation
```

After deploying the necessary Windows Server roles and features, you need to install .NET Framework 4.5.2 and Microsoft Unified Communications Managed API 4.0, Core Runtime 64-bit. The Microsoft web page with prerequisites provides links to these items.

The next page in the Setup Wizard is the Installation Space And Location screen, where you can choose the installation path for the Exchange program files. Once you select an installation path for the Exchange program files, Setup will provide a comparison of the amount of disk space required to the amount that is currently available. The amount required will depend on which roles you chose to install on the previous screen.

When specifying a path for the Exchange program files, remember that by default this is where all Exchange databases and log files will be stored. Most of these you can (and should) move after the installation, but you want to make sure that the volume on which the Exchange program files are stored has at least 30 GB of free space.

CONSIDER DRIVE SPACE ON C:

If you install Exchange 2016 in the default location of the C: drive, you need to ensure that there is enough space available on the C: drive. Many organizations do not allocate enough space for the C: drive and later need to either expand it or move files. This is particularly true in virtualized environments where disk size is intentionally kept small.

During an Exchange 2016 installation, only about 9 GB of data is copied to the install location. However, there are several features that use additional space:

- **Mailbox databases.** The default location for mailbox databases is the Exchange installation directory. You should store mailbox databases and their logs on dedicated drives.

- **Exchange Server diagnostic logs.** Exchange Server is constantly performing internal diagnostics and keeps logs of the results. These logs are stored in the Exchange installation directory and cannot be moved.

- **Transport queues.** The transport queues used by Exchange server for mail delivery are located in the Exchange installation directory by default. On a busy server, the database holding these queues can grow very large and never shrinks automatically. You can move mail.que and the associated log files to a different location after installation.

- **IIS log files.** By default, IIS log files are stored in C:\inetpub\logs. There is no automated mechanism to remove logs after a period of time. You should create a scheduled task to remove older log files or change the location of log files to a different drive.

- **Transport logs.** Exchange has various transport logs that you can use for troubleshooting. These include message tracking logs, protocol logs, and others. These logs can be managed with maximum age and maximum directory size settings by using the Set-TransportService cmdlet.

As a best practice, you should install Exchange Server 2016 on a drive other than the C: drive. This makes it easier to manage drive space in the long run.

If Active Directory has not already been prepared and this is the first Exchange Server, then the Exchange Organization screen is displayed. On this screen, you can enter the name of the Exchange Organization. You can also choose to enable the Active Directory split-permissions security model. This security model is typically used only by large organizations that need to split the management of Active Directory and Exchange. Next, the Malware Protection Settings screen provides the administrator with the ability to disable malware scanning on the Mailbox server role. You might want to do this if you are using a third-party product to handle message hygiene on the server. This setting can also be changed later, after Exchange is installed.

The last screen analyzes all of the selections you have made and uses that information to determine if the server has all of the software prerequisites necessary to proceed with the Exchange installation. If required Windows roles or features are missing and you opted to have Setup install them, it will do so now. If you did not opt to have Setup install them, it will notify you so that you can take the necessary action. If you find anything about the configuration that should be changed, you must resolve those matters before continuing.

One of the nice things about the Microsoft Exchange Server 2016 Setup Wizard is that if it detects a missing component or something that must be done prior to starting the Exchange setup, you can fix the issue and then click the Retry button. The Setup program will recheck the prerequisites and pick up where it left off.

Once the prerequisites have all been met and the readiness check is complete, you must click the Install button to initiate the installation. What you observe on the screen after clicking the Install button will depend on which server roles you opted to install and whether you took previous steps to prepare Active Directory manually or are allowing Setup to do it for you. If this is the first time you are installing Exchange Server 2016 in your environment, you are installing the Mailbox server role, and you are allowing Setup to handle the Active Directory preparations, then you will see a total of 15 steps in a successful installation.

Don't be alarmed if the Setup process appears to be hung during installation. This can be normal, particularly during step 8 (Mailbox role: Transport service). As long as Setup does not return errors or explicitly state that it has failed, be patient. You can also check `ExchangeSetup.log` located in `c:\ExchangeSetupLogs` for more details about what Setup is doing at any given time.

You can also review `ExchangeSetup.log` to verify that setup completed properly. After setup is complete, you can use the `Get-ExchangeServer` cmdlet to verify that the new Exchange server has been installed.

Command-Line Setup

The Exchange Server 2016 Setup program includes a powerful set of command-line options that can help you automate an Exchange server setup or perform custom setup options that you could not do through the GUI. The command-line setup options are broken into six categories:

- Installing Exchange server roles

- Removing Exchange server roles

- Recovering an existing Exchange server

- Preparing Active Directory to support Exchange

- Creating delegated or pre-provisioned servers

- Adding or removing Unified Messaging language packs

For all of these options, you run the same `setup.exe` program that you use for launching the GUI.

 Real World Scenario

THE USEFULNESS OF COMMAND-LINE INSTALLATIONS

A lot of Exchange administrators wonder why the command-line setup options even exist since the graphical user interface is so easy-to-use and has most of the same options. Consider the case of an organization that is installing 30 Mailbox servers.

Due to the organization's requirements for certifying a production IT system, all server builds have to be thoroughly documented prior to being deployed. By generating the installation scripts ahead of time, their Exchange team can ensure that each server is built exactly to the design specifications and with the necessary options. This speeds up the overall installation and ensures that nothing is overlooked.

Command-Line Installation Options

By and large, the server role installation options are probably the most useful for a typical person installing or configuring Exchange. They are certainly the most numerous. Some of these setup.exe options have required parameters. For example, if you use the /mode:install option, you will have to specify which server role or roles you are installing. Table 10.1 lists the command-line installation options in alphabetical order.

TABLE 10.1:   Exchange Server 2016 Command-Line Installation Options

OPTION	OPTIONAL (O) OR REQUIRED (R)	EXPLANATION
/ActiveDirectorySplitPermissions	O	Specifies whether to enable or disable the Active Directory split-permissions mode when preparing the Exchange organization. Disabled by default.
/AnswerFile	O	Allows you to specify a text file that contains answers to some of the advanced setup parameters.
/CustomerFeedbackEnabled	O	Configures Exchange Server to report usage information to Microsoft automatically. All server roles can use this information.
/DbFilePath	O	Specifies the path and name to the default database file. This is used in conjunction with the /Mdbname and the /LogFolderPath switches.
/DisableAMFiltering	O	Allows you to turn off malware scanning on the Mailbox role. Enabled by default.
/DomainController	O	Allows you to specify the NetBIOS name or the FQDN of a domain controller.
/DoNotStartTransport	O	Tells Setup not to allow the Transport service on a Hub Transport or Edge Transport server.

TABLE 10.1:   Exchange Server 2016 Command-Line Installation Options   *(CONTINUED)*

Option	Optional (O) or Required (R)	Explanation
/EnableErrorReporting	O	Configures Exchange Server to report errors automatically to Microsoft. All server roles can use this option. The default is not to enable this feature.
/IAcceptExchangeServerLicenseTerms	R	Specifies that you understand and accept the terms of the Exchange Server license.
/InstallWindowsComponents	O	Allows you to have Setup automatically install any required Windows roles or features.
/LogFolderPath	O	Specifies the path for the log files for the default database when installing a Mailbox server role.
/Mdbname	O	Specifies the name of the default mailbox database when installing a Mailbox server.
/mode or /m	R	Specifies whether the Setup program is installing a new role or removing it. Valid options are as follows: /mode:install /mode:uninstall /mode:upgrade
/OrganizationName	O	Allows you to specify an organization name; this is necessary only if this is the first server being installed in the Active Directory forest and the /PrepareAD step has not previously been done.
/role or /r	R	Specifies which roles are being installed. These are the valid role types: Mailbox, mb ManagementTools, mt, t EdgeTransport, et

TABLE 10.1: Exchange Server 2016 Command-Line Installation Options *(CONTINUED)*

OPTION	OPTIONAL (O) OR REQUIRED (R)	EXPLANATION
/SourceDir	O	Specifies the location for the Exchange installation files.
/TargetDir	O	Allows you to specify an optional path for the Exchange program files rather than the default location on the C:\ drive.
/TenantOrganizationConfig	O	Specifies the path to the file that contains configuration data about your Office 365 tenant. This file is created by running the Export-OrganizationConfig cmdlet in your Office 365 tenant.
/UpdatesDir	O	Specifies a path to a directory that contains updates that should be applied as a part of the installation process.

ABBREVIATIONS AND SHORTCUTS

Most of the command-line switches and options have a long and short option. For example, the following three commands accomplish exactly the same thing (installing the Mailbox role):

◆ setup /m:install /r:mb

◆ setup /m:install /r:Mailbox

In this chapter, we have chosen to spell out the options completely to more clearly illustrate the commands and in the hope that you will remember them more easily. However, once you learn the long version of the options, you will probably find it easier to use the shorter versions. They are just a bit cryptic when you are learning.

Command-Line Server-Recovery Options

There may come a time when you have to recover an Exchange server from a backup. This process will involve rebuilding the Windows server (with the same updates and disk layout) and then reinstalling Exchange Server using the Recover Server mode. This option will read most of the configuration of the server from the Active Directory rather than installing the server from scratch. Several options are available when recovering a server, as shown in Table 10.2.

TABLE 10.2: Exchange Server 2016 Server-Recovery Setup Options

OPTION	OPTIONAL (O) OR REQUIRED (R)	EXPLANATION
/DomainController	O	Allows you to specify the NetBIOS name or the FQDN of a domain controller.
/DoNotStartTransport	O	Tells Setup to not allow the Transport service on a Hub Transport or Edge Transport server to start. This is useful during a recovery if you do not want messages to start flowing until you are sure the server is fully recovered.
/EnableErrorReporting	O	Configures Exchange Server to report errors automatically to Microsoft. All server roles can use this option. The default is set to not enable this feature.
/IAcceptExchangeServerLicenseTerms	R	Specifies that you understand and accept the terms of the Exchange Server license.
/mode:RecoverServer	R	Specifies that the installation mode is to be the Recover Server option.
/TargetDir	O	Allows you to specify an optional path for the Exchange program files rather than the default location on the C:\ drive.
/UpdatesDir	O	Specifies a path to look for updates after the installation is completed.

Command-Line Delegated Server Installation

In some large organizations, the person who is installing the Exchange servers may not have an account with sufficient Active Directory permissions to create the server objects in the Active

Directory. For this reason, someone else may have to create the necessary server objects, and the installer can then set up the servers.

This is where the delegated server installation is handy. The person with the necessary rights to set up the servers can "prestage" the servers in the Active Directory directory. Table 10.3 shows a list of the options available for delegated server setup.

TABLE 10.3:   Exchange Server 2016 Delegated Setup Options

OPTION	OPTIONAL (O) OR REQUIRED (R)	EXPLANATION
/IAcceptExchangeServerLicenseTerms	R	Specifies that you understand and accept the terms of the Exchange Server license.
/NewProvisionedServer or /nprs	O	Creates a new provisioned server with the name specified on the command line, such as this: `Setup.exe / NewProvisionedServer:HNLMBX`
/RemoveProvisionedServer or /rprs	O	Removes a server that was previously configured with the /NewProvisionedServer option.

Installing Language Packs

If you are supporting an Exchange 2016 server for only English-speaking users and administrators, you do not need to worry about installing additional language packs. Exchange Server 2016 automatically includes native support for the U.S. English (en-US) messaging language pack (and it can't be removed), as well as many other languages. For a full list of languages supported by default from both the server and client, please refer to this URL:

`http://technet.microsoft.com/en-us/library/dd298152.aspx`

Depending on the cultural diversity of your environment and users, you should know how to install additional Unified Messaging language packs.

Table 10.4 shows the valid options for installing Unified Messaging language packs. Note that the Unified Messaging language pack options are available only on servers that already have the Mailbox role installed.

TABLE 10.4:   Exchange Server 2016 Language Pack Options

OPTION	OPTIONAL (O) OR REQUIRED (R)	EXPLANATION
/AddUmLanguagePack	R	Adds the specified Unified Messaging language pack. You must specify the language pack name that you want to install; for French, you would use this command: Setup /AddUmLanguagePack:fr-fr Not required if /RemoveUmLanguagePack is used.
/IAcceptExchangeServerLicenseTerms	R	Specifies that you understand and accept the terms of the Exchange Server license.
/RemoveUmLanguagePack	R	Removes the specified Unified Messaging language pack. Not required if /AddUmLanguagePack is used.
/SourceDir	O	Specifies the source folder for the Unified Messaging language pack.
/UpdatesDir	O	Specifies the path for updates for the Unified Messaging language pack.

Removing Exchange Server

Understanding how to remove an Exchange server is as important as understanding how to install Exchange Server. If you don't remove an Exchange server properly, some Active Directory objects are left behind, which will generate errors in event logs and can cause performance problems.

Removing an Exchange server is not difficult, but it needs to be done in an orderly way by uninstalling Exchange Server from the server. You can uninstall by using the graphical interface or the command-line interface, but a proper uninstall needs to be done. The uninstall process removes all Active Directory references to the server. If the uninstall process finds active components such as a mailbox database, you are presented with an error message indicating why removal cannot proceed.

If an Exchange server fails and you decide you no longer need that specific server, the only supported process for properly removing it is to first recover it, and then uninstall Exchange Server. However, if you do a quick Internet search, you'll find that many people reference cleaning up a failed Exchange server by using ADSI Edit in the Configuration partition. Just be aware that this is definitely not supported by Microsoft.

The Bottom Line

Implement important steps before installing Exchange Server 2016. One of the things that slows down an Exchange Server installation is finding out you are missing some specific Windows component, feature, or role. Reviewing the necessary software and configuration components will keep your installation moving along smoothly.

The minimum requirements for the Mailbox server role are at least 30 GB of free space and 8 GB of RAM. However, you need to calculate the proper hardware requirements for your implementation. Ensure that you are using Windows Server 2012 or Windows Server 2012 R2 with the most recent updates. Install the Windows Server roles and features necessary for the Exchange server's role requirements.

Master It You are working with your Active Directory team to ensure that the Active Directory is ready to support Exchange Server 2016. What are the minimum prerequisites that your Active Directory must meet in order to support Exchange Server 2016?

Prepare the Active Directory forest for Exchange Server 2016 without actually installing Exchange Server. In some organizations, the Exchange administrator or installer may not have the necessary Active Directory rights to prepare the Active Directory schema, the forest, or a child domain. Here is a breakdown of the steps involved and the associated group membership requirements to complete each:

◆ Running the Exchange Server 2016 setup.exe program from the command line with the /PrepareSchema option allows the schema to be prepared without installing Exchange. A user account that is a member of the Schema Admins group is necessary to extend the Active Directory schema.

◆ Running the Exchange Server 2016 setup.exe program from the command line with the /PrepareAD option allows the forest root domain and the Active Directory configuration partition to be prepared without installing Exchange. A user account that is a member of the Enterprise Admins group is necessary to make all the changes and updates necessary in the forest root. When preparing a child domain, a member of the Enterprise Admins group or the child domain's Domain Admins group may be used.

Master It You have provided the Exchange 2016 installation binaries to your Active Directory team so that the forest administrator can extend the Active Directory schema. She wants to know what she must do in order to extend only the schema to support Exchange Server 2016. What must she do?

Employ the graphical user interface to install Exchange Server 2016. The graphical user interface can be used for most Exchange Server installations that do not require specialized prestaging or nonstandard options. The GUI will provide all the necessary configuration steps, including Active Directory preparation.

The GUI allows you to install the Mailbox or Edge Transport roles on a server.

Master It You are implementing Exchange Server 2016 for a large organization with strict security requirements. You want to implement the Active Directory split-permissions security model to ensure that Exchange administrators and Active Directory administrators have separate sets of permissions. When you use the GUI to install Exchange Server 2016, this option is not available. Why is this option not available?

Determine the command-line options available when installing Exchange. The Exchange 2016 command-line installation program has a robust set of features that allow all installation options to be chosen from the command line exactly as if you were installing Exchange Server 2016 using the graphical user interface.

Master It You are attempting to use the command line to install an Exchange Server 2016 Mailbox server role. What is the proper command-line syntax to install this role?

Chapter 11

Upgrades and Migrations to Exchange Server 2016 or Office 365

Exchange Server is the de facto standard for business email systems. It is rare to find a large business that does not use Exchange Server. Very few businesses upgrade an email system immediately upon the release of a new version. In fact, many stick with older versions as long as they can. However, at some point businesses need to update Exchange Server to a newer version or consider migrating to Office 365.

You need to know how to move from an older version of Exchange Server to Exchange Server 2016 or Office 365. Depending on the software you have used in the past, you may be used to in-place upgrades, where you have an existing version of the software on a computer, run the installer, and end up with the new version of the software. However, there is no in-place upgrade path for organizations migrating to Exchange Server 2016.

This absence may seem to complicate life, but it actually simplifies the migration path from a legacy version of Exchange Server. Using new Exchange servers means that they are more stable, and it will ease interoperability during the migration.

IN THIS CHAPTER, YOU WILL LEARN TO:

◆ Choose between an upgrade and a migration

◆ Choose between on-premises deployment and Office 365

◆ Determine the factors you need to consider before upgrading

◆ Understand coexistence with legacy Exchange servers

◆ Perform a cross-forest migration

Upgrades, Migrations, Cross-Forest Migrations, and Deployments

Let's take a moment to clear up matters of terminology. Through the release of Exchange Server 2003, it was possible to *upgrade* from one major Exchange Server version to the next—on the same server. Since that time, every major version of Exchange Server has required deployment to new servers and migration of the data from the old servers to the new servers. Some Microsoft documentation (and lots of other documentation as well) makes a strong distinction between *upgrade* and *migration* because of this. That distinction no longer makes any difference. Every Exchange Server upgrade is a migration.

However, when your upgrade involves movement between an existing Exchange Server organization and a new Exchange Server organization, you'll see upgrades referred to as *inter-organizational migrations, cross-forest migrations,* or *transitions.* The terms are interchangeable.

There are two variations you need to know: *deployment* (in which Exchange Server does not connect to Office 365) and *hybrid deployment* (which occurs when you configure your Exchange Server organization to reside both on-premises and in Office 365).

Finally, when we refer to moving data between organizations, we will explicitly say *migration strategy.* This helps us be clear and stay consistent with the documentation provided for Exchange Server 2016.

Factors to Consider before Upgrading

Are you ready to upgrade? Not so fast! Before you pull the trigger and double-click setup.exe from the Exchange Server 2016 installation media, you must take into account a number of factors. Let's take some time to go over them in more detail so that your upgrade is successful.

Prerequisites

Before you can begin upgrading your Exchange Server organization, you have to ensure that the organization meets the prerequisites. We've gone over some of them in previous chapters from the context of a fresh installation of Exchange Server 2016, but let's look at them again, this time keeping in mind how your existing Exchange Server organization may affect your ability to meet those prerequisites.

HARDWARE AND OPERATING SYSTEM

Exchange Server 2016 is available only in a 64-bit version. This means it must run on a 64-bit operating system that is running on 64-bit hardware. The 64-bit hardware must conform to x64 (also known as x86-64) specifications.

Since the operating systems supported by Exchange Server 2016 are available only in 64-bit versions, that does simplify the choices. Do be aware that Exchange Server 2016 does not support the use of Server Core mode in Windows Server. Windows Server 2016 also includes an even smaller mode named Nano Server that is not supported. You must use the full GUI mode operating system.

All modern processors are multicore processors, and Exchange Server 2016 takes full advantage of this. When you calculate the hardware requirements for Exchange Server 2016 by using the Exchange Requirements calculator, the calculator identifies the number of cores required rather than the number of processors required. When using Windows Server 2012 or Windows Server 2012 R2, the licensing is based on processors rather than cores. So, it is to your advantage to have more cores when possible. However, no more than 24 cores is recommended. Also, remember that you should use the Exchange Server Role Requirements Calculator to identify the requirements for your deployment.

You can run Exchange Server 2016 on any edition of Windows Server 2012 or any edition of Windows Server 2012 R2. This means that to reuse existing server hardware, you must have at least one spare server and be prepared to reinstall Windows Server and Exchange Server on your servers as you go. We discuss this topic in more detail in the section, "An Overview of the Upgrade Process," later in this chapter.

As of this writing Windows Server 2016 has not been released, but it is expected that Windows Server 2016 will be a supported operating system for Exchange Server 2016. Be aware that Microsoft has announced that Windows Server 2016 licensing is based on cores. So, it may be to your advantage to get sufficient cores in your hardware without maximizing the number of cores.

ACTIVE DIRECTORY

Because Exchange Server 2016 depends on Active Directory, you should take a good look at the domain controllers and global catalog servers in your Active Directory forest before starting the upgrade process.

Exchange Server 2016 requires all domain controllers that may be accessed by Exchange Server 2016 to have a minimum operating system version of Windows Server 2008. This includes the Schema Master domain controller (usually the first domain controller installed in your Active Directory forest) and all global catalog servers that will be used by Exchange Server 2016. If Exchange Server 2016 cannot find domain controllers at the required versions, then installation fails.

Our recommendation is to upgrade all your domain controllers to at least Windows Server 2008 R2. Windows Server 2008 and Windows Server 2008 R2 are both supported until January 14, 2020, but Windows Server 2008 R2 has Active Directory enhancements such as Active Directory Recycle Bin, which makes standardizing on Windows Server 2008 R2 beneficial over Windows Server 2008. Best practice would be for you to find a way to upgrade your infrastructure all the way to Windows Server 2012 R2.

CHECK THE HEALTH OF YOUR ACTIVE DIRECTORY SITE BEFORE UPGRADING

It is extremely important that Active Directory be healthy before you upgrade to Exchange Server 2016. Among other things, Exchange Server 2016 relies directly on your Active Directory site structure for message-routing information. Most configuration information for Exchange Server 2016 is stored in Active Directory. If there are replication errors in Active Directory, you could see errors during the upgrade process.

Whether you upgrade all your domain controllers or just the minimum number, you need to prepare a list of all the Active Directory domains in which you will either install Exchange Server 2016 or create Exchange Server 2016 recipient objects, such as users, contacts, and distribution groups. For each of these domains, ensure that the domain functional level is set to Windows Server 2008 or higher. The Active Directory forest functional level must also be Windows Server 2008 or higher.

Exchange Server 2016 supports domain functional levels and forest functional levels from Windows Server 2008 all the way to Windows Server 2012 R2. While Exchange Server 2016 does not mandate that you move to higher domain and forest functional levels, there are Active Directory benefits and features that are available if you do so. A major one is the Active Directory Recycle Bin introduced in Windows Server 2008 R2.

Exchange Server performance is directly impacted by Active Directory performance. Therefore, it is important for your domain controllers to perform well. Performance for your domain controllers is enhanced when your domain controllers have enough memory to load the entirety of your Active Directory database (NTDS.DIT) into memory. Also be aware of other applications that are using Active Directory and might impact domain controller performance. Review the current performance of your domain controllers as part of the upgrade planning process.

Technically, installing Exchange Server on a domain controller is supported (although it must be a global catalog server). However, doing so is not recommended. Exchange Server and its ancillary services consume most of the memory available on any server where Exchange Server is installed. This can have a significant negative impact on Active Directory performance. Also, restoring such a combination server, in the event of a catastrophic failure of the server, is much more difficult than restoring a server with just Active Directory or just Exchange Server.

EXCHANGE SERVER 2016 AND DCPROMO

DCPROMO is a part of Active Directory Domain Services (before Windows Server 2012) used either to promote a computer to be a domain controller or to demote a computer from being a domain controller to a normal member computer. After Exchange Server is installed, changing the domain controller status of the computer is *not* supported. That is, you may not promote the computer to a domain controller or demote the computer from being a domain controller with Exchange Server installed. It will break Exchange Server. Don't do it.

LEGACY EXCHANGE

In order to upgrade to Exchange Server 2016 in your current Exchange Server organization, your existing Exchange Server environment must meet certain minimum requirements.

If you have Exchange Server 2010 servers in your organization, they must be upgraded to a minimum of Exchange Server 2010 Service Pack 3 with Update Rollup 11. This includes Edge Transport servers. If you have Exchange Server 2013 servers in your organization, they must be upgraded to a minimum of Exchange Server 2013 Cumulative Update 10. This also includes Edge Transport servers. If you have both Exchange Server 2010 and Exchange Server 2013 servers in your organization, the same minimums apply.

HYBRID DEPLOYMENTS

In a hybrid scenario, some part of your Exchange Server organization is on-premises and another part is in Office 365. For a hybrid deployment, your on-premises Exchange servers must be updated to the same minimum versions as described in the previous section, "Legacy Exchange." This is because Exchange Online in Office 365 is effectively Exchange Server 2016. When you investigate hybrid deployments, you will see the term *hybrid server*. However, there is no specific server role for a hybrid server. A hybrid server is just an

Exchange server that communicates with Office 365 for mail routing and integration of free/busy information. In most cases, the same servers that provide client access for Internet users are also your hybrid servers.

Hybrid mode can be implemented with Exchange Server 2010 or later. However, if your Exchange organization has multiple versions of Exchange, then only the most recent version of Exchange is supported for the Hybrid mode servers. So, if you have a mix of Exchange Server 2010 and Exchange Server 2016, the hybrid servers must be Exchange Server 2016.

OFFICE 365 PLANS SUPPORTING HYBRID DEPLOYMENTS

Any Office 365 plan that supports directory synchronization can be used for Hybrid mode. This includes business, enterprise, academic, and charity plans. You may find some references to business plans not supporting Hybrid mode, but those references are for older business plans that were hosted separate from enterprise plans. Office 365 tenants can now have a mix of business and enterprise licenses.

OFFICE 365 FOR EDUCATION

Microsoft provides Office 365—for academic environments—for free. This is a so-called basic experience. It includes Exchange Online, Skype for Business, SharePoint Online, and Office Web Apps, and is currently known as plan A2. There is also a plan for Alumni, which is also free, that includes only Exchange Online.

Plans with more feature content are available for nominal fees, including Office Pro Plus, home-use rights for five PCs, Exchange voicemail, Exchange archiving, Access, Excel, Infopath, and others.

These plans are discussed at `https://products.office.com/en-us/academic/office-365-education-plan`. If the URL disappears, you can search for "Office 365 education" at `www.microsoft.com`.

To simplify sign-in for Office 365 users, you should ensure that the user principal name (UPN) for users matches their email address. Authentication to Office 365 is done by using the UPN, and it is confusing for users to remember two items that look like email addresses. It will also enable you to deploy single sign-on (SSO) by using Active Directory Federations Services (AD FS) if desired.

You also need to install a directory synchronization tool between your on-premises Active Directory and Office 365. Directory synchronization copies user and group information from your on-premises Active Directory and makes it available to Exchange Online in Office 365. This information is used to ensure that there is a single, unified global address list (GAL) that includes on-premises and Office 365 mailboxes. It also synchronizes the information necessary for message routing.

Microsoft has provided several different tools for directory synchronization. The first tool was DirSync, and many people still use DirSync as a generic term for the latest version of the tool. The most recent directory synchronization tool is Microsoft Azure Active Directory Connect (Azure AD Connect). To avoid needing to upgrade in the future, ensure that you are installing the latest tool because older versions are still available and some instructions provide links to older versions. All support for the older versions ends on April 13, 2017. See https:// azure.microsoft.com/en-us/documentation/articles/active-directory-aadconnect-dirsync-deprecated/ for more information.

Choosing Your Strategy

Now that you are aware of the various preparations that must be completed to upgrade Exchange Server, it is time to figure out how to do it. As we discussed earlier, there are three options in front of us: *upgrade*, *cross-forest migration*, and *hybrid deployment*.

Hybrid deployment is a special case because it involves first performing either an upgrade or a migration and then integrating with Office 365. Because of that, we will discuss upgrades and cross-forest migrations first and then return to discuss integration with Office 365.

If you're like many readers, you probably have at least some preference for your upgrade strategy already in mind. Before you set that choice in stone, though, read through this section and see whether there are any surprises (good or bad) that might allow you to address some aspect of the upgrade that you hadn't previously considered. If, on the other hand, you're not sure which strategy would be best for you, this section should give you enough information to begin making a well-informed decision.

Let's start with an overview of how the two strategies stack up. Table 11.1 lists several points of comparison between the cross-forest migration and upgrade strategies.

TABLE 11.1: Comparison of Exchange Server 2016 Upgrade Strategies

POINT OF COMPARISON	CROSS-FOREST MIGRATION STRATEGY	UPGRADE STRATEGY
Tools	You can perform this type of migration by using only free Microsoft tools, such as the Active Directory Migration Tool and the mailbox move functionality included in Exchange Server. There are also third-party tools available to help simplify the migration process.	You can use the built-in tools in Exchange Server 2016 and Windows Server to control all aspects of the upgrade, including building the new servers, reconfiguring Active Directory, or moving mailbox data.
Hardware	You will usually require a significant amount of new hardware. You may not need to have a complete spare set of replacement hardware, but you'll need enough to have the basic infrastructure of your new Exchange Server 2016 organization in place.	The hardware requirements for Exchange Server 2013 and Exchange Server 2016 are approximately the same. However, Exchange Server 2016 requires significantly more memory and processor cores than Exchange Server 2010. In most cases, you will want to replace older hardware as part of your upgrade process. If the servers are virtualized, just ensure that you've allocated the necessary resources for the new virtual machines.

TABLE 11.1:   Comparison of Exchange Server 2016 Upgrade Strategies   *(CONTINUED)*

POINT OF COMPARISON	CROSS-FOREST MIGRATION STRATEGY	UPGRADE STRATEGY
Active Directory and DNS	You must create a new Active Directory forest. Typically, this means that you cannot reuse the same Active Directory domain names (although you will be able to share the same SMTP domain names).	You can utilize your existing Active Directory and DNS deployment; however, you may need to upgrade your existing domain controllers and global catalogs to meet the prerequisites.
User accounts	You must move your user accounts to the new AD forest or re-create them. In most cases, you also want to synchronize passwords from the old accounts to the new accounts.	Your users will be able to use their existing accounts without any changes.
Message routing	Your SMTP domains must be split between your legacy organization and your new organization; one of them must be configured to be nonauthoritative and to route to the other. This configuration may need to change during the course of the migration. Additionally, you must set up explicit external SMTP connectors between the two organizations or play tricks with name resolution.	Your organization continues to be a single entity, with full knowledge of all authoritative domains shared among all Exchange servers. Message flow between organizations can be controlled by normal Send and Receive connectors along with AD site links.
Outlook profiles	You will need to either create new Outlook profiles (manually or using the tools found in the matching version of the Microsoft Office Resource Kit) or use third-party tools to migrate them over to the new organization. This may cause loss of information, such as any personalizations made to Outlook.	As long as you keep the legacy mailbox servers up and running during an appropriate transition phase, Outlook will transparently update your users' profiles to their new server the first time they open it after their mailbox is moved to Exchange Server 2016.

For the most part, Table 11.1 speaks for itself; if any point requires more in-depth discussion, we address it properly in the detailed sections that follow.

Cross-Forest Migration

From the overview given in Table 11.1, it may seem as if we have a grudge against upgrading to Exchange Server 2016 by using the cross-forest migration strategy. Although we have to admit it's not our favorite strategy, we'll hasten to say that cross-forest migration offers possibilities that a normal upgrade doesn't offer:

◆ It is the only realistic way to consolidate two or more separate Exchange Server organizations into a single organization. This kind of consolidation can happen as the result of a major reorganization inside one company or a merger or acquisition.

◆ It allows you to set up a *greenfield* (a term used to denote the ideal state of implementation) deployment of Exchange Server 2016. No matter how conscientious you are as an admin, any real network is the product of a number of design compromises. After a while, the weight of those compromises and workarounds adds up; the design and structure of your network can reflect imperatives and inputs that no longer exist, or are no longer relevant, in your organization. Although there is some appeal to the idea of wiping the slate clean, it is rarely worth the time and effort to do a cross-forest migration to do an Active Directory cleanup.

◆ It permits you to move your Exchange servers out of your existing Active Directory forest and establish them in their own forest. If you're in an environment that separates administrative control between Active Directory and the Exchange Server organization, having a separate forest for Exchange Server can make it a lot easier to accomplish many of the day-to-day management tasks on your servers. (We don't know about you, but we'd much prefer to have control of the OU structure and Group Policy objects that affect our Exchange servers.) If the benefits of a multiforest deployment outweigh the drawbacks, this configuration may improve the efficiency of the split between directory/account administration and Exchange Server administration.

◆ It gives you the chance to easily define new policies and procedures that apply equally to everyone, from account provisioning to server-naming conventions. With the importance of regulatory compliance and strong internal IT controls and auditing rising on a daily basis, this can be a strong motivator.

◆ It allows you to perform additional configuration and testing of your new organization before you move the bulk of your live data and users to it. Being able to perform additional validation, perhaps with a pilot group of users, gives you additional confidence in the strength of your design and affords you extra opportunities to spot problems and correct them while you can.

Now that we've said that, we should point out that a cross-forest migration strategy usually involves more work, more money, or both. Sometimes, though, it's what you have to do.

Here's what a cross-forest migration might look like:

1. Deploy a new Active Directory forest and root domain, as well as any additional domains. These will probably be named something different from the domains in use in your current network so that you can operate in both environments (and your users can as well). You could be using this forest as an Exchange Server resource forest, or you could be moving all your servers and desktops as well. Because cross-forest migrations don't happen overnight, you'll probably need some sort of forest trust between your forests so that accounts and permissions will work properly while the cross-forest migration is in progress. This step is outside the scope of this book; for more information see: *Mastering Microsoft Windows Server 2012 R2* by Mark Minasi, et al. (Sybex, 2013).

2. Move a suitable set of user accounts to the new forest. Perhaps you're concentrating on one site at one time to minimize confusion; if so, you need to move each user account in the site to the corresponding site in the new Active Directory forest. Again, this step is outside the scope of this book.

3. Install Windows Server 2012 R2 and Exchange Server 2016 on a suitable number of servers to form the core of your new Exchange Server organization. You don't need to have new servers for everything, but you usually should have at least a site's worth of equipment on hand. You'll need to configure SMTP connectors between the two organizations, and you must have some sort of directory synchronization going on

between the two forests. That way, as users get moved into the new forest, each GAL is properly updated to ensure that internal mail is delivered to the right Exchange Server organization.

4. Move the mailbox data for the site from the legacy Exchange servers to the new Exchange Server 2016 servers. Update your users' Outlook profiles so that they can get to their mailboxes, and ensure that the GAL information is updated so that mail follows these users to their new mailbox servers. Once everything is working, you can remove the legacy Exchange servers from this site.

5. Don't forget that you may have to join your users' desktops, as well as any other Windows member servers (such as file/print, database, and web servers) to the new forest if it isn't being used exclusively as an Exchange Server resource forest. This step is outside the scope of this book.

6. Continue this process one site at a time until you've moved all your user accounts and mailbox data into the new Exchange Server 2016 organization and have decommissioned the remaining legacy Exchange servers.

Now you can see why we consider the cross-forest migration strategy to be the labor-intensive route. You don't have the luxury of accepting your existing Active Directory structure and accounts. Although you can move message data over to a new organization, more effort is involved in making sure users' profiles are properly updated. Alternatively, you can rebuild your users' profiles and accept some data loss. You also have the additional worry of whether you need to move the desktop machines into a new forest.

Remember that the Exchange team in your organization cannot arbitrarily decide to create a new Active Directory forest and migrate user accounts without impacting other services. Active Directory is a shared resource, and you need to work with other teams to identify whether a new Active Directory forest is a good idea.

On the other hand, if you have an Active Directory deployment with serious structural problems (whether through years of accumulation or the results of previous mistakes), if you need to extract your Exchange servers into a separate Active Directory resource forest, or if there is some other reason why upgrading your existing organization isn't going to work for you, a cross-forest migration has a lot to offer.

Cross-forest migrations require you to keep track of a lot of details and separate types of information. Although you can move all the important information—mailboxes, public folders, GAL data—using the freely available Microsoft tools, you'll have a harder time migrating some of the smaller details that aren't mission critical but nonetheless can add up to a negative user experience if omitted. If their first experience on the new messaging system is having to reconfigure Outlook with all their preferences, users are going to be less than happy about the experience. The cost of third-party tools may well prove to be a good investment that saves you time, reduces complexity, and gains you the goodwill of your users.

Upgrading Your Exchange Organization

The process of upgrading your Exchange Server organization to Exchange Server 2016 resembles the process required to upgrade from previous versions of Exchange Server. If you have experience in those particular upgrades, relax. All you're doing is moving mailboxes and public folder information, so it's easy—well, as easy as these types of projects get.

Let's take a closer look at the typical upgrade to Exchange Server 2016.

AN OVERVIEW OF THE UPGRADE PROCESS

Whether you are upgrading from Exchange Server 2010 or Exchange Server 2013, the overall upgrade process is the same. At a high level, you install Exchange Server 2016, move mailboxes, and then remove the older Exchange servers. This process allows for coexistence, and when done properly the only effect on users is a prompt to restart Outlook when the mailbox move is completed. Because Exchange Server 2007 cannot coexist with Exchange Server 2013, if you need to upgrade from Exchange Server 2007, you need to first do an upgrade to Exchange Server 2010 or Exchange Server 2013.

For all but the smallest organizations, multiple Exchange servers are used to provide high availability. This requires load balancing for client access services and database availability groups (DAGs) for mailbox databases. In most cases, you want to set up the entire Exchange Server 2016 infrastructure and test the high-availability infrastructure before moving mailboxes. For this reason, it is difficult to reuse existing Exchange servers for an Exchange Server 2016 upgrade.

A typical upgrade process for a single site would look like this:

1. Use the latest version of the Exchange Requirements Calculator to identify hardware requirements. Then purchase the required hardware and install it on site.

2. Ensure that your organization meets all the prerequisites we discussed earlier. Run the PrepareAD step of setup to upgrade the Active Directory forest schema with the Exchange Server 2016 extensions and to create the proper objects in the forest and the root domain.

3. If you have additional Active Directory domains in your forest, prepare each of them by running the PrepareDomain step of setup or PrepareAllDomains.

4. Install all of the Exchange Server 2016 Mailbox servers. This includes configuration of load balancing and database replication in the DAG.

5. Test mail flow and client access services on the new servers. To do this, create a test mailbox and test all of the services, such as Outlook on the web, required by your users. You should also do a test mailbox move.

6. Update external client access to use Exchange Server 2016. At this point, all external client access will be proxied through Exchange Server 2016 to legacy Exchange servers. Before making this change, test the proxying functionality. Using the hosts file on a workstation can help with this process.

7. Update external mail to use Exchange Server 2016. Change the inbound mail flow through your firewalls or antispam device to begin forwarding mail to Exchange Server 2016. You'll also need to create a send connector that uses Exchange Server 2016 as the source for outbound messages.

8. Move mailboxes to Exchange Server 2016. As you move each mailbox, Outlook automatically updates the profile to accessing the mailbox in Exchange Server 2016. If the user is in Outlook when the mailbox move is performed, the user will be prompted to restart

Outlook. Other clients such as ActiveSync do not need to be updated because the external URL has already redirected at the firewall.

9. After all of the mailboxes have been moved, you can remove the legacy Exchange servers. Before removing legacy Exchange servers, verify that no applications or devices such as scanners are still using them. Then uninstall Exchange Server to remove it. Do not simply turn off an Exchange Server to remove it.

PREPARING ACTIVE DIRECTORY

If you are upgrading more than one version of Exchange, you need to be aware of a limit that is in place when you prepare Active Directory. After you prepare Active Directory for the latest version of Exchange Server, you cannot prepare Active Directory for a previous version of Exchange Server. For example, if you have an Exchange organization with Exchange Server 2010 and prepare Active Directory for Exchange Server 2016, then you can't decide later to prepare Active Directory for Exchange Server 2013.

As a best practice, consider preparing Active Directory for all versions of Exchange Server. This ensures that you can add a down-level Exchange Server if required.

Previous versions of Exchange Server required you to install the Client Access server role before the Mailbox server role. Since Exchange Server 2016 does not have separate Client Access server and Mailbox server roles, there is no concern about the order in which to install server roles.

If you are implementing an Exchange Server 2016 Edge Transport server, then you should do so at the same time that you implement the Exchange Server 2016 Mailbox servers. The new Exchange Server 2016 Edge Transport servers are implemented before you change the message flow over to Exchange Server 2016.

When moving mailboxes to Exchange Server 2016 Mailbox servers, you should use only the Exchange Server 2016 Exchange Admin Center New Migration Batch Wizard or the Exchange Management Shell `New-MoveRequest` or `New-MigrationBatch` cmdlets. Do not use the wizard or cmdlets in legacy versions of Exchange Server or you could break the mailboxes.

Public folder migration varies depending on the version of Exchange Server. In Exchange Server 2013 and Exchange Server 2016, public folders are stored in public folder mailboxes. Migrating public folders from Exchange Server 2013 to Exchange Server 2016 is as easy as moving the public folder mailbox. If the public folders are hosted on Exchange Server 2010, the migration process is more involved. Migrating public folders from Exchange Server 2010 to Exchange Server 2016 is covered in Chapter 17, "Managing Modern Public Folders."

If your Exchange organization has multiple sites, then you typically upgrade to Exchange Server 2016 one site at a time. Internet-accessible sites should be upgraded first as they provide proxying functionality. While it is possible for Exchange Server 2013 to proxy connectivity to Exchange Server 2016, it is not possible for Exchange Server 2010 to proxy connectivity to Exchange Server 2016 or Exchange Server 2013. There is more detailed information about proxying client access connectivity in Chapter 21, "Understanding the Client Access Services."

Office 365

We are certainly not here to make a pitch for you to move to Office 365. That being said, for many organizations, a cloud-based communication platform makes sense, and that's primarily what Office 365 is about. Exchange Online provides cloud-based email and scheduling, Skype for Business provides cloud-based instant messaging and videoconferencing, and SharePoint Online provides cloud-based file sharing and rich websites.

The price point, if you exclude licensing of the Office client software, is quite low. In fact, we have to wonder if Microsoft actually makes a profit at it! If you have not yet considered it, it is a fair bet that your management will expect you to soon.

However, for many other companies, cloud-based solutions don't make sense. Moving your operations to the cloud represents a significant loss of control and, potentially, concerns about the security of your data.

The process of moving onto Office 365 from on-premises systems (or other cloud providers) is known as *onboarding*. Similarly, the process of moving off Office 365 to another provider is known as *offboarding*. We suggest that you not onboard your Exchange Server organization without some plan in place to offboard. Some companies have moved and then retired from Office 365 quickly after finding that they cannot accept the restrictions of the services. However, a proper planning process and an understanding of Office 365 features and restrictions mitigates this risk.

Very detailed descriptions of the services are available and a very interesting read. The descriptions include detailed explanations of exactly what is, and is not, available as part of the online services when compared to the on-premises solutions:

```
http://technet.microsoft.com/en-us/library/office-365-service-descriptions.aspx
```

Should that URL disappear, search for "Office 365 service descriptions" on `http://technet.microsoft.com` or your favorite search engine.

Surprisingly, perhaps, preparing for either a hybrid deployment of Exchange Server 2016 with Office 365 or a full transition to Office 365 requires the same steps as for an on-premises deployment of Exchange Server 2016.

Microsoft has invested heavily in making the onboarding process easy—at least as easy as an on-premises upgrade.

Office 365 Options

When moving to Office 365, there are four basic mechanisms to do so:

Hybrid Deployment   We have discussed hybrid deployment as a mechanism to host some mailboxes on-premises and some mailboxes in Office 365. However, hybrid deployment can also be used to migrate all mailboxes from on-premises to Office 365. Because Hybrid mode synchronizes the GAL and provides free/busy integration between on-premises and Office 365, it is well suited to large migrations that will take an extended period of time.

Cutover Exchange Migration   Microsoft recommends a cutover migration only for organizations with fewer than 1,000 mailboxes. All of the mailboxes are moved in a single batch, which limits how many mailboxes can be done in a reasonable period of time. The migration is also limited by the amount of data in the mailboxes and the speed of the Internet connection. To help speed up a cutover migration, most of the data is migrated before the cutover.

At the cutover, only delta data (new messages and deletions) are migrated, which makes the cutover significantly faster. A cutover migration automatically creates the user account in Office 365 based on the source.

Staged Exchange Migration   A staged migration is used to migrate Exchange Server 2003 or Exchange Server 2007 organization that can't use a hybrid migration. Users are moved in batches similar to a hybrid migration, but there is not integration of free/busy data. Directory synchronization is used to prepare users in Office 365. You must take some care to ensure that mail flow works properly.

IMAP Migration   This approach also allows you to move multiple groups of users, across a period of time, to onboard them onto Office 365. The source servers may be any IMAP server. While this type of migration could be used for Exchange Server, it is typically used for non-Exchange email systems such as Gmail. Prior to executing an IMAP Migration to onboard your users, you must use some tool to create users and mailboxes in Office 365. (See the section "Exchange Server Deployment Assistant" later in this chapter.) You must take some care in order to ensure that mailflow works properly.

For all the migration scenarios, mailbox moves can be initiated from Exchange Admin Center in Office 365. If Hybrid mode has been configured, you can also initiate mailbox moves from the on-premises Exchange Admin Center.

Office 365 Coexistence

It is possible to manually configure all of the functionality provided by Hybrid mode with Office 365. You can perform all of the manual steps to configure a trust relationship and organizational sharing policies. You can also create your scripts or programmatic solutions to synchronize user and group information. However, Hybrid mode and the Hybrid Configuration Wizard perform the configuration for you. Each iteration of the Hybrid Configuration Wizard is better and easier to use than the last.

Here are some of the considerations when configuring Hybrid mode:

◆   Some type of directory synchronization is required. Microsoft provides Azure AD Connect for this purpose. However, if you have a complex situation and Azure AD Connect can't do what is required, more advanced Microsoft tools, such as Microsoft Identity Manager, and non-Microsoft tools are available. Regardless, users, groups, contacts, and a significant set of attributes must be copied from the on-premises environment to Office 365.

◆   When you implement Azure AD Connect, you have the option to implement password synchronization from your on-premises Active Directory to Office 365. This makes it easier for your users because they don't need to remember a second password for Office 365. However, this is not true single sign-on because authentication is happening in Office 365.

◆   You have the option to use AD FS to implement true single sign-on. When you implement AD FS, all authentication requests for your users are forwarded to your on-premises ADFS implementation. The main benefit of using AD FS is complete control over authentication. For example, when you disable an on-premises user account, they are no longer able to authenticate to Office 365. However, if your AD FS infrastructure is unavailable, then users can't authenticate to Office 365, which negates one of the benefits of moving to cloud-based services.

- You must have an on-premises Internet-accessible Exchange Server 2016 Mailbox server with Autodiscover DNS records pointing to it. In most cases, you already have this as part of your Exchange Server organization.

- Mailbox servers that will be referenced when using the Hybrid Configuration Wizard must have a valid third-party SSL certificate installed on them, and the Autodiscover and Exchange Web Services (EWS) configured names must be valid subject alternative names on the certificates. Again, this is a best practice for Internet-accessible Exchange organizations.

Before running the Hybrid Configuration Wizard, you should ensure that directory synchronization is working properly. You can do this by reviewing Azure AD Connect and by viewing the synchronized users and groups in Office 365. If you are using AD FS, verify that it is working properly too. You verify the configuration of your on-premises Exchange organization by using the Microsoft Remote Connectivity Analyzer at http://www.testexchangeconnectivity.com.

Once those tests are successful, you are ready to execute the Hybrid Configuration Wizard. To start the Hybrid Configuration Wizard, log in to the Exchange Admin Center on one of your on-premises Mailbox servers or in Exchange Online. Select the Hybrid node and click Configure. This will start the Hybrid Configuration Wizard, and then you simply select the appropriate options for your organization. They are self-explanatory.

When the Hybrid Configuration Wizard successfully completes, your hybrid deployment is live. At this time, you can move mailboxes back and forth between the cloud and on-premises. For more information on that topic, see "Moving Mailboxes" later in this chapter.

Performing a Cross-Forest Migration

This part of this chapter focuses on moving from an Exchange Server 2010 or Exchange Server 2013 organization into a new or separate Exchange Server 2016 organization. This type of migration is somewhat more difficult than an intraorganization upgrade, may be more disruptive for your users, and often leaves you with fewer options than a normal upgrade. However, you may be faced with an organizational configuration that leaves you no choice.

INTRAORGANIZATION VS. CROSS-FOREST UPGRADE

An intraorganization upgrade occurs within your current Exchange Server organization. A cross-forest upgrade (or migration) occurs between your current Exchange Server organization and another Exchange Server organization.

Is Cross-Forest Migration the Right Approach?

A cross-forest migration is quite a bit more complex for both the person handling the migration and the users. The "upgrade" migration is by far the simplest type of Exchange Server 2016 migration. Before you choose a cross-forest migration over an upgrade, you want to make sure you are choosing the right (and simplest) upgrade path.

Most organizations that are moving to Exchange Server 2016 will not need to perform a cross-forest migration. If the following checklist sounds like your organization, you should perform an "upgrade" instead:

◆ You have a single Active Directory forest and no resource forests.

◆ You are running Exchange Server 2010 or Exchange Server 2013.

◆ Your Exchange Server organization is part of your existing Active Directory.

Does this sound like you? If so, go back and read the first part of this chapter because performing a normal upgrade is what you need to do. Because you already have Exchange Server in your Active Directory, there is no need for the extra effort of a cross-forest migration.

So, who needs to perform a cross-forest migration? You might need to perform a cross-forest migration for a number of reasons:

◆ You are consolidating one or more separate Exchange Server organizations.

◆ You are moving Exchange Server resources from a resource forest into your accounts forest.

◆ You are moving from Exchange Server 2007 or earlier to Exchange Server 2016.

◆ You are moving from a different messaging system to Exchange Server 2016.

If you have multiple organizations that you need to consolidate or some other item in the preceding list, you have no choice but to proceed down the cross-forest migration path. Proceeding down this path means different things to different organizations, but most of these cross-forest migrations face a number of challenges:

◆ Finding the tools necessary to perform the migration based on your needs

◆ Moving mail data between two systems

◆ Moving directory data between two systems

◆ Maintaining directory synchronization and messaging between two systems during some period of interoperability

◆ Ensuring that email flows correctly between the email systems during the transition

◆ Figuring out how and when to transition services, such as public folders, MX records, mobile phones, and web mail

Choosing the Right Tools

When you're planning a cross-forest migration, it is important to pick the right tools to help you create accounts, move data, synchronize directories, create forwarders, and perform other migration tasks. Naturally, the most powerful and flexible of these tools are all provided by third parties rather than by Microsoft. However, Microsoft does provide some basic tools that you can use to perform Exchange Server 2007/2010 to Exchange Server 2016 cross-forest migrations.

Active Directory Migration Tool If the user accounts have not yet been created or migrated into your target Active Directory, consider migrating the accounts from their original Active Directory rather than creating new user accounts. The Active Directory Migration Tool (ADMT) is a free tool from Microsoft that will help you migrate users, groups, and computers from one Windows domain or Active Directory to another. The big advantages of this tool are that it preserves the source domain's security identifier (SID) in the target account's SID history attribute and that it preserves group membership.

You can download the Active Directory Migration Tool v3.2 and its associated documentation from the download center of Microsoft's website at `http://microsoft.com/downloads`.

New-MoveRequest and New-MigrationBatch Cmdlets The Exchange Server 2016 New-MoveRequest cmdlet and the `New-MigrationBatch` cmdlet have options that allow you to migrate mailbox data from separate Exchange Server 2007 or newer organizations, and there are automated options for them to create an account for you if one does not exist. We cover these tools in more detail later in this chapter in the section, "Moving Mailboxes."

`Export-Mailbox` AND `New-MailboxImportRequest` CMDLETS

If you have a small number of users (fewer than 50), you might opt to export all their mail from their old mail server using a tool like `Export-Mailbox` (or even ExMerge or Outlook, yikes!) and then use the Exchange Server 2016 `New-MailboxImportRequest` cmdlet to import mail data from these PST files into the users' new mailboxes. This is a basic solution, but it saves you from having to learn the `New-MoveRequest` cmdlet, and you still get to move your users' mail data. Keep in mind, though, that if you use this method, you will lose things like folder rules and delegates that users have assigned to their folders.

Third-Party Tools If you have more than a few hundred users, a lot of public folder data, or very large mailboxes, or if you will need to maintain some level of interoperability between your old Exchange Server 2007 or newer system and your new Exchange Server 2016 system for a long period of time (longer than a few weeks), you should consider a third-party tool. These are often a tough sell after an organization has invested a lot of money in a new mail system, but they can make your migration much easier and allow for better long-term interoperability.

Maintaining Interoperability

During either a true migration or a transition migration from one messaging system to another, the period of interoperability is always one of the biggest headaches. One of the first factors we always want to take into consideration when faced with a cross-forest migration is developing a plan that will minimize the time during which the old system and the new system must coexist.

The transition type of migration is the simplest type if you are going to need two systems to coexist for some period of time. However, this approach is not always an option. In that case, you need to figure out if you can perform an "instant" or light-switch migration or if you must have some period of interoperability.

LIGHT-SWITCH MIGRATIONS

For a relatively small number of users (fewer than 1,000 mailboxes, for example), we try to find a way to perform a *light-switch migration*. On Friday afternoon when a user leaves work, she is using the old system. On Monday morning when she returns to work, she is using the new system. This is a light-switch migration; from the user's perspective, the transition occurs very quickly.

We like the light-switch migration strategy because it usually does not require us to perform any sort of destructive migration on the source system, and everything is migrated all at once. We have performed successful light-switch migrations for 20-user organizations all the way up to 1,500-user organizations. A number of factors will determine if a light-switch migration is possible in your organization. Here are some of the factors to consider:

- Can all of the data be moved in a short period of time?

- Can users' Outlook clients and ActiveSync devices be directed or reconfigured to use the new servers effectively and accurately?

- Are there sufficient help desk and information technology resources to support the user community on "the morning after"?

- If new accounts have to be created for users, can the old passwords be synchronized or can new passwords be distributed to the users?

If you can properly support the light-switch migration, it is best for minimizing interoperability between two systems. The first goal has to be minimizing disruption for the user community, but a long transition between two mail systems can often be more disruptive if the interoperability issues are not properly addressed.

A lot of factors are involved in planning any cross-forest migration strategy, but here is a list of major factors in roughly the order in which they should be done:

- Deploy the new messaging system and test all components, including inbound/outbound mail routing and web components.

- Develop a plan for migrating Outlook profiles such as using Outlook Autodiscover or a script that creates a new profile.

- Create mailboxes and establish email addresses that match the existing mailboxes on the source system.

- Move older data (mailboxes and public folders) if possible.

- Restrict user access to the older mail system and start the migration.

- Switch inbound email to the new mail system.

- Switch Outlook profiles to the new servers.

- Switch over inbound HTTP/HTTPS access to mailboxes.

- Replicate public folder data.

- Move mailbox data; if using a third-party migration tool, try to replicate older mailbox data prior to migration day.

- Keep the old mail system up and running for a month or two just in case you need to retrieve something.

INTEROPERABILITY FACTORS

In migrations, we try to avoid keeping two mail systems operating in parallel for very long. Without the right tools, interoperability is a royal pain in the neck. That being said, you are probably wondering what some of the issues of interoperability are. Here is a partial list of things you need to be concerned about or that your migration utilities should address:

- Email forwarding between domains should work seamlessly; email should be delivered to the right location regardless of whether someone has been migrated.

- Directory/address book synchronization should work seamlessly; users should be able to continue to use the GAL and it should accurately reflect the correct address of the user.

- Mail distribution groups should continue to work properly regardless of where the member is located.

- Users should still be able to reply to email messages that were migrated to the new system.

- Public folder data and free/busy data should be synchronized between the two systems.

- You should have a plan that includes how to transition from one web-based mail system and mobile device system to another.

- Your plan should include migrating users in groups or by department if possible.

- Your plan or migration utilities should also include a mechanism to migrate (or help the user to reproduce) rules, folder permissions, and mailbox delegate access.

Preparing for Migration

You can do some things to get ready for your cross-forest migration; these tasks will make things go more quickly for you. This preparation includes gathering information about what you have to migrate as well as preparing for the actual steps of migration. Here is a partial list:

- Because you are migrating your users from an existing Exchange Server organization to a new Exchange Server 2016 organization, have all the target systems' Exchange Server 2016 servers installed, tested, and ready to use before starting the migration.

- Document everything relevant about your source organization, including connectors, email flow, storage/message size limits, mail-enabled groups, and web access configuration (Outlook on the web/OWA, ActiveSync, IMAP4, POP3).

- Ensure that DNS name resolution between the two Active Directories is working correctly. You may need to configure conditional forwarders or zone transfers to achieve this.

- Make sure there are no firewalls between the two systems; if there are, ensure that the necessary ports are open between the systems.

- Configure trust relationships between the two systems.

- Ensure that you have Domain Administrator and Exchange Administrator permissions in both the source and target systems.

- If you are planning to use the Active Directory Migration Tool (ADMT) to migrate user accounts, you must establish name resolution, a trust relationship, and admin accounts in both domains.

Moving Mailboxes

Exchange Server 2016 includes the `New-MoveRequest` cmdlet, which can be used to move mailboxes either within an organization (intraorganization) or between two different Exchange Server organizations (cross-forest). For cross-forest migrations, `New-MoveRequest` can be used to migrate mailboxes from Exchange Server 2010 or later to Exchange Server 2016.

The `New-MoveRequest` cmdlet is a powerful tool with many parameters and options. In this section, we focus just on its use when moving mail data between one Exchange Server organization and another. Keep in mind that one requirement for using the `New-MoveRequest` cmdlet is that the global catalog servers in both the source and target forests must be running Windows Server 2008 or later.

Exchange Server 2013 introduced the concept of *batches* and of *migration endpoints*. A batch of mailboxes seems fairly self-explanatory—it is simply a group of mailboxes. A batch always connects to a local server and to a migration endpoint. Batch moves are used for cross-forest migrations of every type. The types are discussed in the section, "Office 365 Options," earlier in this chapter. A batch move must always be executed in the target Exchange Server environment (this means that all migrations are "pulled" across from the source environment).

A migration endpoint, which is used only for cross-forest moves, is used to identify the configuration settings and connection mechanism for the source mailboxes that will be used by the batch move request. Therefore, if you are executing a batch move to onboard to Office 365, you will create a migration endpoint and execute a batch move either from the Office 365 Exchange Admin Center or when connected to the Office 365 environment via remote PowerShell.

The cmdlet that is used to create a migration endpoint is `New-MigrationEndpoint`. The cmdlet that is used to create a new migration batch is `New-MigrationBatch`. There are also many other batch-related cmdlets. The cmdlets provide ways to control the movement of mailboxes via batch, including ways to stop a batch from executing, suspend it, get the status and statistics associated with a currently executing batch, and so on. You can find information on all the batch cmdlets at `https://technet.microsoft.com/en-us/library/jj218644(v=exchg.160).aspx` or by searching for "Exchange 2016 move and migration cmdlets" using your favorite search engine.

Migration batches are preferred over the use of `New-MoveRequest` in Exchange Server 2016, but both mechanisms are supported. Migration batches can be fully controlled and monitored from within the EAC, and that is the recommended method for doing so. The batch cmdlets have many options and many different usage scenarios depending on whether you are onboarding or offboarding to Office 365, performing cross-forest moves, doing staged Exchange Server migrations or cutover Exchange Server migrations, or even just performing local (same forest) mailbox moves.

Although some admins are resistant to the Exchange Admin Center at first, they often find that it provides a great interface for executing and monitoring batch moves.

Migrating User Accounts

Using either of the cross-forest move mechanisms (individual move requests or migration batches) requires that a mail-enabled user account be created in the destination forest before the mailbox move is initiated. As noted in our prior section "Office 365 Coexistence," this can be accomplished in a number of different ways. Microsoft currently documents the attributes that *must* be copied and that *may* be copied for Exchange Server 2013, which is also accurate for Exchange Server 2016, at this URL:

    http://technet.microsoft.com/en-us/library/ee633491

If that URL should disappear, then on http://technet.microsoft.com (or your favorite Internet search engine) search for "prepare mailboxes for cross-forest move requests."

Another resource for creating users and copying attributes that we have not previously discussed can be very handy. As part of Exchange Server 2016, the Exchange Server team shipped a script named Prepare-MoveRequest.ps1. This script is located in the $ExScripts directory, normally at C:\Program Files\Microsoft\Exchange Server\V15\Scripts. It is extremely useful if you are planning some type of custom migration where none of the earlier tools are useful, for whatever reason. Using this script (again, for Exchange Server 2013 but accurate for Exchange Server 2016) is discussed at:

    http://technet.microsoft.com/en-us/library/ee861103

Also, you can find the most current link by searching for "prepare mailboxes for cross-forest moves using the Prepare-MoveRequest.ps1 script in the shell."

Permissions Required

When you are moving mailboxes between forests, you need to have accounts in both the source and destination forests that will give you the necessary permissions to move mailbox data between the two organizations. Usually, the accounts you use for the source and target organizations will *not* be the same account. Permissions required are pretty simple: you need to be a recipient administrator for all the accounts you will be moving. In the case of Office 365, in Hybrid mode, you need Recipient Management permissions.

Importing Data from PSTs

A personal folder (PST) file has the ability to hold mailbox data. Outlook uses PST files to store data for POP3 and IMAP accounts. Outlook also uses PST files to archive older messages and lower mailbox size. Most messaging administrators dislike PST files because they are difficult to manage. However, PST files can be useful sometimes during migrations:

- If you are migrating from a POP3 or IMAP email system, you can import the PST files from clients into user mailboxes.

- If you are doing a small cross-forest migration, it might be easier to export mailboxes to a PST and import than to set up the infrastructure to do mailbox moves between the two Exchange organizations.

Exchange Server 2016 has the native (that is, does not depend on Outlook) capability to import personal folder (PST) files into a mailbox. Similar to mailbox batches discussed in the prior section, there is an entire suite of cmdlets controlling this capability. Unlike with mailbox batches, there is a not a nice, pretty interface in the Exchange Admin Center, which is unfortunate.

Regardless, the cmdlets are as follows:

- `Get-MailboxImportRequest`

- `Get-MailboxImportRequestStatistics`

- `New-MailboxImportRequest`

- `Remove-MailboxImportRequest`

- `Resume-MailboxImportRequest`

- `Set-MailboxImportRequest`

- `Suspend-MailboxImportRequest`

Before you begin trying to import PST data into an existing mailbox, make sure that you have the necessary permissions. By default, just because you are an Exchange Server administrator does not mean you can import data. Use the EMS `New-ManagementRoleAssignment` cmdlet to give your account the necessary permissions. Here is an example where we give user Rena. Dauria permission to import or export user data from mailboxes:

```
New-ManagementRoleAssignment -Role "Mailbox Import Export"
-User "Rena.Dauria"
```

Once you have the necessary permissions to the mailbox and have opened an instance of the Exchange Management Shell, you can proceed. Here is an example of importing a PST file called `ARoberts.PST` into the mailbox Andrew.Roberts:

```
New-MailboxImportRequest Andrew.Roberts -FilePath \\Server\PSTshare\ARoberts.PST
```

Unlike in earlier versions of this cmdlet, the dumpster is included by default. You can also specify that you want the data imported into the user's archive versus the main mailbox, the specific folders you want to include and exclude, and many other options. Unfortunately, unlike the `Import-Mailbox` cmdlet that was present in Exchange Server 2010, there is no way to specify a date range.

For more details about the `New-MailboxImportRequest` cmdlet, see

```
http://technet.microsoft.com/en-us/library/ff607310.aspx
```

or search for "Exchange 2016 New-MailboxImportRequest."

Tasks Required Prior to Removing Legacy Exchange Servers

If you are performing an upgrade or are migrating completely to Office 365, the time will come when all of the upgrade and/or migration tasks are complete (at least, we hope so!).

Now you are ready to start removing the old servers. No, you can't just cut them off and be done with it. Exchange Server has hooks deep into your Active Directory, and if you have new servers (or are going to continue with directory synchronization to the cloud), you *must* clean up the remnants of the old servers. If you don't, they are guaranteed to come back and haunt you.

To actually remove an installation of Exchange Server from a server, you need Organization Admin privileges, plus local Administrator privileges on that server.

Before you begin the process of removing Exchange Server, there are some items that you should verify for completeness:

◆ If you are using public folders, you need to ensure that replication has completed and that the migration is completed on the target environment.

◆ If you are not using public folders, you need to ensure that all replicas of both system and normal public folders have been removed from all public folder databases and that the public folder databases have been deleted.

◆ All client access configuration is pointing to Exchange Server 2016 Mailbox servers (including EWS, EAS, Outlook Anywhere, Autodiscover, and the like).

◆ All Send and Receive connectors are pointing to Exchange Server 2016 servers.

◆ All user mailboxes have been moved to Exchange Server 2016.

◆ All system mailboxes have been moved to Exchange Server 2016 (including arbitration and discovery search mailboxes).

◆ All mailbox databases on the legacy servers have been removed.

◆ All Exchange Server 2010 client access arrays have been removed.

◆ All applications that may be using Exchange Server services (SMTP relay, for example) have been reconfigured to use Exchange Server 2016 servers.

Once all of these tasks are complete and verified, you are ready to begin removing legacy Exchange servers.

Removing Exchange Server from a server is as simple as choosing Programs and Features ➤ Exchange Server ➤ Uninstall. Simply follow the Uninstallation Wizard. If you have forgotten to perform any of the steps listed previously, the wizard will let you know. At that point, you should correct the problem and rerun the wizard.

Exchange Server Deployment Assistant

Beginning with Exchange Server 2010, Microsoft made available an online tool to assist in the planning and deployment process for Exchange Server. The web-based tool, known as the

Microsoft Exchange Server Deployment Assistant (EDA), allows a user to specify their starting configuration and desired end result. Then the tool produces a detailed set of instructions for how to reach the desired end result.

EDA, especially with common deployment scenarios, can be a great time-saver. While EDA does not cover every scenario or diagram of everything that must be done, especially when third-party messaging systems or extensions come into play, it does provide extensive links to the relevant TechNet literature. Relevancy is the key. TechNet is a huge repository of data, and determining what is relevant to a particular deployment can be challenging. That is where EDA comes in.

Here's what EDA covers:

◆ On-premises upgrades and transitions from Exchange Server 2010 and Exchange Server 2013 to Exchange Server 2016

◆ Hybrid deployments

◆ Transitions to cloud-only solutions (that is, moving your entire messaging infrastructure to Office 365)

You can find EDA at `https://technet.microsoft.com/en-us/office/dn756393`. Should that link disappear, you can search for "Microsoft Exchange Server Deployment Assistant" on TechNet, using your favorite Internet search engine.

The Bottom Line

Choose between an upgrade and a migration. The migration path that you take will depend on a number of factors, including the amount of disruption you can put your users through and the current version of your messaging system.

Master It Your company is currently running Exchange Server 2010 and is supporting 3,000 users. You have a single Active Directory forest. You have purchased new hardware to support Exchange Server 2016. Management has asked that the migration path you choose have minimal disruption on your user community. Which type of migration should you use? What high-level events should occur?

Choose between on-premises deployment and Office 365. A common choice today is deciding whether to move your mailbox data into the cloud. Office 365 is Microsoft's cloud solution, of which Exchange Online is a part.

Master It You work at a university using Exchange Server 2010 on-premises for 10,000 students. You want to offer the functionality present in Exchange Server 2016 to your students, but you have budgetary constraints and cannot replace all of the required servers. What is your best course of action?

Determine the factors you need to consider before upgrading. Organizations frequently are delayed in their expected deployments due to things that they overlook when preparing for their upgrade.

Master It You are planning your Exchange Server 2016 upgrade from an earlier version. What are some key factors that you must consider when planning the upgrade?

Understand coexistence with legacy Exchange servers. Coexistence with earlier versions of Exchange Server is a necessary evil unless you are able to move all your Exchange Server data and functionality at one time. Coexistence means that you must keep your old Exchange servers running for one of a number of functions, including message transfer, email storage, public folder storage, or mailbox access. One of the primary goals of any upgrade should be to move your messaging services (and mailboxes) over to new servers as soon as possible.

Master It   You are performing a normal upgrade from Exchange Server 2013 to Exchange Server 2016. Your desktop clients are a mix of Outlook 2010 and Outlook 2013. You quickly moved all your mailbox data to Exchange Server 2016. Why should you leave your Exchange Server 2013 servers online for a few weeks after the mailbox moves have completed?

Perform a cross-forest migration.   Cross-forest migrations are by far the most difficult and disruptive migrations. These migrations move mailboxes as well as other messaging functions between two separate mail systems. User accounts and mailboxes usually have to be created for the new organization; user attributes, such as email addresses, phone numbers, and so forth must be transferred to the new organization. Metadata such as "reply-ability" of existing messages as well as folder rules and mailbox permissions must also be transferred.

Although simple tools are provided to move mailboxes from one Exchange Server organization to another, large or complex migrations may require third-party migration tools.

Master It   You have a business subsidiary that has an Exchange Server 2010 organization with approximately 2,000 mailboxes; this Exchange Server organization is not part of the corporate Active Directory forest. The users all use Outlook 2013. You must move these mailboxes to Exchange Server 2016 in the corporate Active Directory forest. What four options are available to you to move email to the new organization?

Part 3

Recipient Administration

Chapter 12

Management Permissions and Role-Based Access Control

In Exchange Server 2016, the methodology for managing access permissions to user and administrative functionality is the same as it was in Exchange Server 2010 and Exchange Server 2013. This technology, called Role-Based Access Control (RBAC), provides more powerful and granular control over what people can do than what was available in earlier versions of Exchange.

To use it effectively, we need to take an in-depth look at how RBAC works and how it differs from the permission model in previous versions of Exchange. Then we'll examine the tools and processes for configuring and managing RBAC. After that, we can dig deeper into the topic of roles and how to assign them to users and administrators.

IN THIS CHAPTER, YOU WILL LEARN TO:

- ◆ Determine what built-in roles and role groups provide you with the permissions you need

- ◆ Assign permissions to administrators using roles and role groups

- ◆ Grant permissions to end users for updating their address list information

- ◆ Create custom administration roles and assign them to administrators

- ◆ Audit RBAC changes using the Exchange Management Shell and built-in reports in the Exchange Administration Center

RBAC Basics

The goal in this section is to give you a broad and high-level understanding of what RBAC is and how it works. As we discuss these various topics throughout this chapter, we will build on this knowledge and you will gain deeper insights into RBAC. This will help you learn what RBAC can do for you and how you can use it.

Differences from Previous Exchange Versions

In the most basic sense, RBAC is the permissions model for Exchange Server 2016. Anyone who has had to customize permissions in Exchange versions prior to Exchange 2010 can understand the inconvenience of making permission changes in Active Directory and keeping track of what permission modifications were made. Prior to RBAC's introduction, access control lists (ACLs) on various Active Directory objects were used to configure permissions. Each object to which you wanted to delegate permissions had its own ACL. Each ACL was further composed of multiple access control entries (ACEs) that defined what permissions each user or group had on that object. To make this process a bit more manageable, Exchange used property sets. A *property set* is a group of attributes that can share a common ACE. For example, instead of setting an ACE on 15 different attributes, those attributes could be added to a property set so that applying the ACE to the property set would update the ACLs on each of the attributes.

RBAC is a significantly different approach to solving this problem. Because the management of Exchange Server 2016 is brokered through PowerShell cmdlets, it makes more sense to apply the permissions at the administrative level instead of on the Active Directory object. RBAC does this by using roles to define which Exchange cmdlets can be run and what parameters can be used with those cmdlets. By moving these permissions to the cmdlet level, you ensure that access control is enforced by PowerShell. This allows Exchange to do some really powerful things, such as presenting administrators with only the cmdlets that they have permissions to run.

AVAILABLE COMMANDS BASED ON ROLE GROUP ASSIGNMENT

If an administrator doesn't have access to run a cmdlet, such as the Set-Mailbox cmdlet, the cmdlet will not be available to that administrator when the Exchange Management Shell (EMS) is used. Not only will the cmdlet not be found if the administrator tries to run it, but it won't be part of tab completion in the EMS.

How RBAC Works

To illustrate how RBAC works, let's look at an example. Suppose that in your Exchange infrastructure, you have a group of people who provide support for your end users. This group is primarily responsible for creating new accounts, mail-enabling users, configuring mailbox properties, and similar tasks. To enable this group of people to do their job, you could assign the Mail Recipients role to their accounts. When these users are assigned this role, they gain the permissions to run the Exchange cmdlets that this role allows. In this example, the users will have access to cmdlets, such as Enable-Mailbox, Set-Mailbox, and Get-MailboxStatistics. Remember that these permissions are used not only for the Exchange Management Shell, but also the Exchange admin console.

The previous example illustrates only one aspect of RBAC: the ability to assign roles to various levels of Exchange administrators. But there is another aspect of RBAC that allows you to assign roles to end users. The types of roles that end users would have are different than the roles that an Exchange administrator would have. Whereas the Exchange administrator's roles are geared toward managing Exchange, the end user's roles are geared toward the end users managing their own contact information, mailbox settings, marketplace apps, team mailboxes, and distribution groups. For example, if you want your users to be able to update their own phone numbers in the global address list (GAL), you can assign them the MyContactInformation or MyPersonalInformation role.

To understand how RBAC defines and distributes roles, you will need to become familiar with a few relevant terms:

Management Role   A management role, also referred to simply as a *role*, represents a grouping of Exchange cmdlets that can be run by people who are assigned the role. These cmdlets are also referred to as management role entries.

Management Role Entry   A management role entry, also known simply as a *role entry*, is the term used to refer to every Exchange cmdlet and parameter that is defined on a role. There is also a special type of role that allows your role entries to be PowerShell scripts or non-Exchange cmdlets.

Management Role Scope   The scope defines the boundary of objects to which a role can be applied. By default, the scope of impact on roles is not very restrictive. However, you can create custom scopes that make the scope of impact for a role more restrictive, such as restricting a role to only an organizational unit (OU) of recipients.

Management Role Group   A role group is a security group in Active Directory that has been assigned management roles. Users that are members of the group have the ability to run the cmdlets defined by the management roles assigned to the group. When management roles are assigned to the group, they can be restricted by a scope. Several default role groups, such as Organization Management, are created during the installation of Exchange Server, but you can also create your own role groups. For example, you could create a role group that allows administration of recipients only in the OU for a remote location. Then help desk staff in the remote location are made members of the role group to allow them to manage local recipients. It is possible to assign roles directly to users, but as with managing other types of permissions, it is generally easier to manage permissions by using groups.

Management Role Assignment   Management role assignments, also known as *role assignments*, are what pull everything together. RBAC defines who (the role group or user account) has what permissions (the roles) and where (the scope) those permissions are in effect. The role assignment pulls this together by assigning a management role to a role group, a user account, or a role assignment policy. A scope can also be attached to each role assignment. Each time a role is assigned to a unique role group, user account, or role assignment policy, a different role assignment is created. Each role assignment assigns only one role to one role group or user account. However, there can be multiple role assignments for a role group or user account.

Role Assignment Policy   A role assignment policy is a collection of management permissions for users to manage themselves. Management role assignments are used to assign end user management roles to the role assignment policy. The management role assignments define the permissions that are allowed. Each mailbox is associated with one role assignment policy that controls the permissions a user has to manage his or her own attributes.

Two different processes define how the RBAC components interact with one another. The process for assigning permissions to Exchange administrators is different than the process for assigning permissions to end users, though there is some overlap. In both instances, management roles are used to define what the assignee can do. Management roles contain management role entries. The difference, however, is in how management roles are assigned.

RBAC FOR ADMINISTRATORS

When assigning roles to administrators, management role groups are the basic method used to define which roles administrators have. These groups are universal security groups in Active Directory. When you want to give an administrator a group of roles, you add the administrator's Active Directory account to the appropriate management role group. Each of these groups is assigned one or more management roles.

Management role assignments allow you to assign one or more management roles to management role groups. For example, the Organization Management role group has several roles associated with it. Each of these roles is associated with the role group by using a unique management role assignment. Within this management role assignment, you can also define the scope of the role. Suppose you want to create a group of administrators who can manage only the mailboxes belonging to the users in the Baltimore OU. You can create a role group called Baltimore Mailbox Administrators and use a management role assignment to assign the Mail Recipients role to that group for only users in the Baltimore OU.

To better illustrate how these components come together, see Figure 12.1. Management role entries are defined on management roles. Management role assignments tie a management role to a management role group. Administrator accounts are added as members of the role group. Once in the group, those administrators have access to the functionality defined by the roles that are assigned to the group.

FIGURE 12.1
The interaction among the RBAC components for granting permissions to administrators

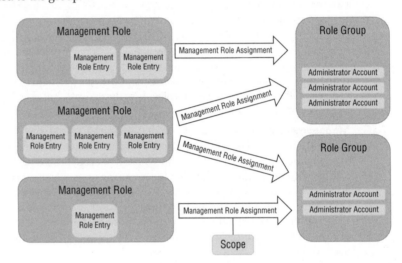

Just as you can assign file permissions directly to a user, you can also directly assign roles to a user account. This is called direct role assignment. However, it is much easier to manage if you use role groups.

RBAC FOR END USERS

The process for assigning roles to end users is different than the process for assigning roles to administrators. End users still use management roles and management role entries. However, the roles are assigned to user accounts using a role assignment policy. The role assignment policy has management roles assigned, just as role groups do. The difference is that role assignment policies aren't groups to which users can be added. Therefore, a user cannot have multiple role assignment policies. Like other types of policies in Exchange, a user account can have only one role assignment policy assigned to it. The roles that users have in Exchange are defined by that policy.

Figure 12.2 describes how this process takes place for user accounts. Contrasting this with Figure 12.1, you can see that each end-user account gains its roles by specifying the policy that takes effect on it, but each administrator account gains its roles by being a part of the role group.

FIGURE 12.2
How RBAC is
used to grant
permissions to end
users

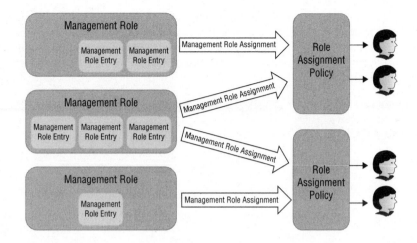

You can assign the roles for users directly to user accounts, but this is not recommended. Role assignment policies are a better way to manage these permissions.

Managing RBAC

As you are managing RBAC, multiple areas need your attention. When you deploy Exchange, you have to manage the various RBAC components. This work consists of assigning the roles, modifying role groups, setting role assignments, and much more. You will also have to manage the role distribution, which consists of managing the role groups and the role assignment policies, and before anyone can manage those things, you must delegate the RBAC management permissions to the appropriate people.

There are primarily two built-in tools you can use to manage these various aspects of RBAC. There is also a downloadable tool from www.codeplex.com named RBAC Manager. In this section, we'll look at these tools and discuss what they enable you to do at a high level. Throughout the remainder of this chapter, we will be using these tools and examining them in more detail.

Exchange Administration Center

The first tool that we will look at is the Exchange Admin Center (EAC). The EAC is a web-based management console used to manage Exchange Server 2016 features and services.

When you sign in to the EAC, you will navigate to the Permissions task in the Feature pane. Notice the two tabs, Admin Roles and User Roles, shown in Figure 12.3. If you don't have these tabs available, you likely don't have the appropriate permissions to manage the roles.

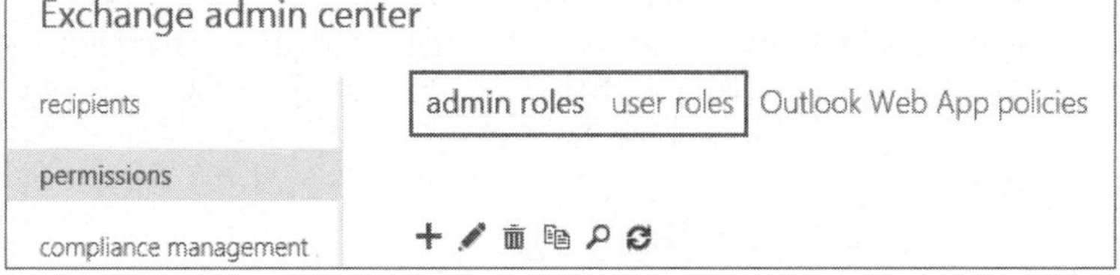

FIGURE 12.3
Managing administrator roles and
user roles in the
EAC

Exchange admin center

recipients	
permissions	**admin roles** user roles	Outlook Web App policies
compliance management	+ ✎ 🗑 📋 🔎 ♻

When you click the Admin Roles tab, the role groups are listed alphabetically. This list includes both the built-in role groups and any custom role groups that you may have created. If you select a role group, the Details pane on the right will display the description of the role group, the roles that the group is assigned, and the members of the group. This is shown in Figure 12.4.

FIGURE 12.4

Viewing role group details in the EAC

You can also create a new role group, delete a role group, copy a role group, and edit the role group. The steps for doing this are described in the "Distributing Roles" section, later in this chapter.

When you click the User Roles tab in the EAC, you are presented with a list of role assignment policies that exist in your organization. In a manner similar to the Admin Roles tab, you can select the role assignment policy from the list and view the details of the policy in the Details pane on the right. You can also edit the user roles that are assigned to this policy, create a new assignment policy, and delete an assignment policy that is not associated with a mailbox. This is covered later in the section, "Distributing Roles." Figure 12.5 shows the information available on the User Roles tab of the EAC.

This is the extent to which you can manage RBAC inside the EAC. If you require more advanced configuration options, such as customized management roles, you must use the EMS or RBAC Manager.

Exchange Management Shell

The EMS is the built-in tool where you will probably be spending most of your time when you are managing RBAC. Table 12.1 lists which cmdlets are available for managing each RBAC component. These cmdlets are further discussed and used throughout the remainder of this chapter.

Figure 12.5
Viewing the user role information in the EAC

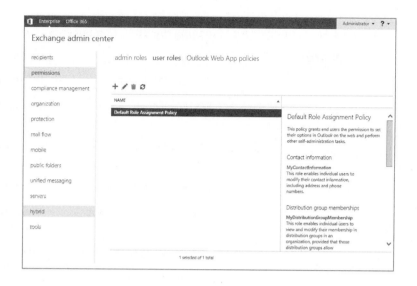

Table 12.1:   Cmdlets for Managing the RBAC Components

Component	Cmdlet	Description
Management role	New-ManagementRole	Creates a new role
	Get-ManagementRole	Gets the list of roles or the properties of a specific role
	Remove-ManagementRole	Deletes a role
Management role entry	Add-ManagementRoleEntry	Adds a role entry to an existing role
	Get-ManagementRoleEntry	Retrieves the list of role entries on a role
	Remove-ManagementRoleEntry	Removes a role entry from a role
	Set-ManagementRoleEntry	Sets the parameters on an already-defined role entry
Role group	Get-RoleGroup	Gets the list of role groups or the properties of a specific role group
	New-RoleGroup	Creates a new role group

TABLE 12.1: Cmdlets for Managing the RBAC Components *(CONTINUED)*

COMPONENT	CMDLET	DESCRIPTION
	Remove-RoleGroup	Deletes a role group
	Set-RoleGroup	Changes the properties of the role group
	Add-RoleGroupMember	Adds an administrator to a role group
	Get-RoleGroupMember	Lists the members of a role group
	Remove-RoleGroupMember	Removes an administrator from a role group
	Update-RoleGroupMember	Modifies the role group membership in bulk
Role assignment policy	Get-RoleAssignmentPolicy	Retrieves the list of role assignment policies or retrieves the details of a specific role assignment policy
	New-RoleAssignmentPolicy	Creates a new role assignment policy
	Remove-RoleAssignmentPolicy	Deletes a role assignment policy
	Set-RoleAssignmentPolicy	Configures the properties of a role assignment policy, including whether the policy is the default policy for the domain
Management role assignment	Get-ManagementRoleAssignment	Retrieves the list of role assignments or the details of a specified role assignment
	New-ManagementRoleAssignment	Creates a new role assignment
	Remove-ManagementRoleAssignment	Deletes a role assignment
	Set-ManagementRoleAssignment	Configures the properties of the role assignment, including the scope that the assignment uses

TABLE 12.1: Cmdlets for Managing the RBAC Components *(CONTINUED)*

COMPONENT	CMDLET	DESCRIPTION
Management scope	`Get-ManagementScope`	Retrieves management scopes, orphaned scopes, and exclusive or regular scopes
	`New-ManagementScope`	Creates a regular or exclusive management scope for recipients or Exchange objects
	`Remove-ManagementScope`	Removes management scopes that are orphaned
	`Set-ManagementScope`	Updates the existing configuration of a management scope

RBAC Manager

RBAC Manager provides a GUI interface to manage the implementation of RBAC within your organization. This tool provides more advanced functionality for managing RBAC than the EAC.

This is an open-source tool (not from Microsoft) that is not actively in development and has not been updated since 2012. The description for the tool states that it works with Exchange Server 2010 and Exchange Server 2013 Preview. However, RBAC Manager does work with Exchange Server 2016.

To install RBAC Manager, you need to have .NET Framework 3.5.1 installed. Because this is not used for Exchange Server 2016, you are better off installing this tool on a workstation rather than a server running Exchange Server 2016. The tool connects to an Exchange server and uses PowerShell remoting to perform its tasks. As long as the cmdlets for managing RBAC remain the same, RBAC Manager should continue to work properly. If you view the log file, you can see the cmdlets that are being used as you perform tasks in the application.

In the RBAC Manager window, there are four tabs that can be used to manage your RBAC configuration:

◆ Show Management Roles

◆ Show Assignment Policies

◆ Show Role Groups

◆ Show Management Scopes

Figure 12.6 shows the tabs available in RBAC Manager—from left to right, they are Show Management Roles, Show Role Assignment Policies, Show Role Groups, and Show Management Scopes.

FIGURE 12.6
Tabs to manage
roles, role
assignment poli-
cies, role groups,
and scopes

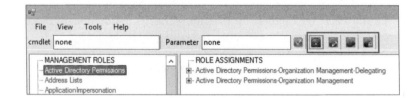

The Show Management Roles tab (brown briefcase image) displays all the built-in management roles that are created during the installation of Exchange Server 2016. Any custom management roles are stored underneath the parent management role. Built-in management roles
are listed in green, and custom management roles are listed in blue.

The Show Role Assignment Policies tab displays all the mailbox role assignment policies in
the right pane. Much like the Show Management Roles tab, the Default Role Assignment Policy
that is created during install is listed in green, and any new role assignment policy is listed
in blue.

To see all the administrators and security groups that have been assigned a role, you can use
the Show Role Groups tab. All security groups that have been assigned a role are displayed as
green, and roles that have been assigned directly to a user are displayed in blue.

The last tab, Show Management Scopes, provides a list of all the custom management scopes
you have created in your organization.

Defining Roles

The management role is the key component of RBAC. This section will go into a little more
detail about roles and show you how to choose an existing role to assign and how to create
a custom role if it's necessary.

What's in a Role?

At the most basic level, a management role is a grouping of Exchange cmdlets and parameters.
Anyone who is assigned the management role has permissions to execute those cmdlets with
those parameters. To illustrate this more clearly, let's examine a management role. The Mailbox
Import Export role is a built-in role in Exchange, meaning that Exchange created this role by
default during setup. There are many built-in roles, but we'll look at Mailbox Import Export in
particular for this example.

The Mailbox Import Export role allows assignees to run the following cmdlets:

◆ `New-MailboxImportRequest`

◆ `Get-MailboxImportRequest`

◆ `Set-MailboxImportRequest`

◆ `Suspend-MailboxImportRequest`

◆ `Resume-MailboxImportRequest`

- `Remove-MailboxImportRequest`

- `Get-MailboxImportRequestStatistics`

- `New-MailboxExportRequest`

- `Get-MailboxExportRequest`

- `Set-MailboxExportRequest`

- `Suspend-MailboxExportRequest`

- `Resume-MailboxExportRequest`

- `Remove-MailboxExportRequest`

- `Get-MailboxExportRequestStatistics`

- `Get-Notification`

- `Set-Notification`

- `Get-Mailbox`

- `Search-Mailbox`

- `Start-AuditAssistant`

- `Write-AdminAuditLog`

- `Get-UnifiedAuditSetting`

- `Set-UnifiedAuditSetting`

- `Set-ADServerSettings`

To get the list of the management role entries for a management role, run this command:

```
Get-ManagementRoleEntry "Mailbox Import Export\*" | fl name
```

Having the `Get-Mailbox` cmdlet as a part of this role is especially important. If you don't have any `Get-*` cmdlets defined in your roles, the assignee cannot retrieve the data they are modifying. With each one of these cmdlets, the role defines which parameters the assignee can use. If the parameter isn't in this list, it can't be used. For example, the Mailbox Import Export role doesn't specify that the assignees can use the `Database` parameter with the `Get-Mailbox` cmdlet. Because of this, the assignee can't list all the mailboxes on a database unless they are assigned another role that has those permissions.

To get the list of the parameters that are available for a specific role entry, run this command:

```
(Get-ManagementRoleEntry "Mailbox Import Export\get-mailbox").parameters
```

Because PowerShell is the underlying command-execution engine in Exchange, you can see how this level of granularity is very powerful. In RBAC terms, these cmdlets are referred to as management role entries. There is another type of management role that allows you to use PowerShell scripts and non-Exchange cmdlets as management role entries, but we'll look at that a little later, in the section, "Unscoped Top-Level Roles: The Exception." Figure 12.7 shows the relationship between management roles and management role entries.

FIGURE 12.7
The relationship between a management role and its management role entries

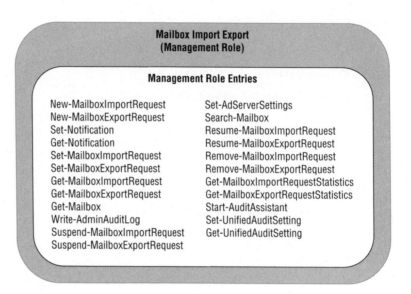

As discussed earlier in this chapter, the RBAC data is stored in Active Directory. Each management role has an associated object of the object type msExchRole in Active Directory. The role objects are stored in the Configuration Naming Context inside the following container: Services\Microsoft Exchange*Org Name*\RBAC\Roles. If you were to examine this in ADSI Edit, you would see something similar to Figure 12.8.

FIGURE 12.8
The role objects in Active Directory

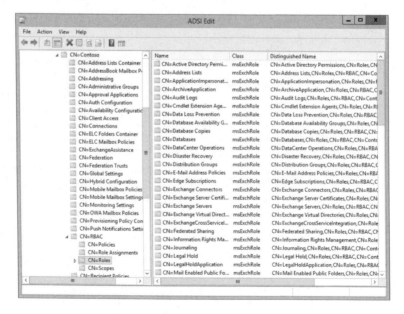

If you were to open the Mailbox Import Export role object (CN=Mailbox Import Export), you would see the Properties dialog shown in Figure 12.9.

FIGURE 12.9
The properties for
the Mailbox Import
Export role object

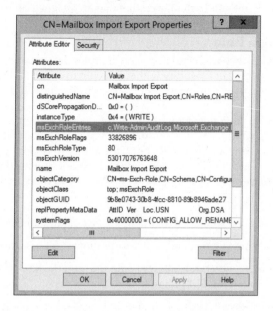

You will notice that one of the attributes on this object is the msExchRoleEntries attribute. This is a multivalued string attribute that lists each management role entry and the parameters that role assignees can run. Figure 12.10 shows the values that the Mailbox Import Export object has for its msExchRoleEntries attributes, as viewed in ADSI Edit.

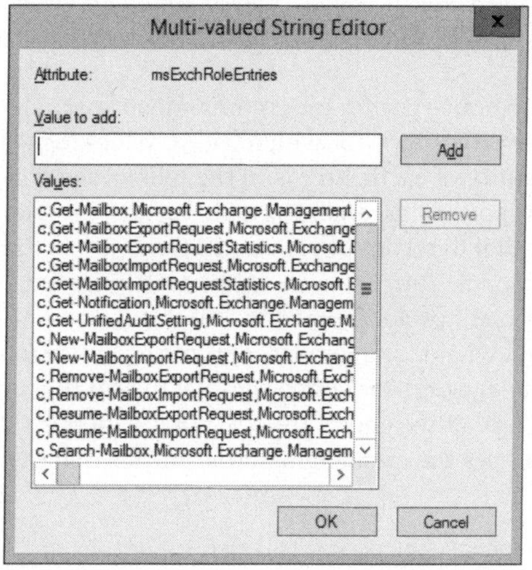

FIGURE 12.10
The management
role entries for the
Mailbox Import
Export role as seen
in ADSI Edit

So as you can see, management role entries are added to management roles as an attribute of the management role. The management role itself is its own object. Each of these management role entries defines an Exchange cmdlet that an assignee can run.

Choosing a Role

Exchange already has several management roles defined out of the box. These defined roles give you a great degree of flexibility without having to create and customize your own management roles. For the sake of simplicity and manageability, these built-in roles should be used whenever possible.

But how do you know which built-in role to use? Let's pretend that you didn't know the Mailbox Import Export role existed. However, you have an ongoing legal investigation and you need to give your lawyer, Richard, the ability to import mail stored on the personal folder store to a specific mailbox. To determine which role you need to assign to Richard, you can use the Get-ManagementRoleEntry cmdlet. With it, you can specify wildcards to determine the following:

♦ Which management role contains a particular management role entry

♦ Which management role entries are allowed for a particular management role

To determine which role allows Richard to run the New-MailboxImportRequest cmdlet, you can run the following EMS command:

```
Get-ManagementRoleEntry "*\New-MailboxImportRequest"
Name                           Role                     Parameters
----                           ----                     ----------

New-MailboxImportRequest       Mailbox Import Export    {AcceptLargeDataLos…
```

As you can see from the command's output, the New-MailboxImportRequest cmdlet is added only to the Mailbox Import Export role. There are no other options by default in Exchange. If you want to use the built-in roles, you must assign the Mailbox Import Export role to Richard.

You will also notice that in the command we specified *\New-MailboxImportRequest as the management role entry for which we were looking. When working with management role entries, the identity of each entry is in the following format: *management role\management role entry*. By specifying a wildcard character (*) in place of the *management role* portion, we told the cmdlet to retrieve every management role that has the New-MailboxImportRequest cmdlet defined on it. You can use wildcards in different places and retrieve different results.

For example, let's pretend that you stumbled across the Mailbox Import Export role and you want to find out what management role entries this management role allows. Again, you can use the Get-ManagementRoleEntry cmdlet to find this information. However, this time you will place the wildcard at the end of the role entry's identity instead of the beginning. The following command retrieves the management role entries that the Mailbox Import Export management role allows:

```
Get-ManagementRoleEntry "Mailbox Import Export\*"
Name                           Role                     Parameters
----                           ----                     ----------
Write-AdminAuditLog            Mailbox Import Export    {Comment, Confirm, ...
Suspend-MailboxImportRequest   Mailbox Import Export    {Confirm, Debug, Do...
Suspend-MailboxExportRequest   Mailbox Import Export    {Confirm, Debug, Do...
```

```
Start-AuditAssistant            Mailbox Import Export    {Identity}
Set-UnifiedAuditSetting         Mailbox Import Export    {Debug, ErrorAction...
Set-Notification                Mailbox Import Export    {Confirm, Debug, Do...
Set-MailboxImportRequest        Mailbox Import Export    {AcceptLargeDataLos...
Set-MailboxExportRequest        Mailbox Import Export    {AcceptLargeDataLos...
Set-ADServerSettings            Mailbox Import Export    {ConfigurationDomai...
Search-Mailbox                  Mailbox Import Export    {Confirm, Debug, De...
Resume-MailboxImportRequest     Mailbox Import Export    {Confirm, Debug, Do...
Resume-MailboxExportRequest     Mailbox Import Export    {Confirm, Debug, Do...
Remove-MailboxImportRequest     Mailbox Import Export    {Confirm, Debug, Do...
Remove-MailboxExportRequest     Mailbox Import Export    {Confirm, Debug, Do...
New-MailboxImportRequest        Mailbox Import Export    {AcceptLargeDataLos...
New-MailboxExportRequest        Mailbox Import Export    {AcceptLargeDataLos...
Get-UnifiedAuditSetting         Mailbox Import Export    {Debug, ErrorAction...
Get-Notification                Mailbox Import Export    {Debug, DomainContr...
Get-MailboxImportRequestSta...  Mailbox Import Export    {Debug, Diagnostic,...
Get-MailboxImportRequest        Mailbox Import Export    {BatchName, Debug, ...
Get-MailboxExportRequestSta...  Mailbox Import Export    {Debug, Diagnostic,...
Get-MailboxExportRequest        Mailbox Import Export    {BatchName, Debug, ...
Get-Mailbox                     Mailbox Import Export    {Anr, Credential, D...
```

By using `Mailbox Import Export\*` in the command, we told the cmdlet to retrieve every management role entry that is defined on the Mailbox Import Export management role. When deciding which roles you need to assign to administrators, it's very important to look at not only what role allows the administrator to do their job but also what other permissions the administrator will gain when using one of the built-in roles.

Customizing Roles

You should always turn to the built-in management roles first and determine if you can use what's already there before attempting to customize your own roles. However, there may be times when the built-in roles offer you too much access. To illustrate this, let's continue with the scenario of your legal struggles. In the previous section, we determined that to give Richard, your lawyer, the ability to import mail stored in PST files, you could assign him the Mailbox Import Export role. This role allows him to run the cmdlets we identified earlier.

Now let's suppose that you run a very tight ship. When you examined the Mailbox Import Export role, you noticed that not only does the role give Richard the ability to import mail, but it also gives him the ability to export it. Knowing this, you've decided that you don't want your lawyer to be able to export mail from people's mailboxes. In this case, you can create a custom management role.

How a Custom Role Works

To create a new custom management role, you must start with an existing management role and copy it. You cannot create a custom management role from scratch (however, there is one exception that we will discuss shortly in the section "Unscoped Top-Level Roles: The Exception"). Each custom role that you create must inherit properties from an existing management role that is already in place. This forms a parent/child relationship between an existing role (the parent) and the custom role (the child). Let's take a closer look at the Mailbox Import Export role to understand this more clearly.

To fulfill the scenario that we just discussed of allowing Richard to only import mail, you would have to create a custom role that is similar to the Mailbox Import Export role but that doesn't have the ability to export mail. Because every custom role must have a parent management role that already exists, we can make the Mailbox Import Export role the parent to our new custom role. We'll call this new role Mailbox Import Only.

When we create the custom role, it will be able to use only the same management role entries that the parent role uses. This will give the Mailbox Import Only role access to the same management role entries defined on its parent role, Mailbox Import Export. We cannot add any role entries to our new custom role that aren't already included in the Mailbox Import Export role. This restriction applies not only to the cmdlets but also to the parameters on the cmdlets. Because of this, the role entries that the child role can have are limited to the role entries defined on the parent. Even though we don't have the ability to add role entries to the Mailbox Import Only role, we do have the ability to remove them. In this case, you would remove access to all the MailboxExportRequest cmdlets.

This leaves the Mailbox Import Only role without any of the MailboxExportRequest cmdlets. Figure 12.11 illustrates the relationship between the parent and child roles.

FIGURE 12.11
The relationship between a parent role and a child role

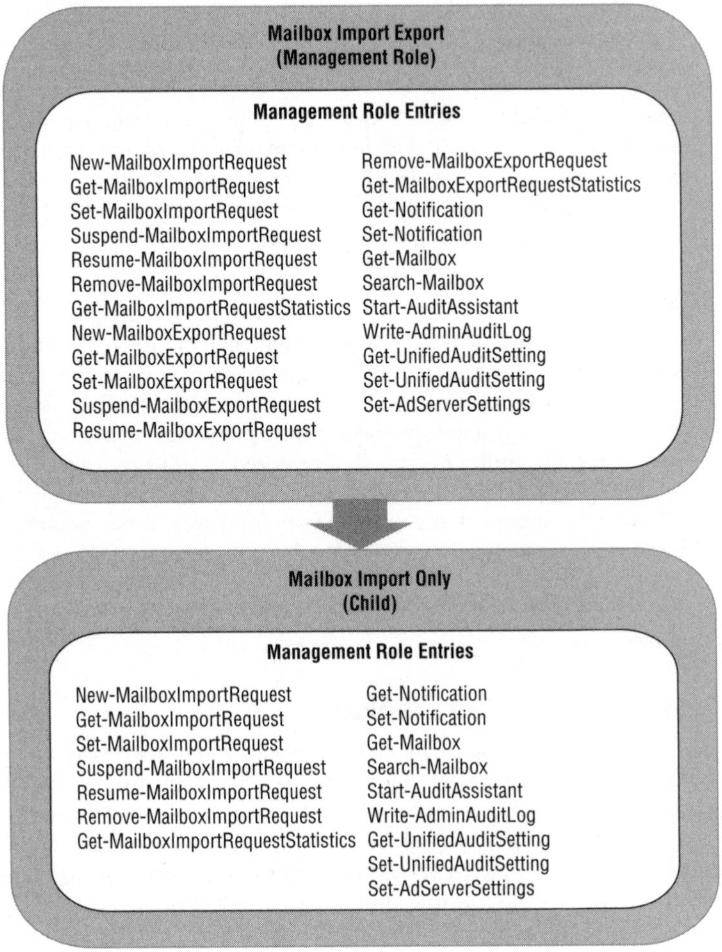

Mailbox Import Export
(Management Role)

Management Role Entries

New-MailboxImportRequest
Get-MailboxImportRequest
Set-MailboxImportRequest
Suspend-MailboxImportRequest
Resume-MailboxImportRequest
Remove-MailboxImportRequest
Get-MailboxImportRequestStatistics
New-MailboxExportRequest
Get-MailboxExportRequest
Set-MailboxExportRequest
Suspend-MailboxExportRequest
Resume-MailboxExportRequest

Remove-MailboxExportRequest
Get-MailboxExportRequestStatistics
Get-Notification
Set-Notification
Get-Mailbox
Search-Mailbox
Start-AuditAssistant
Write-AdminAuditLog
Get-UnifiedAuditSetting
Set-UnifiedAuditSetting
Set-AdServerSettings

Mailbox Import Only
(Child)

Management Role Entries

New-MailboxImportRequest
Get-MailboxImportRequest
Set-MailboxImportRequest
Suspend-MailboxImportRequest
Resume-MailboxImportRequest
Remove-MailboxImportRequest
Get-MailboxImportRequestStatistics

Get-Notification
Set-Notification
Get-Mailbox
Search-Mailbox
Start-AuditAssistant
Write-AdminAuditLog
Get-UnifiedAuditSetting
Set-UnifiedAuditSetting
Set-AdServerSettings

DEFINING CUSTOM ROLES

To create custom roles, you must use the EMS or RBAC Manager. The EAC does not give you the ability to manage custom roles. When defining these roles, you will use the following cmdlets:

New-ManagementRole   Creates a new custom role

Remove-ManagementRole   Deletes a custom role that you previously created

Add-ManagementRoleEntry   Adds a role entry onto an existing role

Remove-ManagementRoleEntry   Removes a role entry that you previously added

Set-ManagementRoleEntry   Adjusts the parameters that can be used on a role entry that has already been added to a role

To continue with the legal scenario, let's create the Mailbox Import Only role using the New-ManagementRole cmdlet. When using the cmdlet, you specify the name of the new role and the parent from which the role is inheriting its management role entries. The following example creates the Mailbox Import Only role that we've been discussing:

```
New-ManagementRole "Mailbox Import Only" -Parent "Mailbox Import Export"
Name                                    RoleType
----                                    --------

Mailbox Import Only                     MailboxImportExport
```

You can run the Get-ManagementRoleEntry cmdlet on this newly created role to see that, by default, the custom role defines all the same role entries that the parent role has:

```
Get-ManagementRoleEntry "Mailbox Import Only\*"
Name                          Role                  Parameters
----                          ----                  ----------
Get-Mailbox                   Mailbox Import Only    {Anr, Credential, D...
Get-MailboxExportRequest      Mailbox Import Only    {BatchName, Debug, ...
Get-MailboxExportRequestSta...Mailbox Import Only    {Debug, Diagnostic,...
Get-MailboxImportRequest      Mailbox Import Only    {BatchName, Debug, ...
Get-MailboxImportRequestSta...Mailbox Import Only    {Debug, Diagnostic,...
Get-Notification              Mailbox Import Only    {Debug, DomainContr...
Get-UnifiedAuditSetting       Mailbox Import Only    {Debug, ErrorAction...
New-MailboxExportRequest      Mailbox Import Only    {AcceptLargeDataLos...
New-MailboxImportRequest      Mailbox Import Only    {AcceptLargeDataLos...
Remove-MailboxExportRequest   Mailbox Import Only    {Confirm, Debug, Do...
Remove-MailboxImportRequest   Mailbox Import Only    {Confirm, Debug, Do...
Resume-MailboxExportRequest   Mailbox Import Only    {Confirm, Debug, Do...
Resume-MailboxImportRequest   Mailbox Import Only    {Confirm, Debug, Do...
Search-Mailbox                Mailbox Import Only    {Confirm, Debug, De...
Set-ADServerSettings          Mailbox Import Only    {ConfigurationDomai...
Set-MailboxExportRequest      Mailbox Import Only    {AcceptLargeDataLos...
Set-MailboxImportRequest      Mailbox Import Only    {AcceptLargeDataLos...
Set-Notification              Mailbox Import Only    {Confirm, Debug, Do...
Set-UnifiedAuditSetting       Mailbox Import Only    {Debug, ErrorAction...
Start-AuditAssistant          Mailbox Import Only    {Identity}
Suspend-MailboxExportRequest  Mailbox Import Only    {Confirm, Debug, Do...
Suspend-MailboxImportRequest  Mailbox Import Only    {Confirm, Debug, Do...
Write-AdminAuditLog           Mailbox Import Only    {Comment, Confirm, ...
```

Now that the role is created, you can remove the `MailboxExportRequest` cmdlets from the list of role entries. To do so, you run the `Remove-ManagementRoleEntry` cmdlet and specify the role entry that you want to remove. Because there are multiple cmdlets with `MailboxExportRequest`, you will first run `Get-ManagementRoleEntry` and pipe the results to `Remove-ManagementRoleEntry`. When you run this command, you will be prompted with a confirmation message that asks you if you are sure that you want to remove the role entry. You can bypass this message by adding the `-Confirm:$False` parameter to the command. The following example demonstrates the command you would use to remove the `MailboxExportRequest` cmdlets from the Mailbox Import Only role, bypassing the confirmation message:

```
Get-ManagementRoleEntry "Mailbox Import Only\*-MailboxExportRequest" | Remove-
ManagementRoleEntry -confirm:$false
```

To verify that the role entry was removed, you can run the `Get-ManagementRoleEntry` cmdlet again to retrieve the management role entries on the management role. You will notice that all the management role entries for `MailboxExportRequest` have been removed:

```
Get-ManagementRoleEntry "Mailbox Import Only\*"
Name                         Role                  Parameters
----                         ----                  ----------
Get-Mailbox                  Mailbox Import Only   {Anr, Credential, D...
Get-MailboxExportRequestSta... Mailbox Import Only {Debug, Diagnostic,...
Get-MailboxImportRequest     Mailbox Import Only   {BatchName, Debug, ...
Get-MailboxImportRequestSta... Mailbox Import Only {Debug, Diagnostic,...
Get-Notification             Mailbox Import Only   {Debug, DomainContr...
Get-UnifiedAuditSetting      Mailbox Import Only   {Debug, ErrorAction...
New-MailboxImportRequest     Mailbox Import Only   {AcceptLargeDataLos...
Remove-MailboxImportRequest  Mailbox Import Only   {Confirm, Debug, Do...
Resume-MailboxImportRequest  Mailbox Import Only   {Confirm, Debug, Do...
Search-Mailbox               Mailbox Import Only   {Confirm, Debug, De...
Set-ADServerSettings         Mailbox Import Only   {ConfigurationDomai...
Set-MailboxImportRequest     Mailbox Import Only   {AcceptLargeDataLos...
Set-Notification             Mailbox Import Only   {Confirm, Debug, Do...
Set-UnifiedAuditSetting      Mailbox Import Only   {Debug, ErrorAction...
Start-AuditAssistant         Mailbox Import Only   {Identity}
Suspend-MailboxImportRequest Mailbox Import Only   {Confirm, Debug, Do...
Write-AdminAuditLog          Mailbox Import Only   {Comment, Confirm, ...
```

UNSCOPED TOP-LEVEL ROLES: THE EXCEPTION

Earlier in this section, we stated that there was an exception to the fact that custom management roles require an existing management role to be the parent. That exception is a special type of management role called the *unscoped top-level role*. This type of role does not have a parent. The unscoped top-level role allows you to define both PowerShell scripts and non-Exchange cmdlets as its role entries. This type of role is highly customized, so it can't have a parent role because there is no starting point for it. You would typically want to use an unscoped top-level role when you want to strictly limit what an administrator can do, such as only giving them access to predefined scripts.

By default, no one has permissions to create unscoped top-level roles. If you want to grant these permissions to an administrator, you will need to assign the role called Unscoped Role Management to the administrator who needs to create unscoped top-level roles.

To create the unscoped top-level role, use the `New-ManagementRole` cmdlet with the `UnscopedTopLevel` parameter. If the `UnscopedTopLevel` parameter isn't available, that means you have not been assigned the Unscoped Role Management role. The following example creates an unscoped top-level role called Run Custom Scripts:

```
New-ManagementRole "Run Custom Scripts" -UnScopedTopLevel
Name                                    RoleType
----                                    --------
Run Custom Scripts                      UnScoped
```

After the role is created, you can use the `Add-ManagementRoleEntry` cmdlet to add custom scripts or non-Exchange cmdlets as role entries on the role. When you run this cmdlet, specify the script with the syntax of *Management Role\Script*. Also specify the type of role entry you are adding (script or cmdlet), and use the `UnScopedTopLevel` parameter. You can also use the `Parameters` parameter to specify what parameters can be used with the script. For example, to add the custom script called `CheckServerHealth.ps1` to the Run Custom Scripts role, you would use the following command:

```
Add-ManagementRoleEntry "Run Custom Scripts\CheckServerHealth.ps1"
-UnScopedTopLevel -Type Script -Parameters CheckServices,CheckLogs
```

Lastly, you need to assign the unscoped role to a security group or a user. The process for assigning roles is discussed later in this chapter.

Distributing Roles

After you have defined the roles you want to use in your RBAC implementation, you must distribute those roles to administrators and end users. This section will discuss the important aspects of role distribution and show you how to distribute roles to both administrators and end users.

Determining Where Roles Will Be Applied

When distributing roles, one important detail that should not be overlooked is where those roles apply. In RBAC, this is referred to as the role's *scope*. The scope defines what objects (such as recipients or servers) the role can impact. As you'll see throughout this section, scopes are extremely flexible. They allow roles to be applied throughout the organization or even restricted to just a particular OU of recipients in Active Directory. Scopes can be used as part of limiting administrative permissions to only what is required.

INHERITED SCOPES

Every role has a scope. When a role is created, it has a default scope, also known as an *implicit* scope. There are two types of implicit scopes: a recipient scope and a configuration scope. The recipient scope defines which recipients the role can impact. The configuration scope defines which configuration components the role can impact. To illustrate how this applies to a role, let's look at our example of the Mailbox Import Export role. We can use the `Get-ManagementRole` cmdlet to view the implicit scope defined on this role:

```
Get-ManagementRole "Mailbox Import Export" | fl *scope*
ImplicitRecipientReadScope  : Organization
ImplicitRecipientWriteScope : Organization
ImplicitConfigReadScope     : OrganizationConfig
ImplicitConfigWriteScope    : OrganizationConfig
```

The first thing you will notice is that there are four scope attributes on the role. Each type of scope (recipient and configuration) has both a read scope and a write scope associated with it. In most cases, the read and write scope are the same. However, there are a few roles where they are different. If you run the following command, you can see the roles that have different read and write scopes defined. As you can tell from the output of the command, the cases where the read and write scope differ make sense. For example, the View-Only Configuration role can read the configuration of Exchange but not write to it.

```
Get-ManagementRole | where {
$_.ImplicitRecipientReadScope -ne $_.ImplicitRecipientWriteScope -or
$_.ImplicitConfigReadScope -ne $_.ImplicitConfigWriteScope} |
fl Name, *scope*
Name                        : Legal Hold
ImplicitRecipientReadScope  : Organization
ImplicitRecipientWriteScope : Organization
ImplicitConfigReadScope     : OrganizationConfig
ImplicitConfigWriteScope    : None

Name                        : View-Only Configuration
ImplicitRecipientReadScope  : Organization
ImplicitRecipientWriteScope : None
ImplicitConfigReadScope     : OrganizationConfig
ImplicitConfigWriteScope    : None

Name                        : View-Only Recipients
ImplicitRecipientReadScope  : Organization
ImplicitRecipientWriteScope : None
ImplicitConfigReadScope     : OrganizationConfig
ImplicitConfigWriteScope    : None

Name                        : MyDistributionGroups
ImplicitRecipientReadScope  : MyGAL
ImplicitRecipientWriteScope : MyDistributionGroups
ImplicitConfigReadScope     : OrganizationConfig
ImplicitConfigWriteScope    : None

Name                        : O365SupportViewConfig
ImplicitRecipientReadScope  : Organization
ImplicitRecipientWriteScope : None
```

```
ImplicitConfigReadScope     : OrganizationConfig
ImplicitConfigWriteScope    : None

Name                        : View-Only Audit Logs
ImplicitRecipientReadScope  : Organization
ImplicitRecipientWriteScope : None
ImplicitConfigReadScope     : OrganizationConfig
ImplicitConfigWriteScope    : None
```

Table 12.2 shows the various types of the scope parameters and what each of these values means.

TABLE 12.2:   Implicit Scope Values

SCOPE	APPLIES TO RECIPIENT SCOPE	APPLIES TO CONFIGURATION SCOPE	DESCRIPTION
MyDistributionGroups	Yes	No	If in the read scope, allows read access to distribution groups owned by the user. If in the write scope, allows users to create or modify distribution lists that they own.
MyGAL	Yes	No	View the properties of recipients in the GAL. Valid only with the read scope.
None	Yes	Yes	Disallows access to the scope to which it's applied.
Organization	Yes	No	If in the read scope, gives users read access to all recipients in the organization. If in the write scope, gives users the ability to create or modify recipients in the organization.
OrganizationConfig	No	Yes	If in the read scope, allows the user to view the configuration of any server in the organization. If in the write scope, the user can modify configuration settings on any server.
Self	Yes	No	If in the read scope, users can view only their own properties. If in the write scope, users can modify their properties.

The implicit scope that is defined on a role cannot be changed. When you define a custom role, the same implicit scopes on the parent role also apply to the custom role, and they cannot be changed. However, the implicit scopes defined on the roles can be overwritten. To overwrite the implicit scopes, you can set an explicit scope on the role assignment, instead of configuring it on the role. *Explicit* scopes are scopes that you apply, as opposed to the implicit scopes that Exchange has already applied. Explicit scopes come in two forms: predefined scopes and custom scopes.

OVERWRITING THE WRITES

Explicit scopes only overwrite the write scopes associated with the role. The read scopes will always apply, regardless of any explicit scope defined in the role assignment. Because of this, you can't specify an explicit write scope that isn't within the read scope of the management role. For example, if the read scope on a role is Self, you can't specify a write scope of Organization.

USING PREDEFINED SCOPES

Predefined scopes are explicit scopes that Exchange makes available to you by default. These predefined scopes apply only to the recipient scope type. Exchange creates the following predefined scopes:

MyDistributionGroups Allows users to create distribution groups and modify the properties of distribution groups where they are defined as the owner.

Organization Allows users that hold the role to modify recipients in the entire organization. For example, if the role allows users to change the recipient display name, this scope would allow the role holders to change it for any recipient in the organization.

Self Allows users to modify only their own properties. For example, if the role allows users to change the recipient display name, this scope would allow the role holder to change only their own display name.

CREATING CUSTOM SCOPES

Aside from using an existing predefined scope, you can create a custom scope that offers more flexibility. Custom scopes are extremely useful because they allow you to narrow down the scope of a role to a very granular level. For example, you can narrow down the scope of recipients to a specific OU or only recipients with a specific attribute set on their accounts. For servers, you can narrow down the configuration scope to a specific site or even name the servers themselves. For databases, you can select a static set of databases or use a filter to manage databases that have a common configuration.

Along with configuring which objects a custom scope is applied to, you can configure if the scope is exclusive or regular. By default, all new scopes are created as regular; however, you can specify that a custom scope be an exclusive scope. An exclusive scope and a regular scope act almost the same. The major difference between them is that an exclusive scope prevents any administrator that is not associated with an exclusive scope from making changes to objects even if the object falls within the boundaries of a regular scope. Once you set a scope as an exclusive scope, the deny action takes effect immediately. For example, if you have a role group named Baltimore IT, with the custom write scope of the Baltimore OU, members of the Baltimore IT group would be able to manage users in the Baltimore OU based on the roles applied to the Baltimore IT group. If you created a new exclusive scope with a filter to include anyone with "Manager" in the Department field, administrators of the Baltimore IT group would not be able to edit users in the Baltimore OU that have "Manager" in the Department field unless they have been associated with the new exclusive scope or an equivalent exclusive scope. Figure 12.12 illustrates the implementation of an exclusive scope (note that the -eq command stands for equal).

FIGURE 12.12

Implementation of an exclusive scope

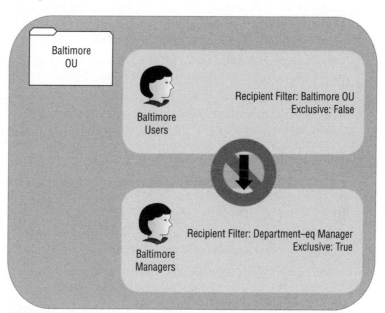

Like predefined scopes, custom scopes are applied to the role assignments and not the roles themselves. However, unlike with predefined scopes, you can specify a configuration scope as well as a recipient scope. You can create a custom scope using the New-ManagementScope cmdlet. When you create the scope, you have several options that give you the ability to narrow the scope as granularly as you want. You have the following options when creating the scope:

DatabaseList   Allows you to specify a list of databases to which this scope applies.

DatabaseRestrictionFilter   Allows you to define a filter based on databases' attributes to which the scope applies. For example, you can filter out databases that match a certain string.

RecipientRestrictionFilter Gives you the ability to define a filter based on attributes on the recipient. For example, you can define a scope whose recipients include only the people on the fourth floor of a specific building.

RecipientRoot Allows you to restrict the scope to an OU in Active Directory.

To illustrate how this works, let's create a couple of custom scopes:

ServerList Allows you to specify a list of servers to which this scope applies.

ServerRestrictionFilter Allows you to define a filter based on server attributes to which the scope applies. For example, you can filter out the servers based on the Active Directory site they are in.

For our first example, we'll say that you want to create a scope that allows you to confine certain roles to only servers in Baltimore. To accomplish this, we'll use the New-ManagementScope cmdlet with the ServerRestrictionFilter parameter. In this parameter, we'll create a filter that specifies only servers in the Baltimore Active Directory site. The following command would be used:

```
New-ManagementScope -Name "Baltimore Site" -ServerRestrictionFilter {
ServerSite -eq "CN=Baltimore,CN=Sites,CN=Configuration,DC=contoso,DC=com"}
```

For the next example, we'll build a custom recipient scope that applies only to users in the Accounting OU in Active Directory. Referring to the preceding list, you can see that you will need to use the RecipientRoot parameter. You are also required to specify a RecipientRestrictionFilter, but you can set this to be all accounts that are user mailboxes. This command creates a scope that includes all user mailboxes in the Accounting OU:

```
New-ManagementScope -Name "Accounting Only" -RecipientRoot
"OU=Accounting,DC=contoso,DC=com" -RecipientRestrictionFilter
{RecipientType -eq "UserMailbox"}
```

You can also create a custom recipient scope based only on a filter. The following command creates a scope that includes only mailboxes that are considered Discovery Mailboxes:

```
New-ManagementScope -Name "Discovery Mailboxes" -RecipientRestrictionFilter
{RecipientTypeDetails -eq "DiscoveryMailbox"}
```

In the last example, you can create a filter for all mailbox databases that start with "Baltimore" in the string and ensure that only administrators assigned this role can manage the Baltimore mailbox databases by using the Exclusive parameter:

```
New-ManagementScope -Name "Baltimore Databases" -DatabaseRestrictionFilter
{Name -Like "Baltimore*"} -Exclusive -Force
```

After the scope is created, you can apply the role assignment. This is discussed in more detail in the next section.

Real World Scenario

GEOGRAPHIC ROLES VS. TIERED ROLES

RBAC gives you great flexibility in designing the access model for your Exchange implementation. There are many models that you can use when defining your roles. The rule of thumb is that the RBAC model you adopt should mirror how you manage your Exchange organization. There are two models in particular that we've frequently encountered in various Exchange organizations.

The geographic management model divides the management of Exchange into different physical regions. Suppose you're working with an organization that wanted to have central control of the Exchange organization maintained from one region but also allow other regions to manage their own Exchange servers and recipients. This organization could use RBAC to define server scopes based on sites and recipient scopes based on regional OUs.

Another organization might use a tiered management model. In this model, the lower tier (Tier 1 in this case) handles basic recipient management tasks. Higher tiers (Tier 2 and Tier 3) handle more advanced tasks. As you get to higher tiers of support, the permissions get less and less restrictive. Eventually, you would reach the top tier of support, providing an administrator or a group of administrators the rights to manage all tasks within the Exchange organization. This organization could also use RBAC to their benefit by creating different role groups for each tier of support and assigning the necessary roles to the appropriate tiers. In this case, the scope of management is the entire organization, so there would be no need to specify an explicit scope.

Assigning Roles to Administrators

The process for assigning roles to administrators is different than the process for assigning roles to end users. The roles that administrators are assigned are inherently different from the roles that users are assigned. Administrators need to have the permissions to manage and configure Exchange. Before we go further and show you how to assign roles to administrators, you should first understand how role assignments work for administrators.

HOW ROLES ARE ASSIGNED TO ADMINISTRATORS

When assigning roles to administrators, you have two options. The first option is to assign the role to a management role group and then add the administrator to the role group. This is the easiest and preferred method of assigning roles to administrators. The second option is to assign the role directly to the administrator's account using a direct role assignment.

Regardless of which method you use, management roles are assigned to either the management role group or the administrator's account using a management role assignment. In Active Directory, an msExchRoleAssignment object is created that represents the role assignment between the account and the role. These role assignment objects are stored in the Configuration

Naming Context under the container `Services\Microsoft Exchange\<Org Name>\RBAC\Role Assignments`.

When these role assignments are created, the default name of the assignment object is the name of the role, followed by a hyphen, followed by the name of the object to which it's being assigned. Figure 12.13 shows an example of a role assignment. Here, the Mail Recipients role is assigned to the Organization Management role group.

FIGURE 12.13
A role assignment object is created in Active Directory when roles are assigned

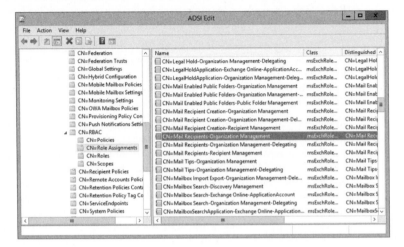

If you were to take a closer look at the role assignment object, you would see that the msExchRoleLink attribute corresponds to the Mail Recipients role's AD object and the msExchUserLink attribute corresponds to the distinguished name of the Organization Management security group (Figure 12.14). This is how a role is united with the assignee.

FIGURE 12.14
A deeper look at the role assignment object in Active Directory

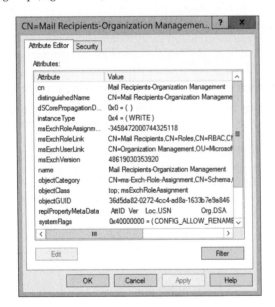

You can retrieve a list of the role assignments in the EMS by running the Get-ManagementRole-Assignment cmdlet with no parameters. Several role assignments are created by default. The following example is only a partial listing:

```
Get-ManagementRoleAssignment
Name                        Role      RoleAssig RoleAssig Assignmen Effectiv
                                      neeName   neeType   tMethod   eUserName

----                        ----      --------- --------- --------- --------
View-Only Configuratio...   View-O... Delega... RoleGroup Direct    All G...
Legal Hold-Discovery M...   Legal ... Discov... RoleGroup Direct    All G...
Mailbox Search-Discove...   Mailbo... Discov... RoleGroup Direct    All G...
User Options-Help Desk      User O... Help Desk RoleGroup Direct    All G...
View-Only Recipients-H...   View-O... Help Desk RoleGroup Direct    All G...
ApplicationImpersonati...   Applic... Hygien... RoleGroup Direct    All G...
Receive Connectors-Hyg...   Receiv... Hygien... RoleGroup Direct    All G...
Transport Agents-Hygie...   Transp... Hygien... RoleGroup Direct    All G...
Transport Hygiene-Hygi...   Transp... Hygien... RoleGroup Direct    All G...
View-Only Configuratio...   View-O... Hygien... RoleGroup Direct    All G...
View-Only Recipients-H...   View-O... Hygien... RoleGroup Direct    All G...
Active Directory Permi...   Active... Organi... RoleGroup Direct    All G...
Active Directory Permi...   Active... Organi... RoleGroup Direct    All G...
...
```

Figure 12.15 illustrates the relationship between management role assignments, scopes, management roles, and management role groups. This figure shows that a management role assignment object is used to assign a role to a role group.

FIGURE 12.15

The relationship between management role assignments, scopes, management roles, and management role groups

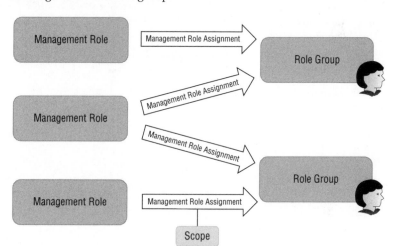

ADDING ADMINISTRATORS TO A MANAGEMENT ROLE GROUP

You can add an administrator's account to a management role group using the EMS, EAC, RBAC Manager or by adding the account directly to the group in Active Directory using a tool, such as

Active Directory Users and Computers. When you add an administrator's account to a management role group, the account gains every role that is specified on the role group. Roles are added cumulatively, so if an administrator's account is a member of another role group, the account will retain those permissions in addition to the permissions assigned by the roles of the new role group.

To add an administrator to a management role group, use the `Add-RoleGroupMember` cmdlet. To use the cmdlet, specify the name of the management role group and the administrator's account in the command. The following example shows the command for adding lawyer Jennifer Fox's account to the Lawyers role group, which has permissions only to export mail from a mailbox:

```
Add-RoleGroupMember "Lawyers" -Member "Jennifer Fox"
```

After you execute this command, you can verify that the administrator was added to the group by enumerating the group membership using the `Get-RoleGroupMember` command and specifying the name of the management role group:

```
Get-RoleGroupMember "Lawyers"
Name                                RecipientType
----                                -------------
Jennifer Fox                        UserMailbox
Richard Alvin                       UserMailbox
```

If you look in the Active Directory security group that represents the Lawyers group, you will also notice that Jennifer Fox's account has been added as a member (Figure 12.16).

FIGURE 12.16
Administrator accounts are added to the AD group that represents management role groups

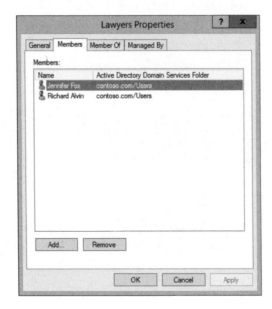

You can also add the administrator's account to the role group through the EAC. This provides a convenient method for modifying permissions without having to open a remote PowerShell connection. You can use the following steps to add an administrator account to a management role group in the EAC:

1. Sign in to EAC by using a web browser to connect to `https://<mailserverFQDN>/ECP`.

2. In the Feature pane, in the left column of the EAC, select permissions.

3. In the toolbar across the top of the EAC, select the Admin Roles tab. The role groups are populated in the list in the center of the EAC, as shown in Figure 12.17.

FIGURE 12.17
The list of management role groups is populated into the EAC

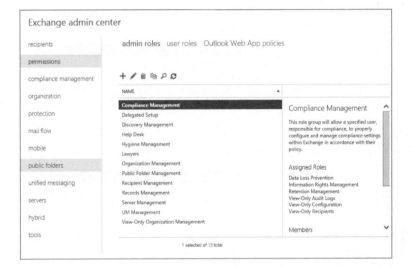

4. Double-click the role group to which you want to add the administrator's account. The management role group's details will be displayed in a separate web browser dialog.

5. In the role group's dialog, click the Add button (+ sign) under the Members list, as shown in Figure 12.18.

6. The Select Members dialog will be displayed, listing the accounts that can be added to the role group. Select the accounts you want to add one at a time, or highlight a group of accounts and click the Add button to add them to the list. After you have added all the accounts in the Select Members dialog, click OK.

7. When you are returned to the Details dialog for the role group, the accounts that you added are displayed in the Members list. Click the Save button to close this dialog and return to the EAC.

Whether you decide to use the EAC to add administrator accounts to management role groups or you use the EMS cmdlets or RBAC Manager, the result is the same: the administrators gain the permissions they need to do their job.

FIGURE 12.18
Click the Add
button to add a
member of a role
group in the EAC

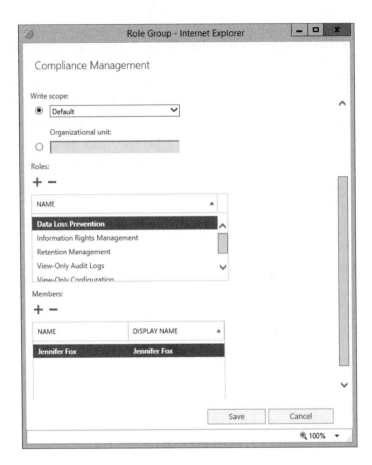

MODIFYING ROLE GROUPS

You may find that a role you want to assign is not available on any of the existing role groups. You can modify the existing role groups or even create your own custom role groups to assign the management roles you want to use. To add a role to an existing role group, you have to create a role assignment for the group.

For example, let's suppose your legal team is a member of the Discovery Management role group. The Discovery Management role group is assigned the roles Legal Hold and Mailbox Search. The legal team needs to be able to search all mail content for users in the Accounting OU over the last six years. The legal team discovers that some of the mail content has been moved to PST files. You need to give the legal team the ability to import messages from the PST files to mailboxes in the Accounting OU. To do this, you can modify the Discovery Management role group and add the Mailbox Import Only role to the group.

To modify an existing role group, use the New-ManagementRoleAssignment cmdlet to create the role assignment between the Mailbox Import Only role and the Discovery Management role group. When running the command, specify the SecurityGroup parameter to indicate that the role is being assigned to a group and to identify the group to which the role is being assigned. The following command demonstrates adding the Mailbox Import Only role to the Discovery Management role group:

```
New-ManagementRoleAssignment -Role "Mailbox Import Only" -SecurityGroup
"Discovery Management"
Name                      Role       RoleAssig RoleAssig Assignmen Effectiv
                                     neeName   neeType   tMethod   eUserName
----                      ----       --------- --------- --------- --------
Mailbox Import Only-Di... Mailbo...  Discov... RoleGroup Direct
```

When assigning a role to a role group, you have the ability to specify the scope that the role impacts. Earlier in this chapter, we showed you how to use explicit scopes and how to create your own custom scopes. If you want to apply a custom scope that you created, specify the `CustomConfigWriteScope` and `CustomRecipientWriteScope` parameters. For example, if you want to apply the Mailbox Import Only role to the users in the Accounting OU, you can use the custom scope called Accounting Only that we created earlier in this chapter. The following command would apply this:

```
New-ManagementRoleAssignment -Role "Mailbox Import Only" -SecurityGroup
"Discovery Management" -CustomRecipientWriteScope "Accounting Only"
```

In most cases, the preferred method is to create a new role group and then use the previous command to create the role assignment to assign the necessary roles to it. To create a role group, use the `New-RoleGroup` cmdlet. Specify the name of the role group you are creating and at least one role that will be assigned to the role group. In the following example, we're creating the role group called Lawyers and assigning the Mailbox Import Only role to it:

```
New-RoleGroup "Lawyers" -Roles "Mailbox Import Only"
Name            AssignedRoles       RoleAssignments      ManagedBy
----            -------------       ---------------      ---------
Lawyers         {Mailbox Import ... {Mailbox Import ...  {contoso.com/Mic...
```

After the role group is created, you can manage it just like any existing role group. If you are using Active Directory Users and Computers to manage groups created by the `New-RoleGroup` cmdlet, the groups are located in the Microsoft Exchange Security Groups OU. For the steps to add administrator accounts to this role group, see the previous section.

DIRECTLY ASSIGNING ROLES TO ADMINISTRATORS

Instead of adding administrator accounts to management role groups, you can assign management roles directly to the administrator's account. Although this method is available, it's not necessarily preferred. When you use this method of assigning permissions, it's harder to track the roles that you delegate to administrators and it's more difficult to manage the access.

Assigning Roles to End Users

When you are assigning roles to end users, the process is a little different than when assigning roles to administrators. User roles serve a different purpose than do administrator roles.

Whereas administrators will need permissions assigned to manage Exchange, users only need to be assigned permissions to modify contact information, mailbox settings, marketplace apps, team mailboxes, and distribution groups. Not only is the scope different between the administrators and users, but users will be managing their own mailboxes instead of other people's mailboxes.

How Roles Are Assigned to End Users

As discussed in the previous section, administrators are assigned to roles either by adding the administrator's account to a management role group that contains the necessary roles or by assigning the management role directly to the administrator's account. This process is quite different for end users.

Roles are assigned to end users using a role assignment policy. Each mailbox can have only one role assignment policy attached to it. Management roles are tied to the role assignment policy with management role assignments. Exchange creates a management role assignment object in Active Directory that links the management role with the management role assignment policy. If you are browsing the management role assignment objects in Active Directory, you will notice that among the assignments that link roles to role groups, you will also find assignments that link roles to assignment policies. Most roles that are assigned to users start with "My"—for example, MyBaseOptions or MyTeamMailboxes. Figure 12.19 shows the MyBaseOptions role assigned to the Default Role Assignment Policy using a role assignment object.

FIGURE 12.19
Role assignment objects are also used for assigning roles to role assignment policies

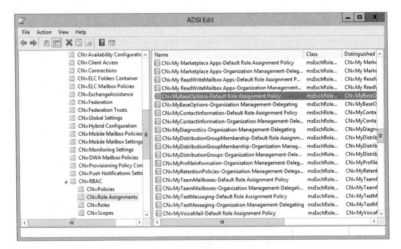

Default User Roles

Every mailbox gets a role assignment policy by default when the mailbox is created. The role assignment policy called Default is created when Exchange is installed and is set to be the default policy for new mailboxes. On this default policy, seven roles are assigned by default, as follows:

MyBaseOptions   Allows users to modify basic mailbox settings for their own mailbox. This includes settings for managing their ActiveSync device, inbox rules, and so on.

MyContactInformation   Gives users the ability to update their contact information in Active Directory.

MyDistributionGroupMembership   Gives users the ability to change their own distribution group memberships. They can use this role to add or remove themselves from distribution groups.

My Custom Apps   Allows users to manage their custom apps.

My MarketPlace Apps   Allows users to manage their marketplace apps.

My ReadWriteMailbox Apps   Allows users to install apps with ReadWriteMailbox permissions.

MyTeamMailboxes   Allows users to create a site mailbox and connect it to SharePoint sites.

MyTextMessaging   Allows users to manage their text messaging settings.

MyVoiceMail   Allows users to change their voicemail settings, which includes the ability to do things like changing their PIN.

The Default Role Assignment Policy doesn't have to remain as the default policy. You can designate a different role assignment policy that you created to be the default policy. When you do this, new mailboxes will use the new policy you defined instead of the one Exchange created. The existing mailboxes that were using the Default Role Assignment Policy will remain with that policy.

To change the Default Role Assignment Policy, use the `Set-RoleAssignmentPolicy` cmdlet with the `IsDefault` parameter. The following EMS command changes the Default Role Assignment Policy to a different policy:

```
Set-RoleAssignmentPolicy "Contact Update Only Policy" -IsDefault
```

WORKING WITH ROLE ASSIGNMENT POLICIES

Role assignment policies can be managed using the EAC, RBAC Manager, or the EMS. In the EAC, you can add and remove certain user-specific roles to and from the role assignment policy. You can do this by performing the following steps:

1. Sign in to EAC by using a web browser to connect to `https://<mailserverFQDN>/ECP`.

2. On the Feature pane of the EAC, select Permissions.

3. In the toolbar across the top of the EAC, select the User Roles tab. The role assignment policies are populated in the list in the center of the EAC.

4. Select the role assignment policy on which you want to assign or unassign roles. When you select the role assignment policy, the Details pane to the right of the list will display some information about the policy.

5. After you have selected the role assignment policy you want to modify, click the Edit button or double-click the role assignment policy.

6. A new window will open displaying the role assignment policy you selected to edit. You can assign or unassign roles by checking or unchecking the roles. The list of roles for the Default Role Assignment Policy will look like Figure 12.20.

FIGURE 12.20
Check and uncheck
the roles that you
want to add to or
remove from the
role assignment
policy

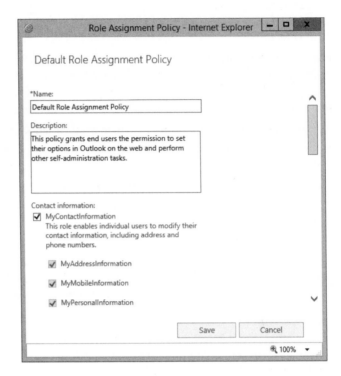

7. After you have chosen the roles you want to assign to the policy, click the Save button at the bottom of the dialog.

   If you are prompted with a Warning dialog indicating that this policy change will affect many users, click Yes to indicate that you want to continue.

Although you can assign roles to role assignment policies in EAC, this option does not give you a lot of flexibility because you can't create or configure role assignment policies. To do this, you must use the EMS or RBAC Manager to manage the role assignment policies.

To start off, you can view a list of the role assignment policies that are currently in existence by running the Get-RoleAssignmentPolicy cmdlet. No parameters are needed to run this command. With a fresh Exchange organization, you should see only the Default Role Assignment Policy. The following example demonstrates the use of this command and the output:

```
Get-RoleAssignmentPolicy | fl Name, IsDefault, Description, RoleAssignments,
AssignedRoles
Name         : Default Role Assignment Policy
IsDefault    : True
Description  : This policy grants end users the permission to set their
               options in Outlook on the web and perform other
               self-administration tasks.
```

```
AssignedRoles : {MyTeamMailboxes, MyDistributionGroupMembership, My Custom
                 Apps, My Marketplace Apps, My ReadWriteMailbox Apps,
                 MyBaseOptions, MyContactInformation, MyTextMessaging,
                 MyVoiceMail}
```

You can view the roles that are tied to the policy by using the `Get-ManagementRole-Assignment` cmdlet with the `RoleAssignee` parameter. Just specify the name of the policy, and the roles will be enumerated for you. The following command demonstrates this by listing all the roles in the Default Role Assignment Policy:

```
Get-ManagementRoleAssignment -RoleAssignee "Default Role Assignment
Policy" | ft Name, Role
Name                                   Role
----                                   ----
MyTeamMailboxes-Default Role Assignm... MyTeamMailboxes
MyDistributionGroupMembership-Defaul... MyDistributionGroupMembership
My Custom Apps-Default Role Assignme... My Custom Apps
My Marketplace Apps-Default Role Ass... My Marketplace Apps
My ReadWriteMailbox Apps-Default Rol... My ReadWriteMailbox Apps
MyBaseOptions-Default Role Assignmen... MyBaseOptions
MyContactInformation-Default Role As... MyContactInformation
MyTextMessaging-Default Role Assignm... MyTextMessaging
MyVoiceMail-Default Role Assignment ... MyVoiceMail
```

If you can't use an existing role assignment policy, you can create a custom policy and add your own set of roles to it. To create the policy itself, use the `New-RoleAssignmentPolicy` cmdlet. The following example creates a new role assignment policy that is similar to the default policy but removes some of the functionality in the `MyBaseOptions` role:

```
New-RoleAssignmentPolicy "Limited Assignment Policy"
```

You can add a role to an existing policy by creating a new management role assignment. This is serviced by the `New-ManagementRoleAssignment` cmdlet in the EMS. Specify the role you are adding to the role assignment policy along with the name of the role assignment policy itself. Let's say that you don't want users to have access to the message-tracking features that come with the `MyBaseOptions` role. Therefore, you've created a custom role based on `MyBaseOptions`, called `MyLimitedBaseOptions`, and removed the message-tracking role entries from the role. The following command adds the `MyLimitedBaseOptions` role to the policy we just created:

```
New-ManagementRoleAssignment -Role "MyLimitedBaseOptions" -Policy
"Limited Assignment Policy"
```

After the role assignment policy is created and configured with the management roles you want to use, you can start applying that policy to end users. To apply a role assignment policy to end users, use the `Set-Mailbox` cmdlet in the EMS. When you do, specify the name of the mailbox to which you are applying the policy as well as the name of the policy you are applying. The following example sets the role assignment policy on Lincoln's account to the Limited Assignment Policy we created previously:

```
Set-Mailbox "Lincoln Alexander" -RoleAssignmentPolicy "Limited Assignment Policy"
```

Auditing RBAC

As the previous sections have illustrated, there are a lot of moving parts in implementing and managing an RBAC deployment. When RBAC is not working as expected, it can be difficult to gather usable information to pinpoint where the problem lies and search the changes made to your RBAC configuration. This section will cover how to reveal what changes were made to your RBAC configuration and find out which roles have been assigned to your users.

Seeing What Changes Were Made

Because RBAC provides administrators with control over an Exchange Server 2016 organization, it is critical that you closely monitor any changes made to the roles assigned to your users. With any administrative change made in your Exchange Server 2016 organization, the change is recorded in the administrator audit log. Using the administrator audit log, you will be able to reveal any modifications made to the RBAC implementation. There are a couple ways to do this.

EXCHANGE ADMIN CENTER

You can generate an administrator role group report through the EAC. This provides a convenient method of retrieving changes made to role groups without having to filter through the administrator audit logs. You can use the following steps to run a role group report in the EAC:

1. Sign in to EAC by using a web browser to connect to https://<mailserverFQDN>/ECP.

2. On the Feature pane of the EAC, select Compliance Management.

3. In the toolbar across the top of the EAC, select the Auditing tab. The built-in reports are populated in the center of the EAC.

4. Select Run An Administrator Role Group Report.

5. A new window will open displaying all changes made to your role groups in the last two weeks. The new window is broken down into four sections:

   ◆ The name and date of the role group(s) modified

   ◆ Lists of changes made against the role group and the user who made the change

   ◆ Date range to search for changes made against role groups

   ◆ The Select Role Groups button, which allows you to search for a specific role group

In Figure 12.21, you can see that the Administrator user changed the group membership of the Compliance Management role group to include Jennifer Fox.

EXCHANGE MANAGEMENT SHELL

The administrator role group report does not provide all the RBAC changes made in your Exchange Server 2016 organization. Using the Search-AdminAuditLog cmdlet, you can search the administrator audit log for a specific cmdlet and parameter. For example, let's use the previous example when we changed the role assignment policy of Lincoln's mailbox to Limited Assignment Policy. To change Lincoln's role assignment policy to Limited Assignment Policy, we used the `Set-Mailbox` cmdlet with the `RoleAssignmentPolicy` parameter. To search the administrator audit log for role assignment policy changes, you can run the following command to search the administrator audit log:

```
Search-AdminAuditLog -Cmdlets Set-Mailbox -Parameters
RoleAssignmentPolicy -StartDate 04/01/2016 -EndDate 04/15/2016


RunspaceId         : df81c2a9-8234-4492-aed6-148468333098
ObjectModified     : contoso.com/Users/Lincoln Alexander
CmdletName         : Set-Mailbox
CmdletParameters   : {RoleAssignmentPolicy, Identity}
ModifiedProperties : {}
Caller             : contoso.com/Users/Administrator
...
```

FIGURE 12.21 Auditing RBAC changes using the EAC

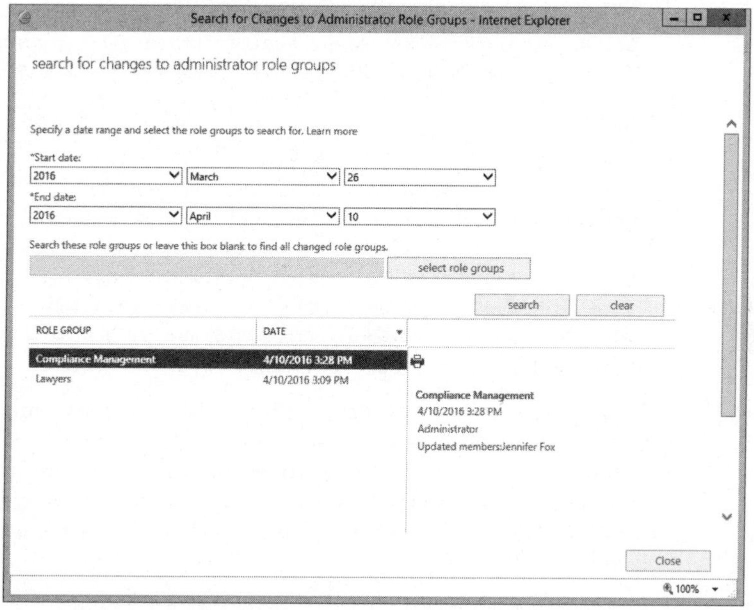

ENABLE ACTIVE DIRECTORY AUDITING

Role groups in RBAC are any security groups that have been assigned a role. When members are added to or removed from a role group using the Exchange Server 2016 tools, the change is recorded in the administrator audit log. However, if a member is added to a role group using Active Directory tools, Exchange Server 2016 does not log the change in the administrator audit logs. To ensure that any members added to a role group are recorded, you must enable Active Directory auditing.

Seeing Who Has Been Assigned Rights

Generating audit logs is a great way to determine what changes have been made, but in many cases you will need to find out what Exchange Server 2016 permissions have already been allocated to users. Using the EMS, you will be able to discover the roles, role groups, and how the permissions have been allocated to your users.

ADMINISTRATOR PERMISSIONS

Using the `Get-ManagementRoleAssignment` cmdlet with the `GetEffectiveUsers` parameter, you can output how each role is assigned to an administrator. In most cases, roles are assigned to administrators through group membership, but an administrator could have a direct assignment or a policy application. In the following example, Jennifer Fox has access to the roles Data Loss Prevention, Information Rights Management, Retention Management, View-Only Audit Logs, View-Only Configuration, and View-Only Recipients because she is a member of the Compliance Management role group. She also has access to the Mailbox Import Only role because she is a member of the Lawyers role group.

```
Get-ManagementRoleAssignment -GetEffectiveUsers | where
{$_.EffectiveUserName -eq "Jennifer Fox"} | ft Name,Role,RoleAssigneeName

Name                      Role                      RoleAssigneeName
----                      ----                      ----------------
Data Loss Prevention-Co... Data Loss Prevention     Compliance Management
Information Rights Mana... Information Rights Mana... Compliance Management
Retention Management-Co... Retention Management     Compliance Management
View-Only Audit Logs-Co... View-Only Audit Logs     Compliance Management
View-Only Configuration... View-Only Configuration  Compliance Management
View-Only Recipients-Co... View-Only Recipients     Compliance Management
Mailbox Import Only-Law... Mailbox Import Only      Lawyers
```

You can also use the `Get-ManagementRoleAssignment` cmdlet with the `GetEffectiveUsers` parameter and search to determine which users have access to a specific role. Using the `Unique` parameter will ensure that each administrator is shown only once, even if they have access to the role through different role assignments. In the following example, all the administrators listed under `EffectiveUserName` have access to the Mailbox Search role group:

```
Get-ManagementRoleAssignment -Role 'Mailbox Search'
-GetEffectiveUsers  | select EffectiveUserName -Unique

EffectiveUserName
-----------------
All Group Members
Administrator
Exchange Online-ApplicationAccount
```

END-USER PERMISSION

When multiple role assignment policies have been created and applied to mailboxes, the `Where-Object` cmdlet can be used to search all mailboxes that have a specific role assignment policy applied. Using the Limited Assignment Policy we created earlier in this chapter, you can search all mailboxes for a specific role assignment policy. By running the following command, any mailbox with the role assignment policy of Limited Assignment Policy will be displayed:

```
Get-Mailbox -ResultSize Unlimited | Where
RoleAssignmentPolicy -eq "Limited Assignment Policy"} | FT -Auto

Name              Alias    ServerName ProhibitSendQuota
----              -----    ---------- -----------------
Lincoln Alexander Lincoln  nyc-ex1    Unlimited
```

The Bottom Line

Determine what built-in roles and role groups provide you with the permissions you need.   Exchange Server 2016 includes a vast number of built-in management roles out of the box. Many of these roles are already assigned to role groups that are ready for you to use. To use these built-in roles, figure out which roles contain the permissions you need. Ideally, determine which role groups you can use to gain access to these roles.

Master It   As part of your recent email compliance and retention initiative, your company hired a consultant to advise you on what you can do to make your Exchange implementation more compliant. The consultant claims that he needs escalated privileges to your existing journal rules so he can examine them. Because you tightly control who can make changes to your Exchange organization, you don't want to give the consultant the ability to modify your journal rules, though you don't mind if he is able to view the configuration details of Exchange. What EMS command can you run to find out what role the consultant can be assigned to view your journal rules but not have permissions to modify them or create new ones? What role do you want to assign to the consultant?

Assign permissions to administrators using roles and role groups.   When assigning permissions to administrators, the preferred method is to assign management roles to role groups and then add the administrators account to the appropriate role group. However, Exchange allows you to assign management roles directly to the administrator's account if you want.

Master It   Earlier in the day, you determined that you need to assign a certain role to your email compliance consultant. You've created a role group called Email Compliance Evaluation and you need to add your consultant to this role group. What command would you use in the EMS to add your consultant, Sam, to this role group?

Grant permissions to end users for updating their address list information.   RBAC doesn't apply only to Exchange administrators. You can also use RBAC to assign roles to end-user accounts so users can have permissions to update their personal information, Exchange settings, and their distribution groups.

Master It   You've decided that you want to give your users the ability to modify their contact information in the global address list. You want to make this change as quickly as possible and have it apply to all existing users and new users coming into your Exchange organization immediately. You determine that using the EAC would be the easiest way to make this change. What would you modify in the EAC to make this change?

Create custom administration roles and assign them to administrators.   If you can't find an existing role that meets your needs, don't worry! You can create a custom role in Exchange Server 2016 and assign the permissions you need to the custom role.

Master It   Your company has asked you to allow administrators in the Baltimore office to manage mailbox settings for all users in the Baltimore OU. Your company does not want the administrators in the Baltimore office to be able to change the mailbox storage limits for individual mailboxes. What would you implement to ensure that administrators in the Baltimore office can only manage mailboxes in the Baltimore OU and are not able to change the mailbox storage limits?

Audit RBAC changes using the Exchange Management Shell and built-in reports in the Exchange Administration Center.   Assigning RBAC permissions is the easy part, determining who has been assigned what permissions can be a bit tricky. Luckily EMS can be used to determine the roles assigned to users.

Master It   Your company has purchased a partner company, which has an administrator named Dave. You have been tasked with providing Dave with the same level of RBAC permissions in your Exchange Server 2016 organization that he has in his Exchange Server 2016 organization. What command would you run in your partner's organization to determine the roles assigned to Dave?

Chapter 13

Basics of Recipient Management

The term *Exchange recipient* defines any mail or mailbox-enabled object in Active Directory used to send or receive email within an Exchange organization.

Depending on the size of your organization, recipient management (handling the user accounts, groups, contacts, public folders, and other resources that can receive email) may consume the vast majority of Exchange administration time. In a small organization, you may be responsible for every aspect of your Exchange server, including creating and managing recipients. In a larger organization with lots of changes, new users, and users leaving the organization, recipient administration will probably be handled by a person or team that is separate from the person or team that manages the Exchange Server infrastructure (message routing, backups, server maintenance, and so on).

This chapter discusses the basics of recipient management. It examines the environment configurations that must exist to support recipient management and the tools you use to manage recipients. It also examines Exchange address lists and how email addresses are defined.

IN THIS CHAPTER, YOU WILL LEARN TO:

◆   Identify the various types of recipients

◆   Use the Exchange Admin Center to manage recipients

◆   Configure accepted domains and define email address policies

Understanding Exchange Recipients

There are different types of users in your organization, as well as different types of needs for message delivery. To account for those differences, Exchange provides various recipient types. Each one fills a specific need within your messaging environment.

User Mailboxes

A user mailbox, which is sometimes referred to as a mailbox-enabled user, has an account in Active Directory and a mailbox on an Exchange server. A user mailbox can send and receive email messages within the Exchange organization and through the Internet—plus it can have access to a personal calendar, contact list, and other services provided by the Exchange server. In most organizations, all corporate users have mailboxes and, therefore, store all emails on the Exchange servers. As you can guess, a user mailbox is the most common type of recipient in Exchange.

Users who have a mailbox can use various client applications to access mailbox content or send emails. For example, they can use Office Outlook, Outlook on the web, or Exchange ActiveSync to access all mailbox content.

Resource and Shared Mailboxes

When you create a user mailbox, you can create multiple types of mailboxes. For example, you can create a standard mailbox that is associated with a user and then used by a company employee to send and receive emails, or you can create a resource mailbox that can be used to represent a company's resources, such as a conference room. Additionally, the concept of the shared mailbox in Exchange Server 2016 provides a more fluid solution for mailbox sharing within the Exchange organization. More detailed information about mailbox-enabled users is available in Chapter 14, "Managing Mailboxes and Mailbox Content."

Mail Users and Mail Contacts

A mail user, which is sometimes referred to as a mail-enabled user, is quite different from a user mailbox—the distinction is more than just a few letters. A *mail user* has a user account in Active Directory and an *external* email address associated with the account. In fact, the mail user has *no* mailbox on an Exchange Server inside your organization.

All mail users who appear in the corporate global address list can receive email from any user inside your organization (assuming there are no restrictions in place to prevent delivery) and can be used to manage certain aspects of those recipients.

So why would a company *not* create a mailbox for a user? Why would they only associate an external email address with their user accounts? The answer is that mail users fill a specific need: the need to make an external *contact* appear in the internal address list. Yes, but there is already an object that fills that need, the *mail contact* (more on that recipient type later in this section). The caveat here is that the external *contact* needs access to internal network resources by using an Active Directory user account. An example of this would be an onsite contract employee who requires access to the network but needs to continue receiving email through their existing external email address. As a result, the mail user appears in the global address list and other users can easily locate and send email to the address, even though the user does not have a mailbox in the Exchange organization. Note also that a mail user *cannot* send or receive email by using the internal Exchange servers. In addition to the mail user, the other recipient type is the mail contact, and the mail contact is exactly that: a *contact* for an individual who is external to your organization. A mail contact is an individual who has neither a security principal in Active Directory nor a mailbox on an internal Exchange server. Mail contacts are visible in the global address list, but they receive all email on an external messaging system. Any internal user can send an email to a mail contact simply by selecting the contact from an address list.

So what is the real-world purpose of a mail contact? Imagine a company that has a large number of suppliers or customers with whom many internal users regularly communicate. You may want to make it easy for your internal users to locate and identify these external contacts; by adding these contacts to Active Directory, you are making them available from a central location and accessible to all internal users. This also provides you with a way to include the suppliers in distribution groups that are used for mass mailings.

Contacts can be created in Active Directory without an Exchange infrastructure in place, but in that case, they are essentially useless. Even after working with Active Directory since 1999, we are still looking for a compelling reason to create *non*-mail-enabled contacts. More information about mail users and mail contacts is available in Chapter 15, "Managing Mail-Enabled Groups, Mail Users, and Mail Contacts."

Table 13.1 shows the core differences between user mailboxes, mail users, and mail contacts.

TABLE 13.1:   User Mailboxes, Mail Users, and Mail Contacts

RECIPIENT	NEEDS ACCESS TO INTERNAL RESOURCES?	NEEDS A MAILBOX IN YOUR EXCHANGE ORGANIZATION?
User mailbox	Yes	Yes
Mail user	Yes	No
Mail contact	No	No

 Real World Scenario

CONTACTS: USED IN A SYNCHRONIZATION SCENARIO

We certainly don't want to oversimplify or minimize the purpose of mail contact recipients. These seemingly minimal objects, which have no access rights, are key elements of some of the most complex Exchange environments. If your organization has long-lasting business relationships with other organizations, you may want to maintain a *somewhat* unified address list where all users from the partner companies appear.

To achieve this goal, your company will create contact objects for all users in the other companies, and vice versa. Though this doesn't actually result in a *single* global address list, it is a way to make the address lists look identical.

Additionally, some organizations that want to extend the feature-rich experience with their on-premises Exchange organization to Office 365 may want to create mail contact objects as part of their hybrid deployment scenario and unified global address list solution.

In scenarios where coexistence between multiple directories is in place, generally a synchronization solution must be deployed. Microsoft Identity Manager 2016 can be used to achieve such coexistence scenarios.

In scenarios of coexistence between on-premises Active Directory infrastructures and an Office 365 tenant, Microsoft Azure Active Directory Connect is used by the hybrid setup to synchronize mail recipient objects, and, therefore, email address lists.

Linked and Remote Mailboxes

Linked mailboxes are user mailboxes that are associated with specific users in a separate, trusted Active Directory forest. When you create a linked mailbox, a disabled user account is created in the Exchange organization, and a user account from a trusted forest is given access to the mailbox. Users with linked mailboxes sign in with the credentials to their local Active Directory domain. Through the Active Directory trust, those credentials are then used to access a mailbox in an Exchange organization in a different forest.

Linked mailboxes are commonly used in the following scenarios:

◆ *Exchange is deployed in a resource forest.* When Exchange is deployed in a resource forest scenario, the Exchange servers are connected to one Active Directory forest. Access to the mailboxes is enabled on user accounts located in one or more trusted forests (called account forests).

◆ *In a merger or acquisition scenario.* In this scenario, both of the organizations will have deployed Exchange before the merger or acquisition. Linked mailboxes provide the opportunity to remove the Exchange Server deployment from one of the organizations. The users from one of the organizations can be configured with linked mailboxes in the other organization. This ensures that users from both organizations are listed in a single GAL, making availability information accessible to all users.

Remote mailboxes are similar to linked mailboxes in that they span multiple environments. A remote mailbox consists of a mail-enabled user in your on-premises Active Directory and an associated mailbox in your cloud-based service (e.g., Office 365). When you create a new remote mailbox, the mail-enabled user is created in your on-premises Active Directory. Then, directory synchronization (e.g., Azure AD Connect) automatically synchronizes the new user object to the cloud-based service. The hosting service recognizes the object and converts it to a user mailbox. Remote mailboxes are typically provisioned as user mailboxes or as resource mailboxes for meeting rooms and equipment. Directory synchronization and mail flow should be provisioned correctly for the mailbox to be provisioned in the hosting service. Also, provisioning of the mailbox in the hosting service is not immediate and depends on the directory synchronization schedule.

Site Mailboxes

Site mailboxes are mailboxes that include both an Exchange mailbox and a SharePoint site. With site mailboxes, the email messages are stored in the mailbox, but the documents are stored on the SharePoint site.

Site mailboxes in Exchange Server 2016 provide an integrated experience for users who need to collaborate. Site mailboxes enable users to access both documents stored on SharePoint Server 2016 and email stored on an Exchange Server 2016 mailbox by using the same client interface—for example, by using Office Outlook and Outlook on the web. The same content also can be accessed directly from the SharePoint site.

With site mailboxes, Exchange stores the email, providing users with the same email conversations that they use every day for their own mailboxes. SharePoint stores the documents and provides advanced document-management tools such as version control. Site mailboxes provide that integration on the user interface layer, while leaving the content in the optimized stores, such as Exchange for email and SharePoint for documents.

Mail-Enabled Groups

A mail-enabled group is an Active Directory group that has been tagged with all the appropriate Exchange mail attributes, including an email address. Once a group has been mail-enabled, any internal or external user can send email to the group (assuming that there are no restrictions preventing message delivery to the group). The group membership can then be modified to configure who receives emails that are sent to the group.

An Active Directory forest that does not include any Exchange organization already uses groups to manage access to resources and permissions. With the integration of an Exchange organization into Active Directory, the same groups (security groups) can be mail-enabled or new groups (distribution groups) that will only be used as a *distribution list* can be created and then mail-enabled.

Active Directory contains two types of groups: distribution and security. Some organizations may decide to mail-enable only distribution groups to prevent the likelihood of mistakenly adding users to a group and assigning them access to secured resources. This decision should be made early or during the architecture and design and governance phases in an Exchange deployment to ensure consistent use of groups.

A mail-enabled group can contain any type of Exchange recipients, including other mail-enabled groups. In Exchange Server 2016, you can mail-enable only groups that are set to the universal group scope. The groups can be either security groups or distribution groups. A unique type of distribution group, called a dynamic distribution group, is a group that has an automatically updated membership and is mail-enabled as well.

More information about mail-enabled groups is available in Chapter 15.

Mail-Enabled Public Folders

A public folder is an electronic version of a bulletin board. Public folders can be used to store messages, contacts, or calendars that must be accessed by multiple users in your organization. Users can create public folders by using Microsoft Outlook, and administrators can create public folders by using the Exchange Administration Center. In Exchange Server 2016, public folders are often referred to as *modern* public folders.

A mail-enabled public folder is one that has been tagged with all the appropriate Exchange mail attributes. Mail-enabled public folders have an email address and can receive email from any internal or external user from your organization (assuming that the appropriate permissions have been configured for the folder).

Mail-enabled public folders are particularly useful if you need to have a "virtual" mailbox shared between multiple users. For example, you may want to have multiple individuals in the HR department review the job applications that are sent to your company. You can create a mail-enabled public folder and provide an email address of hr@yourcompany.com. You would then provide the necessary permissions to individuals in the HR department to review the contents of the folder, without having a large number of emails polluting their inboxes.

While there are not many changes in terms of user access and client functionality for public folders in Exchange Server 2016, the key changes are present in the back end. The main difference is related to public folder storage and public folder replication. Public folders are stored in public folder mailboxes, which reside on mailbox databases. Public folder mailboxes must be created by an administrator from the Exchange Administration Center or the Exchange Management Shell.

It may appear that the shared mailbox recipient type provides the same functionality as a mail-enabled public folder, but there are some distinct differences. Public folders are commonly used for project collaboration or for data archiving. In addition to receiving messages, they can also serve as a main appointment calendar, an elaborate task management structure, or simple document sharing for organizations without SharePoint. The main feature of a mail-enabled public folder is its distribution—once you enable public folders, they are automatically shown in Outlook. On the other hand, a shared mailbox serves well as a common contact mailbox, such as support team or sales representative's email. Commonly, each department in a company has its own shared mailbox with access granted to designated users or groups. In addition to Exchange Server 2016, shared mailboxes also require deploying SharePoint Server 2013 or later or SharePoint Online.

Table 13.2 shows the core differences between mail-enabled public folders and shared mailboxes.

TABLE 13.2: Mail-Enabled Public Folders and Shared Mailboxes

FEATURE	MAIL-ENABLED PUBLIC FOLDERS	SHARED MAILBOXES*
Targeted environments	Small/Medium	Medium/Large
Who can access by default	Anyone in the organization	Designated users or groups
Accessibility in Outlook	Once enabled, appears automatically in all Outlook clients	Each user may have to add the shared mailbox to their Outlook manually
Users can drag and drop files for sharing	Yes	No

Shared mailboxes require deploying SharePoint Server 2013 or later or SharePoint Online.

Defining Email Addresses

Before we discuss how to create mail users, groups, or contacts, we'll first discuss how these objects get their email addresses. The process of creating an email address is just a bit different in Exchange Server 2016 compared with earlier versions of Exchange such as Exchange Server 2003 and 2007. Email addresses are generated for the object at the time the mail-enabled recipient is created, and they are generated by an Exchange Management Shell (EMS) task or the Exchange Administration Center—still with a background EMS task, though. Recipient policies from Exchange Server 2016 have been broken up into two separate concepts:

◆ Email domains for which your organization will accept mail, also known as *accepted domains*

◆ Policies that define the syntax of email addresses, also known as *email address policies*

For addresses that will be assigned to mailboxes on your Exchange Server 2016 servers, you define both an accepted domain and an email address policy.

Accepted Domains

An accepted domain is an SMTP domain name (aka SMTP namespace) for which your Exchange Server 2016 servers will accept email. The servers will either deliver the email to an Exchange mailbox or relay it to internal or external SMTP email servers. If you migrate from a previous version of Exchange Server, the list of accepted domains in Exchange Server 2016 will include all accepted domains from the previous environment. Accepted domains must be defined for all email addresses that will be routed into your organization. Most small- and medium-size organizations will have only a single accepted domain.

ABOUT DOMAIN TYPES

One tricky thing about defining an accepted domain is that you must define how Exchange is to treat a message for the domain. When creating an accepted domain, you can choose from three types of domains:

Authoritative Domains   These are SMTP domains for which you accept the inbound message and deliver it to an internal mailbox within your Exchange organization. In fact, if the recipient of an email does not exist in your Exchange organization, the sender will receive a Non-Delivery Report, or NDR.

Internal Relay Domains   These are SMTP domains for which your Exchange Organization will accept inbound SMTP email, and the Exchange Server may host some, but not all, of the mailboxes for the domain. Often referred to as a "shared SMTP namespace," one common scenario for when you might use an internal relay domain is two companies merging but having yet to consolidate their Exchange environment. After enabling an internal relay domain, if an Exchange server receives an email for the domain but is unable to locate a recipient in the organization, the server will look to the list of Send Connectors to determine where to send the message. The Exchange server then relays the message to another internal email system.

External Relay Domains   These are SMTP domains for which your Exchange organization will accept inbound SMTP email but the Exchange server hosts no mailboxes for the domain. This type of domain is commonly used when one organization is acting as an Internet Service Provider (ISP) for another organization or offering services such as email content filtering (e.g., Exchange Online Protection, or EOP, in Office 365). After enabling an external relay domain, if an Exchange Server receives an email for the domain, then the server will relay the email to an external SMTP email server, usually one that is outside of the organization's boundaries. If Edge Transport servers are deployed in your environment, they will handle external relay domains for the Exchange organization.

SETTING UP AN ACCEPTED DOMAIN USING THE EXCHANGE ADMINISTRATION CENTER

Accepted domains are found within the Mail Flow window. When you choose the Accepted Domains link in the top banner, you will see a list of the accepted domains that have been defined for your organization, such as those shown in Figure 13.1.

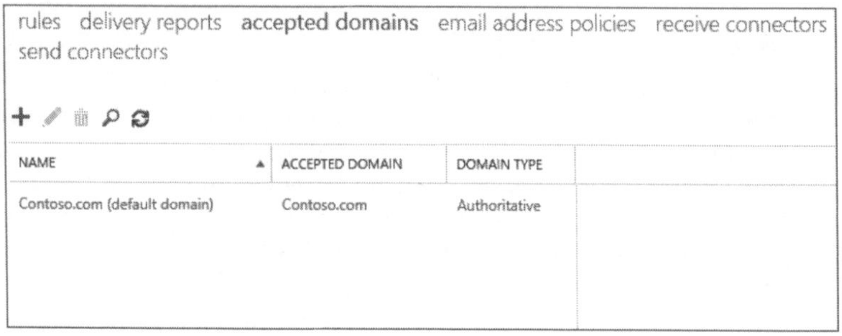

FIGURE 13.1
List of accepted domains

rules   delivery reports   **accepted domains**   email address policies   receive connectors
send connectors

NAME	ACCEPTED DOMAIN	DOMAIN TYPE	
Contoso.com (default domain)	Contoso.com	Authoritative	

When you create an Exchange organization, a single authoritative accepted domain is created automatically and given a name. This is the name of the Active Directory forest root domain; for some organizations, this will not be correct because the naming conventions for Active Directory domain names and SMTP domain names may be different. For example, your Active Directory name may be `Contoso.local`, whereas your public domain name for email is `Contoso.com`.

Accepted domains are simple to create and require little input. To create a new accepted domain, open the New Accepted Domain window by clicking the + (Add) sign in the Actions list. You need to provide only a descriptive name for the accepted domain, the SMTP domain name, and an indication of how messages for this domain should be treated when messages are accepted by Exchange Server 2016 (see Figure 13.2).

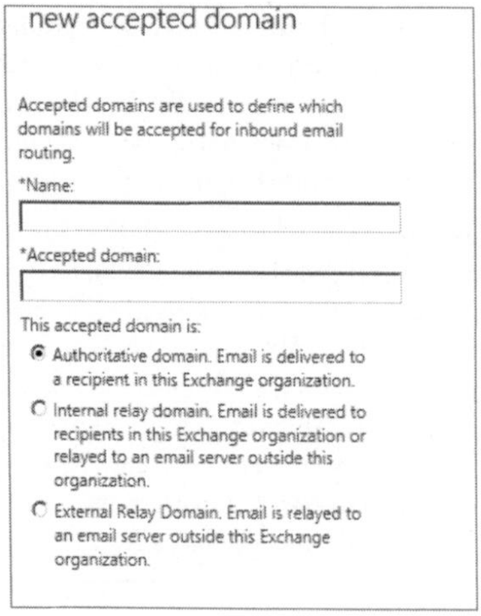

FIGURE 13.2
Creating a new accepted domain

new accepted domain

Accepted domains are used to define which domains will be accepted for inbound email routing.

*Name:

*Accepted domain:

This accepted domain is:

- Authoritative domain. Email is delivered to a recipient in this Exchange organization.
- Internal relay domain. Email is delivered to recipients in this Exchange organization or relayed to an email server outside this organization.
- External Relay Domain. Email is relayed to an email server outside this Exchange organization.

Keep in mind that you cannot change the domain name of an accepted domain once it is created. You can change the domain type, however. If you need to change the domain name of an accepted domain, you will have to remove the domain name and then create a new domain name for the accepted domain.

SETTING UP AN ACCEPTED DOMAIN USING THE EMS

You can also manage accepted domains using the following EMS cmdlets:

- `New-AcceptedDomain`
- `Set-AcceptedDomain`
- `Get-AcceptedDomain`
- `Remove-AcceptedDomain`

For example, to create a new accepted domain for a Canadian division of Contoso, use the following EMS command:

```
New-AcceptedDomain -Name "Contoso Canada" -DomainName "Contoso.ca"
-DomainType "Authoritative"
```

Email Address Policies

For a recipient to send or receive email messages, the recipient must have an email address. Email address policies generate the primary and secondary email addresses for recipients in an Exchange organization so they can send and receive email. Each time a recipient object is modified, Exchange enforces the application of the email address criteria and settings. Also, when an email address policy is modified, all recipient objects associated with the criteria of the email address policy are updated with the appropriate email address.

Using the Exchange Administration Center, you can find email address policies in the Mail Flow window. Select the Email Address Policies tab to see a list of the email address policies in the organization. In Figure 13.3, we have only the default policy assigned by the Exchange Server 2016 organization.

FIGURE 13.3
Email address policies for an Exchange Server 2016 organization

Similar to previous versions of Exchange Server, the default email address policy is the lowest priority policy.

CHANGING AN EXISTING POLICY

When you install Exchange Server 2016, a default email address policy is created by default. The default email address policy defines the email address to consist of the recipient object's alias, which is the local part of an email address that appears before the at sign (@), and the domain name of the Active Directory forest root. Suppose you want to make two changes to the email address policy:

◆ You want to change the SMTP domain name that is on the default policy to something else. For example, this is relevant when the default domain name for the Active Directory forest root is different from the public domain name used for SMTP, and you need to fix this.

◆ You want all email addresses to be generated using the first name, followed by a period, then the last name, and then the domain name.

To perform those tasks, follow these steps:

1. Define an accepted domain. If the default accepted domain is not correct for your organization, you need to create a new accepted domain because Exchange 2016 does not allow you to change an accepted domain. As an example, your Active Directory forest root is named `Contoso.local`, but your public SMTP domain is `Contoso.com`. Under the Accepted Domains tab, create a new authoritative accepted domain for `Contoso.com`.

2. Change the default email address policy so that it uses the new domain name and generates an email address using the *firstname.lastname* format, such as `josh.maher@Contoso.com`. Locate the default policy by clicking the Email Address Policies tab, highlight the default policy, and double-click to edit the policy. On the Email Addresses Format page, you see the list of all domain names used to generate email addresses. Click the domain name you want to modify, in this case `@Contoso.com`, and then click the Edit button to see the SMTP Email Address dialog box. The default setting in the email address policy is to use the user's alias to generate the email. This can be modified to multiple combinations, as Figure 13.4 shows.

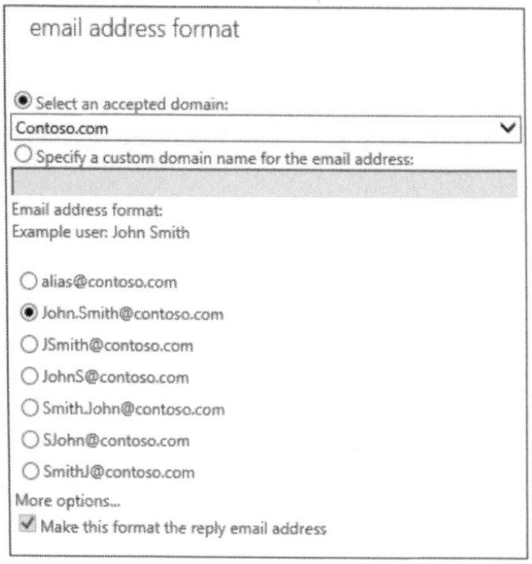

FIGURE 13.4
Changing how the SMTP address is generated

3. Click the Apply To link on the next tab to select the scope of the policy. This setting allows you to choose which recipients will be affected by the email address policy.

Once the email address policy is modified, it will run automatically at its preset interval. The preset interval is immediate once the Active Directory site is updated. In order to force the application of the policy to recipients, an administrator must run the `Update-EmailAddressPolicy` cmdlet.

Of course, you can also create email address policies using the EMS; Table 13.3 shows the EMS cmdlets for creating, deleting, modifying, and updating email address policies.

TABLE 13.3: EMS Cmdlets Used to Manipulate Email Address Policies

EMS CMDLET	DESCRIPTION
New-EmailAddressPolicy	Creates a new email address policy
Set-EmailAddressPolicy	Changes properties of the email address policy specified
Update-EmailAddressPolicy	Updates mail-enabled objects in Active Directory if the conditions of the policy specified apply to those objects
Get-EmailAddressPolicy	Retrieves a list of email address policies and their properties
Remove-EmailAddressPolicy	Deletes the specified email address policy

The following is an example of an EMS cmdlet that would create an email address policy for the domain `Contoso.ca`:

```
New-EmailAddressPolicy -Name 'Contoso Canada' -IncludedRecipients
'MailboxUsers' -Priority '1' -EnabledEmailAddressTemplates 'SMTP:%g.%s@Contoso.ca'
```

Finally, if you want to see the email addresses that have been applied to a mail-enabled object, you can also use an EMS cmdlet to retrieve that information. You could use EAC for this task, but it would require hours of work. Preferably, you would use `Get-Mailbox`, `Get-MailContact`, or `Get-DistributionGroup`. To retrieve the email addresses for a mailbox with an alias that is `Julie.Samante`, for instance, you could type the EMS cmdlet,

```
Get-Mailbox "julie.samante" | Format-List DisplayName,EmailAddresses
```

and see output similar to this:

```
DisplayName    : Julie Samante
EmailAddresses : {smtp:Julie.Samante@Contoso.ca,
SMTP:Julie.Samante@contoso.com}
```

CREATING A NEW EMAIL ADDRESS POLICY

If you have a small- or medium-size organization, you probably support only a single SMTP domain for your users. However, even companies with a handful of mailboxes can sometimes require two or three SMTP domain names. Let's look at an example of an organization that has two divisions, each of which requires its own unique SMTP addresses.

Previously, you changed the default policy for an organization so that all users would get an SMTP address of @Contoso.ca. Let's expand that example further. Let's say that this organization has another division called Volcano Surfboards and its SMTP domain is @volcanosurfboards.com. Any recipient whose company attribute in the Active Directory contains *Volcano Surfboards* should have an SMTP address of *firstname.lastname*@volcanosurfboards.com, and that address should be set as the mailbox default reply address. The default reply address is also known as the primary SMTP address or Reply To address and is typically shown in bold. For SMTP addresses, the reply address will also display "SMTP" in all capital letters in the Type column, whereas the other addresses will be in lowercase letters. Mailboxes can receive email sent to any of the email addresses.

 Real World Scenario

CREATE A NEW EMAIL ADDRESS POLICY OR MODIFY THE DEFAULT EMAIL ADDRESS POLICY?

This is one of the questions we hear the most often: Should I create a new email address list when I need to add a new SMTP domain, or should I simply modify the default email address list?

Let's look at an example to illustrate when you should use one method or the other. Also, keep in mind that only one email address policy can be applied to a recipient in your organization. For example, when you create a new user, Exchange checks to see which email address policy matches the new recipient, based on conditions and filters. If multiple email address policies apply to the user, it will apply only the policy with the highest priority. If there are no custom policies that apply to the user, then the default email address policy is applied. (A policy must always be applied when you create a user mailbox, which is why you cannot remove or delete the default email address policy.)

Now on to our scenario. One of this book's authors was called in because "the Internet was broken and not sending emails." (We love those descriptions!) He quickly noticed that the organization had five different email address policies. Each address policy had a different SMTP domain and was configured to apply to *all users*. So, when a new user mailbox was created, the mailbox received only the highest priority email address policy and was, therefore, assigned only a single SMTP address that matched that policy. The easy fix to this was to simply remove all the custom email address policies and then add the SMTP domains to the default email address policy. After he reapplied the email address policy, all user mailboxes were assigned the correct SMTP addresses.

So now to answer the email address policy question: You should create a custom email address policy when you need to assign a separate SMTP domain to a *subset* of your users. Alternatively, you should modify the default email address policy when you want to add domains to *all users* in your organization.

You should now have enough information for a solution to the Volcano Surfboards division. The first thing you need to do is define `volcanosurfboards.com` as an authoritative accepted domain. If you don't define the accepted domain, you will receive an error message when you try to create an email address policy based on the domain. The accepted domain must always exist first.

Next, you need to create the email address policy. To create a new email address policy, click the + (Add) sign from the Actions list on the Email Address Policies tab in the Mail Flow window. In the New Email Address Policy window, you will configure the name of the policy, the email address format, the sequence of the policy in relation to other policies, and to what types of objects this policy applies.

In this example, the policy is being created for the user mailboxes in the Volcano Surfboards division. To configure the email address format, you will need to click the + (Add) sign from the Actions list under the Email address format. On the Email Address Format window, select the new accepted domain and click the option to use the email address format of `John.Smith@contoso.com`, as shown in Figure 13.5. Click Save to return to the New Email Address Policy window.

FIGURE 13.5
Defining the email address format for the email address policy

You also need the policy to apply only to mailboxes, so you will provide that information on the screen shown in Figure 13.6.

You can further define the conditions that will be used to apply the email address policy by clicking the Add a Rule button. This built-in filter provides more granularity to define the target of the policy. Figure 13.7 shows the conditions available for the rule. You can select such criteria as the state or province, department, or company name of the object.

FIGURE 13.6
Naming the email
address policy

new email address policy

Email address policies generate the primary and secondary email addresses for your
recipients (which include users, contacts, and groups) so they can receive and send email.
Learn more

*Policy name:

Volcano Surfboards

*Email address format:

+ ✏ —

TYPE	ADDRESS FORMAT
SMTP	**John.Smith@VolcanoSurfboards.com**

*Run this policy in this sequence with other policies:

1

*Specify the types of recipients this email address policy will apply to.

○ All recipient types

◉ Only the following recipient types:

☑ Users with Exchange mailboxes

☐ Mail users with external email addresses

☐ Resource mailboxes

FIGURE 13.7
Conditions available
in the email address
policy rules

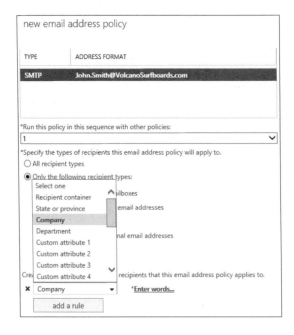

new email address policy

TYPE	ADDRESS FORMAT
SMTP	**John.Smith@VolcanoSurfboards.com**

*Run this policy in this sequence with other policies:

1

*Specify the types of recipients this email address policy will apply to.

○ All recipient types

◉ Only the following recipient types:

- Select one
- Recipient container
- State or province
- Company
- Department
- Custom attribute 1
- Custom attribute 2
- Custom attribute 3
- Custom attribute 4

ailboxes

email addresses

nal email addresses

Cre...   recipients that this email address policy applies to.

✕ Company ▼   *Enter words...

add a rule

In this example, you need the policy to apply to recipients whose company attribute contains *Volcano Surfboards*.

Once you select the Company condition, the Specify Words or Phrases window opens; there you enter the company name (see Figure 13.8). If the Specify Words or Phrases window does not open automatically, simply select Enter Words next to the drop-down menu.

FIGURE 13.8
Specifying words for a rule in an email address policy

After you have entered the necessary company information, click OK to close the window. You can verify that the conditions are defined correctly by clicking the Preview Recipients The Policy Applies To link near the bottom of the New Email Address Policy window. This will open the Preview dialog box; you should see users who have a mailbox and whose company name contains *Volcano Surfboards*. After you verify this information, click Save to create the email address policy.

The Preview Recipients The Policy Applies To link is also helpful in confirming that attributes are being entered correctly in Active Directory. However, in a 10,000-user company, administrators may not recognize if everyone exists in the Email Address Policy Preview dialog box. Fortunately, you can use EMS to get the same information. For example, to retrieve the list of recipients for an email address policy named Volcano Surfboards, use the following EMS command:

```
Get-Recipient -Filter (Get-EmailAddressPolicy "Volcano Surfboards").RecipientFilter
 | sort Name
```

If a user's company name does not contain exactly *Volcano Surfboards*, the policy conditions will not be met and the user's mailbox will include the email addresses from the default email address policy instead.

The Bottom Line

Identify the various types of recipients.   Most recipient types in Exchange Server 2016 have been around since the early days of Exchange. Each serves a specific purpose and has objects that reside in Active Directory.

Master It Your company has multiple Active Directory domains that exist in a single forest. You must make sure that the following needs for your company are met:

◆ Group managers cannot, by mistake, assign permissions to a user by adding someone to a group.

◆ Temporary consultants for your company must not be able to access any internal resources.

Use the Exchange Administration Center to manage recipients. Historically, Exchange administrators mainly used a combination of Active Directory tools and Exchange-native tools to manage Exchange servers and objects. That has all changed with Exchange Server 2016, mainly with the advent of the remote PowerShell implementation of the Exchange Management Shell, but also with the browser-based version of the Exchange Administration Center.

Master It You are responsible for managing multiple Exchange organizations, and you need to apply identical configurations to servers in all organizations. If you are just starting out with Exchange Server 2016 and you are not yet familiar with Remote PowerShell and Exchange Management Shell, you need some guidance regarding the commands that must be used. What should you do?

Configure accepted domains and define email address policies. Accepted domains and email address policies, once a single concept, have been broken up since Exchange Server 2007, and that is still the case in Exchange Server 2016. This gives you more flexibility in managing email address suffixes and SMTP domains that will be accepted by your Exchange servers.

Master It You plan to accept mail for multiple companies inside your organization. Once accepted, the mail will be rerouted to the SMTP servers responsible for each of those companies. What do you need to create in your organization?

Chapter 14

Managing Mailboxes and Mailbox Content

In a small- or medium-sized business, you may be the sole person responsible for all Exchange Server tasks, such as backing up the server, checking the queues, reviewing event logs, and managing mailboxes. In a larger business, you might have a specific task, such as running backups or managing mobile devices.

With any sized business, the common thread for any Exchange Server organization is the day-to-day administrative tasks of mailbox management. The majority of these tasks involve creating mailboxes, moving them to the correct database, setting mailbox properties or policies, and managing email addresses. Other types of tasks may include the management of the mailbox content, such as purging the Deleted Items folder, moving content to other folders, or removing content from a user's mailbox.

IN THIS CHAPTER, YOU WILL LEARN TO:

- ◆ Create and delete user mailboxes
- ◆ Manage mailbox permissions
- ◆ Move mailboxes to another database
- ◆ Perform bulk manipulation of mailbox properties
- ◆ Use Messaging Records Management to manage mailbox content

Managing Mailboxes

This first section on mailbox management tackles the most common tasks: creating, managing, and deleting mailboxes associated with a user account. If you are upgrading from Exchange Server 2007/2010 to Exchange Server 2016, you will immediately notice the absence of the Exchange Management Console and the Exchange Control Panel. Since Exchange Server 2013, all GUI-based management operations are performed via the Exchange Admin Center (EAC).

Enabling a Mailbox Using the EAC

Let's start with a common task: enabling a mailbox for an existing user. You may hear this process referred to as "mailbox-enabling" a user or simply creating a mailbox. Let's say we have a user who requires a mailbox. Her unique location and distinguished name are as follows:

```
contoso.com/Corporate/Amany Bakr
CN=Amany Bakr,OU=Corporate,DC=contoso,DC=com
```

To enable this user mailbox, you must use either the Exchange Management Shell (EMS) or the EAC.

A WIZARD BY ANY OTHER NAME

You had several options available, such as the Exchange Management Console, the Exchange Control Panel, and the venerable Exchange System Manager in earlier versions of Exchange Server. In Exchange Server 2016, you can use the Exchange Management Shell, or you have a unified GUI experience in the EAC to perform an action, enabling you to do your tasks more efficiently and consistently.

Launch the Exchange Admin Center and navigate to the Mailboxes section of the Recipients option on the Feature pane (Figure 14.1). Above the list of recipients you'll notice the + (Add) sign in the Actions bar. This launches the New User Mailbox Wizard, which will allow you to create a user mailbox and associate it with an existing user account, create a new user account with a mailbox, or link a mailbox.

FIGURE 14.1
The Mailboxes section of the EAC's Recipient Configuration work center

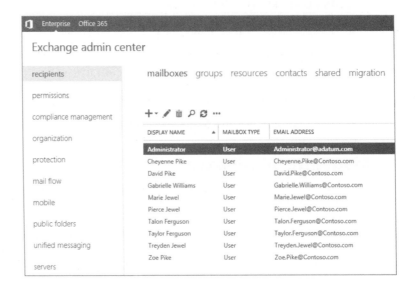

User Mailbox This wizard creates a mailbox for an existing user in the same Active Directory domain. The user could be a new user (without a user account) or an existing user without a mailbox account.

Linked Mailbox This wizard also creates a disabled user account, assigns it a mailbox, and prompts the administrator to provide a user account in a separate, trusted forest. The account in the other forest is considered the owner of this mailbox and has the Associated External Account permissions to the mailbox. This is used in organizations that install Exchange Server in a resource forest. If you are creating linked mailboxes, the user account in your forest must remain disabled.

In this example, you are mailbox-enabling a user account that has no existing mailbox, thereby creating a user mailbox. To proceed, you would click the Browse button to locate the user account that you want to enable with the new mailbox. After you have selected the user account, you can specify the user's Exchange Server alias, define the mailbox database on which the mailbox will be hosted (or allow Exchange Server to select one for you automatically), create an archive, and assign an address book policy to the user if needed. Figure 14.2 shows the wizard.

FIGURE 14.2
In the Mailbox Wizard, you can select a mailbox database for a user, as well as enable an archive mailbox and assign an address book policy

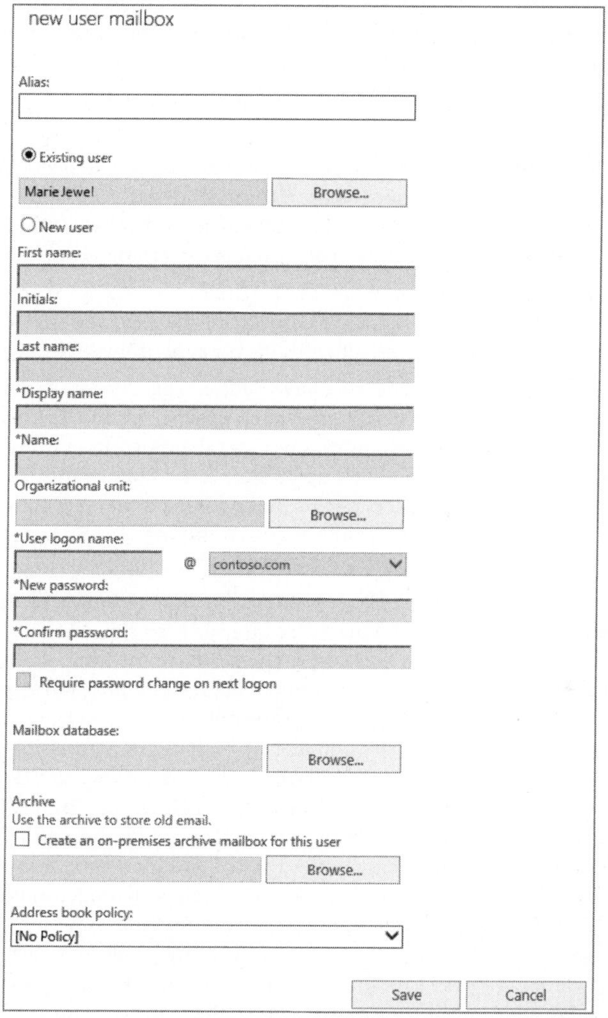

AUTOMATICALLY ASSIGNING A MAILBOX TO A MAILBOX DATABASE

Exchange Server 2010's management tools introduced a great feature that automatically assigned a user to a mailbox database, and Exchange Server 2016 inherited this feature in the EAC. Historically, some mailbox administrators would select the first mailbox database in the list. This feature is a benefit to organizations that have trouble balancing mailboxes on mailbox databases.

Exchange Server 2016 provides you the option of allowing Exchange to choose the mailbox database using automatic mailbox distribution. With automatic mailbox distribution, Exchange uses built-in logic when creating a mailbox, moving a mailbox, or mailbox-enabling an existing user account. Consequently, you don't need to specify a mailbox database name when provisioning a mailbox. The logic in automatic mailbox distribution is as follows:

1. Gather all mailbox databases in the Exchange Server organization.

2. Exclude any mailbox databases that are marked for exclusion from the distribution process.

3. Exclude any mailbox databases that are outside the database management scopes applied to the administrator performing the operation.

4. Exclude any mailbox databases that are not in the same Active Directory site as the provisioning server.

5. From the remaining list of mailbox databases, Exchange will choose a mailbox database at random. Exchange uses the mailbox database if the mailbox database is online and healthy. If the mailbox database is offline or not healthy, another mailbox database is chosen at random. The operation will fail if no online or healthy mailbox databases are found.

If you want to use the automatic mailbox distribution, do not specify a mailbox database when provisioning or moving a mailbox. Microsoft recommends that you balance the distribution of mailboxes and not scope stores with specific types of users.

There are scenarios where you may have defined specific databases on which you do not want automatic distribution of mailboxes (such as when you've enabled journaling on the mailbox database). You can exclude mailbox databases from automatic distribution by changing the properties on the mailbox database via the EMS cmdlet `Set-MailboxDatabase`. In Exchange Server 2016, this cmdlet includes three parameters for controlling automatic mailbox distribution: `IsSuspendedFromProvisioning`, `IsExcludedFromProvisioning`, and `IsExcludedFromProvisioningDueToLogicalCorruption`.

These three parameters provide similar functionality (excluding the mailbox database from automatic mailbox distribution), but one is intended for short-term exclusion and the other two are intended for long-term exclusion. The scenario for `IsSuspendedFromProvisioning` is used when you are temporarily taking a mailbox database or server out of rotation for new mailboxes. The scenario for `IsExcludedFromProvisioning` is used when you have a mailbox database that you want to permanently exclude from provisioning—for example, when the mailbox database is full or is a mailbox database dedicated to VIP personnel. Finally, the scenario for `IsExcludedFromProvisioningDueToLogicalCorruption` is used when you want to exclude a mailbox database because of database corruption. When any of these parameters is enabled, you also need to configure the `IsExcludedFromProvisioningReason` property with the reason for the exclusion. When you enable these parameters on the mailbox database, the `IsExcludedFromProvisioningBy` property is automatically populated with your user account. In addition, the `IsExcludedFromProvisioning` property is automatically enabled when the `IsExcludedFromProvisioningDueToLogicalCorruption` parameter is enabled. The reason for these exclusion distinctions is that you might prefer to distinguish mailbox databases that are permanently excluded from those that are temporarily excluded from mailbox provisioning.

After you have determined to which mailbox database you want to provision the new mailbox or allow for automatic mailbox distribution, there are some additional settings you might need to configure. From the Mailbox Settings page, you need to specify the following information:

Alias   The alias is used to generate the default SMTP addresses as well as other internal Exchange Server functions. The default value of the alias is the user account name, but you can change it if you need it to conform to other standards.

Mailbox Database   This browse list consists of mailbox databases found in the Exchange organization.

Create On-Premises Archive   Exchange provisions an additional on-premises mailbox, also called an Archive mailbox, to which users can move emails that should be saved for longer terms, saving the inconvenience of a local Personal Storage Table (PST) and lost emails. This can be enabled manually or based on retention policies.

Address Book Policy   The address book policy allows you to assign a custom address book for the user, hiding some aspects of the GAL from the user.

When you are convinced that the parameters for the mailbox you are creating are correct, click the Save button on the New User Mailbox screen. The EAC then launches an EMS cmdlet in the background that enables the mailbox by adding the mailbox attributes to the user account in Active Directory that are required by Exchange. The mailbox object is actually created in the mailbox database when the user logs on to the mailbox or receives an email message.

ASSIGNING A MAILBOX TO MORE THAN ONE USER

The EAC does not offer the ability to create or enable multiple mailboxes at the same time. In order to do that, you must use the Exchange Management Shell (the PowerShell command-line tool for Exchange Server). In the next section, "Enabling a Mailbox Using the EMS," we will explore how to do that in detail.

Enabling a Mailbox Using the EMS

In larger organizations, you will probably want to streamline or script the creation of new mailboxes and/or user accounts. The EMS allows you to do this faster than the EAC. For example, let's look at the scenario you just completed from the EAC when you enabled a mailbox for an existing user and assigned the user mailbox to a specific mailbox database. The following cmdlet accomplishes the same task:

```
Enable-Mailbox -Identity ABakr -Alias Abakr -Database MBX-002 -ArchiveName Abakr
-AddressBookPolicy "Engineering AB Policy"
```

If you want to enable the mailbox on a specific mailbox database, you need to specify the mailbox database name. You will need to establish a naming standard for mailbox databases across the Exchange organization, since unique database names are required for Exchange Server 2016. This is because mailbox databases can be moved between Exchange Servers in the organization. In versions of Exchange prior to Exchange Server 2010, the mailbox databases were local to each Exchange Server and only required a unique database name on the local server.

For this reason, we recommend against including the server name as part of the mailbox database name. The active copy of a mailbox database may move from one server to another only if you are using database availability groups.

ASSIGNING PERMISSIONS TO A MAILBOX USING THE EMS

On some occasions, you may need to assign a user the permission necessary to access another user's mailbox. With Exchange Server 2010, you could accomplish this by using the Manage Full Access Permission task in the Actions pane. In Exchange Server 2016, however, you need to open the user's mailbox and navigate to the Mailbox Delegation tab. The permissions available for a selected mailbox are shown in Figure 14.3; they are the Send As, Send on Behalf, and Full Access permissions.

FIGURE 14.3
Available mailbox permissions

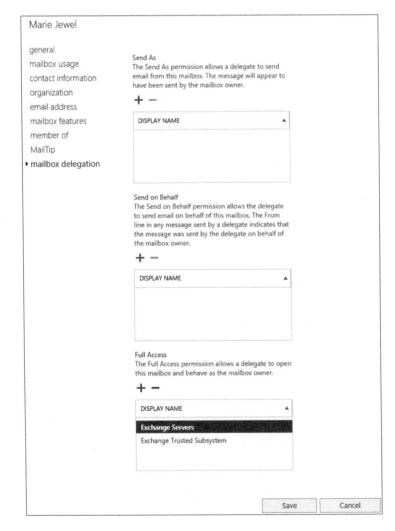

◆ The Full Access permission allows another user, or delegate, to open the mailbox and access the contents, including messages or folders, of the mailbox.

◆ The Send As permission allows a delegate to send a message that appears to have been sent from the mailbox owner.

◆ The Send on Behalf permission allows a delegate to send a message that appears to have been sent by the delegate on behalf of the mailbox owner.

For example, if Terresa Musse (mailbox owner) grants John Rodriguez (delegate) the Send on Behalf permission, the **From** address in any message sent by the delegate appears as if the message had been sent by the delegate on behalf of the mailbox owner. This implies to the recipient that John Rodriguez is authorized to send messages on Terresa Musse's behalf, a common scenario for an executive assistant. On the other hand, the **From** address in any message sent by a delegate with Send As permission to another mailbox will appear to have been sent from the mailbox owner. This grants a degree of impersonation of the mailbox onto the delegate.

FULL ACCESS VS. SEND AS VS. RECEIVE AS PERMISSIONS

Granting a user, or delegate, Full Access permission to another mailbox will allow the user to open the mailbox and access the contents, including messages or folders, of the mailbox. This can be performed in the EAC or in the EMS via the Add-MailboxPermission cmdlet. However, if the user needs to send a message as the mailbox owner, the Send As permission is required. For example, the Send As permission can be used for delegate permission on shared mailboxes to a team or department. However, the team will not have permission to access the shared mailbox contents without granting them Full Access permission as well.

When a user is granted Full Access permissions to other mailboxes, Outlook, through Autodiscover, automatically loads all mailboxes to which the user has Full Access permission. If the user has Full Access permission to a large number of mailboxes, performance issues may occur when starting Outlook. For example, in some Exchange organizations, administrators have full access to all the mailboxes in the organization. In this scenario, it may make more sense to grant Receive As permission to the mailboxes or to the mailbox database. Granting a user Receive As permission to another mailbox will allow the user to open the mailbox and access the contents, including messages or folders, of the mailbox, but the user will not have permission to send messages from the other mailbox. Outlook will not load mailboxes to which the user has Receive As permission.

When using the Add-MailboxPermission cmdlet to grant Full Access permission to a mailbox, you can specify the AutoMapping parameter to ignore the auto-mapping feature in Outlook. You may be asking yourself, when would I grant Receive As permission to a mailbox if I can accomplish the same task by granting Full Access permission with the AutoMapping parameter? You may have missed the earlier reference, but Receive As permission can also be granted to the mailbox database. In this scenario, a user granted Receive As permission to a mailbox database would allow the user to open all the mailboxes on the mailbox database, including current and future mailboxes. This option would enable you to grant full access permission to new mailboxes automatically. Nice, huh?

A few common scenarios when you may choose to grant Receive As permission to the mailbox database include legal review or integration with third-party products. For example, Blackberry Enterprise Server (BES) requires that you grant Receive As and Send As permissions to the BES service account.

You can add Receive As permission by using the `Add-ADPermission` cmdlet and specifying the `-ExtendedRights Receive-As` parameter. You can add Send As permissions through the EAC or by using the `Add-ADPermission` cmdlet and specifying the `-ExtendedRights Send-As` parameter. Full Access permissions can be added through the EAC or by using the `Add-MailboxPermission` cmdlet and specifying the `-AccessRights FullAccess` parameter.

ASSIGNING FULL ACCESS PERMISSION

To assign Full Access permissions to a mailbox, simply select the mailbox to which you want to add more permissions and double-click it to open up the mailbox properties. From the Mailbox Properties interface window (the assigned user appears at the top left), select the Mailbox Delegation option tab from the feature list on the left, and then you can scroll down in the window. You'll notice the Full Access section list. By clicking the + (Add) sign in the Actions list, you can click the plus sign to add the selected user (delegate) to the list of users with Full Access permission to this mailbox.

You could also grant Full Access permission to a mailbox using the EMS cmdlet `Add-MailboxPermission`. In this example, to assign user mJewel Full Access permission to Taylor Ferguson's mailbox, you would use this command:

```
Add-MailboxPermission -Identity tFerguson -User mJewel -AccessRights FullAccess
```

You can remove the Full Access permission using the EMS cmdlet `Remove-MailboxPermission` with the following command:

```
Remove-MailboxPermission -Identity tFerguson -User mJewel -AccessRights
FullAccess
```

If you want to assign an administrator Full Access permission to all mailboxes in your Exchange organization, you can use the Role-Based Access Control (RBAC) management role called Mailbox Import Export. While this management role is commonly used by administrators to import or export mailbox content, it has the distinct advantage of granting full access to all mailboxes in your Exchange organization as well. For example, to assign user mJewel this management role, you would use this command:

```
New-ManagementRoleAssignment -Role "Mailbox Import Export" -User mJewel
```

ASSIGNING SEND AS PERMISSION

To assign Send As permission, you navigate to the same page as for assigning Full Access permission. From the Mailbox Properties window, select the Mailbox Delegation tab from the feature list on the left. The Send As list is located near the top of the page. By clicking the + (Add) sign in the Actions list, you can add the user (delegate) to the list of users with Send As permission to the mailbox.

You could also grant Send As permission to a mailbox using the EMS cmdlet `Add-ADPermission`. In this example, to assign user mJewel Send As permission to Taylor Ferguson's mailbox, you would use this command:

```
Add-ADPermission -Identity tFerguson -User mJewel -ExtendedRight Send-As
```

You can remove the Send As permission using the EMS cmdlet `Remove-ADPermission` with the following command:

```
Remove-ADPermission -Identity tFerguson -User mJewel
-ExtendedRights Send-As
```

ASSIGNING SEND ON BEHALF PERMISSION

To assign Send on Behalf permissions, you would navigate to the same page for assigning Full Access permission. From the Mailbox Properties window, select the Mailbox Delegation tab from the feature list on the left. The Send on Behalf list is located near the middle of the page. By clicking the + (Add) sign in the Actions list, you can add the user (delegate) to the list of users with Send on Behalf permission to the mailbox.

You could also grant Send on Behalf permission to a mailbox using the EMS cmdlet `Set-Mailbox`. In this example, to assign user mJewel Send on Behalf permission to Taylor Ferguson's mailbox, you would use this command:

```
Set-Mailbox -Identity tFerguson -GrantSendOnBehalfTo mJewel
```

If an existing user has Send on Behalf permission to a mailbox, the previous command will overwrite the existing list. However, you can add users to the list using the EMS cmdlet `Set-Mailbox` with the following command:

```
Set-Mailbox -Identity tFerguson -GrantSendOnBehalfTo @{Add="mJewel"}
```

You can remove the Send on Behalf permission using the EMS cmdlet `Set-Mailbox` with the following command:

```
Set-Mailbox -Identity tFerguson -GrantSendOnBehalfTo @{Remove="mJewel"}
```

ASSIGNING FOLDER-LEVEL PERMISSION

All of the previous methods for assigning permission to a mailbox involve modifying permission on the entire mailbox. However, you may need to assign permission selectively to one or more specific folders within the mailbox. Assigning someone else permissions to access individual folders within their mailbox is a common task that an end user can perform using the Outlook client.

For an Exchange administrator, it's not practical to require them to use the Outlook client to assign folder-level permission for an end user. Although using the EAC is not an option, you can assign and manage folder-level permission for an end user using the EMS cmdlet `Add-MailboxFolderPermission`. For example, to assign user mJewel owner permission (equivalent to full-control permission) to the Inbox of Taylor Ferguson's mailbox, you would use this command:

```
Add-MailboxFolderPermission -Identity tFerguson:\Inbox -User mJewel `
  -AccessRights Owner
```

When assigning folder-level permission, there are multiple access rights, as well as roles (a combination of commonly used access rights), that you can use. Refer to the list of available access rights with the corresponding individual permissions in Table 14.1, as well as the list of available roles with the corresponding permissions that they assign in Table 14.2.

TABLE 14.1: Access Rights of Mailbox Folders

ACCESS RIGHTS	MAILBOX FOLDER PERMISSION
CreateItems	The user can create items within the specified folder.
CreateSubfolders	The user can create subfolders in the specified folder.
DeleteAllItems	The user can delete all items in the specified folder.
DeleteOwnedItems	The user can only delete items that they created from the specified folder.
EditAllItems	The user can edit all items in the specified folder.
EditOwnedItems	The user can only edit items that they created in the specified folder.
FolderContact	The user is the contact for the specified public folder.
FolderOwner	The user is the owner of the specified folder. The user can view the folder, move the folder, and create subfolders. The user can't read items, edit items, delete items, or create items.
FolderVisible	The user can view the specified folder but can't read or edit items within the specified public folder.
ReadItems	The user can read items within the specified folder.

TABLE 14.2: Access Rights (Roles) of Mailbox Folders

ROLE (ACCESS RIGHTS)	MAILBOX FOLDER PERMISSIONS
Author	CreateItems, DeleteOwnedItems, EditOwnedItems, FolderVisible, ReadItems
Contributor	CreateItems, FolderVisible
Editor	CreateItems, DeleteAllItems, DeleteOwnedItems, EditAllItems, EditOwnedItems, FolderVisible, ReadItems
None	FolderVisible
NonEditingAuthor	CreateItems, FolderVisible, ReadItems

TABLE 14.2: Access Rights (Roles) of Mailbox Folders *(CONTINUED)*

ROLE (ACCESS RIGHTS)	MAILBOX FOLDER PERMISSIONS
Owner	CreateItems, CreateSubfolders, DeleteAllItems, DeleteOwnedItems, EditAllItems, EditOwnedItems, FolderContact, FolderOwner, FolderVisible, ReadItems
PublishingEditor	CreateItems, CreateSubfolders, DeleteAllItems, DeleteOwnedItems, EditAllItems, EditOwnedItems, FolderVisible, ReadItems
PublishingAuthor	CreateItems, CreateSubfolders, DeleteOwnedItems, EditOwnedItems, FolderVisible, ReadItems
Reviewer	FolderVisible, ReadItems

If you need to change the permission a user has to a folder within a mailbox, you can use the EMS cmdlet Set-MailboxFolderPermission to update the existing permission. In this example, to update the existing permission that user mJewel has for Taylor Ferguson's Inbox folder to Reviewer, you would use this command:

```
Set-MailboxFolderPermission –Identity tFerguson:\Inbox –User mJewel `
  –AccessRights Reviewer
```

You can remove the folder-level permission using the EMS cmdlet Remove-MailboxFolderPermission with the following command:

```
Remove-MailboxFolderPermission –Identity tFerguson:\Inbox –User mJewel
```

Creating a Mailbox Using the EAC and EMS

Previously, you saw how to enable an existing user with a mailbox via the EAC; now we will explore how to create a new user and mailbox at the same time (as shown in Figure 14.4).

In the New User Mailbox window, you select the New User option and provide user account information, such as the first name, middle initials, last name, display name, canonical name, user principal name (or user logon name), and a new password. Because the user account does not exist yet, you must also specify the organizational unit (OU) in which the user account will be created. You must have the necessary Active Directory permissions to create user accounts in the OU.

While most of the New User Mailbox window in the EAC is the same for new and existing users, there are more differences when creating a user mailbox in the EMS. For example, you would use the following commands to create a mailbox and user account at the same time:

```
$password = Read-Host "Enter password" -AsSecureString
New-Mailbox –FirstName Marie -LastName Jewel -DisplayName "Marie Jewel" –Name
mJewel -UserPrincipalName mJewel@contoso.com -SamAccountName mJewel -Database
"MBX-003" -OrganizationalUnit Corporate -Password $password
-ResetPasswordOnNextLogon $true
```

FIGURE 14.4
Creating a user
account and
mailbox from
the Exchange
Administration
Center

You probably noticed the first major difference: the password component of the first command. When creating a user account in Active Directory, you are required to provide a password for the new account. With the first command, you are prompted to input the password for the new user account. As you type the password in the EMS, each character is replaced with an asterisk on the screen to protect the privacy of the password. For additional protection, the string variable of the password will be encrypted in memory to prevent the password from being compromised. In fact, you are required to use an encrypted password when creating a user account in Active Directory.

You will notice the second command is the New-Mailbox cmdlet, as opposed to the Enable-Mailbox cmdlet used in the earlier section, "Enabling a Mailbox using the EMS." While the latter cmdlet enables a mailbox for an *existing* user account, the New-Mailbox cmdlet creates the user account and mailbox at the same time. Further in the command, you will notice the -OrganizationalUnit parameter, which allows you to specify the name of the domain and OU where the new user account is created. If not specified, the user account is created in the default Users container in Active Directory.

The New-Mailbox cmdlet allows you to also provide the -SamAccountName parameters for defining the pre–Windows 2000 account name. Finally, the –Password parameter will accept the encrypted variable you defined earlier. If not specified, the administrator will be prompted to input the password for the new user account.

As an alternative to reading the password from the administrator input, you can convert a string directly in the command. For example, this abbreviated version of the earlier command will use the password, P@ssw0rd, when creating the new user account:

```
New-Mailbox ... -Password (ConvertTo-SecureString -String P@ssw0rd
-AsPlainText -Force)
```

Managing User Mailbox Properties

Many of the user account properties managed through the Active Directory Users and Computers console can now be managed through the EAC or the EMS. For some, using the EAC is a little easier than using the command line, but the EMS is more flexible and more efficient, especially when managing multiple objects.

Using the EAC to Manage User and Mailbox Properties

Let's start with managing user and mailbox properties using the EAC. We'll take a look at a few of the things that you can do and some of the user property pages.

General The General page (Figure 14.5) includes much of the same information provided when creating a mailbox, such as the first name, middle initials, last name, canonical name, display name, alias, and the user logon name.

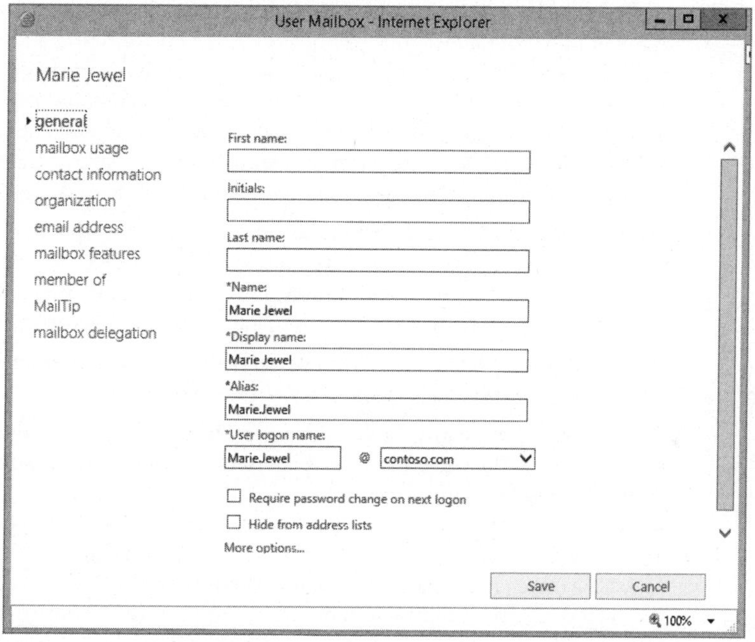

FIGURE 14.5
General properties
page for a mailbox

In addition to the option to require a password change at the next logon, you'll also notice the option to Hide From Address Lists. Exchange will use this setting to prevent the mailbox from appearing in the global address list (GAL) and other custom address lists.

Located near the bottom of the General page, additional information is available by clicking More options. The General page will expand to display more properties such as the Organizational Unit and the Mailbox Database name. The General page also includes a Custom Attributes section that allows you to access all 15 custom attributes (also referred to as extension attributes).

Mailbox Usage   Exchange displays the last time the user signed on to their mailbox in a read-only box under Last Logon. This is useful in determining the frequency of user access. Another read-only item is a percentage bar that shows the total size of the mailbox and the percentage of the total mailbox quota that has been used. You can click More Options to customize the usage settings. The first option allows the administrator to modify the storage quota to override the database quota settings such as when to issue a warning, when to prohibit the user from sending email, and when to prohibit the user from sending and receiving email.

The second storage option allows you to customize the deleted item retention settings for the mailbox. This is the length of time that deleted items are retained before they are permanently deleted from the mailbox and cannot be recovered by the user. Permanently deleted items are any mail items that are deleted from the Deleted Items folder, also known as the recoverable items folder, or hard-deleted. By default, each mailbox database will keep permanently deleted items for 14 days. Another deleted item storage option allows you to prevent mailboxes and email messages from being deleted until after the mailbox database on which the mailbox is located has been backed up.

While it may not have significant impact when customizing a few mailboxes, you should be cautious when increasing storage quotas and the retention of deleted items for many mailboxes. You should keep in mind the original design and goals for the messaging system. If quotas change, the system needs to be reevaluated to determine if more resources are required. Because these adjustments can increase the size of the mailbox database, you should periodically monitor the mailbox database to assess the impact.

Contact Information and Organization   The Contact Information and the Organization pages include many of the user attributes available in AD, such as street, city, state/province, zip code, country/region, work phone, mobile phone, fax, office, home phone, web page, notes, title, department, company, manager, and direct reports.

Email Address   The Email Address page allows you to manage the SMTP addresses (and other address types) that are assigned to the mailbox, as shown in Figure 14.6.

Regardless of how many email addresses are assigned to a mailbox, only one email address will be used as the reply address. A mailbox can receive messages sent to any of the email addresses, but messages sent from the mailbox will use only one email address. When a recipient replies to a message from the mailbox, the message will be sent to the reply address. The reply address is also known as the primary SMTP address or Reply To address. In Figure 14.6, this is the email address shown in bold. For SMTP addresses, the reply address will also show "SMTP" in all capital letters in the Type column, whereas the other addresses will be in lowercase letters. You can change the Reply To address by selecting another email address, clicking the pencil (Edit) sign in the Actions bar, and selecting the option to Make This the Reply Address.

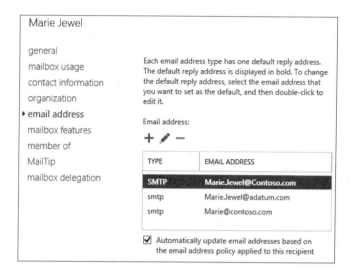

Marie Jewel

general

mailbox usage

contact information

organization

▸ email address

mailbox features

member of

MailTip

mailbox delegation

Each email address type has one default reply address.
The default reply address is displayed in bold. To change
the default reply address, select the email address that
you want to set as the default, and then double-click to
edit it.

Email address:

╋ ✎ ─

TYPE	EMAIL ADDRESS
SMTP	**Marie.Jewel@Contoso.com**
smtp	Marie.Jewel@adatum.com
smtp	Marie@contoso.com

☑ Automatically update email addresses based on
the email address policy applied to this recipient

On the same page, you have the option to Automatically Update Email Addresses Based On The Email Address Policy Applied To This Recipient. When this option is enabled on a mailbox, the email addresses are automatically updated based on changes that are defined in the email address policies in your Exchange organization. Disabling this option allows you to assign a different reply address, as discussed earlier.

Email address policies affect the email addresses assigned to a mailbox. As email address policies are created, additional email addresses will be added to one or more mailboxes based on the scope of the policy. If a policy updates the default SMTP address, the reply address will be updated on mailboxes.

This is a useful feature for organizations that have more than one email domain. Notice in Figure 14.6 that the mailbox for Marie Jewel has addresses from two different domains: `Marie.Jewel@Contoso.com` and `Marie.Jewel@adatum.com`. Email sent to either email address will be forwarded to her mailbox. However, email sent from her mailbox will use `Marie.Jewel@Contoso.com` as the reply address. Although Exchange does not allow users to select which email address to use for the reply address when sending a message, Outlook provides an option for users so they can "have replies sent to" another email address. With the appropriate permission, users can send a message from another mailbox.

Mailbox Features   The Mailbox Features page (Figure 14.7) includes a number of configuration items. Depending on your environment, you may need to customize features for mailboxes.

The Sharing Policy option defines which sharing policy is applied to the mailbox. You can use sharing policies to control how users in your organization share calendar information with users outside your organization. Sharing policies allow users to share calendar information with different types of external users. They support the sharing of calendar information with external federated organizations (such as Office 365 or another Exchange organization), external nonfederated organizations, and individuals with Internet access.

FIGURE 14.7
Mailbox Features
properties of a
mailbox

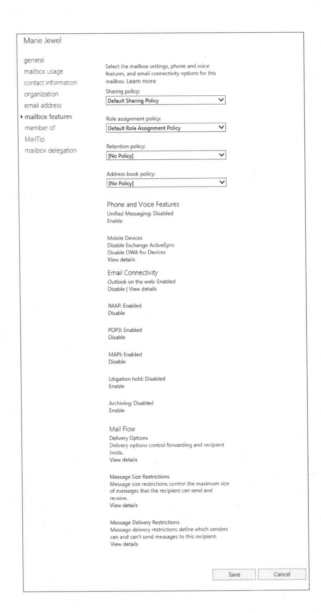

The Role Assignment Policy option defines which role-based access control (RBAC) role is applied to the owner (user) of the mailbox. The RBAC role controls which mailbox and distribution group configuration settings the user can modify. More information about RBAC is available in Chapter 12, "Management Permissions and Role-Based Access Control."

The Retention Policy option defines which retention policy and retention tags are applied to the mailbox. The retention tags control how long messages are kept in the mailbox and what action to take on items that have reach a certain age.

The Address Book Policy option defines which address book policy is applied to the mailbox. An address book policy allows you to provide customized views of the address book to users.

The Phone And Voice Features options allow you to enable the mailbox for Unified Messaging and assign a Unified Messaging mailbox policy to the mailbox. These features allow you to enable the mailbox for Exchange ActiveSync, also known as MobileSync, and enable Outlook on the web for devices. You can also assign a mobile device mailbox policy and manage the mobile devices associated with the mailbox.

Email Connectivity options allow you to:

- Enable Outlook on the web and assign an Outlook on the web mailbox policy.

- Enable users to connect to their mailbox using the IMAP, POP3, and MAPI client protocols.

- Enable Litigation Hold.

- Enable Archiving.

Mail Flow options allow you to:

- Enable Delivery Options, such as forwarding email to another recipient and setting a limit on the number of recipients the user can include on an email.

- Enable Message Size Restrictions to set a maximum message size on messages sent or received.

- Enable Message Delivery Restrictions to identify which senders can and can't send messages to the recipient.

On the Delivery Options page, you can enable the option to deliver messages to an alternative recipient, also known as the forwarding address. The recipient that you specify must be a mailbox in your organization or a mail user or mail contact.

When you select a mail user or mail contact in your organization, any messages sent to the mailbox are forwarded to the external email address of the mail user or mail contact. This is commonly used when someone leaves the company but wants to receive email that was sent to their previous email address.

If you enable the option to Deliver Message To Both Forwarding Address And Mailbox, any messages sent to the mailbox are sent to the mailbox and to the forwarding address. This is commonly used when a manager wants her assistant to receive a copy of her email.

Exchange will prevent users from sending an email to more than 5,000 users if you don't enable the recipient limit, or the maximum number of recipients a user can include on an email. This default global limit provides protection against spammers who may have gained access to your system. You can use the recipient limit to allow VIPs or other authorized users, such as Human Resources personnel, to send messages to large numbers of users.

The Message Size Restrictions allow you to specify the maximum size of messages the user can send or receive. Exchange will use the default global message size restrictions, 25 MB, or the connector message size restrictions, 10 MB, by default if limits are not enabled on the mailbox.

The Message Delivery Restrictions, as shown in Figure 14.8, allow you to restrict who is allowed to send mail to this particular mailbox. For example, you might want to restrict messages sent to a VIP in your organization by defining the list of accepted senders. Conversely, you might want to restrict harassing messages sent to a user in your organization by defining the list of rejected senders.

FIGURE 14.8
Message Delivery
Restrictions
options

By default, all email received from the Internet is received anonymously, in that the senders do not authenticate with your Exchange servers. For some recipients, you may prefer to require that senders authenticate with your Exchange servers. By enabling the option to Require That All Senders Are Authenticated, you can prevent a recipient from receiving email from anonymous senders. This would also reduce exposure for distribution lists that receive email only from users in your organization.

> You will need an Exchange Server enterprise client access license (eCAL) for deploying personal archive mailboxes, personal retention tags, transport journaling, advanced features of ActiveSync, In-Place Hold, Data Loss Prevention (DLP), Information protection and control (IPC) features, and Unified Messaging features.

Using the EMS to Manage User and Mailbox Properties

You can manage mailbox and user properties using EMS. There are three EMS cmdlet pairs that you should be familiar with for managing most of the user and mailbox properties: `Get-User` and `Set-User`, `Get-Mailbox` and `Set-Mailbox`, and `Get-CasMailbox` and `Set-CasMailbox`.

Get-User and Set-User   The Get-User and Set-User cmdlets allow you to manage user account properties that are not directly related to Exchange Server. For example, you would use the following command to update the mobile phone number for Marie Jewel:

```
Set-User Marie.Jewel -MobilePhone "(920) 646-6234"
```

The Set-User cmdlet has many useful parameters for managing user properties (refer to the following partial list). You can retrieve them from within the EMS by typing **Get-Help Set-User.**

City   Sets the city or locality name.

Company   Sets the company name.

Department   Sets the department name.

DisplayName   Updates the user's display name, which appears in the GAL.

Fax   Specifies the fax number.

FirstName   Specifies the given or first name.

HomePhone   Sets the home phone number.

LastName   Specifies the surname or last name.

Manager   Sets the name of the user's manager; the input value must be a distinguished name in canonical name format, such as Contoso.com/Corporate/CJ Leon.

MobilePhone   Sets the mobile/cell phone number.

Phone   Sets the business phone number.

PostalCode   Sets the zip or postal code.

StateOrProvince   Sets the state or province.

StreetAddress   Sets the street address.

Title   Sets the title or job function.

You can retrieve the list of properties for a user with the Get-User cmdlet, specifying a username, and then piping the output to the Format-List cmdlet; an abbreviated alias for this cmdlet is FL. Piping the output of Get-User to Format-List is a great way to enumerate the properties of an object and to learn the property names. Here is an example of some of the properties that are returned with the Get-User cmdlet (some properties have been removed to save space).

```
Get-User Marie.Jewel | FL
IsSecurityPrincipal       : True
SamAccountName            : Marie.Jewel
SidHistory                : {}
UserPrincipalName         : Marie.Jewel@Contoso.com
ResetPasswordOnNextLogon  : False
CertificateSubject        : {}
```

```
RemotePowerShellEnabled  : True
NetID                    :
OrganizationalUnit       : contoso.com/Corporate
AssistantName            :
City                     : Honolulu
Company                  : Somorita Surfboards
CountryOrRegion          :
Department               : Surfboard Design
DirectReports            : {}
DisplayName              : Marie Jewel
Fax                      : (920) 555-6657
FirstName                : Marie
HomePhone                :
Initials                 :
LastName                 : Jewel
Manager                  : CJ Leon
MobilePhone              : (920) 646-6234
Notes                    :
Office                   : Honolulu Surfboard Design
OtherFax                 : {}
OtherHomePhone           : {}
OtherTelephone           : {}
Pager                    : (920) 555-5545
Phone                    : (920) 555-1234
PhoneticDisplayName      :
PostalCode               : 96816
PostOfficeBox            : {}
RecipientType            : UserMailbox
RecipientTypeDetails     : UserMailbox
SimpleDisplayName        : Marie Jewel (Honolulu)
StateOrProvince          : Hawaii
StreetAddress            : 550 Kalakaua Avenue, Suite 201
Title                    : Senior Systems Engineer
UMDialPlan               :
UMDtmfMap                : {emailAddress:62884392665,
lastNameFirstName:26656288439, firstNameLastName:62884392665}
AllowUMCallsFromNonUsers : SearchEnabled
WebPage                  :
TelephoneAssistant       :
WindowsEmailAddress      : Marie.Jewel@Contoso.com
UMCallingLineIds         : {}
IsValid                  : True
ExchangeVersion          : 0.10 (15.01.225.0)
Name                     : Marie Jewel
DistinguishedName        : CN=Marie Jewel,OU=Corporate,
DC=contoso,DC=com
OriginatingServer        : HNLMBX01.contoso.com
```

As you can see from the previous details, the `Format-List` cmdlet allows you to see all the property names. As a result, if you need to update the State attribute of a user, you can review the output from the previous command. After determining that this property is referred to as `StateOrProvince`, you could use the following command to update the user:

```
Set-User Marie.Jewel -StateOrProvince "Oklahoma"
```

With EMS, you can pipe the output of one cmdlet with another cmdlet to perform bulk administration. For example, say that you need to update the office name of all users who are in Honolulu. You can use a combination of `Get-User` and `Set-User` cmdlets to accomplish this, based on criteria defined with the `Where-Object` cmdlet; an abbreviated alias for this cmdlet is `Where`:

```
Get-User | Where {$_.City -eq "Honolulu"} | `
Set-User -Office "Main Office"
```

In this example, we piped the output of the `Get-User` cmdlet to a local filter (using the `Where-Object` cmdlet). This provided us with a subset of only the users whose `City` property is equal to Honolulu. The output was then piped to the `Set-User` cmdlet for updating the `Office` property. You will be amazed at the power of EMS to perform bulk administration in your organization.

Get-Mailbox and Set-Mailbox The `Get-Mailbox` and the `Set-Mailbox` cmdlets allow you to manage the properties of a mailbox. You may have already seen these cmdlets earlier in this book when detailing how to update the mailbox storage limits. Let's review some ways you can use these cmdlets for managing user mailboxes. For example, you would use the following command to update the rules quota for the user Cheyenne Pike:

```
Set-Mailbox Cheyenne.Pike -RulesQuota 128KB
```

The `Set-Mailbox` cmdlet has many useful parameters for managing mailboxes (refer to the following partial list). You can retrieve them from within the EMS by typing **Get-Help Set-Mailbox.**

AntispamBypassEnabled When enabled, the Exchange Server will skip antispam processing of messages sent to the mailbox.

CustomAttribute1 This property allows you to store custom information on the mailbox. The property `CustomAttribute1` is stored as the attribute `ExtensionAttribute1` in Active Directory. Fifteen custom attributes are available through EMS, referred to as `CustomAttribute1` through `CustomAttribute15`.

EmailAddressPolicyEnabled When enabled, the Exchange server will apply an email address policy to the mailbox, which includes defining the email addresses.

ForwardingAddress This property stores the name of the recipient when forwarding email to another recipient is enabled.

HiddenFromAddressListsEnabled When enabled, the Exchange server will remove the mailbox from the address lists.

IssueWarningQuota This property stores the warning threshold for the size of the mailbox. The user receives a warning message when the mailbox reaches or exceeds this size.

MaxReceiveSize   This property stores the maximum size of a message that can be sent to the mailbox. Messages larger than the maximum size are rejected.

MaxSendSize   This property stores the maximum size of a message that can be sent by the mailbox. Users receive a warning message when email messages are larger than the maximum size.

ProhibitSendQuota   This property stores a mailbox size threshold. The user receives a warning message that Exchange is preventing the user from sending new messages when the mailbox reaches or exceeds this size.

ProhibitSendReceiveQuota   This property stores a mailbox size threshold. The user receives a warning message that Exchange is preventing the user from sending and receiving new messages when the mailbox reaches or exceeds this size.

RecipientLimits   This property stores the maximum number of recipients a user can include on a message.

RulesQuota   This property stores the maximum size of Inbox rules for the mailbox.

SCLDeleteEnabled   When enabled, Exchange will silently delete messages that meet or exceed the spam confidence level (SCL) value specified in the SCLDeleteThreshold property.

SCLJunkEnabled   When enabled, Exchange will move, to the Junk Email folder, messages that meet or exceed the spam confidence level (SCL) value specified in the SCLJunkThreshold property.

SCLQuarantineEnabled   When enabled, Exchange will quarantine messages that meet or exceed the spam confidence level (SCL) value specified in the SCLQuarantine Threshold property. Quarantined messages are sent to the quarantine mailbox.

SCLRejectEnabled   When enabled, Exchange will reject messages that meet or exceed the spam confidence level (SCL) value specified in the SCLRejectThreshold property. The Exchange server will send an NDR to the sender of rejected messages.

UseDatabaseQuotaDefaults   When enabled, the mailbox uses the applicable storage quotas defined for the mailbox database on which the mailbox is located. When disabled, the mailbox uses the quotas that are defined on the mailbox. The applicable quota values are CalendarLoggingQuota, IssueWarningQuota, ProhibitSendQuota, ProhibitSendReceiveQuota, RecoverableItemsQuota, and RecoverableItemsWarningQuota.

Similar to the method earlier, you can retrieve the list of properties for a mailbox with the Get-Mailbox cmdlet, specifying a mailbox name, and then piping the output to the Format-List, or FL, cmdlet. Here is an example of some of the properties that are returned with the Get-Mailbox cmdlet (some properties have been removed to save space).

```
Get-Mailbox Marie.Jewel | FL
Database                           : MBX-003
DeletedItemFlags                   : DatabaseDefault
UseDatabaseRetentionDefaults       : True
RetainDeletedItemsUntilBackup      : False
DeliverToMailboxAndForward         : False
```

```
LitigationHoldEnabled                    : False
SingleItemRecoveryEnabled                : False
RetentionHoldEnabled                     : False
EndDateForRetentionHold                  :
StartDateForRetentionHold                :
RetentionComment                         :
RetentionUrl                             :
ManagedFolderMailboxPolicy               :
RetentionPolicy                          :
CalendarRepairDisabled                   : False
ExchangeUserAccountControl               : None
MessageTrackingReadStatusEnabled         : True
ExternalOofOptions                       : External
ForwardingAddress                        :
RetainDeletedItemsFor                    : 14.00:00:00
IsMailboxEnabled                         : True
OfflineAddressBook                       :
ProhibitSendQuota                        : unlimited
ProhibitSendReceiveQuota                 : unlimited
RecoverableItemsQuota                    : unlimited
RecoverableItemsWarningQuota             : unlimited
DowngradeHighPriorityMessagesEnabled     : False
ProtocolSettings                         : {}
RecipientLimits                          : unlimited
IsResource                               : False
IsLinked                                 : False
IsShared                                 : False
ResourceCapacity                         :
ResourceCustom                           : {}
ResourceType                             :
SamAccountName                           : Marie.Jewel
SCLDeleteThreshold                       :
SCLDeleteEnabled                         :
SCLRejectThreshold                       :
SCLRejectEnabled                         :
SCLQuarantineThreshold                   :
SCLQuarantineEnabled                     :
SCLJunkThreshold                         :
SCLJunkEnabled                           :
AntispamBypassEnabled                    : False
ServerName                               : hnlmbx01
UseDatabaseQuotaDefaults                 : True
IssueWarningQuota                        : unlimited
RulesQuota                               : 64 KB (65,536 bytes)
Office                                   :
UserPrincipalName                        : Marie.Jewel@contoso.com
UMEnabled                                : False
```

```
MaxSafeSenders                            :
MaxBlockedSenders                         :
RssAggregationEnabled                     : True
Pop3AggregationEnabled                    : True
WindowsLiveID                             :
ThrottlingPolicy                          :
RoleAssignmentPolicy                      : Default Role Assignment Policy
SharingPolicy                             : Default Sharing Policy
RemoteAccountPolicy                       :
MailboxPlan                               :
ArchiveGuid                               : 00000000-0000-0000-0000-
000000000000
ArchiveName                               : {}
ArchiveQuota                              : unlimited
ArchiveWarningQuota                       : unlimited
QueryBaseDNRestrictionEnabled             : False
MailboxMoveTargetMDB                      :
MailboxMoveSourceMDB                      :
MailboxMoveFlags                          : None
MailboxMoveRemoteHostName                 :
MailboxMoveBatchName                      :
MailboxMoveStatus                         : None
IsPersonToPersonTextMessagingEnabled      : False
IsMachineToPersonTextMessagingEnabled     : False
UserSMimeCertificate                      : {}
UserCertificate                           : {}
CalendarVersionStoreDisabled              : False
Extensions                                : {}
HasPicture                                : False
HasSpokenName                             : False
AcceptMessagesOnlyFrom                    : {}
AcceptMessagesOnlyFromDLMembers           : {}
AcceptMessagesOnlyFromSendersOrMembers    : {}
AddressListMembership                     : {\Mailboxes(VLV),
\All Mailboxes(VLV),\All Recipients(VLV), \Default Global
Address List, \All Users}
Alias                                     : Marie.Jewel
ArbitrationMailbox                        :
BypassModerationFromSendersOrMembers      : {}
OrganizationalUnit                        : contoso.com/Corporate
CustomAttribute1                          :
CustomAttribute2                          :
DisplayName                               : Marie Jewel
EmailAddresses                            : {SMTP:Marie.Jewel@contoso.com}
GrantSendOnBehalfTo                       : {}
HiddenFromAddressListsEnabled             : False
LegacyExchangeDN                          : /o=Contoso
/ou=Exchange Administrative Group (FYDIBOHF23SPDLT)/cn=Recipients /cn=Marie
Jewelclm
```

```
    MaxSendSize                             : unlimited
    MaxReceiveSize                          : unlimited
    ModeratedBy                             : {}
    ModerationEnabled                       : False
    PoliciesExcluded                        : {}
    EmailAddressPolicyEnabled               : True
    PrimarySmtpAddress                      : Marie.Jewel@contoso.com
    RecipientType                           : UserMailbox
    RecipientTypeDetails                    : UserMailbox
    RejectMessagesFrom                      : {}
    RejectMessagesFromDLMembers             : {}
    RejectMessagesFromSendersOrMembers      : {}
    RequireSenderAuthenticationEnabled      : False
    SimpleDisplayName                       :
    SendModerationNotifications             : Always
    UMDtmfMap                               : {emailAddress:62884392665,
      lastNameFirstName:26656288439, firstNameLastName:62884392665}
    WindowsEmailAddress                     : Marie.Jewel@contoso.com
    MailTip                                 :
    MailTipTranslations                     : {}
    ExchangeVersion                         : 0.10 (15.01.225.0)
    Name                                    : Marie Jewel
    DistinguishedName                       : CN=Marie Jewel,OU=Corporate,DC=tsxen,
      DC=com
```

You may notice that some of the properties overlap with the properties returned from the Get-User cmdlet. This is because both cmdlets retrieve many of the same properties stored as attributes on the Active Directory user object.

MODIFYING MAILBOX PARAMETERS

Keep in mind that not all properties can be modified, even with the EMS. Some of the properties shown in the previous examples are system properties and are either created or managed exclusively by the Exchange server.

Get-CasMailbox and Set-CasMailbox   The Get-CasMailbox and Set-CasMailbox cmdlets allow you to manage the client access settings of the mailbox. You can configure settings for ActiveSync, Microsoft Outlook, Outlook on the web, POP3, and IMAP4. Using the same piping method earlier, here is an example of some of the properties that are returned with the Get-CasMailbox cmdlet (some properties have been removed to save space):

```
Get-CASMailbox Marie.Jewel | FL
EmailAddresses                 : {SMTP:Marie.Jewel@contoso.com}
LegacyExchangeDN               : /o=Contoso/ou=Exchange
Administrative Group (FYDIBOHF23SPDLT)/cn=Recipients/cn=Marie Jewelclm
LinkedMasterAccount            :
PrimarySmtpAddress             : Marie.Jewel@contoso.com
```

```
SamAccountName                          : Marie.Jewel
ServerLegacyDN                          : /o=Contoso/ou=Exchange
Administrative Group (FYDIBOHF23SPDLT)/cn=Configuration/cn=Servers
/cn=HNLMBX01
ServerName                              : hnlmbx01
DisplayName                             : Marie Jewel
ActiveSyncAllowedDeviceIDs              : {}
ActiveSyncBlockedDeviceIDs              : {}
ActiveSyncMailboxPolicy                 : Default
ActiveSyncMailboxPolicyIsDefaulted      : True
ActiveSyncDebugLogging                  : False
ActiveSyncEnabled                       : True
HasActiveSyncDevicePartnership          : False
OwaMailboxPolicy                        :
OWAEnabled                              : True
ECPEnabled                              : True
EmwsEnabled                             : False
PopEnabled                              : True
PopUseProtocolDefaults                  : True
PopMessagesRetrievalMimeFormat          : BestBodyFormat
PopEnableExactRFC822Size                : False
PopProtocolLoggingEnabled               : False
ImapEnabled                             : True
ImapUseProtocolDefaults                 : True
ImapMessagesRetrievalMimeFormat         : BestBodyFormat
ImapEnableExactRFC822Size               : False
ImapProtocolLoggingEnabled              : False
MAPIEnabled                             : True
MAPIBlockOutlookNonCachedMode           : False
MAPIBlockOutlookVersions                :
MAPIBlockOutlookRpcHttp                 : False
IsValid                                 : True
ExchangeVersion                         : 0.10 (15.01.225.0)
Name                                    : Marie Jewel
DistinguishedName                       : CN=Marie Jewel,OU=Corporate,
DC=contoso,DC=com
```

Moving Mailboxes

Moving mailboxes from one mailbox database to another is a common task for Exchange Server administrators. Sometimes, mailboxes need to be moved during a transition or migration. You may also need to move all the mailboxes to another mailbox database when decommissioning an Exchange server or mailbox database. Another common scenario is when you discover a corrupted mailbox; moving the mailbox to a different mailbox database won't move the corrupt messages.

Mailbox moves in Exchange Server 2016 are largely the same as they were in Exchange Server 2013 and Exchange Server 2010, using a process known as move requests. The advantages with move requests are that the mailboxes are kept online and available during an asynchronous move from database to database, managed by the Microsoft Exchange Mailbox Replication service (MRS). In Exchange Server 2016, you may enable one or more mailbox servers for MRS and use throttling to manage the MRS performance. For remote mailbox moves over the Internet, you can enable the Microsoft Exchange Mailbox Replication Proxy (MRSProxy) service.

You can use the Exchange Administration Center (EAC) or the New-MoveRequest cmdlet to start a move request. Whichever method you prefer, the Exchange server will use the same process to move the mailbox. The steps for a local move request are as follows:

1. The Exchange administrator submits a new move-mailbox request to the Exchange server.

2. The Exchange server adds the mailbox to be moved to a queue by placing a special message in the system mailbox on the target mailbox database. The status of the move request is *Queued*.

3. All instances of MRS periodically check the system mailbox on every mailbox database in its Active Directory site to verify if there are any queued moved requests. The first MRS instance that discovers the move request will pick it up.

4. If the databases are healthy, the MRS logs into the source mailbox and target mailbox, begins to move the mailbox data from the source mailbox database to the target mailbox database, and updates the mailbox's status in the system mailbox to *InProgress*.

5. Near the end of the move request, the mailbox is temporarily locked while the final mailbox synchronization is completed. At this point, the move request status changes to *CompletionInProgress*.

6. When the move request is completed, the applicable Active Directory attributes are updated, the old mailbox on the source mailbox database is soft deleted, and the new mailbox on the target mailbox database is activated. The move request status changes to *Completed*. Client access to the mailbox will be redirected to the new mailbox database.

7. The Exchange administrator can use the Get-MoveRequestStatistics cmdlet to review the move request statistics and verify detailed information about the mailbox move, such as corrupt messages or large items that are skipped, as well as a very detailed report.

8. The Exchange administrator can use the Remove-MoveRequest cmdlet to clear or remove the move request; the mailbox cannot be moved again until the move request is cleared.

Mailbox move operations may take a considerable amount of time depending on a number of factors, including network bandwidth between servers and server resources such as available CPU and disk I/O. While every environment is different, a typical move request between two servers on LAN-speed network segments may move between 3 GB to 5 GB per hour. Of course, your results may vary.

Also, depending on your Active Directory infrastructure and replication times, Outlook on the web users might not be able to reconnect to their mailboxes for up to 15 minutes after a move request. This may be the result of the home mailbox database attribute needing to be replicated to all domain controllers.

Starting with Exchange Server 2013, a new concept arose for managing move requests, the *migration batch*. Although it still relies on MRS, using migration batches to move mailboxes provides enhanced architectural improvements. For example, you can move multiple mailboxes in large batches, generate move-report email notification after the move is complete, facilitate automatic retry and prioritization of the move requests, move primary and archive mailboxes together or separately, provide the option for manual move-request finalization (allowing you to review your move before you complete it), and perform periodic incremental syncs to update migration changes.

Moving Mailboxes Using the EAC

One of the methods for moving mailboxes is to use the Exchange Administration Center (EAC). Open the Recipients work center of the EAC, select one or more mailboxes, and then select the Move Mailbox To Another Database task in the Details pane. This launches the New Local Mailbox Move Wizard.

NEW LOCAL MAILBOX MOVE WIZARD

The most important information is found on the Move Configuration page of the New Local Mailbox Move Wizard (see Figure 14.9). You can define the migration batch name, the choice for moving the primary and/or archive mailbox, the target database for the mailbox, the target database for the archive mailbox (if one exists), and the bad item limit.

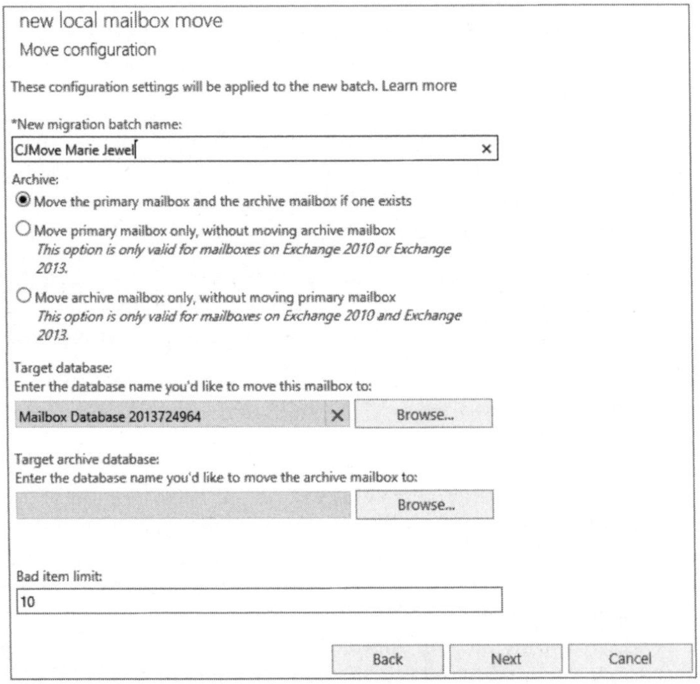

FIGURE 14.9
Move Configuration settings

Occasionally, the properties of a message in a mailbox get corrupted. This occurred more frequently with previous versions of Exchange Server if a pointer between one table and another table was corrupted. These corrupted messages are less common in Exchange Server 2010 and newer, since the single-instance storage (SIS) feature was removed. Nonetheless, the move request will fail if it encounters more than the maximum number of corrupted messages allowed as defined by the bad item limit.

On the next page, you are presented with migration batch settings, including the recipient who will receive a move notification report when the batch is complete, the preferred option of starting the batch automatically or manually, and the preferred option of completing the batch automatically or manually (see Figure 14.10).

FIGURE 14.10
Options for the migration batch

MIGRATION DASHBOARD

The Migration Dashboard (see Figure 14.11) allows you to manage the migration batches in your organization. The dashboard displays helpful information about active and inactive migration batches and their progress.

Figure 14.12 shows a synced migration batch that is waiting to be completed. Frequently, organizations prefer to schedule email migrations over the weekend or during nonbusiness hours. Using the option to delay completion of the migration batch allows an organization to prepare migration for large volumes of email and minimize the time required to complete the email migration. You can complete the migration batch by clicking the Complete This Migration Batch link. This link is available if you select the option to manually complete the migration batch, as shown previously in Figure 14.10.

FIGURE 14.11
The Migration
Dashboard

FIGURE 14.12
Migration progress
in the Migration
Dashboard

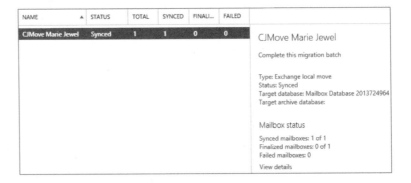

As an alternative to starting a move request as described earlier, you can click the + (Add) sign in the Actions bar to create a migration batch, either to a different database or from another forest.

Most of the options in the New Local Mailbox Move Wizard are similar to the earlier description, with the exception of the first page. Upon starting the wizard, you are provided the option of selecting the users that you want to move or uploading a list of users in a CSV file. The CSV file format is very simple, specifying the user's email address on each line.

After creating a migration batch, you can select the option to stop a batch in progress, resume a suspended or failed batch, or complete (finalize) a batch that has completed initial synchronization. These options are available in the Actions bar or Details pane of a migration batch.

NEW MIGRATION ENDPOINT WIZARD

Exchange Server 2016 uses migration endpoints to capture the remote server information and to store the required credentials for migrating the data as well as the source throttling settings. You can use a migration endpoint for remote and cross-forest moves. You do not need to use a migration endpoint when you are moving mailboxes between two different on-premises Exchange mailbox databases; this procedure is also referred to as a local move. In a cross-forest move, you can move mailboxes between two different on-premises Exchange forests, which requires using an Exchange RemoteMove endpoint.

In a hybrid deployment, mailboxes can be stored on an on-premises Exchange server or hosted on the Internet by Microsoft Office 365. In this environment, a remove move may include *onboarding* or *offboarding* migrations. When onboarding, mailboxes are moved from an on-premises Exchange Server to Exchange Online in Microsoft Office 365, which requires using a RemoteMove endpoint. When offboarding, mailboxes are moved from Exchange Online in Office 365 to an on-premises Exchange Server, which requires using an Exchange RemoteMove endpoint. As you can see, migration endpoints can be either a source or a destination endpoint to facilitate moving mailboxes back and forth between your different environments. Because hybrid deployments can exist indefinitely, their corresponding migration endpoints are kept persistent and used by migration batches to move mailboxes as necessary.

To create a migration endpoint, expand the Actions bar by clicking the ellipsis (More) and select Migration Endpoints. This will open the Migration Endpoints list and display the current endpoints. To add a new endpoint, click the + (New) sign from the Actions bar to start the New Migration Endpoint Wizard.

Creating a new migration endpoint is very straightforward; you need to enter the source-forest email address, the source-forest administrator name, and the source-forest administrator password.

Once you click Next, the wizard will attempt to verify the endpoint settings via Autodiscover. If unsuccessful, the wizard will prompt you to manually enter the FQDN of the Mailbox Replication Service (MRS) server URL.

Moving Mailboxes Using the EMS

Let's say you need to move the mailbox belonging to Gabrielle Williams to a mailbox database named MBX-001, while allowing up to two corrupt messages. You would use the New-MoveRequest cmdlet in the following command to initiate this move request:

```
New-MoveRequest -Identity "Gabrielle Williams" -TargetDatabase MBX-001
-BadItemLimit 2
```

You may notice that this command prompts you to confirm that you want to move the mailbox. To avoid the confirmation prompt, you can include the parameter –Confirm$false in the command. The complete command would look something like this:

```
New-MoveRequest –Identity "Gabrielle Williams" -TargetDatabase MBX-001
-BadItemLimit 2 -Confirm:$false
```

Similar to most EMS cmdlets, you can use piping to create move requests using the New-MoveRequest cmdlet. For example, say that you want to move everyone who is a member of the Executives group to the mailbox database called MBX-001. You would use the Get-DistributionGroupMember cmdlet to enumerate the membership of the Executives group and pipe the output to the New-MoveRequest cmdlet:

```
Get-DistributionGroupMember –Identity "Executives" | New-MoveRequest
-TargetDatabase MBX-001 -Confirm:$false
```

Alternatively, you can move the mailboxes via a migration batch, while adding a little more sophistication to the command. In the following example, you create the batch job using the `New-MigrationBatch` cmdlet with a batch name of `MoveExecutives`. The parameter Local defines the migration batch as a local move (not over the Internet). The parameter CSVData defines the list of mailboxes to migrate using the .NET method `ReadAllBytes()`. The `TargetDatabases` parameter defines the target mailbox databases to move the mailboxes. Finally, the parameter `AutoStart` will start the migration batch automatically.

```
New-MigrationBatch -Name MoveExecutives –Local -CSVData ([System.IO.
File]::ReadAllBytes("C:\Users\Administrator\Desktop\Goldusers.csv"))
-TargetDatabases @(MBX-001,MBX-002) -AutoStart
```

As we discussed earlier, you may need to move all the mailboxes to another mailbox database when decommissioning a mailbox database. In this scenario, you can use the `Get-Mailbox` cmdlet with the `Database` parameter to narrow the scope and pipe the output to the New-MoveRequest cmdlet, as shown in the following example:

```
Get-Mailbox -Database MBX-001 | New-MoveRequest -TargetDatabase MBX-003
DisplayName     Status  TotalMailboxSize      TotalArchiveSize PercentComplete
-----------     ------  ----------------      ---------------- ---------------
Marie Jewel     Queued  59.54 KB (60,966 bytes)                0
Cheyenne Pike   Queued  59.19 KB (60,610 bytes)                0
David Pike      Queued  80.89 KB (82,831 bytes)                0
Treyden Jewel   Queued  59.4 KB (60,822 bytes)                 0
Pierce Jewel    Queued  59.13 KB (60,547 bytes)                0
```

With a little creativity, you can probably figure out a number of other ways to accomplish this task or tasks similar to it.

After submitting move requests, you have several options to check the status of the move requests. The simplest method is the `Get-MoveRequest` cmdlet:

```
Get-MoveRequest
DisplayName                     Status           TargetDatabase
-----------                     ------           --------------
Marie Jewel                     Queued           MBX-001
Pierce Jewel                    Queued           MBX-001
Treyden Jewel                   Queued           MBX-001
Cheyenne Pike                   Queued           MBX-001
David Pike                      Queued           MBX-001
Gabrielle Williams              InProgress       MBX-001
Taylor Ferguson                 InProgress       MBX-001
Talon Ferguson                  InProgress       MBX-001
```

You can use the `Get-MoveRequestStatistics` cmdlet to view detailed information about move requests. The results from the following command display detailed information on the move request for Treyden Jewel, such as the move type (intraorganization), the status, and the progress (percentage):

```
Get-MoveRequestStatistics Treyden.Jewel | FL
UserIdentity                    : contoso.com/Corporate/Treyden Jewel
DistinguishedName               : CN=Treyden Jewel,OU=Corporate,
```

```
        DC=tsxen,DC=com
        DisplayName                         : Treyden Jewel
        Alias                               : Treyden.Jewel
        ArchiveGuid                         :
        Status                              : InProgress
        StatusDetail                        : CreatingInitialSyncCheckpoint
        SyncStage                           : CreatingInitialSyncCheckpoint
        Flags                               : IntraOrg, Pull
        MoveType                            : IntraOrg
        Direction                           : Pull
        IsOffline                           : False
        Protect                             : False
        Suspend                             : False
        SuspendWhenReadyToComplete          : False
        IgnoreRuleLimitErrors               : False
        SourceVersion                       : Version 15.1 (Build 225.0)
        SourceDatabase                      : MBX-001
        TargetVersion                       : Version 15.1 (Build 225.0)
        TargetDatabase                      : MBX-003
        RemoteHostName                      :
        RemoteGlobalCatalog                 :
        BatchName                           :
        RemoteCredentialUsername            :
        RemoteDatabaseName                  :
        RemoteDatabaseGuid                  :
        TargetDeliveryDomain                :
        BadItemLimit                        : 0
        BadItemsEncountered                 : 0
        QueuedTimestamp                     : 06/28/2009 10:45:38 AM
        StartTimestamp                      : 06/28/2009 10:46:55 AM
        LastUpdateTimestamp                 : 06/28/2009 10:47:16 AM
        InitialSeedingCompletedTimestamp    :
        FinalSyncTimestamp                  :
        CompletionTimestamp                 :
        SuspendedTimestamp                  :
        MoveDuration                        : 00:01:42
        TotalFinalizationDuration           :
        TotalSuspendedDuration              :
        TotalFailedDuration                 :
        TotalQueuedDuration                 : 00:01:13
        TotalInProgressDuration             : 00:00:29
        TotalStalledDueToCIDuration         :
        TotalStalledDueToHADuration         :
        TotalTransientFailureDuration       :
        MoveServerName                      : HNLMBX01.contoso.com
        TotalMailboxSize                    : 4.355 MB (4,566,443 bytes)
        TotalMailboxItEACount               : 44
        TotalArchiveSize                    :
```

```
TotalArchiveItEACount         :
BytesTransferred              : 22.55 KB (23,089 bytes)
BytesTransferredPerMinute     : 56.31 KB (57,657 bytes)
ItemsTransferred              : 0
PercentComplete               : 15
PositionInQueue               :
FailureCode                   :
Message                       :
FailureTimestamp              :
IsValid                       : True
ValidationMessage             :
```

You can use the following command to also pipe the output of all move requests, sorting the output on the Status property with the Sort-Command cmdlet; an abbreviated alias for this cmdlet is Sort:

```
Get-MoveRequest | Get-MoveRequestStatistics | Sort Status
DisplayName      Status         TotalMailbox TotalArchive PercentComplete
                                Size         Size

-----------      ------         ------------ ------------ ---------------
Gabrielle Wi... Completed       116.1 KB ...              100
Taylor Fergu... Completed        59.24 KB ...             100
Talon Fergus... Completed        59.24 KB ...             100
Marie Jewel     CompletionInProg...401.6 KB ...           95
Pierce Jewel    InProgress       3.895 MB ...             29
Treyden Jewel   InProgress      272.5 KB ... 3.427 KB (3  89
Cheyenne Pike   Queued          115.4 KB ...              0
David Pike      Queued           59.74 KB ...             0
```

You can also use the Get-MigrationStatistics cmdlet to display the migration batch statistics:

```
Get-MigrationStatistics | FL
RunspaceId            : 8077d2a0-1dd9-43cf-82ab-2aef5c008225
Identity              :
TotalCount            : 8
ActiveCount           : 0
StoppedCount          : 0
SyncedCount           : 0
FinalizedCount        : 3
FailedCount           : 0
PendingCount          : 0
ProvisionedCount      : 0
MigrationType         : ExchangeLocalMove
DiagnosticInfo        :
IsValid               : True
ObjectState           : Unchanged
```

You can also configure existing migration batches to migrate mailboxes during the move using the Set-MigrationBatch cmdlet. A couple of key parameters are available with the Set-MigrationBatch cmdlet:

- ◆ AutoRetryCount. This parameter specifies the maximum number of attempts to automatically restart the migration batch for move requests that encountered errors.

- ◆ AllowIncrementalSyncs. This parameter specifies whether new messages sent to the source mailbox are copied to the corresponding target mailbox of a move request. If enabled, the Exchange server will incrementally synchronize the source mailbox with the target mailbox every 24 hours.

For example, you can use the Set-MigrationBatch cmdlet to update the Executives migration batch with new parameters:

```
Set-MigrationBatch -Identity Executives -AutoRetryCount 5 `
-AllowIncrementalSyncs $true
```

You can use the Stop-MigrationBatch cmdlet to stop the migration batch:

```
Get-MigrationBatch | Stop-MigrationBatch
```

Alternatively, you can use the Remove-MigrationBatch cmdlet to remove the migration batch:

```
Get-MigrationBatch | Remove-MigrationBatch
```

Exchange stores some of the information about a mailbox move in the mailbox object. Here is an example of the move request information available using the Get-Mailbox cmdlet:

```
Get-Mailbox Treyden.Jewel | FL Displayname,*move*
DisplayName               : Treyden Jewel
MailboxMoveTargetMDB      : MBX-001
MailboxMoveSourceMDB      : MBX-003
MailboxMoveFlags          : IntraOrg, Pull
MailboxMoveRemoteHostName :
MailboxMoveBatchName      :
MailboxMoveStatus         : Completed
```

Historical move request information that is stored in a mailbox can be retrieved using the Get-MailboxStatistics cmdlet with the IncludeMoveHistory parameter. Review the MoveHistory property from the following command output:

```
Get-MailboxStatistics Treyden.Jewel -IncludeMoveHistory | FL
AssociatedItEACount     : 12
DeletedItEACount        : 0
DisconnectDate          :
DisplayName             : Treyden Jewel
ItEACount               : 32
LastLoggedOnUserAccount : ITHICOS\Treyden.Jewel
LastLogoffTime          :
LastLogonTime           : 06/28/2009 1:34:31 PM
ObjectClass             : Mailbox
StorageLimitStatus      : BelowLimit
TotalDeletedItemSize    : 0 B (0 bytes)
TotalItemSize           : 4.356 MB (4,568,055 bytes)
Database                : MBX-003
ServerName              : HNLMBX01
```

```
DatabaseName            : MBX-003
MoveHistory             : {(06/31/2009 10:48:01 AM: TargetMDB=MBX-003,
Size=4.355 MB (4,566,443 bytes), Duration=00:02:18), (07/06/2009
11:31:02 PM: TargetMDB=MBX-001, Size=4.301 MB (4,510,383 bytes),
Duration=00:02:03)}
IsQuarantined           : False
IsArchiveMailbox        : False
```

You can remove the completed or queued move requests using the `Remove-MoveRequest` cmdlet when you no longer need information about the move. You are required to remove move requests for mailboxes for which you want to submit an additional move request.

While this cmdlet removes the move status information from Active Directory, it does not remove the move history from the mailbox statistics. To remove user Treyden.Jewel's move request information, use this command:

```
Remove-MoveRequest Treyden.Jewel -Confirm:$false
```

You can also use piping to remove move requests based on criteria. The following command removes the completed move requests from Active Directory:

```
Get-MoveRequest | Where {$_.Status -eq "Completed"} | Remove-MoveRequest
```

 Real World Scenario

MANAGING THE MIGRATION BATCH

When migrating to a new environment, many Exchange architects and consultants spend a great deal of time staring at progress bars or status windows as mailboxes move between databases; this can be extremely frustrating. To avoid wasting time, you should not wait until the environment is completely deployed before you start moving the mailboxes. Rather, create a migration batch and enable it to automatically suspend, providing you with more flexibility regarding when the batch file will complete. In this way, you can complete the deployment of the post mailbox database environment while the mailboxes are migrating.

Once you are ready to complete the migration batch, Exchange will synchronize differences in the mailboxes since the initial sync, or since the last sync if you enabled incremental syncs, and complete the migration batch. Any time you spend learning how to create a migration batch, you will make up for when the migration occurs over hours instead of days.

Retrieving Mailbox Statistics

At various times, Exchange administrators may need to run a report that identifies the amount of storage that each mailbox is consuming. The building blocks of information for this type of report are available using the `Get-MailboxStatistics` cmdlet, which requires one of three parameters:

-Identity Retrieves the mailbox statistics for a specific mailbox

-Database Retrieves statistics for all mailboxes on a specific mailbox database

-Server Retrieves statistics for all mailboxes on a specific server

Here is an example of using the cmdlet to retrieve mailbox statistics for a specific mailbox:

```
Get-MailboxStatistics -Identity Cheyenne.Pike
DisplayName          ItemCount   StorageLimitStatus     LastLogonTime
-----------          ---------   ------------------     -------------
Cheyenne Pike        35          NoChecking             03/15/2009 1:34:31 PM
```

Here is an example of using the cmdlet to retrieve mailbox statistics for all the mailboxes on the mailbox database MBX-003:

```
Get-MailboxStatistics -Database MBX-003
DisplayName               ItemCount StorageLimitStatus    LastLogonTime
-----------               --------- ------------------    -------------
Suriya Supatanasakul      4         BelowLimit            11/25/2009 9:55:28 AM
Online Archive - Chuck... 0         NoChecking            12/15/2009 7:47:41 AM
Michael G. Brown          4         BelowLimit            11/26/2009 9:01:12 AM
Chuck Swanson             9
Jason Crawford            5         BelowLimit            11/27/2009 3:53:09 PM
Jordan Chang              11        BelowLimit
Luke Husky                4         BelowLimit            12/21/2009 5:23:48 PM
Clayton K. Kamiya         35        NoChecking            12/23/2009 6:48:12 AM
Treyden Jewel             32        BelowLimit            12/13/2009 7:13:38 PM
```

The Get-MailboxStatistics cmdlet contains multiple useful properties. You can use these properties to display the necessary information for an administrator, as well as the required fields for a management report. The following are some of the properties that are returned with the Get-MailboxStatistics cmdlet:

DisplayName   Display name of the mailbox.

ItemCount   Total number of items in the mailbox.

TotalItemSize   Total size of all the items in the mailbox except for items in the Recoverable Items folder.

TotalDeletedItemsSize   Total size of all the items in the Recoverable Items folder, previously known as the Dumpster or deleted item cache.

StorageLimitStatus   Status of the mailbox storage limits; the limits you may see are as follows:

-BelowLimit—Mailbox is below all limits.

-IssueWarning—Mailbox storage is above the issue warning limit.

-ProhibitSend—Mailbox is above the prohibit send limit.

-MailboxDisabled—Mailbox is over the prohibit send and receive limit.

-NoChecking—No quota checking

Database   Name of the mailbox database, such as MBX-002, on which the mailbox is located.

ServerName   Name of the mailbox server on which the database is active.

LastLogoffTime   Date and time the last account logged off the mailbox.

LastLogonTime Date and time the last account logged on to the mailbox.

LastLoggedOnUserAccount Name of the last account (domain name and username) logged on to the mailbox. This could be an account with full access permissions to the mailbox, a delegate, or even someone simply checking the Calendar.

DisconnectDate Date and time the mailbox was deleted or disconnected.

IsArchive Indicates if the mailbox is an archive mailbox.

IsQuarantined Indicates if the mailbox is quarantined. An Exchange server will quarantine a mailbox when it detects a client consuming too much of the Store process. This may be caused by corrupt mailbox data or a software bug in either the client or Store process.

MoveHistory Historical information of a completed move request when the -IncludeMoveHistory parameter is used. This information includes status, flags, target database, bad items, start times, end times, duration that the move request was in various stages, and failure codes.

Let's suppose you want to view a mailbox report that includes the display name, the total size of the mailbox, the total number of items, and the storage limit status on the mailbox database MBX-003. You can use the following command to accomplish this and include the Where clause to filter out any mailbox whose name contains the word *system*:

```
Get-MailboxStatistics -Database MBX-003 | Where {$_.DisplayName -notlike
"*System*"} | FT DisplayName,TotalItemSize,ItemCount,StorageLimitStatus
DisplayName          TotalItemSize                    ItemCount StorageLimitStatus
-----------          -------------                    --------- ------------------
Julie R. Samante     372.5 KB (381,396 bytes)                 4 BelowLimit
Suriya Supatanas...  970 MB (1,017,087,604 bytes)             4 BelowLimit
Ken Vickers          7.842 KB (8,030 bytes)                   4 BelowLimit
John Park            5.138 MB (5,387,323 bytes)              11 BelowLimit
Online Archive -...  7.846 KB (8,034 bytes)                   0 NoChecking
Michael G. Brown     8.077 MB (8,469,169 bytes)               4 BelowLimit
Chuck Swanson        4.618 GB (4,958,195,270 bytes)           9
Online Archive -...  2.133 GB (2,289,975,794 bytes)           0 NoChecking
Clarence A. Birtcil  17.4 GB (18,680,008,619 bytes)           4 BelowLimit
Jonathan Core        1.002 GB (1,075,524,880 bytes)           4 BelowLimit
Marie Badeau         15.28 GB (16,404,419,182 bytes)          4 BelowLimit
Kevin Wile           91.02 GB (97,729,567,596 bytes)          4 BelowLimit
Jason Crawford       16.39 KB (16,785 bytes)                  5 BelowLimit
```

As you may have noticed, the unit of measure for the values of TotalItemSize are not consistent; they include KB, MB, and GB. This can be problematic when you need to produce a report for management. Fortunately, you can use PowerShell to convert the mailbox size to a standard unit of measure. Depending on the average size of mailboxes in your environment, you may need to convert the value to kilobytes, megabytes, or gigabytes. For example, you can use the following expression to convert TotalItemSize to megabytes:

```
expression={$_.TotalItemSize.Value.ToMB()}
```

Starting with the previous requirements, you can use the following command that standardizes the TotalItemSize as megabytes and redirects the output to a text file using the > (greater than) character and a filename:

```
Get-MailboxStatistics -Database MBX-003 | Where {$_.DisplayName -notlike
"*System*"} | FT DisplayName, @{expression={$_.TotalItemSize.value.ToMB()};
width=20;label="Mailbox Size(MB) "},ItemCount,StorageLimitStatus
> c:\Mailbox.txt
```

You could also send the data to a CSV, XML, or HTML file by piping the output using the `Export-Csv`, `Export-Clixml`, or `ConvertTo-Html` cmdlet. For more detailed examples of tuning the output of `Get-MailboxStatistics`, look at Chapter 5, "Introduction to PowerShell and the Exchange Management Shell."

Here are a few more examples of common requests you may receive in your organization. Using the PowerShell cmdlet `Get-Date`, you can use the following command to identify the mailboxes that have not been accessed in the last 30 days (subtracts 30 days from the current date):

```
Get-MailboxStatistics -Database MBX-003 | Where {$_.LastLogonTime -lt
(Get-Date).AddDays(-30)} -And $_.DisplayName -notlike "*System*"} |
Format-Table DisplayName,LastlogonTime,LastLoggedonUserAccount,ServerName
```

You can use the following command to identify the mailboxes that have been disconnected over the last seven days on server HNLMBX01:

```
Get-MailboxStatistics -Server HNLMBX01 | Where {$_.DisconnectDate
-gt (Get-Date).AddDays(-7)} | Format-Table DisplayName,ServerName,
DatabaseName,TotalItemSize -Autosize
```

Deleting Mailboxes

Deleting mailboxes might not seem like such a complicated task until you realize there are multiple ways, or options, to delete a mailbox. These options include disconnecting the mailbox from a user account, deleting both the user account and the mailbox, and purging the mailbox.

USE CAUTION WHEN DELETING!

In Exchange Server 2016, the Actions bar in the EAC provides you with the default Delete action, which will delete the mailbox and the user account. If you prefer to delete only the mailbox, ensure you click the ellipsis (More) and select Disable.

Deleting the Mailbox but Not the User

If you choose the Disable option within the EAC, the mailbox is disconnected from the user account, but the user account remains in Active Directory. This is equivalent to using the EMS cmdlet `Disable-Mailbox`. For example, you would use the following command to disable a mailbox:

```
Disable-Mailbox Marie.Jewel
```

When you disable a mailbox, the Exchange attributes are removed from the corresponding Active Directory user account, but the user account is retained. When a mailbox is deleted, Exchange retains the mailbox in the mailbox database and switches the mailbox to a disabled state. Disabled and deleted mailboxes are retained in the mailbox database until the deleted mailbox-retention period expires, which is 30 days by default. After the retention period expires, the mailbox is permanently deleted or purged. Disabled or deleted mailboxes are commonly referred to as *disconnected mailboxes*. In addition to retaining disconnected mailboxes for 30 days, many organizations will commonly keep the disabled user account for 30 days in case they need to be reactivated.

Deleting Both the User and the Mailbox

If you choose the Remove option within the EAC, the mailbox is disconnected from the user account, the Exchange attributes are removed from the corresponding Active Directory user account, *and* the user account is deleted from Active Directory. This is equivalent to using the EMS cmdlet `Remove-Mailbox`. For example, you would use the following command to remove a mailbox:

```
Remove-Mailbox Marie.Jewel
```

When the user account and the mailbox are deleted, the procedure to restore them would require more steps. This is because the objects are stored in separate locations. You would need to restore the mailbox from the mailbox database. The user account would need to be restored from Active Directory (e.g., using the Active Directory Recycle Bin).

Purging the Mailbox

When you permanently delete or purge mailboxes, all mailbox contents are purged from the mailbox database, and the data loss is permanent. The associated user account in Active Directory is also deleted, if it exists. This prevents the mailbox from being recovered.

As noted earlier, a deleted mailbox is permanently deleted or purged after the retention period expires. However, here are two methods to manually purge a mailbox from the mailbox database based on the current status.

If you want to permanently delete the user account and the mailbox, you can use the Permanent parameter. For example, you can use the following command to permanently delete an active mailbox:

```
Remove-Mailbox Marie.Jewel -Permanent:$true
```

There are two types of disconnected mailboxes in Exchange: *disabled* and *soft-deleted*. If you want to permanently delete a disconnected mailbox from the mailbox database, you must specify one of these types when using the `Remove-Mailbox` cmdlet to permanently delete the mailbox. If the type you specify does not match the actual type of the disconnected mailbox, the command will fail.

You can use the `Get-MailboxDatabase` and the `Get-MailboxStatistics` cmdlets to identify whether a disconnected mailbox is disabled or soft-deleted and to retrieve the mailbox GUID value of the disconnected mailbox. This is used by the `Remove-StoreMailbox` cmdlet. In addition to the mailbox GUID, you will need to identify the mailbox database where the mailbox was deleted. For example, you can use the following commands to permanently delete the disconnected mailbox from MBX-003, which was disabled:

```
$Temp = Get-MailboxDatabase | Get-MailboxStatistics | `
    Where {$_.DisplayName -eq "Marie Jewel"} | `
```

```
        fl DisplayName,MailboxGuid,Database,DisconnectReason
Remove-StoreMailbox -Database $Temp.Database `
    -Identity $Temp.MailboxGuid –MailboxState $Temp.DisconnectReason
```

Reconnecting a Deleted Mailbox

Exchange Server allows you to undelete a deleted mailbox, which is commonly referred to as reconnecting a deleted, or disconnected, mailbox. As we noted earlier, there are two types of disconnected mailboxes in Exchange. For reconnection purposes, here is a more in-depth description of each:

◆ *Disabled mailboxes.* When a mailbox is disconnected or removed by using the `Disable-Mailbox` or `Remove-Mailbox` cmdlet, Exchange retains the disconnected mailbox, and the mailbox is switched to a *disabled* state. The Active Directory user account associated with the mailbox is also deleted. With disabled mailboxes, you can recover mailbox data without having to restore the entire mailbox database. In fact, disabled mailboxes are retained in the mailbox database until the deleted mailbox retention period expires, which is 30 days by default, or until the mailbox is permanently deleted.

◆ *Soft-deleted mailboxes.* When a mailbox is moved, Exchange does not completely delete the mailbox from the source mailbox database upon completion of the move request. Instead, the mailbox in the source mailbox database is switched to a *soft-deleted* state. With soft-deleted mailboxes, you can use the `New-MailboxRestoreRequest` cmdlet to access mailbox data during a mailbox restore operation. Soft-deleted mailboxes are retained in the source mailbox database until either the deleted mailbox retention period expires, which is 30 days by default, or until the `Remove-StoreMailbox` cmdlet is used to purge the mailbox.

Until a deleted mailbox is permanently deleted from the mailbox database, you can use the EAC or the Shell to connect a deleted mailbox to an Active Directory user account. You can also use the Shell to restore the contents of the deleted mailbox to an existing mailbox.

RECONNECTING A MAILBOX USING THE EAC

To reconnect a deleted mailbox using the EAC, from the Actions menu of the Mailbox tab, click the ellipsis (More) and then select Connect A Mailbox. In the Connect a Mailbox, select the appropriate mailbox server from the drop-down menu (see Figure 14.13).

FIGURE 14.13
Connecting a disconnected mailbox

connect a mailbox   Help

A disconnected mailbox is a mailbox that isn't associated with a user account or that's been moved to a different mailbox database. You can connect a disconnected mailbox to a user account or restore it to the original mailbox database. Learn more

Select server: LON-EX1   ▾

DISPLAY NA... ▾	IDENTITY	DISCONNECT DATE	DATABASE
Taylor Ferguson	2da37586-6534-4d1a-9cd0-c4dbd686c374	5/11/2016 9:43:17 AM	Mailbox Database 0384961236

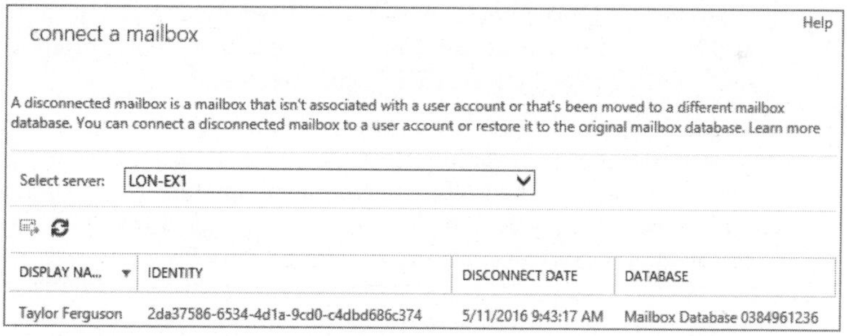

The list of disconnected mailboxes includes disabled mailboxes, deleted mailboxes, and soft-deleted mailboxes. In this example, select the disconnected mailbox for Marie Jewel and click Connect. If the wizard is able to locate the corresponding user account in Active Directory, you will be prompted to connect the mailbox to either the original user account or a different account. If the wizard is unable to locate the corresponding user account in Active Directory, you will be prompted to only connect the mailbox to a different user account in Active Directory.

If you choose to connect the mailbox to a different user account, you will be prompted to select it from the existing user accounts in Active Directory. You will only be shown a list of user accounts that aren't mail-enabled. Next, you will select the type of mailbox that you are reconnecting—User mailbox, Room Resource mailbox, Equipment Resource mailbox, or Linked mailbox.

You can use the following command to generate the same list of disconnected mailboxes by using the Get-MailboxStatistics command with a filter to include only objects with a value for the DisconnectDate property:

```
Get-MailboxStatistics -Server HNLMBX01 | Where {$_.DisconnectDate
-ne $null} | ft DisplayName,DisconnectDate
DisplayName        DisconnectDate
-----------        --------------
Pierce Jewel       12/10/2009 3:13:37 AM
Marie Jewel        12/02/2000 3:13:23 AM
Treyden Jewel      11/25/2009 3:13:55 AM
Cheyenne Pike      11/20/2009 3:13:47 AM
David Pike         11/16/2009 3:13:01 AM
```

NO MORE WORRIES ABOUT DISCONNECTED MAILBOXES

In previous versions of Exchange Server, you needed to run the Clean-MailboxDatabase cmdlet after you deleted a mailbox. This cmdlet cleaned up the mailbox database so disconnected mailboxes would appear in the Disconnected Mailboxes section.

In Exchange Server 2016, the Disable-Mailbox cmdlet runs a cleanup process immediately after you disconnect a user's mailbox, updating the database to reflect the disconnected status.

In some cases, however, the store state for a mailbox may become out-of-sync with the state of the corresponding user account in Active Directory. This can result from Active Directory replication latency. For example, a mailbox-enabled user account is disabled in Active Directory but isn't marked as disabled in the Exchange mailbox store.

In this scenario, you can use the Update-StoreMailboxState cmdlet to synchronize the store state for the mailbox with the state of the corresponding user account in Active Directory and mark the mailbox as disabled in the Exchange mailbox store. This cmdlet is useful for troubleshooting issues when the store state for a mailbox is unexpected or if you suspect that the store state is different from the state for the corresponding Active Directory account.

RECONNECTING A MAILBOX USING THE EMS

To reconnect a deleted mailbox using the EMS, you would use the `Connect-Mailbox` cmdlet. When using this cmdlet, you need to provide the name of the deleted mailbox, the mailbox database name where the mailbox was deleted, and the user account to connect the mailbox.

The identifier for the deleted mailbox should be the unique mailbox GUID, the display name, or the legacy Exchange distinguished name (commonly referred to as LegacyDN). You can also provide a new alias for the mailbox when reconnecting.

In many situations, you may not have the necessary information about the deleted mailbox prior to reconnecting the deleted mailbox. You can use the `Get-MailboxStatistics` cmdlet to enumerate the information you need to reconnect a mailbox:

```
Get-MailboxStatistics -Server HNLMBX01 | Where {$_.DisconnectDate
-ne $null} | FT DisplayName,Database
DisplayName                    Database
-----------                    --------
Marie Jewel                    MBX-001
CJ Jewel                       MBX-002
Pierce Jewel                   MBX-003
Treyden Jewel                  MBX-003
```

With this information, you can use the following command to reconnect the deleted mailbox, Marie Jewel, to the user account Contoso\Marie.Jewel:

```
Connect-Mailbox "Marie Jewel" –Database MBX-001 -User "Contoso\Marie.Jewel"
```

Bulk Manipulation of Mailboxes Using the EMS

Arguably the most beneficial feature of Windows PowerShell and the EMS is the ability to perform bulk manipulation of Exchange-related objects.

Managing Mailbox Properties Using the EMS

Let's say you want to disable Outlook on the web for all the mailboxes in your organization. As you may recall from earlier, you would use the `Set-CASMailbox` cmdlet to configure client access settings on a mailbox. With one line in the EMS, you can retrieve all the mailboxes in your organization and pipe them to the `Set-CASMailbox` cmdlet:

```
Get-Mailbox | Set-CASMailbox -OWAEnabled:$False
```

As you can see from the previous example, these are very powerful and potentially dangerous commands. If not careful, you can easily do something you did not intend to do. Use extreme caution when using the EMS if you are performing any type of bulk administration.

You may want to consider appending the `WhatIf` parameter to any commands performing bulk administration. This option allows you to test what would happen if the script ran without actually making any changes to the environment. Effectively, it provides a preview of the changes.

When beginning to learn EMS, you may not be interested in making changes to every mailbox or user account in your organization. For this reason, you may want to consider starting with smaller groups of users. In many situations, these groups of users may already be members of common groups.

You can use the `Get-DistributionGroup` cmdlet to list all of the distribution groups in the organization:

```
Get-DistributionGroup
Name                DisplayName         GroupType            PrimarySmtpAddress
----                -----------         ---------            ------------------
Operations Group    Operations Group    Global, Security     Ops@contoso.com
Executives          Executives          Global, Security     Execs@contoso.com
Sales Group         Sales Group         Universal, Security  Sales@contoso.com
```

Further, you can use the `Get-DistributionGroupMember` cmdlet to retrieve a list of members of a distribution group (remember that this is not text within the PowerShell environment; these are unique objects that can be piped as input to another cmdlet):

```
Get-DistributionGroupMember –Identity "Executives"
Name                                    RecipientType
----                                    -------------
Marie Jewel                             UserMailbox
Pierce Jewel                            UserMailbox
Treyden Jewel                           UserMailbox
```

Starting with an example we used earlier to override the mailbox quotas for one mailbox, you can use a similar command to set the quota for all members of the Executives group:

```
Get-DistributionGroupMember –Identity "Executives" | `
    Set-Mailbox –ProhibitSendQuota 250MB –IssueWarningQuota 200MB `
    -UseDatabaseQuotaDefaults $false –ProhibitSendReceiveQuota 300MB
```

This cmdlet retrieves the membership list for the Executives distribution group and then passes those objects as input to the `Set-Mailbox` cmdlet.

Another common task you may need to perform is to move all of the mailboxes in the Executives group to the Executives mailbox database:

```
Get-DistributionGroupMember –Identity "Executives" | `
    New-MoveRequest -BadItemLimit 2 – TargetDatabase MBX-003
```

Further, you could use the following command to move all mailboxes on a specific mailbox server by using the `Get-Mailbox` cmdlet with the `-Server` option to help you narrow your list of mailboxes:

```
Get-Mailbox –Server HNLEX04 | New-MoveRequest –TargetDatabase MBX-003
```

Similarly, you could use the following command to move only the mailboxes on a specific mailbox database:

```
Get-Mailbox -Database MBX-004 | New-MoveRequest -TargetDatabase MBX-003
```

As you can imagine, there are multiple ways to accomplish similar tasks in EMS.

Scripting Account Creation

In many organizations, the account provisioning process will create multiple accounts simultaneously. This is also a common task that is used during migrations. The EMS allows you to automate this process by reading the data from a text or CSV file. For example, here's a CSV file of new users:

```
Name,Database,OrganizationalUnit,UserPrincipalName
Marie Jewel,MBX-001,contoso.com/Executives,Marie.Jewel@contoso.com
Treyden Jewel, MBX-001,contoso.com/Executives,Treyden.Jewel@contoso.com
Pierce Jewel, MBX-001,contoso.com/Executives,Pierce.Jewel@contoso.com
Cheyenne Pike, MBX-002,contoso.com/Sales,Cheyenne.Pike@contoso.com
David Pike,MBX-002,contoso.com/Sales,David.Pike@contoso.com
Zoe Pike,MBX-002,contoso.com/Sales,Zoe.Pike@contoso.com
Taylor Ferguson,MBX-003,contoso.com/HR,Taylor.Ferguson@contoso.com
```

Within the CSV file are four columns of attributes, which represent the minimum required attributes to create a user mailbox, along with the password. In your environment, however, you may have additional attributes for new users, such as first name, last name, SAMAccountName, userPrincipalName, alias, and so on. In most scenarios, the parent OU for each user must exist in Active Directory.

A common method for reading information from a CSV file is to use the `Import-CSV` cmdlet. This cmdlet creates table-like custom objects from the items in the CSV file. Each column in the CSV file becomes a property of the custom object, and the items in rows become the property values.

In this scenario, you will use the `New-Mailbox` cmdlet to create a mailbox for each row in the CSV file after you import the file with the `Import-CSV` cmdlet. Here is a sample script for creating mailboxes referenced in the CSV file:

```
# Import the CSV file - save objects to the $Users variable.
$Users = Import-Csv -Path C:\Demo\newaccounts.csv
# Output the contents of the $Users variable - for display only
$Users
# Prompt for a password that will be used for each new user account.
$Password = Read-Host "Please enter a password" -AsSecureString
# Use a Foreach loop to parse each line of the CSV file separately
Foreach ($User in $Users) {
  New-Mailbox -Name $User.Name -Database $User.Database `
    -OrganizationalUnit $User.OrganizationalUnit `
    -UserPrincipalName $User.UserPrincipalName -Password $Password
}
```

Managing Mailbox Content

The need to control mailbox content and size is often due to limited disk space for mailbox databases, but it may also be due to company security policies, email archiving, electronic discovery (eDiscovery) requirements, regulatory compliance, or simply needing to assist your users with cleaning the junk out of their mailboxes. Over the years, there have been multiple third-party solutions for managing mailbox and folder content.

Many organizations deploy email archive solutions that remove content from users' mailboxes and store it in long-term storage, such as tape, optical, network-attached storage (NAS), or storage area networks (SANs). In some cases, archive solutions are put in place merely to reduce the size of the Exchange Server mailbox databases but still allow users long-term access to their old mail data. In other cases, an organization is required to keep certain types of message content, such as financial data, official company communications, and healthcare-related data.

As you can imagine, email archiving has raised new issues and challenges not only for the Exchange Server administrator but for management and users as well. For example, some types of messages may need to be retained for long periods of time, but is one copy of each message sufficient? There has to be some method of determining which messages should be retained or archived. Unfortunately, most of the time this responsibility falls to the user.

Organizations that are concerned about meeting regulatory compliance requirements with respect to message archiving and long-term retention of certain types of messages may also be interested in keeping a journaled copy of messages.

Exchange Server 2007 introduced the basics of mailbox contents management; Exchange Server 2010 leaped forward with retention policies and retention tags. Exchange Server 2013 and Exchange Server 2016 continue with the policies and tags from previous editions but with some advancements and modifications. In this section, we will specifically explore retention policies and retention tags in more detail.

Finally, significant improvements in IOPS for Exchange Server 2016 and in costs for large disks have created opportunities for organizations to provide 100 GB mailboxes on-premises. Along with the cached mode sync slider in Outlook 2013 and Outlook 2016, very large mailboxes are possible for end users.

Understanding the Basics of Messaging Records Management

Before diving into how you would design and deploy Messaging Records Management (MRM), you should become familiar with some basic terminology and behavior. We'll explore possible usage scenarios, what the user would experience, and the basics of getting started.

For starters, Messaging Records Management encompasses management of email content "at rest." This means that you are managing the content while it is sitting in a folder in a mailbox. You shouldn't confuse this concept with transport rules, which are discussed in more detail in Chapter 23, "Managing Transport, Data Loss Prevention, and Journaling Rules."

MESSAGING RECORDS MANAGEMENT AND LICENSING

Exchange Server 2016 licensing for MRM is simple; you can use the default retention policies. Default retention policies are applied to the entire mailbox.

If you want to use personal or custom policies, you will need to purchase an enterprise CAL, or eCAL. The following web pages contain more information:

`http://office.microsoft.com/en-us/exchange/microsoft-exchange-server-licensing-licensing-overview-FX103746915.aspx`

`https://products.office.com/en-us/exchange/microsoft-exchange-server-licensing-licensing-overview`

User Participation

Keep in mind that MRM requires user participation. A popular misconception is that content that should be retained will automatically be moved to the appropriate managed folder in your primary mailbox. Messages in your primary mailbox are *not* organized automatically—users must participate in MRM by moving the relevant content into the appropriate managed folders.

On the other hand, there are some automatic actions that do not require user participation. Automatic actions are limited to deleting (purging) messages or moving messages to the archive mailbox. For example, you can enable the Exchange server to automatically purge messages from the Deleted Items folder or to move messages from the Inbox in your primary mailbox to the same folder in your archive mailbox. However, the real purpose of MRM is for the user to participate in the process. For example, you can enable custom retention tags in the user's mailbox, but it is up to the user to determine where and when to apply those tags. Figure 14.14 shows a sample set of the default and personal retention tags.

FIGURE 14.14
List of the default and personal retention tags

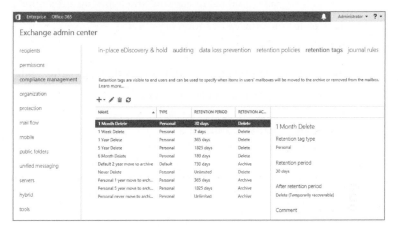

The administrator defines the retention policy name, the retention action, and the retention period (number of days before the retention action should be applied), but it is up to the user to apply those retention tags in their mailbox. Users should be trained to categorize their mailbox content and apply personal retention tags to the content. This will allow the Exchange server to take actions based on the retention policies applied and delete/move items based on the retention tags' settings.

Possible Scenarios

You will find many useful scenarios for MRM, even if your organization does not perform email archiving or is not required to meet regulatory compliance, such as these:

◆ Creating custom retention tags that are used by users to categorize or organize information that must be retained in your organization

◆ Deleting emails in the Junk Email folder and emptying the Deleted items folder

◆ Archiving emails in a shared mailbox

- Enforcing deletion of Inbox messages after the defined retention period
- Archiving or deleting voicemail messages after a period of time

These are just a few of the common scenarios for MRM.

Getting Started with Messaging Records Management

Retention policies and tags can be defined in the EAC or the EMS. In most of our scenarios, we will describe how you can do this in the EAC and follow up with EMS commands as necessary.

The retention policies and tags are located in the Compliance Management section in the EAC. Because of the complexities, you cannot set up Messaging Records Management (MRM) using a single dialog or wizard—multiple steps are required to get started. We'll go into more detail later in the chapter on how to do each of these steps, but for now, let's start with a basic outline of how you would begin creating and applying a retention policy:

1. Create one or more retention tags.

2. Define retention tag settings and actions.

3. Create a retention policy, and link retention tags to the policy.

4. Assign the retention policy to users.

Managing Default Folders

The default folders in a mailbox are the folders that Outlook creates automatically the first time you open a mailbox. The list of default folders is static; you cannot create additional default folders. To prevent conflicting policies, you can enable only one retention tag for a particular default folder within the same retention policy. The following is a list of the default folders in Exchange:

- Calendar
- Conversation History
- Deleted Items
- Drafts
- Inbox
- Journal
- Junk Email
- Notes
- Outbox
- RSS Feeds
- Sent Items
- Sync Issues

Creating Retention Tags

You can use retention tags to apply retention settings to items and folders in the user's mailbox. The applied settings specify how long a message stays in the user's mailbox and what happens when the message reaches its retention age. When a message reaches its retention age, it can be moved to the user's archive mailbox, deleted (moved to the Recoverable Items folder), or permanently deleted (message is unrecoverable). This action depends on the retention tag settings you choose when you create the retention tag. You can also allow users to apply a retention tag to items and folders in their own mailboxes.

When creating the retention tag, you can choose from three types:

Applied Automatically To Entire Mailbox (Default)   Also referred to as default policy tags (DPTs), these retention tags apply to any untagged mailbox items in the entire mailbox. Untagged items are mailbox items that do not have a retention tag applied.

Applied Automatically To A Folder   Also referred to as retention policy tags (RPTs), these retention tags apply retention settings to default folders, such as the Inbox, Deleted Items, or Sent Items. Items within a default folder will inherit the RPT of the folder, if one is assigned. Users cannot change an RPT that is applied to a default folder. They can, however, apply a different personal tag to one or more items in a default folder.

Applied By Users To Items And Folders (Personal)   Commonly referred to as personal tags, these tags are applied manually by users to specific items or folders through Outlook or Outlook on the web. Users can apply personal tags to items even if a different personal tag is already applied. When planning for licensing, your organization will need to acquire enterprise CAL (eCAL) for each user with personal tags.

Three types of actions are available to choose from when you're creating the retention tag:

Delete And Allow Recovery   This option deletes the item from the mailbox and moves it to the Recoverable Items folder. The user can recover these items from there. You can apply this action in DPTs, RTPs, and personal tags.

Permanently Delete   This option purges the item from the mailbox. The user cannot recover these items. You can apply this in DPTs, RTPs, and personal tags.

Move To Archive   This option moves the item to the archive mailbox. If the user has not been enabled with an archive mailbox, no action is taken. You can apply this action in DPTs and personal tags only.

You apply these actions based on when an item reaches a specific retention period. The retention period is the age at which retention is enforced on an item. Based on the action, the age limit corresponds to the number of days from the date the item was delivered, the date an item was created, or the date an item was deleted (see Figure 14.15).

You can also enable a comment on the retention tag, which can display helpful information to the user in Outlook.

By default, Exchange creates the retention policy Default MRM Policy in your on-premises Exchange organization. Although the policy is automatically applied to the mailbox when you provision an archive for the mailbox, you can change the retention policy applied to a mailbox at any time.

FIGURE 14.15
Creating a personal
retention tag

For example, you can modify tags included in the Default MRM Policy by changing the retention age or retention actions, disable a tag, or modify the policy by adding or removing tags from it. The updated retention policy is applied to mailboxes the next time they're processed by the Managed Folder Assistant. Table 14.3 shows the default retention tags contained within the Default MRM Policy.

TABLE 14.3:   Default MRM Policy Retention Tags

NAME	TYPE	RETENTION AGE (DAYS)	RETENTION ACTION
Default 2 years move to archive	Default Policy Tag (DPT)	730	Move to Archive
Recoverable Items 14 days move to archive	Recoverable Items folder	14	Move to Archive
Personal 1 year move to archive	Personal tag	365	Move to Archive
Personal 5 year move to archive	Personal tag	1,825	Move to Archive
Personal never move to archive	Personal tag	Not applicable	Move to Archive

TABLE 14.3:   Default MRM Policy Retention Tags   *(CONTINUED)*

NAME	TYPE	RETENTION AGE (DAYS)	RETENTION ACTION
1 Week Delete	Personal tag	7	Delete and Allow Recovery
1 Month Delete	Personal tag	30	Delete and Allow Recovery
6 Month Delete	Personal tag	180	Delete and Allow Recovery
1 Year Delete	Personal tag	365	Delete and Allow Recovery
5 Year Delete	Personal tag	1,825	Delete and Allow Recovery
Never Delete	Personal tag	Not applicable	Delete and Allow Recovery

While most organizations will simply customize and apply the Default Retention Policy, some organizations require more than one retention policy. Such scenarios requiring multiple retention policies may include different DPTs or different retention requirements for default folders. You may also have different requirements for which you present personal retention tags to users, thereby necessitating more than one retention policy in your organization.

When planning retention tags, you should consider the following:

◆ You can only select a delete action for RPTs—either delete and allow recovery or permanently delete.

◆ You can't create an RPT to move messages to the archive. To move old items to archive, you can create a DPT, which applies to the entire mailbox, or you can enable personal tags, which allows users to apply in Outlook or Outlook on the web.

◆ Messages with a personal tag applied take precedence over any other retention tag that may also be applied to the message.

◆ You can only add one RPT for a particular default folder to a retention policy. For example, if a retention policy has a Deleted Items tag, you can't add another RPT of type Deleted Items to that retention policy.

◆ You cannot apply RPTs to the Contacts folder.

◆ Retention policies are applied to mailbox users. The same policy applies to the user's mailbox and archive.

◆ The DPT also applies to the Calendar and Tasks default folders. Consequently, this may result in items being deleted or moved to the archive inadvertently based on the DPT settings. To prevent the DPT settings from deleting items in these folders, create RPTs with retention disabled, as this will take precedence over the DPT. To prevent the DPT settings from moving items to the archive, you can create a disabled personal tag with the move to archive action, add it to the retention policy, and then have users apply it to the default folder.

Real World Scenario

KEEPING THE DELETED ITEMS FOLDER CLEAN WITH RETENTION TAGS

One pet peeve of many Exchange Server administrators is that users will delete messages from their Inbox or Sent Items folder but never empty the Deleted Items folder. It is not uncommon to find hundreds of megabytes of message content in a user's Deleted Items folder. In the following example, you set up conditions on the Deleted Items folder so that items older than seven days are deleted from the Deleted Items folder, but users can recover the deleted message from the Recoverable Items folder.

Let's create a new retention tag to purge items older than seven days from the Deleted Items folder. To do this through the EAC, choose Compliance Management ➤ Retention Tags and create a new tag that is automatically applied to a default folder. Select the Deleted Items folder and specify the retention action to permanently delete after seven days.

> new tag applied automatically to a default folder
>
> *Name:
> Remove Items from the deleted items after 7 days
>
> Apply this tag to the following default folder:
> Deleted Items ▾
>
> Retention action:
> ○ Delete and Allow Recovery
> ● Permanently Delete
>
> Retention period:
> ○ Never
> ● When the item reaches the following age (in days):
> 7
>
> Comment:
>
> [Save] [Cancel]

Here is the EMS command to define this managed-content setting:

```
New-RetentionPolicyTag -Name "Remove Items from the deleted items
after 7 days" -Type "DeletedItems" -RetentionAction PermanentlyDelete
-RetentionEnabled $True -AgeLimitForRetention 7.00:00:00
```

Managing Retention Policies

After creating the retention tags, you assign them to mailboxes with a retention policy. A retention policy is simply a collection of one or more retention tags that can be applied to a mailbox. You can assign the policy to one or more mailboxes.

One Retention Policy per Mailbox

Each mailbox can have only one retention policy assigned to it.

Creating Retention Policies

Retention policies are found in the Retention Policies section of the Compliance Management work center. By default, there is one policy; it contains all the default tags created in Exchange Server 2016 during the installation.

A retention policy has few properties. When you launch the New Retention Policy Wizard, you are asked to provide a name for the policy, and you must provide the retention tags that will be assigned through this policy. Figure 14.16 shows the New Retention Policy page of the wizard.

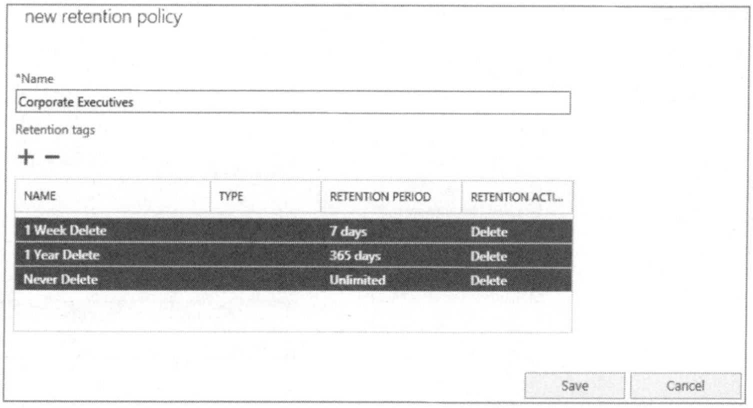

FIGURE 14.16
Creating a retention policy

When creating retention policies, you must remember that only one retention policy can be assigned to a user, so you should design your policies carefully. However, you can create multiple retention policies for different groups of users.

You can use the `New-RetentionPolicy` cmdlet in the following command to create a retention policy:

```
New-RetentionPolicy -Name "Corporate Executives" -RetentionPolicyTagLinks "1 Week
Delete", "1 Year Delete", "Never Delete"
```

The following retention tags can be included in a retention policy:

♦ One or more retention tags for supported default folders

♦ One DPT with the Move To Archive action

- ◆ One DPT with the Delete And Allow Recovery or Permanently Delete action

- ◆ One DPT for voicemail messages with the Delete And Allow Recovery or Permanently Delete action

- ◆ Any number of personal tags

ASSIGNING RETENTION POLICIES TO USERS

After you define a retention policy, the next step is to apply it to a mailbox. You can do this in one of two ways. The first method is to apply the retention policy to a mailbox in the EAC after the mailbox is created. Figure 14.17 shows the Mailbox Features page of the mailbox's properties. You can open the drop-down list and select the policy you want to assign for that use.

The second method is to apply the retention policy to a mailbox by using one of these EMS cmdlets: Enable-Mailbox, Set-Mailbox, or New-Mailbox. With any of these cmdlets, you can use the RetentionPolicy parameter to apply the appropriate retention policy to a mailbox. For example, you can use the following command to apply the retention policy when you enable a mailbox:

```
Enable-Mailbox -Identity "Marie Jewel" -Alias Marie.Jewel
-Database MBX-001 -RetentionPolicy "Corporate Executives Policy"
```

FIGURE 14.17
Assigning a retention policy to a user's mailbox

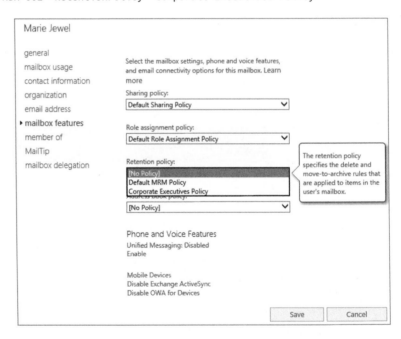

If the mailbox already exists, you can use the following command to assign the retention policy:

```
Set-Mailbox "Marie Jewel" -RetentionPolicy "Corporate Executives Policy"
```

If you know that you have to apply a retention policy to a group of mailboxes, it may be easier using the EMS. For example, you can use the following command to apply the retention policy to all the users in the Executives group:

```
Get-DistributionGroupMember –Identity "Executives" | Set-Mailbox
-RetentionPolicy "Corporate Executives Policy"
```

In another common scenario, you have been tasked with identifying the mailboxes with the Corporate Executives Policy applied. You can use the following command to filter the objects using the Where cmdlet:

```
Get-Mailbox | Where {$_.RetentionPolicy -like "*Executive*"}
| Format-Table Name,RetentionPolicy
Name                       RetentionPolicy
----                       ---------------------------
Marie Jewel                Corporate Executives Policy
Pierce Jewel               Corporate Executives Policy
Treyden Jewel              Corporate Executives Policy
```

ENABLING MESSAGING RECORDS MANAGEMENT ON THE MAILBOX SERVER

The Managed Folder Assistant is a process that runs on every Mailbox server in your organization and is responsible for making MRM work. The Managed Folder Assistant processes mailboxes that have a retention policy applied, and it will stamp each item with the appropriate retention tag. The Managed Folder Assistant will also take appropriate actions on the items, including moving to archive and deleting.

With earlier versions of Exchange Server, you had to manage the schedule for when mailbox servers should run the Managed Folder Assistant, preferring nonbusiness hours and during times when availability of resources was minimal. However, in Exchange Server 2016, the Managed Folder Assistant is a throttle-based assistant, which means that it is always running and does not need to be scheduled. Because the Managed Folder Assistant is throttled on the amount of system resources it can consume, Exchange defines the frequency for how often mailboxes are processed for MRM. By default, the work cycle for the Managed Folder Assistant is one day.

You can use the following command to view the default Managed Folder Assistant settings on each mailbox server:

```
Get-MailboxServer | fl name,*managedFolder*
Name                                    : EX2016MBX1
ManagedFolderWorkCycle                  : 1.00:00:00
ManagedFolderWorkCycleCheckpoint        : 1.00:00:00
ManagedFolderAssistantSchedule          :
LogPathForManagedFolders                : C:\Program Files\Microsoft\Exchange
 Server\V16\Logging\Managed Folder Assistant
LogFileAgeLimitForManagedFolders        : 00:00:00
LogDirectorySizeLimitForManagedFolders  : Unlimited
LogFileSizeLimitForManagedFolders       : 10 MB (10,485,760 bytes)
RetentionLogForManagedFoldersEnabled    : False
JournalingLogForManagedFoldersEnabled   : False
```

```
FolderLogForManagedFoldersEnabled        : False
SubjectLogForManagedFoldersEnabled       : False
```

While the Managed Folder Assistant is automated, you can also run it manually. You can use the `Start-ManagedFolderAssistant` cmdlet in the following command to immediately start processing the specific mailbox for MRM:

```
Start-ManagedFolderAssistant -Identity Marie.Jewel
```

The Bottom Line

Create and delete user mailboxes.   Exchange Server 2016 supports the same types of mail-enabled users as previous versions of Exchange Server. These are mailbox-enabled users who have a mailbox on your Exchange server and the mail-enabled user account. The mail-enabled user account is a security principal within your organization (and would appear in your global address list), but its email is delivered to an external email system.

There are four different types of mailbox-enabled user accounts: a User mailbox, a Room Resource mailbox, an Equipment Resource mailbox, and a Linked mailbox. You can perform mailbox management tasks via either the Exchange Administration Center or the Exchange Management Shell.

Master It   Your Active Directory forest has a trust relationship to another Active Directory forest that is part of your corporate IT infrastructure. The administrator in the other forest wants you to host their email. What type of mailboxes should you create for the users in this other forest?

Master It   You must modify user Marie Jewel's office name with Honolulu. You want to do this using the Exchange Management Shell. What command would perform this task?

Master It   You need to increase the maximum number of senders that can be included in the safe senders list for Pierce Jewel's mailbox from 1,024 to 4,096. You want to make this change using the Exchange Management Shell. What command would you use?

Manage mailbox permissions.   A newly created mailbox allows only the owner of the mailbox to access the folders within that mailbox. An end user can assign someone else permissions to access individual folders within their mailbox or to send mail on their behalf using the Outlook client. The administrator can assign permissions to the entire mailbox for other users. Further, the administrator can assign a user the Send As permission to a mailbox.

Master It   All executives within your organization share a single administrative assistant whose username is Cheyenne Pike; all of the executives belong to a mail distribution group called Executives. All of the executives want you to grant user Cheyenne Pike access to all of the folders within their mailboxes. Name two ways you can accomplish this.

Move mailboxes to another database.   Exchange Server 2016 implements a way to move mailbox content from one mailbox database to another. Although you initiate the move using the administrative tools (i.e., the EAC and the EMS cmdlet New-MoveRequest), the Microsoft Exchange Server Mailbox Replication service (MRS) that runs on each Mailbox server manages the moves and migrates the data.

Master It   You want to use the EMS to move the mailbox for Treyden Jewel from mailbox database MBX-001 to MBX-002. The move should ignore up to three bad messages before it fails. What command should you use?

Master It   You have submitted a move request for user Treyden Jewel. You want to check the status and statistics of the move request to see if it has completed; you want to use the Exchange Management Shell to do this. What command would you type?

Perform bulk manipulation of mailbox properties.   By taking advantage of piping and the EMS, you can perform bulk manipulation of users and mailboxes in a single command that previously might have taken hundreds of lines of scripting code.

Master It   You want to move all of your executives to a single mailbox database called MBX-004. All of your executives belong to a mail distribution group called Executives. How could you accomplish this task with a single command?

Use Messaging Records Management to manage mailbox content.   Messaging Records Management provides you with control over the content of a user's mailbox. Basic MRM features allow you to automatically purge old content, such as deleted items or junk email. You can create new managed folders within the user's mailbox as well as move content to these folders.

Master It   You are managing an Exchange Server organization that was transitioned from Exchange Server 2010. You have found that many of your users are not emptying the contents of their Deleted Items and Junk E-mail folders. You want to automatically purge any content in these folders after 14 days. What are the steps you should take to do this?

Chapter 15

Managing Mail-Enabled Groups, Mail Users, and Mail Contacts

At this point, you should be well aware of the different recipient types that are available in Exchange Server 2016. (If you need a refresher, review Chapter 13, "Basics of Recipient Management.")

While most administrators are familiar with the concept of groups in Active Directory, mail-enabled groups are simply groups with all the necessary attributes to be listed in the Exchange-specific directories and to be identified as a recipient object. All the benefits of groups, as Active Directory objects, still apply to mail-enabled groups. The largest benefit of mail-enabled groups is that you can use them to apply permissions to resources as well as to send email messages to the same group of users.

IN THIS CHAPTER, YOU WILL LEARN TO:

◆ Create and mail-enable user and contact objects

◆ Manage mail users and mail contacts in a messaging environment

◆ Choose the appropriate type and scope of mail-enabled groups

◆ Create and manage mail-enabled groups

◆ Explore the moderation features of Exchange Server 2016

Understanding Mail-Enabled Groups

If your organization is like most organizations today, you make significant use of mail groups. You may refer to these as mail-enabled groups, distribution groups, or distribution lists. The official term for a mail group, though, is *mail-enabled group*—essentially, a group that resides in Active Directory but is managed as a mail-enabled object from the Exchange Server administrative tools. Within Active Directory are two primary types of groups—security groups and distribution groups:

Security Groups   These groups can be assigned permissions to resources or rights to perform certain tasks. Security groups can be mail-enabled and can be used for addressing mail by Exchange Server recipients.

Distribution Groups   These groups are not security principals; they have no security identifier and, therefore, cannot be assigned any rights or permissions. Distribution groups are intended for use with a mail system that integrates with Active Directory, such as Exchange Server.

Dynamic Distribution Groups These groups are a subset of distribution groups. The membership of a dynamic distribution group (DDG) is dynamic, based on criteria defined by the administrator. DDGs are managed by using the Exchange Administration Center or the Exchange Management Shell. Similar to distribution groups, these groups cannot be assigned any rights or permissions.

When you create a new group using the Active Directory Users and Computers interface, you must provide a scope for the group in addition to defining the group type (see Figure 15.1).

FIGURE 15.1

Creating a new group using Active Directory Users and Computers

All mail-enabled groups in Exchange Server 2016 must be configured with a Universal group scope. With this scope type, Active Directory will replicate the membership list attribute for the group to all global catalog servers in the organization.

In earlier versions of Exchange Server, such as Exchange Server 2007, you could mail-enable groups configured with a global or domain local group scope. However, this could cause mail-delivery problems in organizations with multiple Active Directory domains, because the membership of a global group, for example, was not replicated to a global catalog server. As you can imagine, this resulted in lost emails.

Naming Mail-Enabled Groups

When creating mail-enabled groups, an important consideration should be made with regard to a standard for the display names. Choose a standard that will work for your organization and that your users will clearly understand. The key is to identify a naming convention that represents static units (based on geography or department) and that is, therefore, less likely to need to be modified.

Using a naming standard also allows them to all be grouped together in the global address list. Because address lists are sorted alphabetically, users can easily locate the correct mail-enabled group, even if they are unaware of the group beforehand.

To assist with this endeavor, you can create a distribution group naming policy. A group naming policy allows you to standardize and manage the names of distribution groups created by users in your organization. For example, you can require that a specific prefix and suffix be added to the name of a distribution group when it's created, and you can block specific words from being used, thereby minimizing the use of inappropriate words in group names.

With a group naming policy, you can:

◆   Enforce a consistent naming strategy for groups created by users.

◆   Identify distribution groups in the shared address book.

◆   Suggest the function or membership of the group.

◆   Identify the type of users who are likely members of the group.

◆   Identify the geographic region in which the group is used.

◆   Block inappropriate words in group names.

Creating Mail-Enabled Groups

The simplest method to create and manage mail-enabled groups is to use the Exchange Admin Center. Using only Active Directory Users and Computers will not define the mail attributes required by Exchange.

To create a mail-enabled group, launch the Exchange Admin Center, navigate to the Recipients area work center, select Groups, and then click + (Add) from the Actions menu. Select one of the three group types from the list of available group types: distribution group, security group, or dynamic distribution group, as shown in Figure 15.2.

FIGURE 15.2
Viewing the group choices in the Exchange Admin Center

Selecting a group type launches the New Group window. For example, selecting the group type Distribution Group opens the New Distribution Group window, as shown in Figure 15.3. In this window, you can create a distribution group with the following options:

Display Name: The name of the group that is visible from the Exchange Admin Center and the global address list.

Alias: The alias will be used to generate the group's email address.

Notes: The description can be used to provide context for the group and is visible from the global address list and Active Directory Users and Computers.

Organizational Unit: The location where the group will be created in Active Directory.

Owners: Owners of the group are users who can change the membership of the group by using Microsoft Outlook or Outlook on the web. Additionally, any user that has the appropriate Recipient Management role assigned can modify the membership of a group.

Members: Members of the group can be any recipient type, including other mail-enabled groups. This section also includes options that control the membership of the group.

For example, you can enable the group to allow users to join the membership of a group. Group membership requirements can be set to Open, Closed, or Owner Approval. Only distribution groups can be enabled for Open or Closed. Because of the risk of inadvertently granting unnecessary permissions to users, security groups can only be set to Owner Approval.

FIGURE 15.3
Opening the New
Distribution Group
window

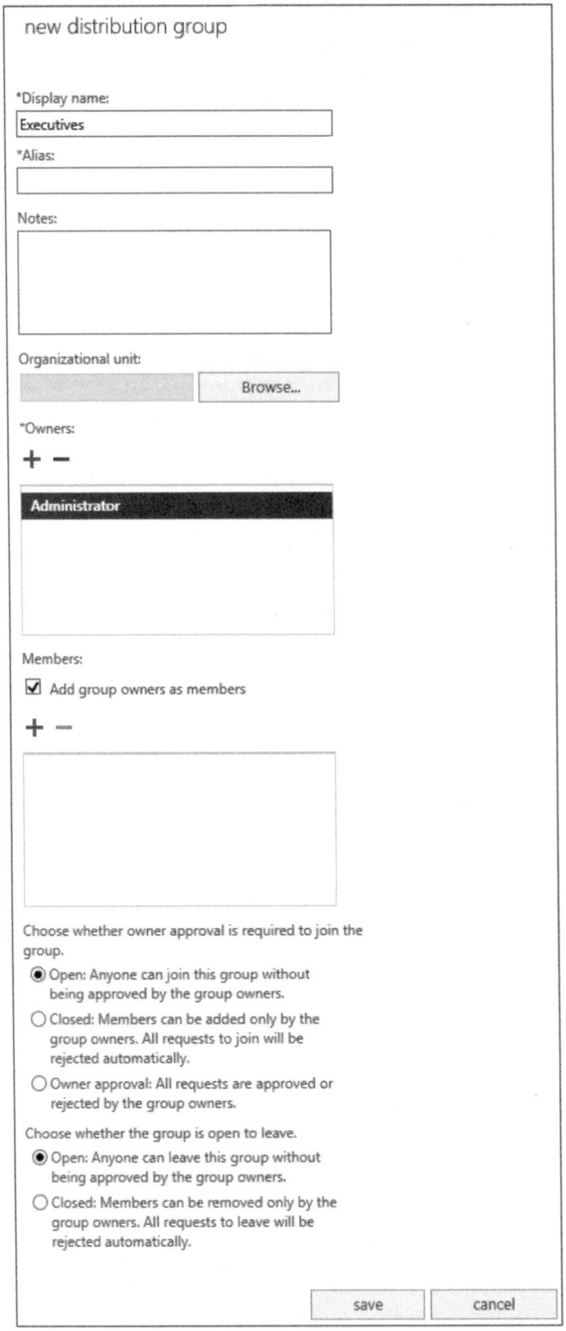

In the event you want to mail-enable an existing distribution group or security group, you must use the Exchange Management Shell (EMS). You can use the following command to mail-enable the existing Executives group:

```
Enable-DistributionGroup –Identity Executives -DisplayName Executives
-Alias Executives
```

 Real World Scenario

MAIL-ENABLED GROUPS: WHAT NOT TO DO

While groups allow administrators to efficiently manage resource permissions and provide users with a simple method of sending email messages to multiple recipients, there are many examples of companies that misuse or overuse groups. In most of these scenarios, inappropriate management of group permissions, as well as the lack of a standard naming convention, can have unforeseen consequences for administrators and users.

In an example, one organization's Active Directory infrastructure had lost all default and standard security provisions for minimizing administrative rights. Their lack of a security policy allowed everyone in the company to have domain administrator permission. Beyond the obvious security implications, this issue had snowballed into a messaging problem where the global address list included more than 50,000 objects for a company of fewer than 200 users.

Upon further inspection, a large group of support users was in charge of creating mail-enabled groups for anyone who requested them. Requests came from everyone, with little more reason than, "I need a group for Project X. Please add me to that group. We need to send emails to each other as well." Because the company lacked a standard group-naming convention, it was difficult to identify the purpose of each group. To complicate the situation, groups were never purged from Active Directory. Most of them had been stale for many years, and all were mail-enabled.

This example illustrates the consequences of improper planning when designing and implementing Active Directory and Exchange Server. A large offline address book, a security risk (when mail-enabled security groups are mistaken for distribution groups), and an inefficient Active Directory structure are only some of the impacts of improper group management.

CREATING DYNAMIC DISTRIBUTION GROUPS

With many medium and large organizations, you may discover a problem with keeping the membership of your distribution groups up to date. In most scenarios, you may consider using dynamic distribution groups (DDGs) as an alternative solution. DDGs are distribution groups whose membership is based on specific recipient filters rather than a defined set of recipients. When an email is sent to a DDG, Exchange will query Active Directory and identify the recipients based on one or more criteria, such as organizational unit, city, or department. The benefit to using a DDG is that when Active Directory properties are changed, the DDG membership updates dynamically. Similar to distribution groups, DDGs cannot be security groups—they cannot be used to assign permission to resources.

The process to create a DDG is a little different than other mail-enabled groups because you need to define the recipient filters and the conditions of the mail-enabled group. Exchange provides pre-canned filters to make it easier for you to create the recipient filters for DDGs. In addition, you can specify a list of conditions that the recipients must meet.

To create a DDG, launch the Exchange Admin Center, navigate to the Recipients area work center, select Groups, select + (Add) from the Actions menu, and then click Dynamic Distribution Group. In the New Dynamic Distribution Group window, provide the information required for the new group, including the organizational unit in which the object will be created, the display name, and the Exchange alias of the group. Located near the bottom of the window are the filter settings for defining the types of recipients to include in the membership list and the list of conditions for defining the rules for membership in the group (Figure 15.4).

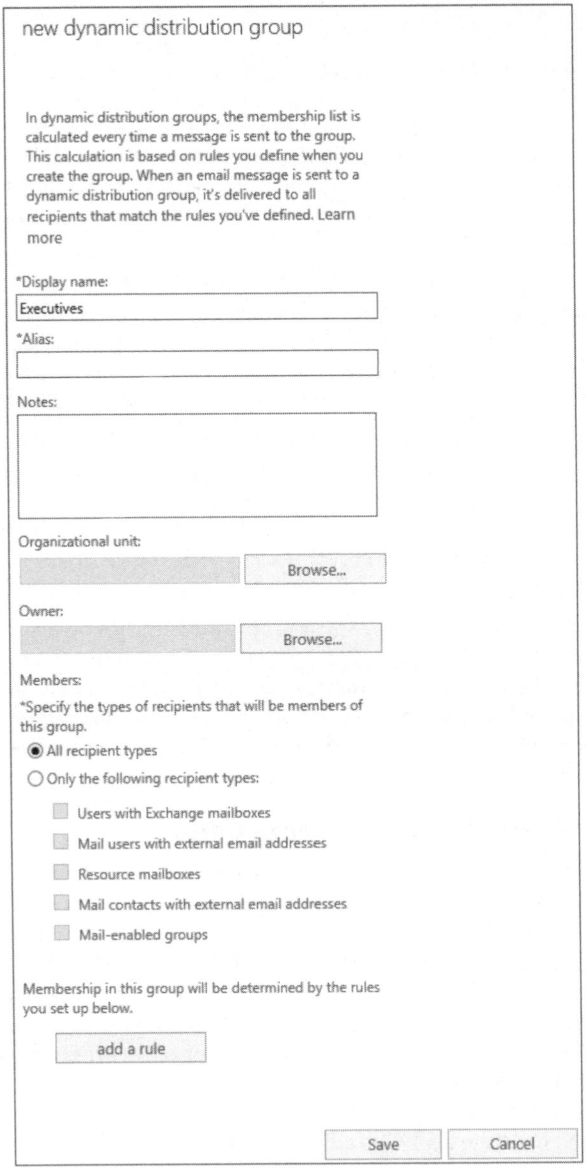

FIGURE 15.4
Filter settings and conditions for a dynamic distribution group

new dynamic distribution group

In dynamic distribution groups, the membership list is calculated every time a message is sent to the group. This calculation is based on rules you define when you create the group. When an email message is sent to a dynamic distribution group, it's delivered to all recipients that match the rules you've defined. Learn more

*Display name:

Executives

*Alias:

Notes:

Organizational unit:

Browse...

Owner:

Browse...

Members:
*Specify the types of recipients that will be members of this group.

⦿ All recipient types

◯ Only the following recipient types:

☐ Users with Exchange mailboxes

☐ Mail users with external email addresses

☐ Resource mailboxes

☐ Mail contacts with external email addresses

☐ Mail-enabled groups

Membership in this group will be determined by the rules you set up below.

add a rule

Save   Cancel

The following recipient types can be included in the filter settings:

◆ All recipient types

◆ Users with Exchange mailboxes (mailbox-enabled users)

◆ Mail users with external email addresses (mail-enabled users)

◆ Resource mailboxes (room and equipment)

◆ Mail contacts with external email addresses (mail-enabled contacts)

◆ Mail-enabled groups

After selecting the recipient type and OU scope for the DDG, you can further refine the scope of the group membership by adding conditional rules. To add these, click the Add A Rule button and then select the appropriate filter based on the keywords of a specific attribute. For example, if you have populated a custom attribute on all recipients in Active Directory, you may consider using a filter on this attribute for membership of the DDG. The following attributes can be used to filter DDG membership with the rules in the new dynamic distribution group:

◆ Recipient container

◆ State or province

◆ Company

◆ Department

◆ Custom attribute 1 through 15

After the DDG is created, you can use the Preview button to confirm that your scope and rules are defined properly. This button will open the Dynamic Distribution Group Preview dialog box and display the membership of the group based on the current attributes in Active Directory.

As with most actions in the Exchange Admin Center, you can also create DDGs by using the EMS. You can use the following command to create a DDG that includes all mailboxes and mail users in the Recipients OU with the State attribute of Washington.

```
New-DynamicDistributionGroup -Name "Everyone in Washington"
 -IncludedRecipients "MailboxUsers, MailUsers"
 -ConditionalStateOrProvince "Washington"
 -OrganizationalUnit "Contoso.com/Users"
 -Alias "EveryoneInWashington"
 -RecipientContainer "Contoso.com/Recipients"
```

Managing Mail-Enabled Groups

Once a group has been mail-enabled, you can configure the properties for additional mail settings. Though the core function of a group is to facilitate the delivery of mail messages to multiple users, and its subsequent management, there are many specific group features that you can configure.

KNOWING WHEN TO USE A SHARED MAILBOX INSTEAD

The shared mailbox provides functionality similar to a mail-enabled group. Both of these recipient types are often used by groups of users to provide a single entry point for emails. However, there are multiple differences between shared mailboxes and mail-enabled groups. In addition to receiving email, a shared mailbox provides a shared calendar. Also, recipients have a central location for managing email content. More information about the shared mailbox is available in Chapter 14, "Managing Mailboxes and Mailbox Content."

Let's start with Delivery Management (Figure 15.5). Available from the group's properties, Delivery Management includes two components you can configure: whether the group can receive email messages only from senders inside the organization or whether the group can receive email messages from any sender, inside and outside the organization. You can also configure the group to receive email messages only from a predefined list of senders. The sender must already exist in the global address list to include them in the predefined list of senders. For example, if you need to add a specific sender outside your organization to the list, you must create the sender as a mail contact or mail user in the organization. With many medium and large organizations, you should consider restricting who is allowed to send email messages to large mail-enabled groups or groups that contain VIPs. This will minimize senders inadvertently sending email to a large number of recipients and restrict unwanted email sent to your VIPs.

FIGURE 15.5
The Delivery
Management
window of a
Distribution
Group object

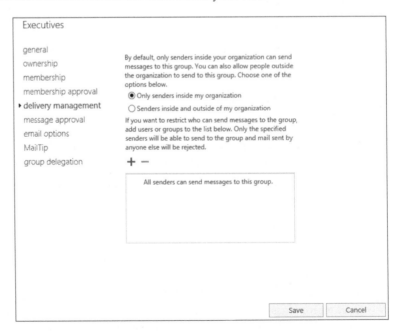

The Email Options properties page displays the email addresses that can be used when addressing a message to the group. You can edit the existing addresses or add new addresses by using the Exchange Management Shell.

The Reply address, commonly referred to as the Reply To address, will not be particularly important for a distribution group that is used primarily within your organization. However, the Reply address is very important for a distribution group used internally and externally; keep in mind that the Reply address will be the SMTP address used by people outside the organization.

One very common example is when a user inside your organization sends an email to recipients outside your organization and includes the address of a distribution group within your organization. You should be aware of the Reply address for the distribution group if recipients outside your organization reply to all the recipients of the email. Frequently, users will notify you that senders outside your organization were not able to reply to an email that includes the distribution group. You should consider whether the distribution group should be enabled to receive email from senders outside your organization or the users inside your organization should be educated on when to include the distribution group as a recipient on email messages.

Other settings that you can configure from the General properties of a distribution group include the option to Hide This Group From Address Lists. Unchecked by default, this setting allows you to prevent a mail-enabled group from being displayed in the address lists. This option may be useful for specialized groups that are used only for mail distribution by an automated system or for users who only send emails to the SMTP address.

Browsing through the other group options, you'll quickly realize that some settings are not available from the Exchange Admin Center. Some settings, such as the Message Size restrictions, must be set from the Exchange Management Shell. Message Size restrictions can help prevent misuse of distribution groups or the accidental distribution of large files. With the `Set-DistributionGroup` cmdlet, you can use either the `MaxRecieveSize` parameter to prevent large messages from landing in the mailbox of each recipient in the group or the `MaxSendSize` parameter to prevent the group from being used as the sender of large messages.

Another setting that is not available from the Exchange Admin Center and requires using EMS is the Expansion Server setting, which is used via the `Set-DistributionGroup` cmdlet. Message expansion is the process of enumerating the members of a mail-enabled group and determining where each member is, either within your organization or externally. As you can imagine, expansion of large mail-enabled groups can be a pretty intensive process for an Exchange server as well as the Active Directory global catalog server that the Exchange server is using.

By default, the Expansion server is set to any server in the organization. This means the first Exchange Server Mailbox server that receives the message is responsible for expanding the membership of the mail-enabled group. In some environments, you may prefer to configure which Exchange server expands the mail-enabled group, especially environments where multiple versions of Exchange Server will be responsible for mail delivery or environments where the Exchange servers have different hardware specifications.

If you need to configure a preferred expansion server, you should choose the appropriate Exchange server based on the following recommendations:

- Is running the latest version of Exchange Server

- Has a reliable and rapid connection to domain controllers

- Has enough resources available to manage the additional demand for group expansion

Some organizations choose to identify a dedicated expansion server for all distribution groups to facilitate the troubleshooting process and provide clear process flow should mail delivery problems arise.

Managing Moderation for Distribution Groups

With some distribution groups, your organization may require a second set of eyes on a message before it's delivered to the group members. You can enable this moderation process, also referred to as message approval, on a distribution group and define one or more moderators, as well as exceptions to the moderation process. Figure 15.6 displays the message approval configuration options on the Message Approval page. A group owner or an administrator who has been assigned the necessary RBAC role can also enable groups for moderation and add multiple moderators from the Exchange Control Panel.

By default, moderation is disabled on all groups. To enable the feature, you will need to configure one or more moderators for the group. When an email message is sent to the moderated group, the moderator receives an email with a request to approve or reject the message. The text of the message includes buttons to approve or reject the message, and the attachment includes the original message to review. Messages are not delivered to the members of the group until a moderator of the group has approved the message. While you can define multiple moderators, you can assign only users, not groups, as moderators.

FIGURE 15.6
Configuration options for moderated groups

An administrator can also exempt the moderation process on messages from specific senders. Users listed in the Senders Who Don't Require Message Approval list are able to send email messages to the group without being moderated.

Near the bottom of the Message Approval page, you can choose how senders are notified when messages aren't approved. The Select Moderation Notifications settings will notify or silently drop unapproved messages sent to the group. If you choose to notify senders of unapproved messages, you can choose to notify only internal senders or all (internal and external) senders.

You should be aware that moderation is not limited to groups; an administrator can also enable moderation for email messages sent to mailboxes or mail contacts. In addition, you can create a mail flow rule as an alternative moderation method. With the mail flow rule, you can require approval for messages that match specific criteria or that are sent to a specific person. You can also enable exceptions to the moderation process in the mail flow rule.

CONVERTING GLOBAL OR LOCAL DISTRIBUTION GROUPS TO UNIVERSAL GROUPS

In earlier versions of Exchange Server, groups created as global or domain local may experience problems with group expansion. If the Exchange server that expanded the group was using a domain controller from a domain that did not contain the membership list for a domain local or global group, the distribution group would not be expanded and the message would not be delivered to the intended recipients. Even more problematic, the sender may not receive a notification that the message was not delivered.

For this reason, Microsoft now requires that all mail-enabled groups created in Exchange are universal groups. If you create a domain local or global group using Active Directory Users and Computers and then attempt to mail-enable the group using the EMS, the group will not appear in the list of available groups.

For organizations that were upgraded or transitioned from an earlier version of Exchange to Exchange Server 2016, you may find that some mail-enabled groups are not universal groups. Fortunately, you can manage these groups using either the Exchange Admin Center or the Exchange Management Shell.

You can modify an existing group to a universal group using Active Directory Users and Computers. On the General properties page of the mail-enabled group, as shown in Figure 15.7, select the Universal radio button and click OK to update the group.

You can also use the Set-Group command to modify an existing group to a universal group:

```
Set-Group "Operations Group" -Universal
```

For multiple groups, you can use the Get-DistributionGroup cmdlet, with the Where-Object filter, in the following command to identify all of the mail-enabled groups that are not universal groups:

```
Get-DistributionGroup | Where {$_.RecipientType -eq "MailNonUniversalGroup"}


Name                DisplayName         GroupType          PrimarySmtpAddress
----                -----------         ---------          ------------------
Operations Group    Operations Group    Global, Security…  OperationsGroup@…
Executives and …    Executives and …    Global, Security…  ExecutivesandVIP…
Field Research G…   Field Research G…   Global, Security…  FieldResearchGro…
Failure Analysis…   Failure Analysis…   Global             FailureAnalysisT…
```

FIGURE 15.7
Converting a group to a universal group using Active Directory Users and Computers

This results in a list of all mail-enabled groups that are not universal groups. You can use the following command to update all of the groups to universal groups by piping the list above to the Set-Group cmdlet:

```
Get-DistributionGroup | Where {$_.RecipientType
-eq "MailNonUniversalGroup"} | Set-Group -Universal
```

As you may discover, this command does not change the group type: security group and distribution group.

MANAGING GROUPS USING THE EXCHANGE MANAGEMENT SHELL

To assist with daily administrative tasks of group management, here is a summary review of the cmdlets that are available for managing and manipulating mail-enabled groups. Table 15.1 lists the EMS cmdlets you can use to manage groups and mail-enabled groups.

TABLE 15.1:   EMS and PowerShell Cmdlets for Group Management

CMDLET	FUNCTION
Get-Group	Retrieves information about all Active Directory groups.
Set-Group	Sets information about an Active Directory group; this will work for any Active Directory group, not just mail-enabled ones.
Get-DistributionGroup	Retrieves information related to mail-enabled groups.

TABLE 15.1:   EMS and PowerShell Cmdlets for Group Management   *(CONTINUED)*

CMDLET	FUNCTION
Set-DistributionGroup	Sets properties of mail-enabled groups.
New-DistributionGroup	Creates a new group in Active Directory and mail-enables that group.
Enable-DistributionGroup	Mail-enables an existing group that was previously created in Active Directory.
Disable-DistributionGroup	Removes mail attributes from a mail-enabled group but does not remove the group from Active Directory.
Remove-DistributionGroup	Deletes the mail attributes of a mail-enabled group and removes the group from Active Directory.
Get-DistributionGroupMember	Retrieves membership list information from a mail-enabled group.
Add-DistributionGroupMember	Adds members to a mail-enabled group.
Remove-DistributionGroupMember	Removes members from a mail-enabled group.
Get-DynamicDistributionGroup	Retrieves information about a dynamic distribution group.
Set-DynamicDistributionGroup	Sets properties for dynamic distribution groups.
New-DynamicDistributionGroup	Creates a new dynamic distribution group.
Remove-DynamicDistributionGroup	Removes mail properties from a dynamic distribution group and deletes the group from Active Directory.

For our purposes in this chapter, we'll focus on only a few of the cmdlets listed in Table 15.1 and some common properties that can be used with them. The best method to illustrate how these cmdlets function is with some real-world examples.

In our first scenario, you have a universal group in the Corporate OU in Active Directory called Finance. You want to configure this group as a distribution group. Because the group already exists in Active Directory, you will want to use the Enable-DistributionGroup cmdlet. You can use the following command to assign the group an Exchange Server alias and a display name:

```
Enable-DistributionGroup –Name Finance -DisplayName Finance
-Alias Finance
```

If the group does not exist in Active Directory and you want to create the group and mail-enable it, you will want to use the `New-DistributionGroup` cmdlet. You can use the following command to create the Finance group in the Corporate OU:

```
New-DistributionGroup -Name Finance -Type Distribution
-OrganizationalUnit "contoso.com/Corporate"
-SamAccountName Finance -DisplayName Finance
-Alias Finance
```

You may have observed that additional parameters were used in this example compared with the previous. This is because the `OrganizationalUnit` parameter is required for new groups and the `SamAccountName` parameter is required for mail-enabled security groups.

To add members to a group, you will want to use the `Add-DistributionGroupMember` cmdlet. For example, you can use the following command to add Marie Jewel to the Finance group:

```
Add-DistributionGroupMember -Identity Finance -Member "Marie.Jewel"
```

Conversely, you can use the `Remove-DistributionGroupMember` cmdlet to remove members from a group.

To enumerate the members of a group, you will want to use the `Get-DistributionGroupMember` cmdlet. For example, you can use the following command to retrieve a list of the members in the Finance group:

```
Get-DistributionGroupMember -Identity Finance
Name                RecipientType
----                -------------
Marie Jewel         UserMailbox
```

You will want to use the `Set-DistributionGroup` cmdlet to modify the properties of a distribution group. For example, you can use the following command to enable moderation for a group and then configure the moderators, along with the exceptions and the notification settings:

```
Set-DistributionGroup -Identity Finance -ModerationEnabled $true
-ModeratedBy "Maries.Jewel@contoso.com","Pierce.Jewel@contoso.com"
-ByPassModerationFromSendersOrMembers "Administrators"
-SendModerationNotifications Internal
```

Table 15.2 lists some of the common properties that you can define for a mail-enabled group.

TABLE 15.2:   Common Mail-Enabled Group Properties

PROPERTY	FUNCTION
`Alias`	Sets the Exchange Server alias for the group. By default, the alias is used when SMTP addresses are generated.
`CustomAttribute1` through `CustomAttribute15`	Sets 1 of the 15 custom attributes (aka extension attributes).

TABLE 15.2: Common Mail-Enabled Group Properties *(CONTINUED)*

PROPERTY	FUNCTION
DisplayName	Sets the display name of the mail-enabled group; the display name is what is visible in address lists.
HiddenFromAddressLists Enabled	Sets whether the group will be displayed in address lists. The default is that the objects are visible. You can set this to $True and the group will be hidden from the address lists.
MaxReceiveSize	Sets the maximum size of a message that can be sent to the group.
ModerationEnabled	Enables or disables moderation for a group.

You can use the Get-DistributionGroup cmdlet to view the properties of a group, or use the Set-DistributionGroup cmdlet to modify the properties of a group.

Finally, if you no longer need a group, you can use the Remove-DistributionGroup cmdlet to delete a group, which includes the group object in Active Directory. Alternatively, you can use the Disable-DistributionGroup cmdlet to disable a group, which removes the mail attributes from the group but leaves the group object in Active Directory.

In addition to distribution groups, you can create and manage dynamic distribution groups, in the same way, using the EMS. For example, you can use the following command to create a dynamic group in the Research OU that includes only mailbox-enabled users with the name of All Research:

```
New-DynamicDistributionGroup -Name "All Research"
 -IncludedRecipients 'MailboxUsers'
 -ConditionalDepartment 'Research'
 -OrganizationalUnit 'contoso.com/Research'
 -Alias 'AllResearch'
 -RecipientContainer 'contoso.com/Corporate'
```

After provisioning the dynamic group, you can use the following command to configure the maximum receive size of the group to 750 KB:

```
Set-DynamicDistributionGroup -Name "All Research"
 -MaxReceiveSize 750KB
```

ALLOWING END USERS TO MANAGE GROUP MEMBERSHIP

As your organization expands, you may consider delegating the management of distribution groups to your users. With the appropriate permissions, users can manage the membership of distribution groups in the global address list of Outlook. Figure 15.8 shows the Outlook interface that allows you to manage the membership of a distribution group.

FIGURE 15.8
Managing group
membership from
within Outlook

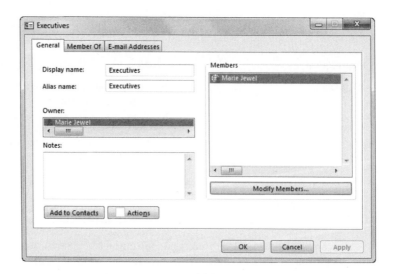

FIGURE 15.8
Managing group
membership from
within Outlook

Note that only mail-enabled groups can have their membership managed by an Outlook client. This feature is not available for dynamic distribution groups.

Within the properties of a distribution group is the owner or manager of the group. In earlier versions of Exchange Server, you only needed to define a user as the owner for them to manage the membership of a group. However, in Exchange Server 2016, the ability to manage a distribution group membership is delegated through management roles. As a result, not only do you need to configure the distribution group owner, but you also need to assign the appropriate role assignment policy to the owner. The necessary role assignment policy should contain the My Distribution Groups and My Distribution Group Membership roles to manage the membership of a distribution group. (Management roles and role-based access control are covered in more detail in Chapter 12, "Management Permissions and Role-Based Access Control.")

In addition to Outlook, users can manage the membership of distribution groups using the control panel in Outlook on the web. Once a user is delegated the appropriate permissions, users can create new distribution groups and manage existing distribution groups, including group membership. Figure 15.9 shows how a user can modify the membership of an existing distribution group.

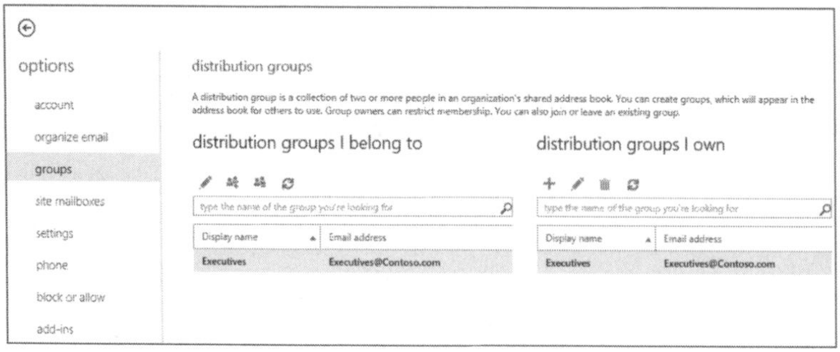

FIGURE 15.9
Managing group
membership from
within the control
panel

Other options for managing the membership of distribution groups are the Exchange Admin Center or the Exchange Management Shell. These options are more commonly used by administrators, but end users can leverage the same tools after they are delegated the necessary permissions. With the Exchange Admin Center, you can locate the group in the Groups list and modify the members in the Membership properties of the group. With the Exchange Management Shell, you can use the Add-DistributionGroupMember and Remove-DistributionGroupMember cmdlets to modify the members of the distribution group. For example, you can use the following command to add four users to the distribution group Executives:

```
Add-DistributionGroupMember -Identity Executives
 -Member "Marie.Jewel@contoso.com, Cheyenne.Pike@contoso.com,
Zoe.Pike@contoso.com, Taylor.Ferguson@contoso.com"
```

Creating and Managing Mail Contacts and Mail Users

If your company's users frequently correspond with other organizations, you may consider publishing the email addresses from other organizations as mail contacts in the Exchange Server address lists. This would provide accessibility of the mail contacts to all of your users, rather than requiring users to maintain them in their personal contacts. Although mail contacts appear in your organization's address lists, they direct email messages to mail systems outside of your organization.

Although you can create a contact object in Active Directory using the Active Directory Users and Computers snap-in, it will not be mail-enabled and, therefore, will not appear in the Exchange Server address lists. In earlier versions of Exchange Server, you could mail-enable a contact using the snap-in. However, in Exchange Server 2016, the process of mail-enabling a contact may require a second step when using the snap-in, as described later in the section "Managing Mail Contacts and Mail Users Using the EMS."

When using the Active Directory Users and Computers snap-in, you can create a contact object in Active Directory with minimal information; simply specify the contact's name information. Figure 15.10 illustrates the options when creating contact objects using the Active Directory Users and Computers snap-in.

FIGURE 15.10
Creating a new contact object using Active Directory Users and Computers

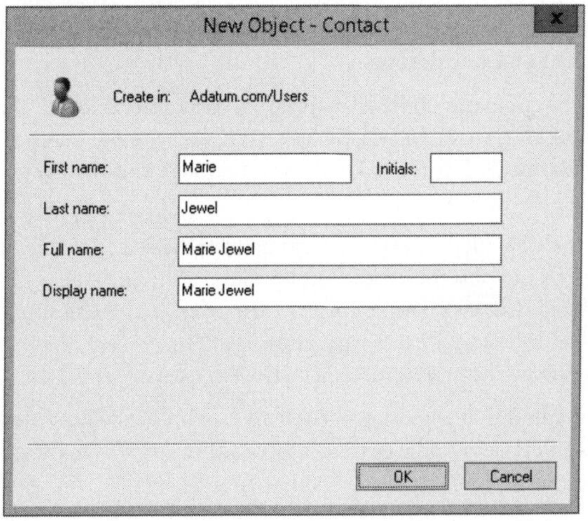

After you create a contact, you may notice the E-mail property of the contact in Active Directory Users and Computers (shown in Figure 15.11). However, Exchange Server does not use only this property to mail-enable a contact; additional mail attributes are required for a mail contact.

FIGURE 15.11
Contact information
in Active Directory
Users and Computers

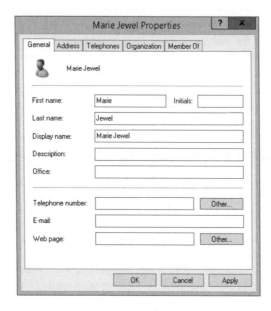

To properly mail-enable a contact for use with Exchange Server, you must use the Exchange Admin Center or the Exchange Management Shell.

MAKING THINGS EASY FOR YOUR USERS

We worked with a company that had a large number of external suppliers—contacts—that were often used in communications by internal users. Users often shared this contact information with one another by forwarding emails and using old-fashioned pen and paper. That solution was inefficient and error prone.

Using the company's billing system, we were able to locate the list of suppliers in an existing electronic format, within a SQL Server database. The next step was to export the database using SQL tools. We decided to use a SQL Server database `export` command to export to a comma-separated value (CSV) file.

With the CSV file, we were able to use the Active Directory export/import tool, `CSVDE.exe`, to create contact objects for all the suppliers. The next step was to mail-enable the contacts. Once we completed this task, the contact information for all the suppliers was available to the users in the global address list. In retrospect, we could have used one Exchange Management Shell cmdlet to create the mail contact, instead of the two steps.

Keep in mind that when a user copies a contact to their personal contacts, the contact then becomes a *local* object; any updates that may occur in Active Directory will not be downloaded to the local object.

Managing Mail Contacts and Mail Users Using the EAC

You can use the Exchange Admin Center and the Exchange Management Shell to create and manage a mail contact. From within the Exchange Admin Center, navigate to the Recipients work area of the Exchange Admin Center, and select Contacts. Displayed on the page will be a list of all mail contacts and mail users in the organization. Although the page is labeled Contacts, this is the location from which you can view and manage all mail contacts and mail users.

As described earlier in Chapter 13, the *mail contact* is an object that appears in Active Directory and the Exchange Server address lists, but it is not a security principal. You cannot add the mail contact to a security group nor assign it permissions because it does not have a security identifier. This type of contact is useful when you need to make an external email address available from your address lists and does not require permissions in your organization.

The *mail user* is a user account in your organization but not one for which you host a mailbox. For example, you might need to create a user account for an external auditor who will be working from one of your workstations. Your accountants may need to correspond with the auditor and prefer that the auditor is available from the Exchange Server address lists, but the auditor's mailbox is hosted outside of your organization.

You may be wondering what the difference is between a mail-enabled user, or mail user, and a mailbox-enabled user, or user mailbox. The answer is that you are *not* responsible for a mail user's email storage, but you are responsible for a user mailbox's email storage.

These recipient types are covered in more detail in Chapter 13, but here is a short list describing the three principal recipients in Exchange Server 2016 and how they differ:

- User mailbox

  - User exists *inside* your organization.

  - Mailbox exists *inside* your organization.

  - Recipient appears in your address lists by default or can be hidden.

- Mail user

  - User exists *inside* your organization.

  - Mailbox exists *outside* your organization.

  - Recipient appears in your address lists by default or can be hidden.

- Mail contact

  - User exists *outside* your organization.

  - Mailbox exists *outside* your organization.

  - Recipient appears in your address lists by default or can be hidden.

To create a mail contact in the Exchange Admin Center, navigate to the Recipients work area, select Contacts, click the + (Add) icon from the Action menu, and then select Mail Contact. The New Mail Contact window allows you to specify basic information about the contact you want to create, as shown in Figure 15.12.

FIGURE 15.12
Creating a mail-
enabled contact

Alternatively, you can use the Exchange Management Shell to manage your contacts. For example, you can use the following command to mail-enable a contact for an external user named Marie Jewel:

```
Enable-MailContact -Identity "contoso.com/Users/Marie Jewel"
-ExternalEmailAddress "SMTP:mJewel@adatum.com" –Alias mJewel
```

Creating a mail user in the Exchange Admin Center is similar to creating a mail contact. Navigate to the Recipients work area, select Contacts, click the + (Add) icon from the Action menu, and then select Mail User. In addition to the basic information when creating a mail contact, the New Mail User window allows you to specify information about the user account, including the logon name and password.

Alternatively, with the Exchange Management Shell, you can use the following command to create a new mail user:

```
New-MailUser -Name "Marie Jewel" -Alias mJewel
-OrganizationalUnit "contoso.com/Users"
-UserPrincipalName "mJewel@contoso.com"
-SamAccountName mJewel -FirstName Marie -LastName Jewel
-Password 'System.Security.SecureString' -ResetPasswordOnNextLogon $false
-ExternalEmailAddress 'SMTP:mJewel@adatum.com'
```

Most properties of a mail contact or a mail user are similar to those you have seen in previous chapters for mailboxes. In fact, one of the benefits is that you can add a mail contact or a mail user as a member of a distribution group.

Managing Mail Contacts and Mail Users Using the EMS

With medium and large organizations, you should consider using the EMS for most of your Exchange Server management tasks. Table 15.3 shows the cmdlets that can be used to manipulate mail contacts and mail users.

TABLE 15.3:   Exchange Management Shell Cmdlets for Mail Contacts and Mail Users

CMDLET	DESCRIPTION
New-MailContact	Creates a new contact in Active Directory and mail-enables that contact
Enable-MailContact	Mail-enables a previously existing contact
Set-MailContact	Sets mail properties for a mail-enabled contact
Get-MailContact	Retrieves properties of a mail-enabled contact
Remove-MailContact	Removes the mail properties from a contact and deletes that contact from Active Directory
Disable-MailContact	Removes the mail properties from a contact
New-MailUser	Creates a new user in Active Directory and mail-enables that user
Enable-MailUser	Mail-enables a previously existing user
Set-MailUser	Sets mail properties for a mail-enabled user
Get-MailUser	Retrieves properties of a mail-enabled user
Remove-MailUser	Removes the mail properties from a user and deletes that user from Active Directory
Disable-MailUser	Removes the mail properties from a user

Here are a few scenarios to demonstrate some of these cmdlets. For example, David Pike is a contractor who occasionally works for your company. While onsite, he uses a network application hosted from one of your servers. His manager has requested that all of the users should readily have access to his external email address, David.Pike@adatum.com. Because the contractor already has access to Active Directory, you need to use the following command to mail-enable his user account:

```
Enable-MailUser "David Pike" -Alias "David.Pike"
-ExternalEmailAddress "SMTP:David.Pike@adatum.com"
```

In a different scenario, Cheyenne Pike is a new contractor who will occasionally work for your company and won't require access to any network applications. The manager of the contractor has requested that all of the users should readily have access to her external email address, Cheyenne.Pike@adatum.com. Because the contractor won't request access to Active Directory, you need to use the following command to create a new mail contact:

```
New-MailContact
-ExternalEmailAddress "SMTP:Cheyenne.Pike@adatum.com"
-Name "Cheyenne Pike" -Alias "Cheyenne.Pike"
-OrganizationalUnit "Contoso.com/Users"
-FirstName "Cheyenne" -LastName "Pike"
```

When configuring the properties of a mail contact or a mail user, you should keep in mind some of their more useful properties. Table 15.4 shows some of the common properties that these two object types share.

TABLE 15.4: Useful Properties of Mail Contact and Mail User Objects

PROPERTY	DESCRIPTION
Alias	Sets the object's Exchange Server alias.
CustomAttribute1 through CustomAttribute10	Sets custom attributes 1 through 10; these are also known as the extension attributes.
DisplayName	Sets the display name of the object.
ExternalEmailAddress	Sets the address that is to be used to deliver mail externally to the user or contact.
HiddenFromAddressLists Enabled	Specifies whether the object is hidden from address lists. The default is $False, but it can be set to $True.
MaxSendSize	Sets the maximum size of a message that can be sent to this recipient.

The Bottom Line

Create and mail-enable contact objects.   In some cases, you should *not* create a mail user but instead choose an object with fewer privileges—a mail contact. Mail contacts can be used to provide easy access to external email contacts by using your internal address lists. Mail users can be used to provide convenient access to internal resources for workers who require an externally hosted email account.

Master It   You periodically update the email addresses for your Active Directory contacts. However, some users report that they are not seeing the updated contact address in the address list and that they receive nondelivery reports (NDRs) when sending email to some contacts. What should you do?

Manage mail-enabled contacts and mail-enabled users in a messaging environment.
All Exchange Server–related attributes for mail users and mail contacts are unavailable from Active Directory Users and Computers. To manage all Exchange Server–related attributes, you must use the Exchange Admin Center or the EMS tools.

> **Master It**   Whether you want to manage users in bulk, need to create multiple users in your domain or multiple mail contacts in your organization, or simply want to change the delivery restrictions for 5,000 recipients, which tool should you use?

Choose the appropriate type and scope of mail-enabled groups.   Although you can modify your group scope or group type at any time after the group has been created, it's always a best practice to create all groups as universal groups in an environment that hosts Exchange servers.

> **Master It**   Your company needs to ensure that if an administrator adds a user to a distribution list, that user will not get any unnecessary access to resources on the network. How should you ensure that this type of administrative mistake does not impact the security of your networking environment?

Create and manage mail-enabled groups.   Creating and managing distribution groups can mostly be done from the Exchange Admin Center, with only limited options that require the Exchange Management Shell.

> **Master It**   You want to simplify the management of groups in your organization. You recently reviewed the functionalities of dynamic distribution groups and decided that this technology can provide the desired results. You need to identify the tools that should be used to manage dynamic distribution groups. What tools should you choose?

Explore the moderation features of Exchange Server 2016.   Moderation and moderated groups are one of the self-service features of Exchange Server 2016 that allow a user to review messages sent to an email address on your server.

> **Master It**   You need to enable moderation of email messages sent to particular recipients in your organization. You recently reviewed the multiple methods to enable moderation of distribution groups and other recipients in Exchange Server 2016. Which moderation method should you use based on each option's advantages and limitations?

Chapter 16

Managing Resource Mailboxes

Resource mailboxes play an important role in the scheduling of various tools and facilities—conference rooms, projectors, laptop computers, smart boards, company vehicles, and any other sort of location or tool that is in demand but may have limited availability. To that end, it's important to maintain a calendar for these resources, as well as define who can schedule access. Exchange Server 2016, Outlook on the web, and Microsoft Outlook allow you to view the availability of resources and schedule them easily.

In some respects, managing resource mailboxes is the same as managing user or shared mailboxes. However, there are some features and settings that are unique to resource mailboxes and enhance their functionality.

IN THIS CHAPTER, YOU WILL LEARN TO:

- ◆ Understand how resource mailboxes differ from other types of mailboxes
- ◆ Create resource mailboxes
- ◆ Configure resource scheduling policies
- ◆ Convert resource mailboxes

The Unique Nature of Resource Mailboxes

As mentioned in Chapter 13, "Basics of Recipient Management," there are multiple types of mailboxes. Some of these types include user mailbox, room mailbox, equipment mailbox, linked mailbox, shared mailbox, and site mailbox. We covered user and linked mailboxes in Chapter 14, "Managing Mailboxes and Mailbox Content." In this chapter, we'll focus on room mailboxes and equipment mailboxes.

Room Mailbox   A room mailbox is a resource mailbox assigned to a physical location, such as a conference room, a training room, or an auditorium. Meeting organizers can reserve conference rooms by including room mailboxes in meeting requests as resources.

Equipment Mailbox   An equipment mailbox is a resource mailbox assigned to a resource that is not location specific, such as a projector, a portable computer, specialty A/V equipment, or a company car. Like room mailboxes, equipment mailboxes can be included in meeting requests as resources.

Like all mailbox types, resource mailboxes have an associated user account in Active Directory. However, there should never be a need to log in to Active Directory with the user account. For this reason, the corresponding user account of a resource mailbox is disabled in Active Directory.

In contrast, the icons associated with resource mailboxes in the global address list are different than the icons associated with user mailboxes and mail-enabled groups. Further, additional attributes are included on resource mailboxes that allow them to be utilized as resources. Outside of these differences, resource mailboxes are the same as user mailboxes and their corresponding user accounts in Active Directory.

Exchange 2016 Resource Mailbox Features

Resource mailboxes are very useful for reserving or booking resources, such as conference rooms or equipment, such as projectors. In Exchange Server 2016, resource mailboxes for conference rooms allow you to accept or decline meeting requests sent from meeting organizers. The properties of a room mailbox can include information about the seating capacity as well as information about permanent items in the room, such as whiteboards and video teleconferencing tools. Likewise, the properties of resource mailboxes for equipment can provide descriptions about those resources, such as the make and model for a laptop computer or a company car. Various clients, including Microsoft Outlook, Outlook on the web, and mobile clients, schedule resource mailboxes using the Calendar and Availability services, the same way attendees are invited to meeting requests,.

Multiple customizations for booking are available with resource mailboxes. You can enable a booking policy to accept or decline meeting requests automatically. Based on the policy criteria you configure, valid meeting requests automatically reserve the room. In contrast, you can configure policy criteria to automatically decline meeting requests if there's a scheduling conflict with an existing reservation or if the booking request violates the scheduling limits of the resource.

With a booking policy, you can enforce rules to define the maximum time a resource can be reserved, who can reserve it, and what actions to perform on some of the information within meeting requests. For example, you can restrict meeting requests to business hours only or allow meeting requests only from meeting organizers in your organization. With a policy, you can also ensure that attachments are automatically removed from meeting requests sent to the resource mailbox or that non-calendar messages are deleted automatically.

For organizations with less standardization of meeting requests, you can enable delegation of resource mailboxes. Delegation allows you to configure resource delegates who are responsible for accepting or declining meeting requests sent to the resource mailbox. Even with delegation enabled, you can configure a list of meeting organizers who are allowed to reserve the resource outside of the defined policies.

Creating Resource Mailboxes

You will discover that creating resource mailboxes is very similar to creating other types of mailboxes. Using the same tools, the Exchange Administration Center (EAC) or the Exchange Management Shell (EMS), you can provision a resource mailbox by including a parameter to define the mailbox as a resource mailbox.

Creating and Configuring Resource Mailboxes

Let's begin by creating a resource mailbox for the conference room *Conference Room South*. Within the EAC, navigate to Recipients from the Feature pane, select the Resources tab, click + (Add) from the Actions menu, and then select Room Mailbox. In the New Room Mailbox Wizard (shown in Figure 16.1), fill in the appropriate information.

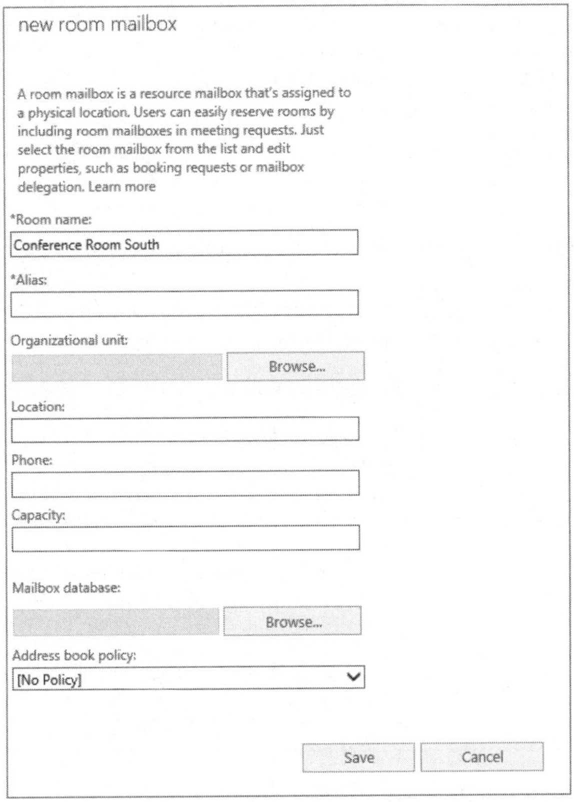

FIGURE 16.1

Defining general information for a conference room mailbox

new room mailbox

A room mailbox is a resource mailbox that's assigned to a physical location. Users can easily reserve rooms by including room mailboxes in meeting requests. Just select the room mailbox from the list and edit properties, such as booking requests or mailbox delegation. Learn more

*Room name:

Conference Room South

*Alias:

Organizational unit:

Browse...

Location:

Phone:

Capacity:

Mailbox database:

Browse...

Address book policy:

[No Policy]

Save   Cancel

If an organizational unit (OU) is not defined when a resource mailbox is provisioned, the corresponding user account will be placed in the Users container in Active Directory. Alternatively, you can click the Browse button next to Organizational Unit in the New Room Mailbox Wizard to define the appropriate OU to locate the corresponding user account.

The remaining mailbox settings in the wizard are the same as for other types of mailboxes. When you create a resource mailbox in the EAC, the corresponding user account is also created in Active Directory as a disabled account.

Within the EMS, you will use the `New-Mailbox` cmdlet with the `Room` parameter to create a conference room resource mailbox. For example, you can use the following to create the conference room *Conference Room South*:

```
New-Mailbox -Name 'Conference Room South' -Room
-OrganizationalUnit "contoso.com/Resource Mailboxes"
-DisplayName "Conference Room South"
```

In Exchange Server 2016, you may notice properties that are unique to resource mailboxes. Some of these properties include `RecipientTypeDetails`, `ResourceType`, `ResouceCapacity`, `IsResource`, and `ResourceCustom`. For example, you can use the `Get-Mailbox` cmdlet to display information about a resource mailbox, such as in the following code (some properties have been removed to save space):

```
Get-Mailbox "Conference Room South" | FL Name,*recipient*,*resource*
Name                 : Conference Room South
RecipientType        : UserMailbox
RecipientTypeDetails : RoomMailbox
IsResource           : True
ResourceCapacity     :
ResourceCustom       : {}
ResourceType         : Room
```

Table 16.1 provides details about these attributes for resource mailboxes.

TABLE 16.1:   Recipient-Related Attributes for Resource Mailboxes

ATTRIBUTE	VALUE/PURPOSE
RecipientType	Always set to UserMailbox, regardless of whether the mailbox is a user mailbox or resource mailbox
RecipientTypeDetails	Set to either RoomMailbox or EquipmentMailbox
IsResource	For indicating whether the mailbox is a resource mailbox
ResourceCapacity	For defining room capacity to assist when planning the number of attendees
ResourceCustom	For defining additional properties of a resource mailbox
ResourceType	Set to either Room or Equipment

Exchange Server will use the information in these attributes for specific handling of meeting requests and providing information for meeting organizers. For example, Exchange will display conference room resource mailboxes in the exclusive address list All Rooms (as shown in Figure 16.2).

FIGURE 16.2
Viewing room resources in the Address Book using Outlook

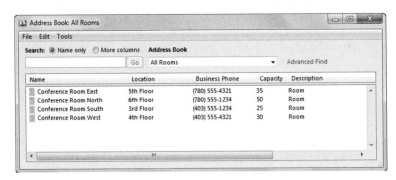

As you can imagine, this provides a simplified view of conference rooms to meeting organizers without the clutter of the entire global address list.

Configuring Advanced Resource Mailbox Features

With Exchange Server 2016, you can specify additional attributes of the resource mailbox to aid meeting organizers when scheduling meetings: the `ResourceCapacity` and `ResourceCustom` attributes. The `ResourceCapacity` attribute allows you to define the maximum capacity of a conference room, as shown in Figure 16.2, which can certainly help meeting organizers when planning the number of attendees.

To define the `ResourceCapacity` of a resource mailbox using the EAC, select the resource mailbox from the Resources tab, and then click the pencil icon (Edit) from the Actions menu. On the General tab, type the appropriate number in the Capacity box, as shown in Figure 16.3.

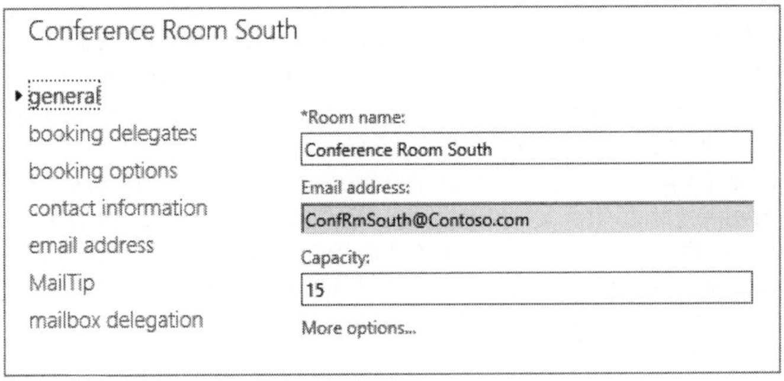

FIGURE 16.3
Entering the room capacity for a resource mailbox

The resource capacity of a resource mailbox can also be defined within the EMS. You can use the `Set-Mailbox` cmdlet in the following command to define the room capacity of *Conference Room North*:

```
Set-Mailbox "Conference Room North" -ResourceCapacity 15
```

In most scenarios, meeting organizers need more information than room capacity when planning a meeting; information about equipment in the conference room can also be helpful. In most organizations, each conference room is equipped with different equipment. Some rooms may have a TV, while other rooms provide a projector. Likewise, conference rooms may have different teleconferencing systems and audio/video equipment. For this reason, Exchange provides the custom resource properties.

Custom resource properties can help users select the most appropriate conference room or equipment by providing additional information about the resource. For example, you can create a custom property for room mailboxes called *Audio/Video Teleconferencing*. After you create this resource property, you can add the property to all conference rooms with audio and video teleconferencing equipment. When scheduling a meeting, organizers can identify which conference rooms have audio/video teleconferencing equipment.

Resource properties are stored as resource object attributes in the Active Directory schema. Before you can add the resource properties to resource mailboxes, you need to create the necessary attributes using the `Set-ResourceConfig` cmdlet. Unfortunately, using the Set-ResourceConfig cmdlet overwrites all existing attributes in the schema; the cmdlet doesn't add a new entry to the list. As a result, you should use the `Get-ResourceConfig` cmdlet to query the existing entries in the schema and then append them to the list. For example, you can use the following command to retrieve the existing list of attributes (the default configuration does not include entries):

```
Get-ResourceConfig | FL Name,ResourcePropertySchema
Name                  : Resource Schema
ResourcePropertySchema : {}
```

With no existing entries in the list, you can use the following command to add the resource properties Audio Video Equipment, or AV, and Teleconferencing Equipment, or TeleConf, to the list in Active Directory (entries must begin with either Room/ or Equipment/ to indicate the resource mailbox type with which they associate):

```
Set-ResourceConfig -ResourcePropertySchema("Room/AV","Room/TeleConf")
```

The process to add entries to the list of resource attributes will change after the first time you populate the list. Although you could add new entries by typing the existing and new attributes to the list with the previous command, you should consider using operators or methods that are native to Windows PowerShell to minimize typos.

For example, say that you want to define the additional resource properties TV, Projector, and Speakerphone for associating to room mailboxes and the resource properties Laptop, Van, and Car for associating to equipment mailboxes. Similar to the previous example, you will use the `Set-ResourceConfig` cmdlet in the following command to add new entries to the existing list (two options are shown here; choose only one):

```
$ResourceConfig = Get-ResourceConfig

# Option 1 using a Method
$ResourceConfig.ResourcePropertySchema.Add("Room/TV","Room/Projector", "Room/
Speakerphone","Equipment/Computer","Equipment/Van","Equipment/Car")

# Option 2 using an Operator
$ResourceConfig.ResourcePropertySchema.+=("Room/TV","Room/Projector",  "Room/
Speakerphone","Equipment/Computer","Equipment/Van","Equipment/Car")

Set-ResourceConfig –ResourcePropertySchema    $ResourceConfig.
ResourcePropertySchema
```

In the previous example, we retrieved the current list of entries and stored them in a variable (more specifically, an array). In both of the options, we added the entries to the array. In the last line, we configured the resource attributes in the Active Directory schema with the existing and new resource properties.

What if you decide that a resource property is no longer needed and you want to remove it from the list of available properties? For example, you need to replace the resource property Computer with Desktop. You will use similar options in the following command to update (remove/add) entries in the existing list (two options are shown here; choose only one):

```
$ResourceConfig = Get-ResourceConfig

# Option 1 using a Method
```

```
$ResourceConfig.ResourcePropertySchema.Remove("Equipment/Computer")
$ResourceConfig.ResourcePropertySchema.Add("Equipment/Desktop")

# Option 2 using an Operator
$ResourceConfig.ResourcePropertySchema.-=("Equipment/Computer")
$ResourceConfig.ResourcePropertySchema.+=("Equipment/Desktop")

Set-ResourceConfig -ResourcePropertySchema     $ResourceConfig.
ResourcePropertySchema
```

As you may have noticed in the previous example, the method and operator are very similar to the first example. Of course, it's not necessary to add a resource property to the list after you remove a resource property from the list; these actions are independent of one another. When you want to confirm the list of attributes after creating them, you can use the `Get-ResourceConfig` cmdlet with the `ResourceCustom` attribute

After creating all of the required resource properties, you will use the `Set-Mailbox` cmdlet to associate specific properties with the resource mailbox. For example, you can use the following command to inform meeting organizers that the resource mailbox `Conference Room North` has audio/video equipment, a desktop computer, and a room capacity of 15:

```
Set-Mailbox "Conference Room North" -ResourceCustom ("AV","Desktop")
-ResourceCapacity 15
```

To confirm the changes, you can use the `Get-Mailbox` cmdlet, as shown in the following command:

```
Get-Mailbox "Conference Room North" | FL Name, *resource*
Name             : Conference Room North
IsResource       : True
ResourceCapacity : 15
ResourceCustom   : {AV, Desktop}
ResourceType     : Room
```

Exchange Server will update the resource mailbox in the address book with this information so Outlook may display the details for meeting organizers. For example, Outlook displays the resource attributes for conference room resource mailboxes in the address list as shown in Figure 16.4.

FIGURE 16.4
Viewing the custom attributes of room resources in the Address Book using Outlook

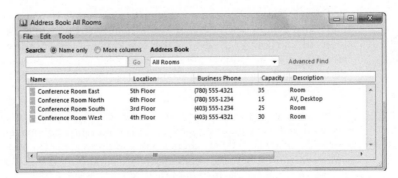

Configuring Resource Scheduling Policies

In Exchange Server 2016, the processing of meeting requests is considered the most important feature of resource mailboxes. With the appropriate policies deployed, most of the processing should be automated, requiring minimum actions from admins and users alike.

Among the options available, you can customize who can book resources automatically or via a delegate, how to handle conflicting requests, and when meetings can be scheduled and for how long. Exchange Server 2016 allows you to manage these options using the Exchange Admin Center (EAC) and the Exchange Management Shell (EMS).

CONFIGURING RESOURCE SCHEDULING POLICIES USING THE EAC

After opening the properties of a resource mailbox in the EAC, you can use two of the five tabs to manage the resource scheduling configuration: Delegates and Booking Options.

Delegates You can use this section to view or change how the conference room mailbox handles reservation requests and to define who can accept or decline meeting requests, if this is not done automatically. An example of the Delegates is shown in Figure 16.5.

FIGURE 16.5
Delegates for a
resource mailbox

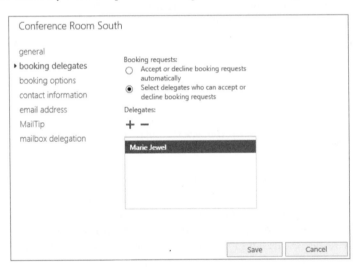

Booking Options You can use this section to view or change the settings for the booking policy that defines when the conference room can be scheduled, how long the room can be reserved, and how far in advance the room can be reserved. You can also define whether recurring meeting requests are allowed, enable message replies to meeting organizers, and perform many other advanced scheduling options. An example of the Booking Options is shown in Figure 16.6.

Although some of the common resource scheduling configuration of a resource mailbox can be managed using the EAC, most of the configuration options require using the EMS with the Set-CalendarProcessing cmdlet. Table 16.2 provides a list of the most commonly used resource scheduling, or booking, configuration options for resource mailboxes. Along with a brief description, this table includes information on whether you can configure the option in the EAC or the EMS and the corresponding parameter name of each option.

FIGURE 16.6
Booking Options
for a resource
mailbox

FIGURE 16.6
Booking Options
for a resource
mailbox

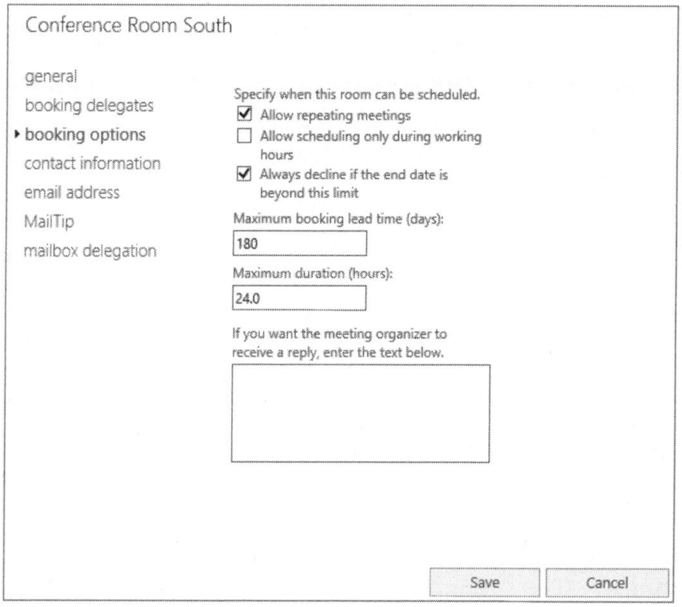

TABLE 16.2: Booking Options and EMS Equivalents

EAC PARAMETER	EMS PARAMETER	DESCRIPTION
(Not available in EAC)	AllowConflicts	Specifies whether to allow conflicting meeting requests. If enabled, this will allow multiple meetings to be accepted for the same date and time. The default value is $false.
Allow repeating meetings (Booking Options)	AllowRecurringMeetings	Specifies whether to allow recurring meetings. When enabled, recurring meeting requests, such as those for every Monday at 9 A.M., are accepted. The default value is $true.
(Not available in EAC)	AutomateProcessing	Enables calendar processing on the mailbox. The default value on a resource mailbox is AutoAccept, and the default value on a user mailbox is AutoUpdate.
Maximum booking lead time (days) (Booking Options)	BookingWindowInDays	Specifies the maximum number of days in advance that the resource can be reserved. Valid input is 0 through 1080. When set to 0, the resource can be reserved at any date in the future. The default value is 180 days.

TABLE 16.2: Booking Options and EMS Equivalents *(CONTINUED)*

EAC PARAMETER	EMS PARAMETER	DESCRIPTION
(Not available in EAC)	ConflictPercentageAllowed	Specifies the maximum percentage of meeting conflicts for new recurring meeting requests. Valid input is 0 through 100.
		If a new recurring meeting request conflicts with existing reservations for the resource more than the specified percentage allowed, the recurring meeting request is automatically declined. When set to 0, no conflicts are permitted for new recurring meeting requests. The default value is 0.
(Not available in EAC)	EnforceSchedulingHorizon	Enforces an end date for recurring meetings based on the BookingWindowInDays setting. The default value is $true.
(Not available in EAC)	ForwardRequestsToDelegates	Specifies whether to forward incoming meeting requests to the delegates defined for the mailbox. The default value is $true.
(Not available in EAC)	MaximumConflictInstances	Specifies the maximum number of conflicts for new recurring meeting requests when the AllowRecurringMeetings parameter is enabled. Valid input is 0 through 2147483647.
		If a new recurring meeting request conflicts with existing reservations for the resource more than the maximum number of instances specified, the recurring meeting request is automatically declined. When set to 0, no conflicts are permitted for new recurring meeting requests. The default value is 0.
Maximum duration (hours) (Booking Options)	MaximumDurationInMinutes	Specifies the maximum duration (in minutes) allowed for incoming meeting requests. Valid input is 0 through 2147483647.
		When set to 0, the maximum duration of a meeting is unlimited. For recurring meetings, this value applies to the length of an individual meeting instance. The default value is 1440 (24 hours).
		(Note: This value is specified in hours in the EAC, whereas the value is specified in minutes in the EMS).

TABLE 16.2:   Booking Options and EMS Equivalents *(CONTINUED)*

EAC PARAMETER	EMS PARAMETER	DESCRIPTION
(Not available in EAC)	`ProcessExternalMeetingMessages`	Specifies whether to process meeting requests from outside the Exchange organization. The default value is $false.
Delegates (Booking Delegates)	`ResourceDelegates`	Specifies a list of users who are resource mailbox delegates. Resource mailbox delegates can approve or reject requests sent to this resource mailbox.
Allow scheduling only during working hours (`Booking Options`)	`ScheduleOnlyDuringWorkHours`	Specifies whether to allow meetings to be scheduled outside work hours. If checked, meeting requests for times outside the mailbox's working hours will be rejected. The default value is $false.

In addition, you can configure scheduling options to help in standardizing how meeting requests appear in the resource mailbox calendar. These settings are listed in Table 16.3, which includes information on whether you can configure the option in the EAC or the EMS and the corresponding parameter name of each option.

TABLE 16.3:   Resource Information Settings and Their EMS Equivalents

EAC PARAMETER	EMS PARAMETER	DESCRIPTION
`Open text box` (Text box in the `Booking Options`)	`AdditionalResponse` (`AddAdditionalResponse`)	Specifies the additional information to be included in responses to meeting requests (requires that the `AddAdditionalResponse` parameter is set to `$true`).
(Not available in EAC)	`AddNewRequestsTentatively`	Specifies whether to mark new meeting requests as tentative on the calendar until a Delegate can accept or decline the meeting request.
(Not available in EAC)	`AddOrganizerToSubject`	Specifies whether the meeting organizer's name is used as the subject of the meeting request.
(Not available in EAC)	`DeleteAttachments`	Specifies whether to remove attachments from all incoming messages.

TABLE 16.3:   Resource Information Settings and Their EMS Equivalents   *(CONTINUED)*

EAC PARAMETER	EMS PARAMETER	DESCRIPTION
(Not available in EAC)	DeleteComments	Specifies whether to remove any text in the message body from incoming meeting requests.
(Not available in EAC)	DeleteNonCalendarItems	Specifies whether to remove all non-calendar items received by the resource mailbox.
(Not available in EAC)	DeleteSubject	Specifies whether to remove the subject of incoming meeting requests.
(Not available in EAC)	EnableResponseDetails	Specifies whether to include the reasons for accepting or declining a meeting in the response email message.
(Not available in EAC)	OrganizerInfo	Specifies whether to have the resource mailboxes send organizer information when a meeting request is declined because of conflicts.
(Not available in EAC)	RemoveForwarded MeetingNotifications	Specifies whether forwarded meeting notifications are moved to the Deleted Items folder after processed by the mailbox.
(Not available in EAC)	RemoveOldMeetingMessages	Specifies whether old and redundant updates and responses are removed by the mailbox.
(Not available in EAC)	RemovePrivateProperty	Specifies whether to clear the private flag for incoming meeting requests.

Using the automated booking policies, you can define which meeting requests are automatically approved to schedule resources, which requests are automatically declined, and which are subject to delegate approval. Meeting requests sent to the resource mailbox are categorized as either *in-policy* meeting requests or *out-of-policy* meeting requests.

In-policy meeting requests are requests that do not violate any of the resource scheduling options. Some of the resource scheduling options are detailed in the earlier tables; they can include the available hours of a conference room, the maximum duration of a meeting, whether recurring meetings are allowed, and so forth.

The booking policies for meeting requests that are in compliance with the resource scheduling options, or *in-policy* meeting requests, are listed in Table 16.4. Depending on the policy you choose, the scope of the meeting organizers can include specific users or everyone in the organization. (Policies can only be assigned using the EMS.)

TABLE 16.4:   EMS Parameters of In-Policy Booking Policies

EMS PARAMETER	DESCRIPTION
AllBookInPolicy	Specifies whether to automatically approve in-policy requests from all users.
AllRequestInPolicy	Specifies whether to allow all users to submit in-policy requests. These meeting requests require approval from a resource mailbox delegate, unless AllBookInPolicy is enabled.
BookInPolicy	Specifies a list of users who are allowed to submit in-policy meeting requests. In-policy meeting requests from these users are automatically approved.
RequestInPolicy	Specifies a list of users who are allowed to submit in-policy meeting requests. In-policy meeting requests from these users require approval from a resource mailbox delegate.

On the other hand, the booking policies for meeting requests that are not in compliance, or *out-of-policy* meeting requests, are listed in Table 16.5. Similar to in-policy meeting requests, the scope of the meeting organizers can include specific users or everyone in the organization, depending on the policy you choose. (Policies can only be assigned using the EMS.)

TABLE 16.5:   EMS Parameters of Out-of-Policy Booking Policies

EMS PARAMETER	DESCRIPTION
AllRequestOutofPolicy	Specifies whether to allow all users to submit out-of-policy requests. These meeting requests require approval from a resource mailbox delegate.
RequestOutOfPolicy	Specifies a list of users who are allowed to submit out-of-policy requests. Out-of-policy meeting requests from these users require approval from a resource mailbox delegate.

CONFIGURING RESOURCE SCHEDULING POLICIES USING THE EMS

In contrast to the EAC, you can use the EMS to view and configure all of the resource schedule policy settings. For example, you can use the Get-CalendarProcessing cmdlet to view the resource scheduling policy settings of a resource mailbox, as shown in the following command:

```
Get-CalendarProcessing -Identity "Conference Room South" | FL
RunspaceId                    : 53135a92-3a51-4db4-a0aa-7a45c231fb91
AutomateProcessing            : AutoAccept
```

```
AllowConflicts                         : False
BookingWindowInDays                    : 180
MaximumDurationInMinutes               : 1440
AllowRecurringMeetings                 : True
EnforceSchedulingHorizon               : True
ScheduleOnlyDuringWorkHours            : False
ConflictPercentageAllowed              : 0
MaximumConflictInstances               : 0
ForwardRequestsToDelegates             : True
DeleteAttachments                      : True
DeleteComments                         : True
RemovePrivateProperty                  : True
DeleteSubject                          : True
AddOrganizerToSubject                  : True
DeleteNonCalendarItems                 : True
TentativePendingApproval               : True
EnableResponseDetails                  : True
OrganizerInfo                          : True
ResourceDelegates                      : {}
RequestOutOfPolicy                     :
AllRequestOutOfPolicy                  : False
BookInPolicy                           :
AllBookInPolicy                        : True
RequestInPolicy                        :
AllRequestInPolicy                     : False
AddAdditionalResponse                  : False
AdditionalResponse                     :
RemoveOldMeetingMessages               : True
AddNewRequestsTentatively              : True
ProcessExternalMeetingMessages         : False
RemoveForwardedMeetingNotifications    : False
Identity                               : Contoso.com/Res MBs/Conference Room South
```

Using the Set-CalendarProcessing cmdlet to update resource scheduling policy settings is fairly straightforward. For example, you can use the following command to add the resource delegate Marie Jewel to the resource mailbox Conference Room South:

```
Set-CalendarProcessing "Conference Room South"
-ResourceDelegates "Marie Jewel"
```

In another example, you can use the following command with other EMS commands, and you can supply multiple attributes in one command. If you want to, say, add a delegate and also add the meeting organizer's name to the subject, you could use this:

```
Set-CalendarProcessing "Conference Room South" -ResourceDelegates
"Alex Bossio" -AddOrganizerToSubject $true
```

A complete description of each of the attributes is listed in Tables 16.2 through Table 16.4 earlier in this chapter.

CONFIGURING MAILBOX CALENDAR USING THE EMS

All mailboxes in Exchange Server 2016 provide Calendar configuration settings that allow users to customize the look of their calendar and the way reminders work in Outlook on the web. These settings also impact how meeting invitations, responses, and notifications are sent to the user. For user mailboxes, most of these settings are configured either the first time the user signs into Outlook on the web or when the mailbox is provisioned.

Similar to user mailboxes, resource mailboxes use the same Calendar configuration settings with the same impact on meeting invitations, responses, and notifications. Unfortunately, because the corresponding user accounts of resource mailboxes are disabled by default, the Calendar settings for resource mailboxes may not be configured correctly.

Luckily, Exchange Server 2016 enables you to configure the Calendar configuration settings of resource mailboxes using the EMS. With the Get-MailboxCalendarConfiguration cmdlet, you can configure the Calendar settings noted earlier, as well as the working (or business) hours and days, the time zone, and the default reminder settings. As you may recall, some of these settings are used in determining whether meeting requests violate any of the resource scheduling options, such as the available hours/days of the resource (refer to the booking policies of *in-policy* and *out-of-policy* meeting requests described earlier in this chapter for more information).

To demonstrate Calendar configuration settings, you can use the following command to view the current Calendar configuration of the resource mailbox Conference Room South:

```
Get-MailboxCalendarConfiguration -Identity "Conference Room South" | FL
RunspaceId             : 53135a92-3a51-4db4-a0aa-7a45c231fb91
WorkDays               : Weekdays
WorkingHoursStartTime  : 08:00:00
WorkingHoursEndTime    : 17:00:00
WorkingHoursTimeZone   : Central Standard Time
WeekStartDay           : Sunday
ShowWeekNumbers        : False
FirstWeekOfYear        : FirstDay
TimeIncrement          : ThirtyMinutes
RemindersEnabled       : True
ReminderSoundEnabled   : True
DefaultReminderTime    : 00:15:00
Identity               : Contoso.com/ResMBs/Conference Room South
IsValid                : True
```

When updating the Calendar configuration settings of a mailbox, you use the Set-MailboxCalendarConfiguration cmdlet. For example, you can use the following command to update the working hours time zone to Eastern Standard Time and to increase the working hours start and end time by one hour:

```
Set-MailboxCalendarConfiguration -Identity "Conference Room South"
-WorkingHoursTimeZone "Eastern Standard Time"
-WorkingHoursStartTime 07:00:00 -WorkingHoursEndTime 18:00:00
```

A complete list of the available parameters for the Set-MailboxCalendarConfiguration cmdlet is shown in Table 16.6.

TABLE 16.6:   Set-MailboxCalendarConfiguration Parameters

PARAMETER	DESCRIPTION
WorkDays	Specifies which days are defined as workdays in the Outlook on the web calendar
WorkingHoursStartTime	Specifies the start of the workday in hours, minutes, and seconds
WorkingHoursEndTime	Specifies the end of the workday in hours, minutes, and seconds
WorkingHoursTimeZone	Specifies the time zone used to determine the working start and end times (e.g., WorkingHoursStartTime and WorkingHoursEndTime)
WeekStartDay	Specifies which day of the week is the start of the work week
ShowWeekNumbers	Specifies whether the week number is displayed in the Outlook on the web calendar
FirstWeekOfYear	Specifies the first week of the year
TimeIncrement	Specifies the scale that the Outlook on the web calendar uses to show time
RemindersEnabled	Specifies whether reminders are enabled for items in the Outlook on the web calendar
ReminderSoundEnabled	Specifies whether a sound is played along with the reminder
DefaultReminderTime	Specifies the length of time before a meeting or appointment when the reminder is first displayed

Automatic Processing: AutoUpdate vs. AutoAccept

Automatic processing of meeting requests is enabled by a property on resource mailboxes called AutomateProcessing. By default, this property on a user mailbox is set to AutoUpdate. However, when a resource mailbox is created or an existing user mailbox is converted to a resource mailbox, this property is updated to AutoAccept. The value of this property will determine if the resource mailbox validates meeting requests using the booking policy settings.

Resource mailboxes use the *Resource Booking Attendant* to accept or decline resource requests based on policies you create. Although users could manually accept meeting requests, many organizations choose to deploy an automated method whereby Exchange Server can process meeting requests automatically based on many different configuration options. If the Resource Booking Attendant is enabled, the property is set to AutoAccept, and it uses the booking policies to determine if incoming requests will be accepted or declined. If the Resource Booking Attendant is disabled, the property is set to AutoUpdate, and the resource mailbox's delegate must accept or decline all requests.

In rare situations, you may need to change the `AutomateProcessing` attribute on a resource mailbox. Fortunately, changing this attribute is simple; you can use the EMS or Outlook on the web. To change this attribute, sign in to Outlook on the web as the resource mailbox. Near the top-right of the window, select Settings. On the Resource tab, update the setting for *Automatically Process Meeting Requests And Cancellations*.

Using the EMS, you set the `AutomateProcessing` attribute using the `Set-CalendarProcessing` cmdlet. For example, you can use the following command to enable the Resource Booking Attendant for the resource mailbox `Conference Room South`:

```
Set-CalendarProcessing -Identity "Conference Room South"
-AutomateProcessing AutoAccept
```

In another example, you can use the following command to enable the Resource Booking Attendant on all resource mailboxes:

```
Get-Mailbox -filter {IsResource -eq $true} |
Set-CalendarProcessing -AutomateProcessing AutoAccept
```

Configuring Resource Calendar Permissions

Typically, when meeting organizers create a meeting invitation, they review the availability of the conference room in the Scheduling Assistant via Outlook on the web, Microsoft Outlook, mobile app, or mobile Outlook on the web. By default, the availability of a conference room calendar will display the existing meetings as busy or tentative, as shown in Figure 16.7. For this reason, the availability of the calendar is commonly referred to as `Free/Busy`.

FIGURE 16.7
Availability of resource mailbox in Outlook

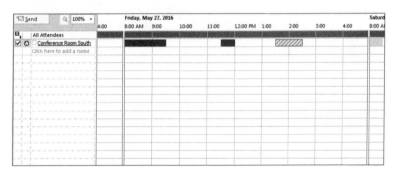

Frequently in organizations, there are some meeting organizers who prefer to see more than the availability of a conference room calendar when scheduling a meeting. A common justification may be their need to contact other meeting organizers for rescheduling. Regardless of the reasons, you can use the EMS to configure the calendar permissions.

Configuring permissions on the conference room calendar is similar to configuring folder permissions in other types of mailboxes. While there are multiple access rights, as well as roles (a combination of commonly used access rights), for mailbox folders in Exchange Server 2016, a subset of the roles are commonly used for Calendar folders (as shown in Table 16.7).

TABLE 16.7: Access Rights (Roles) of Calendar Folders

ROLE (ACCESS RIGHTS)	CALENDAR PERMISSIONS
None	No permissions
AvailabilityOnly (Default)	Availability (free/busy) of existing meetings
LimitedDetails	Availability (free/busy), subject, and location of existing meetings
Reviewer	Availability (free/busy), subject, location, attendees, and description of existing meetings
Editor or Owner	In addition to Reviewer, user can create new meetings and change/delete existing meetings

Similar to configuring folder permissions for other types of mailboxes, you will use the Add-MailboxFolderPermission cmdlet to add new permissions to the conference room Calendar folder. For example, you can use the following command to provide Marie Jewel with the subject and location of existing meetings to the conference room Conference Room South:

```
Add-MailBoxFolderPermission "ConfRmSouth:\Calendar" -User Marie.Jewel
-AccessRights LimitedDetails
```

Some organizations prefer that all the users have different permissions to the conference room calendar. Instead of adding permissions to the calendar for each user, you can use the Set-MailboxFolderPermission cmdlet to configure the Calendar permissions for the default object. For example, you can use the following command to provide all the users in your organization with the subject and location of existing meetings to the conference room Conference Room South:

```
Set-MailBoxFolderPermission "ConfRmSouth:\Calendar" -User default
-AccessRights LimitedDetails
```

When a user's role changes in a company, you can use the Remove-MailboxFolderPermission cmdlet to remove existing permissions for the conference room calendar. For example, you can use the following command to remove permission for Marie Jewel for the conference room Conference Room South:

```
Remove-MailBoxFolderPermission "ConfRmSouth:\Calendar" -User Marie.Jewel
```

Creating Room Lists

If meeting organizers want to search for a conference room's availability when they're creating a meeting invitation, they need to add all the possible conference rooms to the meeting request and then use the Scheduling Assistant to view the available conference rooms. As you can imagine, this requires a considerable amount of work in medium to large organizations.

Alternatively, in Exchange Server 2016, you can create *room list* distribution groups to provide lists of conference rooms to meeting organizers. Room lists are specially marked distribution groups that contain resource mailboxes as members. In Outlook on the web and Microsoft Outlook, users can select uniquely named room lists and receive information about the availability of multiple conference rooms (as shown in Figure 16.8).

FIGURE 16.8
Availability using
room lists in
Outlook

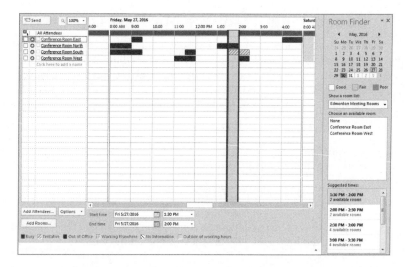

When planning your room lists, you should consider the preferences of your meeting organizers and the size of your organization. For small to medium organizations, you may consider creating a room list for each location or for each building. For medium to large organizations, you may consider creating a room list for each building or for groups of floors within a building. Because room lists can contain other room lists, you may consider creating a hierarchy of room lists (e.g., room lists for groups of floors within rooms lists for each building within room lists for each location).

While you can access room lists as you would other distribution lists, you can only create room lists using the EMS. For example, you can use the following command to create a room list for all the conference rooms in the Edmonton office:

```
New-DistributionGroup -Name "Edmonton Meeting Rooms" -RoomList
```

After creating the room list, you add the conference rooms to the room list. For example, you can use the following command to add the conference room Conference Room South to the room list:

```
Add-DistributionGroupMember -Identity "Edmonton Meeting Rooms"
-Member "Conference Room South"
```

With large room lists, you may consider using the Filter PowerShell function to populate the membership of the room lists. For example, you can use the following commands to create a room list that includes all of the conference rooms in the MacDonald building:

```
$Members = Get-Mailbox -Filter {(RecipientTypeDetails -eq "RoomMailbox")
-and (CustomAttribute1 -eq "MacDonald Building")}

New-DistributionGroup -Name "MacDonald Meeting Rooms"
-OrganizationalUnit "Contoso.com/Rooms" -RoomList -Members $Members
```

For existing lists, you can use the following command to convert a distribution list to a room list:

```
Set-DistributionGroup -Identity "Edmonton Meeting Rooms" -RoomList
```

Converting Resource Mailboxes

In most situations, you enable a resource mailbox during provisioning. However, you can also convert an existing user mailbox or shared mailbox to a resource mailbox and vice versa. Using the Set-Mailbox cmdlet with the Type parameter, you can convert a mailbox to Room, Equipment, Shared, and Regular. For example, you can use the following command to convert the mailbox Conference Room South to a conference room resource mailbox:

```
Set-Mailbox "Conference Room South" -Type Room
```

After converting to a resource mailbox, you should enable the conference-room resource mailbox to automatically process appointments, as shown here:

```
Get-Mailbox "Conference Room South" |
Set-CalendarProcessing -AutomateProcessing AutoAccept
```

Once the resource mailbox is converted, you can use the standard tools for managing the resource mailbox: EAC, EMS, and Outlook on the web.

 Real World Scenario

ELIMINATING CONFERENCE ROOM HIJACKING

Organization KLMN is a large community church; it is not like most churches. With more than 400 staff, volunteers, and interns, there are constant meetings, conferences, and gatherings in the building's five conference rooms. To complicate matters, the scheduling process for the conference rooms was antiquated and inconvenient. Three-ring binders for every conference room were in the building's lobby. Each binder contained pages for every calendar day. Someone who wanted to reserve a conference room had to go to the lobby, look through the binder for the desired conference room, and try to decipher sometimes-cryptic entries. Additionally, when meetings were cancelled, meeting organizers didn't always remove the entry in the binder to allow the conference room to be rescheduled. Because some of KLMN's staff worked outside the main building, the process was even more cumbersome when trying to find a conference room that was available. The process was so inconvenient that many would just hijack a conference room without scheduling it. This sometimes led to "musical conference rooms" and a lot of user frustration.

When KLMN moved to resource mailboxes in Exchange Server, users could immediately reserve conference rooms by merely adding the conference room to the meeting request. Additionally, because the conference-room resource mailboxes were configured with room capacity and other special features defined, it became much easier to locate a conference room that best fit the needs of the users. After deployment, the organization discovered that remote users had the same experience as local users, and the number of conference room "hijackings" dropped to nearly zero.

This process has improved the adoption of using Microsoft Outlook Calendar meeting requests and the process of booking conference rooms. Users no longer have to walk to the other end of the building or go down three floors just to find out when a conference room might be reserved. They can simply open Microsoft Outlook, Outlook on the web, or a mobile device to schedule their meetings, invite attendees, and reserve conference rooms and any necessary equipment. In addition, third-party vendors provide devices that are mounted to the wall outside the conference rooms to display scheduling information. Commonly, these devices retrieve the scheduling information directly from Exchange Server.

The Bottom Line

Understand how resource mailboxes differ from regular mailboxes.   Resource mailboxes serve a different purpose in Exchange Server 2016 than user mailboxes and, therefore, have different features and capabilities. Understanding how resource mailboxes are different, including what added features are provided, can help improve the end-user experience and increase adoption rate.

Master It   You are planning to create resource mailboxes to support conference rooms and other resource scheduling. Identify how the resource mailboxes are different from user mailboxes.

Create resource mailboxes.   Creating resource mailboxes is easy with the tools in Exchange Server. Users need resource mailboxes for conference rooms and equipment to allow for easier, more informative scheduling.

Master It   What tools are available to create resource mailboxes and to define additional schema properties for resource mailboxes?

Configure resource mailbox booking and scheduling policies.   Properly configured resource mailboxes help users find the correct resource and determine whether it is available when needed. When the resource mailbox is properly configured, users can quickly and easily find conference rooms that have the proper capacity and features needed to hold a meeting.

Master It   You need to configure a resource mailbox to handle automatic scheduling. What tools can you use?

Convert resource mailboxes.   Converting mailboxes from one type to another allows your organization to be flexible. As business requirements change, you can ensure that the right types of resource mailboxes are available.

Master It   After provisioning a shared mailbox for a team within your organization, you have received clarification that they only require a calendar resource with automated booking. You need to convert this mailbox to an Exchange Server 2016 resource mailbox. What steps should you take?

Chapter 17

Managing Modern Public Folders

Public folders are a major part of many Exchange Server deployments. Public folders are a powerful way to share knowledge and data with users throughout an organization. They've been a staple of Exchange Server since 1996.

Back in Exchange Server 2007, there were rumors that public folders might not exist in subsequent editions because they used a separate management and replication architecture that was difficult to scale. In Exchange Server 2013 and 2016, Microsoft dramatically changed the public folder architecture to make it more scalable, making it possible to support public folders for many years to come. Public folder technology introduced in Exchange Server 2013 is part of Exchange Server 2016 as well.

IN THIS CHAPTER, YOU WILL LEARN TO:

◆ Understand the architectural changes made to public folders

◆ Manage public folders

Understanding Architectural Changes for Modern Public Folders

Despite rumors of their demise, public folders are alive and well, and, in some ways, they're better in Exchange Server 2013 and Exchange Server 2016 than they ever have been.

In Exchange Server 2013, Microsoft changed the public folder architecture, branding them as "modern public folders." This change enabled Microsoft and those implementing Exchange Server 2013 and Exchange Server 2016 to easily support and scale the infrastructure, overcoming the challenges and limits from previous editions.

MODERN PUBLIC FOLDERS AND EXCHANGE SERVER 2016

Before Exchange Server 2013, the public folder database stored public folders. In addition, public folders used a separate replication architecture known as *PF replication*.

To scale and simplify the public folder architecture, Microsoft decided to move away from the legacy public folder database and public folder replication. In Exchange 2013 and Exchange Server 2016, public folders are stored in a special type of mailbox called a *public folder mailbox*, but in essence those public folder mailboxes are normal mailboxes and Exchange Server treats them as it does users' mailboxes.

> Because mailboxes now store public folders, public folder replication is no longer based on a multi-master model. The database availability group (DAG) replicates public folder mailboxes and their contents as it does any other mailbox in the organization. Therefore, there is no need to manage and troubleshoot public folders separately or use different procedures to troubleshoot public folder replication.

In Exchange Server 2016, as we explained, mailboxes store public folders and mailboxes are hosted on a mailbox database. End users do not see any difference; they use public folders the same way they used them in previous versions of Exchange Server. What has changed is how public folders are stored and replicated.

To create a public folder, first you need to create a public folder mailbox that will host the public folder's hierarchy and content. There can be only one primary hierarchy in an organization. The primary hierarchy is writable, and the secondary hierarchy copies are read-only. The primary hierarchy mailbox is the first public folder mailbox created in the Exchange Server organization, although the hierarchy can be replicated to every public folder mailbox.

The primary hierarchy holds the public-folder tree hierarchy and folder structure, which helps identify permissions on the folders and the parents and children of that folder.

When users connect, they connect to their home hierarchy, which contains a copy of the primary hierarchy (in read-only format if they are not connecting to the primary hierarchy), and they access public folder contents located on a mailbox hosting the contents in their site via their local client access services. If they are accessing content that resides in a different public folder mailbox, the client access services will connect the user to that public folder mailbox directly, even if the content is remote or on a different site, since there is no local copy of this content.

Modern Public Folders and Replication

Modern public folders do not use public folder replication as previous Exchange Server versions did; because public folders are stored in mailboxes, the DAG must replicate the mailboxes. However, there is a mentality shift here; there is only one writable copy of the contents at any time. Contents in every public folder mailbox are not writable as they were previously.

From a high-availability point of view, public folder mailboxes are treated as normal mailboxes; they are replicated via the database continuous replication that runs on Exchange servers that are members of the DAG. In case of failure, the passive copy of the mailbox database that holds the public folder mailbox in the DAG will take ownership and serve the users. We will explore in detail the high-availability considerations for modern public folders later in this chapter.

If there are no changes to the hierarchy, the hierarchy will be replicated to every public folder mailbox every 24 hours. If there is a change to the hierarchy, the replication is triggered immediately via the incremental-change synchronization process, which helps monitor the mailbox contents. When users are connected to content mailboxes, the synchronization occurs every 15 minutes. If the node hosting the hierarchy is part of a DAG, it will fail over to the database passive copy within the DAG should the mailbox database with the public-folder primary hierarchy fail.

Modern Public Folder Limitations and Considerations

If you have been using public folders for years, you are probably already aware of their limitations. However, there are new considerations for modern public folders:

- The maximum recommended mailbox size is 100 GB, and the maximum recommended mailbox database size is 2 TB. You might need to consider splitting your public folder into multiple public folder mailboxes, keeping in mind limits of 100 public folder mailboxes and 2,000 concurrent users per public folder mailbox. End users will see the same folder structure regardless of how the public folders are stored.

- The total number of public folders in a hierarchy is limited to 1 million, and the folder depth is limited to 300.

- The maximum individual public folder size is 10 GB, and the maximum number of messages per public folder is 1 million.

- There is no more public folder replication; therefore, public folder replication does not replicate contents independently. Mailbox database replication in DAG replicates public folder mailboxes. There is only one writable copy of the content, and users must connect to this copy to update that content.

- You must use Outlook 2010 or later to access modern public folders on Exchange Server 2016.

- Users cannot delete public folders from Outlook on the web, but they can perform any other operation.

- You cannot apply retention policies to public folder mailboxes.

Moving Public Folders to Exchange Server 2016

If you are migrating from Exchange Server 2010 to Exchange Server 2016 and you are planning to continue to use public folders, you will need to download public folder migration scripts from the following URL: `https://www.microsoft.com/en-us/download/details.aspx?id=38407`. Next, you will need to extract the public folder statistics via `Export-PublicFolderStatistics .ps1`, create a mapping between public folders and public folder mailboxes, and create a migration request to move the public folders, as detailed in these steps:

1. To document the current public folder hierarchy, run the following command from your Exchange Server 2010 server to export the public folder structure to CSV:

    ```
    Get-PublicFolder -Recurse | Export-CliXML C:\PFMigration\EX2010_PFHierarchy.xml
    ```

2. To document the current folders' sizes, items, and owners, run the following command from your Exchange Server 2010 server:

    ```
    Get-PublicFolderStatistics | Export-CliXML C:\PFMigration\EX2010_PFStatistics
    .xml
    ```

3. To document the current public folder permissions, run the following command from your Exchange Server 2010 server:

```
Get-PublicFolder -Recurse | Get-PublicFolderClientPermission | Select-Object
Identity,User -ExpandProperty AccessRights | Export-CliXML C:\PFMigration\
EX2010_PFPermissions.xml
```

4. Next, you should locate and rename public folders that contain a backslash (\) in the name, because a backslash in the name during the migration process will cause public folders to be created in the parent public folder.

   a. To locate the public folders that contain a backslash in the name, run the following command on the Exchange Server 2010 server:

   ```
   Get-PublicFolderStatistics -ResultSize Unlimited | Where {$_.Name -like
   "*\*"} | Format-List Name, Identity
   ```

   b. If the previous command returns public folders that contain a backslash in their names, rename them by running the following command on the Exchange Server 2010 server:

   ```
   Set-PublicFolder -Identity <public folder identity> -Name <new public
   folder name>
   ```

5. Now you should generate a CSV file that will map the folder name to the folder size for each migrated public folder. The CSV file will contain two columns, FolderName and FolderSize, where FolderSize numbers will represent bytes. In order to generate the CSV file, run the following script on the Exchange Server 2010 server:

   ```
   .\Export-PublicFolderStatistics.ps1  "\\Server\SharedFolder\PFStatistics.csv"
   "EX2010.contoso.com"
   ```

6. Create a folder-to-mailbox mapping using the following script, which imports the file and configures the maximum size of the public folder mailbox to 100 GB. The script will create the Mapping.csv file that you will use in step 7. You can always open the map file and edit the folder-to-mailbox mapping:

   ```
   .\PublicFolderToMailboxMapGenerator.ps1 100000000000 \\Server\SharedFolder\
   PFstatistics.csv \\Server\SharedFolder \EX2016PFmap.csv
   ```

7. Create the public folder mailboxes by running the Create-PublicFolderMailboxesForMigration.ps1 script. This script will create a target mailbox for each mailbox that was generated in the CSV file in step 6 for every mailbox.

   ```
   .\Create-PublicFolderMailboxesForMigration.ps1 -FolderMappingCsv Mapping.csv
   -EstimatedNumberOfConcurrentUsers:<estimate>
   ```

8. On the Exchange Server 2016 server, in the Exchange Management Shell, run the following script to create the pubic folder migration batch:

   ```
   New-MigrationBatch -Name PFMigration -SourcePublicFolderDatabase (Get-
   PublicFolderDatabase -Server EX2010) -CSVData (Get-Content "\\Server\
   SharedFolder\EX2016PFmap.csv " -Encoding Byte)
   ```

9. On the Exchange Server 2016 server, run the following script to kick off the migration:

```
Start-MigrationBatch PublicFolderMigration
```

Once the migration starts, you can use `Get-PublicFolderMigrationRequest` to see how the migration is progressing.

You will know the migration is working when it changes from `Created` to `Syncing` status. Once it reaches `Synced`, that will mean the migration request is completed. Proceed to the next step.

10. To prevent users from accessing the old public folder, on the Exchange Server 2010 server, issue the following command to lock it down. During this time, downtime will be required, since users will not be able to access public folders:

```
Set-OrganizationConfig -PublicFoldersLockedForMigration:$true
```

NOTE   If the migration batch file still displays **PublicFolderMigrationComplete** with status **False** after step 10, restart the Information Store on the Exchange Server 2010 server.

11. At this point, on the Exchange Server 2016 server, you need to run the following command to change the Exchange 2016 deployment type to `Remote`:

```
Set-OrganizationConfig -PublicFoldersEnabled Remote
```

12. Now it is time to complete the public folder migration by running the following command that will cause Exchange to perform a final synchronization between Exchange Server 2010 and Exchange Server 2016 and that will change the status of the migration batch from `Completing` to `Completed`:

```
Complete-MigrationBatch PublicFolderMigration
```

13. To unlock the public folders on the Exchange Server 2016 server, run the following command:

```
Get-Mailbox -PublicFolder | Set-Mailbox -PublicFolder
-IsExcludedFromServingHierarchy $false
```

14. On Exchange Server 2010 server, run the following command, which will mark the public folder migration as complete:

```
Set-OrganizationConfig -PublicFolderMigrationComplete:$true
```

15. As a final step, run the following command on the Exchange Server 2016 server:

```
Set-OrganizationConfig -PublicFoldersEnabled Local
```

Congratulations! Now that you've have completed your public folder migration, it is safe to remove public folders and public folder databases from Exchange Serve 2010.

Now that your public folders are on Exchange Server 2016, we'll show how you can manage them.

Managing Public Folder Mailboxes

In the previous section, we discussed the process of creating public folder mailboxes, but here we will discuss how to create them from the Exchange Administration Center (EAC) and control their properties.

You can create a dedicated public folder mailbox for every folder or group of folders you want, but keep in mind the public folder mailbox limits mentioned earlier in this chapter. As with other public folder changes, this will not affect end users' experience; they will still see the public folders in the hierarchy you specified.

You can use the EAC or PowerShell to create public folders. To create a public folder mailbox from the EAC, open the EAC, browse to Public Folder Mailboxes, and click the + (Add) sign to open the Public Folder Mailbox window (see Figure 17.1 and Figure 17.2).

If this is your first public folder mailbox, it will contain the primary hierarchy, as shown in Figure 17.3. Keep in mind that you cannot create a primary hierarchy mailbox when you are migrating from Exchange Server 2010 because it must be created with the HoldForMigration status.

To edit the public folder, click the Edit button, which opens the public folder mailbox's properties. On the General page, shown in Figure 17.4, you can rename the mailbox and view its organizational unit and the mailbox database that hosts that mailbox.

FIGURE 17.1
The Public Folder
Mailboxes screen

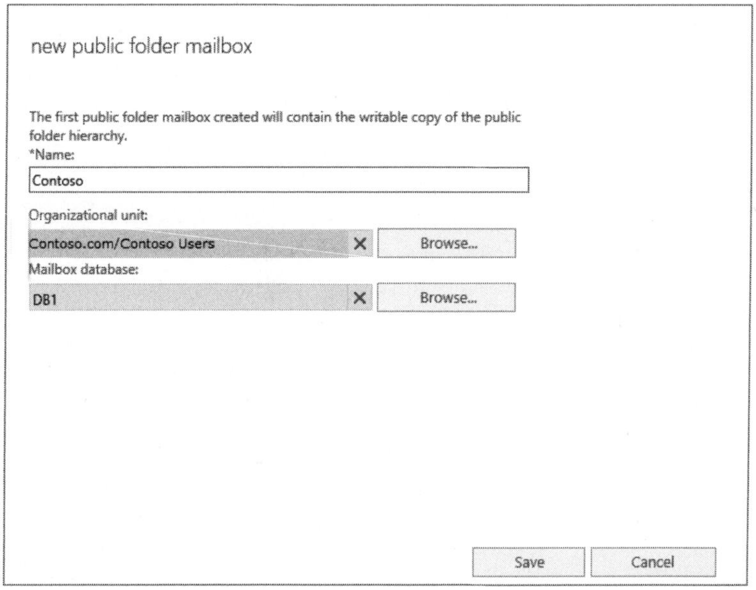

FIGURE 17.2
Creating a new
public folder
mailbox

new public folder mailbox

The first public folder mailbox created will contain the writable copy of the public folder hierarchy.
*Name:

Contoso

Organizational unit:

Contoso.com/Contoso Users ✕   Browse...

Mailbox database:

DB1 ✕   Browse...

Save   Cancel

FIGURE 17.3
Primary hierarchy
public folder mailbox

Enterprise   Office 365   Administrator ▾ ? ▾

Exchange admin center

recipients

permissions   public folders   public folder mailboxes

compliance management

organization   + ✎ 🗑 ⟳

protection   NAME   ▲ CONTAINS

mail flow   Contoso   Primary Hierarchy

mobile

public folders

unified messaging

servers

hybrid

tools

1 selected of 1 total

FIGURE 17.4
Public Folder
Mailbox properties

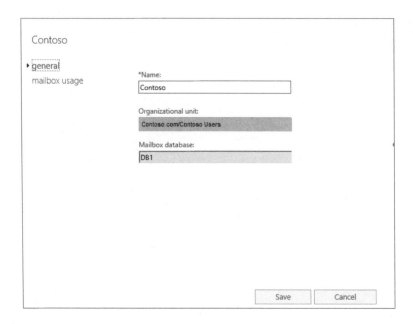

The Mailbox Usage page displays the mailbox size limit and how much it consumes, and it defines the mailbox limits, including the following:

◆ Issue Warning at (MB): Defines when the public folder users will receive a warning when it reaches a certain size

◆ Prohibit Post at (MB): Defines a size at which users will not be able to post to the public folder

◆ Maximum Item Size (MB): Defines the maximum size of items that can be sent to that public folder

You can set this configuration via PowerShell. The following cmdlets are used to create and manage a public folder mailbox:

New-Mailbox -PublicFolder   Creates a new public folder mailbox

Set-Mailbox -PublicFolder   Sets the properties of a public folder mailbox

Get-Mailbox -PublicFolder   Retrieves a list of public folder mailboxes and their properties

Remove-Mailbox -PublicFolder   Deletes a public folder mailbox

Managing Public Folders

Now that you have created a public folder mailbox, let's look at creating the public folders within the public folder mailbox using the EAC.

To add a folder to the public folder mailbox, navigate to the public folders and click the + (Add) sign to add a public folder to the root. The New Public Folder screen will open, as shown in Figure 17.5. You use the New Public Folder screen to fill in two attributes of the public folder—the name of the public folder, and the path of the public folder should it be nested in a public folder hierarchy.

FIGURE 17.5

Adding a new public folder

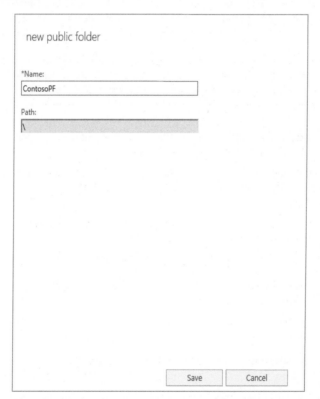

new public folder

*Name:

ContosoPF

Path:

\

Save   Cancel

To mail-enable the public folder, which will allow users to post to that public folder via email, click the Enable link under the Mail Settings section on the right side of the EAC. This will launch a wizard, which will ask if you are sure you want to enable the public folder. Click Yes to enable the public folder for emails. The email address will be taken from the name of the public folder and the default email address policy for the organization. If you have created a public folder and given it a name that includes a space, the space will be removed when the folder's email address is created. Given that we started with a public folder named Sales, and our default email address domain is contoso.com, we can now send email to this folder from outside the organization by addressing mail to sales@contoso.com after the email address has been enabled.

PUBLIC FOLDER PROPERTIES

The default permissions on a folder deny anonymous users to contribute to a folder. The permissions can be viewed by selecting the Manage button beneath the Folder Permissions section of the Details pane in the EAC, or by using the EMS to run the Get-PublicFolderClientPermission cmdlet. To look at the client permissions on a folder called Sales, you would run the following cmdlet:

```
Get-PublicFolderClientPermission "\Sales"
```

In this example, the path is listed as "\Sales", indicating that the folder was created at the root of the public folder mailbox. If there were a parent folder named Departments in which the Sales folder was nested, the path would be "\Departments\Sales".

To view the public folder's properties, click the Edit icon to open the public folder's properties page, which is divided into several subpages:

General Displays the public folder's general information such as name, item count, and the database hosting the public folder mailbox that hosts the public folder, as shown in Figure 17.6.

Statistics Displays the item counts, deleted items, total items sizes, and the like. Figure 17.7 shows the Statistics properties page.

Limits Sets the public folder limits, including the following (see Figure 17.8):

- **Issue Warning At (MB):** Defines when the public folder users will receive a warning about the folder reaching a certain size.

- **Prohibit Post At (MB):** Defines a size at which users will not be able to post to the public folder.

- **Maximum Item Size (MB):** Defines the maximum size for items sent to that public folder.

- **Deleted Item Retention:** Allows you to use the global organization's settings or specify the maximum number of days deleted items are kept; by default, it is five days.

- **Age Limits:** Allows you to use the global organization settings and to instruct the database to delete any item in any folder on this database that exceeds the specified age limit. This is useful if you want to delete or age out older content, but it is probably better to apply this property on a folder-by-folder basis.

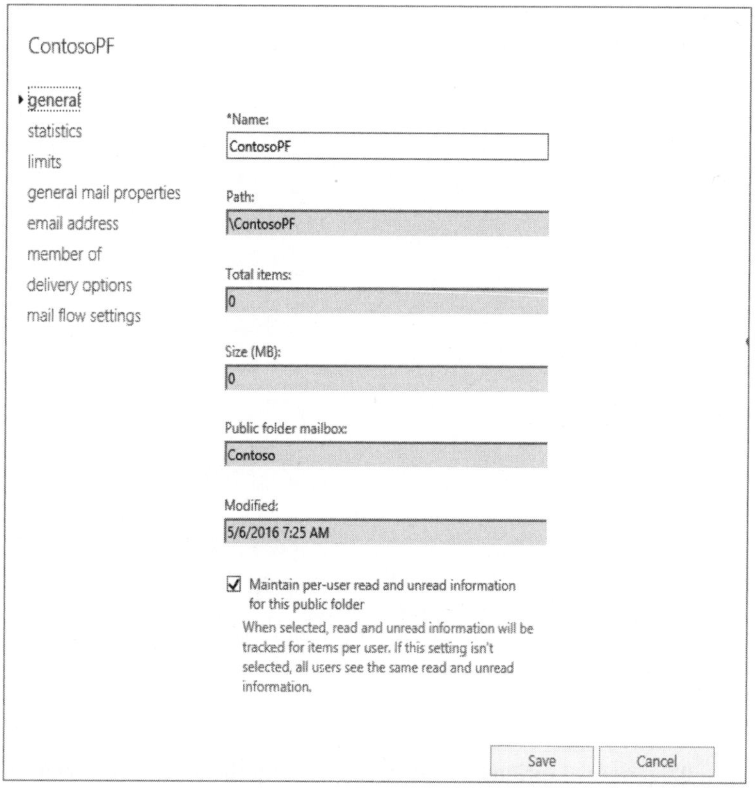

FIGURE 17.6

The Public folder's General properties page

General Mail Properties Defines the various general properties, including alias and display name, in the global address list (GAL). You can change them to meet your requirements and how you want the public folder to be displayed in the GAL. You can also hide the public folder from the GAL if necessary or define custom attributes that will be used in your organization.

Email Address Lets you change the public folder's email address or add additional email addresses. Each email address can be used by users (internally or externally) to post to the public folder. By default, the email address will be updated based on the email address policy defined in the organization; however, you can disable that to define the email address(es) for that public folder.

Member Of Shows the distribution lists (DLs) in which this public folder is a member. Public folder distribution groups are a very cool way to archive DL conversations.

FIGURE 17.7
The Public folder's
Statistics properties
page

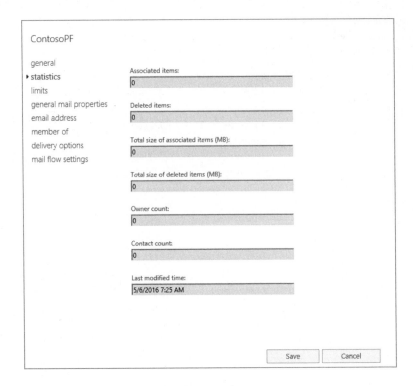

Delivery Options   Allows you to grant the following permissions:

◆ Send As: Allows you to grant a user or a group the permissions to send email as that
public folder.

◆ Send on Behalf: Allows you to grant send-on-behalf permissions to a user or group.

◆ Forward To: Lets you forward all the emails sent or received via this public folder to
another DL, mailbox, or public folder.

Additionally, you can define the maximum sending and receiving message sizes in MB, and
you can define whether this public folder will receive emails from all senders or from specific
senders or groups. You can also specify specific senders who will be rejected.

Message Flow Settings Allows you to manage the following settings (see Figure 17.9):

◆ Message Size Restrictions for Maximum Sending Message Size and Maximum Receive Message Size

◆ Message Delivery Restrictions (Accept), defining whether to accept messages from All Senders or only senders listed in the list gathered from the global address list

◆ Message Delivery Restrictions (Reject), defining whether to reject message from All Senders, or only senders listed in the list gathered from the global address list

The Message Delivery Restrictions (Accept) option allows you to require that users be authenticated before their messages will be accepted by the public folder.

FIGURE 17.8
The Public folder's Limits properties page

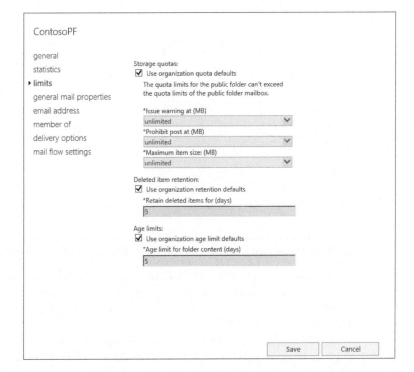

FIGURE 17.9
Mail flow settings

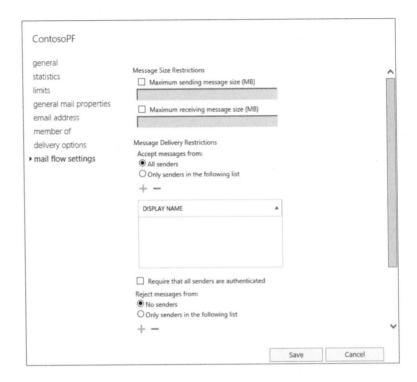

All of the public folder properties can be managed from the Exchange Management Shell.

WHEN PUBLIC FOLDERS PROVIDE EASY BUSINESS SOLUTIONS

Public folders have been around for a while. Organizations of various sizes have been using them to provide easy solutions to sometimes complex problems. Sometimes, it seems that using a public folder is truly the easiest solution to a business requirement. Maybe that is the secret to the longevity of this technology.

The simplest aspect of public folders—and one that some companies forget to implement—is the ability to send and receive mail on a public folder. You can mail-enable a public folder and then configure it to receive emails. This solution is typically used for public folders that must receive information from external senders or users who do not use a client application that supports public folder access.

For example, we encountered a company that needed a solution for collecting resumes for job postings. The company needed to be able to accept resumes from external individuals applying for positions. The specific need was for external individuals to be able to send an email by using the external email address. The solution was easy. All we did was mail-enable a public folder, thereby converting the folder into an email recipient. Whenever an email came into the public folder, internal HR employees responsible for selecting applicants could review the attached resume.

A user must have permissions to post to the folder to successfully send a message to the folder's email address. If you are setting up a mail-enabled public folder that will receive email from outside your organization, make sure that anonymous users have Contributor permissions to the public folder. The Contributor role contains two rights: the right to post to a folder and the right to see the folder in a folder list.

Suppose we select a folder called Sales in the List View pane and then click the Manage Folder Permissions task from the Details pane. This will open the Public Folder Permissions screen and will allow us to add/remove user permissions based on different levels of permissions, as shown in Figure 17.10.

FIGURE 17.10
Opening the folder permissions

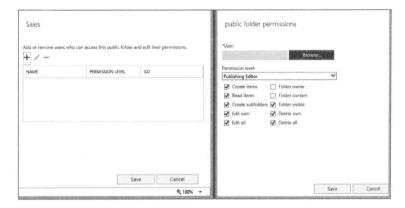

The client permissions in Exchange Server 2016 are the same as in the previous versions (Owner, Contributor, Editor, and so on). In our example, we will assign a user the Owner permissions on the Sales folder.

DEFINING THE DEFAULT PUBLIC FOLDER SERVER

In previous versions of Exchange Server, you had to specify the default public folder database for users by setting the default public folder on the user's mailbox database. In Exchange Server 2016, this is no longer required because Exchange Server calculates the public folder mailbox to be accessed based on the site this user belongs to and the hierarchy information.

Defining Public Folder Administrators

In a small- or medium-sized organization, one or two administrators are responsible for all Exchange Server administrative tasks, including managing the public folders. However, in very large organizations, you may need to delegate the public folder administration tasks to a different person or group. Exchange Server 2016 automatically creates a group in the Microsoft Exchange Security Groups OU called Public Folder Management. Members of this group can manage the Exchange Server public folder attributes and perform public folder operations, including these tasks:

- Creating public folders
- Creating top-level public folders
- Modifying public folder permissions
- Modifying public folder administrative permissions
- Modifying public folder properties, such as content expiration times, storage limits, and deleted item retention time
- Modifying public folder replica lists
- Mounting and dismounting public folder databases
- Mail-enabling/disabling public folders

Using the Exchange Management Shell to Manage Public Folders

Exchange Server 2016 includes the Exchange Management Shell (EMS) and the ability to manage public folders from the command line. Because there have been many changes to the way public folders can be implemented in Exchange 2016, the EMS has been updated as well to reflect those changes.

PERFORMING GENERAL PUBLIC FOLDER TASKS

These cmdlets apply to the entire public folder hierarchy at once and provide broad control of your public folder infrastructure:

Get-PublicFolderStatistics This cmdlet provides a detailed set of statistics about the public folder hierarchy on a given server:

```
Get-PublicFolderStatistics -Server "MBX01"
```

If the -Server parameter is not specified, the cmdlet will default to displaying the statistics on the local server.

Suspend-PublicFolderMigrationRequest This cmdlet suspends all public folder content migration. You may want to suspend public folder migration if, for example, a huge amount of network traffic occurs or you want to pause it during working hours.

Resume-PublicFolderMigrationRequest This cmdlet reenables all public folder content migration from previous versions if it has been suspended.

New-PublicFolderMoveRequest This cmdlet creates a new public folder move request, and moves public folders from one public folder mailbox to another. You must specify the public folders you want to move, as well as the public folder mailbox that is the destination, as in this example:

```
New-PublicFolderMoveRequest -Folders \Departments\Sales -TargetMailbox
ManagedPublicFolders -Name \PublicFolderMove
```

Suspend-PublicFolderMoveRequest This cmdlet suspends the public folder move from one mailbox to another. As move requests can be given names, you can reference the name in the cmdlet. If you have not given the original move request a name, it is referred to as \PublicFolderMove, as referenced in the example:

```
Suspend-PublicFolderMoveRequest –Identity \PublicFolderMove
```

Resume-PublicFolderMoveRequest This cmdlet resumes the public folder move from one mailbox to another mailbox. Here's an example:

```
Resume-PublicFolderMoveRequest –Identity \PFMoveRequest1
```

You may want to move a specific public folder to another mailbox to reduce the size of the original mailbox or move it to another mailbox database.

MANIPULATING INDIVIDUAL PUBLIC FOLDERS

These cmdlets are designed to work with a specific public folder:

Get-PublicFolder This cmdlet retrieves the properties for the specified public folder:

```
Get-PublicFolder -Identity "\Jobs\Posted" -Server "MBX01"
```

If you don't name a public folder by specifying a value for the -Identity property, it will default to the root public folder.

By default, the Get-PublicFolder cmdlet returns the values for only a single folder. The -Recurse switch changes the behavior to report on all subfolders as well:

```
Get-PublicFolder -Identity "\Jobs\Posted" -Server "MBX01" -Recurse
```

If you want to see system folders, you'll need to set the -Identity property to a value beginning with the string \NON_IPM_SUBTREE:

```
Get-PublicFolder -Identity \NON_IPM_SUBTREE –Recurse
```

New-PublicFolder This cmdlet creates a new public folder. The -Path property is required and provides the name and location of the new public folder:

```
New-PublicFolder -Name New -Path "\Jobs" -Server "MBX01"
```

Remove-PublicFolder This cmdlet deletes a public folder. The -Path property is required and provides the name and location of the public folder to be deleted:

```
Remove-PublicFolder -Path "\Jobs\Old" -Server "MBX01"
```

By default, the Remove-PublicFolder cmdlet removes only the named public folder. The -Recurse switch will delete all subfolders as well, which is handy for removing an entire group of folders at once.

Set-PublicFolder This cmdlet allows you to set most of the properties for the named public folder, such as limits, replicas, replication schedules, and more:

```
Set-PublicFolder -Identity "\Jobs\Posted" -Server "MBX01"
```

You cannot use the Set-PublicFolder cmdlet to mail-enable a public folder or to change its mail-related attributes. See the next section, "Manipulating Public Folder Mail Attributes," for the cmdlets to use for these tasks.

Update-PublicFolderMailbox This cmdlet starts the hierarchy-synchronization process for the named public folder mailbox. The -Identity property is required:

```
Update-PublicFolderMailbox -Identity "PF Mailbox2"
```

MANIPULATING PUBLIC FOLDER MAIL ATTRIBUTES

These cmdlets are designed to work with a specific public folder, mail-enable it, and modify the attributes it receives when it is mail-enabled:

Enable-MailPublicFolder This cmdlet renders an existing public folder mail-enabled. The optional -HiddenFromAddressListsEnabled switch allows you to hide the folder from your address lists:

```
Enable-MailPublicFolder -Identity "\Jobs\New"
-HiddenFromAddressListsEnabled $true -Server "MBX01"
```

Disable-MailPublicFolder This cmdlet renders an existing mail-enabled public folder mail-disabled:

```
Disable-MailPublicFolder -Identity "\Jobs\New"
```

You set the mail-related attributes separately using the Set-MailPublicFolder cmdlet.

Get-MailPublicFolder This cmdlet retrieves the mail-related properties for the specified public folder:

```
Get-MailPublicFolder -Identity "\Jobs\Old" -Server "MBX01"
```

If you don't name a public folder by specifying a value for the -Identity property, it will default to the root public folder.

Set-MailPublicFolder This cmdlet allows you to set the mail-related properties for the named public folder, such as an alias, email addresses, send and receive sizes, permitted and prohibited senders, and so on:

```
Set-MailPublicFolder -Identity "\Jobs\Posted" -Alias PostedJobs
-PrimarySmtpAddress jobs@contoso.com
```

Keep in mind that to be able to modify the mail-related attributes for a public folder, you must first mail-enable it using the Enable-MailPublicFolder cmdlet.

MANAGING PUBLIC FOLDER MAILBOXES

These cmdlets allow you to manage the public folder mailbox:

Get-mailbox -PublicFolder This cmdlet provides the functionality used by the EAC and allows you to view the properties of existing public folder databases:

```
Get-Mailbox -Publicfolder -Server "MBX01"
```

This cmdlet takes one of two parameters: -Identity or -Server. The parameters are not compatible with each other. Use only one of them to narrow your selection.

New-mailbox -PublicFolder This cmdlet allows you to create a new public folder mailbox.

```
New-Mailbox -Publicfolder -Name "PF MB1"
```

Remove-Mailbox -publicfolder This cmdlet deletes an existing public folder mailbox from the active configuration of the server:

```
Remove-Mailbox -PublicFolder -Identity "PF Mailbox2"
```

If this mailbox is a hierarchy mailbox and there are other mailboxes below it in the hierarchy, you will have to delete the other mailboxes first and then delete the primary hierarchy mailbox.

MANAGING PUBLIC FOLDER PERMISSIONS

These cmdlets allow you to modify and monitor the permissions on your public folders. You can control the client permissions as well as the administrative permissions through EMS. The Exchange Server 2016 documentation contains the list of specific permissions you can apply.

Add-PublicFolderClientPermission   This cmdlet lets you add a client permission entry to a given public folder. You can specify a single access right or list multiple rights at once using the syntax shown here:

```
Add-PublicFolderClientPermission -User John.Doe -Identity "\Jobs\Posted"
-AccessRights CreateItems, DeleteItems
```

Get-PublicFolderClientPermission   This cmdlet lets you view the client permission entries on a given public folder:

```
Get-PublicFolderClientPermission  -Identity "\Jobs\Posted"
```

Remove-PublicFolderClientPermission   This cmdlet lets you remove a client permission entry from a given public folder:

```
Remove-PublicFolderClientPermission -User John.Doe -Identity "\Jobs\Posted"
-AccessRights CreateItems
```

USING ADDITIONAL SCRIPTS FOR COMPLICATED TASKS

Although the cmdlets described in the preceding sections are certainly great for single-folder operations, performing common operations on entire groups of folders starts getting sticky. Because most of us aren't scripting gurus, Exchange Server 2016 provides some example EMS scripts that allow you to perform more complicated server and management tasks that affect groups of folders:

- ◆ `AddUsersToPFRecursive.ps1` allows you to grant user permissions to a folder and all folders beneath it.

- ◆ `Export-MailPublicFoldersForMigration.ps1` exports all mail-enabled public folders to an XML file.

- ◆ `Export-PublicFolderStatistics.ps1` generates a CSV file with public folder sizes.

- ◆ `Import-MailPublicFoldersForMigration.ps1` imports a list of mail-enabled public folders from the XML file.

- ◆ `Merge-PublicFolderMailbox.ps1` merges the content of a given public folder with the destination public folder mailbox.

- ◆ `Move-PublicfolderBranch.ps1` moves a branch public folder and all its subfolders to another mailbox.

- ◆ `PublicFolderToMailboxMapGenerator.ps1` creates a mapping between branch public folders and mailboxes; we used this script in the migration steps earlier in the "Moving Public Folders to Exchange Server 2016" section.

◆ `RemoveUserFromPFRecursive.ps1` removes the given user's access permissions from the given public folder and all its subfolders.

◆ `ReplaceUserPermissionOnPFRecursive.ps1` replaces existing user permissions with a new set of permissions for the folder provided as well as all folders beneath that folder when you run the script.

◆ `ReplaceUserWithUserOnPFRecursive.ps1` copies one user's access permissions on a given public folder and all its subfolders to a second user while retaining permissions for the first user.

You can find these scripts in the Scripts subfolder of the Exchange Server 2016 installation folder, which is by default located on $Drive$:`\Program Files\Microsoft\Exchange Server\ v15\Scripts`, where $Drive$ represents the logical disk where Exchange binaries are installed. The Scripts folder location may also be displayed using the $exscripts$ variable in Exchange Management Shell. Note that with the default Windows PowerShell configuration, you just can't click these scripts and run them; you must invoke them from within the EMS, usually by navigating to the folder and calling them explicitly.

Using Outlook to Create a Public Folder

Mailbox-enabled users can also create Exchange Server public folders in their email clients. Here are the steps for doing so in Outlook:

1. Open Outlook and make sure the folder list is displayed.

2. Double-click Public Folders in the folder list, or click the + (Add) icon just in front of Public Folders. Notice that the + (Add) icon becomes a – (Minus) icon when a folder is expanded to show the folders within it.

   You've now expanded the top-level folder for public folders, which contains two subfolders: Favorites and All Public Folders.

3. Expand the All Public Folders folder. If your organization uses public folders, you probably have many subfolders listed here.

4. Right-click All Public Folders, select a child folder, and select New Folder from the menu that pops up. This brings up the Create New Folder dialog box (see Figure 17.11).

5. Enter a name for the folder. We've given ours the name Sales because it will be a new Sales unit and will require a dedicated public folder.

   Note that the folder will hold two different kinds of items:

   ◆ Email items that are messages.

   ◆ Posted items that contain a subject and text. You can post an item in a folder designed to hold posts without having to deal with messaging attributes, such as to whom the item is sent. To post an item, click the down arrow near the New icon on the main Outlook window, and select Post In This Folder from the drop-down menu.

6. When you've finished creating your folder, click OK.

   If you're told that you don't have sufficient permissions to create the folder, you need to have those permissions assigned using one of the other Exchange Server public folder management tools. If you have Exchange Server administrative permissions, you can make this change yourself.

The new public folder now shows up under the All Public Folders hierarchy. If you can't see the full name of your new folder, make the Folder List pane a little wider.

FIGURE 17.11
Creating a new folder

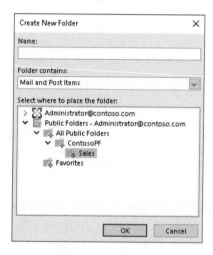

7. To set additional properties for your folder, right-click your new folder and select Properties from the context menu.

The properties dialog box for the Sales folder is shown in Figure 17.12.

FIGURE 17.12
The Outlook client's properties dialog box for a public folder

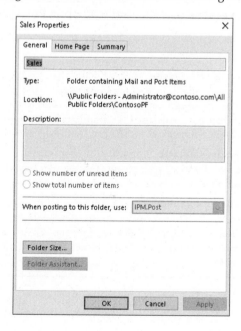

Among other things, mailbox owners use a public folder's properties dialog box to do the following:

◆ Add a description for other mailbox owners who access the folder.

◆ Make the folder available on the Internet.

◆ Set up a default view of the folder, including grouping by such things as the subject or sender.

◆ Set up administrative rules on folder characteristics, access, and such.

◆ Set permissions for using the folder.

If your Exchange Server organization has a large number of public folders, you can drag the ones that you use a lot to your Favorites subfolder. This makes them easier to find. Folders in the Favorites folder are also the only ones that are available when you work offline without a connection to your Exchange server. Only public folders that are in a user's Favorites folder, and that have been selected by the user, will be downloaded when working in Local Cache mode.

Understanding the Public Folder Hierarchy

A public folder hierarchy, or public folder tree, is a list of public folders and their subfolders that are stored in the default public folder database on the Exchange servers in an Exchange Server organization. The hierarchy also includes the name of the server on which a copy of each folder resides. The hierarchy does not contain any of the actual items in your various public folders. There is one organization-wide public folder hierarchy object.

THE THREE PIECES OF THE PUBLIC FOLDER PUZZLE

The public folder hierarchy can be confusing, so here's an overview of the objects and components that make up public folders.

Public Folder Hierarchy As outlined earlier, the hierarchy is essentially the list of public folder names available in your organization. This list is viewed from the Exchange Server 2016 Exchange Admin Center (EAC) or from the Outlook client when viewing all public folders. When you are delegating administrative permissions over Exchange Server public folders, the hierarchy is the target of the permissions.

Public Folder Content These are the items that are contained in the folder. These items could be files, emails, posts, or any other content type that Outlook supports. When you are delegating client permissions to public folders, the content is the target of the permissions.

Public Folder Recipient Object When a public folder is mail-enabled, a recipient object is created for the folder. Because the recipient must be added to the Exchange Server address lists, this object is created in Active Directory. When you delegate recipient management permissions over Exchange Server objects, the permissions will apply to a public folder recipient object.

Exploring Public Folder High Availability

As we stated earlier, there is no specific public folder replication architecture in Exchange Server 2016. Public folder high availability shifted from public folder replication to mailbox database replication in the DAG, as you have seen. Public folders are hosted in mailboxes, which are hosted in mailbox databases. Therefore, they are treated as any other mailbox and replicated via mailbox database replication running on the servers that are members of the DAG architecture, with no special configuration or separate administration needed.

This could be challenging when migrating from the existing public folder implementations with multiple geographical locations to Exchange Server 2016. In Exchange Server 2010 and previous versions, people were redirected to their local replica, where they could perform different operations (read, write, and delete), and changes were synchronized later according to the synchronization schedule. Because there is only one writable replica in modern public folders, user traffic might traverse the WAN in an undesired manner to access the writable contents. Therefore, you need to pay close attention when moving public folders from Exchange Server 2010 to Exchange Server 2016 and reconsider your public folder structure.

Here are some factors to consider when you're planning Exchange Server 2016 public folder for high availability:

♦ The size of your public folder has impacts on the total size of the database and whether it will be hosted on a shared database with other mailboxes or on a separate database replicated to designated mailbox servers and whether you will use the same DAG for mailboxes or a different DAG.

♦ Based on the new architecture, there is only a single writable instance of the public folder. Mailboxes are replicated via DAG, and if a mailbox or a mailbox database fails, one of the passive copies becomes active on another member of the DAG.

♦ Because there is only a single writable instance of the public folder, the write operations are performed on a single mailbox hosted on a designated server; the write operation is single-master (not multimaster as it was previously). If you were distributing your mailbox contents geographically before, this will no longer work. Users might have to cross the WAN to access their contents, so you might need to reconsider your public folder mailbox architecture and how users will access the public folders.

♦ You need to carefully plan for DAG failover. Failing over a mailbox database will have a great effect on users' access to public folders.

♦ You no longer add public folder replicas; you add a replica of the mailbox database that hosts the public folder mailbox. You need to plan this as part of your DAG deployment strategy and allocate space accordingly.

⊕ **Real World Scenario**

HIGH AVAILABILITY—A PRACTICAL EXAMPLE

A multinational company has three branches in the United States, the United Kingdom, and Australia. The company currently has three datacenters distributed among the branches running Exchange Server 2010 SP3 RU12.

The sales team heavily uses public folders across the three branches; they use public folders to share weekly and monthly reports, as well as other information. The administrators configured one top-level Sales public folder and three subfolders—one for each branch underneath it. They also configured a single Exchange Server public folder database that holds a replica of the three folders in each site; therefore, users from each site access the local replica and can see the three folders. They can post as they wish in collaboration with the other teams. Data in the public folders is replicated via public folder replication after working hours.

When designing the migration to Exchange Server 2016, IT team decided to create three public folder mailboxes, each hosting a single public folder mailbox and each public folder mailbox holding a public folder. After reviewing that design, they realized that there will be some impact on the network because there is a single writable copy of a public folder; users will see the data, but they must cross the WAN when they access the other countries' sales folders.

For example, when the U.S. team works with the Australian team on a new lead, the U.S. team can post to the Australia public folder in their replica, and vice versa. In the new system, there is no local replica, so the U.S. team will have to cross the WAN to post to the Australia Sales public folder.

For the DAG design, they decided to create two mailbox database copies, one local and one in the closest datacenter. Therefore, the U.S. public folder mailbox database will have two copies—one local and one in the U.K., and vice versa. The Australia public-folder mailbox database will have two copies—one local and one in the U.K.

Managing Public Folder Permissions

You can manage folder permissions in one of two ways. The simplest is just to use Outlook. Navigate to the public folder, right-click to display its properties, and select the Summary tab (shown in Figure 17.13).

Of course, when you are using Outlook, your user account must be one of the owners of the folder. Otherwise, the Permissions properties page will not be displayed. The Permissions properties page shows the permissions that the groups (mail-enabled groups) or users have to the folder.

You can use the Permissions properties page to assign specific folder access rights to Exchange Server users and distribution groups, who can then work with a public folder using their Outlook client. For emphasis, we'll restate what we just said in a somewhat different form: *You grant public folder access permissions to Exchange Server recipients, not to Active Directory users and groups.* Once access to a public folder is granted, Exchange Server recipients access the folder in their Outlook client while connected to their mailbox.

FIGURE 17.13
Managing public
folder permissions
via Outlook

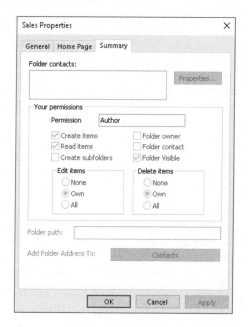

For a graphic reinforcement of this point, click Add +, on the Public Folder Permissions page, to start adding a new user or group who will have access to this public folder. This action opens a dialog box that looks very much like the Outlook address book that you use to select message recipients.

If a user has the correct permissions on a public folder, that user can change access permissions on the folder for other users. Permissions on a public folder can be modified only from within the Outlook client using the Permissions properties page for a public folder.

There is a group named Default that includes all Exchange Server recipients not separately added to the Name List box. When the folder is created, this group is automatically given the default role of Author. Authors can edit and delete only their own folder items, but they do not own the folder and cannot create subfolders.

To make assigning permissions easier, Microsoft has created predefined roles. Each role has a specific combination of permissions to the folder. The roles are Owner, Publishing Editor, Editor, Publishing Author, Author, Nonediting Author, Reviewer, Contributor, and Custom—each with a different combination of client permissions.

Comparing Public Folders, Site Mailboxes, and Shared Mailboxes

Exchange Server 2016 continues the revamped public-folder architecture that was introduced in Exchange Server 2013. This public folder architecture is scalable for most uses. It also includes another collaboration feature known as site mailboxes, which rely on SharePoint 2013 and SharePoint 2016 to display documents and email in Outlook.

When you design a collaboration solution, you must understand the capabilities and limitations of each option to provide the best solution for your organization. When you want to implement a mailbox that needs to be accessible to a number of users located in the same site, it is hard to decide whether public folders, site mailboxes, or shared mailboxes should be used, but the following points will help you decide:

◆ Public folders provide a great way to share knowledge and archive that knowledge within the organization. For example, they fit well for HR as a method for receiving resumes via email, and they can be used to document conversations between distribution list members or to host a small forum.

◆ Site mailboxes provide a group of users working on a shared pool of resources (documents and emails) with a shared area where related documents and emails are stored in a single location and viewed via Outlook. This setup is perfect for a group of users working on the same project or task. You need to be aware that site mailboxes require SharePoint 2013 and SharePoint 2016, which has its own infrastructure and servers to manage and operate.

◆ Shared mailboxes fit virtual entities such as sales or support, which need to receive shared emails and respond on behalf of the entity.

The Bottom Line

Understand the architectural changes made to public folders. If you're coming new to Exchange Server 2016 or don't have a lot of investment in public folders in your current Exchange Server organization, you will need to learn the modern public folder architecture. Thorough understanding on how modern public folders work will allow you to design an efficient collaboration solution for your organization.

Master It You are the administrator of a distributed messaging environment that runs Exchange Server 2016. You plan to deploy a collaboration solution, and you are currently evaluating public folders as well as site mailboxes and shared mailboxes. You need to identify the potential strengths of this approach and present recommendations to your company's executives. What information should you present?

Manage public folders. You are managing a large distributed Exchange Server infrastructure, and you want to create a hierarchy of public folders to reflect the organizational structure of your enterprise environment. How can you do it in Exchange Server 2016?

Master It Start with the public folder mailbox, and then define the various departments within your folder structure. You can add various nested folders underneath the Departments parent folder, manage the folder structure underneath, and modify the permission structure to reflect the needs of the organization.

Chapter 18

Managing Archiving and Compliance

Since the rise of archiving systems in business more than a decade ago in response to storage concerns on Exchange servers, the technology has gone through some very impressive growth and technological improvements. The need for archiving systems is also growing with increasingly stringent regulations and litigation procedures.

Messaging systems such as Microsoft Exchange Server 2016—Microsoft's latest version of Exchange Server—have also seen their share of changes and improvements in archiving and compliance.

IN THIS CHAPTER, YOU WILL LEARN TO:

◆ Understand the basic principles of email archiving

◆ Ensure your company complies with regulations

◆ Enable Exchange Server 2016 in-place archiving

◆ Use Exchange Server 2016 retention policies

◆ Use Exchange Server 2016 In-Place eDiscovery and Hold

Introduction to Archiving

Over time, archiving products have evolved significantly. They have gone from simple storage-size-reduction software to sophisticated enterprise content-management systems that not only offer storage management for Exchange servers but have moved beyond email to managing file-systems, SharePoint, third-party email and collaboration solutions, and even databases. Don't be intimidated by archiving products; they can resolve many pain points in your organization; in some ways, they can even be seen as an insurance policy.

One of the main things to understand is that the way business communications are handled has drastically changed over the last 20 years or so. In the past, most communications and even most business contracts were transacted using either fax or paper records. Nowadays, more than 90 percent of business communications take place by electronic means—email and instant messaging (IM), for instance—and this number is increasing on an annual basis.

A couple of famous corporate failures in the past have sparked massive lawsuits. Some of the world's most well-known companies and institutions have lost their credibility due to evidence that was brought up through email in different cases. Even some financial institutions and banks have suffered similar fates and have been forced to pay millions in penalties after evidence surfaced from emails about illegal activities performed by their own employees. And the list of these cases goes on, with different companies having gone through public court cases over information in emails. Because of lawsuits/litigations, external compliance investigations, and even internal human resources (HR) investigations, *eDiscovery* (that is, the discovery of electronic information) has become entrenched in current business.

In the United States, all these cases have resulted in the courts deciding that organizations have to retain and be able to recover emails within a "reasonable" time frame and also to prove, when these records are provided, that the emails have not been tampered with and are complete.

To clarify this process, amendments were made to the Federal Rules of Civil Procedure (FRCP). These amended rules went into effect on December 1, 2006, and require that companies create, document, and enforce policies to retain emails or dispose of them as part of their operating procedures. One of the most important parts of the new FRCP rules is that, as mentioned already, organizations must now discover and disclose relevant information and emails within a reasonable time frame, so stalling tactics no longer work.

Archiving systems are used throughout the world in many different scenarios, largely depending on industry and country. Some of the scenarios are as follows:

- Storage management of Exchange Server

- Simple compliance data capture by using journaling

- Complete data capture using journaling and archiving

- EDiscovery and litigation support

- Enterprise content management (beyond just Exchange Server)

Benefits of Archiving

Archiving generally refers to the process of removing data from its primary storage location and moving it to another, cheaper storage location. Archived data is accessed less frequently, compared to the frequency of access for nonarchived data. Archiving systems can be tailored or tweaked for use with specific scenarios.

Retention

These days it is an accepted fact that business email is considered a record or controlled record and that these records need to be archived under either your corporate policy or government regulatory requirements. A defined email-retention policy informs employees as to what email must be archived and for how long. For an email-retention policy to be effective, you have to distribute this policy in written format to all employees. A written retention policy should include several of these details:

Effective Date   This leaves no doubt as to whether the policy is currently in effect or is an old one that should be discarded.

Last Change Date and Changes Made   This information confirms the policy's authenticity and appropriateness because regulations change over time.

Person or Department Responsible for the Policy   This gives employees or their managers someone to contact with questions regarding the policy.

Scope/Coverage   This includes the geographic limits of the policy (if any), affected departments and offices, and a definition of what company information is covered.

Purpose of the Policy/Policy Statement   This can include a company philosophy statement about the business, legal, or regulatory reasons for records retention.

Definitions   This area defines what constitutes business records and applicable exceptions.

Responsibilities   This area covers the following:

- Business units, subsidiaries, and special departments (such as the legal department)
- General employees
- Records-retention coordinators
- Procedures for retention and deletion of email and attachments (if no automated email-archiving system is employed)
- How the emails should be stored
- Instructions on organizations to not use PST as a form for archiving/compliance
- How often those files should be cleaned out
- How duplicate and convenience copies are treated

Consequences   This describes what happens if the policy isn't adhered to.

Appendix A   This appendix should include litigation-hold and stop-destruction policies, including a backup procedure.

Appendix B   Appendix B should include a current list of department records-retention coordinators and contact information.

A manually managed email-retention policy relies on employees understanding and following the policy. The obvious fact is that each employee will interpret the policy a little differently, so in practice organizations will have many different email-retention policies. This fact is the main reason you need to adopt an automated email-archiving solution.

The benefits of automating your email-retention policy are multifold:

Regulatory Compliance   Email retention for some companies' regulatory compliance isn't a choice but a requirement. The only choice is how you meet the requirements: manually or with email-archiving automation. Automating your email-retention policy lowers your overall risk of noncompliance and ensures that you are keeping your email for the required time period.

Legal-Risk Management   When you can show the court that you keep your email-retention policy current and enforce it, you can demonstrate retention intent and that you might not have purposely destroyed information in case of litigation.

Document Retention for Corporate Governance   Businesses rely on the generation, use, and reference of data to make ongoing business decisions. The data the business generates has a value to the business if that data can be used efficiently. An effective retention policy ensures that valuable information is available for some period of time, and an automated email-archiving system allows for quick search and reference.

Discovery

Organizations that have regulatory compliance requirements also use electronic discovery, also known as *eDiscovery*. This refers to the process of finding electronically stored information for litigation reasons and generally isn't restricted to searching for email. While it is very common for emails, including attachments, to be requested as a part of an eDiscovery case, it is almost just as likely for general office productivity documents not specifically involved in email transmissions to also be requested (which means Word and Excel files on your file server and desktops are part of the litigation). Metadata does play an important role in this process and is referred to as *chain of custody*—a verifiable record of who had access to the data and whether the data could have been altered or changed during the eDiscovery process.

Eliminating PST Files

It is our opinion that there are no good reasons to have PST files in a corporate environment other than handing them over to a lawyer for review. Starting to see the trend here? Archiving systems can be your friend, but you will start working closely with your HR and legal people. PST files have become popular because of mailbox quotas, which were implemented to help curb the growth of Exchange Server databases. These easy-to-implement policies were for the longest time the only option an Exchange Server administrator had to gain some sort of control over this growth. Now the problem is that the quotas have a nasty side effect: end users who are unable to find the Delete key on their keyboards are forced to groom their inboxes for old email messages to delete when they hit their mailbox limit.

They then naturally create PST files. In the past, this approach was encouraged by Exchange Server administrators. These files were created either locally on the desktop or laptop or on the file server, where they would take up valuable storage space. PST files use up more storage than if the data were kept in Exchange Server in the first place. We could probably write an entire book on eliminating PST files, but here's the gist: Large mailboxes, together with an archiving feature in Exchange, can be your best allies here, helping you find the PST files and helping you bring them back under control, which ultimately reduces the storage footprint of PST files in your environment.

Reducing Storage Size

Reducing the storage size of production Exchange Server databases was the first reason the practice of archiving systems became popular. In the late 1990s, Standard editions of Exchange Server still had a 16 GB mailbox-store limit, and having a 5 or 10 MB mailbox limit was extremely common. People were looking for other ways to offload content from their mailbox stores, not only to keep database storage limits in line but also to reduce backup times. Smaller backup sizes also mean shorter recovery times, which is something you start to appreciate once you have gone through a full-blown Exchange Server disaster recovery. Archiving systems can offload email to the archiving storage system, while either leaving a shortcut behind to open up the archived email or simply removing the entire message. Doing this can substantially reduce the size of your Exchange Server databases; however, it adds complexity to Exchange management and can affect user experience.

Disaster Recovery

You are probably wondering what disaster recovery has to do with archiving. The whole idea is related to storage management. A substantial amount of the older data stored in Exchange Server databases is never accessed again by end users; however, this data is backed up daily to either tape or disk, and in the event of a disaster this data will also have to be restored. Archiving can help you remove this data from Exchange Server and, therefore, reduce not only the backup time but also the amount of time it would take to recover a database.

Compliance

Compliance makes most people cringe, but you need to understand it. The odds are that your company is subject to some regulation that requires you to retain records. Some industries—especially healthcare and finance—face stricter and more complex rules than others. Regulatory compliance is either already part of your daily Exchange Server life or soon will be. Let's briefly go over some of the current laws that might be applicable to your organization:

Federal Rules of Civil Procedure The Federal Rules of Civil Procedure (FRCP) implemented in 2006 impact how companies retain, store, and produce electronic data, including email for litigation. The rules that most often affect organizations are as follows:

Rules 16 and 26 These rules call for organizations to "give early attention to issues relating to electronic discovery, including the frequently recurring problems of the preservation of the evidence…." This means being ready to discuss a strategy for dealing with electronically stored evidence at the very first meeting with other parties in litigation.

Rule 34(b) This rule requires organizations to produce electronically stored information in its native format with its metadata intact and to prove chain of custody. While the duty to preserve evidence is narrowed only to relevant data, the potential repercussions are great. For example, if a defensible process is not demonstrated, opponents may be granted access to an organization's network.

Rule 37(f) This rule provides a "safe harbor" for data destruction. *Safe harbor* means that organizations face no penalties for deleting electronically stored information in keeping with routine operation of IT systems if the party took "reasonable" steps to preserve it. However, any destruction must be the result of routine operation and done in good faith, a systematic framework must be in place, and this systematic framework must have integrated litigation hold procedures.

Sarbanes-Oxley Act The Sarbanes-Oxley Act (SOX) was passed mostly in response to the front-page news headlines of corporate corruption and financial scandals (namely Enron and WorldCom) in the early part of the last decade. SOX provides severe criminal penalties, including jail sentences for corporate executives who knowingly destroy business documents and other information that is used in the daily operations of their organization. It also describes specific records that need to be retained and requires a records retention period of seven years.

Financial Industry Regulatory Authority   The Financial Industry Regulatory Authority (FINRA) rules (formerly known as SEC Rules 17a-3 and a-4) focus on brokers and traders, and they require these people to retain and store specific records, such as customer communications and customer-account trading activities, for a specific period of time on nonrewritable electronic media and to make them ready for easy review by the SEC within a reasonable time frame, typically 24 hours.

Health Insurance Portability and Accountability Act   One part of the Health Insurance Portability and Accountability Act (HIPAA) requires that an organization's patient records and related data (including related email) be archived and retained in a secure manner that ensures privacy and content integrity for at least two years after the death of the patient.

ISO 15489 (Worldwide)   This standard offers guidelines on the classification, conversion, destruction, disposition, migration, preservation, tracking, and transfer of records.

Title 17 Code of Federal Regulations Part 1   This regulation allows record keepers for futures-trading companies to store information either on electronic media or on micrographic media. This regulation also requires that "record keepers store required records for the full five-year maintenance period" while continuing to provide commission auditors and investigators with timely access to a reliable system of records.

Federal Energy Regulatory Commission Part 125   This rule sets specific retention periods for the public utilities industry and states that the records must have a life expectancy equal to or greater than the specified retention periods.

National Archives and Records Administration Part 1234   The National Archives and Records Administration (NARA) regulations specify which government agency records are kept, for how long, and in what form and how they are to be accessed.

Freedom of Information Act   The Freedom of Information Act (FOIA)—which applies to federal agencies—allows for the full or partial disclosure of previously unreleased information and documents controlled by the U.S. government. The act, which relies on the NARA regulations, defines federal agency records subject to disclosure and outlines mandatory disclosure procedures and, under certain circumstances, time frames for response.

The USA PATRIOT Act   The USA PATRIOT Act (fully named Uniting and Strengthening America by Providing Appropriate Tools Required to Intercept and Obstruct Terrorism) requires the Secretary of the Treasury to prescribe regulations "setting forth the minimum standards for financial institutions and their customers regarding the identity of the customer that shall apply in connection with the opening of an account at a financial institution." Broker-dealers must have a fully implemented customer identification program that includes procedures for making and maintaining a record of all information obtained.

Federal Employment–Related Regulations   Largely unknown to many Exchange Server administrators, federal employment regulations exist that require some sort of records retention, and they apply to all companies with employees. Some of the best-known are as follows:

- Title VII of the Civil Rights Act of 1964
- Age Discrimination in Employment Act
- Americans with Disabilities Act

- ◆ Family and Medical Leave Act

- ◆ Equal Pay Act of 1963

- ◆ Vocational Rehabilitation Act

- ◆ Employee Retirement Income Security Act of 1974

- ◆ National Labor Relations Act

- ◆ Fair Labor Standards Act

Each of these regulatory acts introduces its own set of requirements for data retention and stewardship, for which the employer is responsible. So, any company that employs people should be familiar with these and consider email archiving as a way to meet these regulations.

The regulatory requirements listed are the relatively well-known U.S. federal government drivers for record retention and cover quite a bit, including email data. However, this is not a complete list. There are more than 10,000 records-retention regulations effective in the United States, and many of these are state-mandated, so reviewing the regulations in the states your company operates in is a great idea.

 Real World Scenario

IMPLEMENTING ARCHIVING

An organization was using Microsoft Exchange Server for its email-communication infrastructure. However, due to ever-increasing messaging volume, the network was slowly becoming unmanageable. One of the reasons was that employees were retaining all of their email dating back to the early 1990s outside their mailboxes in PST files. This practice strained the company's backup and storage capacity to the limit. Because many state and local governments do business electronically, and with the paperless initiatives taking off, the problem was only getting worse. Efforts to bring the PST sprawl under control manually by asking employees to clean up were futile. Because end users continued to save all their email in local PST files, the problems reached a boiling point when the PST files started to experience corruption and monopolized costly storage space on file shares, desktops, and laptops.

To ensure that data was preserved, retained, and protected properly, the organization decided to move ahead and implement archiving. A project was initiated to locate all the PST files in the environment and bring them under centralized control. This strategy ensured that legal counsel, general counsel, and officials could perform retention management and search all the email content easily for discovery when the organization received a request for public records. This allowed the organization to comply with the U.S. Department of State Freedom of Information Act requirements.

Industry Best Practices

Organizations that are planning to deploy an archiving system in their environment soon realize that deployment can be a daunting task. Email archiving is a critical application for driving down the cost of managing email for corporate governance, litigation support, and regulatory compliance. Doing something wrong can result in some serious trouble. So, in this chapter we want to give you some insight into the industry's best practices (that is, guidelines for doing things right the first time).

Storage Management

One of the main reasons that many organizations want to use archiving is storage management. Think of offloading old email messages as filing away your IRS tax records. You don't keep your IRS records on the table forever; you file them away where you have easy access to them. In the years that we've been working with and deploying archiving solutions, one thing has stood out when it comes to storage management: nearly all emails older than six months are never accessed again, and then you start to wonder why you keep them on your Exchange server.

Most administrators mistakenly think that the performance of the Exchange Server database is related to the size of the database or the size of the mailbox. Microsoft Knowledge Base article 2768656 "Outlook performance issues when there are too many items or folders in a Cached mode .ost or .pst file folder" (`https://support.microsoft.com/en-us/kb/2768656`) describes how Microsoft Office Outlook users experience poor performance when they work with a folder that contains many items on a server that is running any version of Exchange Server. You can now have about 100,000 items per folder before performance degradation starts to take place, so these issues will arise a lot less. You can help avoid performance degradation in Outlook by managing the number of items in heavily used folders, including Inbox, Sent Items, and Calendars.

In order to improve Outlook performance when running in Cache mode, you might use the "Mail to keep offline" setting in Outlook 2013 and Outlook 2016. With this option, you might choose to keep an offline copy in the `.ost` file for the email that is old (1, 3, 6, 12, or 24 months) instead of keeping an offline copy of your entire mailbox. Furthermore, Outlook 2016 has an option to keep email that is old (3 days, 1 week, and 2 weeks). For more information about this Outlook feature, visit the knowledge base "Only a subset of your Exchange mailbox items are synchronized in Outlook 2016 or 2013," which is located on `https://support.microsoft.com/en-us/kb/2733062`.

Archiving solutions reduce the storage footprint, but traditionally administrators perform archiving only because they want to allow end users to have transparent access to data. When that happens, you will run into the item-limit counts, because even though the stubbed archived messages are only a few kilobytes in size, they count toward the item limits.

A few storage-management options are available; here we'll go over two that we've seen work at organizations:

Time Based With this option, you archive data pretty much from day one, but you don't create stubs in the mailbox; instead, you delete all data from the mailbox that's older than a specific age. The philosophy behind this approach is that you don't want to possibly confuse the end user with stubbed or archived messages. The time frame in which you want to delete the older data depends on how users use email in your organization, but deleting anything older than six months or a year is generally safe. You have to realize that even though you delete it from the mailbox, the data is in the archiving system, so end users can access the data if they need to do so. In some situations, however, organizations deploy an organizational archive and do not allow end users to access the data.

Stub and Time Based This option combines the first one—deleting data older than six months or a year—with stubbing or archiving messages. This means that you can squeeze out a bit more storage savings by replacing the large emails that are younger than six months or so.

We can't tell you exactly what will work in your environment; however, don't create a stubbing policy that acts on data that is younger than a few days. Not only would that create frustration for your end users, but it would also result in data ping-pong, because end users would constantly want to restore archived data to their mailboxes.

Archiving PSTs

PSTs are notoriously bad for your environment. We often compare them to those pesky blackberries in your garden that take over the entire yard if you don't keep them in line. Most administrators know what PST files are because we've been using them daily since we started to use Exchange Server and Outlook. Archiving these days has almost become a standard practice as part of a process to get the messaging data under centralized management.

Two versions of PST files are available. Originally, PSTs created by Outlook 2002 or earlier used the American National Standards Institute (ANSI) format, which has an overall size limit of 2 gigabytes (GB). Today, the most common and current version, known as Unicode, has a theoretical 32 TB file size limit. In the real world, however, the Unicode PST file could cause performance degradation beyond 5 GB in file size if you do not have adequately performing hardware. Beyond 10 GB, according to Microsoft, you will encounter short pauses on almost all hardware (see the article "You may experience application pauses if you have a large Outlook data file" at `https://support.microsoft.com/en-us/kb/2759052` for more details).

For more than a decade, users controlled the creation and location of PST files. The lack of centralized management tools played a major role in the sprawl of PST files. A company we worked with reported that it had close to 300 TB of data in PST files that were spread across desktops, laptops, servers, and backup tapes. Some users' PST file storage far exceeded what would be considered feasible to make available via an Exchange Server primary mailbox, which is 100+ GB of data stored in a user's primary mailbox, archiving mailbox, and recoverable data. The company needed to consider segregating the data into an archive mailbox in order to bring the data under centralized management.

An archiving system can make your life easier. To comply with laws and regulations, you can't simply ignore and delete PST files. It fascinates us that organizations often spend a small fortune protecting their messaging infrastructure with data-leak-prevention software to block sensitive data from leaving the organization unchecked. By forgetting about PST files, they have neglected to close a major security leak. One of the most common ways for end users to take their mailbox data with them is to simply export all the contents of their mailbox to a PST file and store it on a thumb drive or even MP3 player. They then can walk out the door with your company's sensitive information, contracts, and intellectual property, all unchecked.

Even if you have managed to retain the information in your infrastructure, the cost of storing data in PST files is enormous. The file format itself is so bloated that it uses more storage than if the data were kept in the Exchange Server database.

So how do you effectively eradicate PST files from your environment? We recommend implementing a multistep process:

1. Write a project plan.

   A project plan will come in handy, particularly for large companies. A project plan allows you to prepare and think about exceptions that you didn't consider. For instance, what are you going to do with data from employees who have left your organizations? How are you going to handle password-protected PST files? A good plan will save you time.

2. Prevent further growth of the problem.

   Some good Microsoft system management (Group Policy object) policies are available; they allow you to restrict users from creating PST files. You can download them from `https://www.microsoft.com/en-us/download/details.aspx?id=49030`. Use them. We love, for instance, the option "Prevent Users From Adding New Content To PST Files." This option allows end users to open their PST files but prevents them from adding any new content.

3. Discover all existing PST files.

   This task probably will take up the most time, because you will have to find *all* the files on your network. If you run scripts to do this, ensure that you don't do an all-out search, because it will saturate your network with network traffic. It takes such a long time because you'll find PST files on servers, tapes, laptops, and workstations. Think about how you are going to deal with people who work remotely. (See the sidebar, "The Microsoft Exchange Server PST Capture 2.0 Tool.")

4. Archive PST data.

   Archiving PST data allows you to bring the data back under your control. One of the reasons you shouldn't bring it into Exchange Server directly is because there is a good chance that you might not have the required storage available. A big advantage is that if the data is in an archive, it allows you to set retention and gives you additional benefits when it comes to eDiscovery, risk management, and early case assessment.

THE MICROSOFT EXCHANGE SERVER PST CAPTURE 2.0 TOOL

This tool can assist search for PST files across your network and import them into Exchange Server 2010 or 2013 before you upgrade to Exchange Server 2016. The tool consists of a central service, a console, and agents (the latter of which can be pushed out to all the computers in your organization). The agents can be scheduled to search for PST files and send them back to the server, where the central service is running, for import into Exchange Server. The Microsoft Exchange Server PST Capture 2.0 Tool is available at `http://www.microsoft.com/en-us/download/details.aspx?id=36789`.

5. Give end users access to their archived PSTs.

Taking away PST files from end users and not giving them access to their own data is the quickest way to start a revolt. Give end users access to the archived data—they need access to the data for productivity reasons.

AVOID EXCESSIVE USE OF STUBS

Stub files are shortcuts in the mailbox pointing to the archived item that now resides in the archive—it's no longer on Exchange Server. Excessive use of stubs can create problems on Exchange Server with whitespace, fragmentation, and major I/O overhead.

---

6. Disable PST file creation.

This final step is important because, after all, what good would it do if you bring everything under control and then you do not prevent your users from creating PST files again? Use the policies that we referred to in step 2.

Retention Policies

Deciding on your retention categories or how long you want to retain information within the archive will probably take up the most planning time. This process will involve most of the departments in your organization, from the storage team to the Exchange Server team, management, legal counsel, and even HR.

Retention controls the creation, filing, storage, and disposal of records in a way that is not only legally correct but also administratively possible. Retention has to serve multiple purposes, fulfill the operational needs, and provide a way to preserve an adequate historical record of the information. It is very important to implement and practice proper retention management, because it allows your organization to accomplish the following:

- Reduce compliance and litigation risks by proactively managing the retention and disposition of all potentially discoverable information.

- Reduce storage costs by storing only important and relevant information in the archive.

- Have only the relevant information in the archive, which will also make it easier and faster to find relevant information.

- Increase the reliability of information by managing the appropriate versions of information assets and ensuring that they have high value as evidence if they are needed in a court of law.

There are significant benefits to developing your retention policies before automating and implementing an archiving solution:

More Effective Regulatory Compliance   You don't have a choice when it comes to email retention for regulatory compliance; it is an absolute requirement. The only choice your company has is in how you meet the requirements: manually or with an email-archiving automation system. Creating and automating your email-retention policy lowers your overall risk of noncompliance and ensures that all required email is kept for the required time period.

Better Legal Risk Management   The ability to show a court an updated and regularly enforced email-retention policy can demonstrate retention policy intent and counter the claims of "spoliation," or purposeful destruction of evidence, by the plaintiff's attorney.

More Consistent Corporate Governance   Organizations these days rely on the active generation, use, and leverage/reference of data for business processes and decisions. The data that a business generates has value to the business if that data can be used efficiently. An effective retention policy will ensure that this information will remain available for some period of time, and an email-archiving system allows for quick search and reference.

More information about retention policies, and how they are used specifically within Exchange Server 2016, will be discussed later in this chapter.

Archiving with Exchange Server 2016

Microsoft has made several key improvements to the archiving, retention, search, and hold capabilities in Exchange Server 2016. These features allow granular control over how information is preserved and accessed, while also allowing end users to manage their mailboxes according to their own filing habits.

The following messaging and compliance features are included in Exchange Server 2016:

◆   Preservation of mailbox data based on specific criteria, known as *query-based hold*

◆   Preservation of mailbox data based on a date range, known as *time-based hold*

◆   Ability to conduct searches across SharePoint 2016, Skype for Business 2015, and Exchange Server 2016 from one interface

◆   GUI for conducting In-Place eDiscovery and Hold operations

◆   Support for Calendar and Tasks folders when creating retention tags

Exchange In-Place Archive vs. Third-Party Enterprise Archives

When evaluating archiving solutions, organizations should compare their regulatory compliance and business requirements in order to choose a product that best suits their needs. Many organizations decide to use Exchange archiving instead of investing in expensive third-party solutions.

When should you use the In-Place Archive (previously known as "personal archive") feature that is available in Exchange Server 2016, and when should you use an enterprise archive solution available through third parties? In essence, the decision has to be made based on the requirements and functionality offered by these solutions. In-place archiving in Exchange enables organizations to get rid of PST files, implement large mailboxes, and provide advanced search. Once they're implemented, users will see the archive mailbox as an additional mailbox in Outlook or Outlook on the web. For the users, working with the archive mailbox is the same as working with the primary mailbox, and they can copy and move messages between their primary mailbox and their archive mailbox.

You have an option to create users' primary and archive mailboxes on the same mailbox database or on a different mailbox database in the same Active Directory site. If your organization has deployed Exchange in a hybrid configuration, you may also choose to create archive mailboxes in the cloud.

Some organizations need additional features, such as records management or preservation of electronic information beyond Exchange Server or support for write-once, read-many (WORM) storage. Organizations that have strict requirements to retain information beyond email or that need to store information on WORM storage should look at an enterprise archive solution. Some organizational archiving requirements go beyond the scope of the In-Place Archive and deliver full mailbox capture for all users, full single-instance storage across all data, and advanced search and case-management tools for eDiscovery.

By way of comparison, a typical third-party email-archival solution can be expected to deliver all or a portion of the following key functions in addition to the In-Place Archive functionality in Exchange Server 2016:

- Logs, WORM, read-only

- Single instancing/compression

- Regulatory accreditation

- Federated discovery, retention, and reporting across multiple content sources

- Data mining and visualization

- Content monitoring and supervisory tools

Many organizations will find the archiving features of Exchange Server 2016 satisfactory to reduce the strain on storage growth and eliminate PST files. Likewise, many organizations will find native Exchange archiving to be helpful as an email retention and eDiscovery solution.

Retention Policies and Tags

The technology used in Exchange Server 2016 to maintain records management is called Message Records Management (MRM) and helps organizations reduce legal risks associated with email and other communications. It is much easier to make an organization comply with company policies and regulatory needs with MRM, and within Exchange Server 2016 this is accomplished with retention policies. Each mailbox can have one retention policy assigned to it, and each retention policy can have multiple retention tags. Exchange Server 2016 has multiple types of retention tags available for maintaining and moving data between the primary and archive mailboxes:

Default Policy Tag   Default policy tags (DPTs) are used to apply retention policies to untagged mailbox items. Untagged items are mailbox items that either didn't receive a retention tag from the folder that they are located in or didn't get a policy applied explicitly by the user. DPTs are created by specifying the type All.

A retention policy should not contain more than one DPT with the MoveToArchive action and one DPT with the DeleteAndAllowRecovery or PermanentlyDelete action. Also, if both a deletion tag and an archive tag exist on a retention policy, the archive tag should always have the shorter retention period.

Personal Tags Personal tags are available to users in their mailbox as part of their retention policy, and they can apply these tags to folders they create themselves or to individual items. This allows end users to tag information they consider critical and, therefore, apply a longer retention period to it.

Retention Policy Tag A retention policy tag (RPT) applies retention settings to the default folders (Inbox, Deleted Items, and Sent Items) in a mailbox, and all items that are in these default folders inherit the folders' policy tag. Users are not able to change the tag that is applied to a default folder, but they can apply a different tag to individual items in one of the default folders. You can create RPTs for the following default folders:

- Calendar
- Conversation History
- Deleted Items
- Drafts
- Inbox
- Journal
- Junk Email
- Notes
- Outbox
- Recoverable Items
- RSS Subscriptions
- Sent Items
- Sync Issues
- Tasks

In Exchange Server 2016, RPTs support the Calendar, Journal, Notes, and Tasks folders. However, you still cannot use the MoveToArchive retention action with RPTs. The MoveToArchive action is reserved for use with default policy tags and personal tags only, both of which we will discuss next.

You can define retention tags with the following actions:

Move To Archive Automatically moves messages from the primary mailbox to the personal archive. The DPT created by Exchange Server setup has a retention action of MoveToArchive and a retention period of 730 days (two years), but any number of days or Never can be configured. This policy can help keep the mailbox under quota. The policy works like the Outlook Auto-Archive functionality without creating the PST file and will create a folder name that matches the primary mailbox folder name from which the item was moved. This action can only be applied to default policy tags or personal tags; it cannot be applied to retention policy tags. Any policy tag that uses this action is referred to as an *archive tag*.

Delete And Allow Recovery Emulates the behavior when the Deleted Items folder is emptied or the user deletes a message using Shift+Delete. Messages move to the Recoverable Items folder when deleted item retention is configured for either the mailbox database or the user. Recoverable Items, also known as the *dumpster*, gives the user another chance to recover deleted messages. Any policy tag that uses this action or the Permanently Delete action is known as a *deletion tag*.

Permanently Delete Permanently deletes a message. A message is purged from the mailbox when this policy is applied; this is similar to a deleted message being removed from Recoverable Items. Once this happens, the user can no longer recover the message (although when single-item recovery or legal hold is enabled, the item is placed in the Purges folder of Recoverable Items and, therefore, can be recovered by administrators).

The priority in which policies take effect is pretty simple. Explicit policies have a higher priority over default policies, and longer-term policies apply over shorter-term policies. Remember that you can't apply a managed folder policy to a mailbox that has an archive mailbox enabled. During setup, Exchange Server creates a default retention policy, called Default MRM Policy, which includes several archive tags, as shown in Table 18.1.

TABLE 18.1: Default Archive Tags

RETENTION TAG NAME	TAG TYPE	DESCRIPTION
Default 2-Year Move To Archive	Default	Applies to items in the entire mailbox that do not have a retention tag applied explicitly or inherited from the folder. Messages are automatically moved to the archive mailbox after two years.
Personal 1-Year Move To Archive	Personal	Messages are automatically moved to the archive mailbox after 365 days.
Personal 5-Year Move To Archive	Personal	Messages are automatically moved to the archive mailbox after five years.
Personal Never Move To Archive	Personal	Messages are never moved to the archive mailbox.
Recoverable Items 14 days Move To Archive	Recoverable Items Folder	Messages are moved from the Recoverable Items in the user's primary mailbox to the Recoverable Items folder in the archive mailbox after 14 days.

The default retention policy is automatically assigned to each mailbox that has archiving enabled. The tags will be made available to the mailbox user after the Managed Folder Assistant has processed the mailbox. The user can then use these tags and apply them to folders or messages.

MOVING ITEMS BETWEEN FOLDERS

When an item is moved from one folder to another, it inherits the retention tag from the new folder location. If no retention policy tags are active on that particular folder, the item automatically gets the default policy tag. However, when the item has a specific personal tag assigned to it, this tag will travel with the item and always take priority over any folder-level tags or the default tag.

SETTING A RETENTION TAG

You can assign retention policies directly to a mailbox or to all mailboxes that are members of a distribution group. When assigning a retention policy to a distribution group, keep in mind that any new members added to a distribution group after the fact will not automatically receive that given retention policy, and you should run the distribution group policy cmdlet at regular intervals. The following example applies the Finance retention policy to John Doe's mailbox:

```
Set-Mailbox "John Doe" -RetentionPolicy "Finance"
```

The next example applies the Finance retention policy to members of the distribution group Seattle-Finance:

```
Get-DistributionGroupMember -Identity "Seattle-Finance" | Set-Mailbox
-RetentionPolicy "Finance"
```

It is also possible to use the EAC to assign a retention policy to one or more mailboxes simultaneously. To assign a retention policy to a single mailbox, follow these steps:

1. Log on to EAC and navigate to the Recipients ➤ Mailboxes pane.

2. In the list view, select the mailbox to which you want to assign a retention policy and click the Edit button.

3. In the properties of the mailbox, click Mailbox Features.

4. From the Retention Policy drop-down menu, select the policy you want to assign and then click Save (see Figure 18.1).

To assign a retention policy to multiple mailboxes simultaneously, use these steps:

1. Log on to EAC and navigate to the Recipients ➤ Mailboxes pane.

2. In the list view, use the Shift or Ctrl keys to select the mailboxes to which you want to assign the policy.

3. In the Details pane, click More Options.

4. Under Retention Policy, click Update.

5. In the Bulk Assign Retention Policy dialog box, select the retention policy that you want to assign from the drop-down menu and then click Save.

FIGURE 18.1
Assigning
a retention
policy to a single
mailbox

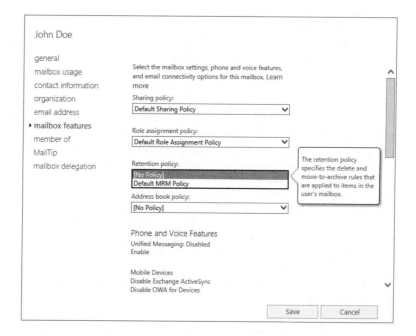

CHANGING A RETENTION POLICY

You can also change the policy that is applied to mailboxes in a new policy. The following two-step example applies the new retention policy "New-Retention-Policy" to all mailboxes that have the old policy "Old-Retention-Policy":

```
$OldPolicy=(Get-RetentionPolicy "Old-Retention-Policy"}.distinguishedName
Get-Mailbox -Filter {RetentionPolicy -eq $OldPolicy} -Resultsize Unlimited |
   Set-Mailbox -RetentionPolicy "New-Retention-Policy"
```

DELETING AND REMOVING A RETENTION TAG

When you remove a retention tag from the retention policy that is applied to the mailbox, it is no longer available to the user and, therefore, can no longer be applied to items in the mailbox. Items that have been specifically stamped with this tag, however, will continue to be processed by the Mailbox Assistant with these settings.

Removing a tag using the Remove-RetentionPolicyTag cmdlet will not only remove the retention tag from being available to the user but will also remove the tag from Active Directory. The next time the Mailbox Assistant runs, it will restamp all the items that had the removed policy applied and apply the default policy tag. If you remove the tag from a large number of mailboxes and items, this could result in a significant increase in resource consumption on your mailbox servers.

RETENTION HOLD

Retention policies might cause actions to be taken on new email messages before intended recipients can get to them if they are away or unable to access email due to vacations or other reasons. Depending on the policies that may be active and applied to the user, this could mean that messages may have been moved from the primary mailbox to the archive or even deleted. For these users, you have the option to temporarily suspend the retention policies from processing the mailbox for a set amount of time by placing the mailbox on a retention hold. You can specify a retention comment that will notify and inform the user (or another user who might have access to the mailbox) about this hold and explain when it begins and ends. These retention holds are visible only in supported Outlook clients, however, and they can be localized in the language of the user's preferred language setting.

Applying a retention hold will not modify or change the mailbox quota limits if they are applied. If end users are leaving for an extended period of time, you might want to increase or remove their mailbox quotas. Also, it might take users a while to catch up on email after they return, so give them time to go through their messages before you remove the retention hold status when they return. Retention hold works in a similar fashion to litigation hold but with some distinct differences, such as the fact that users on retention hold can proactively purge data from the mailbox permanently. Litigation hold will be discussed in more detail later in this chapter.

PLACING A MAILBOX ON RETENTION HOLD

In Exchange Server 2016, when you place a mailbox on retention hold, the Managed Folder Assistant stops processing the retention tags on the retention policy that exists on that particular mailbox. End users can still log on to their mailbox as they normally would during a legal hold and send, delete, or change emails. However, when the user searches her mailbox, she will not be able to find items that were older than the retention time period because they are stored in the Purges folders of Recoverable Items. You can configure Exchange Server to leave a comment when you place a mailbox on retention hold. This comment will be displayed in supported versions of Outlook.

You can only use PowerShell to place a mailbox on retention hold. The following example places John Doe's mailbox on retention hold from June 2, 2015, until June 12, 2015:

```
Set-Mailbox "John Doe" -RetentionHoldEnabled $true -StartDateForRetentionHold
"6/2/2015" -EndDateForRetentionHold "6/12/2015"
```

This example removes the retention hold from John Doe's mailbox:

```
Set-Mailbox "John Doe" -RetentionHoldEnabled $false
```

Enabling In-Place Archiving

You have two ways to archive-enable a mailbox:

◆ Through the Exchange Admin Center (EAC)

◆ Through PowerShell

To enable an existing mailbox for archiving within the EAC, follow these steps:

1. In the Feature pane on the left, click Recipients, click the Mailboxes tab, and then select the mailbox you want to enable.

2. Select the Edit button from the toolbar.

3. Click Mailbox Features and scroll down until you see the Archiving option.

4. Click Enable.

5. In the dialog box, you can optionally specify the database where you would like the archive mailbox to reside.

6. Click Save.

To enable new users that are created through the EAC with the wizard, you simply select the Enable option under Archiving: Disabled section, where you will need to choose a mailbox database for the archive mailbox(see Figure 18.2).

FIGURE 18.2
Select the Create
An On-Premises
Archive Mailbox
For This User option

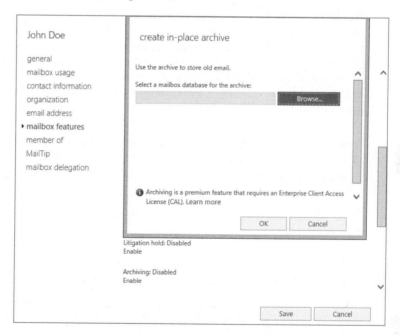

You can use PowerShell to enable it as well, and your cmdlet would look like this:

```
Enable-Mailbox "John Doe" -archive
```

Disabling a mailbox from being archive-enabled can be done in the same way: by navigating to the properties of the mailbox in the EAC and selecting Disable Archiving, or by selecting the Disable Archiving option in the Details pane on the right side of the EAC when you highlight the mailbox. If you want to do it with a cmdlet, the command will look like this:

```
Disable-Mailbox "John Doe" -archive
```

Disabling ensures that the data remains but that no new data can be added. This is basically the same as disconnecting a primary mailbox from an account.

The Remove command will delete the archive mailbox from Exchange Server, and the command looks like this:

```
Remove-Mailbox "John Doe" -archive
```

Using the Exchange Server 2016 In-Place Archive

For an end user to access to his archived data with Exchange Server 2016, he will either have to use Outlook on the web or have Outlook 2010 or later installed. An end user can drag and drop email from his PST files directly into the personal archive, but mail in the primary mailbox can also be moved automatically using retention and archive policies that can be set on the mailbox, folder, or item level.

You can set a quota on the archive mailbox separately from the primary mailbox, as we'll discuss next.

Archive Quotas

Many organizations enforce quotas on users' mailboxes, and archive mailboxes are designed to allow users to store historical data outside their primary mailboxes. Mailbox quotas are one of the primary reasons end users have started using PST files. To attempt to remove end users' desire and need to use PST files, you must ensure that the archive mailbox has enough storage available for end users to store all of their data. However, organizations may want to cap the growth of archive mailboxes for cost reasons or storage-expansion planning. You can configure an end user's archive mailbox with two options:

ArchiveWarningQuota   When an end user's archive mailbox exceeds this limit, an event is logged in the Application event log. The default is 45 GB.

ArchiveQuota   When an end user's archive mailbox exceeds this limit, moving data to the archive mailbox is prohibited. The default is 50 GB.

As with most of the archiving functionality in Exchange 2016, you have two ways to configure quotas:

◆   Through the EAC

◆   Through PowerShell

To set personal archive quotas within the EAC, select Recipients from the Feature pane on the left, click the Mailboxes tab, and select the mailbox you would like to configure. In the Details panes, under In-Place Archive, click View Details. Fill in the storage values in gigabytes, or choose an option from the drop-down menu.

You can configure both the ArchiveQuota and ArchiveWarningQuota settings with PowerShell. To set an ArchiveQuota of 20 GB and an ArchiveWarningQuota of 18 GB for an end user, use this command:

```
Set-Mailbox -Identity "John Doe" -ArchiveQuota 20GB -ArchiveWarningQuota
18GB
```

Offline Access

Most users have Outlook configured to synchronize their mailbox with Exchange Server using an Offline Storage Tables (OST) file. This gives users an offline cache so that they can still read their email when they are not connected to the network. The archive mailbox is not integrated with the OST file, which means that when data has been moved from a user's mailbox to their archive, the data will not be in the offline cache. If the user requires access to this data, the user has two options: get access through Outlook on the web or move the data back to the user's primary mailbox.

Understanding Litigation and In-Place Hold

Organizations use litigation hold to preserve all forms of relevant information when litigation is reasonably anticipated. It prevents deletions and preserves record changes to mailbox items in both the user's primary mailbox and archive mailboxes.

Exchange Server 2016 includes two types of holds: Litigation Hold and In-Place Hold. Litigation Hold sets the LitigationHoldEnabled property of a mailbox, and once Litigation Hold is enabled, all primary and archive mailbox items are placed on hold. In-Place Hold preserves only items that correspond to the results of the search query created in the In-Place eDiscovery tool. Therefore, multiple In-Place Holds can be configured for a mailbox, while Litigation Hold can be enabled or disabled for a mailbox. In-Place Hold and Litigation Hold can have a duration period configured to hold items. If a duration isn't configured, items are on hold with no time limit or until the hold is disabled for that mailbox.

When you're upgrading from Exchange Server 2010 and Exchange Server 2013, moving a mailbox that has Litigation Hold enabled on the previous Exchange Server version will not affect the Litigation Hold setting on a mailbox. Litigation Hold will be still be enabled once the mailbox is moved to Exchange Server 2016.

There is very tight integration within the EAC between placing a mailbox on In-Place Hold and eDiscovery. Both are handled using the same wizard, which you will see.

Placing a Mailbox on In-Place Hold

A lot of improvements have been made to the legal-hold functionality in Exchange Server 2016. With Exchange Server 2010, it was only possible to place *everything* in the mailbox on hold for an indefinite period of time, until the hold was removed. This could result in a lot of unnecessary data retention and misused storage. Now administrators and compliance officers can search one or more mailboxes for data based on a very specific set of criteria and place only those items on hold. Those criteria can include keywords, date ranges, sender, recipient, and message type. Additionally, you can define how long the items should be kept on hold, in terms of days since they were received or created in the mailbox. When you place a mailbox on In-Place Hold, policies are still acted on and applied, but the relevant data is never purged from the mailbox. End users can log on to their mailbox as they normally would during a legal hold and send, delete, or change emails. However, when the user searches her mailbox, she will not be able to find items that are older than the retention time period. Any messages that are modified by the user will have a copy of the original saved to a hidden folder within the mailbox that is inaccessible to the mailbox owner but remains subject to searches. This is known as copy-on-write (COW).

Although litigation hold can still be enabled on a mailbox through PowerShell using the `Set-Mailbox` cmdlet with the `-LitigationHoldEnabled` parameter, this is discouraged in Exchange Server 2016. Instead, a new tool called the In-Place eDiscovery & Hold Wizard is available in the EAC, and it can be used to perform both single- and multi-mailbox searches, as well as to implement In-Place Holds. We will walk through the wizard later in this chapter, in "Using the In-Place eDiscovery & Hold Wizard."

Implementing eDiscovery

The ability to search for relevant content within mailboxes is provided in Exchange Server 2016 through the eDiscovery feature. These searches are common practice within organizations that are dealing with litigations and lawsuits or that want to ensure they are in compliance with organizational rules, rules that are enforced by their business bylaws, or rules that are enforced on their business by legislation.

The eDiscovery functionality uses the existing content indexes created by Exchange Search, which has been revamped in Exchange Server 2016 to use Microsoft Search Foundation rather than Windows Search. Microsoft Search Foundation offers significant improvements in the areas of indexing and query performance. There is now an easy search interface, but behind the scenes it is still a PowerShell cmdlet (`Search-Mailbox`, `New-MailoxSearch`). One of the reasons for this change is that it is fairly rare to find a lawyer or HR person who is fluent in PowerShell, and the GUI is much more suited for them.

WHEN DO YOU USE EDISCOVERY?

There are a few scenarios for which you would use the eDiscovery option. The main usage scenarios are as follows:

Legal eDiscovery   More and more organizations are forced to provide information to support litigation or lawsuits. Traditionally, you had to manually search multiple servers, and if you were lucky you could use some of the PowerShell cmdlets. No matter what you used, it was a time-consuming and costly exercise. Exchange Server 2016 eDiscovery fills a niche; you can search across your entire organization without using cmdlets (which is important for HR or legal people).

HR   Corporate human resources departments commonly must respond to requests to research and monitor email content or complaints. For instance, in a case where an employee feels that the email content he has received from peers is offensive in content and in violation with HR policies, HR should investigate this matter.

SAFEGUARDING AGAINST UNWARRANTED MAILBOX ACCESS

Because cross-mailbox and cross-server search is a powerful right to have (that is, you technically could look in everyone's mailbox), it is a restricted permission. Add nontechnical personnel to the Discovery Management security group to grant them the Role-Based Access Control permissions necessary to perform eDiscovery searches without disclosing administrative permissions.

Organizational Investigations   Many organizations are involved in legal matters that involve an external party. In such cases, the internal legal department will respond to a formal request for information as part of a legal matter and will have a limited amount of time to respond to this request.

USING THE IN-PLACE eDISCOVERY & HOLD WIZARD

To use the Exchange Server 2016 In-Place eDiscovery & Hold Wizard, a user should be added to the Discovery Management role group. By default, this group does not have any members. Administrators who have the Organizational Management role are restricted from doing any In-Place eDiscovery searches without being added to the Discovery Management role group. In-Place eDiscovery is a powerful feature that potentially allows anyone with the appropriate permissions to access all the email records and public folders stored in your entire organization. Therefore, it is critical to control and monitor who gets access to the Discovery Management role and keep a close eye on the In-Place eDiscovery actions.

You can use PowerShell to add a user to the Discovery Management role group. To add, for instance, user John Doe, the cmdlet looks like this:

```
Add-RoleGroupMember "Discovery Management" -User Jdoe
```

After you have obtained permission, you can open the Discovery Manager console by going to https://servername.contoso.com/ecp and logging in with your credentials (see Figure 18.3).

FIGURE 18.3
The Exchange
Server 2016
In-Place eDiscovery
& Hold Console

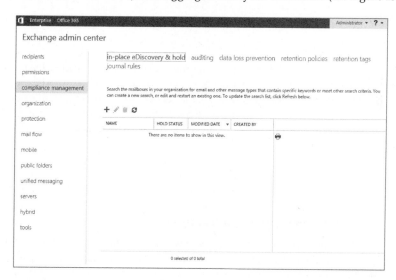

Once logged in, you can create a new In-Place eDiscovery search or In-Place Hold by clicking Compliance Management in the Feature pane and then selecting the In-Place eDiscovery & Hold tab. Give the search a name that is descriptive, so that it will make sense to you and others later; you will be sharing this view of the console with others in the Discovery Management group. Select what you want to search. You have the option to search all mailboxes, specific mailboxes, or mailboxes that belong to a distribution group and all public folders. In Figure 18.4, we are searching a specific mailbox, as well as mailboxes for all members of the Sales Group, as well as all public folders content.

FIGURE 18.4

Selecting mailboxes, distribution groups, and public folders in the In-Place eDiscovery & Hold Wizard

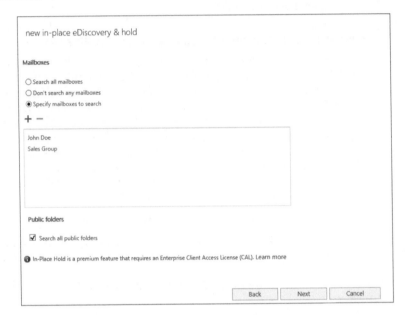

On the Search Query page, define the content you want to locate. You can search the entire mailbox, or you can narrow your search by selecting keywords, message types, To and From addresses, date ranges, and specific senders or recipients. To filter based on keywords, as in Figure 18.5, you can simply type basic words—or to be more specific, you can build complex queries based on Keyword Query Language. The Message Types to Search screen is shown in Figure 18.6.

If you want to preserve the results of your search, check the box to place the matching content on hold (see Figure 18.7). You have the option to put the contents on hold indefinitely or for a specific number of days. After you click Finish, Exchange Server will queue the search.

VIEWING THE SEARCH RESULTS

Once the search is completed, you will be able to see a summary of the results in the Details pane of the EAC, including the total number of items, aggregate size, and keyword statistics. Next, you can preview the results within the browser or export them to a Discovery Search mailbox. Be aware of the amount of data you are exporting, the mailbox you are exporting to, and the database and volume where that mailbox resides. You don't want to cause an outage because you filled up the drive with exported data. You can select the default Discovery Search mailbox, or you can create additional ones and use them. There are also export options for whether to include unsearchable items and to enable deduplication and thread compression.

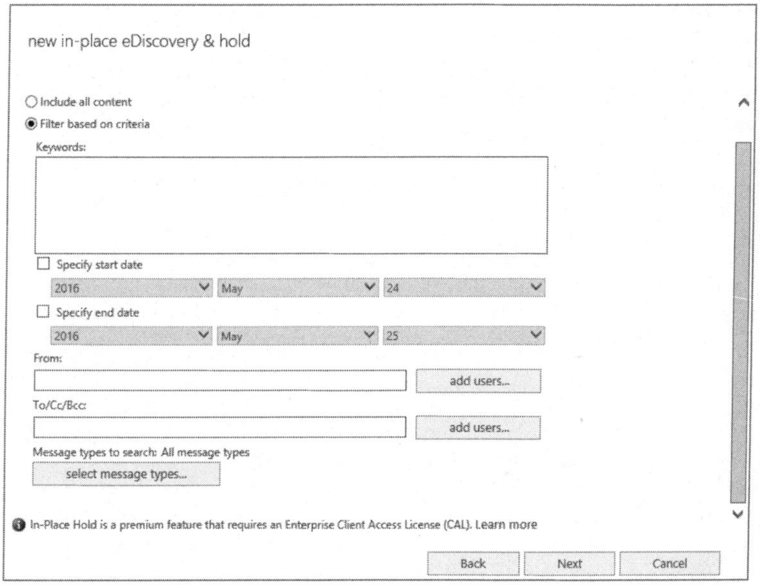

FIGURE 18.5
Defining a search query

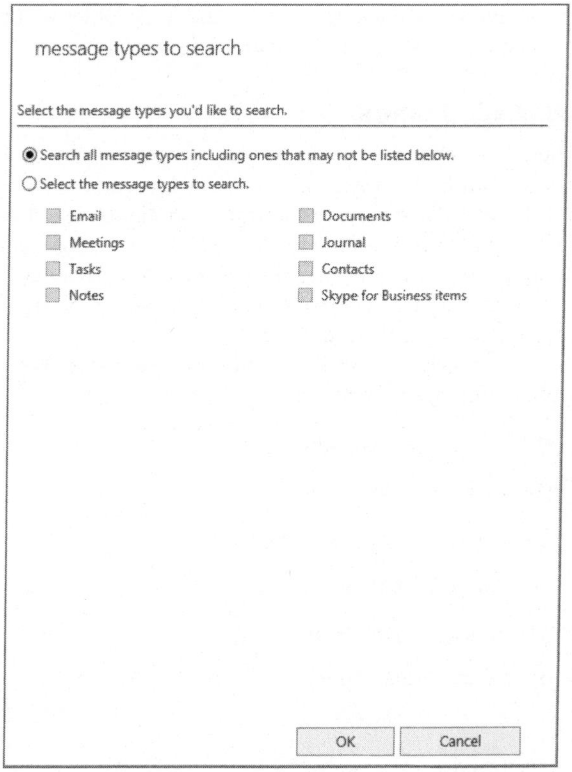

FIGURE 18.6
Defining the message types to search

FIGURE 18.7
Using the In-Place
Hold settings to
place search results
on hold

During the export, In-Place eDiscovery will create a new folder in the target mailbox that has the same name you gave to the search, and a subfolder will be created below that for each mailbox that had information that matches the search query.

COMPLIANCE SEARCH

Exchange Server 2016 includes a new eDiscovery search tool named Compliance Search. Compliance Search can be used to search a large numbers of mailboxes in a single search. You can run simultaneously one or multiple compliance searches. Compliance Search has better performance capabilities than the In-Place eDiscovery tool. For example, In-Place eDiscovery can search up to 10,000 mailboxes in a single search with a maximum of two In-Place eDiscovery simultaneous searches, whereas Compliance Search has no limits on the number of searches that can run at the same time.

You can manage and run the Compliance Search tool only in Exchange Management Shell by using the following commands:

- `Get-ComplianceSearch`
- `New-ComplianceSearch`
- `Remove-ComplianceSearch`
- `Set-ComplianceSearch`
- `Start-ComplianceSearch`
- `Stop-ComplianceSearch`

For example, to create a new search for all the members of a distribution group named "Sales Group" in Exchange Management Shell, run the following command:

```
New-ComplianceSearch -Name "Sales Group Search" -ExchangeLocation "Sales Group"
```

To start the search you have just created, in Exchange Management Shell, run the following command:

```
Start-ComplianceSearch -Identity "Sales Group Search"
```

To review the details about the search you have just started, in Exchange Management Shell, run the following command:

```
Get-ComplianceSearch -Identity "Sales Group Search" | Format-List
```

Requirements and Considerations

There are many important factors to consider before you implement Exchange Server 2016 to address archiving, compliance, and data management within your organization. As we've discussed throughout this chapter, while the native functionality available within Exchange Server has matured greatly over the past several releases of the product and may suit many companies, it still might not have all of the features necessary to meet your needs. Make sure you understand the laws and regulations that impact your organization's business and what your obligations are in terms of data retention and stewardship. Here are some other factors to consider before moving forward with any strategy.

Licensing

As a starter, the archiving functionality requires an enterprise client access license, also known as an eCAL, which adds some cost on top of the regular Exchange Server licensing fees. Also, it is recommended that you install at least Outlook 2013 to take advantage of the full archiving and compliance capabilities. Of course, you can use Outlook on the web for lots of the functionality, but deploying Exchange Server 2016 in combination with Outlook 2016 is recommended.

Server Storage

When it comes to archiving, proper storage planning is important, and Exchange Server 2016 comes with a few additional "curve balls."

When you import PST files with Exchange Server 2016, you need to ensure that additional capacity is available. The problem gets more interesting when you start deploying database availability groups and replicate data. You will replicate not only the primary mailbox but also the archived data in the personal archive. This could mean that your storage requirements grow exponentially. There is a reason Microsoft provides the option to put the archive mailbox on the same or different database as the primary mailbox it belongs to: Microsoft spent a lot of time making Serial Advanced Technology Attachment (SATA) storage a viable option beginning with Exchange Server 2010 and continuing to Exchange Server 2013 and Exchange Server 2016 for both performance and capacity. If you decide to go with SATA, there is no reason to split the personal archive and primary mailbox onto separate databases because you are already on the cheapest disks out there. In addition, keep in mind that disk capacity is continuing to increase while performance isn't; this means that if you continue to split the data onto different drives, you are not maximizing the efficiency of the drives (either capacity or performance).

If your organization is going to extensively use the in-place archiving functionality, be prepared for the additional storage requirements as well. A rapid increase in storage needs could occur when someone creates a large search result set that is copied to the Discovery Search mailbox. When you quickly export those results and provide them to the legal team, this might be only a short-term problem.

Client Requirements

As mentioned earlier, it is recommended that you install Outlook 2013 or later or use Outlook on the web to be provided full MRM capabilities. First, searches across both primary and archive mailboxes are not supported. Selecting All Mailbox Items when conducting a search will return results only from the mailbox you are searching, primary or archive. Second, users are not able to apply personal tags to items in their primary mailbox. However, administrators are still able to move data to the archive through default and retention tags, and users can manage personal tags via Outlook on the web as an alternative.

The Bottom Line

Understand the basic principles of email archiving. An archiving solution not only provides a way to ease the pain of storage problems on Exchange Server whether they are with the databases or with PST files but also assists in helping organizations become compliant and make discovery of email easier.

Master It How can government organizations actively comply with regulations and open-records laws?

Ensure your company complies with regulations. It is extremely important that your messaging system be configured in such a way that email data is managed according to laws and regulations.

Master It Which laws and regulations are in effect in your business, and what does it mean for your organization?

Enable Exchange Server 2016 in-place archiving. Exchange Server 2016 allows for efficient management of the user's primary mailbox by enabling the mailbox for archiving and using policies to move the content between the mailbox and the archive.

Master It How does archiving allow older email content to be moved automatically from the primary mailbox to the In-Place Archive?

Use Exchange Server 2016 retention policies.   Retention policies define how long data must be retained before it is automatically removed when the time setting has been met.

   Master It   You can create as many policies as you need; however, in many organizations, retention policies will be created per department (for instance, finance).

Use Exchange Server 2016 In-Place eDiscovery and Hold.   In certain situations, you may need to prevent email from being deleted for a period of time while an end user is away and unable to attend to their mailbox.

   Master It   Without retention hold, and depending on the policies that may be active and applied to the user, messages may have been moved from the primary mailbox to the archive or even deleted. What is the cmdlet to put a mailbox on retention hold?

Part 4

Server Administration

Chapter 19

Creating and Managing Mailbox Databases

The considerations for creating and managing mailbox databases have evolved over the years. Older versions of Exchange Server required high performance disks, but each user had relatively small mailboxes. Today, users demand large mailboxes and store multiple years of emails for reference. To accommodate this, the database engine for Exchange Server has been optimized to use disks that are larger, slower, and less expensive. However, you still need to understand the basic concepts for managing mailbox databases.

IN THIS CHAPTER, YOU WILL LEARN TO:

- ◆ Identify the core components of Exchange Server databases
- ◆ Plan for disk storage requirements for Exchange Server databases
- ◆ Manage mailbox databases

Getting to Know Exchange Server Databases

To end users, Exchange Server is all about sending and receiving email. For the administrator, it's about making sure users' email is available and up-to-date. Of course, there's a lot more to it than that, but the basic job of Exchange Server is to store and process messages for users. To this end, it is important to understand how the database technology works "under the hood."

Exchange Server 2010

Exchange Server 2010 introduced a version of Extensible Storage Engine (ESE) that was reengineered to denote years of customer feedback, experience, and the reality of larger user-mailbox requirements. The changes in Exchange Server 2010 were mostly the kind of changes that most administrators would not notice when working with middle-of-the-range servers or hardware. However, for administrators who manage Mailbox servers with 500 or more mailboxes, the importance of the changes became very real, very fast.

Online defragmentation running at runtime, new database tables, a larger page size, and an aggressive compression solution were just few of the architectural changes in storage for Exchange Server 2010. Exchange Server 2010 vastly reduced random disk access, which reduced IOPS (input/output operations per second) requirements by up to 90 percent (when compared to Exchange Server 2003). Many administrators had to rethink their strategy for disk storage, because it brought about the possibility of using cheaper, lower-performance JBOD (Just a Bunch of Disks) in many scenarios.

Exchange Server 2013

Several years of lessons learned from experience accrued in Exchange Server 2010 environments led Microsoft to further improve how mailbox databases are handled in Exchange Server 2013 and Exchange Server 2016. Database schema changes have been introduced, and resource utilization for disk access has been decreased further, improving overall performance. We've seen some numbers floating around that indicate disk utilization has decreased by over 97 percent from the days of Exchange Server 2003. Although those numbers are really impressive, they are only marginally more than what Exchange Server 2010 was already able to achieve, even though Exchange Server 2013 offered an improvement of up to 50 percent over Exchange Server 2010. It is important to note that many of the improvements are unseen by the administrator but are notable in disk and server sizing.

Exchange Server 2016

Microsoft continues to implement performance improvements in the mailbox database schema for Exchange Server 2016, but they are incremental changes that have a minor impact on performance. A mailbox database in Exchange Server 2016 requires approximately the same disk I/O as a mailbox database in Exchange Server 2013. Instead, the schema changes are focused on improving features. For example, replicated mailbox databases in Exchange Server 2016 now have database divergence detection to identify when database copies become corrupted. Many changes in database management also provide enhanced failover experiences and replication mechanisms within database availability groups. Refer to Chapter 20, "Creating and Managing Database Availability Groups," to review many of those changes.

Basics of Storage Terminology

In this section, we'll visit the basics of storage terminology and explain why these terms should be relevant to you in a discussion on storage.

MAILBOX DATABASE

In Exchange Server 2016, the mailbox database is the configuration object that provides management for all database settings. From the mailbox database properties, an administrator can configure the location of the database file, the transaction log file settings, and some settings that apply to mailboxes stored in the mailbox database.

Each Exchange Server 2016 server that has the Mailbox server role installed has a mailbox database named Mailbox Database <GUID> (the GUID suffix is there to ensure that the database name is unique; we'll discuss that in more detail later in this chapter).

This database is created during the installation process and has an EDB (Exchange database) file named `Mailbox Database <GUID>.edb`, stored in the default Mailbox folder in the Exchange Installation directory. (The EDB file may also be renamed and stored in an alternative location if you use the `/MdbName` and `/DBFilePath` parameters during installation.) On an Exchange Server 2016 Standard Edition Mailbox server, an administrator can create up to 5 mailbox databases; Enterprise Edition allows creation of up to 100 mailbox databases (though most administrators will likely *not* need or want to create so many).

Administrators often ask me why they would ever need to create more than one Exchange database, especially since the maximum mailbox database size is *unlimited*. Later in this chapter, we will discuss the organizational and business reasons why having multiple mailbox databases might be the right solution for your Exchange Server environment.

Microsoft Exchange Information Store Service

Exchange databases are mounted and managed by the Microsoft Exchange Information Store Service. If you ever see documentation references to the Extensible Storage Engine (ESE), this is the database that is used for Exchange Server and is implemented by the Information Store Service. If you stop the Information Store Service, all databases on the server are dismounted.

Starting with Exchange Server 2013, each database is managed by a separate worker process. This improves overall Exchange Server stability because problems with one database now affect only that database. When there was only a single worker process, a single problem could cause all mailbox databases to stop responding.

Restarting the Information Store Service is still a valid solution when a worker process is hung, but you also have the option to kill only the hung worker process and then remount the database. All of the worker processes appear in Task Manager as `Microsoft.Exchange.Store.Worker`, but you can use the process ID from `Get-MailboxDatabase` to identify which worker process corresponds to which mailbox database.

Transaction Logs

Transaction logging is obscure to most administrators. It is easy to forget about transaction logging, since it all occurs automatically (or *automagically*). For every transaction that enters your messaging server (new email, deleted email, a change to an email message, a modified attachment, and so on), the information is written to a transaction log file before the database is updated. When transaction log files are filled up with data, new transaction log files are created in a perpetual fashion that bears resemblance to a factory production line.

Transaction log files always have the same size, 1 MB. We compare them to milk containers (whether empty or full, they are always one-gallon containers, or one-liter containers for those using the metric system). Transaction log files are created at the 1 MB size and then filled to capacity. These files are persistent on the hardware. Later in this chapter, we will discuss the recommended methods for administrators to purge or remove older transaction log files.

 **Real World Scenario**

Who Owns the Storage?

The databases are more than physical files on the hard drive. The databases store information, and the properties of these databases have to be configured and managed according to the purpose they serve. One way to better understand how Exchange Server manages them is to compare them to a rental property. The organization is the top-level entity in Exchange Server. It is the name that describes the configuration boundary for Exchange Server, much as a forest describes the boundary for Active Directory.

Databases are created and managed at the organization level. They are effectively "owned" by the landlord, the organization, much as a building would be. Databases can have one or more copies on individual mailbox servers. These servers are in effect leasing the database from the landlord, because the organization is still the point of management. We'll discuss database management in more depth shortly.

Storage in Exchange Server 2016

There are many notable characteristics of database storage and architecture in Exchange Server 2016. They are important to point out because they have a far-reaching impact on Exchange Server deployments and the overall strategy that an organization takes with its messaging infrastructure. Let's look at some of those characteristics—or at least the ones most relevant to Exchange Server administrators:

♦ Most write transactions to the Exchange Server databases are performed as sequential writes rather than traditional *random* writes. Why should you care? Well, it means that the hard disk arm does not move; the disk is spinning, but the arm is not moving. This characteristic, which may seem like a detail at first, is significant in reducing the number of IOPS for Mailbox servers and improving overall database access performance. (Note that some write transactions are still performed as random writes as required, but they are greatly reduced.)

♦ Each version of Exchange Server has an updated database schema. This allows Exchange Server to support new features. Cumulative updates also can update the database schema, but you should review the release notes to be sure. (By the way, this new database schema is the main reason you cannot perform an in-place upgrade from previous versions of Exchange Server.)

♦ Well, it can't all be good. Single instance storage (SIS) was removed as a database feature as of Exchange Server 2010. (Keep in mind that SIS was effectively gone in Exchange Server 2007 when it no longer applied to email attachments.) SIS had become decreasingly important, to the point that it would be detrimental to performance to attempt to implement this solution at the database level.

♦ The database page (each transaction resulting in new data creates at least one database page) size is 32 KB. In essence, this means that a 5 KB message will require a 32 KB block of space in the database. However, a 16 KB message is now stored in a single page, rather than two pages as in versions of Exchange Server previous to Exchange Server 2010.

♦ Database pages are compressed to mitigate the risk of an increased database size potentially caused by the new larger page size and other new database architectural changes.

 **Real World Scenario**

HOW SHOULD I THINK ABOUT STORAGE?

Wouldn't it be great if you could walk into your boss's office and get the budget to give every user a 100 GB mailbox so they would never (well, not for a while at least) have to delete anything? Then you could create as many databases on your Exchange server as possible before your fingers went numb. Users could go to town.

Unfortunately, we all have constraints we have to live within; that goes for system administrators, end users, and our VIP users. So, thinking about adding more storage and allowing larger mailboxes or databases, what are some of the constraints that we face? Some of them are technological in nature and some are budgetary or political. We're hoping that you already know most of these and can skim right through them:

◆ Exchange Server 2016 Standard Edition supports a maximum of five mailbox databases.

◆ Exchange Server 2016 Enterprise Edition supports a maximum of 100 mailbox databases.

◆ Exchange Server 2016 has approximately the same disk I/O performance as Exchange Server 2013. However, this is vastly improved over legacy Exchange Server versions such as Exchange 2003. The relatively low disk I/O in Exchange Server 2016 supports the use of relatively slow disks such as 7200 RPM near line storage.

◆ Large mailboxes can lead to large databases. The maximum database size you allow should be based on the time to backup and restore during disaster recovery. For typical backups of Exchange Server databases, the restore time will be twice as long as the backup time. If you create multiple replicated databases in a Database Availability Group (DAG), you may not need backups at all.

◆ Microsoft recommends a maximum Exchange Server database of 2 TB when you have multiple replicated copies of your databases. This assumes you will not need to restore the database. A 200 GB limit is recommended for databases that may need to be restored from backup.

◆ You need to plan for 7 to 10 days' worth of transaction logs; a good starting point for estimating how much space transaction logs will consume is about 9 GB of transaction logs for every 1,000 average users. However, we will discuss later, in "Managing Mailbox Databases," how some organizations will want to enable circular logging and, therefore, not require additional disk space to store transaction logs.

◆ If you implement database replication with a database availability group and multiple replication partners, remember that log files will only purge after a successful replication (even when circular logging is enabled). Therefore, you must account for network outages where replication will fail and transaction log files can queue on your physical disks. Depending on the time necessary to troubleshoot or repair the problem that is preventing successful replication, enough disk space must be available before databases will begin to shut down.

◆ You should assume that each database needs to contain 10 to 15 percent additional space for deleted items (known as the recoverable item space or the database dumpster), deleted mailboxes, and for database whitespace. Also, note that whitespace can continue to grow if the online maintenance process does not complete. However, this is unlikely to be an issue because Exchange Server 2016 performs online maintenance as a background task whenever resources are available.

An Additional Factor: Archive Mailboxes

An archive mailbox is what we call the "Siamese" mailbox to a user's primary mailbox. It's a secondary mailbox that is "joined at the hip" to a user's primary mailbox and provides a second location for storing older, rarely accessed emails. We'll briefly discuss archive mailboxes in this chapter, since it does have an effect on the overall storage solution. Let's look at some of the features unique to archive mailboxes:

- An archive mailbox is created by using the `Enable-Mailbox <mailbox> -Archive` command, or you can use `Enable-Mailbox <mailbox> -RemoteArchive` if you plan to create an archive mailbox in Office 365 for a user who has a mailbox in an on-premises deployment of Exchange Server 2016.

- An archive mailbox and a primary mailbox for a user do not have to be stored in the same mailbox database.

- The archive mailbox cannot be cached locally on an Outlook client through an offline store (OST).

- An archive mailbox cannot be accessed by all editions of Outlook. In general, stand-alone versions of Outlook and volume licensed versions of Outlook can use archive mailboxes. Outlook 2013 and Outlook 2016 in Microsoft Office bought at retail cannot access archive mailboxes.

- Archive mailboxes can allow administrators to provide larger storage solutions for users, while still providing access to all email.

- Do not confuse an archive mailbox with a personal folder. Personal folders, or PSTs, are containers for email messages and other Outlook content. PSTs are always stored on client computers, are portable, and can be used as a means of backup by individual users.

For older versions of Outlook, your entire mailbox was cached in a local OST file for cached mode. A smaller OST file was one motivation for implementing archive mailboxes. This is much less of a concern now because current versions of Outlook cache only recent data (a configurable time frame) and not an entire mailbox. Online connectivity is required to access older data just as if the data were moved into an archive mailbox.

A second motivation for implementing archive mailboxes was to put archive mailboxes on slower disks. Again, this is much less of a concern than it once was because Microsoft recommends large (and relatively slow) disks for all Exchange Server storage. This is why they've put so much effort into reducing the IOPS required.

So, the only remaining rationales for implementing archive mailboxes are to reduce mailbox clutter and for flexible backups. A smaller main mailbox is just intuitively appealing to some users and organizations even if it's not a technical requirement. For backups, if active mailboxes are smaller, the databases holding them can be restored faster during disaster recovery. Then, databases with archive mailboxes can be restored later.

Disk Size vs. I/O Capacity

Historically, Exchange Server was limited by the performance of its disks rather than by the space available on those disks. In Exchange Server 2010, there was somewhat of a role reversal between those two characteristics, and Exchange Server 2016 has continued to improve this situation. The improvements and reductions in I/O requirements permit administrators to use low-speed high-capacity disks, such as SATA disks or near-line SAS disks. Many organizations find that there is internal resistance to using large, slow, relatively inexpensive disks rather than high performance disks, but Exchange Server is designed for this. You will also see that storage vendors still recommend using a SAN even when it isn't required.

The performance required by the disk subsystem is normally measured (and planned) in terms of the IOPS profile of the users who will use the system. The Exchange Server team at Microsoft has done much research into the type of load that users place on an Exchange server, and they have incorporated this into the Exchange Server Role Requirements Calculator. This is the tool that you should start with when planning CPU, memory, and storage for your Exchange Server deployment. It generates the expected IOPS for the user profile you select and shows whether various disk configurations would be acceptable.

Note that the reductions in IOPS in recent Exchange Server versions are significant, to the point that an Exchange Server 2016 deployment requires only a small fraction (a few percentage points) of the IOPS required by a server that ran Exchange Server 2003. IOPS is one of the least significant disk and hardware elements used in calculating server size for Exchange Server 2016.

What's Keeping Me Up at Night?

We spend quite a bit of time wondering if we have our storage configuration optimized. Ask yourself these questions about your own environment:

- Am I giving my users enough mailbox space to store enough historical information to do their jobs? Or am I giving them (*shudder*) too much space?

- Are users wasting mail storage on personal or non-work-related content, such as MPG files of cats playing the piano (`http://www.youtube.com/watch?v=npqx8CsBEyk`)?

- Should I employ an email archival solution to move older content off the mailbox database and onto alternative storage? Should I use the built-in archive mailbox solution or a third-party solution? If I use either solution, how much "recent" content should be left on the Exchange server versus moved out to the archive?

- Do I need to keep copies of certain types of messages (such as for regulatory, legal, or business reasons)?

- Are my databases growing so fast that I might run out of disk space before I notice?

- Do I have the right balance of databases, size of disk, frequency of backups, and deployment of redundancy?

Planning Mailbox Database Storage

When estimating mailbox database size for a given configuration, as a worst-case scenario, we once estimated that a single database could grow to 1.3 TB in size. Although Exchange Server can technically support a database that large, it would take forever to back up, and worse, it would take forever to restore. (Okay, maybe not forever but longer than what would make operational sense.) Even if you are using snapshot technologies, if the snapshot backup software performs database verification, the verification would take far too long. So a database size of 1.3 TB is just not practical in organizations that have not yet implemented a DAG with replication.

Maximum Database Sizes

Microsoft recommends that you keep each mailbox database under about 200 GB if you are not using replication technology. If you are using a DAG and maintaining at least three copies of each database, you can consider allowing a maximum database size of 2 TB. In practical terms, there are very good reasons to keep it far smaller, such as the time necessary to back up and restore the files and the time necessary to repair the files, but this number is only a general idea of what you should attempt to stay under.

These numbers are based on some simple principles. Consider that if you *don't* use replication for your mailbox databases, you have to account for the time necessary to restore a database and the impact of a restore operation. A smaller database, in the case of loss or hardware failure, can be restored quickly, ensuring minimal impact on users. When database replication is put in place, the replica of the database in essence acts as a backup and, depending on the number of mailbox database copies, may never be used in a restore operation. In that case, a large database is more efficient, because it simplifies administration by reducing the number of databases in the organization.

We urge you to consider your existing environment when you think about these maximum sizes. Ultimately, you need to consider how much time it will take to restore one of these databases from a backup; if the absolute longest time you can take to restore a database from your backup media is two hours, and your system restores at a rate of 30 GB per hour, then the largest database size you should consider supporting is 60 GB. Your company's recovery time objective/recovery point objective (RTO/RPO) will most likely dictate recovery time and, therefore, will help you calculate what your maximum database sizes should be.

Replication technologies in Exchange Server 2016 provide options for quicker access to a mailbox database, in the event of a server or disk failure. Naturally, this requires a proper implementation and configuration of a DAG.

Determining the Number of Databases

The primary determinant for the number of mailbox databases is the RTO for disaster recovery. Having multiple smaller databases provides you with flexibility during recovery so that you can restore databases with important mailboxes first to get them up and running again quickly. Even in a scenario where you are using DAG replication, smaller databases can be reseeded faster when a disk is lost.

From a performance perspective, the number of databases only matters if you are spreading those databases across multiple disks. In an installation that does not use DAG replication, you should use some type of RAID to provide disk-level redundancy. If you are using RAID, the server typically has a single large pool of disks for storing the databases, and there is no performance change regardless of whether you have one database or ten.

When creating additional mailbox databases that do not use database replication with a DAG, you should plan to place each database's transaction logs on separate disk spindles from the database files. This can help improve performance (due to the nature of the I/O differences), though it mainly improves recoverability. If you are using a DAG and have two copies or more, you can safely place the transaction logs and the database files on the same spindles or disks.

PLANNING FOR MAILBOX DATABASES

A company named ABC is planning to migrate their existing messaging infrastructure to Exchange Server 2016. ABC has 1,200 users who connect to a server farm in the company's main office. During their planning process, administrators are attempting to determine the number of databases required to support their requirements.

They have identified the following requirements:

◆ Minimize the time necessary to perform a restore in the event of a single disk failure.

◆ Minimize the time necessary to perform an offline operation on the database files.

◆ Provide all users with at least 1 GB of storage but support even much larger mailboxes. (Today, it's becoming the norm for users to expect mailboxes that have unlimited storage; the new generation of users is increasingly familiar with cloud storage and cheap disk storage.)

After looking at each requirement, ABC has determined that they should design the following storage solution:

Create Multiple Mailbox Databases   By having multiple mailbox databases, ABC feels that they will be able to split up the 1,200 users and, therefore, keep the database files to a manageable size. With smaller database files, database restore and offline database repair or defrag times are minimized.

Configure Mailbox Size Limits   To ensure that a user or a group of users does not over-run the amount of disk space used, ABC has decided to implement mailbox size limits on the mailbox databases. Hard disk drives have been purchased to support up to 5 GB of storage for each user. For now, administrators plan to configure users to receive a warning message when their storage reaches 4 GB.

Although a single Mailbox server can support the company's users, ABC has also determined that they should plan for mailbox resiliency by using a DAG and database replication across multiple Mailbox servers.

Note that this scenario does not take into consideration the performance requirements of the mailbox databases. ABC must also analyze the backup/restore needs, service-level agreements, and user profiles and then provide a storage configuration that will meet the I/O and performance requirements.

Allocating Disk Drives

The Microsoft preferred architecture recommends large, relatively slow storage with multiple databases per disk. This recommendation is based on the experience of customers and Microsoft's own experience managing Office 365. The low per-mailbox I/O needs for Exchange Server 2016 support this.

The Microsoft preferred architecture also recommends JBOD (Just a Bunch of Disks) for the disk configuration. JBOD is literally just disks attached to a storage controller. A battery-backed cache is recommended for the storage controller to improve performance (disk-level cache should be off), but no RAID is recommended because RAID increases complexity and your disk cost per server by having redundant storage. It is assumed that you have a DAG and replicated databases.

Most organizations should have a DAG with replicated databases. However, if you don't, you should use RAID in your servers to provide redundancy at the storage level. Then if a disk fails, the server continues operating while the disk is replaced. As a best practice, have a hot spare in the same server to automatically rebuild the RAID array by using an unused disk. Don't forget to monitor your servers to identify when a disk in a RAID array has failed. If you don't notice when multiple disks fail, you'll have to restore from backup.

Also, if you don't use replicated databases, you should separate your databases and transaction logs onto different physical disks for recovery. Then if the disk holding a database fails, you can restore the database and replay the transaction logs to minimize data loss.

Many larger organizations have standardized on SAN-based storage, either iSCSI or Fibre Channel. Regardless of the type of SAN, it tends to be more expensive and complex than direct attached storage (DAS). However, a SAN is designed for high availability and you may decide to have fewer database copies when using a SAN when compared to DAS. For example, for a two-site DAG, you may have only a single server in each site, but the databases are stored on a SAN with high availability. When using DAS without the SAN, you may have had two database copies per site.

The SAN is usually some aggregation of a large number of disks in a RAID 5, RAID 1+0, or another redundant configuration. The person who manages the SAN (hereafter known as one of the SAN people) carves up the amount of storage you request from that large aggregation of disk space and assigns it to you as a logical unit number (LUN) of disk space. You then configure your Windows server to connect to those LUNs across the iSCSI or Fibre Channel network (or fabric).

While Exchange Server 2016 is designed to work well with cheaper storage, there are some benefits to using a SAN for storage. The ability to combine large numbers of disks into a very large volume and then allocate pieces of that large volume to the applications (such as Exchange Server) that need disk space can help reduce your storage costs and allow you to take advantage of technologies, such as snapshot backups and improved recoverability features. Further, because some of the storage is not physically connected to the server, a disaster that befalls the server hardware may not affect the storage system.

If you are a SAN user, you should ask your SAN people for two LUNs for each mailbox database. One LUN should be sized to hold a mailbox database's transaction log files, and the other should be sized to hold that database file—that is, of course, for a Mailbox server role and does not account for the backup requirements. By putting one database and one transaction log on each LUN, you ensure that the granularity of snapshot solutions is per database. Dedicating LUNs to specific tasks helps you isolate I/O for those tasks; you should avoid placing the data for other applications on those LUNs that would affect I/O. This also allows you to configure the LUN characteristics to suit that data type. For example, RAID 1 would be more suited to transaction logs, whereas RAID 5 would be more suited to database files.

Those of you who think about disks and disk performance may be wondering about all of those LUNs being carved out of the same logical disk. If your SAN is improperly sized and does not have enough spindles, performance can be a problem. A properly engineered SAN solution should provide enough total I/O capacity for all the LUNs and the applications that will use those LUNs to function correctly.

You should also consider the file system you are using to store your mailbox databases. Beginning with Windows Server 2012, you can use ReFS (Resilient File System) instead of NTFS for data storage (but the operating system still needs to boot from NTFS). ReFS is designed for very large disks and to be more resilient to errors than NTFS. Disk repair operations are much faster, and larger files are supported. This means that you can have mailbox databases larger than 2 TB if it makes sense for your organization (although this is not commonly needed). The preferred architecture for Exchange Server 2016 recommends using ReFS, but you need to disable Integrity Streams.

Another supported option for Exchange Server 2016 is using BitLocker to encrypt mailbox databases and transaction logs. Mailbox databases and their associated transaction logs often contain sensitive information. If someone were able to remove a disk from an Exchange server, they could quite easily gain access to the contents of the mailboxes stored on the disk. Implementing BitLocker introduces a minor performance decrease (about 10 percent slower) but ensures that data in mailboxes remains private.

If you are implementing Exchange Server 2016 by using Hyper-V, using dynamic VHDX files is now supported. A dynamic VHDX file is a virtual disk that dynamically expands as data is added to it. This allows for the most efficient use of disk space on the Hyper-V host. In the past, dynamically expanding VHD files had about a 20 percent performance hit, whereas dynamic VHDX files have only about a 2 percent performance loss.

Related to Hyper-V, you may see some documentation stating that SMB 3.0 is supported for mailbox databases. This is true, but it needs to be clarified. SMB 3.0 or later is the file-sharing protocol in Windows Server 2012 and newer. You cannot store a mailbox database directly on a file share. However, Hyper-V supports using a file share to store the VHDX file that stores a mailbox database, and that VHDX can be attached to a virtual machine running Exchange Server 2016. This seems like splitting hairs, but the difference is important. Just remember that using SMB 3.0 to access a VHDX over the network should be done on an isolated network that you are effectively configuring as a SAN.

Managing Mailbox Databases

You can create and manage mailbox databases by using both the Exchange Admin Center (EAC) and Windows PowerShell cmdlets. It is useful to be aware of both methods. If you work with Exchange Server 2016 only occasionally, you will probably prefer the graphical interface provided by the EAC. If you work with Exchange Server 2016 daily, you will begin to appreciate the ability of the Windows PowerShell cmdlets to show you all of the information you need quickly. However, for simplicity, the examples in this section deal with only a single mailbox database.

Viewing Mailbox Databases

You can view the current mailbox database for each server using the EAC, or you can use the Get-MailboxDatabase cmdlet to list all the mailbox databases stored on an Exchange server, as shown here:

```
Get-MailboxDatabase -server NYC-EX1
Name                  Server        Recovery       ReplicationType
----                  ------        --------       ---------------
Mailbox Database 1    NYC-EX1       False          None
Mailbox Database 2    NYC-EX1       False          None
```

The Get-MailboxDatabase cmdlet has an -IncludePreExchange2013 parameter. This parameter instructs the cmdlet to return information for all mailbox databases in the organization, including those on servers that run on Exchange Server 2010. For example, the following command will return all mailbox databases in a mixed organization:

```
Get-MailboxDatabase -IncludePreExchange2013
```

You can also query the mailbox databases from just a single server:

```
Get-MailboxDatabase -Server NYC-EX1
```

Creating Mailbox Databases

To create a new mailbox database in EAC, on the left pane, select Servers. In the middle pane at the top, click Database. Then click the + (Add) to create a new database. This launches the New Database screen, shown in Figure 19.1. To create a new database, provide a name for the database and then enter the name of the server that will store the database; the path will automatically be completed and the database's EDB file will be put in the same path as the transaction logs. The paths can always be changed later to ensure that the database files are in the correct location.

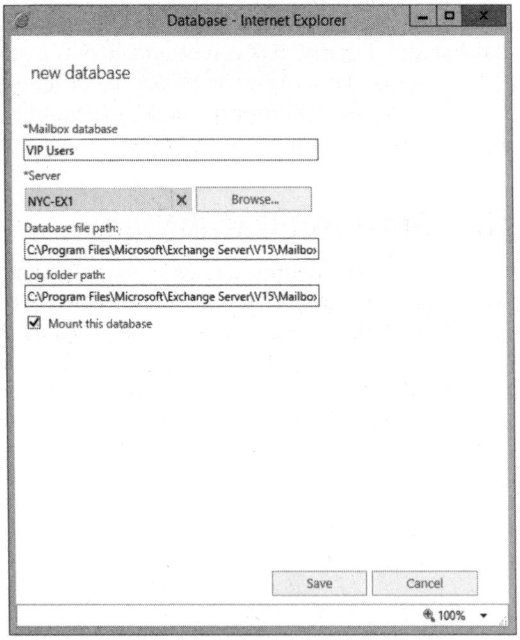

FIGURE 19.1
Creating a new database using the Exchange Admin Center

When creating a new database, name it something that is standardized and descriptive but unique in the entire organization. Note that a mailbox database can be activated and then mounted on any Mailbox server in your organization, if it's part of the same DAG and you've created mailbox database copies. This functionality introduced in Exchange Server 2010 created the requirement for unique mailbox database names within an organization. Also, making sure the filename matches the display name of the database will ensure that it's easier to manage. For example, a database name of MBX-Sales-NYC-01 can adequately describe the mailboxes stored in the database, as well as include a numerical trailer to accommodate growth in the Sales department.

Normally, you would modify the database file and transaction log paths and select the correct location for the mailbox database now, but we will show you how to move the mailbox database in the next section. You should not store your mailbox databases in the default location on the C: drive!

The EAC creates and then mounts the database. The new database file is empty and ready for you to add mailboxes. In the background, the New-MailboxDatabase cmdlet is used in the command to create the database, and the Mount-Database cmdlet is used to mount the database. You can do it manually in the Exchange Management Shell (EMS) as follows:

```
New-MailboxDatabase -Name 'VIP Users' -EdbFilePath
'C:\Program Files\Microsoft\Exchange Server\V15\Mailbox\VIP Users\VIP Users.edb'
-Server NYC-EX1.Contoso.com
Mount-Database -Identity 'VIP Users'
```

Sometimes, when you create a mailbox database by using the EAC, it won't mount correctly. This is typically due to Active Directory replication latency. One domain controller is used when creating the database, and another is read when trying to mount it. When this happens, just wait a few seconds and try mounting the database again.

Moving the Mailbox Database EDB File

We created the database in the default path (see Figure 19.1) so we could illustrate the process of moving it. Using EMS, you can move the database by using the Move-DatabasePath cmdlet. Here's an example:

```
Move-DatabasePath -Identity 'VIP Users' -EdbFilePath 'F:\VIP\VIP Users.edb'
```

When you specify that you want to move the database files, you are warned that the database will be dismounted while the files are being copied and that it will be inaccessible. The amount of time that it takes to move the database file depends both on the size of the database file and the speed of the disk subsystem.

If the mailbox database is replicated in a DAG, you cannot change the path of the database file or the transaction logs. To change the path, you need to remove all database copies except for one, and then you can change the path. In a DAG, the path is the same for all mailbox database copies.

Moving the Mailbox Database Log Files

When you move the database, you probably also want to move the transaction logs. The same method using the EMS outlined in the previous section can be used to move the Transaction log folder location for a database. Administrators of earlier versions of Exchange Server remember that the Transaction log folder location was tied to a storage group. By using the

Move-DatabasePath cmdlet, you can also modify the Transaction log folder path. You are also warned that a dismount must occur. Here's an example:

```
Move-DatabasePath -Identity 'VIP Users' -LogFolderPath F:\VIP\Logs
```

As you have seen for the last two commands, the database must be taken offline to perform these actions. It is, therefore, better to plan ahead and implement the desired paths at the time of database creation to avoid downtime in the future or to plan to modify the database path before you move mailboxes to your database.

Properties of a Mailbox Database

Now let's look at some of the properties of a mailbox database. Figure 19.2 shows the General section of the mailbox database's properties dialog box. At the top is the display name of the mailbox database. From here, you can rename the database if you need to conform to a new database-naming standard. The path to the database is shown, but you cannot change the path here; you must use the Move-DatabasePath cmdlet.

FIGURE 19.2
General section of the mailbox database's properties dialog box

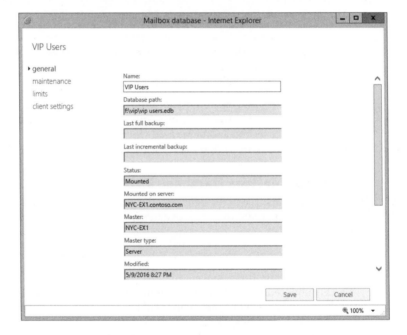

A lot of dynamic state information resides on the General tab as well, including the following:

Last Full Backup Indicates the last time a full or normal Exchange Server–aware VSS backup was performed. Transaction logs would have also been purged at that time.

Last Incremental Backup Indicates the last time an incremental backup was run. This backup type will back up the database's transaction logs and then purge them.

Status Indicates if the database is mounted or dismounted.

Master Indicates if the copy of the database is the master copy in a DAG deployment.

Master Type   Indicates the type of master copy of the database that exists on the server.

Modified   Shows the date and time the database properties in Active Directory were last changed.

This information (including the dynamic information) can be retrieved using the `-Status` parameter of the `Get-MailboxDatabase` cmdlet. The output for the following example database has never been backed up:

```
Get-MailboxDatabase 'VIP Users' -Status | FL Name,*last*,Mounted
Name                            : VIP Users
SnapshotLastFullBackup          :
SnapshotLastIncrementalBackup   :
SnapshotLastDifferentialBackup  :
SnapshotLastCopyBackup          :
LastFullBackup                  :
LastIncrementalBackup           :
LastDifferentialBackup          :
LastCopyBackup                  :
Mounted                         : True
```

The next section in the mailbox database's properties screen is Maintenance, shown in Figure 19.3. Here you find a potpourri of various configurations that relate to overall database file and content management.

FIGURE 19.3
The Mailbox database's Maintenance settings

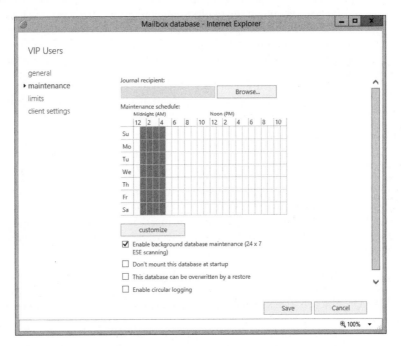

The Journal Recipient option allows you to specify a journaling recipient for all mailboxes located on this mailbox database. If this is enabled, a copy of any message or delivery receipt sent or received by a mailbox on this system will be sent to the journal mailbox.

The Maintenance Schedule settings allows you to schedule online maintenance for this particular database.

The Enable Background Database Maintenance (24 × 7 ESE Scanning) option, which is enabled by default, ensures that database maintenance occurs at runtime. If you disable this option, database maintenance will run only during the maintenance schedule.

The Don't Mount This Database At Startup check box allows you to prevent the database from being mounted after the Information Store Service is restarted. This might be useful when you are restarting an Exchange server multiple times during maintenance.

The This Database Can Be Overwritten By A Restore check box is used when you must restore a database file from a backup. An attempt to restore a database without this checked will result in a failure of the restore procedure.

The Enable Circular Logging check box is used to automatically purge transaction log files on the disk after they have been committed to the database. When this option is not enabled, transaction logs are purged only after a successful full or incremental backup. For mailbox databases that are not replicated in a DAG, circular logging should be off to aid in disaster recovery after a restore. However, you might disable circular logging temporarily during a period of high activity, such as during mailbox moves when many logs are generated and there might not be enough disk space. When a mailbox is not replicated, you need to dismount and remount a database for this setting to take effect.

In a DAG deployment scenario, we recommend that you enable circular logging if you are using mailbox database replication as a backup solution. When circular logging is enabled in a DAG, transaction logs are purged only after they are replicated to all database copies.

The next section on the mailbox database properties screen is Limits, shown in Figure 19.4. This tab allows you to specify the amount of storage that each mailbox is allowed to have. Administrators familiar with earlier versions of Exchange Server will be relieved that newly created mailbox databases have defaults. *Everyone* will appreciate the actual default values:

◆ Issue Warning At (GB) is set to 1.9 GB. When a mailbox reaches this limit, users will receive an email message informing them that they have reached a limit on their mailbox and they should clean up some data in it.

◆ Prohibit Send At (GB) is set to 2 GB. Once the mailbox hits this limit, the user will be unable to send new messages or reply to existing messages. Both Outlook and Outlook on the web will inform users if they try to send a message while they are over this limit.

◆ Prohibit Send And Receive At (GB) is set to 2.3 GB. When a mailbox exceeds this limit, the mailbox is closed or disabled. Even though the user can access the mailbox, the server will not allow the user to send new messages or reply to existing messages. In addition, the mailbox will not receive any incoming mail from other Exchange Server users or from outside the organization.

Outlook has a neat feature that will inform users of how close they are to their limit or if they are over their limit. Simply right-click the bottom bar in Outlook, and select Quota Information On. You can then see in the bottom-left corner the quota utilization, as shown in Figure 19.5.

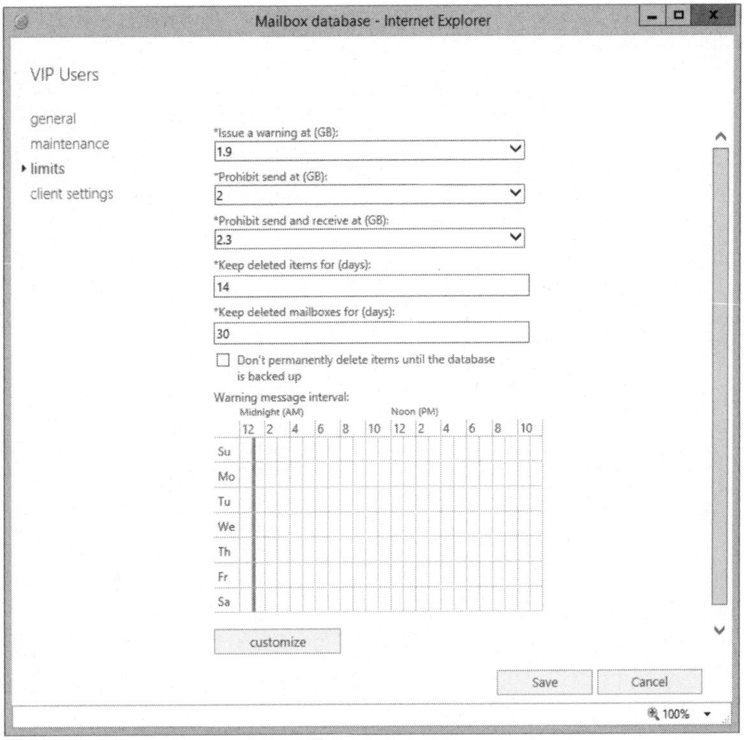

FIGURE 19.4
The Mailbox database's Limits settings

FIGURE 19.5
Quota limit in Outlook

An administrator can also determine mailbox utilization using the EAC by selecting a user from Recipients in the left pane and then clicking Mailbox Usage on the properties for that user, as shown in Figure 19.6.

In the properties of a mailbox database, the Warning Message Interval determines the interval at which Exchange Server generates a warning message informing users that they are over their Issue Warning limit. By default, this is sent once daily at 1:00 AM local time. You can customize this to be another time or to run more often. However, be careful about how often you schedule it. Too many warning messages will seem like spam to your users.

FIGURE 19.6
Quota limit in EAC

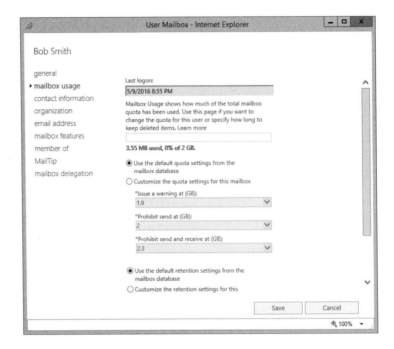

USE CAUTION WITH SCHEDULE BOXES

When using any schedule box that has both a 1-hour view and a 15-minute view, switch to the 15-minute view to set a schedule. If you select an entire hour, whatever process you are scheduling will run four times per hour. In this case, if you select an entire hour, a warning message will be sent to all mailboxes over their warning limit four times per hour. The users will *not* be amused.

The deletion settings of the Limits section allows you to configure how long the server will retain deleted items for this mailbox and how long the server will retain a mailbox once it is deleted. The Keep Deleted Items For (Days) option specifies how many days the Exchange server will keep items that have been deleted either from the Deleted Items folder or via a hard delete (Shift+Delete) from another folder. Once a message has been in the Recoverable Items folder for longer than this period (14 days by default for Exchange Server 2016), the user will no longer be able to retrieve the message using the Recover Deleted Items feature.

The Keep Deleted Mailboxes For (Days) option specifies how long the mailbox database will keep a deleted mailbox in a disconnected state before it is permanently purged. The default is 30 days, which is reasonable for most organizations. A mailbox that has been deleted but not purged can be recovered using EAC's Connect a Mailbox feature or via the Exchange Management Shell's Connect-Mailbox cmdlet.

The Don't Permanently Delete Items Until The Database Is Backed Up check box tells the server that it should not permanently purge an item or a mailbox until the mailbox database has been backed up. This ensures that a copy of the deleted item or deleted mailbox could be recovered from backup media if necessary.

The Client Settings section (shown in Figure 19.7) allows you to specify which offline address book (OAB) an Outlook client should download. Clients that work in offline mode or cached mode use an OAB. The default OAB contains the default global address list and is sufficient for most small- and medium-size businesses. If you do not specify an OAB for a mailbox database, then the default OAB is used.

FIGURE 19.7
The Client Settings properties of a mailbox database

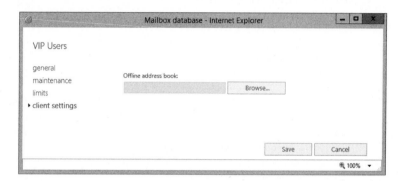

The properties you have just examined using the graphical user interface can also be examined using the Get-MailboxDatabase cmdlet. The following example retrieves mailbox database properties and sends them to a formatted list:

```
Get-MailboxDatabase 'VIP Users' | FL
RunspaceId                                          : bc95a45f-bfe6-4ff8-b8fd-
aff97670e0b7
JournalRecipient                                    :
MailboxRetention                                    : 30.00:00:00
OfflineAddressBook                                  :
OriginalDatabase                                    :
PublicFolderDatabase                                :
ProhibitSendReceiveQuota                            : 2.3 GB (2,469,396,480
bytes)
ProhibitSendQuota                                   : 2 GB (2,147,483,648 bytes)
RecoverableItemsQuota                               : 30 GB (32,212,254,720
bytes)
RecoverableItemsWarningQuota                        : 20 GB (21,474,836,480
bytes)
CalendarLoggingQuota                                : 6 GB (6,442,450,944 bytes)
IndexEnabled                                        : True
IsExcludedFromProvisioning                          : False
IsExcludedFromProvisioningReason                    :
IsExcludedFromProvisioningBy                        :
IsExcludedFromProvisioningBySchemaVersionMonitoring : False
IsExcludedFromInitialProvisioning                   : False
IsSuspendedFromProvisioning                         : False
IsExcludedFromProvisioningBySpaceMonitoring         : False
```

```
IsExcludedFromProvisioningForDraining            : False
IsExcludedFromProvisioningByOperator             : False
IsExcludedFromProvisioningDueToLogicalCorruption : False
MailboxLoadBalanceMaximumEdbFileSize             :
MailboxLoadBalanceRelativeLoadCapacity           :
MailboxLoadBalanceOverloadedThreshold            :
MailboxLoadBalanceUnderloadedThreshold           :
MailboxLoadBalanceEnabled                        :
DumpsterStatistics                               :
DumpsterServersNotAvailable                      :
ReplicationType                                  : None
AdminDisplayVersion                              : Version 15.1 (Build 225.42)
AdministrativeGroup                              : Exchange Administrative
Group
                                                   (FYDIBOHF23SPDLT)

AllowFileRestore                                 : False
BackgroundDatabaseMaintenance                    : True
ReplayBackgroundDatabaseMaintenance              :
BackgroundDatabaseMaintenanceSerialization       :
BackgroundDatabaseMaintenanceDelay               :
ReplayBackgroundDatabaseMaintenanceDelay         :
MimimumBackgroundDatabaseMaintenanceInterval     :
MaximumBackgroundDatabaseMaintenanceInterval     :
BackupInProgress                                 :
DatabaseCreated                                  : True
Description                                      :
EdbFilePath                                      : f:\vip\vip users.edb
ExchangeLegacyDN                                 : /o=Contoso/ou=Exchange
Administrative Group (                             FYDIBOHF23SPDLT)/
cn=Configuration/cn=Servers/                       cn=NYC-EX1/cn=Microsoft
Private MDB
DatabaseCopies                                   : {VIP Users\NYC-EX1}
InvalidDatabaseCopies                            : {}
AllDatabaseCopies                                : {VIP Users\NYC-EX1}
Servers                                          : {NYC-EX1}
ActivationPreference                             : {[NYC-EX1, 1]}
ReplayLagTimes                                   : {[NYC-EX1, 00:00:00]}
TruncationLagTimes                               : {[NYC-EX1, 00:00:00]}
RpcClientAccessServer                            : NYC-EX1.contoso.com
MountedOnServer                                  :
DeletedItemRetention                             : 14.00:00:00
SnapshotLastFullBackup                           :
SnapshotLastIncrementalBackup                    :
SnapshotLastDifferentialBackup                   :
SnapshotLastCopyBackup                           :
LastFullBackup                                   :
LastIncrementalBackup                            :
```

```
LastDifferentialBackup                  :
LastCopyBackup                          :
DatabaseSize                            :
AvailableNewMailboxSpace                :
MaintenanceSchedule                     : {Sun.1:00 AM-Sun.5:00 AM,
Mon.1:00

                                          AM-Mon.5:00 AM, Tue.1:00
AM-Tue.5:00 AM,

                                          Wed.1:00 AM-Wed.5:00 AM,
Thu.1:00

                                          AM-Thu.5:00 AM, Fri.1:00
AM-Fri.5:00 AM,

                                          Sat.1:00 AM-Sat.5:00 AM}
MountAtStartup                          : True
Mounted                                 :
Organization                            : Contoso
QuotaNotificationSchedule               : {Sun.1:00 AM-Sun.1:15 AM,
Mon.1:00

                                          AM-Mon.1:15 AM, Tue.1:00
AM-Tue.1:15 AM,

                                          Wed.1:00 AM-Wed.1:15 AM,
Thu.1:00

                                          AM-Thu.1:15 AM, Fri.1:00
AM-Fri.1:15 AM,

                                          Sat.1:00 AM-Sat.1:15 AM}
Recovery                                : False
RetainDeletedItemsUntilBackup           : False
Server                                  : NYC-EX1
MasterServerOrAvailabilityGroup         : NYC-EX1
WorkerProcessId                         :
CreationSchemaVersion                   :
CurrentSchemaVersion                    :
RequestedSchemaVersion                  :
AutoDagExcludeFromMonitoring            : False
AutoDatabaseMountDial                   : GoodAvailability
DatabaseGroup                           :
MasterType                              : Server
ServerName                              : NYC-EX1
IssueWarningQuota                       : 1.899 GB (2,039,480,320
bytes)
EventHistoryRetentionPeriod             : 7.00:00:00
Name                                    : VIP Users
LogFolderPath                           : f:\vip\logs
TemporaryDataFolderPath                 :
CircularLoggingEnabled                  : False
LogFilePrefix                           : E01
LogFileSize                             : 1024
```

```
LogBuffers                              :
MaximumOpenTables                       :
MaximumTemporaryTables                  :
MaximumCursors                          :
MaximumSessions                         :
MaximumVersionStorePages                :
PreferredVersionStorePages              :
DatabaseExtensionSize                   :
LogCheckpointDepth                      :
ReplayCheckpointDepth                   :
CachedClosedTables                      :
CachePriority                           :
ReplayCachePriority                     :
MaximumPreReadPages                     :
MaximumReplayPreReadPages               :
DataMoveReplicationConstraint           : None
IsMailboxDatabase                       : True
IsPublicFolderDatabase                  : False
MailboxProvisioningAttributes           : ServerName=NYC-
EX1;DatabaseName=VIP Users;
MetaCacheDatabaseVolumesRootFolderPath  : C:\ExchangeSSDVolumes
MetaCacheDatabaseRootFolderPath         : C:\ExchangeMetaCacheDbs
MetaCacheDatabaseMountpointFolderPath   : C:\ExchangeMetaCacheDbs\VIP
Users
MetaCacheDatabaseFolderPath             : C:\ExchangeMetaCacheDbs\VIP
Users\VIP

                                          Users.mcdb
MetaCacheDatabaseFilePath               : C:\ExchangeMetaCacheDbs\VIP
Users\VIP

                                          Users.mcdb\VIP Users-mcdb.

edb
CafeEndpoints                           :
AdminDisplayName                        : VIP Users
ExchangeVersion                         : 0.10 (14.0.100.0)
DistinguishedName                       : CN=VIP
Users,CN=Databases,CN=Exchange

                                          Administrative Group
                                          (FYDIBOHF23SPDLT),CN=Admini

strative

Groups,CN=Contoso,CN=Microsoft Exchange,CN=Se

                                          rvices,CN=Configuration,DC=

contoso,DC=com
Identity                                : VIP Users
Guid                                    : 89d85728-08f3-4833-9a3f-
5d315d692e47
ObjectCategory                          : contoso.com/Configuration/
Schema/ms-Exch-Priv

                                          ate-MDB
```

```
ObjectClass                            : {top, msExchMDB,
msExchPrivateMDB}
WhenChanged                            : 5/9/2016 6:27:12 PM
WhenCreated                            : 5/9/2016 5:56:19 PM
WhenChangedUTC                         : 5/10/2016 1:27:12 AM
WhenCreatedUTC                         : 5/10/2016 12:56:19 AM
OrganizationId                         :
Id                                     : VIP Users
OriginatingServer                      : NYC-DC1.contoso.com
IsValid                                : True
ObjectState                            : Changed
```

Some of these properties can be changed through the EMS using the `Set-MailboxDatabase` cmdlet. For example, to change the Prohibit Send At (KB) quota to 100 MB, you would type this:

```
Set-MailboxDatabase 'VIP Users' -ProhibitSendQuota:100MB
```

Not all of the properties that you see in the output of the `Get-MailboxDatabase` cmdlet can be changed. Some of them are system properties.

The Bottom Line

Identify the core components of Exchange Server database storage. The ability to identify the components of your Exchange servers that provide storage functionality will allow you to properly plan and troubleshoot storage.

Master It When you plan the storage configuration for your server, you need to accurately identify the messaging requirements and patterns of your users. After you have done so, how do you identify an acceptable storage solution?

Plan for disk storage requirements for Exchange Server databases. A major paradigm shift has occurred in the Exchange Server messaging world. Up to now, administrators have been focused on their IOPS and the capacity of their disks to handle the client requests. Today, administrators have to rethink the way they plan for server storage, though they still need to think about IOPS and capacity, storage capabilities, and limits.

Master It When planning for storage requirements for Exchange, you must take many factors into consideration. Many of them have to do with storage type, capacity, load, and redundancy. However, many administrators don't always plan for the number of databases that need be created and opt for a reactionary approach to mailbox database creation. What are the considerations for determining the number of mailbox databases to create?

Manage Mailbox Databases. You can use either the EAC or EMS to create and manage mailbox databases. Some of the more advanced options are available only in EMS by using Windows PowerShell cmdlets.

Master It One of the options you can configure for a mailbox database is circular logging. Circular logging purges mailbox database transaction logs after they are committed to the database. When should circular logging be used and not be used?

Chapter 20

Creating and Managing Database Availability Groups

Messaging services for most organizations are deemed business-critical and need to be online with minimal to no data loss during a variety of failure scenarios. Organizations are also looking for more flexibility in managing a Mailbox server during business hours while minimizing the impact on end users. To assist organizations with these requirements, Exchange Server 2007 and later versions include new solutions for high availability. Through a process called *continuous replication,* a mailbox database can be copied to one or more Mailbox servers and the database is kept up-to-date through transaction log shipping and replay into the passive copy (or copies) of the database. In Exchange Server 2010, this continuous-replication process matured as database availability groups (DAGs).

You add Mailbox servers into the DAG as members, and then you can determine which databases will be replicated to which member servers. The value here is simple. If the Mailbox server hosting the active database were to fail or if maintenance is going to be performed on a Mailbox server, a copy of that mailbox database can be activated on a different Mailbox server with minimal to no interruption of mailbox services to the end users.

Long before the DAG is created and Mailbox servers are added, a design is created laying out the configuration of the DAG. The configuration should be built around business and technical requirements while taking into consideration the limitations of the existing environment. For many organizations, the business and technical requirements drive the configuration of the DAG to be stretched across multiple datacenters, which requires additional implementation and management considerations.

A single misstep in the configuration of a component can have catastrophic effects, ranging from prolonged outages to loss of email data. This chapter covers the essential components of a DAG and how they operate together.

IN THIS CHAPTER YOU WILL LEARN TO:

◆ Understand database replication

◆ Manage a database availability group

◆ Understand Active Manager

◆ Understand DAG maintenance

◆ Understand site resiliency for Exchange Server 2016

Understanding Database Replication in Exchange Server 2016

In Exchange Server 2007, Microsoft introduced continuous replication. The concept of continuous replication was enhanced in Exchange Server 2010 with the introduction of a database availability group (DAG) and has been incrementally improved in Exchange Server 2013 and Exchange Server 2016. A DAG is the means to replicate database content between Mailbox servers. By default, Mailbox servers that are members of a DAG and have copies of the same mailbox database use continuous replication, which is performed by the Microsoft Exchange Replication Service, to seed or reseed a mailbox database copy and to replicate transaction logs between the active mailbox copy and the passive mailbox copies.

When a passive mailbox database is added to a Mailbox server that is a member of a database availability group, continuous replication kicks in. The Mailbox server that was added as a passive database copy opens a TCP connection to the Mailbox server hosting the active database copy, and the mailbox database is seeded from the source server to the target server. Once the mailbox database has been seeded, continuous replication uses the same procedure to replicate transaction log information between the source and the target Mailbox servers.

The TCP port used to connect the target and source replication services can be changed. If Windows Firewall is enabled on the Mailbox server, you must add the updated replication port in the Windows Firewall settings. The default port used is TCP 64327; the replication port can be changed by running this command:

```
Set-DatabaseAvailabilityGroup –Identity (name of DAG) –ReplicationPort (new
    replication port)
```

One major improvement for DAGs in Exchange Server 2016 is search indexing for mailbox databases. Mailbox servers with a copy of a mailbox database maintain an index for that database. In Exchange Server 2013, the indexing service on a server holding a passive copy of the database performed its indexing on the active database copy. If your WAN links were slow, this placed an extra burden on them. In Exchange Server 2016, all indexing is performed on a local mailbox database copy, which can significantly reduce WAN utilization in an organization with high email volume. These indexes are important because they are used when users perform searches. When a passive mailbox database copy is activated, you want it to have an up-to-date search index.

Local search indexing for passive databases was announced by Microsoft before the release of Exchange Server 2016, but it was not included at release. As of Exchange Server 2016 CU2, this feature is still not released but is on the product roadmap.

File Mode vs. Block Mode

Before we dig into File mode and Block mode, you need to understand how transactions are stored on a Mailbox server. As you know by now, Exchange Server stores transaction log files and the corresponding mailbox database on disk. The contents in the transaction log files are played into the mailbox database. We will not cover this process in great detail. What is important to understand for this chapter is how content is written to a transaction log. Every database, both the active copy and passive copies, stores transactions in a memory location called the *log buffer*. When the log buffer is flushed from memory, it is written to a transaction log.

Now that you know where transactions are stored on a Mailbox server, let's take a look at the two types of continuous replication. *File mode* is used to replicate closed transaction logs to all Mailbox servers that hold a passive mailbox database copy, where the transaction logs are played against the passive database. Because transaction log files are only 1 MB in Exchange Server 2016, if replication falls behind by a couple logs and a failure occurs, the impact of the data loss will be minimal. In Exchange Server 2007 and the RTM version of Exchange Server 2010, the only way to replicate database changes between Mailbox servers that held a database replica was using File mode.

Microsoft wanted to improve how content was replicated between mailbox copies so they introduced *Block mode* in Exchange Server 2010 SP1. This feature has been carried over to Exchange Server 2013 and 2016. As mentioned earlier, File mode must be up-to-date before Block mode is used. As updates are written to the log buffer of the active copy, the log buffer content is sent to the log buffer of all passive copies. When the log buffer is full, each database copy commits the log buffer content from memory to disk in the form of a transaction log file. By replicating changes in the log buffer, the passive copies have the latest changes performed against a mailbox database. To limit the amount of data loss during an unexpected failure of the active database copy, Block mode replication is used by default when File mode replication is up-to-date.

To determine whether a passive copy is using Block mode or File mode, you can use the `Get-Counter` cmdlet to retrieve the value of the Continuous Replication - Block Mode Active counter. The value 1 indicates the Mailbox server holding a passive copy is using Block mode, and the value 0 indicates the Mailbox server holding a passive copy is using File mode. The following command returns values for all mailbox databases hosted on a Mailbox server:

```
Get-Counter -ComputerName NYC-EX1 -Counter
 "\MSExchange Replication(*)\Continuous replication - block mode Active"
```

The Anatomy of a Database Availability Group

A DAG is a grouping of up 16 Mailbox servers that uses components of Windows Failover Clustering and continuous replication to provide a high-availability solution for mailbox databases. Once a DAG is formed and Mailbox servers are added as members, those member Mailbox servers can be assigned active and passive copies of mailbox databases to provide fault tolerance during a datacenter outage, network interruption, storage subsystem failure, Mailbox server failure, database failure, or a component failure of the Mailbox server, thereby allowing for higher levels of availability.

You can create a DAG using the EAC or EMS. Creating a DAG in the EAC or EMS is a straightforward process and can be performed with minimal effort. Before creating a DAG, however, let's discuss the Microsoft requirements and recommendations to which a DAG configuration should adhere:

◆ Mailbox servers that are members of the same DAG must be in the same domain.

◆ Microsoft doesn't support adding a Mailbox server to a DAG that is installed on domain controllers. (Note that Exchange Server roles should not be installed on domain controllers anyway.)

◆ The DAG name must be 15 characters or fewer.

◆ You can add a mix of Mailbox servers running Exchange Server 2016 Standard and Exchange Server 2016 Enterprise to the same DAG, but you normally would not do so because there would be an imbalance in the number of databases that can be hosted on each server.

◆ At least one network adapter on each Mailbox server must be able to communicate to all other DAG members. In the same site, they should be on the same subnet.

◆ All DAG members should have the same number of network adapters.

◆ If more than one adapter is used on a Mailbox server, each network adapter must be on a different network subnet.

◆ The round-trip latency between DAG members should be no more than 500 milliseconds.

◆ A Mailbox server that is a member of a DAG should not be used as the file-share witness.

You can use either the Standard or Datacenter editions of Windows Server 2012 or Windows Server 2012 R2 for the operating system in DAG. All of these operating systems allow you to install and use Failover Clustering, which is required for a DAG. In previous versions of Exchange Server that supported Windows Server 2008 R2, the operating system edition needed to be Enterprise or Datacenter to include the Failover Clustering feature. This is no longer a concern.

A DAG requires that all Mailbox servers be running the same operating system version. So, before you create a DAG, verify that all of your Mailbox servers are running Windows Server 2012 or Windows Server 2012 R2, and not a mix of both.

When you create a DAG in Exchange Server 2016, the default configuration is an IP-less DAG without an administrative access point. This sounds bad, but it's not. It means that Exchange Server is responsible for all management of Failover Clustering and you can't view a cluster node by using the Failover Clustering management tools. In general, this is best, because you should not manually configure the DAG by using Failover Clustering management tools anyway. Windows Server 2012 R2 is required for an IP-less DAG.

If you choose to create a DAG with an administrative access point and if the DAG members are running Windows Server 2012, the Cluster Name Object (CNO) must be prestaged before adding members to the DAG. For instructions on how to prestage a CNO, search for "Prestage the Cluster Name Object for a Database Availability Group" on the Technet website. The web page may indicate that the instructions apply to Exchange Server 2013, but they are also valid for Exchange Server 2016. If you are using Windows Server 2012 R2, you do not need to prestage the CNO.

Now that you've met all the prerequisites and created a DAG, let's review the steps performed when a Mailbox server is added to the DAG and it is the first Mailbox server added to the DAG. The following changes occur:

◆ Windows Failover Clustering is installed on the Mailbox server.

◆ If you added an IP address for the DAG, the CNO object is created in Active Directory (if the CNO object wasn't already prestaged).

◆ If you added an IP address for the DAG, an A (host) record is created in DNS with the IP address and the name of the DAG.

- The DAG AD object is updated with the Mailbox server that was added to the DAG.

- Any mailbox databases mounted on the Mailbox server added to the DAG are updated in the cluster database.

- If you added an IP address for the DAG, a failover cluster is created using the DAG name.

Once a DAG has been populated with a Mailbox server, any additional Mailbox servers that are added to the DAG run through the following changes:

- Windows Failover Clustering services are installed on the Mailbox server.

- The DAG Active Directory object is updated with the Mailbox server that was added to the DAG.

- Any mailbox databases mounted on the Mailbox server added to the DAG are updated in the cluster database.

- The Mailbox server is added as a node in the cluster.

- The quorum model of the DAG automatically changes (discussed further in a moment).

After creating the DAG and adding Mailbox servers to it, the availability of the DAG is based on maintaining *quorum*. Quorum is maintained when a majority of the Mailbox servers are online. A simple formula of N / 2 + 1 can be used to determine how many voting servers are needed to maintain quorum. For example, if you have a seven-node DAG, four voters are needed to maintain quorum (7 / 2 = 3.5; always round down, so 3 + 1 = 4). Using this example, a DAG that contained seven Mailbox servers (remember all Mailbox servers that are members of a DAG are also members of the same cluster) could sustain a loss of three Mailbox servers. If another Mailbox server were to go offline, quorum would be lost and the cluster would be marked as offline, and all the databases would be dismounted.

As Mailbox servers are added and removed as members of a DAG, the cluster's quorum model changes. When an even number of mailbox servers are members of a DAG, the quorum model is set to Node and File Share Majority. When an odd number of Mailbox servers are members of a DAG, the quorum model is set to a Node Majority. The main difference between the two models is that the Node and File Share Majority model uses a witness server as a tiebreaker when quorum is in question.

DYNAMIC QUORUM

Enabled by default, dynamic quorum is a feature that was introduced in Windows Server 2012 and Windows Server 2012 R2. Dynamic quorum enables the cluster to dynamically manage the number of votes needed to maintain cluster services. This is done by adjusting the number of votes needed to maintain quorum after a node fails. This has the potential to make Exchange Server more resilient to multiple node failures, even maintaining the cluster with one final "last-man-standing" node.

Let's return to our earlier example. If three of the seven Mailbox servers were to fail, the cluster would adjust the number of votes needed to maintain quorum to three. If another server were to fail, the cluster would again adjust the number of votes needed to maintain quorum.

It's important to keep in mind that this is a newer feature, and it does have some limitations. For example, it's required that servers fail sequentially, not all at once. Sequential failures allow the cluster to readjust as opposed to simultaneous failures of a majority of voting members.

To verify that dynamic quorum is enabled, run the following command:

```
Get-Cluster | fl dyn*

DynamicQuorum : 1
```

HEARTBEATS

After the server has been added to a DAG, the cluster monitors the availability of the Mailbox server by issuing a heartbeat request. A cluster heartbeat is a network communication sent between the nodes within a cluster to validate that the cluster service is online and responding. It's like a ball being bounced back and forth. If you throw the ball and it doesn't come back, you assume there is a problem. In a similar line of reasoning, if the heartbeat request goes unanswered after five requests, the node representing the Mailbox server in the cluster is marked as offline. Although it is technically possible to modify the heartbeat thresholds, you shouldn't do so. To view the heartbeat thresholds, run this command from a DAG member:

```
Get-Cluster | fl cross*,same*

CrossSubnetDelay     : 1000
CrossSubnetThreshold : 5
SameSubnetDelay      : 1000
SameSubnetThreshold  : 5
```

File-Share Witness

A witness server is a domain-joined computer that is not part of a DAG and can be used to maintain quorum when a DAG contains an even number of Mailbox servers. As discussed earlier in this chapter, a DAG with an even number of Mailbox servers uses the Node and File Share Majority quorum model. This model uses the witness server as a tiebreaker when half the Mailbox servers are either offline or can no longer communicate with the other half. The witness server doesn't actually get to vote for the cluster quorum; what happens is that a Mailbox server that has placed a lock on the witness.log file has a weighted vote. In scenarios where a DAG is stretched across two datacenters and an even number of Mailbox servers are located at each datacenter, the location of the witness server will determine which datacenter will hold quorum if communication between the two datacenters were to fail. For example, a DAG is stretched across two datacenters and each datacenter houses four Mailbox servers (for a total of eight members of the DAG). The quorum formula would require five voters to maintain quorum (8 / 2 + 1 = 5). The Mailbox server that can lock the witness.log file gets an "extra" vote and is able to maintain quorum and stay online. Only the datacenter with this Mailbox server remains up. Mailbox servers in the other datacenter stop providing Exchange services.

Even though the witness server is not used to maintain quorum when a DAG contains an odd number of Mailbox servers, the witness server is still configured within the DAG. DAG members can fluctuate due to an administrator adding or removing Mailbox servers from the

DAG. Once the number of DAG members changes from even to odd or odd to even, the DAG cluster automatically switches the quorum model.

In some disaster-recovery scenarios, you may need to have an alternative file-share witness in the secondary datacenter. You can specify an alternative file-share witness in the properties of a DAG. The alternative file-share witness is never used automatically when the original file-share witness is unavailable. The alternative file-share witness is used only when you perform a recovery operation that specifies that it should be used.

Creating a Database Availability Group Using the EAC

Before you establish your DAG and include member servers, you will want to have a few design and deployment concepts and configurations in mind. You obviously want to know how many Mailbox servers you will be adding to your DAG and what kind of design for resiliency you are planning. You want to configure the network adapters properly to ensure that both replication and MAPI traffic stay organized. To learn more about this, see the section, "Managing a DAG Network."

In the Exchange Admin Center (EAC), you can create, edit, or remove a DAG, add a new DAG network, or manage DAG membership. You need to perform several steps on a Mailbox server before adding a server as a DAG member. If there are multiple network adapters, they should be configured before the DAG is created. It's also simpler to have storage configured before creating the DAG, but it can be done afterward.

FILE-SHARE WITNESS PERMISSIONS

Before creating a DAG, you need to determine which server will be the file-share witness. Because the witness server cannot be one of your Mailbox servers in the DAG, you can select any other Windows server. The DAG-creation process automatically creates a file share on the witness server for the DAG members to access. For the file-share creation process to work properly, you need to add the Exchange Trusted Subsystem group as a member of the local Administrators group on the witness server. This gives Exchange Servers permission to manage the witness server as necessary for the witness share. Not assigning the correct permissions for Exchange Trusted Subsystem is a common mistake when creating a DAG.

To make a domain controller a file-share witness, you need to make Exchange Trusted Subsystem a member of the domain local group Administrators. This provides Exchange Trusted Subsystem with access to all domain controllers and not just the one you've selected as the file-share witness. For this reason, a member server is preferred for use as a file-share witness.

To create a DAG from the EAC, use the following steps:

1. On your client computer, open Internet Explorer and browse to the Exchange Admin Center URL. For example, for Contoso, the EAC URL might be `https://mail.contoso.com/ECP`.

2. When you're prompted with the Authentication page, type in your name and password and sign in.

3. In the Feature pane, on the left column of the EAC, select Servers.

4. In the toolbar across the top of the EAC, select the Database Availability Groups tab. Any existing DAGs will be listed below.

5. Click the + (Add) button to create a new DAG. Remember, if the DAG includes servers running Windows Server 2012, you must prestage the CNO.

6. In the New Database Availability Group window, enter the name of the DAG in the Database Availability Group Name text box. If you prestaged a CNO, this name should match the CNO.

7. Specify a server by entering the server name in the Witness Server text box, as displayed in Figure 20.1. If you do not specify a witness directory, one is automatically selected.

8. In the Database Availability Group IP Addresses text box, enter the IP address or addresses that will be associated with the DAG. Or, if you are creating an IP-less DAG, then leave this blank. If you enter 0.0.0.0, then DHCP is used.

9. Click Save when you've added all the required details.

FIGURE 20.1
Creating a new DAG in the EAC

10. After the DAG has been created, you can add the first Mailbox server to the DAG by highlighting the DAG and selecting the Manage DAG Membership icon (the one with the small gear in front of the rectangle).

11. In the Manage Database Availability Group Membership window, click the + (Add) button.

12. Highlight the Mailbox server that will be added to the DAG, click the + (Add) button, and click OK. You can add multiple servers or just one at a time. If you add multiple servers, they are added sequentially.

13. Once you add a Mailbox server, click the Save button.

14. After the Failover Clustering service is installed and saving is complete, click Close.

Creating a Database Availability Group Using EMS

The New-DatabaseAvailabilityGroup cmdlet is used to create a new DAG in EMS. The same options that are available in the EAC are available when you're creating a new DAG in the EMS. The following command creates a new DAG using NYC-FS1 as the witness server:

```
New-DatabaseAvailabilityGroup -Name NYC-DAG -WitnessServer NYC-FS1
 -WitnessDirectory C:\DAG1 -DatabaseAvailabilityGroupIpAddresses 192.168.1.44
```

Once the DAG has been created, Mailbox servers can be added to the DAG using the Add-DatabaseAvailabilityGroupServer cmdlet:

```
Add-DatabaseAvailabilityGroupServer -Identity NYC-DAG -MailboxServer NYC-EX1
```

Managing a Database Availability Group

Once you've created a DAG and added Mailbox servers to it, you can modify multiple settings within the DAG and those Mailbox servers to meet the business and technical requirements of your organization. Covering all the settings that can be modified within a DAG falls outside the scope of this book. Instead, we'll concentrate on some of the common changes made after a DAG has been formed and some of the DAG features included in Exchange Server 2013 and 2016.

Managing a DAG in EMS

Using the Exchange Management Shell, you can create, edit, or remove a DAG, modify DAG-specific changes on a Mailbox server or mailbox database, and modify the state a of DAG member. For a full list of the parameters for each of the following cmdlets, please reference the Exchange Server 2016 help file.

Set-DatabaseAvailabilityGroup Modifies the settings of an existing DAG. In the example here, BOS-FS1 has been added as the alternative file-share witness for NYC-DAG:

```
Set-DatabaseAvailabilityGroup -Identity NYC-DAG -AlternateWitnessDirectory C:\
DAGFileShareWitnesses\BOS-FS1.contoso.com -AlternateWitnessServer BOS-FS1
```

Remove-DatabaseAvailabilityGroup Removes the DAG after all Mailbox servers have been removed from a DAG. The following example removes NYC-DAG from the organization:

```
Remove-DatabaseAvailabilityGroup NYC-DAG
```

Set-MailboxServer Helps manage the configuration of Mailbox servers in a DAG. The following example sets the maximum number of active mailbox databases on NYC-EX1 to 50:

```
Set-MailboxServer NYC-EX1 -MaximumActiveDatabases 50
```

Set-MailboxDatabase Changes the mailbox database settings for databases that are part of a DAG. In the following example, a single database copy alert is turned off for DB4:

```
Set-MailboxDatabase DB4 -AutoDagExcludeFromMonitoring $False
```

Add-DatabaseAvailabilityGroupServer Adds Mailbox servers to a DAG. The following command adds NYC-EX2 to NYC-DAG and bypasses the validation of the DAG quorum model and the health check for the witness server:

```
Add-DatabaseAvailabilityGroupServer -Identity NYC-DAG
 -MailboxServer NYC-EX2 -SkipDagValidation
```

Remove-DatabaseAvailabilityGroupServer To remove a Mailbox server from a DAG use this cmdlet. NYC-EX2 will be removed from NYC-DAG when this command completes:

```
Remove-DatabaseAvailabilityGroupServer NYC-DAG -MailboxServer NYC-EX2
```

Stop-DatabaseAvailabilityGroup Marks a Mailbox server, that is a member of a DAG, as failed so no Exchange Server resources can be activated on this server. Mailbox server NYC-EX2 is offline. Using the ConfigurationOnly switch, NYC-EX2 can be marked as failed even though the server is offline:

```
Stop-DatabaseAvailabilityGroup NYC-DAG -MailboxServer NYC-EX2
           -ConfigurationOnly
```

Restore-DatabaseAvailabilityGroup Performs a datacenter switchover process when quorum is lost. The following command starts the restore of DAG services in the Boston AD site:

```
Restore-DatabaseAvailabilityGroup NYC-DAG
 -ActiveDirectorySite Boston
```

Start-DatabaseAvailabilityGroup Reinstates a DAG member to the DAG. Here Mailbox server NYC-EX2 is reinstated in NYC-DAG:

```
Start-DatabaseAvailabilityGroup NYC-DAG -MailboxServer NYC-EX2
```

Multiple Databases per Volume

Managing and planning for a DAG goes beyond configuring parameters in EAC and EMS. Part of managing and planning a DAG is determining the placement of databases on physical spindles. Exchange Server 2010 did not support having multiple databases on the same physical disk. This limitation was a big drawback for organizations that were planning a JBOD (Just a Bunch of Disks) storage solution (see Figure 20.2).

Two problems are apparent in Figure 20.2. The first is the size of the mailbox database; 200 GB is much less than the disk size, 2 TB, which means the organization is wasting available storage. In this example, 1.8 TB are left over. Even with additional space taken by transaction logs, there will still be a lot of unused capacity. Second, each Mailbox server has a dedicated disk for a passive copy. The IOPS load is unevenly dispersed between the physical disks, again wasting the resources of the physical disk. A JBOD storage solution for a DAG in Exchange Server 2010 left a lot to be desired.

FIGURE 20.2
Exchange Server 2010 JBOD configuration

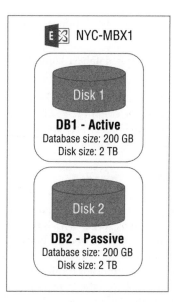 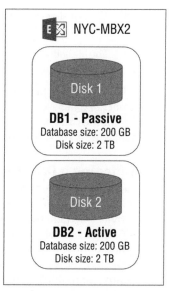

Starting with Exchange Server 2013 and continuing in Exchange Server 2016, Microsoft not only supports multiple databases per physical disk, but recommends it. The recommended number of databases per physical disk in a JBOD configuration is four, with one active and three passive. This works well with very large disks, such as 8 TB. You can have four large databases and their log files on the same disk.

Now a JBOD deployment is a more appealing storage solution because an organization can squeeze the resources out of each physical disk. Before running to your storage team demanding they purchase a JBOD storage solution, you must consider the number of database copies and database placement of those copies. A good rule of thumb to follow is the number of copies of each database should be equal to the number of database copies per physical disk. This type of design is referred to as symmetrical design. Take the example in Figure 20.3. All four Mailbox servers host four database copies on a single disk, and each database has four copies.

FIGURE 20.3
Mailbox databases symmetrically placed between the Mailbox servers

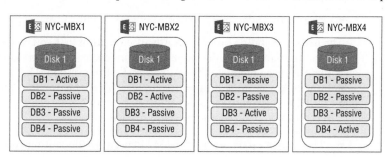

Microsoft has made the following recommendations for deploying multiple databases on the same physical disk:

◆ There should be a single logical disk partition per physical disk.

◆ The number of copies of each database should be equal to the number of database copies per physical disk.

◆ The activation preference of each database copy should be balanced between the Mailbox servers in the DAG.

They key thing to remember about multiple databases per disk is that the database size and number of databases do not affect the overall IOPS. The IOPS are influenced by the number of mailboxes and how busy those mailboxes are. These factors are taken into account by the Exchange Server Role Requirements Calculator.

Managing a DAG Network

Creating a DAG and adding the first Mailbox server to it establishes a DAG network. A DAG network consists of one or more subnets that are used for continuous replication and client connectivity (MAPI network). If a Mailbox server with a single network adapter is added to the DAG, the subnet of that network adapter is used for both client connectivity and continuous replication. The preferred architecture for Exchange Server 2016 specifies that DAG members should have only a single network adapter for replication and MAPI communication. Network teaming for multiple network adapters on the same network is not recommended. This provides simplicity, particularly for multisite configurations. The preferred architecture is all about simplicity and stability rather than optimization.

If you do choose to have a separate replication network, it is important to set up the network adapters on a Mailbox server beforehand. As stated previously, only one adapter can be used for client communication. This adapter is often referred as the MAPI adapter. Any other adapter can be used for replication. These adapters are often referred to as the replication adapters. The MAPI adapter should be configured as follows:

◆ Configure the default gateway.

◆ Enable File and Printer Sharing for Microsoft Networks.

◆ Enable Client for Microsoft Networks.

◆ Register in DNS.

◆ Use the first adapter listed in the network binding order (see Figure 20.4).

The network binding order is an Advanced Setting that you can access from Network Connections. In the Network Connections window, press Alt to display the menu bar, and then click the Advanced menu and the Advanced Settings option. The network binding order is found under Advanced Settings for your network adapter on the Adapters and Bindings tab, and this helps determine the order accessed by network services.

The replication NICs should be configured as follows:

◆ Use a subnet separate from the MAPI network (no routing between them).

◆ Do not configure the default gateway (configure static routes if required for routing on the replication network).

◆ Disable File and Print Sharing for Microsoft Networks.

◆ Disable Client for Microsoft Networks.

◆ Do not register in DNS.

It's useful to note that even with multiple network adapters, there is no redundancy for the MAPI network on a DAG member. There can be only one MAPI network. There can be multiple replication networks. In fact, if all of the replication networks fail, the MAPI network will be used for replication.

FIGURE 20.4
The network bind-
ing order that
should be in place
before adding a
Mailbox server to
a DAG

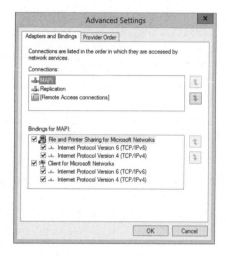

AUTOMATIC DAG NETWORK MANAGEMENT

Starting with Exchange Server 2013, DAG networks are managed automatically by the system; this feature is enabled by default. When the system manages DAG networks, the network adapters of the Mailbox servers that are added to the DAG are checked, and based on the configuration of each network adapter, the system determines if the network adapter can be used for client connectivity, replication, or both.

There are two types of DAG networks: a single subnet and a multi-subnet. When all members of the DAG are in the same subnet, this normally means the DAG is not stretched across multiple datacenters, and the DAG is considered a single subnet. When members of the DAG are in different subnets, this normally means the DAG is stretched across two or more datacenters, and the DAG is considered a multi-subnet.

When a multi-subnet DAG is configured and the automatic management of DAG networks is enabled, the system pairs the proper network subnets for client connectivity and continuous replication based on the configuration of the network adapters.

One of the downsides of having automatic DAG network configuration enabled is that the DAG network settings—including managing the DAG network settings through the EAC—are disabled. But again, it's about simplicity. If you are using a single network as recommended in the preferred architecture, it's unlikely that you'll need to perform any manual network configuration.

MANAGING A DAG NETWORK FROM EMS

You can use EMS to manage, add, and remove DAG networks and manage DAG network settings in the DAG via the following cmdlets:

Set-DatabaseAvailabilityGroup   Changes DAG settings. To disable the automatic management of the DAG networks by the system, run the following command:

```
Set-DatabaseAvailabilityGroup NYC-DAG -ManualDagNetworkConfiguration $true
```

New-DatabaseAvailabilityGroupNetwork Creates a new DAG network. Automatic network configuration must be turned off to run this cmdlet. To create a DAG network that will be used for replication, run this command:

```
New-DatabaseAvailabilityGroupNetwork -DatabaseAvailabilityGroup NYC-DAG
 -Name ReplNet -Subnets 10.1.0.0/16 -ReplicationEnabled:$true
```

Set-DatabaseAvailabilityGroupNetwork Helps manage the DAG networks. Automatic network configuration must be turned off to run this cmdlet. Replication for the MAPI network will be disabled in this example:

```
Set-DatabaseAvailabilityGroupNetwork NYC-DAG\MapiDagNetwork
     -ReplicationEnabled:$false
```

Remove-DatabaseAvailabilityGroupNetwork Deletes a DAG network. In this example, the DAG network ReplNet will be removed from NYC-DAG:

```
Remove-DatabaseAvailabilityGroupNetwork -Identity NYC-DAG\ReplNet
```

Get-DatabaseAvailabilityGroupNetwork Retrieves the DAG networks. To see all the DAG networks, run this command:

```
Get-DatabaseAvailabilityGroupNetwork
Identity                ReplicationEnabled    Subnets
--------                ------------------    -------
NYC-DAG\Mapi    True                          {{192.168.0.0/16,Up}}
NYC-DAG\ReplNet True                          {{10.1.0.0/16,Up}}
```

---

iSCSI and DAG Networks

Any network adapter on a Mailbox server is discovered and exposed as a DAG network. This is a problem when iSCSI storage is configured on a Mailbox server. You don't want Exchange Server 2016 to start replicating mailbox databases across your iSCSI networks. Microsoft recommends that any network adapter used for iSCSI must be excluded from the DAG network. The following example shows how to exclude a network name iSCSI from the DAG:

```
Set-DatabaseAvailabilityGroupNetwork NYC-DAG\iSCSI
 -ReplicationEnabled:$false -IgnoreNetwork:$true
```

Adding a Mailbox Database to a DAG

Developing a database layout is part of the process of adding mailbox databases in a DAG. It consists of spreading the database copies across Mailbox servers and determining the activation preference of each database copy. For example, in Figure 20.5, there are four Mailbox servers and each mailbox database is replicated to each Mailbox server.

The Activation Preference Number of each database copy is used during the Best Copy and Server Selection process, which is covered later in this chapter. However, it's important to note that the Activation Preference Number is used as a tiebreaker *only* when Active Manager chooses which database copy to activate. For example, if *all things were equal* for the mailbox database copy of DB1 on NYC-MBX1 and NYC-MBX2, Active Manager would activate DB1 on NYC-MBX1 because MBX1 has the lowest mailbox database preference. In addition to the Activation Preference, many other factors are taken into account during a database failover. So, while you want to establish the activation preference that makes sense to you with regard to the order in which you would like Mailbox servers to host the active database copy, your preference is not considered of primary importance during the failover process.

FIGURE 20.5

Mailbox database layout

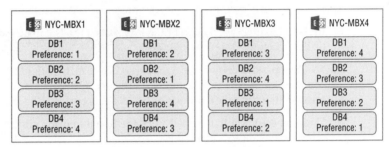

FAILOVER VS. SWITCHOVER

When you read DAG documentation, you will see the terms failover and switchover. You should understand what both terms refer to because there is a distinct difference between the two.

A *switchover* is a process that you initiate while the system is functioning properly. For example, when you move an active database from NYC-EX1 to NYC-EX2, that process is a switchover. Because there is proper communication between all of the servers, a switchover is performed in an orderly way with no data loss.

A *failover* is, by definition, unplanned. A failover occurs when an Exchange server or database fails and databases need to be mounted on another server. In such cases, there is a chance of data loss at the replication level because the original active data source is not healthy (even though missing messages will be recovered from SafetyNet).

MANAGING MAILBOX DATABASE COPIES IN THE EAC

Adding a new mailbox database into a DAG is exactly the same as creating a mailbox database outside of a DAG. However, after adding the first mailbox database copy on a server, you can add passive copies of the mailbox database on other DAG members.

Before you begin creating mailbox databases, you should plan out your storage for hosting the databases. All copies of a mailbox database use the same file paths for the database and logs on each host. So, if the first copy of DB1 is created in E:\DB\DB1, then any DAG member holding a mailbox database copy must also have this path available. To simplify server configuration, it is best to have identical storage on all DAG members.

To add passive copies from the EAC, use the following steps:

1. On your client computer, sign in to the EAC.

2. In the Feature pane, on the left column of the EAC, select Servers.

3. In the toolbar across the top of the EAC, select the Databases tab. Mailbox databases will be listed below.

4. To add a passive copy of a database (Figure 20.6), highlight the mailbox database, click the More button (a row of three dots), and select Add Database Copy. (After a new database is created, it might take a minute or two for this option to become available.)

5. Under Specify Mailbox Server, click the Browse button and choose the Mailbox server to which you want to add a replica.

6. In the drop-down box under Activation Preference Number, select a number—the lower the number, the higher the preference.

7. To see additional (optional) settings, click More Options.

   ◆ Use the Replay Lag Time (Days) text box if you want to make this database a lagged database copy.

   ◆ Postpone Seeding delays the copying of the mailbox database to the Mailbox server being added as a replica. This is used when you manually seed a database copy.

When you click Save, a copy of the mailbox database is seeded (copied) to the Mailbox server you selected. The information in the DAG and Active Directory are also updated to reflect this change. After the database is seeded, transaction logs are replicated to catch up the changes since the seeding operation began.

If you are adding copies of a newly created or very small database, the process is very fast. However, if you are adding a copy of a large mailbox database, the seeding of the database can take an extended period of time, particularly if you are seeding to a disaster-recovery site with limited bandwidth. In some cases, with a very large database and/or very slow network connectivity, it is preferable to preseed the database.

When you preseed a database, you take a copy of the mailbox database (from a backup or dismounted database) and transfer it by file copy. In some cases, transferring a database by file copy over the same network link is significantly faster than letting Exchange Server perform the seeding. You can also copy the database to physical media and ship it to the remote location. However, if you find yourself in a scenario where you need to preseed the database, you might want to consider reducing the size of your databases.

FIGURE 20.6

Adding a mailbox database to a Mailbox server

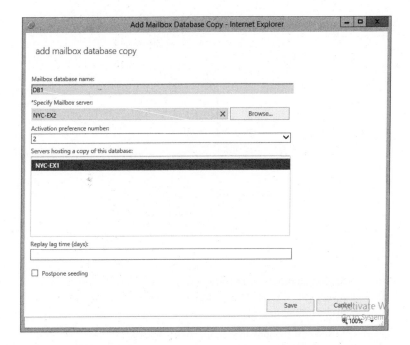

If you are placing a mailbox database in a disaster-recovery site and you never want it to be automatically mounted, you can prevent this copy of the mailbox database from automatically being activated by Active Manager during a mailbox database or Mailbox server failover, by enabling activation block:

1. Highlight the mailbox database to which you just added a replica.

2. In the Details pane, select Suspend (see Figure 20.7) on the mailbox database copy on which you want to enable the activation block.

3. In the Suspend Database Copy window, check the box next to "This copy can only be activated by manual intervention" and click Save.

   When Active Manager builds the list of databases available for activation after a failover, the mailbox copy with activation block enabled will be excluded from the list.

You can use EAC to manually activate a database on another server. In Figure 20.7, you can see that for passive database copies, there is an option to activate the copy. When you activate a database on another server, users are automatically connected to the active database in the new location.

MANAGING A MAILBOX DATABASE IN THE EMS

Using the Exchange Management Shell, you can specify unique settings to each database copy, validate the health of each database copy, pause and resume replication, reseed a database copy, or remove a database copy. For a full list of the parameters for each of the following cmdlets, please reference the Exchange Server 2016 Help file.

FIGURE 20.7
Database options
from the Details
pane in EAC

```
DB1

Database availability group:
NYC-DAG

Servers
NYC-EX1
NYC-EX2

Database copies
DB1\NYC-EX1
Active Mounted
Copy queue length: 0
Content index state: Healthy
View details

DB1\NYC-EX2
Passive Healthy
Copy queue length: 0
Content index state: Healthy
Suspend | Activate | Remove
View details
```

Add-MailboxDatabaseCopy   Adds a replica to an existing mailbox database. The Mailbox server NYC-EX2 will be added as a passive copy of DB6 and will postpone the seeding of the mailbox database:

```
Add-MailboxDatabaseCopy DB6 -MailboxServer NYC-EX2
-ActivationPreference 2 -SeedingPostponed
```

Suspend-MailboxDatabaseCopy   Enables activation block and stops the copying and replay of transaction logs from the active database copy. To suspend replication of DB6 on Mailbox server NYC-EX2, run this command:

```
Suspend-MailboxDatabaseCopy DB6\NYC-EX2 -SuspendComment
   "Taking storage offline"
```

Resume-MailboxDatabaseCopy   Removes activation block or resumes the copying and replaying of transaction logs from the active database copy. Replication will resume for DB6 on the Mailbox server NYC-EX2:

```
Resume-MailboxDatabaseCopy DB6\NYC-EX2
```

Remove-MailboxDatabaseCopy   Removes a mailbox database copy from a Mailbox server. The replica of DB6 will be removed from Mailbox server NYC-EX2:

```
Remove-MailboxDatabaseCopy DB6\NYC-EX2
```

Update-MailboxDatabaseCopy   Seeds or reseeds a mailbox database. This cmdlet can be used to update both the database and content index or just the database or content index. DB6 on NYC-EX2 will seed the mailbox only from All-3 and remove any existing database files:

```
Update-MailboxDatabaseCopy -Identity DB6\NYC-EX2 -SourceServer
      All-3 -DeleteExistingFiles -DatabaseOnly -Network MapiDagNetwork
```

Set-MailboxDatabaseCopy   Changes a mailbox database copy to a lagged copy or changes the activation preference. To change the activation preference to 1 for DB6 on Mailbox server NYC-EX2, run this command:

```
Set-MailboxDatabaseCopy DB6\NYC-EX2 -ActivationPreference 1
```

Move-ActiveMailboxDatabase   Changes the server on which the active mailbox database copy is hosted. In the following example, DB6 is being activated on Mailbox server NYC-EX2:

```
Move-ActiveMailboxDatabase DB6 -ActivateOnServer NYC-EX2
```

Get-MailboxDatabaseCopyStatus   Shows the replication status of all the mailbox databases homed on the Mailbox server from which the cmdlet was run:

```
Get-MailboxDatabaseCopyStatus -ConnectionStatus
```

The Get-MailboxDatabaseCopyStatus cmdlet is very useful in determining the replication state of each mailbox database on a specific Mailbox server. (For more information on mailbox database replication, please see the "Understanding the Best Copy and Server Selection" section, later in this chapter.) To see a list of all copies for a mailbox database, provide the database name:

```
Get-MailboxDatabaseCopyStatus DB1
Name          Status CopyQueueLength ReplayQueueLength
----          ------ --------------- -----------------
DB1\NYC-EX1 Healthy               0                 0
DB1\NYC-EX2 Mounted               0                 0
```

Set-MailboxServer   Applies global settings to all databases homed on a specific Mailbox server. The following example prevents any database from automatically being activated on NYC-EX2:

```
Set-MailboxServer NYC-EX2 -DatabaseCopyAutoActivationPolicy Blocked
```

IMPLEMENTING LAGGED MAILBOX DATABASE COPIES

A lagged mailbox database copy is not a new concept in Exchange Server 2016, but significant changes have been made since Exchange Server 2010 that directly impact lagged databases. A *lagged mailbox database copy* is a passive database copy that delays committing the transaction logs to the database.

A *lagged copy* is defined by the replay lag time setting of a mailbox database copy. The replay lag time specifies how long after the inspection of the transaction log the Mailbox server will wait before committing the changes in the transaction log into the copy of the mailbox database. Having the database hold off on committing changes immediately gives you the ability to restore the mailbox database copy to a specific point in time without restoring from backup. The idea is that after bad changes have occurred to the database, you use the lagged database to recover to a point in time before those bad changes had happened. The lag time needs to be long enough for you or the users to notice that the bad changes have occurred and react to them.

Another parameter that you can manipulate on a lagged database is the *truncation lag time*. The truncation lag time defines when the transaction log files will be deleted from disk after they are committed to the database. The default truncation lag time is 0, which means that logs are deleted immediately after they are committed to the database. However, if you want to retain the transaction logs for use in restoring backups, you can do so. For example, maybe you only do a weekly backup of your Exchange databases. If you have a lagged copy that doesn't commit logs for five days, you should keep logs for another two or three days to ensure that you can replay the transaction logs against a restored database for disaster recovery.

When you implement lagged copies, there is a significant impact on disk utilization. Because the transaction logs are not deleted immediately, they use more disk space. A longer lag replay uses more disk space. When you use the Exchange Server Role Requirements Calculator, it accounts for this as part of the calculation process.

You can set the truncation and replay lag times on a lagged database by using the Add-MailboxDatabaseCopy and Set-MailboxDatabaseCopy cmdlets. The following examples set the replay lag time and truncation lag time to one day.

The following sets the replay and truncation lag times using the Add-MailboxDatabaseCopy cmdlet:

```
Add-MailboxDatabaseCopy -Identity DB1 -MailboxServer NYC-EX2
        -ReplayLagTime 1.00:00:00 -TruncationLagTime 1.00:00:00
            -ActivationPreference 4
```

The following sets the replay and truncation lag times by using the Set-MailboxDatabaseCopy cmdlet:

```
Set-MailboxDatabaseCopy -Identity DB4\NYC-EX2 -ReplayLagTime 1.00:00:00
    -TruncationLagTime 1.00:00:00
```

The introduction of Safety Net, which is covered in Chapter 22, "Managing Connectivity with Transport Services," has replaced the functionality of the transport dumpster that was used in Exchange Server 2007 and 2010. When an email message has been delivered to the active copy of the mailbox database, a copy of the message is stored in the queue. Each active mailbox database retains its own queue. By default, the messages stored in the Safety Net queue are retained for two days.

The use of lagged databases in an organization will directly impact the configuration of the Safety Net. The duration of time set in the ReplayLagTime parameter on a lagged database copy, should match the duration of time Safety Net stores email messages. For example, if you set a lagged database to play transaction logs after five days, messages should be removed from the Safety Net queue after five days. This allows you to use a lagged database copy for recovery from database corruption and obtain any newer messages from Safety Net rather than replaying transaction logs, which may reintroduce the corruption from which you are recovering.

If you have multiple lagged database copies throughout your organization, set the Safety Net threshold to the highest ReplayLagTime value. It is important to note that the longer you set the Safety Net queue, the more storage you will need for it.

Exchange Server 2016 can bypass the Replay Lag Time setting, in certain scenarios, by automatically replaying log files into the mailbox database. This process is referred to in the Microsoft documentation as *play down* of log files and is done to ensure the integrity of data in mailbox databases. To ensure that there is no impact on users, play down is a low priority and will back off when disk activity is high. The following scenarios invoke play down of log files:

◆ When there are fewer than three healthy databases copies (active or passive) for more than 24 hours

◆ When page patching is needed to fix physical corruption of the mailbox database

◆ When free disk space falls below the defined free-disk-space percentage threshold

By default, lagged-copy play down is disabled on a DAG. Using the `Set-DatabaseAvailabilityGroup` cmdlet with the `ReplayLagManagerEnabled` parameter, you can enable lagged copy play down:

```
Set-DatabaseAvailabilityGroup DAG1 -ReplayLagManagerEnabled $true
```

Once the `ReplayLagManagerEnabled` parameter has been set to true on a given DAG, you can modify the Registry on the Mailbox server hosting a lagged copy to change the number of available database copies and the free-disk-space threshold before play down occurs.

The following sets the number of available database copies:

```
HKLM\Software\Microsoft\ExchangeServer\v15\Replay\Parameters\
ReplayLagManagerNumAvailableCopies
```

And this sets the free-disk-space percentage:

```
HKLM\Software\Microsoft\ExchangeServer\v15\Replay\Parameters\
ReplayLagPlayDownPercentDiskFreeSpace
```

Automatic Reseed (aka AutoReseed)

During the lifetime of a DAG, it is almost inevitable that a database copy will enter into a failed state. In Exchange Server 2010, if resuming continuous replication didn't fix the problem, reseeding the mailbox was required to bring the replica back to a healthy state. Reseeding the mailbox database from a healthy copy was a manual process in Exchange Server 2010. In Exchange Server 2013, new parameters have been added to the DAG to allow automatic reseeding.

Automatic reseed does not just force a reseed of a corrupted database. It can also allocate spare volumes to replace failed volumes. This feature is well suited to JBOD disk configurations. When a JBOD disk fails, a spare volume is allocated and the databases that were on the failed disk are automatically reseeded on the new disk. The configuration of Automatic Reseed involves premapping volumes and using mount points. To start with, let's review the Automatic Reseed process flow:

1. The Exchange Replication Service checks for mailbox database copies that have a status of FailedAndSuspended.

2. When the Exchange Replication Service finds a database copy with a status of FailedAndSuspended, prerequisite checks are performed to determine if there is single-copy situation, if a spare disk is available, and if the system can perform an Automatic Reseed.

3. If the all checks pass, the Exchange Replication Service starts the Automatic Reseed process by allocating and remapping a spare drive.

4. Seeding is performed on the failed mailbox database.

5. Once seeding has finished, Exchange Replication Service checks to see if the seeded database is in a healthy state.

Configuring and implementing Automatic Reseed can be a bit tricky the first time through. To ease the pain, Figure 20.8 illustrates an Automatic Reseed configuration for a single database.

Starting from the top, two folders are created on the root of the C:\ drive, ExVols and ExDBs. ExVols contains the folder Vol1. This folder is used as a mount point for a physical disk. This disk is a spare JBOD disk that can be allocated by Automatic Reseed.

The folder C:\ExDBs contains mount points for physical disks (DbDisk1 and DbDisk2) that hold the databases and log files. On each of these disks is one or more database copies that you have placed there.

Now that the mount points are in place, what's next? Parameters within the DAG must be updated to reflect the Automatic Reseed design in Figure 20.8. The following parameters need to be changed:

AutoDagVolumesRootFolderPath   The mount point that contains all of the available volumes (C:\ExVols)

AutoDagDatabasesRootFolderPath   The mount point that contains all of the databases (C:\ExDBs)

AutoDagDatabaseCopiesPerVolume   The number of database copies per volume (one database copy on Disk 1 and one database copy on Disk 2)

FIGURE 20.8
Automatic Reseed
configuration

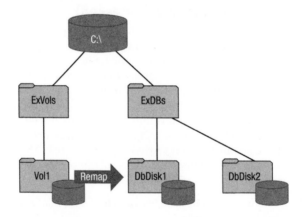

Now Automatic Reseed is ready. If a database copy on DbDisk1 fails, Automatic Reseed will attempt to reseed the copy, if necessary, to restore redundancy. If the hard disk mounted to DbDisk1 fails, Automatic Reseed will remap the hard disk mounted to Vol1 to the DbDisk1 mount point to replace it. Then, the database copies that were stored on the DbDisk1 mount point will be reseeded to restore redundancy.

Understanding Active Manager

Active Manager runs on all Mailbox servers inside the Microsoft Exchange Replication Service and is responsible for many aspects of mailbox availability. Each Mailbox server is designated with an Active Manager role. When the Mailbox server is a member of a DAG, there are two Active Manager roles, Primary and Standby. Only one server in the DAG can hold the Primary Active Manager (PAM) role at a time; all the other Mailbox servers in the DAG hold the Standby Active Manager (SAM) role. When a Mailbox server is not a member of a DAG, the Active Manager role is set to stand-alone. If a stand-alone server is added to the DAG, the Mailbox server will update its role to SAM. The Mailbox server in the DAG that is designated as the PAM always has ownership of the cluster quorum resources. If the PAM server were to fail, another Mailbox server in the DAG would pick up the PAM role. To determine the Mailbox server that holds the PAM role, run either one of these commands:

```
Get-DatabaseAvailabilityGroup NYC-DAG -Status | FL pri*

PrimaryActiveManager : NYC-EX2
```

Or, from one of the DAG members, you run the command Get-ClusterGroup. Cluster Group identifies the primary active manager, as shown here:

```
Get-ClusterGroup

Name               OwnerNode    State
----               ---------    -----
Available Storage  NYC-EX2      Offline
Cluster Group      NYC-EX2      Online
```

The PAM role can be moved to another Mailbox server by using the Move-ClusterGroup cmdlet. The Mailbox server that is taking on the PAM role will record the process, shown in Figure 20.9 and Figure 20.10, in the Operational log found underneath Event Viewer\ Applications and Service Logs\Microsoft\Exchange\HighAvailability.

FIGURE 20.9
Event 227 shows that a configuration change was detected.

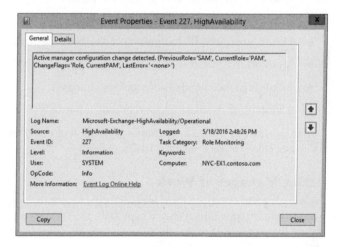

To move the PAM role to a different Mailbox server, run this command:

```
Move-ClusterGroup "Cluster Group" -Node NYC-EX1

Name                 OwnerNode        Status
--------------------  --------------- ------
Cluster Group        NYC-EX1          Online
```

FIGURE 20.10
Event 111 shows
that the change to
PAM is complete.

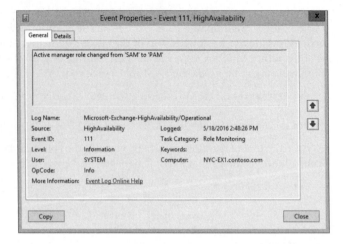

Mailbox servers that hold the SAM role provide information to the PAM. The SAM notifies the PAM of databases that are active on the local server. If a database or a component were to fail, the SAM would communicate to the PAM to start a failover to a passive database copy. If a Mailbox server were to fail, the Mailbox server holding the PAM role would mark the server as down in cluster resources and start the process of activating the mailbox databases on different Mailbox servers. The server that owns the PAM role has several responsibilities, including the following:

◆ Determining which Mailbox server has the active copy of each mailbox database

◆ Monitoring and acting on failures

◆ Notifying DAG members of topology changes

◆ Maintaining database and server state information

Active Manager makes a resubmission request of email messages that are stored in the queue database. This process is covered in Chapter 22.

Active Manager at Work

As already mentioned, the PAM is responsible for controlling the failover process when an active database copy fails. When a copy fails, the PAM selects and activates the best available remaining copy based on a number of factors. This Best Copy and Server Selection (BCSS) process is described in the next section.

The steps performed by Active Manager to find the best database copy to mount are recorded in the Operational log found under `Event Viewer\Applications and Service Logs\Microsoft\Exchange\HighAvailability`. The following process describes the actions of the PAM when a failover occurs in NYC-DAG. There are three database copies of DB1 on NYC-EX1, NYC-EX2, and NYC-EX3. NYC-EX1 is the PAM and NYC-EX2 is the active copy of the database.

1. When NYC-EX1 and NYC-EX3 lose communication with NYC-EX2, NYC-EX2 is marked as down in the Windows failover cluster.

2. Active Manager starts the process of moving DB1 from NYC-EX2 to a different Mailbox server.

3. Active Manager checks the health of key components on Mailbox servers NYC-EX1 and NYC-EX3.

4. DB1 on NYC-EX1 is deemed the best copy, and Active Manager automatically mounts DB1 on NYC-EX1. (The next section of this chapter provides more insight on the process for best copy and server selection.)

5. As part of the failover process, Active Manager tries to copy any missing transaction logs from the Mailbox server that last held the active copy to the Mailbox server the database is moving to. In this example, since NYC-EX2 was the last server to hold the active copy of DB1, this process fails to copy transaction logs to NYC-EX1 because NYC-EX2 is offline (Figure 20.11).

6. After DB1 is mounted, Active Manager requests Safety Net to resubmit messages that it doesn't have because of the failover. (Figure 20.12)

FIGURE 20.11
An attempt to copy remaining transaction log files

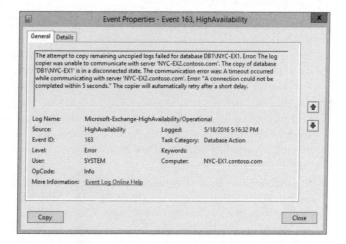

Understanding the Best Copy and Server Selection Process

The Best Copy and Server Selection (BCSS) process is the same in Exchange Server 2016 as it was in Exchange Server 2013. If a failure is detected or an administrator performs a switchover without specifying a target server, the Mailbox server holding the PAM role will evaluate the best passive database to mount.

FIGURE 20.12
Messages requested
from Safety Net

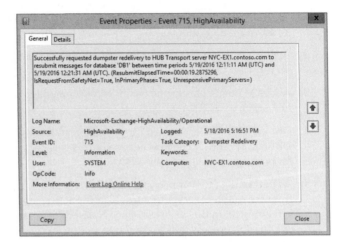

AutoDatabaseMountDial

When you are mounting a passive database, the `AutoDatabaseMountDial` parameter of the Mailbox server is one of the things you should consider. This setting defines how many log files can be lost as part of the switchover or failover process to a passive database. If the setting is not met, then a passive database is not automatically mounted on the server. Instead, you must force it to mount.

Your first instinct might be that no transaction logs can be lost during the failover process and that the setting should be set to Lossless. However, if you do this, during an unexpected failover when a DAG member fails, the database will never mount automatically on a new server because some log data will be missing. However, Lossless is a good selection when you manually activate a passive database copy.

The default value for `AutoDatabaseMountDial` is GoodAvailability, which allows six log files to be lost. You can also select BestAvailability, which allows 12 log files to be lost. Missing log files do not mean that you lose recent messages. The missing data is retrieved from Safety Net so that there is no data loss.

The process to mount a passive database is as follows:

1. A failure is detected by Managed Availability or Active Manager, or an administrator performs a switchover without specifying a target server.

2. The PAM Mailbox server starts the BCSS algorithm.

3. Once the BCSS has determined which mailbox database to activate, the Attempt Copy Last Log (ACLL) process is kicked off. ACLL tries to copy any missing logs from the Mailbox server that hosted the active mailbox database.

4. Once the ACLL process has completed, the value of the copy queue length is compared against the `AutoDatabaseMountDial` parameter of the mailbox database.

5. If the number of missing transaction logs is greater than the value allowed by `AutoDatabaseMountDial`, Active Manager will try to mount the next-best database copy. If there are no other acceptable database copies, the database is left offline.

6. If the number of missing transaction logs is less than or equal to the value allowed by `AutoDatabaseMountDial`, a mount request is issued from the PAM to the Mailbox server that is hosting the passive copy over RPC.

7. If the mount request works, the passive copy of the mailbox database becomes the active copy and end users are able to access their mail content again.

The process of determining which passive database to activate starts with health checks that are part of the Managed Availability monitoring component. During the BCSS process (step 2 from the preceding list), Active Manager performs four additional checks in the order listed here:

1. All Healthy—All monitoring components are in a healthy state.

2. Up to Normal Healthy—All monitoring components with a normal priority are in a healthy state.

3. All Better Than Source—All monitoring components are in a better health state on a Mailbox server to which the database is being moved than they are on the Mailbox server from which the database is being moved.

4. Same As Source—All monitoring components are in the same health state on the Mailbox server to which the database is being moved as they are on the Mailbox server from which the database is being moved.

After the health checks are performed, Active Manager begins the best copy selection by building a list of available database copies. Any database that is unreachable or has its activation block enabled is not added to the database list. If `AutoDatabaseMountDial` is set to Lossless, all transaction logs must be present before the database is mounted on a different Mailbox server and Active Manager sorts the list of available database copies in ascending order by activation preference. When `AutoDatabaseMountDial` is set to anything other than Lossless, Active Manager sorts the available database copies by copy queue length. If multiple database copies have the same copy queue length, the list is sorted a second time using activation preference as a tiebreaker.

Active Manager also looks at the state of the replay queue length, which defines the number of logs that have been copied to a passive Mailbox server but haven't been written to the mailbox database.

Next, Active Manager processes each database copy against 10 sets of criteria to determine which database copy is the best database to mount. Active Manager attempts to find database copies with a replication status of Healthy, DisconnectedAndHealthy, DisconnectedAndResynchronizing, or SeedingSource; and it evaluates the databases against 10 sets of criteria. Each passive mailbox copy goes through the evaluation process to determine the best-suited database to mount. If multiple databases fall within the same criteria, then the Active Manager tries to activate the first mailbox database in the database list. Each database is evaluated against the 10 sets of criteria in Table 20.1.

WHAT HAPPENS WHEN A FAILOVER IS ISSUED

It is worth noting that if a failover is issued by a health service, some of the 10 steps in Table 20.1 are not performed. For example, if the failover is issued because the index status is in a failed state, Active Manager will not activate a database copy on a Mailbox server that also has a failed database index.

TABLE 20.1: Active Manager Evaluation of Each Database Copy

CRITERIA SET	DESCRIPTION
1	Content index is in a Healthy state.
	Copy queue length is less than 10.
	Replay queue length is less than 50.
2	Content index is in a Crawling state.
	Copy queue length is less than 10.
	Replay queue length is less than 50.
3	Content index is in a Healthy state.
	Replay queue length is less than 50.
4	Content index is in a Crawling state.
	Replay queue length is less than 50.
5	Replay queue length is less than 50.
6	Content index is in a Healthy state.
	Copy queue length is less than 10.
7	Content index is in a Crawling state.
	Copy queue length is less than 10.
8	Content index is in a Healthy state.
9	Content index is in a Crawling state.
10	The database copy status is Healthy, DisconnectedAndHealthy, DisconnectedAndResynchronizing, or SeedingSource.

If none of the databases meets the 10 criteria sets, the mailbox database will not be automaticity mounted on a passive Mailbox server. If a passive copy of the database is found that matches one of the 10 criteria sets and the copy queue length is less than the amount of acceptable logs loss, specified by the `AutoDatbaseMountDial` parameter, the chosen passive mailbox database is mounted.

Examples of Best Copy and Server Selection

Before we look at some examples of the BCSS process, let's consider something more important. In general, if your database replication and content indexing are working properly, activation will occur based on Activation Preference. This is because when all other things are equal, Activation Preference is used. You should not be developing a complex plan related to BCSS. It's an automatic process that only becomes complex when your environment is not completely healthy.

As a rule of thumb, the copy queue length for local copies will probably be shorter than copies in a secondary datacenter. This results in local passive copies being preferred over remote passive copies during failover. However, if your connectivity between datacenters is very good, this might not be the case.

Let's use some real-world examples to better understand the details of how the BCSS process works. As we go through the examples, it is important to note that the order listed in Table 20.1 is the order Active Manager uses to determine which Mailbox server should be used to mount the mailbox database.

Our fictional company has deployed four Mailbox servers ranging from MBX1 to MBX4. The Mailbox server MBX1 has three active mailbox databases, DB1 through DB3, and each database is replicated to the other three Mailbox servers. In this example, let's say that MBX1 has a hardware failure. Active Manager must now evaluate each Mailbox server and its corresponding passive database copy to determine which database will be activated. To simplify the BCSS process, none of the databases are set to Lossless and all protocols are in a healthy state. Tables 20.2 through 20.4 provide the status of the passive copies before MBX1 failed. After each table a description is provided of which database would be activated and why.

TABLE 20.2: DB1 Replication Status

DATABASE COPY	ACTIVATION PREFERENCE	COPY QUEUE LENGTH	REPLAY QUEUE LENGTH	CONTENT INDEX STATE	DATABASE STATE
MBX2\DB1	2	9	37	Healthy	Healthy
MBX3\DB1	3	5	0	Crawling	Healthy
MBX4\DB1	4	2	15	Healthy	DisconnectedAndHealthy

Sorting databases on copy queue length

MBX4\DB1

MBX3\DB1

MBX2\DB1

Databases in order of the criteria state they are related to based on Table 20.1

MBX4\DB1 - Criteria Set 1

MBX3\DB1 - Criteria Set 2

MBX2\DB1 - Criteria Set 1

Result

Active Manager would try to activate the database copy MBX4\DB1 because it is missing the fewest transaction logs (copy queue length) and meets the first set of criteria.

TABLE 20.3: DB2 Replication Status

DATABASE COPY	ACTIVATION PREFERENCE	COPY QUEUE LENGTH	REPLAY QUEUE LENGTH	CONTENT INDEX STATE	DATABASE STATE
MBX2\DB2	4	4	39	Healthy	Healthy
MBX3\DB2	2	5	0	Healthy	Healthy
MBX4\DB2	3	4	15	Healthy	Healthy

Sorting databases on copy queue length *and* activation preference

(Here activation preference is used as the tiebreaker because two of the databases have the same copy queue length.)

MBX4\DB2

MBX2\DB2

MBX3\DB2

Database results of the criteria sets

MBX4\DB2 - Criteria Set 1

MBX2\DB2 - Criteria Set 1

MBX3\DB2 - Criteria Set 1

Result

Active Manager would try to activate the database copy MBX4\DB2 because it is missing the fewest transaction logs (copy queue length), is the preferred activation preference, and meets the first set of criteria.

TABLE 20.4: DB3 Replication Status

Database Copy	Activation Preference	Copy Queue Length	Replay Queue Length	Content Index State	Database State
MBX2\DB3	3	41	67	Failed	Healthy
MBX3\DB3	4	13	107	Crawling	Healthy
MBX4\DB3	2	27	51	Healthy	DisconnectedAndHealthy

Sorting databases on copy queue length

MBX3\DB3

MBX4\DB3

MBX2\DB3

Database results of the criteria sets

MBX3\DB3 - Criteria Set 9

MBX4\DB3 - Criteria Set 8

MBX2\DB3 - Criteria Set 10

Result

None of the DB3 copies can be automatically mounted. Even if the database is configured to use BestAvailability, only 12 log files can be lost. In this case, an administrator will need to manually mount MBX3\DB3. MBX3\DB3 is the best choice because it has the shortest copy queue length. However, search performance may be inconsistent because the content index is not complete.

DAG and Database Maintenance

One of the awesome things about Exchange Server 2016 is the number of maintenance tasks it performs for you in the background. Exchange Server 2016 does things like look for database corruption and fixes automatically. In some cases, Exchange Server 2016 does such a good job that it can mask hardware issues and leave them undetected if you are not actively monitoring your Exchange servers.

Incremental Resync

When a failover occurs and transaction logs are lost, there is divergence between the failed database copy and the newly activated database copy. You didn't lose any data because the missing messages were recovered from Safety Net, but the two databases do not have the same transaction log data anymore. When you repair the failed server, one way to fix this would be to reseed the entire database, but that is not very efficient when most of the data is already there. Instead, Exchange Server 2016 can do an incremental resync and use the existing mailbox database as a starting point.

Incremental resync reviews the active database and the divergent copy on the failed server. This process identifies where divergence in the log files occurred and analyzes which data is different between the two databases. When the differences are identified, the necessary log files are copied to the divergent database copy and replayed to make the two databases consistent. This is typically much faster and requires much less data transfer than reseeding a database.

Page Patching

The most common type of database corruption is physical corruption caused by storage subsystem problems. A tiny glitch on a disk results in invalid data for a database page. The corruption is identified because the checksum for the database page is no longer valid. The question is, how do you fix it?

Assuming that you don't have a DAG implemented, if you are lucky, the database is still mounted (or can be mounted) and you can move the mailboxes from the corrupted database to a new database. If you can't mount the database, then you need to restore from backup or try to repair it by using eseutil.exe. There are also many tools for extracting data from corrupted mailbox databases and exporting it to PST.

When you have a DAG, recovering from physical corruption is much easier. One of the little-known DAG features that has been available since Exchange Server 2010 is page patching. *Page patching* fixes corrupt database pages in the active copy of a database by copying the database page from an uncorrupted passive copy. You don't need to do anything to implement page patching. It's an automatic process.

You should monitor event logs to identify that page patching is occurring regularly. A single page patching event is likely not a cause for concern. Multiple page patching events over time might signal impending storage failure.

Database Divergence Detection

Unlike physical corruption, which can be identified by mismatched checksums, logical corruption is valid from the perspective of the database. Logical corruption is bad data, but it is not randomly corrupted. Or, at least, it is not randomly corrupted in a way that is detected by a checksum.

In the context of lagged copies, logical corruption is any unwanted change to a mailbox database, and logical corruption is replicated through the transaction logs. For example, a third-party archiving solution might remove data from the database. In such a case, you'd use the lagged copy to get the data before those transaction logs are played against the lagged copy.

Exchange Server 2016 has added new database-divergence checking scans to detect logical corruption that is not introduced by replicating logs. With this new feature, the active database copy is scanned and a log of database pages and their checksums is generated. Those logs are shipped to the passive database copies and evaluated there. If the passive copy has a different checksum for a database page, then there is logical corruption. Previous versions of Exchange Server did not detect this type of corruption.

The logical corruption identified by database divergence checking usually occurs when the storage system loses a write for a database page. This can occur on either the active or passive copy of a database. The write times for the page in the active and passive databases are compared to identify which copy is behind. When divergence is detected, Microsoft recommends that you move all mailboxes to a new database. You can identify divergence from event logs.

Applying Updates

Applying updates to Exchange Server 2016 and the host operating system in a timely way is important. Updates resolve known issues that can impact stability and security. While Exchange Server 2016 performs many maintenance tasks automatically for you, you need to apply your own cumulative updates.

Administrators in some smaller organizations do not have a specific process for applying updates, and they install updates without any preparation. This is suboptimal because it can result in inconsistent service for clients. During the update process for a DAG member, you should prevent the services on the DAG member from being available to clients. For the DAG, this means you should block automatic activation of databases on the DAG you are updating. From a client-access perspective, you should update your load-balancing solution to avoid directing clients to the server being updated.

The process for putting Exchange Server 2016 into Maintenance mode is exactly the same as it was for Exchange Server 2013. At the time of this writing, Microsoft has not yet explicitly documented how to put Exchange Server 2016 into Maintenance mode. References to the Exchange 2013 documentation can be found here: `https://technet.microsoft.com/en-us/library/dd298065%28v=exchg.150%29.aspx#Pm`.

Database Schema Updates

Mailbox databases have a schema that defines the data they hold. Different versions of Exchange Server have different database schemas, but the schema can also be upgraded when you apply updates.

As an example, back when Exchange 2010 Service Pack 1 was released, it was awkward to implement because it upgraded the database schema. Databases were upgraded to the new schema when they were mounted on an updated server. But after that point, the databases could not be mounted on a server without the updates. This meant that you needed to carefully plan the order in which you applied Service Pack 1 to Exchange 2010 servers to ensure that you didn't lose redundancy.

The process for database schema upgrades in Exchange Server 2013 and 2016 has been improved. In Exchange Server 2016, the database schema is not upgraded until all DAG members have the cumulative update applied. This ensures that you are never in a situation where mailbox databases cannot be mounted on a server due to updates.

The database schema is not upgraded immediately after all DAG members are updated. Instead, after all DAG members are updated, the database schema for an individual database is upgraded the next time that database is mounted.

Understanding Site Resiliency for Exchange Server 2016

A DAG within a single site is great because it can protect you from server and storage failure. However, the real brilliance of a DAG becomes apparent when you start to implement site resiliency. With site resiliency, you can have an entire datacenter go offline, and Exchange Server

2016 will continue to provide services to clients. When it's properly designed, clients won't even notice.

Site resiliency for Exchange Server 2016 is approximately the same as it was for Exchange Server 2013. Unlike Exchange Server 2010, clients use HTTP-based protocols that handle failover better than RPC. Clients connect to a namespace that can exist in multiple datacenters. The concept of an `RpcClientAccessServer` no longer exists.

There is no longer a dependency between the location of client access and the mailbox database. Clients can communicate with client access services in the primary datacenter and access a mailbox that is mounted in a secondary datacenter. The configuration options for client access will be covered in detail in Chapter 21, "Understanding the Client Access Services." For now, we only need to be concerned with how mailbox databases failover between multiple locations.

DAG Preferred Architecture

A critical consideration for site-resilient DAGs is the placement of database copies and the process that occurs when a single server or network link fails. Microsoft provides a preferred architecture that incorporates best practices for high availability. The preferred architecture is not a requirement, but it is a good starting point for you in examining site resilience for Exchange Server 2016. You can view a detailed explanation of the preferred architecture at `https://blogs.technet.microsoft.com/exchange/2015/10/12/the-exchange-2016-preferred-architecture/`.

The preferred architecture for Exchange Server 2016 (Figure 12.13) has the following characteristics:

◆ Two datacenters have Exchange servers.

◆ Two Exchange servers are in each datacenter.

◆ Active database copies are evenly distributed among Exchange servers in both datacenters

◆ Two passive database copies are evenly distributed among Exchange servers in both datacenters.

◆ A lagged database copy for each mailbox database is evenly distributed among Exchange servers in both datacenters.

◆ A witness server is located in a third location or Microsoft Azure.

To implement the preferred architecture, you must have high-speed connectivity between the two datacenters. This configuration does not optimize client connectivity to databases and can result in significant network activity between the two datacenters. You can use the Activation Preference for mailbox databases to set preferred servers, but this is no guarantee that mailbox databases will be mounted there all of the time.

The database copies are distributed evenly among the Exchange servers to even out disk utilization on all servers. In our scenario, there are four mailbox databases with one active copy on each Mailbox server. The active databases generate more disk activity than passive databases and lagged copies.

The witness server is located in a third location or Microsoft Azure to provide better tolerance for datacenter failures. The witness server will always be accessible to the remaining datacenter and, therefore, able to maintain a quorum. If the witness server is in datacenter 1 and datacenter 1 fails, then Exchange servers in datacenter 2 will not be able to obtain quorum and the DAG will require manual intervention to start again.

FIGURE 20.13
Exchange Server
2016 preferred
architecture

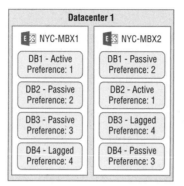

Datacenter 1

EⓍ NYC-MBX1	EⓍ NYC-MBX2
DB1 - Active Preference: 1	DB1 - Passive Preference: 2
DB2 - Passive Preference: 2	DB2 - Active Preference: 1
DB3 - Passive Preference: 3	DB3 - Lagged Preference: 4
DB4 - Lagged Preference: 4	DB4 - Passive Preference: 3

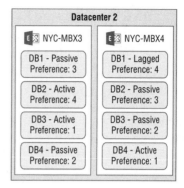

Datacenter 2

EⓍ NYC-MBX3	EⓍ NYC-MBX4
DB1 - Passive Preference: 3	DB1 - Lagged Preference: 4
DB2 - Active Preference: 4	DB2 - Passive Preference: 3
DB3 - Active Preference: 1	DB3 - Passive Preference: 2
DB4 - Passive Preference: 2	DB4 - Active Preference: 1

Datacenter 3

File Share Witness

If you can meet the requirements for the preferred architecture, then it is a good way to go. However, there are other variations you can consider.

🌐 Real World Scenario

BYE-BYE, BACKUPS

Ever wonder what it would be like to never have to worry about backups again? Well, that is a possibility with Exchange Server 2013 and 2016; by using lagged database copies, page patching, litigation hold, and single-item recovery, you can take the worry down a notch.

When evaluating Exchange Native Data Protection features to maintain email content, you must review all possible failure scenarios and the process to recover email content in each scenario. It is also critical to review all single points of failure in the Exchange Server 2013 and 2016 design. Using shared storage or a shared enclosure could be a single point a failure. You never want one catastrophic failure to vaporize a mailbox database.

Along the lines of reviewing single points of failure, choosing the number of database copies and deciding where to place them are important decisions. You want to maintain email content during failure events. In the past, Microsoft recommended a minimum of three database copies when using Native Data Protection, but they now include a fourth lagged database copy in the preferred architecture. And never, never consider native backup without replicating to a second location. That second location is your offsite backup in case of fire or other physical disaster.

Lastly, your design should include other native Exchange Server features, such as single item recovery, changing the deleted item retention window, enabling continuous replication circular logging, using In-Place Archive, In-Place Hold, and so on. Utilizing these features will help you meet the customers' requirements for long-term data storage and recovery after an accidental deletion.

Previously, one of the major drawbacks to not using traditional backups was the inability to account for logical database corruption. You needed to identify the logical corruption, when the corruption occurred, and then attempt to get uncorrupted data from a lagged copy. Database-divergence detection now helps to mitigate this risk.

DAG for Disaster Recovery

Some organizations do not want high availability and automatic failover between sites. Instead, they want a DAG in a secondary site only for disaster recovery. Figure 20.14 shows a scenario for a very small organization that wants site resilience. There is a single Exchange server in the primary site and a single Exchange server at the disaster-recovery site. The witness server is in the primary site.

FIGURE 20.14

A simple DAG

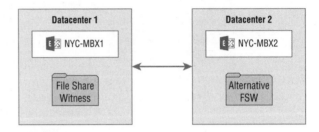

Let's consider a few scenarios:

◆ If network communication is lost between the two sites, the Exchange server in the disaster-recovery site does not have a quorum and cannot mount databases.

◆ If the Exchange server in the primary site fails, the mailbox database automatically mounts in the disaster-recovery site because there is still connectivity to the witness server to maintain a quorum.

◆ If the primary site is lost, then manual steps are required to bring up the disaster-recovery site because it does not have a quorum.

This scenario can also be enhanced by adding a second Exchange server in the primary site. This provides local high availability, and you can then consider configuring the database copy at the disaster-recovery site as a lagged copy for enhanced recoverability.

Multiple DAGs

If you implement the preferred architecture for Exchange Server 2016, you configure the network in such a way that you don't care which datacenter your user mailboxes are in. In many cases, this also avoids the need to carefully manage which database a specific mailbox is located in. All mailbox databases are treated as equal.

Some organizations have a strong preference to keep mailboxes for users close to where the users are physically located. This is typically due to concerns about network speed and reliability between locations. In such cases, you can implement multiple DAGs to ensure that the quorum for each DAG is maintained at a specific location, as shown in Figure 20.15.

In this configuration, if the network connection between the two datacenters is lost, each DAG maintains the quorum in one datacenter. The mailboxes would be stored in the datacenter closest to the users. So, there would be a set of users with mailboxes primarily located in the first datacenter and a second set of users associated with the second datacenter.

This configuration accomplishes the goal of keeping mailboxes closer to the users, but at the cost of increased complexity. Compared to the preferred architecture, you now need to manage which mailboxes are in the appropriate database. You also have eight servers to manage instead of four servers for the same number of mailboxes. In the case of a datacenter failure, you will need to perform manual steps for recovery. In general, you are probably better off improving your network connectivity and using the preferred architecture instead.

FIGURE 20.15
Multiple DAGs

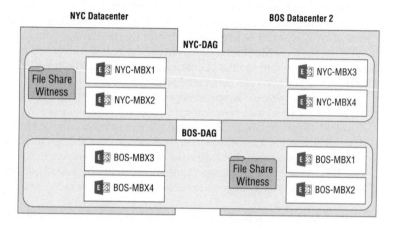

Datacenter Activation Coordination

Microsoft recommends that any DAG with three or more members that have been deployed in a multi-datacenter configuration should have Datacenter Activation Coordination (DAC) mode enabled, since it is disabled by default. In most deployments, a majority of the quorum voters will be placed in the primary datacenter. If a single DAG is used to service active users in two datacenters, the file-share witness is typically located where the majority of your users' mailboxes reside, although it can be placed in a third datacenter. In a scenario where a majority of voters are offline, the DAG will be marked as offline and all mailbox databases will be dismounted. When a DAG is offline, there are two options: wait for the majority of voters to be brought back online or manually restore the DAG service.

When choosing to manually restore the DAG service, DAC mode is used to prevent split-brain syndrome. *Split-brain syndrome* occurs when the nodes in each datacenter own a version cluster quorum. Without DAC mode, Active Manager does not communicate with all the other active Mailbox servers before mounting a database copy. Without communicating to the other Mailbox servers, split-brain syndrome could occur, allowing the same mailbox databases to be mounted in multiple datacenters.

Consider an organization that has deployed a DAG between two datacenters and didn't enable DAC mode. In this example, assume that a majority of the nodes are in the primary datacenter. During a catastrophic event, the WAN connection failed and all the Exchange servers in the primary datacenter lost power for an extended period of time, forcing this organization to restore DAG services in the secondary datacenter. All mailbox databases are now mounted on Mailbox servers in the secondary datacenter. Once power has been restored in the primary datacenter, all the Mailbox servers in the primary site are brought online. Because a majority of the cluster nodes are homed in the primary datacenter, the cluster in the primary site has quorum and Active Manager starts mounting databases on those Mailbox servers. Each database is mounted twice; one instance is mounted in the primary datacenter, and the other instance is mounted in the secondary datacenter. Because multiple instances of a database are mounted, divergence has been introduced into the organization.

DAC mode uses the Datacenter Activation Coordination Protocol (DACP) to find the state of the DAG and determine if Active Manager can mount a mailbox database on the Mailbox server. When Active Manager starts on a Mailbox server, DACP is set in memory as a bit with the value of 0. The value of 0 informs Active Manager not to mount any mailbox databases on the local Mailbox server. Active Manager does not update the bit value in memory from 0, Don't Mount Mailbox Databases, to 1, Mount Mailbox Databases, until another Active Manager in the DAG can be located with the value of 1.

Continuing with our example, suppose that this time the organization enabled DAC mode before the catastrophic event occurred. Once power is restored in the primary datacenter and the Mailbox servers are brought online, Active Manager on the Mailbox servers in the primary datacenter will not mount any mailbox database even though the cluster is online in the primary datacenter. This is because none of the Mailbox servers in the primary datacenter have a DACP value of 0. Active Manager will not allow mailbox databases to be mounted on the local server until the WAN connection between the datacenters has been restored and PowerShell cmdlets have run.

The other major benefit of enabling DAC mode is that only EMS cmdlets are needed to perform a datacenter switchover. DAC mode can be enabled on a DAG by running the following command:

```
Set-DatabaseAvailabilityGroup NYC-DAG -DatacenterActivationMode DAGonly
```

The Bottom Line

Understand database replication.   Mailbox databases can be replicated between Mailbox servers in different AD sites. Replicating databases between AD sites ensures mailbox services could be online and available if the Mailbox server in the primary site were to fail.

Master It   Your company has a DAG that is stretched across two datacenters. All databases should be mounted in the primary datacenter where the end users are located. Last week, a server had a hardware failure, causing all the databases on that Mailbox server to failover. After the failover, you noticed that some of the databases were mounted on Mailbox servers in the secondary datacenter. What solution should be put in place to prevent mailbox databases from being activated in the secondary datacenter?

Manage a database availability group.   Lagged database copies maintain an older database state by suppressing when transaction logs are written to the mailbox database. A lagged database can be used to restore mailbox content that has been removed or manipulated.

Master It   A user has reported that email messages are missing from her Inbox today that were present yesterday. After checking the client and the Recoverable Items folder, the messages are still missing. Unfortunately, single-item recovery is not enabled. The user's mailbox is on a mailbox database that has a passive lagged copy that delays committing logs for seven days. What steps should you perform to restore the lagged database copy?

Understand site resiliency for Exchange Server 2016.   When you are designing a DAG, Service Level Agreement (SLA), Recovery Time Objective (RTO), Recovery Point Objective (RPO), business requirements, and technical requirements should be used to model how the DAG is implemented.

> **Master It**   Your company has three datacenters spread across the continental United States. Each datacenter has a low-latency, high-throughput WAN connection to the other datacenters. Users are located in two of the three datacenters. Management requires that mailbox services must be online if the power fails in one of the datacenters. Due to budget restrictions, the solution must use the minimum number of servers. How would you design a DAG solution to meet management's requirements?

Chapter 21

Understanding the Client Access Services

In Exchange Server 2016, the Client Access server role has been removed and its functionality has been combined with the Mailbox server role. Although you can't refer to Client Access server anymore, its functionality is still there in Exchange Server 2016. Now, it's referred to as client access services.

Client access services provide the connectivity needed for clients such as Microsoft Outlook, web browsers, and mobile devices to access information in Exchange Server. These clients can access not only their mailboxes, but also additional services such as Autodiscover, free/busy searches, and offline address books. Without client access services, all you have is a mailbox that nobody can access.

If you are familiar with Exchange Server 2010, most of the services provided are similar, but they are architected differently to provide more flexibility for load balancing. How the services are provided in Exchange Server 2016 is virtually unchanged from Exchange Server 2013, with the exception of the new MAPI over HTTP protocol for Outlook clients.

This chapter introduces the client access services and shows you the steps you'll need to follow to get the most out of them.

IN THIS CHAPTER, YOU WILL LEARN TO:

- ◆ Understand the purpose and architecture of client access services
- ◆ Plan namespaces for client access services
- ◆ Configure connectivity for Outlook clients
- ◆ Configure connectivity for non-Outlook clients
- ◆ Configure calendar sharing
- ◆ Implement coexistence with previous Exchange Server versions

Client Access Services Overview

Understanding client access services is a critical part of implementing and maintaining Exchange Server 2016. If client access services are misconfigured, users can lose access to their mailboxes. Or, just as bad, clients will start getting certificate warning errors in Outlook and flood the help desk with calls about security warnings.

There is no RPC connectivity from any clients directly to mailboxes. In Exchange Server 2007 and earlier, Outlook clients used RPC to connect to the Information Store service. In Exchange Server 2010, RPC connectivity was changed to the RPC Client Access to support DAG failover. Starting with Exchange Server 2013, RPC connectivity to mailbox servers is no longer available. Instead, Outlook clients use client access services such as Autodiscover, Outlook Anywhere, and MAPI over HTTP to connect with mailboxes.

We'll look at most of these client access services in more depth later in the chapter, but here is a quick list of the web-based client access services in Exchange Server 2016:

- Outlook on the web (formerly Outlook Web Access). A web-based interface for accessing mailboxes.

- Exchange Admin Center. A web-based interface for managing Exchange Server 2016. It is also used by users to manage the options for their mailbox.

- ActiveSync. The web service used by mobile devices, such as phones and tablets, to access mailboxes.

- Outlook Anywhere (formerly RPC over HTTP). A web service that can be used by Outlook clients to access mailboxes.

- MAPI over HTTP. A newer and more efficient protocol that can be used by Outlook clients to access mailboxes.

- Exchange Web Services (EWS). Outlook for Mac uses EWS to access mailbox information. Windows-based Outlook clients use EWS for free/busy lookups.

- Autodiscover. A service used by clients to obtain configuration information. Outlook clients use this service to identify the URLs to which they should connect.

- Offline Address Book. Outlook clients download the offline address book from this service.

- PowerShell. A web service used by the Exchange Management Shell and Exchange Admin Center to run the cmdlets for managing Exchange Server 2016. If this web service is unavailable, you cannot manage Exchange Server 2016.

Client Access Services Architecture

Starting with Exchange Server 2013, the client access services were composed of a front-end proxy and a back-end service. The proxying functionality does not perform any content rendering or authentication. The back-end services are responsible for all work related to the service. Clients communicate with the front-end proxy and the front-end proxy relays the request to the back-end server hosting the user's mailbox. This process remains unchanged in Exchange Server 2016.

Using a front-end proxy and back-end service architecture simplifies load balancing for the client access services. While hardware-based load balancing is used by most organizations, it is now possible to use simple layer 4–based load balancing such as DNS round robin. The proxying process is completely stateless because the state of all connections is maintained by the back-end services. Communication with the front-end proxy services can change from one server to another server without any data loss. Figure 21.1 shows how the front-end and back-end services communicate.

FIGURE 21.1
Communication between front-end and back-end services

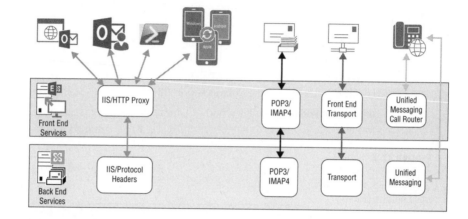

Front-End Transport Services

As with the web-based client access services, there is also a front-end transport service. All communication with clients for SMTP delivery is done by the front-end transport service. Message delivery to Exchange Server from external email systems (such as from the Internet) is also done through the front-end transport service.

The receive connectors for the front-end transport service listen on ports 25 and 587 by default. Port 25 is used for server-to-server email delivery. Port 587 is used to support IMAP and POP3 clients that need to send messages. We'll discuss the front-end transport service and configuration of mail routing in much more detail in Chapter 22, "Managing Connectivity with Transport Services."

Unified Messaging

The final component of client access services is the Unified Messaging (UM) call router. Like transport, UM has both front-end and back-end components. However, unlike the web services, the front-end is not a simple proxy. It is a server called the UM call router. Its role is to accept the incoming connection from IP Private Branch Exchange (PBX) gateways or Skype for Business and determine where to redirect the connection.

The Microsoft Exchange Unified Messaging Call Router service (`Microsoft.Exchange .UM.CallRouter.exe`) listens on port 5060 (unsecured) or 5061 (secured) by default, but it can be configured with the `Set-UMCallRouterSettings` PowerShell cmdlet. Once it determines which Mailbox server should handle the call, it issues a `SIP 302 REDIRECT` message. From there the call is handed off to the back-end UM services, as depicted in Figure 21.2.

All of the configuration settings that applied to the Unified Messaging role in previous versions are still available; however, they are split between the client access services and back-end services. Very few configuration options are available for the UM Call Router service.

The UM Call Router service is configured using the `Set-UMCallRouterSettings` cmdlet. The following parameters are available for this cmdlet:

DialPlans Multivalued property used to specify the dial plan used by the Unified Messaging if integrating with Skype for Business. It can be set to `$null` to remove existing values.

SipTCPListeningPort Specifies the TCP port the UM Call Router service is listening on for nonsecured connections; the default is port 5060.

SipTLSListeningPort Specifies the TCP port the UM Call Router service is listening on for secured connections; the default is port 5061.

UMStartupMode Specifies whether Unified Messaging is running in TCP, TLS, or Dual mode.

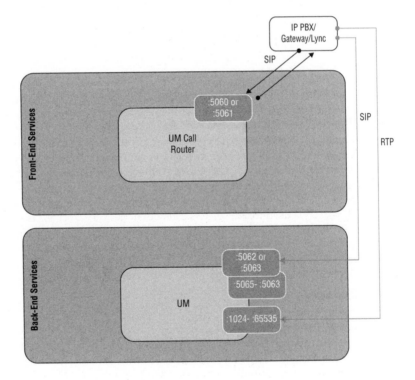

FIGURE 21.2
Exchange Server 2016 Unified Messaging architecture and ports

Namespace Planning

When you design an implementation of Exchange Server 2016, the namespaces are the URLs and fully qualified domain names (FQDNs) that will be used to access Exchange services. There are several different ways to design namespaces, depending on whether all of the sites have Internet connectivity. Microsoft's recommendations for namespaces have evolved over time to be simpler, using a single unbound namespace. However, using an unbound namespace requires a significant investment in infrastructure that not all organizations can make.

Namespaces Within a Site

Let's start by talking about a smaller organization with a single physical location. This organization has two Exchange servers in a database availability group (DAG) for redundancy. By default, the client access services are configured with URLs containing the server name. This configuration works fine for an organization with a single Exchange server, but not when there are multiple Exchange servers.

When there are multiple Exchange servers, you need to implement load balancing for the client access services. There are multiple options for implementing load balancing; but for the moment, let's assume that we've chosen to use a hardware load balancer. To implement load balancing for client access services, we need to select a single namespace that will be shared by all of the Exchange servers. For example, our organization could use `mail.contoso.com` as the namespace. The FQDN `mail.contoso.com` will resolve to a virtual IP address (VIP) that has been configured on the load balancer, as shown in Figure 21.3. Client requests are sent to the load balancer, and the load balancer distributes those requests to client access services on the two Exchange servers. If one of the Exchange servers fails, the load balancer automatically sends all client requests to the remaining, functional Exchange server.

FIGURE 21.3

Single namespace in a site

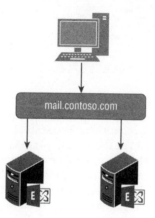

mail.contoso.com

To ensure that clients are directed to the VIP configured on the load balancer, you need to update the URLs for the client access services to use the new namespace. So, you update the URLs to use `mail.contoso.com` instead of the default server names.

Namespaces across Multiple Sites

If you expand the Exchange organization to use two physical locations, then you have the option to use bound namespaces or unbound namespaces. Bound namespaces are site-specific namespaces. For example, you might have `nycmail.contoso.com` and `bosmail.contoso.com`. An unbound namespace is used across multiple sites.

When you use bound namespaces, as shown in Figure 21.4, it allows clients to be directed to the site where mailbox database containing their mailbox is active. If Susan's mailbox is in a mailbox database mounted in New York, then the URLs provided by Autodiscover will be for `nycmail.contoso.com`. If the mailbox database containing Susan's mailbox is activated in Boston, then the URLs provided by Autodiscover will be for `bosmail.contoso.com`. Assuming that Susan is accessing her mailbox from the Internet or the site where her mailbox is located, this is more efficient for network connectivity because Susan's Outlook connects directly to the datacenter where her mailbox is located. If clients are coming in from the Internet, it avoids unnecessary WAN traffic between the two sites. However, during disaster recovery between the two sites, manual steps are required to direct all clients to the remaining datacenter.

FIGURE 21.4
Bound namespaces

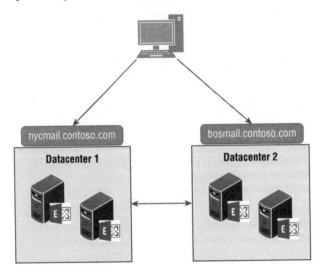

The preferred architecture for Exchange Server 2016 uses a single unbound namespace, as shown in Figure 21.5. In our example, both the New York and Boston servers would be configured to use mail.contoso.com. There would still be a separate VIP configured in each location, but DNS round robin would be used to allow mail.contoso.com to resolve to both addresses. It is possible that a user in New York could be connected to the VIP in Boston that is accessing the mailbox on an Exchange server in New York. As you can see, this system assumes that we have high-speed network connectivity between our locations. The WAN between sites needs to be fast enough that we almost consider the site irrelevant.

FIGURE 21.5
Unbound
namespace

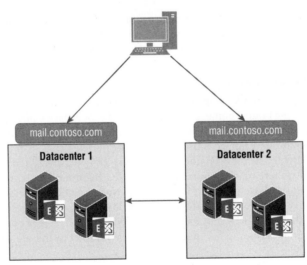

An unbound namespace operates similarly from the Internet. Externally, DNS round robin would also be used to distribute incoming requests between the two locations. A user with a mailbox in New York might connect to the VIP in Boston and be proxied to access the mailbox data from an Exchange server in New York. Again, there could be a high level of network traffic between the sites.

The main benefits of using an unbound namespace are simplicity and automatic failover during disaster recovery. There is no need to make manual DNS changes if one of the sites becomes unavailable. The downside to an unbound namespace is it requires high-speed network connectivity between the sites.

Even though bound namespaces are not in the preferred architecture, they do make sense for a low-powered disaster recovery site. If there is limited bandwidth between the two locations, then an unbound namespace is not an option. In this case, you understand that during disaster recovery, there will be manual activation steps for the disaster recovery site. That is okay, as long as everyone understands that requirement and is willing to wait 30 minutes for a few manual steps to be completed.

Internal and External URLs

For each of the client access services, you can configure internal and external URLs. Intuitively, you understand that internal URLs are used when accessing client access services from the internal network and external URLs are used when accessing client access services from outside the organization over the Internet. What is less intuitive is that by configuring an external URL for a service, you are indicating to Exchange Server that the service can be accessed directly from the Internet.

This is important for Outlook on the web and the Exchange Admin Center (the ECP virtual directory). If you have different external URLs configured for Outlook on the web or the Exchange Admin Center, then clients are redirected to those external URLs instead of being proxied.

Most organizations use the same namespace internally and externally to keep the configuration simple. To support this, you need to use split DNS where the namespace resolves to a different IP when resolved internally or externally. Internal DNS resolves the namespace to an internal IP address for the VIP. External DNS resolves the namespace to a valid Internet-accessible IP address for the VIP.

Load Balancing

A major concern for load balancing in Exchange Server 2010 was how to maintain session affinity. That is, how to keep a client connected with a specific Client Access server. There were several different methods and the preferred method varied depending on the type of clients. The good news is that starting in Exchange Server 2013 and continuing in Exchange Server 2016, session affinity is no longer required for load balancing. So, all we need to worry about is ensuring that our load balancer is directed to the Exchange servers. Then the front-end services on the Exchange server proxy the connections to back-end services where the active mailbox database is located.

WINDOWS NETWORK LOAD BALANCING

Before we go any further, let's eliminate Windows Network Load Balancing (WNLB) as a viable option for load balancing with Exchange Server 2016. WNLB is not very scalable. It was suitable for smaller environments with less than eight Client Access servers in previous versions of Exchange Server. The main drawback for WNLB is that it cannot coexist with the Failover Clustering feature that is required for DAGs. In previous versions of Exchange Server, you could have dedicated Client Access servers to get around this problem. That is not possible for Exchange Server 2016.

DNS ROUND ROBIN

DNS round robin is a system where a single FQDN resolves to multiple IP addresses. When a client resolves the namespace, the DNS server provides the client with a list of IP addresses for that FQDN. The client attempts to connect to the first IP address in the list, and if that fails, attempts to connect to the next IP address in the list. The DNS server rotates the list of IP addresses so that not all clients connect to the same IP address. Figure 21.6 shows what the host records look like in DNS for `mail.contoso.com`.

FIGURE 21.6
Host records for
DNS round robin

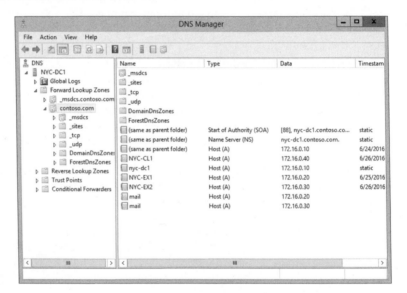

There are a few concerns with DNS round robin. First, you are relying on the client software to understand how to handle failover to the second or third IP address in the list. Outlook is specifically designed to perform properly with DNS round robin, but other software might not be.

Also, DNS round robin has no method for monitoring server nodes and automatically taking them out of service if they have failed like a load balancer would. So, if the failed Exchange server is first in the list, then initial connectivity will be slow. If the Exchange server will be down for an extended period of time, you need to manually remove the IP of that server from the namespace in DNS.

For external access from the Internet, you will need to have an external IP address for each server. Or, you'll need to implement a reverse proxy that can load balance between the Exchange servers.

Our experience implementing Exchange Server indicates that DNS round robin actually works better than most people expect. In environments where cost is a concern, it is a reasonable approach.

Hardware Load Balancers

The preferred solution for load balancing is hardware load balancers (or a virtual load balancer in a virtual machine with the same functionality), as shown in Figure 21.7. Hardware load balancers provide health monitoring of nodes. If a node becomes unhealthy, the load balancer stops directing requests to that node.

FIGURE 21.7
Hardware load balancer

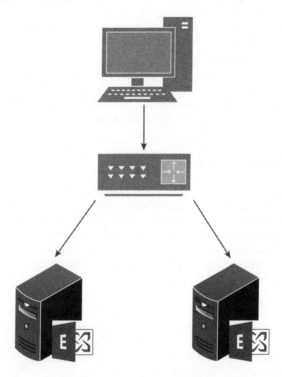

You've undoubtedly read that you can use either layer 4 or layer 7 load balancers with Exchange Server 2016. Those layers are based on the Open Systems Interconnect (OSI) model, but you don't need the details of the OSI model to understand what that means for load balancing Exchange Server.

Layer 7 of the OSI model is the application layer. If a load balancer works at layer 7, then the load balancer can monitor and work with the specific client access services. It can identify requests for the different client access services based on the URL. The main benefit of this is better health monitoring.

A layer 7 load balancer can be configured to monitor each client access service separately. Then, if a specific client access service such as Outlook on the web becomes unhealthy, the load balancer stops directing Outlook on the web requests to that server. Because other services on that server are still healthy, the load balancer continues directing requests to those services.

Layer 4 of the OSI model is the transport layer where TCP and UDP are implemented. So, a layer 4 load balancer can uniquely identify an IP address and port combination, but it won't look at specific URLs. Effectively, this means that none of the web-based client access services can be monitored independently. The client access services are monitored as a unit. Depending on the load balancer, monitoring is done by verifying that a TCP connection can be created with the server or with a single URL that can verify the functionality of only one web service. The problem with monitoring as a unit is that it can be inaccurate. If Outlook on the web is being monitored by the load balancer and ActiveSync is failing, the load balancer continues to direct clients to the failed ActiveSync service. Alternatively, if you are monitoring based on simple TCP connectivity, a failed service is not identified. Effectively, this means you are doing host-based monitoring instead of service-based monitoring.

Each client access service has a URL on each server that can be used for health monitoring. You access it at `https://`*ServerFQDN*`/protocol/healthcheck.htm`. For example, to check Outlook on the web on `NYC-EX1.contoso.com`, you would access `https://nyc-ex1.contoso .com/owa/healthcheck.htm`. If accessing the URL returns 200 OK, then the service is healthy. A load balancer can be configured to use these URLs for monitoring.

SOURCE IP LOGGING

One potential concern with hardware load balancers is the loss of the source IP address for incoming packets. If the hardware load balancer is not acting as the default gateway for the Exchange servers, then most load balancers replace the source IP address in incoming packets with their own IP address. This ensures that responses go back to the load balancer, where IP addresses can be translated as required. In this configuration, the Exchange server is unaware of the IP address of the clients, and all client access logs contain only the IP address of the load balancer. This can make it more difficult to troubleshoot issues.

To work around this problem, the HTTP protocol has an optional X-Forwarded-For header. The load balancer can add the X-Forwarded-For header to each request, and this header contains the original source IP address of the client. However, Internet Information Services (IIS) does not log the X-Forwarded-For information by default. You need to enable logging of X-Forwarded-For. The following link provides instructions for logging X-Forwarded-For: `http://www.iis.net/learn/ get-started/whats-new-in-iis-85/enhanced-logging-for-iis85`.

Certificates

One of the subjects that tend to intimidate a lot of Exchange administrators is certificates. If certificates are not configured correctly, users will be unable to connect with some services and will be get security warnings when connecting to others. This makes incorrect certificate configuration high risk, and because most Exchange administrators don't work with certificates on a regular basis, they find certificate configuration nerve wracking.

The good news is that if you understand the namespaces used for Exchange Server, then certificate configuration is pretty straightforward. You just need to make sure the certificate includes all of the necessary namespaces. If you are renewing an existing certificate, you can verify the required namespaces by looking at the existing certificate.

CERTIFICATE TRUST

We all know that certificates are used to set up encrypted communication between hosts. For example, HTTPS uses a certificate to secure communication when accessing a website. In addition to encrypting communication, certificates are also used to verify the identity of the remote host. For identity verification to work properly, the certificate needs to be trusted.

Certificates are trusted by a client only if the certification authority (CA) issuing the certificate is trusted by the client. How you generate a certificate has implications for whether clients trust the certificate. Table 21.1 describes the trust ramifications for the different certificate-generation methods.

TABLE 21.1:   Certificate Generation Methods

GENERATION METHOD	DESCRIPTIONS
Public CA	Public CAs, such as Digicert or Comodo, are automatically trusted by clients. That is the benefit you get by paying for a certificate from a public CA.
Internal CA	If your organization has an internal CA, the clients inside the organization are likely configured to trust the internal CA. However, external clients, such as a mobile phone, will not automatically trust certificates from an internal CA.
Self-signed	Self-signed certificates are not automatically trusted by any clients. All clients need to be configured to trust the certificate.

When you install Exchange Server 2016, two self-signed certificates are generated during the installation process, shown in Figure 21.8. The WMSVC certificate shown in Figure 21.8 is used by Windows Server 2012 R2 but is not part of Exchange Server 2016 and is not assigned to any Exchange services. The certificate named Microsoft Exchange Server Auth Certificate is used to authenticate SMTP communication between Exchange servers in your organization. This certificate is valid for five years, and you should renew it before it expires. If this certificate is removed or expires, then mail flow between Exchange servers in your organization will be interrupted.

FIGURE 21.8
Default certificates
in Exchange Server
2016

The second self-signed certificate is named Microsoft Exchange. This certificate is assigned to SMTP, IIS, POP, and IMAP. This certificate is used by client-facing services and should be replaced with a certificate from a public CA. It is simply not worth the time involved to try and save a few dollars by using an internal CA or a self-signed certificate. The time you spend performing configuration is worth far more than the cost of the certificate.

MULTI-NAME CERTIFICATES

Even though you are load balancing a single namespace for client access services in a site, you probably need a second namespace for Autodiscover. For example, if you are using `mail .contoso.com` as the main namespace, you will also have `autodiscover.contoso.com` for external clients. For the connection to be trusted properly, both of these names need to be included in the certificate installed on your Exchange servers.

The way to solve this problem in Exchange Server is to use a certificate that allows you to use multiple names. Two types of certificates allow you to do this:

◆   Wildcard certificates

◆   Subject Alternative Name (SAN) certificates

Wildcard certificates allow you to specify a wildcard character in the name. For example, a wildcard certificate for `*.contoso.com` will allow you to use `mail.contoso.com`, `nyc-ex1 .contoso.com`, `mail.europe.contoso.com`, and so forth. Wildcard certificates tend to be a more expensive option, so many organizations choose the second option, SAN certificates.

SAN certificates have an additional field in the certificate called Subject Alternative Names. You input several other names in this field with which you want the server to be accessed. Certificates that support Subject Alternative Names are also referred to as Unified Communications Certificates (UCC). To find certificate authorities that will issue this type of certificate, search the Internet for "Subject Alternative Name" or "Unified Communications

Certificates." Microsoft also maintains a list of certificate authorities that it has partnered with to provide Exchange Server–specific websites for issuing the right certificates: `http://support.microsoft.com/kb/929395`.

When specifying the common name for a SAN certificate, you should use the name that will most frequently be used from the Internet, such as `mail.contoso.com`. Figure 21.9 shows a SAN certificate with a couple of entries in the Subject Alternative Names field. Keep in mind that you need to include in the certificate-only names that will be used to access the server over SSL. The FQDN for individual servers does not need to be included in the certificate because users access services only through the load-balanced name. If this certificate will also be used for SMTP, that name also needs to be included. It is often easier to have a separate certificate for secure SMTP.

FIGURE 21.9
A SAN certificate

GENERATING CERTIFICATES FOR EXCHANGE

The first thing to realize about certificates for Exchange Server is that it doesn't matter how they are generated. As long as the certificate is valid, you can assign it to Exchange Services and begin using it. Exchange Server does not have a separate certificate store in Windows Server. The certificates used for Exchange Server are accessible by using the Certificates snap-in for the Microsoft Management Console.

Some ways you can obtain a certificate for Exchange Server include:

◆ Generate a certificate request from the Exchange Admin Center.

◆ Generate a certificate request by using cmdlets in the Exchange Management Shell.

◆ Generate a certificate request by using the Certificates snap-in.

◆ Use a certificate request-generation tool from a public CA.

The method for certificate generation that is easiest for Exchange administrators to use is the Exchange Admin Center. The Exchange Admin Center has a wizard that guides you through the process for creating a certificate request and suggests names that should be part of the request. The wizard identifies the names to include from the internal and external URLs that you have configured for client access services. Figure 21.10 shows URLs detected by the wizard.

FIGURE 21.10
The New Exchange
Certificate Wizard

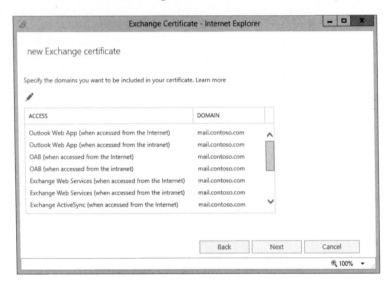

While the wizard does a pretty good job of suggesting certificate names, we find that it often adds names that are unnecessary. In many cases, this is because some services, such as POP or IMAP, are unused and contain invalid information that is detected by the wizard. So, it's still incumbent on you to know your namespaces and ensure that the certificate has the correct names. Most of the time only two names are required: one name for Autodiscover and one for the namespace on the load balancer.

After you generate a certificate request, you submit it to the CA. The CA then provides a certificate response that you import. When the import is complete, the fully formed certificate is on your server and can be assigned to services, as shown in Figure 21.11. You can now also export the certificate from the server you created it on and import it on the other Exchange servers. All Exchange servers should share the same certificate.

It is significantly more awkward to use the Exchange Management Shell for managing certificates, but it is possible. The following cmdlets can be used for certificate management:

◆ `New-ExchangeCertificate`

◆ `Import-ExchangeCertificate`

◆ `Enable-ExchangeCertificate`

FIGURE 21.11
Assigning services
to a certificate

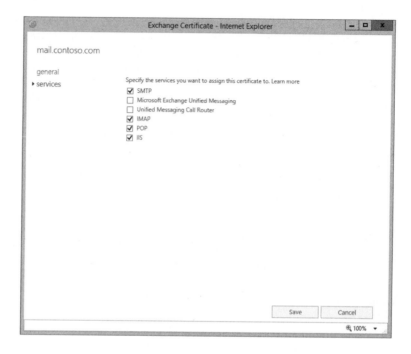

Connectivity for Outlook Clients

The most commonly used client software for accessing Exchange mailboxes from a desktop computer or laptop is Outlook. The popularity of other access methods, such as Outlook on the web or ActiveSync, has grown immensely over the years, but Outlook is still the primary interface that most people use to access their Exchange Mailbox.

Because Outlook has been around for many years, you might think that not much has changed since earlier versions of Exchange Server. However, there have actually been many changes to how Outlook communicates with Exchange Server. In Exchange Server 2013, support for MAPI connectivity was dropped and only Outlook Anywhere was used for connectivity. Then, in Exchange Server 2013 SP1, a new protocol called MAPI over HTTP was introduced. Also new for Outlook 2016, clients must be configured by using Autodiscover. Manual configuration of Outlook 2016 clients for connectivity to an Exchange mailbox is not possible.

Autodiscover

Configuring an Outlook client is not as simple as providing an FQDN for the Exchange server. There are multiple web services that an Outlook client needs access to for downloading the offline address book and free/busy lookups. Autodiscover is used to facilitate configuring

Outlook clients with all of this information. Outlook contacts the Autodiscover web service for configuration information during initial configuration and also periodically after that time.

Configuration information from Autodiscover is provided to Outlook as an XML file. The XML file contains a list of services provided by Exchange and the URLs where they should be accessed. Most of the time you have no need to see this information directly. However, it can be useful when you are troubleshooting. To view the Autodiscover information that can be retrieved by Outlook, perform the following steps:

1. On a computer with Outlook, in the notification area, press Ctrl+right-click the Outlook icon and click Test E-mail AutoConfiguration.

2. In the Test E-mail AutoConfiguration window, enter the email address and password for the user and click OK.

3. On the Results tab, shown in Figure 21.12, review the URLs provided for the services.

4. On the XML tab, review the raw XML provided in the Autodiscover response.

5. On the Log tab, review any errors that may be generated.

FIGURE 21.12

Test E-mail AutoConfiguration

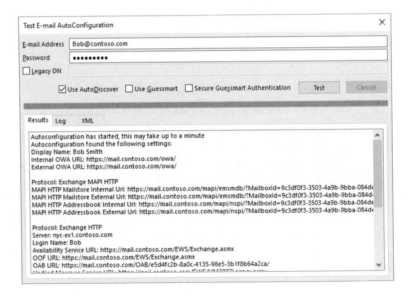

INTERNAL AUTODISCOVER

For clients that are domain-joined, Autodiscover is located by using Active Directory. For each Exchange server, a service connection point object (SCP) is created in Active Directory to represent Autodiscover on that server. The SCP object contains the URL to access Autodiscover. The default URL configured on the SCP object is `https://ServerFQDN/Autodiscover/Autodiscover.xml`. Notice that this uses the name of the server and not the namespace for the load balancer.

If you leave the default configuration, Outlook users will begin getting security warnings about an untrusted certificate. This occurs because the server FQDN is not included in the certificate you have installed on the Exchange servers. To avoid security warnings from an incorrectly configured Autodiscover URL, you should set it immediately after installing a new Exchange server. The URL should be changed to use the load-balanced VIP that you have configured for client access services. The following command sets the Autodiscover URL for LON-EX1:

```
Set-ClientAccessService LON-EX1 -AutoDiscoverInternalUri https://mail.contoso
.com/Autodiscover/Autodiscover.xml
```

The Autodiscover virtual directory is a common point of confusion. The external URL for Autodiscover is configured there. Even though the Autodiscover virtual directory has an internal URL property, that property has no effect and does not need to be configured.

EXTERNAL AUTODISCOVER

Clients outside of the internal network do not have access to domain controllers and the data in Active Directory. These clients can still use Autodiscover, but they locate Autodiscover by using DNS instead. There are several ways that DNS can be used to provide the location of the Autodiscover service. DNS-based location of Autodiscover is also used by clients on the internal network that are not domain-joined.

When external clients create a profile for Exchange Server, the users are prompted for an email address and password. The domain name in the email address is used to identify potential locations for Autodiscover. For example, if the email address is Susan@contoso.com, DNS records will be queried in `contoso.com`.

The two locations searched first are

- `https://emaildomain/Autodiscover/Autodiscover.xml`

- `https://autodiscover.emaildomain/Autodiscover/Autodiscover.xml`

If neither of these locations responds back with the appropriate information, Outlook queries an SRV record that identifies the URL for Autodiscover. The SRV record for `contoso.com` would be

- Service: _Autodiscover

- Protocol: _tcp

- Port: 443

- Target: *hostname*`.contso.com`

The main benefit of configuring an SRV record is that you get to define the FQDN for Autodiscover. Outlook supports using an SRV record to find Autodiscover, but most mobile devices do not use an SRV record. However, you can manually configure most mobile devices quite easily with the server name for ActiveSync.

INTERNAL AUTODISCOVER FOR MULTISITE ORGANIZATIONS

The SCP object for each Exchange server has a scope setting that can be used to control which internal clients use the URL defined in the SCP object. By default, the scope for an SCP object is configured as the local site only.

If an Outlook client is in an Active Directory site that is scoped by an SCP object, the client generates an in-site list of URLs for Autodiscover. Then any of the URLs in the in-site list are queried. The Outlook client does not query URLs defined by SCP objects that are out-of-site. If all in-site queries fail, the external DNS-based methods are used.

If an Outlook client is not in an ActiveDirectory site that is scoped by an SCP object, the client generates an out-of-site list of URLs for Autodiscover. The out-of-site list contains the URL for all SCP objects. Any of the URLs in the out-of-site list are queried. If none of the out-of-site URLs respond, then the external DNS-based methods are used.

Outlook Anywhere

Starting with Exchange Server 2013, support for direct RPC connectivity from Outlook clients to Exchange servers was dropped. One benefit of this design choice is that it greatly simplified the load-balancing configuration for Exchange Server. With RPC connectivity removed, the only protocol used by Outlook clients was Outlook Anywhere. Outlook Anywhere is still supported in Exchange Server 2016.

Outlook Anywhere encapsulates RPC communication in HTTPS packets. This allows RPC communication, which typically uses randomized port numbers, to more easily pass through firewalls by placing the RPC communication in HTTPS packets that only use port 443. Initially, this was introduced for remote connectivity to Exchange Server.

For Outlook Anywhere, you set an internal FQDN and an external FQDN instead of URLs, but the concept is the same as with other client access services. The Outlook Anywhere FQDN settings are in the server properties, as shown in Figure 21.13, rather than a virtual directory. A common mistake when configuring new Exchange servers is to forget about setting the FQDN for Outlook Anywhere because it is in a different location.

You can also use the `Set-OutlookAnywhere` cmdlet to configure the Outlook Anywhere FQDN. The following command sets the internal and external FQDN as `mail.contoso.com`:

```
Set-OutlookAnywhere -Identity "NYC-EX1\rpc (Default Web Site)" -InternalHostname
mail.contoso.com -ExternalHostname mail.contoso.com
```

FIGURE 21.13
Outlook Anywhere
FQDN

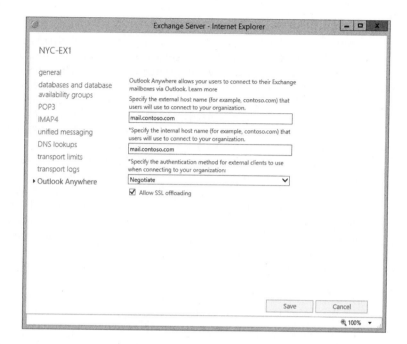

OUTLOOK ANYWHERE AND WILDCARD CERTIFICATES

Some organizations prefer to use a wildcard certificate for Exchange Server rather than using a SAN/UCC certificate. A wildcard certificate for contoso.com would have a subject of *.contoso.com and match any name in the contoso.com domain. This wildcard certificate could then be used for any server in the contoso.com domain.

When you use a wildcard certificate with Outlook Anywhere, you will get a warning about the certificate name not matching the internal or external host name. To prevent this warning, you need to modify the Outlook Anywhere settings that are sent to the clients during Autodiscover with Set-OutlookProvider. The following command configures the Outlook Anywhere settings to support using a wildcard certificate for contoso.com:

```
Set-OutlookProvider -Identity EXPR -CertPrincipalName msstd:*.contoso.com
```

MAPI over HTTP

Outlook Anywhere was a better solution for connectivity than RPC, but it still has flaws because the MAPI commands are in RPC, which can have timing issues with firewall timeouts. Starting with Exchange Server 2013 SP1 and continuing with Exchange Server 2016, MAPI over HTTP is available. The protocol is more efficient than Outlook Anywhere because MAPI commands are placed directly inside HTTPS packets and RPC is not used at all.

MAPI over HTTP can be used by Outlook 2016, Outlook 2013, and Outlook 2010 clients. However, for Outlook 2013 clients, you need to install Service Pack 1. For Outlook 2010 clients, you need to install Service Pack 2, KB2956191, and KB2965295.

If you create a new Exchange Server 2016 organization in a new domain, then MAPI over HTTP is enabled by default. MAPI over HTTP is also enabled by default when Exchange Server 2016 is added to an existing Exchange Server 2010 organization. When Exchange Server 2016 is added to an existing Exchange 2013 organization, MAPI over HTTP is not enabled automatically. To begin using MAPI over HTTP, you need to enable MAPI over HTTP at either the organization level or for individual mailboxes. When both levels are configured, mailbox settings override the organizational setting.

To enable MAPI over HTTP for the Exchange organization, use the following command:

```
Set-OrganizationConfig -MapiHttpEnabled $true
```

To enable MAPI over HTTP for a mailbox, use the following command:

```
Set-CasMailbox -Identity mailbox -MapiHttpEnabled $true
```

Like other client access services, you need to configure internal and external URLs for MAPI over HTTP. These settings can be configured by using the Set-MapiVirtualDirectory or in Exchange Admin Center.

The following example sets the MAPI over HTTP internal and external URLs on the server LON-EX1:

```
Set-MapiVirtualDirectory -Identity "LON-EX1\mapi (Default Web Site)" -InternalUrl
https://mail.contoso.com/mapi -ExternalUrl https://mail.contoso.com/mapi
```

Exchange Web Services

Exchange Web Services (EWS) is seldom talked about, but it provides some of the core services you expect in Exchange Server. For vendors writing applications that access Exchange Server data, EWS can be used to access mailbox data as an alternative to MAPI over HTTP and Outlook Anywhere. The Outlook for Macintosh client uses EWS for accessing mailboxes. Windows-based Outlook clients also use EWS. EWS provides the functionality for free/busy searches and MailTips. EWS provides the services for inter-organizational sharing of calendar information, too.

You can configure the internal and external URL for EWS by using the Exchange Admin Center in Virtual Directories. You can also use the Set-WebServicesVirtualDirectory cmdlet as shown here:

```
Set-WebServicesVirtualDirectory -Identity "NYC-EX1\EWS(Default Web Site)"
-InternalUrl https://mail.contoso.com/EWS/exchange.asmx
-ExternalUrl https://mail.contoso.com/EWS/exchange.asmx
```

Modern Attachments

Email attachments have been the same basic technology for decades. When you send a traditional email attachment, the file you attach is sent as a separate copy. Every user you send the attachment to gets a copy of the file. If you receive comments from recipients, you'll get multiple responses back and will need to combine the responses into a single document. Also, you will have multiple outdated files in mailboxes that could be forwarded with incorrect information.

The argument for modern attachments is like the argument for a centralized file server. Everyone is better off if there is a single authoritative copy of the document. Whenever changes are made, all recipients should see the changes in the centrally stored copy.

Another pain point for attachments is the maximum message size. Every Exchange administrator has at least one story about a user who wanted to send an email attachment of several hundred megabytes. Most organizations don't allow attachments that large. So, even if you allowed it for your users, the recipient email system wouldn't let it in.

Modern attachments are a new feature in Exchange Server 2016 and Outlook 2016. A central store for attachments is implemented in either on-premises SharePoint or OneDrive for Business in Office 365. Attachments are no longer included with the email message. Instead, the email message provides a link to a document in SharePoint or OneDrive for Business. You can select whether recipients have the ability to modify the document or just view it.

Versions of Outlook older than Outlook 2016 do not recognize modern attachments. Instead, older versions display a link to the file in SharePoint or OneDrive for Business. Non-Outlook email clients also display a link. Functionally, you still get the same benefits, but it is not quite as seamless for users.

To use modern attachments in Outlook 2016, you just attach a file from SharePoint or OneDrive for Business. Outlook automatically recognizes those locations as suitable for modern attachments.

To use modern attachments in Outlook on the web, you need to configure Outlook on the web to recognize the storage location. If you are using on-premises Exchange Server 2016 with OneDrive for Business in Office 365, then authentication for modern attachments is configured automatically when you configure Hybrid mode. Then to set the URL for modern attachments, use the following command to configure an OWA mailbox policy that is applied to mailboxes:

```
Set-OwaMailboxPolicy PolicyName -InternalSPMySiteHostURL https://TenantName-my
.sharepointonline.com -ExternalSPMySiteHostURL https://TenantName-my
.sharepointonline.com
```

For an internal SharePoint deployment, you can use the same command, but you use the internal and external URLs for your SharePoint deployment. You also need to configure OAuth authentication between Exchange Server 2016 and SharePoint 2016.

To configure OAuth authentication in SharePoint, run the following command on the SharePoint server:

```
New-SPTrustedSecurityTokenIssuer -Name Exchange -MetadataEndPoint https://
ExchangeVIP/autodiscover/metadata/json/1
```

To configure OAuth authentication in Exchange Server 2016, run the following script from C:\Program Files\Microsoft\Exchange Server\V15\Scripts:

```
.\Configure-EnterprisePartnerApplication.ps1 -AuthMetadataUrl https://
SharePointServer/_layouts/15/metadata/json/1 -ApplicationType SharePoint
```

Connectivity for Non-Outlook Clients

Inside an organization, the majority of clients use Outlook. This is the preferred interface for most users. Many users also use Outlook externally by using Outlook Anywhere or MAPI over HTTP. However, many users expect to access their email from anywhere, at any time, without having a company-issued laptop. To support these users, there is Outlook on the web and ActiveSync. For some legacy clients, POP3 and IMAP are also required.

Outlook on the Web

Outlook on the web is the browser-based access to mailboxes in Exchange Server 2016. In previous versions of Exchange Server, this feature was known as Outlook Web App (Exchange Server 2013) and Outlook Web Access (Exchange 2010 and earlier). Each new version of Exchange Server improves web-based access to mailboxes, and the web interface offers an almost equivalent experience.

Early versions of this interface worked well only with Internet Explorer. Outlook on the web now explicitly supports a wide range of web browsers, including Internet Explorer, Microsoft Edge, Mozilla Firefox, Google Chrome, and Apple Safari. The version of each browser supported changes as Exchange Server 2016 updates are released. So, if your users are experiencing issues such as pages not rendering correctly, ensure they are using a current version of the browser.

> **OFFLINE ACCESS**
>
> Although Outlook on the web provides excellent accessibility, many users prefer a laptop with the full Outlook client to take advantage of the cached mailbox when disconnected from the Internet. However, in Exchange Server 2016, Outlook on the web can be set up with offline access, which functions like Cached mode in the full Outlook client. Users can access their mailbox to read messages and send new messages when disconnected from Exchange Server.
>
> Offline access is available by default for all users. You should take care to educate users only to configure offline access when using a trusted computer. Cached mail should not be left on untrusted computers because there is a potential for the data to be accessed.

CONFIGURING THE OWA VIRTUAL DIRECTORY

As with other client access services, you can configure an internal URL and an external URL for Outlook on the web in the virtual directories of the Exchange Admin Center, as shown in Figure 21.14. You can also use the Set-OwaVirtualDirectory cmdlet, as shown in the following command:

```
Set-OwaVirtualDirectory -Identity "ServerName/owa (Default Web Site)" -InternalURL
https://ExchangeVIP/owa -ExternalURL https://ExchangeVIP/owa
```

FIGURE 21.14
URLs for Outlook
on the web

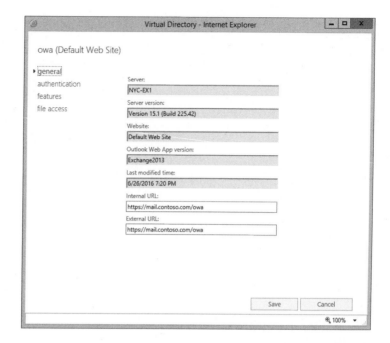

When you configure the URLs for Outlook on the web, you also need to configure the URLs for the Exchange Admin Center in the ecp virtual directory (earlier versions of Exchange called this Exchange Control Panel). The URLs for Outlook on the web and the Exchange Admin Center need to match because they are integrated. When users select the options for their mailbox, they are directed to the ecp virtual directory. The following command sets the URLs for the ecp virtual directory:

```
Set-EcpVirtualDirectory -Identity "ServerName/ecp (Default Web Site)" -InternalURL
https://ExchangeVIP/ecp -ExternalURL https://ExchangeVIP/ecp
```

The other common item that is configured for Outlook on the web is authentication. You can do this in the Exchange Admin Center as shown in Figure 21.15. In almost all cases, you want to use forms-based authentication, which presents a web page for users to enter their credentials. However, some organizations configure integrated Windows authentication because this allows user credentials to be passed automatically from the workstation to Outlook on the web, and the user does not need to type in credentials.

FIGURE 21.15
Outlook on the
web authentication
settings

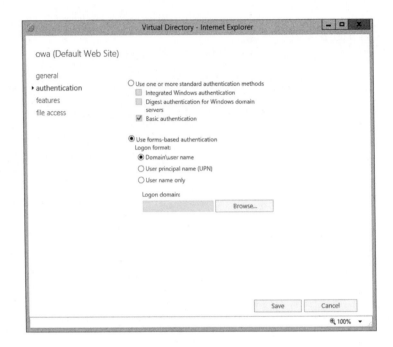

Table 21.2 describes the logon format options for forms-based authentication.

TABLE 21.2: Forms-Based Authentication Logon Formats

LOGON FORMAT	DESCRIPTION
Domain\username	This is the default configuration for the logon format. This format works well for multidomain environments where the same username may exist in multiple domains. Most users are familiar with this format from signing in to their computer.
User principal name (UPN)	A UPN is unique throughout an Active Directory forest, so it is also well suited for use in multidomain environments. Only use this logon format if the UPNs for users match their email addresses. The format of a UPN looks like an email address, and it is confusing for users if they don't match.
User name only	In a single domain environment, you can use this option to remove the requirement to enter the domain name. This simplifies sign-in for users. When you select this option, you also need to select the domain that authentication will be performed against.

You can also enable or disable Outlook on the web features in the properties of the owa directory. If you configure these settings in the virtual directory, you need to ensure that all servers in a site have the same settings. They are not synchronized automatically. In most cases, you are better off using Outlook Web App policies to configure these settings.

OUTLOOK WEB APP POLICIES

Even though Outlook Web App has been renamed to Outlook on the web, the policies used to configure Outlook on the web are still called Outlook Web App policies. These policies contain settings that are applied to individual mailboxes; this provides greater flexibility than configuring virtual directories.

A single Outlook Web App policy named Default is created when you install Exchange Server 2016. This policy is not applied to any mailboxes by default. You can create multiple Outlook Web App policies and apply them to mailboxes as required to meet organizational needs.

By default, users have access to all Outlook on the web features. You can use Outlook Web App policies to disable features that your users do not need, as shown in Figure 21.16. For example, if your organization doesn't need the unified messaging or journaling functionality in Outlook on the web, you can disable it to remove it from the user interface.

FIGURE 21.16
Outlook Web App
policy

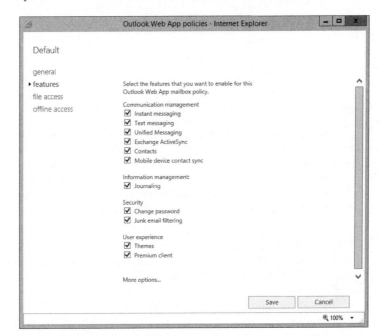

Outlook Web App policies can also control direct file access, as shown in Figure 21.17. Direct File Access controls access to attachments. It is enabled by default but can be disabled. You can control Direct File Access separately for access from public computers and also from private computers and OWA for devices.

FIGURE 21.17
File Access settings in an Outlook Web App policy

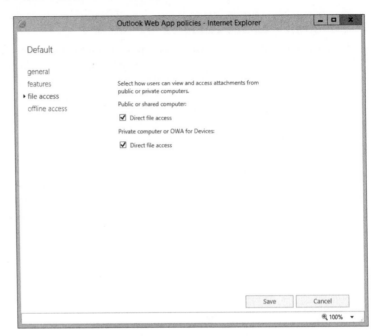

The setting for public computers is not required because Exchange Server 2016 does not provide that option as part of the sign-in process anymore. Older versions of OWA allowed users to select public or private. It's possible to reenable the option in the Outlook on the web sign-in screen, but most organizations never used the setting anyway.

You can also use Outlook Web App policies to control whether users can enable offline access for Outlook on the web. Users are allowed to enable offline access by default.

ActiveSync

ActiveSync is the protocol used by mobile devices to access Exchange mailboxes. It is supported by a wide variety of devices' operating systems, including Windows phones, iOS devices, and Android devices.

The only commonly configured settings for the ActiveSync virtual directory are the internal and external URL. There are also authentication settings, but they are typically left as default, which uses basic authentication and does not use client certificates for authentication. The internal and external URL can be configured by using the Set-ActiveSyncVirtualDirectory cmdlet as shown here:

```
Set-ActiveSyncVirtualDirectory -Identity "ServerName/Microsoft-Server-ActiveSync
(Default Web Site)" -InternalURL https://ExchangeVIP/Microsoft-Server-ActiveSync
-ExternalURL https://ExchangeVIP/Microsoft-Server-ActiveSync
```

OUTLOOK MOBILE APPS

To enhance the experience of accessing Exchange and Office 365 mailboxes from mobile devices, Microsoft has created Outlook apps specifically for iOS and Android. You can download them from iTunes and the Google Play store, respectively. For Windows mobile devices, Outlook is already included.

The Outlook apps for mobile devices provide a more complete Outlook experience on mobile devices than the native mail applications. The native applications provide basic mail and calendar functionality, but the Outlook apps have extra features such as the ability to access shared mailboxes.

As an alternative, mobile devices can access their mailboxes through a web browser. Exchange Server 2016 includes a mobile-optimized experience named OWA for Devices. This feature is enabled by default on mailboxes. It optimizes Outlook on the web for mobile devices by changing the layout and making it less cluttered. In many ways, it works as well as a dedicated app.

MOBILE DEVICE MAILBOX POLICIES

One of the major concerns with mobile devices is security. It is easy for small devices to be lost or stolen. To ensure that data on those devices is secure, you can use mobile-device mailbox policies to enforce security settings. By default, there is one policy named Default that applies to all mailboxes. You can create additional mobile-device mailbox policies as required and apply them to individual mailboxes.

The security settings for the Default policy, shown in Figure 21.18, are not very secure. There is no requirement for a password. You should review the available security settings and configure policies that meet the security requirements of your organization. At a minimum, you should enforce a password and require sign-in after the device has been idle for a few minutes. This ensures that an unattended device locks so that it cannot be accessed by an unauthorized user. You should also consider wiping the device after a number of incorrect sign-in attempts.

The other important option in mobile-device mailbox policies is "Allow mobile devices that don't fully support these policies to synchronize." This option is in the General settings of the policy and should be disabled for most organizations. If you don't disable this option, devices that do not enforce the policy requirements will be able to synchronize, which creates a security risk.

Additional policy options are available if you use the `New-MobileDeviceMailboxPolicy` or `Set-MobileDeviceMailboxPolicy` cmdlets. However, many of the additional options are not widely supported by device manufacturers. If you implement additional options by using the Windows PowerShell cmdlets, be sure to verify that the mobile devices your organization uses actually support the options.

AUTHORIZING DEVICES

Mobile Device Access Settings, shown in Figure 21.19, are used to allow, quarantine, or block mobile devices that connect by using ActiveSync. The default configuration allows all mobile devices, but you can change the default action to block or quarantine devices. When you quarantine devices, you then manually approve the quarantined devices. If you block by default, you need to create device rules to identify which devices will be allowed. Typically, you use device rules to allow only the specific mobile devices provided by your organization.

FIGURE 21.18
Security settings for the Default Mobile-Device Mailbox Policy

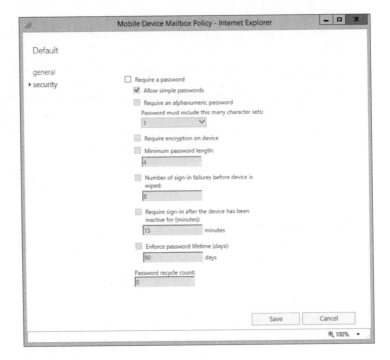

FIGURE 21.19
Mobile Device Access Settings

DOMAIN ADMIN PROBLEM

It is a best practice to have separate user accounts for day-to-day use and for administration. That said, it's pretty common for organizations to temporarily assign a high level of privileges to a standard user account to perform a specific task. This causes a problem for ActiveSync because when you make a user a member of a protected group such as Domain Admins, inheritance is disabled on the user object in Active Directory. When inheritance is disabled, the permissions that Exchange Server needs to create the device association for a new device are blocked.

An event will appear in the Application event log indicating that permissions are the issue. To add that new device association, you need to enable inheritance in Active Directory for the user object. However, if the user is still a member of a protected group, inheritance will be removed again soon. You might be lucky and finish adding the device before that happens, but as a best practice, you should permanently remove the user from all protected groups and use a separate administration account instead.

For more information about protected groups, see https://technet.microsoft.com/en-us/magazine/2009.09.sdadminholder.aspx.

POP3/IMAP

At this time, POP3 and IMAP are considered legacy protocols for accessing email. They are pretty primitive when compared with the other methods you use for accessing an Exchange mailbox. For example, POP3 doesn't allow multiple folders in the Inbox, and neither POP3 nor IMAP have calendaring functionality.

You also need to be aware that POP3 and IMAP are protocols for reading email messages. The clients using POP3 and IMAP still need to send messages by using SMTP. You should use the Client Frontend receive connector that listens on port 587 for this purpose. The Client Frontend receive connector is already configured for user authentication, and port 587 is allowed by most Internet service providers (ISPs). Many ISPs block outbound port 25 for home Internet users.

Even though, most users have no need for POP3 or IMAP, there are some applications that need to read messages in mailboxes. For example, there may be a ticketing system that reads mail messages and incorporates them into the tickets. This type of application typically uses POP3 or IMAP to read the messages rather than an Exchange Server–specific protocol.

Exchange Server 2016 includes support for POP3 and IMAP, but the services are disabled by default. To enable POP3 and IMAP, you need to configure the following services to start automatically:

- Microsoft Exchange POP3
- Microsoft Exchange POP3 Backend
- Microsoft Exchange IMAP4
- Microsoft Exchange IMAP4 Backend

Sharing between Organizations

We all expect to be able to share calendar and contact information with other users in our own Exchange organizations. You may not realize that Exchange Server 2016 has functionality that allows you to share calendar information and contacts with users outside your own Exchange organization. You will often see this referred to as *federated sharing* because in most scenarios a federation trust is configured with Microsoft. However, some scenarios do not require a federation trust and can be implemented by the user from within Outlook.

In general, you can control sharing by using organization relationships or sharing policies. Organization relationships configure settings that apply between two Exchange organizations. Sharing policies configure settings that control user-to-user sharing.

When you configure Hybrid mode between Exchange Server 2016 and Office 365, it integrates free/busy lookups between the two. That integration of free/busy lookups is made possible because a federation trust and an organization relationship are created when you configure Hybrid mode. However, the Hybrid Configuration Wizard takes care of most of the details. When you want to share with another organization, you need to do more manual configuration.

Federation Trust

To share information with another organization, you need to be able to verify their identity. Verifying identity can be a complicated process, which can lead you to avoid sharing information between organizations. Microsoft created federated trust to simplify identity verification between organizations.

To share information with another organization, you don't need to trust that organization directly. Instead, you create a federated trust with Microsoft that requires Microsoft to verify your identity. The other organization also creates a federated trust with Microsoft. Then there is a transitive trust between the two organizations because both organizations trust Microsoft to verify the identity.

The trust relationship does not provide permissions between organizations. It just provides the opportunity to verify the identity of the other organization and provide permissions if desired. Setting up a federated trust is the first step for sharing data between organizations because it allows the other organization to be verified. The Exchange Admin Center doesn't even give you the options for establishing organization relationships or sharing policies until a federated trust is configured.

You configure a federation trust based on a certificate. This certificate is used for authentication of the federated trust. The Federated Trust Wizard in the Exchange Admin Center creates a self-signed certificate for this purpose, and using a self-signed certificate is recommended by Microsoft to simplify configuration.

After creating the federation trust, you add federated domains. For each domain that you add, you need to provide proof of ownership by creating a DNS record in that domain. When you add the domain in the Exchange Admin Center, it provides a value that needs to be created for a TXT record in the domain. However, in some organizations, creating a DNS record takes a long time because it is the responsibility of another group or an external vendor. For this reason, it can be useful to obtain the necessary values ahead of time by using the Get-FederatedDomainProof cmdlet after the federated trust is created. The following example shows how to get the TXT record value for the contso.com domain:

```
Get-FederatedDomainProof contoso.com
```

If your organization has multiple domains for email, you typically add all of them to the federation trust. If you don't, only users with email addresses in the federated domains can participate in the federation trust.

Organization Relationships

An organization relationship is used to configure the sharing of free/busy information between two Exchange organizations. As previously mentioned, both organizations must have a federation trust in place. Table 21.3 describes some of the properties that can be defined when you create an organization relationship using the New-OrganizationRelationship cmdlet. A full description of the available parameters is found in the documentation for the New-OrganizationRelationship cmdlet.

TABLE 21.3:   Properties of an Organization Relationship

PROPERTY	DESCRIPTION
Name	You need to provide a name for each organization relationship. Select a naming standard that is meaningful for you and your colleagues.
Domains	The domains for which the organization relationship is used. These domains represent the external organizations.
FreeBusyAccessEnabled	This enables or disables sharing of free/busy information with the specified domains.
FreeBusyAccessLevel	This defines what free/busy information is available to the external organization. These operate like share permissions, and the default permissions for an individual mailbox can further restrict access. Valid values are None, AvailabilityOnly, or LimitedDetails.
FreeBusyAccessScope	This defines the security group that contains members whose information is shared over the organization relationship.
MailTipsAccessEnabled	This enables or disables access to MailTips for users in your organization for the specified domains.

You can also create organization relationships in the Exchange Admin Center after the federation trust is created. The Exchange Admin Center only allows you to define the domains and the free/busy access information.

After you create an organization sharing policy, users don't need to specifically share their calendar with anyone in the other organization. The organization policy defines which users in your organization (based on security group) are able to be accessed by the other organization. The users in the other organization access the calendars just as if they were part of their own organization. For example, when creating a meeting, you add the user and the availability information will be visible. The communication for an organization relationship is performed between the Exchange servers in each organization.

Sharing Policies

Individual users can also share calendars and contacts with external users. Figure 21.20 shows the options available for calendar sharing in Outlook 2016. The E-mail Calendar option does not require any configuration in Exchange Server and is controlled entirely by Outlook. The other sharing options are controlled by the use of sharing policies.

FIGURE 21.20
Calendar sharing
options in Outlook

When a user selects the E-mail Calendar option, a new email message is created with calendar information attached. The calendar information is attached as an .ics file that can be viewed or imported. This calendar information is static and has no link back to the data in Exchange Server. When the .ics file is generated, the user is prompted for a data range of items and the level of detail that should be included, as shown in Figure 21.21.

FIGURE 21.21
The Send A
Calendar Via E-mail
settings

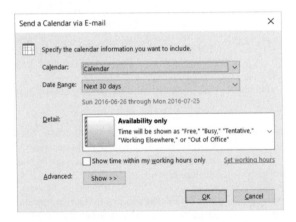

Sharing policies are used to control sharing with federated domains or Internet users. In Outlook, the Share Calendar option is for federated domains. To control sharing with federated domains, you need to have created a federation trust, but no organization relationship is required. Sharing with Internet users (anyone who is not in a federated domain) is anonymous sharing. It is anonymous sharing because the requests to view calendar information are not authenticated and could be viewed by anyone using the correct URL. In Outlook, this is the Publish Online option.

One sharing policy named Default Sharing Policy is present after installing Exchange Server 2016. This policy has the Default attribute set to True. This policy applies to all users unless another policy is specifically applied.

The permissions for a policy are set in the Domains attribute. This attribute contains a list of federated domains and the permissions for those domains. If you are allowing Internet sharing, then the permissions for Internet sharing are set for the Anonymous domain. Table 21.4 describes the permissions that can be configure.

TABLE 21.4: Sharing Policy Permissions

PERMISSION	DESCRIPTION
CalendarSharingFreeBusySimple	Allows sharing of only the free/busy hours. The user is not allowed to see any information about the appointments or meetings, just whether the person is busy or not busy.
CalendarSharingFreeBusyDetail	Allows sharing of the free/busy hours plus the subject and location of appointments or meetings. Content in the body of the appointment or meeting is not visible.
CalendarSharingFreeBusyReviewer	Allows sharing of all information about the meeting or appointment, including content in the body.
ContactsSharing	Allows sharing of personal contacts. This permission is typically combined with a permission for free/busy sharing.

The Default Sharing Policy allows all meeting or appointment information to be shared for Internet-connection sharing. It also allows free/busy hours to be viewed by all federated domains. When you view the Domains attribute for the Default Sharing Policy, it has the following setting:

```
Domains: {Anonymous:CalendarSharingFreeBusyReviewer,
*:CalendarSharingFreeBusySimple}
```

It's important to remember that the permissions provided in the sharing policy are still limited by the permissions that users configure on their own calendars. So, even though the default permission for Internet users in the policy allows access to all calendar details, the individual users do not share any information by default and can share less than the full details, as shown in Figure 21.22.

FIGURE 21.22
Settings for
calendar publishing

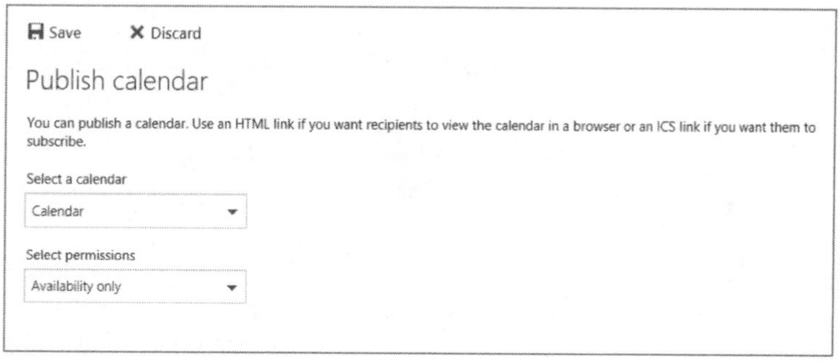

To share with Internet users, in addition to setting permissions for Anonymous in a sharing policy, you also need to enable calendar publishing on the owa virtual directory. To enable calendar publishing for all owa virtual directories in the Exchange organization, you can use the following command:

```
Get-OwaVirtualDirectory | Set-OwaVirtualDirectory -CalendarPublishingEnabled
$true
```

After users publish their calendars, two links are available below the publishing settings. One link is a publicly accessible HTTPS link to access the calendar through Outlook on the web. The second link is to an .ics file that creates a subscription to the calendar. When the .ics file is used to add the shared calendar in Outlook, the contents of the calendar are kept up-to-date by the subscription. Users need to provide the appropriate link to any Internet users they want to view their calendars.

Securing External Access

Client access services for Exchange need to be accessible from outside your organization. Some extremely security-conscious organizations only allow external access to Exchange when users are connected through a VPN. However, that is not typical and is generally not necessary. That said, security is all about how paranoid you want to be.

Most organizations have strict rules about not allowing traffic from the Internet directly into the internal network. Instead, a perimeter network (or DMZ) is placed between the Internet and the internal network. In previous versions of Exchange, client access services were part of a separate Client Access role. This inevitably led to someone in the security group wanting to place the Client Access role in the perimeter network and the Mailbox role on the internal network. This was not supported by Microsoft and led to many contentious meetings during Exchange design. Fortunately, Exchange Server 2016 does not have separate server roles anymore and the whole discussion is avoided. However, this does still leave us with the question of where Exchange servers should be placed and still meet the security needs of the organization.

The traditional answer for isolating an Exchange request from the Internet is to use a reverse proxy in the perimeter network, as shown in Figure 21.23. Connections from the Internet are terminated at the reverse proxy, and the reverse proxy creates new requests to Exchange servers on the internal network. This generally meets the needs of security groups because there is no direct connectivity from the Internet to Exchange servers.

FIGURE 21.23
Using a reverse proxy to secure access

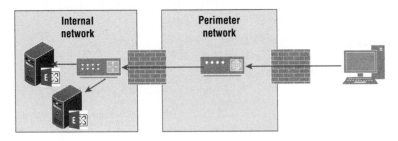

So, we have one good working solution, but we can consider simplifying this even more. Most load-balancing solutions effectively provide this reverse proxy functionality already. So, to avoid the expense of an additional reverse proxy, you can put the load balancer in a perimeter network (usually its own), as shown in Figure 21.24. Then internal and external clients both get access to that perimeter network. Now that client access for Exchange Server uses static port numbers, it's easy to configure the firewalls for client access.

FIGURE 21.24
Load balancer in a
perimeter network

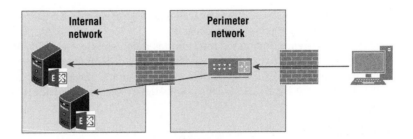

Another variation would be to put both the Exchange servers and the load balancer in a perimeter network. This reduces the risk to the internal network because clients need limited access to the Exchange servers. Just remember that the Exchange servers need unrestricted access to domain controllers.

Another consideration for external access is pre-authentication. Pre-authentication is an option on a reverse proxy to authenticate users before their requests are passed on to Exchange servers on the internal network. It sounds like a good idea, but it can often be tricky to implement with a minimal increase in security. Because the reverse proxy is rebuilding packets for delivery to Exchange servers, the pre-authentication really only protects you against an attack that can be accomplished anonymously before login—for example, a denial of service attack due to high levels of requests—which your firewall might be able to prevent anyway. There are also some scenarios such as federated sharing that fail if pre-authentication is enabled.

The one interesting option that is added by pre-authentication by some reverse proxies is two-factor authentication. Two-factor authentication can require external users to have not just a username and password, but also some physical device to prove their identity. However, it should be noted that there are also two-factor authentication products that integrate directly into Exchange Server.

One other good reason to use pre-authentication is to prevent account lockouts. If your organization has account lockouts enabled for user accounts in Active Directory, then logon attempts through Outlook on the web can trigger account lockout. If you set the account lockout threshold high enough, this won't be a problem during ordinary use, but could be triggered by a password attack which will then prevent the user from working. Most pre-authentication solutions can block logon attempts before reaching the account lockout threshold that you've set in Active Directory.

For a lively discussion about the value of reverse proxies and pre-authentication, see the following TechNet blog post: `https://blogs.technet.microsoft.com/exchange/2013/07/17/life-in-a-post-tmg-world-is-it-as-scary-as-you-think/`. The blog post was written for Exchange Server 2013 but is still valid for Exchange Server 2016.

Coexisting with Previous Exchange Server Versions

In previous versions of Exchange Server, the migration process for client access services was quite complex. Before beginning your migration process, you needed to map out how each service was going to be accessed. In some cases, you needed to generate new certificates that included a new legacy namespace for accessing services on the previous version of Exchange server during the migration process.

Coexistence during the migration is much simpler now because Exchange Server 2016 can proxy connectivity to Exchange Server 2013 or Exchange Server 2010. As long as clients are directed to use Exchange Server 2016 for client access services, all mailboxes can be accessed, as shown in Figure 21.25. This allows the existing namespace to be moved to Exchange Server 2016.

FIGURE 21.25
Coexistence with previous Exchange Server versions

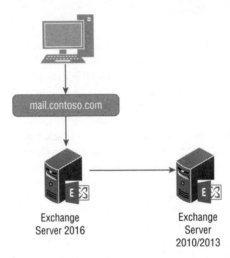

mail.contoso.com

Exchange
Server 2016

Exchange
Server
2010/2013

When you add Exchange Server 2016, you need to create a new load-balanced VIP for the servers running Exchange Server 2016. You can't have Exchange Server 2016 and previous versions using the same virtual IP address.

The basic steps for the migration of client access services are listed here:

1. Install at least one Exchange Server 2016 Mailbox role.

2. Create a VIP for the servers running Exchange Server 2016.

3. Export the certificate from the previous version of Exchange Server.

4. Import the certificate on Exchange Server 2016.

5. Set the URLs for client access services on Exchange Server 2016.

6. Test Exchange Server 2016 functionality.

7. Redirect the namespace to Exchange Server 2016.

8. Set the external URLs on the previous version of Exchange server to $null.

If you are migrating from Exchange Server 2010 to Exchange Server 2016, you need to enable Outlook Anywhere in Exchange Server 2010. Most organizations already have this enabled; but if it's not, it must be configured or functionality like free/busy lookups between Exchange Server 2010 and Exchange Server 2016 might not work properly. See `https://blogs.technet`

`.microsoft.com/exchange/2015/10/26/client-connectivity-in-an-exchange-2016-coexistence-environment-with-exchange-2010/` for a detailed explanation of connectivity scenarios.

Before beginning a migration to Exchange Server 2016, you should use the Exchange Server Deployment Assistant to plan out the specific steps to follow. The Exchange Server Deployment Assistant creates a detailed plan for performing the migration based on information you provide about your environment. You can access the Exchange Server Deployment Assistant at `https://technet.microsoft.com/en-us/office/dn756393.aspx`.

The Bottom Line

Understand namespaces.   A namespace is the FQDN that is used to access Exchange services. The internal URLs for various services are configured to use the local hostname after installation. This means that each server is assigned its own namespace.

> **Master It**   Your colleague has configured several Exchange Server 2016 deployments with a single server. In these deployments, he left the namespace at the default value and everything worked properly. You are both working on a project with four Exchange servers in the first site. How does the namespace need to be configured differently with multiple servers?

Understand certificates.   Certificates are installed on Exchange server to secure communication with clients. The names in the certificate are also used to verify the identity of the server. If a client accesses a namespace that is not included in the certificate, an error is displayed to the client.

> **Master It**   You have installed a new server running Exchange Server 2016. You selected the namespace `mail.contoso.com` and have configured all of the virtual directories to use this namespace by using the Exchange Admin Center. You have also obtained a SAN certificate from a public CA that is trusted by all of your clients. The SAN certificate has been assigned to the SMTP and IIS services. When you test connectivity to the server by using Outlook on a domain-joined computer, you are getting certificate errors. What is the most likely cause of these errors?

Understand calendar sharing.   Exchange Server 2010 includes several ways to share calendar information. You can implement organization relationships and sharing policies to control the information that is shared.

> **Master It**   Your company has recently purchased a competitor. Your company is using Exchange Server 2016 and the recently purchased company is using Exchange Server 2013. It will be an extended period of time before the email systems are merged. In the meantime, you need to configure both systems to allow free/busy information sharing. What steps are required to do this?

Chapter 22

Managing Connectivity with Transport Services

Exchange Server's primary purpose is to send, receive, and store messages. In Exchange Server versions 2007 and 2010, message delivery was handled by an Exchange server running the Hub Transport role. A message would be generated on a Mailbox server, the Mailbox server would notify a Hub Transport server that a new message was ready, and the Hub Transport server would pick up the new message for processing.

In Exchange Server 2013, the responsibility for moving messages from one mailbox to another moved to the Mailbox and Client Access roles; in Exchange Server 2016, the Mailbox role performs all the transport services.

IN THIS CHAPTER, YOU WILL LEARN TO:

- ◆ Understand the improvements in Exchange Server 2016 mail routing

- ◆ Create and manage Send connectors and Receive connectors

- ◆ Configure antispam and anti-malware technologies

Understanding the Transport Improvements in Exchange Server 2016

Before we delve into how internal email routing works, it's worth noting a few of the many improvements Exchange Server 2016 delivers in comparison to Exchange Server 2010.

Prior to Exchange Server 2013, all messages were processed by a dedicated server role named Hub Transport. This approach worked well for many years, but having a separate server just for mail routing wasn't always practical. In fact, many companies would consolidate the Hub Transport and Client Access roles or the Hub Transport, Client Access, and Mailbox roles onto the same server. Due to many changes in Exchange Server 2013 (described in this and other chapters), Microsoft removed the Hub Transport server role from Exchange Server 2013 and moved most of the core email routing functionality to the Mailbox role; in Exchange Server 2016, all transport functionalities are moved to the Mailbox role. The Client Access role in Exchange Server 2013 is now running as client access services in the Mailbox role in Exchange Server 2016; it also plays an important part in email routing.

In Exchange Server 2007 and Exchange Server 2010, mail routing was based on Active Directory (AD) sites. If the source server and the target server of an email message were located in different AD sites, the AD site of the target server was used as the next hop for the email messages. As part of the new transport improvements, Exchange Server 2013 and Exchange Server 2016 include the concept of *delivery groups*. The delivery group is the primary unit used to define a routing topology. AD sites are defined as a type of delivery group. Furthermore, if multiple Mailbox servers are members of the same DAG, those servers are considered to be in their own delivery group. This remains true even if a DAG spans multiple AD sites.

When routing an email message, a Mailbox server does not take into consideration the cost of AD site links when sending to another Mailbox server that is a member of the same DAG, even if that Mailbox server is in a different AD site. This change in routing architecture means that routing topologies in Exchange Server 2016 are significantly different than in Exchange Server 2010, especially for those that have a considerable amount of intra-organization email exchanges.

Another notable change is the introduction of the Safety Net feature in Exchange Server 2013, which is also present in Exchange Server 2016. In Exchange Server 2007 and Exchange Server 2010, the transport dumpster was used as a fail-safe mechanism to capture email messages that might have been otherwise lost during a lossy failover. Exchange Server 2013 and Exchange Server 2016 have replaced the transport dumpster with the Safety Net. When Safety Net is enabled, which it is by default, messages are stored in a separate database called the *queue database* on each Mailbox server. The queue database will hold messages based on the Safety Net value, by default for two days. A Mailbox server will query the queue database of the Safety Net feature to restore any email messages that are missing from a mailbox database after a lossy failover.

Message Routing in the Organization

Again, the most significant change in transport in Exchange Server 2016 compared to Exchange Server 2010 is the removal of the Hub Transport server role. The Transport service that ran on the Hub Transport role has been moved to the Mailbox server role. As well, two additional transport services have been added to the Mailbox server: the Mailbox Transport Delivery service and the Mailbox Transport Submission service. Another notable service is the Front End Transport service that has been added to Exchange Server 2016 Mailbox server role.

Not only are there new services in Exchange Server and Exchange Server 2016, but compared to Exchange Server 2010, Microsoft has completely re-architected mail routing for both internal and external message deliveries. The overall design change of mail routing is based on the introduction of delivery groups (discussed in depth in this chapter).

In this chapter, we'll dig into the nuts and bolts of the email flow process, email delivery, and email queuing. Before we do, you should understand a few important points about the basics of Exchange Server 2016 message routing:

◆ All email messages are processed by the Transport service, Mailbox Transport Delivery service, and the Mailbox Transport Submission service. All services reside on the Mailbox servers.

◆ Inbound and outbound email messages exchanged with the Internet are *passed* through the Front End Transport service that is part of the client access services on the Mailbox Server role.

The Mailbox server role is at the center of the message-routing architecture for messages being delivered internally, as well as messages leaving the organization. Though messages enter your organization through the client access services, all messages are processed by the Mailbox server role regardless of whether they are being delivered locally or remotely. Figure 22.1 shows the components of the Mailbox server that handle message delivery.

FIGURE 22.1

The Mailbox server transport components

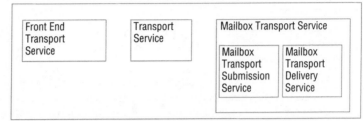

Exchange Server 2016 Mailbox Server Role

The Mailbox server role handles categorization, rule processing, transport-level journaling, and delivery for email messages that are intended for delivery to a local mailbox. Essentially, any email message sent by any recipient to any other internal or external recipient is always handled by the transport services that reside on the Mailbox servers.

The Exchange Server 2016 Mailbox server handles message categorization as well. Categorization is handled by a component of the Transport service called the *message categorizer*. The message categorizer component figures out where an email message needs to go next when it is received by a Mailbox server, otherwise known as the *next delivery hop*. Here are some of the steps involved in message categorization:

◆ Expand distribution lists by querying the global catalog.

◆ Resolve recipient addresses to determine which recipients are local to that server, remote on another server, or outside the organization.

◆ Examine the message sender, recipients, message header, body, and attachments, and apply message transport rules that apply to that message.

◆ Convert the message to the appropriate message format (Summary-TNEF, MIME, or UUencode), depending on the destination of the message.

◆ Determine the next hop for the message.

◆ Place the message into an appropriate queue.

When a message is transmitted from one Mailbox server to another inside the same Exchange Server organization, the Mailbox servers transport the message by using SMTP, the servers authenticate each other by using Kerberos, and the message data stream is encrypted by using Transport Layer Security (TLS). When messages are transmitted from a Mailbox server to an Exchange Server 2016 Edge Transport server, SMTP is used for message transfer, the servers authenticate each other by using mutual authentication using certificates, and the message data stream is encrypted by using TLS. Optionally, an organization that is sending messages to another Exchange Server organization that also contains Edge Transport servers can configure authenticated connections and TLS encryption. By default, messages delivered to other organizations are not encrypted, similarly to any email messages delivered between servers on the Internet.

Before we dig deep into routing, let's continue with a basic explanation of the services on the Mailbox servers. During the installation of the Mailbox server, the following transport services are installed:

Front End Transport Service   Proxies inbound email messages from the Internet to a Mailbox server and can be configured to relay outbound email messages from a Mailbox server to the Internet.

Transport Service   The Transport service is responsible for such tasks as mail queuing, categorization, protocol agents, and routing agents. Any message that is passed through the Exchange Server organization must go through the Transport service.

Mailbox Transport Submission Service   Using RPC, the Submission service connects to mailbox databases to retrieve outgoing email messages. The Mailbox Transport Submission service retrieves the message and sends the email message to the Transport service over SMTP.

Mailbox Transport Delivery Service   The Mailbox Transport Delivery service accepts email messages from the Transport service over SMTP and converts the email message to RPC for delivery to the mailbox database.

An essential part of message routing is determining the next hop in a delivery path. The identification of a next hop is driven by the delivery groups. The following delivery groups exist in Exchange Server 2016:

Routable DAG Delivery Group   A collection of Mailbox servers that are members of the same DAG.

Version Routing Delivery Group   A collection of Exchange servers that are determined by their version of Exchange Server.

AD Site Delivery Group   A collection of Exchange servers that are not members of the same DAG and that are not members of any DAG. An AD Site delivery group normally occurs when there is a hub site along the least-cost route.

Connector Source Server Delivery Group   A collection of Exchange Server 2016 Mailbox servers, Exchange Server 2013 Mailbox servers, or Exchange Server 2010 Hub Transport servers that are scoped as source servers for a Send connector.

Distribution Group Expansion Server Delivery Group   An Exchange Server 2016 Mailbox server, Exchange Server 2013 Mailbox server, or Exchange Server 2010 Hub Transport server that is set as the expansion server for a distribution group.

Exchange Server 2016 prefers certain delivery groups over other delivery groups. Figure 22.2 shows four Mailbox servers: EX1, EX2, EX3, and EX4. The servers are located in two different sites. Incoming mail has been received by EX1, yet the preferred delivery group for servers is the DAG boundary, because the mail is delivered to the server EX4 in another site, where the user's mailbox is located on the active copy of the mailbox database.

Figure 22.2
Mail flow between
DAG members

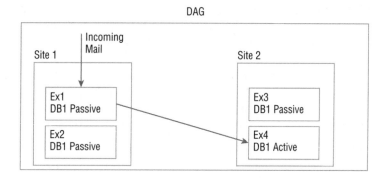

The Mailbox Transport Delivery service accepts email messages over SMTP from other Exchange servers and delivers them to an appropriate mailbox database in the same delivery group by using RPC.

The reverse process will happen when an email message is sent from the Mailbox server. Sending an email message is the responsibility of the Mailbox Transport Submission service. The service retrieves the email from the mailbox database by using RPC and then sends the email to the Transport service on the appropriate Mailbox server. The Mailbox Transport Submission service directly communicates with the Transport service on any Exchange Server 2016 server inside or outside its own delivery group.

For detailed information on mail routing, visit `https://technet.microsoft.com/en-us/library/aa998825(v=exchg.160).aspx`.

Real World Scenario

CUSTOMIZING ROUTING

In Exchange Server 2013 and 2016, hub sites are not evaluated when message delivery occurs between DAG members. There is a good reason for this: a hub site must always be within a *least-cost route* for message delivery to be considered in the delivery path. However, with Exchange Server 2013 and 2016, Mailbox servers that are members of the same DAG all share the same routing cost. Therefore, a hub site can never have a differing cost for any mailbox server in the DAG, so it will never have a least-cost route. Although the hub site least-cost-path functionality is not new to Exchange Server 2013 and Exchange Server 2016, the evaluation of delivery groups is new, and the DAG Member Delivery group definitely introduces a design consideration for administrators involved in implementing message routing in an organization where hub sites are used.

Sending and Receiving Email

Mail routing to and from the Internet has not changed in Exchange Server 2016. In Exchange Server 2013 and Exchange Server 2010, the Edge Transport role was an available option to accept email messages from the Internet. However, Exchange Server 2016 Mailbox servers can still be used to accept email messages from a current and previous version of Edge Transport, accept email from third-party SMTP gateways, or accept email from the Internet directly.

Receiving Email from the Internet

When you are configuring Exchange Server to receive email from the Internet, what do you need to know? This might not seem like such a hard question, but there are a number of variables that you should consider so that you reliably receive email:

◆ You must determine the public- or Internet-facing IP address of all hosts that will accept mail for your organization. In small- and medium-sized businesses, this may be only one or two IP addresses at the same location. For large businesses, this may be multiple IPs spread across several physical locations.

◆ If you are using a managed provider or other external service to handle inbound mail, contact the provider to determine what you need to know.

◆ If you want to implement high availability for SMTP traffic, use a hardware load balancer to balance SMTP traffic between multiple Edge servers or multiple Mailbox servers, depending on the configuration.

◆ You must determine if inbound mail will pass directly through your firewall to your Edge servers and Mailbox servers, or if inbound mail will be routed to a third-party message-hygiene system.

◆ For each host that will accept inbound email for your organization, ensure that your Internet-facing DNS has a public host (A) record registered. For example, if your organization (contoso.com) has two Edge servers, third-party SMTP gateways, or Mailbox servers that will accept email, create two public host records for those servers. The actual host record names do not need to correspond to the actual server names. Here is an example for two servers that accept email from the Internet, where Public IP address 1 and Public IP address 2 are the public IP addresses that correspond to these servers:

```
mail1.contoso.com      IN      A       Public IP address 1
mail2.contoso.com      IN      A       Public IP address 2
```

◆ Ensure that the public DNS zone for your company's domain contains mail exchanger (MX) records for the host records. MX records should point to A records, not CNAME records. For the contoso.com example, the MX records would look something like this:

```
contoso.com      MX      10      mail1.contoso.com
contoso.com      MX      10      mail2.contoso.com
```

One of the practices mentioned earlier suggests that for each server that will receive email for your organization, you should create a separate host record and then create an MX record that points to the associated host record. This works best when you are trying to set multiple levels of priority so that certain hosts will accept mail only if servers with a lower preference value are not available. However, this does not necessarily work well if you are trying to load balance multiple servers that should all have equal value. In the previous example, the contoso.com domain has two MX records that have equal preferences values. Many SMTP servers will not properly load balance or "round robin" between these two different servers (`mail1.contoso.com` and `mail2.contoso.com`). Therefore, one of these two servers will always be much busier than the other.

If you are trying to allow for round-robin load balancing across multiple inbound mail servers, there is a simple solution that most DNS servers will support. The solution requires that you configure the DNS servers to perform round-robin name resolution. First, create a single MX record like this:

```
contoso.com      MX      10        mail.contoso.com
```

Then create a single host record that has two IP addresses; to match the preceding example, the record should contain both public IP addresses.

The MX record resolves to the host `mail.contoso.com`. When the TCP/IP address of the host `mail.contoso.com` is resolved, the DNS name server rotates the IP address values that are returned. By using this solution, DNS ensures that `mail.contoso.com` hosts are round-robin'ed and used equally for inbound mail. Also, this solution provides better control of your email infrastructure by ensuring that a single server is not overused by hosts on the Internet that *insist* on always connecting to the same server.

PRACTICE GOOD DNS RECORD MANAGEMENT FOR INBOUND MAIL

Poor DNS management contributes to many of the inbound mail problems organizations experience. Sometimes these things are a matter of simple oversight, and sometimes they are a result of lack of Exchange Server technical training. Your Internet-facing DNS servers should be configured to provide all the necessary information for someone who needs to send you email, but they should be maintained so that stale information is removed. Here are some tips for proper management:

◆ All Internet-facing mail servers should have an A record.

◆ MX records should point to your mail server's A records.

◆ Not all SMTP servers will use the MX record's weighting value. You may think that by setting your mail servers to an equal value you are load balancing the inbound mail flow; however, creating a single A record with multiple IP addresses (one for each of your inbound mail servers) will provide better inbound-mail load balancing.

◆ Keep your MX records up-to-date and remove records that are no longer active.

Don't confuse your external and internal DNS records. For most organizations, internal MX records are not necessary.

Receive Connectors

The Receive connector is the point where inbound SMTP mail is received by client access services on a Mailbox server. Client access services on a Mailbox server have three Receive connectors created by default:

Client Frontend   Accepts email messages from authenticated client using TLS over TCP port 587.

Default Frontend   Accepts anonymous email messages from external SMTP server over TCP port 25.

Outbound Proxy Frontend   Accepts email messages from Mailbox servers over TCP port 717 for outbound delivery.

The Mailbox server also has two Receive connectors that are created during the installation:

Client Proxy   Accepts email messages from authenticated clients that are proxied through the client access services over TCP port 465.

Default   Accepts email messages from the client access services over TCP port 2525 for inbound delivery. The Transport service hosted by the Mailbox server role will listen on TCP port 2525 instead of TCP 25, since TCP 25 will already be hosted by the Receive connector of the client access services. (Remember, two services cannot listen to the same port on the same IP, on the same server.)

The interaction between the Mailbox Receive connectors and the client access services Receive connectors is important to understand. Figure 22.3 illustrates the relationship between the connectors that run on the servers, and Figure 22.4 illustrates the Receive connectors in the Exchange Admin Center.

The Client Frontend Receive connector listens on TCP port number 587, not TCP port 25. TCP port 587 is the alternative port for POP3/IMAP4 clients to access SMTP, as per RFC 2476. The Client Frontend Receive connector is intended to receive email from non-RPC over HTTPS clients, such as POP3 and IMAP4 clients. You would have to change the client's outbound SMTP port to use this connector for older clients, although most new POP3/IMAP4 client applications default to TCP port 587. The Client Frontend Receive connector passes the client traffic over TCP port 465 to the Client Proxy Receive connector that runs on Mailbox servers.

FIGURE 22.3

Receive connectors

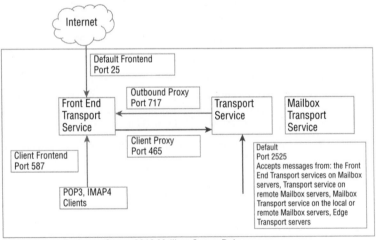

Exchange Server 2016 Mailbox Server Role

The Default Frontend Receive connector is used to receive inbound SMTP mail from SMTP servers outside the organization. In Exchange Server 2007 and Exchange Server 2010, a Receive connector had to be manually created to accept email messages from anonymous senders. This is no longer the case in Exchange Server 2013 and Exchange Server 2016; similarly to Exchange Server 2003, receiving email messages from the Internet happens out of the box. In Figure 22.5 the Permission Groups properties of the Default Frontend Receive connector are shown. These permissions are the required set of permissions for receiving email messages anonymously from the Internet.

FIGURE 22.4

Receive connectors in the Exchange Admin Center

FIGURE 22.5

Default Frontend Receive connector permissions

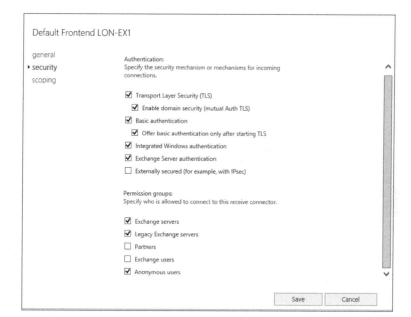

The Frontend Transport service, which is the service that is associated with the Default Frontend Receive connector, performs several actions on incoming email messages before starting an SMTP session to a Mailbox server. The client access services must perform these actions quickly because the client access services do *not* queue any email messages. Queuing occurs only on the Mailbox server.

One of the tasks performed by the client access services is looking up the recipients of the email messages in Active Directory. Once the recipient is successfully looked up, the message is accepted by the Default Frontend Receive connector, and it is passed along to the Default Receive connector running on a Mailbox server. The client access services choose the *best* Mailbox server to relay the email message. The *best* Mailbox server will vary. If the recipient of the email message is a distribution group, the client access services will pass the message to a Mailbox server in the same AD site. If the recipient's mailbox is located on a previous version of Exchange Server, the client access services pass the email message to an Exchange Server 2016 Mailbox server. The client access services never communicates directly to an Exchange Server 2010 server, but it can communicate directly with Exchange Server 2013.

You can view the properties of a Receive connector by using the `Get-ReceiveConnector` cmdlet. Here is an example that displays all the properties of the Default Frontend Receive connector:

```
Get-ReceiveConnector "MBX1\Default Frontend MBX1" | fl
RunspaceId                          : c8f636cc-caa8-4031-b72d-a952b2771c67
AuthMechanism                       : Tls, Integrated, BasicAuth,
BasicAuthRequireTLS, ExchangeServer
Banner                              :
BinaryMimeEnabled                   : True
Bindings                            : {[::]:25, 0.0.0.0:25}
ChunkingEnabled                     : True
DefaultDomain                       :
DeliveryStatusNotificationEnabled   : True
EightBitMimeEnabled                 : True
BareLinefeedRejectionEnabled        : False
DomainSecureEnabled                 : True
EnhancedStatusCodesEnabled          : True
LongAddressesEnabled                : False
OrarEnabled                         : False
SuppressXAnonymousTls               : False
ProxyEnabled                        : False
AdvertiseClientSettings             : False
Fqdn                                : MBX1.contoso.com
ServiceDiscoveryFqdn                :
TlsCertificateName                  :
Comment                             :
Enabled                             : True
ConnectionTimeout                   : 00:10:00
ConnectionInactivityTimeout         : 00:05:00
MessageRateLimit                    : Unlimited
MessageRateSource                   : IPAddress
```

```
MaxInboundConnection                      : 5000
MaxInboundConnectionPerSource             : 20
MaxInboundConnectionPercentagePerSource   : 2
MaxHeaderSize                             : 128 KB (131,072 bytes)
MaxHopCount                               : 60
MaxLocalHopCount                          : 8
MaxLogonFailures                          : 3
MaxMessageSize                            : 36 MB (37,748,736 bytes)
MaxProtocolErrors                         : 5
MaxRecipientsPerMessage                   : 200
PermissionGroups                          : AnonymousUsers, ExchangeServers,
ExchangeLegacyServers
PipeliningEnabled                         : True
ProtocolLoggingLevel                      : Verbose
RemoteIPRanges                            : {::-ffff:ffff:ffff:ffff:ffff:ffff:ffff:
ffff, 0.0.0.0-255.255.255.255}
RequireEHLODomain                         : False
RequireTLS                                : False
EnableAuthGSSAPI                          : False
ExtendedProtectionPolicy                  : None
LiveCredentialEnabled                     : False
TlsDomainCapabilities                     : {}
Server                                    : MBX1
TransportRole                             : FrontendTransport
SizeEnabled                               : Enabled
TarpitInterval                            : 00:00:05
MaxAcknowledgementDelay                   : 00:00:30
AdminDisplayName                          :
ExchangeVersion                           : 0.1 (8.0.535.0)
Name                                      : Default Frontend MBX1
DistinguishedName                         : CN=Default Frontend MBX1,CN=SMTP Receive

Connectors,CN=Protocols,CN=MBX1,CN=Servers,CN=Exchange Administrative Group
                                (FYDIBOHF23SPDLT),CN=Administrative
Groups,CN=First
                                Organization,CN=Microsoft
Exchange,CN=Services,CN=Configuration,DC=contoso,DC=com
Identity                                  : MBX1\Default Frontend MBX1
Guid                                      : 775e96c4-469b-4d51-bc9d-b4c462236380
ObjectCategory                            : contoso.com/Configuration/Schema/
ms-Exch-Smtp-Receive-Connector
ObjectClass                               : {top, msExchSmtpReceiveConnector}
WhenChanged                               : 4/8/2016 10:45:13 PM
WhenCreated                               : 4/8/2016 9:18:03 PM
WhenChangedUTC                            : 4/9/2016 2:45:13 AM
WhenCreatedUTC                            : 4/9/2016 1:18:03 AM
OrganizationId                            :
```

```
OriginatingServer                          : DC1.contoso.com
IsValid                                    : True
ObjectState                                : Unchanged
```

The properties of the Default Receive connector are as follows:

```
Get-ReceiveConnector "MBX1\Default MBX1" | fl
RunspaceId                                 : c8f636cc-caa8-4031-b72d-a952b2771c67
AuthMechanism                              : Tls, Integrated, BasicAuth,
BasicAuthRequireTLS, ExchangeServer
Banner                                     :
BinaryMimeEnabled                          : True
Bindings                                   : {[::]:25, 0.0.0.0:25}
ChunkingEnabled                            : True
DefaultDomain                              :
DeliveryStatusNotificationEnabled          : True
EightBitMimeEnabled                        : True
BareLinefeedRejectionEnabled               : False
DomainSecureEnabled                        : False
EnhancedStatusCodesEnabled                 : True
LongAddressesEnabled                       : False
OrarEnabled                                : False
SuppressXAnonymousTls                      : False
ProxyEnabled                               : False
AdvertiseClientSettings                    : False
Fqdn                                       : MBX1.contoso.com
ServiceDiscoveryFqdn                       :
TlsCertificateName                         :
Comment                                    :
Enabled                                    : True
ConnectionTimeout                          : 00:10:00
ConnectionInactivityTimeout                : 00:05:00
MessageRateLimit                           : Unlimited
MessageRateSource                          : IPAddress
MaxInboundConnection                       : 5000
MaxInboundConnectionPerSource              : Unlimited
MaxInboundConnectionPercentagePerSource    : 100
MaxHeaderSize                              : 128 KB (131,072 bytes)
MaxHopCount                                : 60
MaxLocalHopCount                           : 8
MaxLogonFailures                           : 3
MaxMessageSize                             : 35 MB (36,700,160 bytes)
MaxProtocolErrors                          : 5
MaxRecipientsPerMessage                    : 5000
PermissionGroups                           : ExchangeUsers, ExchangeServers,
ExchangeLegacyServers
PipeliningEnabled                          : True
ProtocolLoggingLevel                       : Verbose
```

```
RemoteIPRanges                          : {::-ffff:ffff:ffff:ffff:ffff:ffff:ffff:
ffff, 0.0.0.0-255.255.255.255}
RequireEHLODomain                       : False
RequireTLS                              : False
EnableAuthGSSAPI                        : False
ExtendedProtectionPolicy                : None
LiveCredentialEnabled                   : False
TlsDomainCapabilities                   : {}
Server                                  : MBX1
TransportRole                           : HubTransport
SizeEnabled                             : EnabledWithoutValue
TarpitInterval                          : 00:00:05
MaxAcknowledgementDelay                 : 00:00:30
AdminDisplayName                        :
ExchangeVersion                         : 0.1 (8.0.535.0)
Name                                    : Default MBX1
DistinguishedName                       : CN=Default MBX1,CN=SMTP Receive
Connectors,CN=Protocols,CN=MBX1,CN=Servers,CN=Exchange Administrative Group
                                (FYDIBOHF23SPDLT),CN=Administrative
Groups,CN=First
Organization,CN=Microsoft Exchange,CN=Services,CN=Configuration,DC=contoso,DC=com
Identity                                : MBX1\Default MBX1
Guid                                    : 410eca52-bd30-46a6-897b-ca72dc934b32
ObjectCategory                          : contoso.com/Configuration/Schema/
ms-Exch-Smtp-Receive-Connector
ObjectClass                             : {top, msExchSmtpReceiveConnector}
WhenChanged                             : 4/23/2016 10:55:00 AM
WhenCreated                             : 4/8/2016 9:40:47 PM
WhenChangedUTC                          : 4/23/2016 2:55:00 PM
WhenCreatedUTC                          : 4/9/2016 1:40:47 AM
OrganizationId                          :
OriginatingServer                       : DC1.contoso.com
IsValid                                 : True
ObjectState                             : Unchanged
```

CREATING A RECEIVE CONNECTOR

With few exceptions, you will usually not need to create additional Receive connectors, nor will you need to make many changes to the existing Receive connectors. The most common situation that should involve creating new Receive connectors is when you need to accommodate the needs of a custom application or server that needs to route email through your Exchange servers. For example, you may have a monitoring server that needs to send email internally to your server administrators. In this case, you could use the Default Receive connectors but would then have to customize them for that need. To avoid messing around with the Default Receive connectors, most organizations choose to create a new Receive connector that has a custom IP address range (which would allow only the monitoring server to communicate) and custom permissions (which would allow the monitoring server to relay email through the Receive connector). This solution minimizes the risk of inadvertently preventing an organization from receiving email because of misconfigurations on the Default Receive connectors.

Creating a Receive connector in Exchange Server should be carefully planned. An Exchange Server will have all of the Default Receive connectors created for the Mailbox server role. On top of the Default Receive connectors that are created, all the transport services for the Mailbox servers will be running on the same server. This could cause a problem since the new Receive connector will listen on port 25 and will use the Transport service. If you recall from earlier in the chapter, the Transport service on a Mailbox server normally listens to port 2525 and the Frontend Transport service listens to port 25. To create a new Receive connector that listens on port 25 and uses the Frontend Transport service, you can run the following:

```
New-ReceiveConnector -Name "Anonymous Relay" -Usage Custom -AuthMechanism
ExternalAuthoritative -PermissionGroups ExchangeServers -Bindings 192.168.1.20:25
-RemoteIpRanges 192.168.5.77 –TransportRole FrontendTransport
```

In Exchange Server 2016, the EMS session is running against a Mailbox server. To create a new Receive connector on a Mailbox server, you use the following steps:

1. Open Windows PowerShell as an administrator.

2. Create your new Receive connector by using the New-ReceiveConnector cmdlet.

Sending Email from Your Servers

Making sure that users on the Internet can send you email is fairly simple, but making sure they can receive email you send is a bit more challenging. Many of these challenges are because there are so many different types of antispam and antispoofing systems on the Internet. Unfortunately, these message-hygiene systems don't all follow the same set of rules. Why might a remote email server reject a connection from your public-facing server?

◆ The public IP address of your sending server may be on a real-time block list (RBL). This could be because that IP address had been a source of spam at one time, it could have been an open SMTP relay, or the IP address could be listed as part of a DHCP or dial-up IP address range.

◆ The public IP address of your sending server may not have a pointer (PTR) record registered in DNS. Some mail servers will not accept a connection from you unless your public IP has a PTR record.

◆ Your email domain may be missing or have an invalid Sender Policy Framework (SPF) DNS record. You must take care during infrastructure changes and when your outbound IP addresses change; you must remember to keep your SPF record up-to-date, as well. While outright rejects because of this are not common yet, more organizations are using SPF as a way to protect against spoofing.

◆ The name that your sending server uses to introduce itself in the SMTP HELO or EHLO command may be an invalid domain name or may not match an existing DNS record.

To ensure that remote servers will accept connections from your email servers, there are a number of things you should do for your connections and in your public-facing DNS servers:

♦ Use a tool such as the Microsoft Remote Connectivity Analyzer (`www.testexchange connectivity.com`) or the DNSBL spam database lookup tool (`www.dnsbl.info`). If you find that your public-facing IP is on one of spam database lists, the list will usually have information on how to remove your IP. If the reason your IP is on the list is because they consider your IP part of a dial-up or DHCP range (common with cable service providers), you will need to work with your ISP to ensure you are removed from the list.

♦ Ensure that each public-facing IP address has a PTR record associated with it. Try to use the same name that the server uses for `EHLO` or `HELO` commands, such as `mail1.contoso .com`. The owner of the IP address range will need to register the PTR records for you; this is usually the ISP.

♦ Create an SPF record in DNS that identifies the SMTP hosts that are authorized to send email for your domain. For small organizations, this will be a simple matter of determining the public-facing IP addresses of your email servers. If you use a managed provider to deliver all of your outbound mail, you will need to contact the provider to get the information necessary to create SPF records for you. In the previous example for the mail servers for `contoso.com`, the following SPF record indicates that only the listed host is authorized to send mail for `contoso.com`:

```
contoso.com   text = "v=spf1 mx ip4:192.168.244.10 ip4:192.168.244.11 -all"
```

 Real World Scenario

INCONSISTENT EMAIL DELIVERY FAILURES

A company that one of the contributors to this book worked with had been reliably sending email to the Internet for a number of years. The users rarely reported nondelivery reports (NDRs) or other outbound email problems.

During an upgrade of the speed of their Internet connection, the company changed their public IP addresses. The mail server and DNS manager dutifully changed the address and MX records on their public-facing DNS server. After the DNS changes took effect, they tested email to and from various domains. All their tests succeeded.

Because the IP address switch-over was so successful, it was quickly forgotten. Therefore, their administrators and their help desk were not quick to make a connection between the IP address change and occasional mail-delivery problems that the users were experiencing. Most of the NDR messages that the users were receiving were not very helpful and usually very cryptic.

Only after looking at the SMTP logs on their outbound smart host did the company determine that a few remote systems were rejecting mail because there were no PTR records for the IP addresses.

The mail administrator contacted their ISP and asked the ISP to create the necessary PTR records for the IP subnet. This resolved the problem.

AOL is particularly strict on requiring IP addresses to have PTR records, but most organizations will accept mail from you regardless. Because only a small fraction of your outbound email is being rejected, it can make troubleshooting this problem more difficult.

Send Connectors

Whereas Receive connectors are configured for each server, Send connectors are organizational connectors that you can assign to a number of different Mailbox servers. This is an important distinction from some of the earlier versions of Exchange Server. Send connectors in Exchange Server 2010, Exchange Server 2013, and Exchange Server 2016 are configured at the organization level and do not inherit settings from any specific server or site.

THE LOWDOWN ON IMPLICIT SEND CONNECTORS

Each Mailbox server in an Exchange Server 2016 organization has an implicit Send connector, but that connector is used only for transferring email messages to other Mailbox servers. The implicit Send connector is not visible in the Exchange Admin Center or in the Exchange Management Shell. There are no properties that can be set for the implicit Send connector, and it cannot be used to deliver messages directly to the Internet or to an external host. This connector is actually *implicitly* created on demand whenever email messages need to be delivered to another mailbox server and then removed from the organization. You cannot configure this connector; so now that I've discussed it and you know it, you can forget about it!

Send connectors accept only Mailbox servers as source servers, though proxying can be enabled on Send connectors. Proxying will mean that outbound email messages will be passed through client access services before leaving the Exchange Server organization. In that case, the Mailbox server establishes an SMTP session with the client access services to deliver the email message. Once a proxy is enabled on a Send connector, the source Mailbox server will look for client access services only in the same AD site as proxy servers for outbound SMTP connections.

Send connectors are managed in the EAC under the Send Connector tab when Mail Flow is selected from the Feature pane. Figure 22.6 shows a custom Send Connector named Internet in the Exchange Admin Center.

FIGURE 22.6
Send connector in the Exchange Admin Center

The Source Server properties page is where you designate which Mailbox server will deliver messages for a Send connector. When you assign more than one Mailbox server as a source server, the outbound messaging load will be balanced among the source servers.

You can also view the properties of a Send connector using the EMS cmdlet `Get-SendConnector`; here is an example:

```
Get-SendConnector "Internet" | FL
[PS] C:\Windows\system32>Get-SendConnector "Internet" | FL
AddressSpaces               : {SMTP:*;1}
AuthenticationCredential    :
CloudServicesMailEnabled    : False
Comment                     :
ConnectedDomains            : {}
ConnectionInactivityTimeOut : 00:10:00
DNSRoutingEnabled           : False
DomainSecureEnabled         : False
Enabled                     : True
ErrorPolicies               : Default
ForceHELO                   : False
Fqdn                        :
FrontendProxyEnabled        : False
HomeMTA                     : Microsoft MTA
HomeMtaServerId             : MBX1
Identity                    : Internet
IgnoreSTARTTLS              : False
IsScopedConnector           : False
IsSmtpConnector             : True
MaxMessageSize              : Unlimited
Name                        : Internet
Port                        : 25
ProtocolLoggingLevel        : None
RequireOorg                 : False
RequireTLS                  : False
SmartHostAuthMechanism      : None
SmartHosts                  : {[192.168.1.171], [192.168.1.172]}
SmartHostsString            : [192.168.1.171],[192.168.1.172]
SmtpMaxMessagesPerConnection : 20
SourceIPAddress             : 0.0.0.0
SourceRoutingGroup          : Exchange Routing Group (DWBGZMFD01QNBJR)
SourceTransportServers      : {MBX1}
TlsAuthLevel                :
TlsCertificateName          :
TlsDomain                   :
UseExternalDNSServersEnabled : False
```

Because Exchange Server 2016 does not have a default SMTP connector for outbound mail, you will need to create at least one Send connector. Most organizations that have only one site will need to create only a single Send connector; this connector will be used to send email directly to the Internet, to an Edge Transport server, or to an SMTP smart host.

CREATING A SEND CONNECTOR

This section goes through an example of creating a Send connector that will be responsible for sending email to the Internet. To start, select Mail Flow from the Feature pane. Choose the Send Connector tab and click the + (Add) icon. This launches the New Send Connector window shown in Figure 22.7. On the Introduction page, you must provide the name of the connector and its type (that is, its intended use).

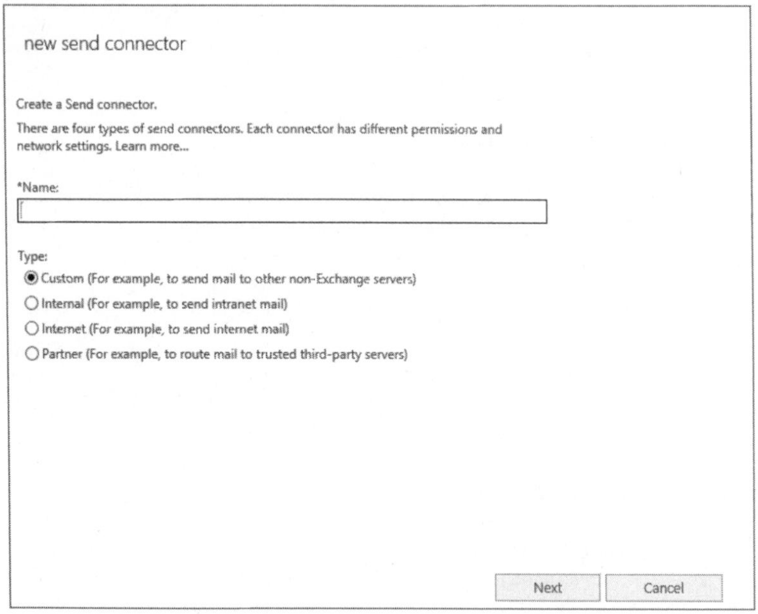

FIGURE 22.7
The Introduction page of the New Send Connector window

new send connector

Create a Send connector.

There are four types of send connectors. Each connector has different permissions and network settings. Learn more...

*Name:

Type:
- ● Custom (For example, to send mail to other non-Exchange servers)
- ○ Internal (For example, to send intranet mail)
- ○ Internet (For example, to send internet mail)
- ○ Partner (For example, to route mail to trusted third-party servers)

Next   Cancel

The New Send Connector window will allow you to create four types of Send connectors. You should note that these types of connectors are nothing more than predefined configuration settings that can be changed at any point after the connector is created. Think of these connector types as templates, nothing more. The four types of Send connectors are listed here:

Custom Allows you to manually configure all the configuration settings and has no preconfigured settings.

Internal Allows you to configure a connector that connects to Edge Transport servers in your organization or servers in another organization. Because all internal mail routing is automatic, you usually will not need to create an internal Send connector to another server in your organization.

Internet Used to send mail to the Internet by using DNS MX records.

Partner Used to send mail to specific Internet domains and to configure certificate authentication and TLS encryption.

On the Network Settings properties page, you can configure a smart host for external delivery. Or, you can select the Use Domain Name System (DNS) "MX" Records To Route Mail

Automatically setting to configure the Send connector to use name resolution to locate external hosts.

In a setting called the *address space,* you must also specify the specific SMTP domains to which a Send connector will deliver email messages. The address space with a value of * represents all SMTP domains that are not explicitly defined on another connector. (If a more precise address space, such as adatum.com, is specified on another connector, that connector will be used instead of the connector that has the more general address space.)

The Source Server page allows you to specify the Mailbox servers that will deliver mail for this Send connector. If you have more than one Mailbox server, you should use additional servers for redundancy and load balancing.

Once you click the Finish button on the New Send Connector page, the EAC will execute the command necessary to create the new Send connector:

```
New-SendConnector -Name 'Internet Connector' -Usage 'Internet'
-AddressSpaces 'smtp:*;1' -DNSRoutingEnabled $true
-UseExternalDNSServersEnabled $false -SourceTransportServers 'EX1'
```

Once you have created the connector, you should set one additional configuration option. On the Scoping tab of the Send connector, enter the public name of the FQDN for this server, such as mail.contoso.com.

This is the name that the Send connector uses to *announce* itself in the EHLO or HELO command when it connects to a remote SMTP system. If you don't specify an FQDN for the connector to use, the connector will use the default FQDN for the server. Often, this is an internal name that is not recognized on the Internet. Some Internet hosts will reject a connection if the name cannot be resolved to a host record in your company's DNS zone.

Securing Mail Flow

One of the most common concerns with Exchange Server is how email messages are secured in transit. Out-of-the-box mail flow between Exchange servers within an organization is secured by using TLS. If a sniffer is placed between source and destination servers, the traffic will be encrypted and unreadable. Not only is server-to-server communication secured by default, but so is all SMTP communication between transport services and SMTP clients, which is authenticated by default.

So, if internal communication is secured by default, where does that leave us regarding communication to hosts on the Internet or third-party SMTP servers? Well, in short, it depends. Several options are available to secure email messages that are coming into or leaving your Exchange Server organization. Several of the most common options are covered in this section.

OPPORTUNISTIC TLS

The Frontend Default Receive connector is set to accept TLS connections from any source SMTP server. If a sending server accepts the SMTP verbs used to announce supportability for TLS, a TLS connection is established between target and source servers. Opportunistic TLS is efficient, but the servers are not validating the certificate being used to secure the SMTP session. Exchange Server *cares* only that a TLS session is established and that the traffic between source and target servers is encrypted.

DOMAIN SECURE TLS

Unlike opportunistic TLS when a certificate is not validated, domain secure TLS requires source and target servers to have valid certificates installed. When domain secure TLS is enabled, sending and receiving servers exchange certificates. The subject name or subject alternative name of a certificate must match the FQDN set on the Send connector of the source organization. In the target organization, the subject name or subject alternative name of the certificate must match the FQDN set on the Receive connector. If the FQDN of the connector does *not* match any of the names on the certificate or if the certificate is not valid, email messages will not be exchanged between the organizations.

TRANSPORT RULE

Another method of enforcing TLS is through a transport rule action that allows Exchange Server 2016 to require TLS to be established before transmitting any SMTP data. The transport rule action is called Require TLS Encryption. As Figure 22.8 illustrates, the action can be added to a transport rule.

FIGURE 22.8
Adding the Require
TLS Encryption
action to a
transport rule

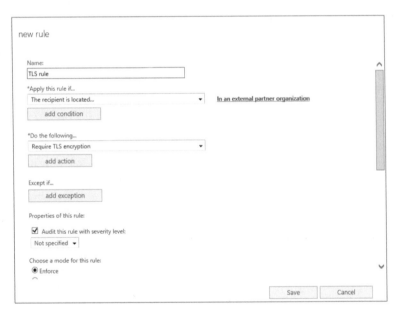

Accepted Domains

An accepted domain is an SMTP domain name (aka SMTP namespace) for which your Exchange Server 2016 organization will accept email messages. The servers in your organization will either deliver an email message to an accepted domain to an internal Exchange Server mailbox or relay it to another SMTP server. During a migration from Exchange Server 2010 or 2013 to Exchange Server 2016, the accepted domains will be inherited in Exchange Server 2016. Accepted domains must be defined for all email addresses that will be routed into your organization by your Exchange Server 2016 servers. Many small- and medium-sized organizations have only a single accepted domain.

SETTING UP AN ACCEPTED DOMAIN USING THE EAC

Accepted domains are found by choosing the Mail Flow tab in the Feature pane and selecting the Accepted Domains tab in the Results pane; you will see a list of the accepted domains that have been defined for your organization, such as those shown in Figure 22.9.

FIGURE 22.9

List of accepted domains

Accepted domains are simple to create and require little input. To create a new accepted domain using the EAC, click the + (Add) icon and you will see the New Accepted Domain window (shown in Figure 22.10). You then need to provide a descriptive name for the accepted domain, the SMTP domain name, and the domain type (how messages for this domain should be treated when messages are accepted by Exchange Server 2016).

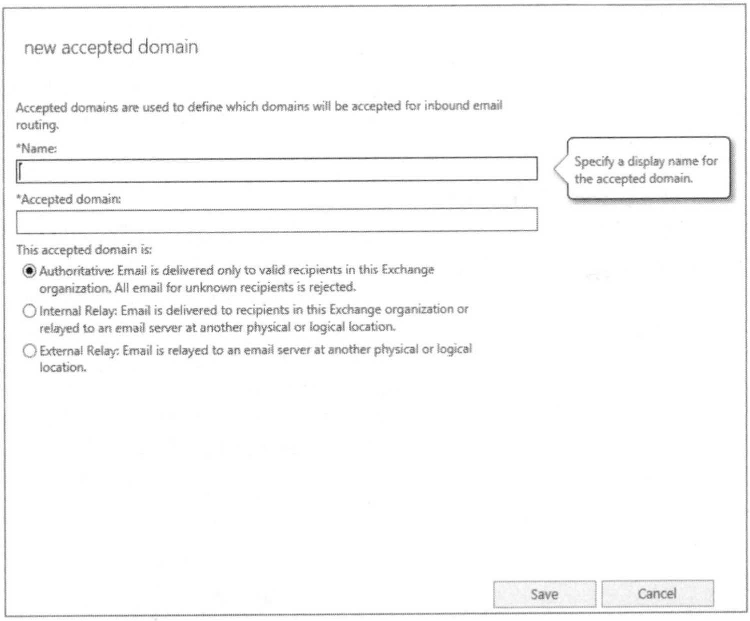

FIGURE 22.10

Creating a new accepted domain

> new accepted domain
>
> Accepted domains are used to define which domains will be accepted for inbound email routing.
>
> *Name:
>
> [   ]   Specify a display name for the accepted domain.
>
> *Accepted domain:
>
> [   ]
>
> This accepted domain is:
>
> ◉ Authoritative: Email is delivered only to valid recipients in this Exchange organization. All email for unknown recipients is rejected.
>
> ○ Internal Relay: Email is delivered to recipients in this Exchange organization or relayed to an email server at another physical or logical location.
>
> ○ External Relay: Email is relayed to an email server at another physical or logical location.
>
> [Save]   [Cancel]

Keep in mind that you cannot modify the domain name of an accepted domain once it is created. (You can change the domain type, however.)

SETTING UP AN ACCEPTED DOMAIN USING THE EMS

You can also manage accepted domains by using the following EMS cmdlets:

◆ `New-AcceptedDomain`

◆ `Set-AcceptedDomain`

◆ `Get-AcceptedDomain`

◆ `Remove-AcceptedDomain`

For example, to create a new accepted domain, use the following EMS command:

```
New-AcceptedDomain -Name 'Contoso' -DomainName
'contoso.com' -DomainType 'Authoritative'
```

ABOUT DOMAIN TYPES

One tricky thing about defining an accepted domain is that you must define how Exchange Server is to treat a message addressed to that domain. You can choose from three types of domains when creating an accepted domain:

Authoritative Domain These are SMTP domains for which you accept the inbound message and deliver it to an internal mailbox within your Exchange Server organization.

Internal Relay Domain These are SMTP domains for which your Exchange server will accept inbound SMTP mail. The Exchange server must have mail-enabled contacts that specify forwarding addresses for users in those domains. The Exchange server then relays the message to another internal mail system. Internal relay domains are used when two Exchange organizations are using federation.

External Relay Domain These are SMTP domains for which your Exchange Server organization will accept inbound SMTP mail and then relay that mail to an external SMTP mail server, usually one that is outside the organization's boundaries. If Edge Transport servers are used, the Edge Transport servers handle the external relay domains.

Remote Domains

When sending mail outside your organization, Exchange Server will make certain assumptions about message formatting and out-of-office replies. These types of settings can be controlled by creating remote domains. For a fresh installation of Exchange Server 2016, a single remote domain configuration is used for all outbound mail. To review the remote domains in your organization, you just need to run `Get-RemoteDomain`.

Creating a new remote domain provides an organization with the ability to define the content that is shared with the remote domain and how email messages from the remote domain are processed by Exchange Server 2016 servers. Here are some of the common configurations the organization may use when creating remote domains:

AllowForwardEnabled   Allows auto forwards of email messages.

CurrentType   Specifies the message content type and format that are accepted by the remote domain.

IsInternal   Recipients in the remote domain are considered internal recipients. This setting will alter how transport rules and transport agents are applied to these recipients.

You can also create the remote domain from an EMS prompt by typing the following command:

```
New-RemoteDomain -Name "Adatum" -DomainName "adatum.com"
```

When an Exchange Server 2016 organization and Office365 are in a hybrid configuration, a new remote domain is created in the Exchange Server 2016 organization for the Office365 domain. Using the Get-RemoteDomain cmdlet, you can view the remote domain settings of an Office365 remote domain:

```
Get-RemoteDomain hy* | fl
RunspaceId                             : c8f636cc-caa8-4031-b72d-a952b2771c67
DomainName                             : contoso.mail.onmicrosoft.com
IsInternal                             : False
TargetDeliveryDomain                   : True
ByteEncoderTypeFor7BitCharsets         : Undefined
CharacterSet                           :
NonMimeCharacterSet                    :
AllowedOOFType                         : External
AutoReplyEnabled                       : True
AutoForwardEnabled                     : True
DeliveryReportEnabled                  : True
NDREnabled                             : True
MeetingForwardNotificationEnabled      : False
ContentType                            : MimeHtmlText
DisplaySenderName                      : True
PreferredInternetCodePageForShiftJis   : Undefined
RequiredCharsetCoverage                :
TNEFEnabled                            :
LineWrapSize                           : Unlimited
TrustedMailOutboundEnabled             : False
TrustedMailInboundEnabled              : False
UseSimpleDisplayName                   : False
NDRDiagnosticInfoEnabled               : True
MessageCountThreshold                  : 2147483647
AdminDisplayName                       :
ExchangeVersion                        : 0.1 (8.0.535.0)
Name                                   : Hybrid Domain - contoso.mail.onmicrosoft.com
DistinguishedName                      : CN=Hybrid Domain - contoso.mail.
onmicrosoft.com,CN=Internet Message
                                         Formats,CN=Global Settings,CN=First
Organization,CN=Microsoft
```

```
Exchange,CN=Services,CN=Configuration,DC=contoso,DC=com
Identity                          : Hybrid Domain - contoso.mail.onmicrosoft.com
Guid                              : 019edd86-1861-43d8-ad96-0cfebea78cad
ObjectCategory                    : contoso.com/Configuration/Schema/ms-Exch-
Domain-Content-Config
ObjectClass                       : {top, msExchDomainContentConfig}
WhenChanged                       : 4/19/2016 2:55:37 AM
WhenCreated                       : 4/19/2016 2:55:21 AM
WhenChangedUTC                    : 4/19/2016 6:55:37 AM
WhenCreatedUTC                    : 4/19/2016 6:55:21 AM
OrganizationId                    :
OriginatingServer                 : DC1.contoso.com
IsValid                           : True
ObjectState                       : Unchanged
```

Messages in Flight

How does Exchange Server 2016 ensure that messages in flight are not lost during a server failure? Microsoft has taken lessons learned from Exchange Server 2007, 2010, and 2013 and expanded on their high-availability solutions for messages in flight. In this section, we will cover the concepts of shadow redundancy and Safety Net. Even if you are familiar with Exchange Server 2010 shadow redundancy, please don't skip over this section, because Microsoft has made some changes to shadow redundancy in Exchange Server 2013 and Exchange Server 2016.

Understanding Shadow Redundancy

Shadow redundancy protects organizations in the event of a Mailbox server or queue database loss. The main principle behind shadow redundancy is maintaining a copy of a message on the previous delivery hop until the server verifies that the email message has been successfully delivered. Think about it as a fail-safe mechanism that waits for the recipient server to *confirm* that a message has been received instead of the sender server *assuming* that the message was successfully delivered. Inside the Exchange Server organization, before an email message is accepted by a receiving Mailbox server, a shadow copy of the email message is created on the sending Mailbox server. The shadow message is stored in a shadow queue.

An important thing to note here is that shadow redundancy is not unique to Exchange Server. This functionality is actually common among other third-party messaging systems.

Before diving into shadow redundancy, let's talk about some of the terminology that will be used in this section:

Primary Message   An original email message

Shadow Message   A copy of an original email message

Primary Server   Mailbox server holding a primary email message

Shadow Server   Mailbox server holding a shadow email message

Once a message has been accepted by a Mailbox server, the Mailbox server processes the message and delivers the email message to the appropriate mailbox database. After the message has been successfully delivered, the primary mailbox server notifies the Mailbox server holding the shadow copy to discard the message from the shadow queue.

The transport boundary for shadow redundancy is *Mailbox servers within the same delivery groups*. If an organization has two DAGs, shadow redundancy will occur within each delivery group.

A shadow message is not identical to a primary message. Since the receiving Mailbox server creates a shadow message before the message is accepted, the shadow message is an unprocessed message. This means that the email message has not yet gone through the transport pipeline. If the shadow message is ever called upon, the email message would have to go through the transport pipeline before being delivered.

Shadow redundancy is configured using `Set-TransportConfig`. It is enabled by default and should not be disabled unless you are troubleshooting specific email delivery issues. You can also view all the shadow redundancy settings by using the `Get-TransportConfig` cmdlet, the default settings of shadow redundancy are shown here:

```
Get-TransportConfig | fl *shadow*
ShadowRedundancyEnabled              : True
ShadowHeartbeatTimeoutInterval       : 00:15:00
ShadowHeartbeatRetryCount            : 12
ShadowHeartbeatFrequency             : 00:02:00
ShadowResubmitTimeSpan               : 03:00:00
ShadowMessageAutoDiscardInterval     : 2.00:00:00
RejectMessageOnShadowFailure         : False
ShadowMessagePreferenceSetting       : PreferRemote
MaxRetriesForLocalSiteShadow         : 2
MaxRetriesForRemoteSiteShadow        : 4
```

An important issue to note is that Exchange Server 2010 performed shadow redundancy by issuing the `XSHADOW` SMTP verb. Exchange Server 2016 servers do not issue an `XSHADOW` verb; therefore, Exchange Server 2010 does not perform shadow redundancy when sending mail to Exchange Server 2016. However, when an Exchange Server 2016 server submits a message to an Exchange Server 2010 Hub Transport server in the same site, it will create a shadow copy of the message until it receives a notification of successful delivery.

For a detail architecture of shadow redundancy and all of the configuration parameters, review this TechNet article at `http://technet.microsoft.com/en-us/library/dd351027(v=exchg.150).aspx`. Even though this is article is specifically about Exchange Server 2013, its principles also apply to Exchange Server 2016.

Understanding Safety Net

In Exchange Server 2007, Microsoft introduced the concept of holding email messages that haven't been delivered to their final destination in the queue database. The queue database is an Extensible Storage Engine (ESE) database, the same database type as a mailbox database, created on Hub Transport servers. As well as keeping copies of messages, the queue database took part in the transport dumpster. Hub Transport servers stored email messages in the queue database based on the transport dumpster settings and database replication. The transport dumpster was a big step forward for transport high availability, something that had long been criticized as being the Achilles' heel of high availability in Exchange Server. The transport dumpster, though, still had big gaps in its functionality.

In Exchange Server 2013 and also in Exchange Server 2016, Microsoft has moved away from the transport dumpster and Safety Net has now taken its place. The queue database is no longer stored on Hub Transport servers; it's now stored on Mailbox servers, the only place where email messages can be queued.

Much like the transport dumpster, Safety Net utilizes the queue database to store email messages that have been successfully delivered. Unlike in legacy versions of Exchange Server, Safety Net defines how long email messages are retained in the queue database, by default for two days. So, all messages that pass through the transport pipeline are stored in the queue database for two days after having been successfully delivered.

Another improvement that Safety Net offers over the transport dumpster is that each message now has two copies, each copy stored in a different queue database. To modify the amount of time that a message is retained in the queue database for Safety Net, change the value of the `SafetyNetHoldTime` parameter by using the `Set-TranportConfig` cmdlet.

It's nice that these messages are stored in the queue database, but how are those copies of email messages actually used? Well, for that to happen, Safety Net has to be invoked. When a database is mounted after a lossy failover, Active Manager generates a resubmit request to all Mailbox servers in its delivery group. The requesting server will always prefer the server that has the primary email message. If the Mailbox server holding the primary message is unavailable for 12 hours, Active Manager will make a request to the Mailbox server that holds the secondary or shadow copy of the original email message. The shadow copy of the message has not yet gone through the transport pipeline, so if there is a large quantity of email messages in the queue, you may notice a spike in transport service usage.

After 24 hours, a resubmit request will expire. To review the resubmit requests in your organization, you can use the `Get-Resubmit` cmdlet.

It's best if the Windows Server 2012 drive that contains the Safety Net database is configured as RAID 1 storage. As well, you should note that if you implement a lagged database copy in the organization, Microsoft recommends setting the `SafetyNetHoldTime` parameter and the `ReplayLagTime` parameter to the same value.

Using Exchange Server 2016 Antispam/Anti-Malware Tools

Microsoft has continued to improve the antispam capabilities of Exchange Server over the past few years. On top of the antispam agents that can be enabled on an Exchange Server 2016 server, an anti-malware solution is built into Exchange Server 2016. Unlike many third-party solutions, the downside of the built-in anti-malware solution is that it contains only one scanning engine.

During the installation of Exchange Server 2016, you can choose to disable or enable anti-malware measures. If you choose to enable antispam functionalities, you can enable them after the installation of Exchange Server 2016.

Microsoft also recommends the use of Exchange Online Protection, which provides cloud-based antispam protection before the message reaches your Exchange Server organization. There are plenty of third-party vendors that also supply on-premises or cloud solutions to assist with antispam and anti-malware. Every organization, no matter the size, should consider placing an antispam and anti-malware solution in front of Exchange servers. It's simply irresponsible to allow spam into your organization and malware onto your network.

Updating Anti-Malware Engines

After the installation of Exchange Server 2016, anti-malware engines and definitions can be updated by using the EMS. The following example uses the `Update-MalwareFilteringServer .ps1` script to download the latest updates:

```
& $env:ExchangeInstallPath\Scripts\Update-MalwareFilteringServer.ps1 -Identity
all-1
```

Once the PowerShell script completes, you can confirm that the latest updates have been downloaded by looking for event 6033 in the Application logs. If no new updates were found, you will see event 6023, as shown here, in the Application log.

```
Log Name:       Application
Source:         Microsoft-Filtering-FIPFS
Date:           6/20/2016 1:06:23 AM
Event ID:       6023
Task Category:  None
Level:          Information
Keywords:
User:           NETWORK SERVICE
Computer:       EX1.contoso.com
Description:
MS Filtering Engine Update process has not detected any new scan engine updates.
 Scan Engine: Microsoft
 Update Path: http://forefrontdl.microsoft.com/server/scanengineupdate
```

Administrators sometimes forget this. You should update the anti-malware engines and definitions before placing production mailboxes on a Mailbox server.

Anti-Malware Policy

An anti-malware policy is a collection of settings that are used to define how an email message with malware is handled within your organization. Unlike the antispam features in Exchange Server 2016, anti-malware policy can be *managed* through EAC. However, from the EAC you cannot *create* a new anti-malware policy. To create a new policy, you must use the `New-MalwareFilterPolicy` command.

The core settings of the anti-malware policy are listed under the Settings tab, as shown in Figure 22.11.

FIGURE 22.11
Default anti-
malware settings

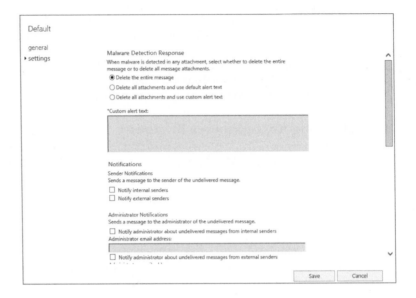

The Malware Detection Response can be set to three possible settings:

Delete The Entire Message   Deletes the email message, thereby preventing the message from being delivered. This is the default setting.

Delete All Attachments And Use Default Alert Text   Removes all attachments from the email message. Adds a text file as an attachment that informs the recipients that all attachments have been removed from the email message because malware was detected.

Delete All Attachments And Use Custom Alert Text   Removes all attachments from the email message. Adds a text file that contains the custom text created in the anti-malware policy.

The Notifications section defines the sender types that will be notified if malware is detected. There are two notification options:

Notify Internal Senders   Send notifications that malware was detected when the sender of the email message is within the organization.

Notify External Senders   Send notifications that malware was detected when the sender of the email message is outside the organization.

The Administrator Notifications section is used to send email messages to an SMTP recipient, most likely a distribution group containing your Exchange Server administrators, for undelivered messages. You can use a semicolon to separate multiple recipients.

The last option in the anti-malware policy is to create custom notifications. The custom notification is sent to the sender or administrator when a message is not delivered. This notification is used only when the entire email message has been deleted from the database.

To test the malware settings and the malware agent, you can download the EICAR (www.eicar.org) anti-malware test file, which masks itself as malware. Send the downloaded EICAR as an attachment to an internal recipient. Once the message is sent, you can use the message-tracking logs to review the actions taken by the malware agent, such as removing the email message from the transport pipeline. In the output shown here, notice that the malware agent detected the presence of malware and removed the infected email message:

```
Get-TransportService | Get-MessageTrackingLog -MessageSubject "Virus2" -event
fail | fl
RunspaceId              : c52ed2d3-e433-40e1-8038-9428479cb5d1
Timestamp               : 4/23/2016 12:44:57 PM
ClientIp                :
ClientHostname          : EX1
ServerIp                :
ServerHostname          :
SourceContext           : Malware Agent
ConnectorId             :
Source                  : AGENT
EventId                 : FAIL>
Recipients              : {john@contoso.com}
RecipientStatus         : {550 4.3.2 QUEUE.TransportAgent; message deleted by
transport agent}
```

Managing Anti-Malware Protection

For many organizations, the use of a third-party anti-malware application is preferred over the built-in Exchange Server solution. In these cases, anti-malware protection should be disabled on the Mailbox server. To disable anti-malware scanning, run the following command on each Mailbox server:

```
& $env:ExchangeInstallPath\Scripts\Disable-Antimalwarescanning.ps1
```

The following command will enable anti-malware scanning:

```
& $env:ExchangeInstallPath\Scripts\Enable-Antimalwarescanning.ps1
```

Once you enable or disable anti-malware scanning, the Transport service must be restarted on the Mailbox server for the change to take effect.

When email messages are lost due to false positives that occur in anti-malware scanning, you can temporarily bypass filtering. Bypassing anti-malware filtering should be done with caution because the Mailbox server will no longer scan an email messages for malware. Enabling and disabling bypassing of malware filtering can take up to 10 minutes to take effect. To enable bypassing of anti-malware scanning, use this command:

```
Set-MalwareFilteringServer -BypassFiltering $true
```

Using the Set-MalwareFiltering cmdlet, you can specify how malware filtering is configured within your organization. We already talked about bypassing malware filtering; you can also change settings, such as the update frequency of the malware engine. You can use the Get-MalwareFilteringServer cmdlet to see the settings that can be modified:

```
Get-MalwareFilteringServer | fl
ForceRescan             : False
BypassFiltering         : False
PrimaryUpdatePath       : http://forefrontdl.microsoft.com/server/
scanengineupdate
```

```
SecondaryUpdatePath          :
DeferWaitTime                : 5
DeferAttempts                : 3
UpdateFrequency              : 60
UpdateTimeout                : 150
ScanTimeout                  : 300
ScanErrorAction              : Block
MinimumSuccessfulEngineScans : 1
```

Enabling Antispam Agents

The Exchange Server 2016 antispam transport features are not enabled out of the box. Microsoft has included PowerShell scripts to enable antispam features in the Exchange Server script directory. Specifically, you will find two PowerShell scripts (`Install-AntispamAgents.ps1` and `Uninstall-AntispamAgents.ps1`) in the folder `C:\Program Files\Microsoft\Exchange Server\v15\scripts`.

On each of your Mailbox servers earmarked to use the antispam agents, you must run the `Install-AntispamAgents.ps1` script. This script needs to be run only on the Mailbox servers that will receive inbound email from outside your organization.

To run the installation script, open the EMS, and change to the scripts folder (again, `C:\Program Files\Microsoft\Exchange Server\v15\scripts`) by typing CD `$exscripts`, and then type this command: `.\Install-AntispamAgents.ps1`. After you run this command, you will need to restart the Microsoft Exchange Transport service for the change to take effect.

If you are familiar with managing antispam in Exchange Server 2010, you will quickly notice that in Exchange Server 2016 you can no longer manage antispam settings from a GUI management interface. All antispam settings are managed through the EMS. The IP Allow lists' and IP Block lists' agents are not available in the Exchange Server 2016 Mailbox server role. To use the IP Allow lists and IP Block lists, you must use an Edge server role.

The most relevant antispam agents are discussed in the next sections.

Connection Filtering

As we mentioned before, connection filtering that was available in Exchange Server 2010 is now available only if it is used with the Edge Transport server role and is the first filtering applied to a receiving message. Connection filtering evaluates a message source and then allows or blocks the receiving email. A connection filter makes its decisions based on the IP address of the connecting mail server; it decides whether any action needs to be taken regarding the inbound message. The decision is made based on a list of allowed and blocked IP addresses. The source IP address may be configured to be specifically allowed, specifically blocked, or analyzed to be evaluated against IP Allow providers or IP Block providers. If none of the above filters apply, the message is evaluated by using the other antispam agents, such as sender-recipient filtering.

You can use the following commands in the Exchange Management Shell on Edge Transport server role to configure connection filtering:

◆   To enable connection filtering, run the following commands:

```
Enable-TransportAgent "Connection Filtering Agent"
Restart-Service MSExchangeTransport
```

◆ To enable an IP block list, run the following command:

```
Set-IPBlockListConfig -Enabled $true
```

◆ To disable an IP block list, run the following command:

```
Set-IPBlockListConfig -Enabled $false
```

◆ To configure an IP block list, run the following command:

```
Set-IPBlockListConfig [-ExternalMailEnabled <$true | $false>]
[-InternalMailEnabled <$true | $false> -MachineEntryRejectionResponse "<Custom
response text>"] [-StaticEntryRejectionResponse "<Custom response text>"]
```

◆ To add IP block list entries, run the following command:

```
Add-IPBlockListEntry <-IPAddress IPAddress | -IPRange IP range or CIDR IP>
[-ExpirationTime <DateTime>] [-Comment "<Descriptive Comment>"]
```

◆ To enable all IP block list providers, run the following command:

```
Set-IPBlockListProvidersConfig -Enabled $true
```

◆ To disable all IP block list providers, run the following command:

```
Set-IPBlockListProvidersConfig -Enabled $false
```

◆ To configure all IP block list providers, run the following command:

```
Set-IPBlockListProvidersConfig [-BypassedRecipients <recipient1,recipient2...>]
[-ExternalMailEnabled <$true | $false>] [-InternalMailEnabled <$true | $false>]
```

◆ To add an IP block list provider, run the following command:

```
Add-IPBlockListProvider -Name "<Descriptive Name>" -LookupDomain <FQDN>
[-Priority <Integer>] [-Enabled <$true | $false>] [-AnyMatch <$true | $false>]
[-BitmaskMatch <IPAddress>] [-IPAddressesMatch <IPAddressStatusCode1,IPAddress
StatusCode2...>] [-RejectionResponse "<Custom Text>"]
```

Content Filtering

Content filtering is an Exchange Server 2016 feature that was formerly known as the Intelligent Message Filter in Exchange Server 2003. The content filter examines a message's content based on keyword analysis, message size, and other factors; it then assigns the message a spam confidence level (SCL) ranking, a score essentially. This ranking is from 0 to 9. A message with an SCL ranking of 0 is not very likely to be spam, and a message with an SCL ranking of 9 is very likely to be spam. Based on the SCL value of a message, the Exchange server takes one of three possible actions:

◆ **Delete messages that meet or exceed a specific SCL threshold**. This is the most drastic action. The sender is not notified that this has occurred, and you can't later evaluate whether the message really was spam.

◆ **Reject messages that meet or exceed a specific SCL threshold**. The Mailbox server accepts the message, analyzes it, and kicks it back to the sender with text indicating that the message was rejected because it looks like spam.

◆ **Quarantine messages that meet or exceed a specific SCL threshold**. Any messages with the specified SCL value or higher will be sent to an SMTP address where you can analyze them to determine whether they are truly spam.

NEGATIVE SCL VALUES?

Is it possible to have an SCL value of –1? Yes, actually it is. For any message that is sent to your server via an authenticated connection, or if the sender's email address is on your safe senders list, the SCL value of the message is set to –1. So if one of your trusted senders is sending you a short message about low-interest-rate mortgages, you will still get the message.

If you are interested in seeing the SCL value that is assigned to any given message in your mailbox, you can use the column-filtering features of Outlook. Simply add the column named SCL to your view. The new column will display the score of each email message in the view.

You can activate none, one, two, or all three of the actions, but the SCL values must progress downward in accordance with the severity of the action. For example, you could set a reject value of 8 or higher and a quarantine value of 7 or higher. In that case, any messages with an SCL value of 8 or 9 will be rejected; messages with an SCL value of 7 will be sent to the quarantine email address. However, you cannot set a quarantine value of 9 but then delete everything with an SCL value greater than or equal to 7.

In Exchange Server 2016, a global value named the SCL Junk Threshold is set to 8 by default. This value determines that the Information Store must place any messages with a spam confidence level of 8 or higher into a user's Junk Email folder. Users can then review the contents of the Junk Email folder to determine whether a message was correctly identified as spam. However, if you set the quarantine value on the Mailbox server to 3, then only messages with an SCL value of 4 or higher will reach the Junk Email folder.

For most organizations, a global SCL Junk Threshold of 8 is sufficient, but depending on your business model and the types of email messages you receive, you might want to lower it. You can lower the SCL value to 5 or 6. To lower the Junk Email threshold for all users, type the following command:

```
Set-OrganizationConfig -SCLJunkThreshold 6
```

You can view the organization configuration using the `Get-OrganizationConfig` cmdlet. Here is an example:

```
Get-OrganizationConfig | FL SCLJunk*
SCLJunkThreshold : 8
```

In some cases, a specific user may need a different set of SCL values than the Mailbox server provides. The values the Mailbox server provides can be customized on a user-by-user basis. In the following command, we have disabled the `Quarantine` and `Reject` parameters for a particular user, and we have specified that this user's Junk Email threshold is 4:

```
Set-Mailbox "John Doe" -SCLRejectEnabled $False -SCLQuarantineEnabled
$False  -SCLJunkThreshold 4 -SCLJunkEnabled $True
```

You can view the resulting configuration for the mailbox with the Get-Mailbox cmdlet. Here is an example:

```
Get-Mailbox "John Doe"  |  FL Name,*scl*
Name                      : John Doe
SCLDeleteThreshold        :
SCLDeleteEnabled          :
SCLRejectThreshold        : 7
SCLRejectEnabled          : False
SCLQuarantineThreshold    : 9
SCLQuarantineEnabled      : False
SCLJunkThreshold          : 4
SCLJunkEnabled            : True
```

 Real World Scenario

WAY TOO MANY VALID EMAILS BEING FLAGGED AS SPAM

A company can set up filters to allow specific messages to pass through the antispam filters. Take, for example, a real estate services company. Much of their communication with customers and prospective customers is via email. When they started using the content filter, they found that many of their customers' emails were being flagged as spam because of keywords in the message body.

They decided to use the content filter's custom-words feature to specify some words or phrases that the content filter would not block. These included words and phrases such as *mortgage*, *interest rates*, *real estate*, and *assessment*. The thought behind this was that it was better to possibly receive a few extra spam messages that use these words than it was to reject a message from a real customer.

You can enable two types of word lists. If the message contains words in the first list, even if the message appears to be spam, the message is accepted. If the words in the second list are contained in a message, the message is blocked unless it contains words from the first list. Using Add-ContentFilterPhrase, you can create a good or bad word list as shown here:

```
Add-ContentFilterPhrase -Influence BadWord -Phrase "Really bad"
```

The list with words and phrases that are always accepted can be particularly useful if legitimate messages to your company will frequently contain a particular word or phrase that might otherwise be filtered (see the "Way Too Many Valid Emails Being Flagged as Spam" sidebar).

Recipient Filtering

When recipient filtering is enabled, the Mailbox server is configured to reject email messages intended for any SMTP address that is not found in the Active Directory or to reject email messages intended for specific SMTP addresses. This reduces the number of *garbage* messages that your Exchange Server organizations accepts, for which it has to issue nondelivery reports. The cmdlet `Get-RecipientFilterConfig` can be used to get the recipient filtering settings:

```
Get-RecipientFilterConfig
BlockedRecipients         : {}
RecipientValidationEnabled : False
BlockListEnabled          : False
Enabled                   : True
ExternalMailEnabled       : True
InternalMailEnabled       : False
```

If you are performing recipient filtering, newly created mailboxes may have their mail rejected by the Mailbox server until the new mailbox has been replicated throughout the organization.

Tarpitting

An Exchange Server can use tarpit to combat dictionary-spamming and directory-harvest attacks. The tarpit feature tells the SMTP server to wait a specified number of seconds (five seconds by default) before responding to a request to send a message to an invalid recipient. For example, if the recipient marketing@contoso.com is an invalid recipient in your organization, but someone's mail server sends a message to that address, your server will wait five seconds and then respond with this error:

```
550 5.1.1 User unknown
```

You may wonder why this feature is even worth mentioning. Spammers often hijack people's home (or work) computers with agents that send mail on their behalf. These "bots" can offer the spammer an almost unlimited supply of SMTP clients, all sending email. They can locate your domain and then go through a dictionary of common names and try to send mail to each one—for example, sending to info@contoso.com, then contact@contoso.com, then sales@contoso .com, and so on. An Exchange server without a tarpit could send back dozens of 550 error messages each second. This makes dictionary spamming more practical. Another evil part of the dictionary-spamming attack is that the spammer can note which addresses are valid and use them in the future. This is called directory harvesting.

A five-second tarpit slows the spammer down by a factor of maybe 500 (depending on your server's speed and your Internet connection speed) by rejecting all the invalid delivery attempts. Most spammers' software programs can't handle the rejects, and they disconnect after some period of time.

You can view your Receive connector's tarpit interval by using the `Get-ReceiveConnector` cmdlet. For example, if you want to change the EX1 Default Receive connector's tarpit interval to 30 seconds, type this command:

```
Set-ReceiveConnector "EX1 Default" -TarpitInterval 00:00:30
```

We recommend that you do not set this value to more than about 30 seconds on any of your Exchange servers because it could start to impact delivery times of email messages to your organization.

Sender Filtering

Sender filtering is one of the oldest antispam features in Exchange Server; it is probably also the least effective. The premise is that you provide a list of SMTP addresses or domains that must be prevented from sending email messages to recipients in your organization. The problem is that most spammers rarely use the same email address twice, so this type of filtering is becoming less relevant to the needs of the users. To get the configuration of the sender filtering agent, you can run the Get-SenderFilterConfig cmdlet:

```
Get-SenderFilterConfig
BlockedSenders                 : {}
BlockedDomains                 : {}
BlockedDomainsAndSubdomains    : {}
Action                         : Reject
BlankSenderBlockingEnabled     : False
RecipientBlockedSenderAction   : Reject
Enabled                        : True
ExternalMailEnabled            : True
InternalMailEnabled            : False
```

A more interesting sender-filtering antispam technique blocks a few pieces of mail by enabling the BlankSenderBlockingEnabled parameter. If a message does not have a sender (and it should), this feature will reject the message.

You can either reject the message entirely or stamp the message as having a blocked sender and allow it through by changing the Action value. If you stamp a message as being from a blocked sender, the content filter will rank the message as spam.

SENDER ID FILTERING—ANTISPOOFING

Earlier in this chapter, we talked a bit about Sender Policy Framework (SPF) records and DNS, and how to make sure that yours are registered properly. Contrary to popular misconception, Sender ID is not an antispam technology but rather an antispoofing technology. Quite simply, to implement Sender ID, each organization on the Internet that sends email should register a Sender Policy Framework record in their public DNS server. This SPF record contains a list of the servers authorized to send mail on behalf of their domain.

When an SMTP server receives a message from a particular domain, it analyzes the message to determine the actual sender and determines which server sent it. If the message originated from an authorized server, it is probably not being spoofed. If it is accepted from a server that is not in the DNS SPF record, the message might be from a spoofed sender.

Using the Get-SenderIDConfig cmdlet, you can export the settings of Sender IP using EMS:

```
Get-SenderIdConfig
SpoofedDomainAction    : StampStatus
TempErrorAction        : StampStatus
BypassedRecipients     : {}
BypassedSenderDomains  : {}
Name                   : SenderIdConfig
Enabled                : True
ExternalMailEnabled    : True
InternalMailEnabled    : False
```

Sender Reputation

Sender reputation is a nice feature of Exchange Server 2016 when it comes to reducing the amount of spam you receive. Why? First, let's outline the problem. Much of the spam that is received today is sent by bot or zombie networks. Spammers have joined forces with virus writers; the virus writers have written malware that infects hundreds of thousands of users' computers. Periodically, these computers check in with the spammer and download a new batch of spam. Blocking a single IP address becomes impractical because the spammers have so many of these computers all over the Internet. However, these zombie networks are usually not using correct SMTP commands and are not RFC compliant. A lot of spammers also use SMTP proxies by sending email messages through a proxy on the Internet.

Sender reputation allows Exchange servers to analyze the connections that are coming in to a Mailbox server and look for things, such as the number of protocol errors, invalid delivery attempts, and the number of messages from the same sender. These can be used to determine if a specific IP address is sending spam, which would give that IP address a bad reputation! Sender reputation can be managed using the `Get-SenderReputationConfig` cmdlet:

```
Get-SenderReputationConfig
MinMessagesPerDatabaseTransaction : 20
SrlBlockThreshold                 : 7
MinMessagesPerTimeSlice           : 100
TimeSliceInterval                 : 48
OpenProxyDetectionEnabled         : True
SenderBlockingEnabled             : True
OpenProxyRescanInterval           : 10
MinReverseDnsQueryPeriod          : 1
SenderBlockingPeriod              : 24
MaxWorkQueueSize                  : 1000
MaxIdleTime                       : 10
Socks4Ports                       : {1081, 1080}
Socks5Ports                       : {1081, 1080}
WingatePorts                      : {23}
HttpConnectPorts                  : {6588, 3128, 80}
HttpPostPorts                     : {6588, 3128, 80}
TelnetPorts                       : {23}
CiscoPorts                        : {23}
TablePurgeInterval                : 24
MaxPendingOperations              : 100
ProxyServerName                   :
ProxyServerPort                   : 0
ProxyServerType                   : None
Name                              : Sender Reputation
MinDownloadInterval               : 10
MaxDownloadInterval               : 100
SrlSettingsDatabaseFileName       :
ReputationServiceUrl              :
Enabled                           : True
ExternalMailEnabled               : True
InternalMailEnabled               : False
```

The default value for the Sender Reputation Level (SRL) block threshold is 7; we recommend keeping it at this slightly moderate value and then monitoring to see if the value can be changed to a more aggressive number. If so, you can increase it slightly, but keep in mind that as you get more aggressive with this value, the possibility of valid connections getting rejected becomes greater, also known as *false positives*.

From the properties of the Sender Reputation settings, the Threshold Action section provides the ability to specify how long a sender is retained on an IP block list once the sender has been determined to be suspicious. The default is 24 hours, and we recommend that you keep that value.

Also as part of Sender Reputation checks, Exchange Server can test for open proxies and determine if the source of a connection is an open proxy. If a connecting SMTP host is identified as an open proxy, it will be added to the IP block list for the time specified. Run the following command to test for an open proxy:

```
Set-SenderReputationConfig - ProxyServerName All-1 -ProxyServerPort 80
-ProxyServerType HttpConnect
```

Troubleshooting Email Routing

Every Exchange Server administrator is involved in regular troubleshooting tasks. When troubleshooting transport, you often have to behave like an investigator trying to trace the path of a message and understanding what went wrong. Sooner or later, that process will lead you to transport logs. There are many transport-related logs, and the protocol logging feature will increase the amount of information collected in those logs. Protocol logging can be enabled on the Mailbox server, Send connector, and Receive connector.

You can enable protocol logging using the following commands:

```
Get-TransportService | Set-TransportService-IntraOrgConnectorProtocolLoggingLevel
verbose
Get-FrontendTransportService | Set-FrontendTransportService-IntraOrgConnectorProt
ocolLoggingLevel verbose
Get-ReceiveConnector | Set-ReceiveConnector -ProtocolLoggingLevel verbose
Get-SendConnector | Set-SendConnector -ProtocolLoggingLevel verbose
```

You will find the log files in the following locations:

◆ The Set-TransportService command creates protocol logs under this path:

```
C:\Program Files\Microsoft\Exchange Server\V15\TransportRoles\Logs\Mailbox\
ProtocolLog
```

◆ The Set-FrontEndTransportService command creates protocol logs under this path:

```
C:\Program Files\Microsoft\Exchange Server\V15\TransportRoles\Logs\FrontEnd\
ProtocolLog
```

◆ The Set-ReceiveConnector command creates protocol logs under this path:

```
C:\Program Files\Microsoft\Exchange Server\V15\TransportRoles\Logs\Hub\ProtocolLog
```

◆ The Set-SendConnector command creates protocol logs under this path:

```
C:\Program Files\Microsoft\ExchangeServer\V15\TransportRoles\Logs\Hub\ProtocolLog
```

The Bottom Line

Create and manage Send connectors and Receive connectors. All messages delivered by an Exchange server are routed through Exchange connectors. The source servers of Send connectors are always Mailbox servers.

Master It You've been called in to deploy Exchange Server 2016 in a "greenfield" deployment, where no messaging system is present. Installing Exchange Server is pretty easy, even for the least experienced IT consultants.

But surprise! After your successful installation, you notice that emails cannot be sent to the Internet. You need to connect this new organization to the Internet. What configuration will allow your customer to book his golf games by email?

Master It You need to plan for the deployment of an Exchange Server 2016 organization. You quickly notice that the organization is concerned about reducing the number of physical servers. Of course, virtualized installation of Exchange Server is always possible, but this customer has very little expertise in virtualization technologies.

They ask you a very important question: do they really need an Edge Transport server on their network?

Chapter 23

Managing Transport, Data Loss Prevention, and Journaling Rules

In spite of the extra features it offers, Exchange Server provides messaging as its core functionality. Messaging systems have been part of the business environment for years—long enough for the novelty of electronic messaging to wear off and for it to become a staple of the office. Email is ubiquitous; right or wrong, your users think of it in the same class as utilities, such as electricity or telephone service. Because of this perception, the majority of messaging administrators must deal with issues, such as regulatory compliance, that once were the province of only a few types of businesses.

Legacy versions of Exchange Server were not equipped with the tools and technology to allow administrators to effectively deal with these sorts of issues out of the box. Electronic discovery, regulatory compliance, leak prevention of sensitive data, long-term message data archiving, and effective retention policies—the basic Exchange Server architecture was designed without these needs in mind. But in today's business world, they are very real problems that some administrators may face. The solution has traditionally been the implementation of expensive, complicated, third-party software suites.

When setting the design goals for Exchange Server 2016, Microsoft wanted to ensure that it was better adapted for modern needs and problems. To combat the ever-growing needs for compliance, protection of sensitive data, archiving, and retention, Exchange Server 2016 has features that will allow administrators to design compliance solutions for the enterprise.

This chapter covers all the elements that work with a transport environment and allow you to control your messages as they flow through your environment. Whether it is to retain message information or to delete messages automatically, Exchange Server 2016 provides many options to administrators.

IN THIS CHAPTER YOU WILL LEARN TO:

- ◆ Create and manage message classifications to control message flow
- ◆ Control message flow and manipulate messages by using transport rules
- ◆ Protect sensitive information by creating data loss prevention policies

Introducing the Exchange 2016 Transport Architecture

In Exchange Server 2007 and 2010, most of the transport functionality had been moved to two distinct roles, Hub Transport and Edge Transport. Messages sent to any mailbox, no matter if the recipient was on the same mailbox database as the sender, were processed by a server with the Hub Transport role first and then delivered to the server with the Mailbox role holding the mounted copy of the mailbox database. This ensured that all messages would be processed by the Microsoft Exchange Transport service.

In contrast, the Mailbox role in Exchange Server 2013 was responsible for the majority of the transport functionality, where Exchange Server 2016 is responsible for the complete transport functionality. The Edge server role is still present, with the same functionality as in previous Exchange versions, sending and receiving email to Internet. The Hub Transport role was removed in Exchange Server 2013, and it doesn't exist in Exchange Server 2016 either. So how does mail flow work now that the Hub role has been deprecated? Let's take a look:

1. When a message is submitted for delivery from an Exchange user, the Mailbox Transport Submission service on the Mailbox server connects to a local database over RPC and captures the pending email message for delivery.

2. The Mailbox Transport Submission service submits the email message over SMTP to the Transport service on the local server or a remote Mailbox server.

3. After the message has been processed by the Transport service, the Mailbox Transport Delivery service on the Mailbox server receives the SMTP messages from the Transport service and delivers the messages using RPC to the local database.

All Messages Pass Through the Mailbox Server

Yes, you read that correctly. Because there is only one server role in the internal Exchange infrastructure (the Mailbox role), every single message you send in Exchange Server 2016 passes through the Microsoft Exchange Transport service, which is now a service on the Mailbox role. Although this might seem inefficient at first glance, the reality is that the resulting benefits make this a great design change. Mainly, and more importantly, it ensures that every single message can be captured by Exchange Server's transport components, which can then act on that message. See Chapter 22, "Managing Connectivity with Transport Services," for more information about this design change and the underlying benefit.

This chapter covers four principal transport capabilities in Exchange Server 2016 in detail:

Message Classifications   These are annotations to an email message that mark it as belonging to a designated category of information that Exchange Server and Outlook may need to treat in a special fashion. These annotations are exposed as properties of the message, allowing clients to display them visually for the users as well as permitting them to be exposed to the rules engine for automated processing. As an example, all messages with certain keywords can be classified as being confidential.

Transport Rules   These are server-side rules that allow you to create and apply messaging policies throughout the entire Exchange Server 2016 organization. Much like Outlook rules, transport rules contain conditions, actions, and exceptions. Every message that passes through the transport pipeline is processed by your organization's transport rules.

Data Loss Prevention   Data loss prevention (DLP) entails identifying, monitoring, and protecting your organization from accidentally exposing sensitive information. A DLP policy combines transport rules, policy tips, and reporting. Each component of a DLP policy can be configured to meet regulatory or business requirements by protecting sensitive information sent through the transport pipeline and by notifying the sender before submitting an email message that contains sensitive information.

Message Journaling   This is the process of capturing complete copies and histories of specified messages within your organization. Journaled message reports are generated and sent to specified recipients, which can be within the Exchange Server organization or some external entity. Journaling may not be exciting or useful by itself, but it's one of the main ways to get messaging data into an external archival system. Note that Exchange Server 2016 also offers content archiving through the personal archive functionality, retention tags, retention policies, and many other technologies designed around the compliance needs of an organization. These features are discussed in the chapters that focus on Mailbox server and data storage technologies.

Setting Up Message Classifications

At their heart, message classifications are simply labels that are set on certain messages. These labels in turn allow other software, such as Outlook and Outlook on the web, to display a visual warning for the user and, optionally, take special action when processing the message with rules.

Message classifications have four principal properties:

◆   The *display name* determines how the classification is displayed in the client user interface and is scanned by the mailbox rules engine.

◆   The *sender description* allows the client interface to tell the sender the purpose of this classification if it isn't clear from the display name alone.

◆   The *recipient description* allows the client interface to tell the recipient the purpose of this classification.

◆   The *locale* is a code that defines the localized version of a classification.

Figure 23.1 illustrates how Outlook 2016 displays a message classification on a message by means of the additional field directly above the To line. In this instance, the message is "R + D Internal Only—This message may contain confidential Research and Development information. Do not forward to external parties without department lead approval."

Out of the box, Exchange Server 2016 comes with three message classifications: Attachment Removed, Originator Requested, and Partner Mail. By default, these classifications are informational only; no associated rules enforce them, and their purpose is simply to display text to recipients. The default message classifications are not published to Outlook on the web or Outlook by default. Additional configuration is needed on the Outlook client and the Exchange servers for the clients to see the default message classifications.

You can modify these default classifications and create new ones to suit your business needs (see the message classifications shown in Figure 23.2). No GUI exists for creating and managing classifications; you must use the Exchange Management Shell (EMS). However, once the classifications are created, you can use the EAC, which is covered later in the section "Setting Up Mail Flow (Transport) Rules," to apply them using transport rules.

FIGURE 23.1
A message classification displayed in Outlook 2016

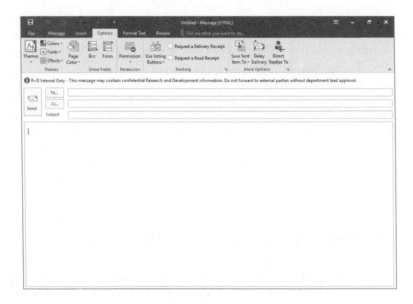

FIGURE 23.2
A sample list of message classifications

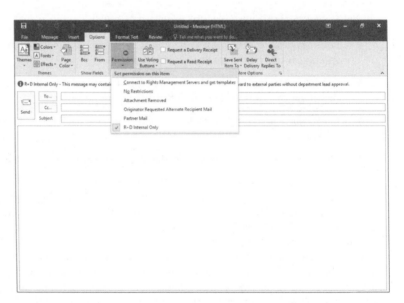

In addition to the basic classification properties, you can set some other properties:

◆ You can specify the precedence, which determines the order in which a given classification is applied to a message if multiple classifications are set. You have nine values (Highest, Higher, High, MediumHigh, Medium, MediumLow, Low, Lower, and Lowest) from which to choose.

◆ You can specify whether a given classification should be retained on the message if it is forwarded or replied to; some classifications, such as Attachment Removed, would make little sense when applied to a forwarded copy of a message or to its replies.

◆ You can create localized versions of message classifications if you are working in a multilingual organization. When working with localizations, Outlook 2016 and Outlook on the web will display the accurate classification based on the localization settings configured on the client.

By default, Outlook on the web supports the display and manual selection of message classifications. To use them in Outlook 2016, you must manually deploy them, which is covered in "Deploying Message Classifications" later in this chapter.

ADVANCED USERS AND MESSAGE CLASSIFICATION

Advanced users (those with admin permissions) can control permissions on message classifications and, therefore, restrict the use of some classifications to a subset of users.

Modifying and Creating Message Classifications

To customize the properties of existing classifications or create new classifications, you must use the Get-MessageClassification, Set-MessageClassification and New-MessageClassification cmdlets in the Exchange Management Shell.

Get-MessageClassification This cmdlet shows you the existing message classifications in your organization:

```
Get-MessageClassification
```

Set-MessageClassification This cmdlet modifies the properties of an existing classification. The following example takes an existing classification named NewMC, sets its precedence to High, and sets the RetainClassificationEnabled property so that the classification will be retained across forwards and replies:

```
Set-MessageClassification -Identity NewMC -DisplayPrecedence High
-RetainClassificationEnabled $True
```

New-MessageClassification This cmdlet creates a new message classification in your organization, configuring it on your Exchange Server 2016 servers and registering it in Active Directory:

```
New-MessageClassification -Name "RandDInternal" -DisplayName "R+D
Internal Only" -RecipientDescription "This message may contain
confidential and/or proprietary information. If you have received
this message in error, please delete it."  -SenderDescription "This
message may contain confidential Research and Development information.
Do not forward to external parties without department lead approval. "
```

Deploying Message Classifications

When you create or modify classifications, they are automatically visible to Outlook on the web users. In what is a particularly painful oversight, the same is not true for Outlook 2016 users. If you want your Outlook 2016 users to benefit from message classifications, you have two tasks to complete:

1. Export the message classifications from Exchange Server 2016 to an XML file.

2. Configure Outlook 2016 to use the XML file that contains the classification information.

These steps must be performed every time you add new classifications or modify the display properties of existing classifications. Just to make it even more annoying, these tasks are completely manual.

The following sections cover these steps in greater detail.

EXPORTING CLASSIFICATIONS FROM EXCHANGE

If you're looking for an EMS cmdlet to export all your classifications, stop. You have to use EMS, but no built-in cmdlet exists to perform this task. Here's how to do it:

1. Navigate to the Scripts subdirectory of the folder into which you installed Exchange Server 2016 (by default, this folder is located at `C:\Program Files\Microsoft\Exchange Server\V15\Scripts`) or just type **cd $ExScripts**.

   Microsoft has provided several useful and complex EMS scripts in this folder; the one you want is named `Export-OutlookClassification.ps1`. Though you can use the `Export-OutlookClassification.ps1` script to export a single classification, you will probably want to export all classifications and configure Outlook to use them.

2. To export all of the classifications to a file called `c:\Classifications.XML`, type the following command:

   ```
   .\Export-OutlookClassification.ps1 > c:\Classifications.xml
   ```

OUT-OF-SYNC CLASSIFICATIONS

If the XML file that Outlook uses is out of sync with the actual classifications specified on the Exchange server, Outlook will not display the classifications that are missing from the file. It will, however, retain them if they can be retained, and they will still be on the messages (and can be viewed in Outlook on the web). Once the file is updated, they will become visible to the user.

IMPORTING CLASSIFICATIONS IN OUTLOOK

This task has two parts: creating the necessary Registry entries and copying over the XML file from the Exchange server on which you ran the `Export-OutlookClassification.ps1` script. Once you've created the Registry settings on a given client, you don't need to keep setting them when you update the classifications XML file.

Copying the XML file to the desired location on all local workstations running a support version of Outlook is simple; you can do it manually, via a batch script, or through your existing desktop-management solution. If you are going to change the classifications on a regular basis, you might want to configure some sort of automated deployment system to minimize the need for manual involvement. For example, you might consider the use of a logon script to ensure that the latest copy of the classifications XML file is pushed out to your clients. If you've deployed Microsoft System Center Configuration Manager (or some third-party equivalent) in your environment, you can also use that mechanism.

PUBLISHING MESSAGE CLASSIFICATION TO VARIOUS VERSIONS OF OUTLOOK

Outlook reads the file in when it starts, so if the file is updated while Outlook is open, it will not use the updated information until it is next restarted.

The following Registry key and values must be created on all Outlook computers with users who have mailboxes on Exchange Server 2016 servers and who are going to be sending message classifications. Until these Registry entries are created, classifications will not be displayed in Outlook, even though they exist on messages.

For Outlook 2016, in the HKCU\Software\Microsoft\Office\16.0\Common key, create a new key named Policy.

For Outlook 2013, in the HKCU\Software\Microsoft\Office\15.0\Common key, create a new key named Policy.

For Outlook 2010, in the HKCU\Software\Microsoft\Office\14.0\Common key, create a new key named Policy.

Within this new key, create the following values:

```
"AdminClassificationPath"="C:\Path\To\Filename.xml"
"EnableClassifications"=dword:00000001
"TrustClassifications"=dword:00000001
```

You should set the values of these keys accordingly:

AdminClassificationPath Specifies the full path and filename of the XML file you copied from the export process. Though this path can be on a network share, it might cause problems for laptop users or other users who lose network connectivity. The file is small, so there's no harm in copying it to the local hard drive.

EnableClassifications Allows you to toggle whether message classifications are read and honored in Outlook on a per-user basis. The value 1 enables classifications, and the value 0 disables them.

TrustClassifications Allows you to toggle whether Outlook actually trusts classifications on messages that are sent to users on legacy Exchange Server Mailbox servers. The value 1 enables trust; 0 disables it.

Keep in mind that there are other options as well. The Office Customization Tool allows you to specify additional Registry keys that will be installed when Office is installed on a machine. If you want to ensure that message classification is universally deployed and supported in your organization, you might want to include these Registry settings in your configuration when creating your installation scripts.

Setting Up Mail Flow (Transport) Rules

The mail flow rules, also known as transport rules, in Exchange Server 2016 give you the ability to define and automatically enforce messaging policies within your organization. In Exchange Server 2016, the Transport Rule agent is triggered while the message is passing through the Transport service on the Mailbox role. The transport rules are enforced on the OnResolvedMessage transport event. You can use transport rules to append disclaimers to messages, search messages for certain types of content, require messages to be transmitted using Transport Layer Security (TLS), append classifications, insert text into a message, apply Rights Management Service templates, and more.

You can create and manage transport rules in both the Exchange Admin Center and the Exchange Management Shell. In the EAC, select Mail Flow from the Feature pane and then select the Rules tab, as shown in Figure 23.3.

Transport rules are similar to Outlook rules, but they are created using Exchange Server 2016 management tools. Like Outlook rules, transport rules have three parts:

FIGURE 23.3
Locating the transport rules in the Exchange Admin Center

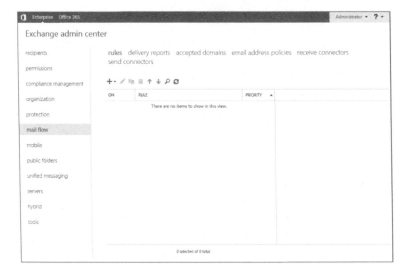

- ◆ Conditions identify the message properties that trigger the application of the rule to a given message. If you define no conditions, the rule will apply to all messages.

- ◆ Exceptions identify message properties that exempt a given message from being processed by the rule even if it matches the defined conditions. Exceptions, like conditions, are optional.

♦   Actions modify the properties or delivery of messages that match the conditions without matching the exceptions defined by the rule. In a given rule, there must be at least one action, and you can have multiple actions.

Transport rules are defined and stored in Active Directory; each server with the Mailbox role in the organization sees the entire set of defined rules and attempts to match them against all messages. This allows you to define a single, consistent set of message policies throughout your organization. Technically, you can define an unlimited number of transport rules. However, you should balance the number of transport rules against the server resources and latency of message delivery.

TRANSPORT EXPANDED GROUP CACHE IN EXCHANGE SERVER 2016

The Transport service on each Mailbox server maintains a list of the mail objects of each distribution group in memory; this is referred to as the expanded group cache. The Transport agent and Journaling agent use the expanded group cache to apply transport rules and journaling rules. The cache is maintained to minimize further queries to Active Directory. By default, the expanded group cache is refreshed every four hours. This information can be particularly useful when troubleshooting transport rules that are not applied consistently in your organization.

The expanded group cache settings can be updated. To change the expanded group cache interval, you need to modify the `AppSettings` section of the `EdgeTransport.Exe.Config` file on each Mailbox server. Modify the value for the `Transport_IsMemberOfResolver_ExpandedGroupsCache_ExpirationInterval` property. You must restart the Microsoft Exchange Server Transport service on all Exchange Server 2016 servers with the Mailbox role installed after making this change.

Transport Rules Coexistence

Transport rules can be a bit of a headache to manage and support during coexistence with legacy versions of Exchange Server. In this section, we will cover how Exchange Server 2010 and 2013 transport rules interact with Exchange Server 2016.

Automatic migration is performed during Exchange Server 2016 setup. If the Setup program detects the existence of legacy rules, those rules are copied to Exchange Server 2016. Manual migration is performed by exporting and importing transport rules between the two messaging platforms or manually re-creating the rules using the Exchange Server 2016 management tools. Automatic migration of transport rules is only performed during the initial installation of an Exchange Server 2016 server, so new transport rules created after the setup process has run will not be read by Exchange Server 2010 servers.

Just as with Exchange Server 2013, when transport rules are created using the Exchange Server 2010 Exchange Management Console or the Exchange Management Shell, the transport rules are stored in the TransportVersioned container, which is represented under the Configuration name context as: `CN=TransportVersioned, CN=Transport, CN=Rules, CN=Transport Settings, CN=<org name>, CN=Microsoft Exchange, CN=Services`.

During the coexistence with Exchange Server 2010, Exchange Server 2016 will apply the transport rules created in the Exchange Server 2010 management tools. However, Exchange

Server 2010 can't always apply transport rules created using Exchange Server 2016 management tools. Certain transport rules, especially those created for DLP, cannot be applied by an Exchange Server 2010 server. Each transport rule has a version associated with the transport rule; the version defines which version of Exchange can be used to manage the transport rule. The transport rule version is stored in the msExchTransportRuleXml property and can be viewed in the EMS, as shown in Figure 23.4. The number 14.x refers to a version of Exchange Server 2010 and the number15.x refers to a version of Exchange Server 2013 and Exchange Server 2016.

FIGURE 23.4

Transport rule version in the EMS

Similarly, transport rules created using the Exchange Server 2010 management tools can be managed using the EAC or the Exchange Server 2016 EMS, but some transport rules created using the Exchange Server 2016 management tools cannot be managed by Exchange Server 2010 management tools. This again is dependent on the version of the transport rule.

In hybrid deployments, transport rules are not replicated between Office 365 and your on-premises Exchange Server 2016 organization. The only way to ensure that the same transport rules are applied to all email messages is to create a matching pair of transport rules in your Office 365 organization and your on-premises organization. At the time of this writing, Office 365 has a limit of 300 transport rules and 100 recipients added to a message by all transport rules.

Transport Rules and Server Design Decisions

A number of factors come into play when you are sizing the server hardware and making server design decisions for your Exchange Server 2016 organization. One of the things to take into account is the number of transport rules you plan to implement. For example, an organization that sends 2,000 messages per hour and has 10 transport rules will need far less computing power than an organization that sends 10,000 messages per hour and has a few hundred transport rules.

Because rules are stored in Active Directory, modifications to your transport rules are subject to your normal AD replication. Depending on your site topology, it may take some time before your current changes replicate fully throughout your organization.

Another design decision point for Exchange Server 2016 transport rules is one of those features that requires previous implementation of non–Exchange Server components. Specifically, a Windows Server 2012 R2 server with the Active Directory Rights Management Service role needs to be available to provide enhanced security through message encryption and authorization. Exchange Server 2016 is Active Directory Rights Management Server (RMS or AD RMS)–aware, ensuring that an administrator can create transport rules that can leverage built-in or custom RMS templates.

Selecting Conditions and Exceptions

Because conditions and exceptions are both involved in identifying whether a given message should be processed by the rule, it should be no surprise that they give you the same set of options.

TRANSPORT CONDITIONS AND EXCEPTIONS

The conditions of the rule define the circumstances under which the rule will apply. Conditions and exceptions are stored as parameters of a transport rule. To get a list of the conditions and exceptions of a transport rule, use the `Get-TransportRule` cmdlet. A condition is represented as parameters within a transport rule.

The following parameters support the implementation of Data Loss Prevention (DLP) in Exchange Server 2016, which will be covered later in this chapter.

`AttachmentExtensionMatchesWords`   Use if you want to search for attachments with certain extensions, such as `.JPG` or `.PNG`.

`AttachmentHasExecutableContent`   Use to find an attachment that contains executable content.

`HasSenderOverride`   Use to determine if the sender overrode a DLP policy through a Policy Tip. (See the section "Understanding DLP Policies" later in this chapter.)

`MessageContainsDataClassifications`   Used to find sensitive information types within an email message.

`MessageSizeOver`   Applies to all messages that exceed a certain size.

`SenderIPRanges`   Condition is met when the IP of the sender matches the value of this condition.

As with conditions and exceptions, your choice of possible actions is vast enough to meet most business needs. The Exchange 2016 Server help files contain detailed descriptions of each condition and exception.

TRANSPORT ACTIONS

The actions of the transport rule specify what the rule will do to the message (or what it will do *about* the message). Figure 23.5 shows some of the actions available for transport rules.

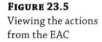

FIGURE 23.5
Viewing the actions from the EAC

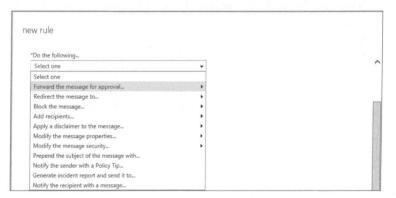

Some of the actions in Exchange Server 2016 include:

GenerateIncidentReport Incident reports are generated when a DLP policy is triggered.

NotifySender This action is used to inform the sender that their email message contains sensitive information through a DLP Policy Tip.

StopRuleProcessing This action prevents further transport rules from processing this email message.

RedirectMessageTo This action redirects the message to the specified recipient.

RouteMessageOutboundRequireTLS Any message that meets the requirements of this transport rule must be delivered from a TLS SMTP session.

HTML DISCLAIMERS IN EXCHANGE SERVER 2016

In Exchange Server 2016, an administrator can create HTML disclaimers as a transport rule action. When using HTML disclaimers, a Mailbox server inserts disclaimers into email messages using the same message format as the original message. For example, if a message is created in HTML, the disclaimer is added in HTML. If the message is created as plain text, HTML tags are stripped from the HTML disclaimer text and the resulting disclaimer text is added to the plaintext message.

Exchange Server 2016 HTML disclaimer text can include HTML tags. This allows you to create messages with rich functionality available in HTML code. For example, HTML tags can include inline Cascading Style Sheets. Messages sent in the HTML format can then display rich disclaimer messages.

More importantly, in Exchange Server 2016 you can add images to an HTML disclaimer by using IMG tags. You cannot actually drag and drop image files directly into the transport rule; you have to place the image files on a publicly accessible web server. Once you have verified that the image is available by using a URL, you can add the path to the disclaimer action in the transport rule, as in this example:

```
<IMG src="http://Server.contoso.com/images/logo.gif"
```

Creating New Rules with the Exchange Admin Center

Creating a transport rule in the EAC is similar to creating a transport rule in the Exchange Management Console in Exchange Server 2010. One of the striking differences from Exchange 2010 is that all the transport rule options are listed on a single screen instead of going through a wizard. To create a transport rule, you can use the following steps in the EAC:

1. On your client computer, open Internet Explorer and browse to the ECP URL. This URL should be the name of your Mailbox server with /ECP appended to the end. If you don't know the URL for EAC, you can use the Outlook on the web URL and specify **/ECP** instead of **/owa** at the end of the URL. For example, for Contoso, the EAC URL might be https://mail.contoso.com/ECP.

2. When prompted with the authentication page, type in your name and password and log in.

3. In the Feature pane, on the left column of the EAC, select Mail Flow.

4. Tabs are listed across the top of the EAC; select the Rules tab. The transport rules should be listed below.

5. Click the + (Add) button to create a new transport rule. If you select the arrow next to the + (Add) button, a list of the most common transport rules will be displayed, as shown in Figure 23.6. These options provide the groundwork you use to build a transport rule.

FIGURE 23.6
Templates to create
new transport rules

Create a new rule...

Apply rights protection to messages...

Apply disclaimers...

Bypass spam filtering...

Filter messages by size...

Generate an incident report when sensitive information is detected...

Modify messages...

Restrict managers and their direct reports...

Restrict messages by sender or recipient...

Send messages to a moderator...

Send messages and save a copy for review...

6. In the New Rule window shown in Figure 23.7, select More Options to see the version in Figure 23.8, which contains more options for creating a new transport rule.

FIGURE 23.7
The New Rule
window for EAC

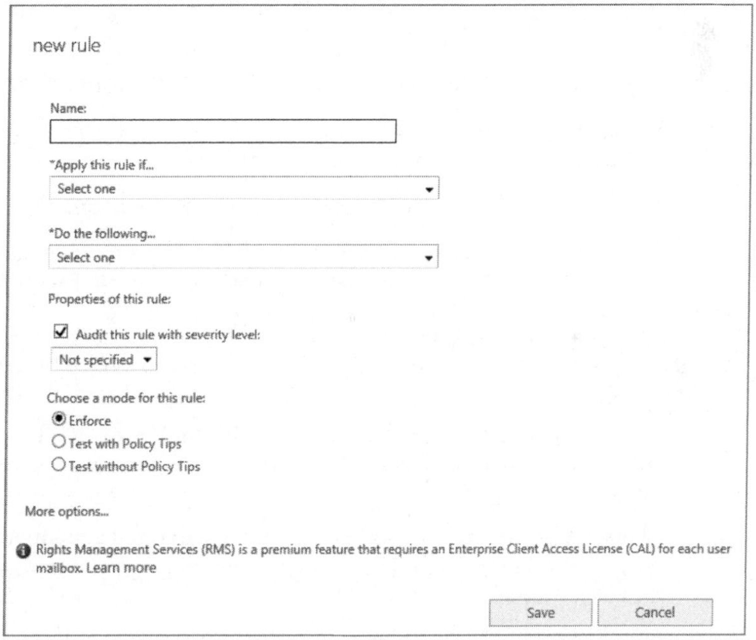

new rule

Name:

*Apply this rule if...

Select one ▼

*Do the following...

Select one ▼

Properties of this rule:

☑ Audit this rule with severity level:

Not specified ▼

Choose a mode for this rule:
● Enforce
○ Test with Policy Tips
○ Test without Policy Tips

More options...

ⓘ Rights Management Services (RMS) is a premium feature that requires an Enterprise Client Access License (CAL) for each user mailbox. Learn more

Save   Cancel

FIGURE 23.8
The New Rule
window for
EAC with more
options

FIGURE 23.8
The New Rule window for EAC with more options

7. Provide a name for the new transport rule in the Name field.

8. To add a condition, select the drop-down box underneath Apply This Rule If, and choose the condition you want to apply to the transport rule.

9. To add an action, select the drop-down box underneath Do The Following.

10. To exclude the transport rule from applying to certain email messages, click Add Exception and select the drop-down box underneath Except If.

Up to this point, creating a new transport rule in Exchange Server 2016 is very similar to creating one in Exchange Server 2010. Now it's time to look at the new bells and whistles that Microsoft added to Exchange Server 2013 and 2016:

Audit This Rule With Severity Level   This topic will be covered more in the "Introducing Data Loss Prevention" section. This option defines the audit severity level of the transport rule.

Choose A Mode For This Rule   This topic will be covered more in the "Introducing Data Loss Prevention" section. This setting allows you to test a transport rule without enforcing the rule on email messages.

Stop Processing More Rules   A priority is associated with each transport rule. The Transport Rule agent analyzes messages against the transport rule with the lowest priority first and moves on to the transport rule with the next-lowest priority until the message has been analyzed by all the transport rules. If you enable this option, no subsequent transport rule will be processed against this email message.

Activate This Rule On The Following Date This property is used to specify when the transport will begin processing email messages.

Deactivate This Rule On The Following Date This property is used to specify when the transport will stop processing email messages.

TRANSPORT RULES: MORE FAMILIAR THAN YOU MIGHT REALIZE

Transport rules are always fun to describe to customers because they have a familiar point of reference. We simply tell them that they are similar in experience to what they create with the Outlook Rules Wizard, except that these rules have many more available settings and run completely server-side.

One of the things that we often run into when we start diving a bit deeper is the ability to get *creative* around transport rules. Specifically, we had a customer who needed to define a disclaimer based on the user's department. This customer created a disclaimer transport rule in an Exchange Server 2010 organization and had not yet upgraded to Exchange Server 2016. So for users in the legal department, the outbound disclaimer had to state the legal requirements regarding client communication, while the sales department disclaimer had to state the company's warranty information.

Our first reaction was, "Sure, basic stuff!" So we fired up the New Transport Rules Wizard and found out quickly that creating a transport rule that applies based on the Department property in Active Directory cannot be done using Exchange Server 2010 management tools. Ouch!

Exchange Server 2013 and Exchange Server 2016 include pretty much every Exchange Server recipient attribute as an available transport rule condition. So today, in Exchange Server 2016, we can create a new rule for this customer simply by selecting the Department attribute.

Creating New Rules with the Exchange Management Shell

The following Exchange Management Shell commands let you add, change, remove, enable, or disable transport rules that are used by the Transport Rule agent:

Get-TransportRule This cmdlet shows you the existing transport rules in your organization:

```
Get-TransportRule
```

Enable-TransportRule This cmdlet sets an existing transport rule as enabled, which means it will be applied to messages:

```
Enable-TransportRule -Identity MyTransportRule
```

Disable-TransportRule This cmdlet sets an existing transport rule as disabled, which means that it will still be present in the configuration but will not be applied to messages:

```
Disable-TransportRule -Identity MyTransportRule
```

The `Disable-TransportRule` cmdlet is useful for troubleshooting problems with transport rules. You can also disable all transport rules with this command:

```
Get-TransportRule | Disable-TransportRule
```

Remove-TransportRule   This cmdlet allows you to delete an existing transport rule:

```
Remove-TransportRule -Identity MyTransportRule
```

Set-TransportRule   This cmdlet allows you to modify the parameters of an existing transport rule:

```
Set-TransportRule Project-X -Priority 3
```

New-TransportRule   This cmdlet allows you to create a new transport rule. Creating a new rule from the EMS is beyond the scope of this book, but it follows the same principles as the `Set-TransportRule` example. From the EMS, issue the following command for a full description of the cmdlet, including examples:

```
Help New-TransportRule -full
```

You can retrieve a list of the actions by using the `Get-TransportRuleAction` cmdlet and get a list of the conditions by using the `Get-TransportRulePredicate` cmdlet. Each transport rule has parameters defining the conditions, exceptions, and actions. Parameters are created based on the properties of a predicate. When using the `Get-TransportRulePredicate` and `Get-TransportRule` cmdlets, you can see the correlation between the transport rule parameter SentTo and the properties of the predicate SentTo.

```
Get-TransportRulePredicate SentTo
RunspaceId        : 6fc02408-b4c0-4e3d-9891-ee220f30dae4
Addresses         :
RuleSubTypes      : {None, Dlp}
Name              : SentTo
Rank              : 0
LinkedDisplayText : sent to <a id="SentTo">people</a>
Identity          :
IsValid           : False
ObjectState       : New
```

The property `LinkedDisplayText` holds two functions. First, it provides a description of the predicate, and second, the required properties are placed between `<a>` and `</a>`. Using the SentTo example, `people` represents any mail-enabled recipient.

Introducing Data Loss Prevention

One shortcoming in Exchange Server 2010 and earlier versions is the inability of the product to deeply analyze the content of an email message using a content engine to determine if the message contains sensitive information. To prevent sensitive information from being mishandled in Exchange Server 2010, you could create a transport rule with a regular expression. A regular expression searches for a specific pattern within the email message. For example, you could create a regular expression that searches for the format of Social Security numbers. If a pattern in the email message matches the regular expression, the action within the transport rule will execute against the email message. A regular expression can be useful in certain circumstances, but in many cases it isn't flexible or advanced enough to meet business needs.

Microsoft answered this problem with the introduction of Data Loss Prevention in Exchange Server 2013 and continuing in Exchange Server 2016. DLP is designed to analyze, monitor, report, and prevent sensitive information from being exposed to unwanted parties. The classification of sensitive information varies for each company and region. For example, the United States uses Social Security Number as an identifier, but Canada uses Social Insurance Number as an identifier. DLP has been designed with the understanding that sensitive information is unique to each organization.

Understanding DLP Policies

The functionality of DLP is stored within a DLP policy. The DLP components are bound together in a DLP policy. The settings of the DLP policy and the components within the DLP policy define:

◆ The sensitive information to scan within an email message and attachments

◆ The actions performed against an email message

◆ The level of reporting within the policy

◆ Whether or not the DLP policy is enforced

◆ How to notify the end user that an email message they are composing falls in line with a DLP policy

Armed with a sensitive information-detection engine that runs under the Transport agent, DLP provides in-depth content analysis of an email message and certain types of attachments. The results of the content analysis are compared against sensitive information defined in a DLP rule. If sensitive content is found within the email message or attachment, the action specified in the transport rule is performed against the email message. Actions of a DLP rule can range from redirecting the email message to a compliance office to notifying the sender that the message contains sensitive information before the sender presses the Send button.

The file types that DLP can scan are shown in Table 23.1. Microsoft OneNote and Publisher are not supported file types unless the IFilters Filter Pack is registered on all the Mailbox servers. Attachments that are password-protected cannot be scanned by DLP.

TABLE 23.1:   Exchange Server 2016 DLP-Scannable File Types

CATEGORY	FILE EXTENSION
Office 2016, 2013, and 2010	DOCM, DOCX, PPTM, PPTX, PUB, ONE, XLSB, XLSM, XLSX
Additional Office files	RTF, VDW, VSD, VSS, VST
Adobe PDF	PDF
HTML	HTML

TABLE 23.1:   Exchange Server 2016 DLP-Scannable File Types   *(CONTINUED)*

CATEGORY	FILE EXTENSION
XML/OpenDocument	XML, ODP, ODS, ODT
Text	TXT, ASM, BAT, C, CMD, CPP, CXX, DEF, DIC, H, HPP, HXX, IBQ, IDL, INC, INF, INI, INX, JS, LOG, M3U, PL, RC, REG, TXT, VBS, WTX
Image	JPG, TIFF
	Note: GIF and PNG are unsupported file types but the AttachmentIsUnsupported action will not execute against GIF and PNG files. The workaround to this problem is to create a transport rule explicitly looking for these file types.
Archive	ZIP, CAB, GZIP, RAR, TAR, UU Encode, TNEF, MSG

The Mode setting within a DLP policy defines how a DLP policy is applied to email messages within the organization and if end users are notified of the DLP policy using Policy Tips. Because every message is subject to DLP policies, a misconfiguration can cause havoc in an organization. Using the Test DLP modes allows you to test a new DLP policy before enforcing the DLP policy against all email messages. The three available modes are described here:

Enforce If an email message meets the conditions of a DLP policy, the actions of the DLP policy are enforced. Content is added to the message-tracking log and Policy Tips are displayed to the sender.

Test DLP Policy With Policy Tips If an email message meets the conditions of a DLP policy, the actions of the DLP policy are *not* enforced. Content is added to the message-tracking log and Policy Tips are displayed to the sender.

Test DLP Policy Without Policy Tips If an email message meets the conditions of a DLP policy, the actions of the DLP policy are *not* enforced. Content is added to the message-tracking log and Policy Tips are *not* displayed to the sender.

The first part of preventing a leak of sensitive data is informing the sender through a Policy Tip that the email message they are composing contains sensitive data and violates a DLP policy. Policy Tips are similar to MailTips, in that a notification is provided to the sender before the sender submits the email message for delivery. A DLP policy can also be overridden through a Policy Tip. Within a DLP rule, you can specify if the rule can be overridden by the sender. You can also impose that a justification be provided when the sender overrides a DLP rule. The justification is registered and can be sent in an incident report.

The clients that support Policy Tips are Outlook 2016, Outlook 2013, and Outlook on the web. Using EWS, the Outlook 2016 client downloads policies and classifications from servers. Policy definitions are downloaded on the local workstation running Outlook 2016 policy definition files (PolicyNudgeClassficationDefinitions<GUID>.XML and PolicyNudgeRules<GUID>.XML) and stores the files under Users\<User>\Appdata\Local\Microsoft\Outlook. The Policy Tip notifies the end user that the content of the email message hit a DLP policy, and the policy will prevent the delivery of the email message unless an override is specified.

To take some of the complexity out of creating DLP policies, Microsoft has provided out-of-the-box DLP templates. A DLP template packages together transport rules and Policy Tips to identify, alert, and monitor sensitive information. Each built-in template is designed to cover a certain area of sensitive information. For example, let's say you create a new DLP policy from the U.S. Personally Identifiable Information (PII) Data template. The DLP policy will be composed of rules that will search email content for anything that matches U.S. taxpayer identification numbers, U.S. Social Security numbers, and U.S./U.K. passport numbers. The Exchange Server 2016 help file provides a list and description of each template.

Most DLP templates consist of similar rules. Continuing with the example, let's look at the rules created when using the DLP template U.S. Personally Identifiable Information (PII) Data. Figure 23.9 shows the rules created and the list following describes each rule:

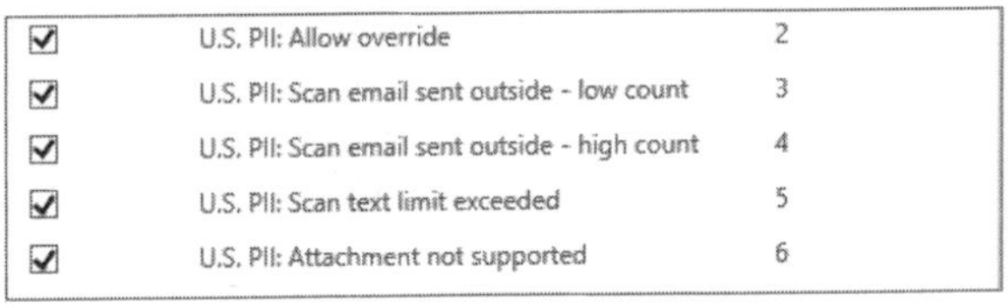

FIGURE 23.9

Rules created from DLP template U.S. Personally Identifiable Information (PII) Data

☑	U.S. PII: Allow override	2
☑	U.S. PII: Scan email sent outside - low count	3
☑	U.S. PII: Scan email sent outside - high count	4
☑	U.S. PII: Scan text limit exceeded	5
☑	U.S. PII: Attachment not supported	6

Allow Override If the word *override* is in the subject of the email message, the DLP rules will be exempt from applying to the email message.

Scan Email Sent Outside – Low Count During the evaluation of an email message, a record is kept each time sensitive information is found. If the total count of sensitive information is between one and nine, the user is notified via a Policy Tip that the message contains sensitive data but is allowed to send the email message.

Scan Email Sent Outside – High Count The High Count rule is configured the same way as the Low Count rule except if the message exceeds nine sensitive items, the message will be blocked unless a business justification is provided by the sender.

Scan Text Limit Exceeded If the DLP engines and Transport agent don't complete scanning the email message, the email message will be audited.

Attachment Not Supported If the email message contains an attachment that cannot be scanned, the email message will be audited.

We have covered the option of creating DLP policies from the Microsoft-provided templates. You can also create a DLP policy by importing your own template or a template provided by a third-party vendor. Using the `New-ClassificationRuleCollection` cmdlet, you can import an XML file that you created or was given to you by a third-party vendor, as shown here:

```
New-ClassificationRuleCollection -FileData ([Byte[]]$
    (Get-Content -Path "C:\rulepack.xml" -Encoding Byte -ReadCount 0))
```

The other way to create a new DLP policy is by creating a custom DLP policy. A custom DLP policy does not contain any default DLP rules; it is a blank canvas that you can use to create your own DLP policy based on the available DLP rules.

A custom DLP policy is a good option when none of the default templates meet your business requirements. For example, you may want to create a DLP policy that blocks U.S., German, and Japanese passport numbers. After selecting the sensitive information type, like Passport Number (U.S./U.K.), you can configure the options of the sensitive information. Figure 23.10 displays the options for sensitive information type Passport Number (U.S./U.K.), and the following list describes each option.

FIGURE 23.10
Options for sensitive information type Passport Number (U.S. / U.K.)

U.S. / U.K. Passport Number

Define the requirements for this type of sensitive information.

- ☑ Minimum count:
  `10`
- ☐ Maximum count:
- ☐ Minimum confidence level:
  `%`
- ☑ Maximum confidence level:
  `100` %

[Save] [Cancel]

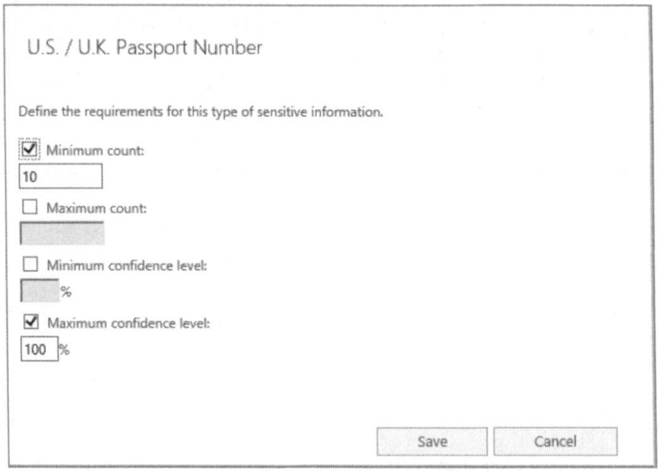

Minimum Count   The minimum number of times that data within the email message matches a message classification, such as Social Security numbers.

Maximum Count   The maximum number of times that data within the email message matches a message classification, such as Social Security numbers.

Minimum Confidence Levels   The lowest acceptable percentage used to count syntax as sensitive information.

Maximum Confidence Levels   The highest acceptable percentage used to count syntax as sensitive information.

Another part of the prevention process is being informed when an email message containing sensitive data was sent. A transport rule action, GenerateIncidentReport, can be used to generate an incident report to a specific recipient. An incident report contains information regarding why the email message was flagged for containing sensitive information.

Message ID   Shows the Message ID of the message sent.

Sender   Shows the sender of the email message.

Subject   Shows the subject of the email message.

To   Lists the recipients of the email message.

Severity   Shows the highest severity of any of the DLP policies that this email message triggered.

Override   The sender can override the DLP policy by providing a justification for sending an email message containing sensitive information. The justification will be shown in the Override field.

False Positive Shows if the information worker reports the message as a false positive.

Data Classification Indicates the type of data that was found within the email message.

Count Gives the number of times that data within the email message matches a message classification, such as Social Security numbers.

Confidence Indicates the confidence level that the sensitive information found in the email message met the data classification in the DLP rule.

Recommended Minimum Confidence Indicates the minimum confidence level that will enforce the DLP rule.

Rule Hit Shows the name of the DLP rule that was applied to the email message.

Action Shows the action that was performed against the email message.

ID Match Shows the type of message classification that was found in the email message.

Value Shows the syntax that was found that matched a message classification.

DLP incidents are recorded in the message-tracking logs. As we talked about earlier in this chapter, when setting the mode of the DLP policy to test, the rules of the DLP policy are not applied to the email message. Instead, you can review the message-tracking logs to see if the DLP policy was applied to an email message. Using the Get-MessageTrackingLog cmdlet, you can export the transport rules that applied to an email message and the actions that were performed on the email message:

```
Get-TransportServer | Get-MessageTrackingLog -MessageSubject SSN |
     where {$_.source -eq 'agent'}
Source    : AGENT
EventData : {[TRA, DC|dcid=a44669fe-0d48-453d-a9b1-2cc83f2cba77|count=1|conf=85],
[TRA,
ETRP|ruleId=5f4d29e2-4e12-411b-907c-a38ccb807ee5|ExecW=335|ExecC=15], [TRA,
ETR|ruleId=f31d282e-59e1-4505-aa6f-8b845dc2fcc2|st=3/1/2016 9:30:25
PM|action=ApplyHtmlDisclaimer|sev=1|mode=Enforce], [TRA,
ETR|ruleId=9ffe0714-b4de-4da0-8fc5-3e0d2c159a3f|st=3/3/2016 2:17:25 AM|action=Set
AuditSeverity|action=NotifySender|action=GenerateIncidentReport|sev=2|mode=Enforc
e|dlpId=0ebf8e62-c10c-478a-ad4a-a205fd33cfeb|dcId=a44669fe-0d48-453d-a9b1-
2cc83f2cba77], [TRA, ETR|ruleId=67c4a4bf-46ff-4bc8-98f77bede9a907b4|st=3/1/2016
9:30:26PM|action=GenerateIncidentReport|sev=1|mode=AuditAndNotify|dlpId=1d4bb7
4b-1001-4919-b8e0-cc6ee4cb0eea|dcId=a44669fe-0d48-453d-a9b1-2cc83f2cba77]}
```

The output contains a lot of useful information. TRA in the output stands for Transport Rule agent. The ruleId is the GUID of the transport rule, which can be found using the Get-TransportRule cmdlet. The actions performed against this email message are registered under action. More information about message tracking can be found in Chapter 22.

Exchange Server 2016 includes several improvements in DLP compared to Exchange Server 2013 that include:

◆ A new condition: **Any attachment has these properties, including any of these words.** When this condition is applied, a mail flow rule can search for messages where the specified property of the attached Office document matches specified words. This condition enables administrators to integrate Exchange mail flow rules and DLP policies with

SharePoint Server and Windows Server 2012 R2 File Classification Infrastructure (FCI). Moreover, this condition enables administrators to integrate Exchange mail flow rules with classification system products from third-party vendors.

♦ A new action: **Notify the recipient with a message.** This action allows a mail flow rule to send a notification to the recipient with the text specified by the administrator. For example, the message may contain information about the reason for rejecting the email.

♦ Updated action: **Generate incident report and send it to.** This action now can be configured to send the incident report to multiple distribution lists.

Creating DLP Policies

DLP policies can be created, managed, and removed using the Exchange Server 2016 management tools.

Managing DLP Settings in the Exchange Admin Center

In the EAC you can create a new DLP policy from a template, import a DLP policy, and create a custom DLP policy. To create a DLP policy from a template in the EAC, use the following steps:

1. On your client computer, open Internet Explorer and browse to the ECP URL. This URL should be the name of your Mailbox server with /ECP appended to the end. If you don't know the URL for EAC, you can use the Outlook on the web URL and specify **/ECP** instead of **/owa** at the end of the URL. For example, for Contoso, the EAC URL might be https://mail.contoso.com/ECP.

2. When prompted with the authentication page, type in your name and password and log in.

3. In the Feature pane, on the left column of the EAC, select Compliance Management.

4. In the toolbar across the top of the EAC, select the Data Loss Prevention tab. The DLP policies should be listed below.

5. Click the + (Add) button to create a new DLP policy from a template. To import a DLP policy or create a custom DLP policy, select the arrow next to the + (Add) button; a drop-down will display those options.

6. In the DLP Policy From Template window, which contains all the built-in templates for DLP, select U.S. Financial Data (see Figure 23.11).

7. In the Name text box, type **U.S. Financial Data**.

8. At the bottom of the DLP Policy From Template window, select More Options.

9. Under Choose A Mode For The Requirements In This DLP Policy, select the Enforce radio button.

10. Click Save to create the new DLP policy.

FIGURE 23.11
The DLP Policy
From Template
window from EAC

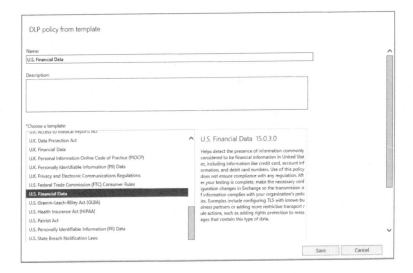

11. Highlight the U.S. Financial Data policy and select the Policy Tip Settings icon (the check box with the gear in the foreground).

12. In the Policy Tips window, click the + (Add) button.

13. In the drop-down box under Action, choose Allow The Sender To Override.

14. Select English from the drop-down underneath Locale.

15. Type **To override this policy add the word Override to the subject** in the Text box.

   The Policy Tip for the DLP policy U.S. Financial Data should look like the one in Figure 23.12.

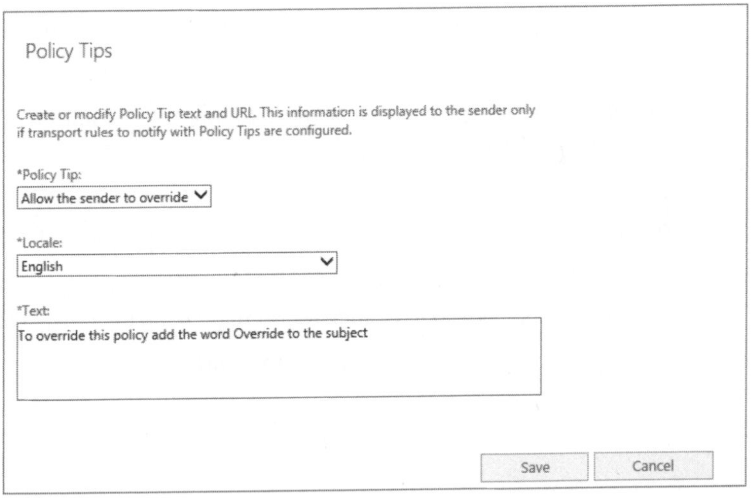

FIGURE 23.12
Policy Tip for
DPL policy U.S.
Financial Data

> Policy Tips
>
> Create or modify Policy Tip text and URL. This information is displayed to the sender only if transport rules to notify with Policy Tips are configured.
>
> *Policy Tip:
> [Allow the sender to override ▾]
>
> *Locale:
> [English ▾]
>
> *Text:
> [To override this policy add the word Override to the subject]
>
> [Save] [Cancel]

16. In the Feature pane, in the left column of the EAC, select Mail Flow.

17. In the toolbar across the top of the EAC, select the Rules tab. The transport rules should be listed below.

18. Highlight the transport rule, U.S. Financial: Scan Email Sent Outside – High Count.

In the Display pane on the right side of the EAC, the types of sensitive information this rule is searching for are Credit Card Number, U.S. Bank Account Number, or ABA Routing Number (see Figure 23.13).

FIGURE 23.13
The sensitive information types covered by the U.S. Financial transport rule: Scan Email Sent Outside – High Count

> U.S. Financial: Scan email sent outside - high count
>
> If the message...
>
> Is sent to 'Outside the organization'
> and The message contains these sensitive information types: 'Credit Card Number' or 'U.S. Bank Account Number' or 'ABA Routing Number'
>
> Do the following...
>
> Set audit severity level to 'High'
> and Notify the sender that the message can't be sent, but allow the sender to override and provide justification. Include the explanation 'Unable to deliver your message. You can override this policy by adding the word 'override' to the subject line.' with status code '5.7.1'

MANAGING DLP SETTINGS IN THE EXCHANGE MANAGEMENT SHELL

The following Exchange Management Shell commands let you manage DLP policies and settings:

Get-DLPPolicy   Shows you the existing DLP policies in your organization:

```
Get-DLPPolicy
```

Get-DLPPolicyTemplate   Shows the DLP policy templates that can be used when creating a DLP policy from a template:

```
Get-DLPPolicyTemplate
```

New-DlpPolicy   Used to create new DLP policy within your organization:

```
New-DlpPolicy -Name "Patriot Act" -Template "U.S. Patriot Act"
```

Set-DlpPolicy   Used to change the configuration of an existing DLP in your organization:

```
Set-DlpPolicy "Patriot Act" -Mode Enforce
```

`Remove-DlpPolicy` Removes a DLP policy from the organization:

```
Remove-DlpPolicy "Patriot Act"
```

`Export-DlpPolicyCollection` Used to export the DLP policy collection from your organization into an XML file. You can use this cmdlet to back up your DLP policies or to export the configuration in a lab environment and import it into a production environment. The `$ExportDLPpolicies` is a variable used in the following example to capture the `Export-DlpPolicyCollection` cmdlet:

```
$ExportDLPpolicies = Export-DlpPolicyCollection
Set-Content -Path C:\DLP\DLPpolicies.xml -Value
$ExportDLPpolicies.FileData -Encoding Byte
```

The contents of the XML file created by running the `Export-DlpPolicyCollection` will look similar to the output shown in Figure 23.14.

`Import-DlpPolicyCollection` Allows you to import a DLP policy collection from an XML file into an organization. Using this cmdlet will create the DLP policies and transport rules from an XML file:

FIGURE 23.14 Contents of the XML after running `Export-DlpPolicyCollection`


```
<?xml version="1.0" encoding="UTF-8" standalone="true"?>
- <dlpPolicies>
  - <dlpPolicy id="9548c9bc-85a5-4196-bdcd-fbc9646695ed" mode="Audit" state="Enabled"
    version="15.0.3.0">
      <name>dgwe</name>
      <contentVersion>4</contentVersion>
      <publisherName>Microsoft</publisherName>
      <description>Helps detect the presence of information commonly subject to U.S. Patriot
        Act, including information like credit card numbers or tax identification numbers.
        Use of this policy does not ensure compliance with any regulation. After your
        testing is complete, make the necessary configuration changes in Exchange so the
        transmission of information complies with your organization's policies. Examples
        include configuring TLS with known business partners or adding more restrictive
        transport rule actions, such as adding rights protection to messages that contain
        this type of data.</description>
      <keywords/>
    - <policyCommands>
      - <commandBlock>
          <![CDATA[New-TransportRule -Name 'U.S. Patriot Act: Allow override' -DlpPolicy
          9548c9bc-85a5-4196-bdcd-fbc9646695ed -Mode Audit -SubjectMatchesPatterns
          'override' -ExceptIfHasSenderOverride $true -SetHeaderName 'X-Ms-Exchange-
          Organization-Dlp-SenderOverrideJustification' -SetHeaderValue 'TransportRule override']]
          >
        </commandBlock>
      - <commandBlock>
          <![CDATA[New-TransportRule -Name 'U.S. Patriot Act: Scan email sent outside - low
          count' -DlpPolicy 9548c9bc-85a5-4196-bdcd-fbc9646695ed -Mode Audit -SentToScope
          NotInOrganization -MessageContainsDataClassifications @{'Name'='Credit Card Number';
          'MinCount'=1; 'MaxCount'=9; 'MinConfidence'=-1; 'MaxConfidence'=100}, @
          {'Name'='U.S. Bank Account Number'; 'MinCount'=1; 'MaxCount'=9; 'MinConfidence'=-1;
          'MaxConfidence'=100}, @{'Name'='U.S. Individual Taxpayer Identification Number
```


```
Import-DlpPolicyCollection -FileData ([Byte[]]$(Get-Content -Path
C:\DLP\ DLPpolicies.xml -Encoding Byte -ReadCount 0))
```

`Import-DlpPolicyTemplate` Used to add a DLP template into an organization. Most of the time the imported templates will be provided by third-party applications:

```
Import-DlpPolicyTemplate -FileData ([Byte[]]$(Get-Content -Path
"C:\DLP\DLPTemplate.xml" -Encoding Byte -ReadCount 0))
```

New-TransportRule Used to create rules within a DLP policy. If the specified DLP policy doesn't exist, a new DLP policy will be created:

```
New-TransportRule -Name "Prevent Bank Account Numbers"
-MessageContainsDataClassifications @{Name="U.S. Bank
Account Number"} -NotifySender RejectUnlessExplicitOverride -Mode
 Enforce -GenerateIncidentReport HR@contoso.com
```

Introducing Journaling

A lot of people confuse *journaling*, which is the process of capturing a set of communications for future use, with *archiving*, which is the practice of removing infrequently accessed or old message data from the message store in favor of a secondary storage location.

Archiving is all about getting stuff—usually old and bulky messages and attachments—out of your mailboxes, so you can reduce the performance hit on your comparatively expensive Mailbox server storage systems and reduce your backup windows. Archival solutions are discussed in Chapter 19, "Creating and Managing Mailbox Databases."

Journaling is record keeping; you're defining a set of users whose traffic you must keep track of, and Exchange Server dutifully captures faithful copies of every message they send or receive. As stated before, journaling is one of the main strategies that compliance and archival vendors use to get messaging data into their solutions.

Although you may not have any explicit applicable regulatory language that forces you to implement journaling, journaling can still be one of the easiest ways to meet the requirements you do have. As compliance becomes more of an issue, the ability to quickly and easily put your hands on complete and accurate records of messaging communications will become critical.

Exchange Server 2016 journaling capabilities are essentially identical to those in Exchange Server 2013 and 2010. The base journaling mechanism used by Exchange Server 2016 is envelope journaling, which captures all recipient information (even Bcc: headers and forwards). However, you have two options for journaling:

◆ Standard journaling (aka per-mailbox database journaling) uses the Journaling agent on a Mailbox server where the Hub Transport service resides, to journal all messages sent to and from recipients and senders whose mailboxes are homed on specified mailbox databases.

◆ Premium journaling (aka per-recipient journaling) also uses the Journaling agent on a Mailbox server where the Hub Transport service resides, but it's more granular. It offers you the ability to design journaling rules for groups or even specific users if needed.

You must have an Exchange Enterprise Client Access License (CAL) to use premium journaling.

Implementing Journaling

The Journaling agent, which is executed on the OnSubmittedMessage and OnRoutedMessage events, is responsible for detecting whether a given message falls under your journaling rules. Since the Transport service has been moved to the Mailbox role, all journaling is performed by servers with the Mailbox role installed. When you use standard journaling, you enable it for an entire mailbox database. Any messages sent to or by recipients whose mailboxes are located on a journal-enabled database will be detected by the Journaling agent and copies will be sent to a designated *journal recipient*. This journal recipient can be another recipient in the Exchange Server organization—if it is an Exchange Server mailbox, it must be dedicated to the purpose— or an SMTP address on another messaging system.

Journaling to an external recipient may seem like a crazy idea at first blush. However, this allows Exchange Server 2016 to be used with compliance and archival solutions that are not part of the Exchange Server organization or even with hosted solution providers.

If you use an external journal recipient, you should ensure that your SMTP transport connections to the external system are fully secure and authenticated. Exchange Server 2016 supports the use of the Transport Layer Security (TLS) protocol; see Chapter 22 for details on how to configure TLS connections to specific domains and how to enable SMTP authentication.

When you use premium journaling, you create journal rules that define a subset of the recipients in your organization. Premium and standard journaling rules are stored in Active Directory and retrieved by all servers with the Mailbox role, depending on the normal AD replication mechanism. The Journaling agent detects that the rule matches a given message and sends a copy of the message to the journaling recipient. Premium journaling rules are found under the Journal Rule tab of the compliance-management feature in the EAC.

Journaling rules can have three scopes, which helps the Journaling agent decide whether it needs to examine a given message:

- The Internal scope matches messages where all senders and recipients are members of the Exchange Server organization.

- The External scope matches messages where at least one sender or recipient is an external entity.

- The Global scope matches all messages, even those that may have already been matched by the other scopes.

To create a new journaling rule, run the New Journal Rule Wizard found on the Actions pane.

This same operation can be performed by using the Exchange Management Shell. The following command creates a new journal rule that will capture all messages for the members of the VIP distribution groups and send the journaled message to the Journal1 mailbox:

```
New-JournalRule -Name 'Journal VIP mail' -JournalEmailAddress
'Journal1' -Scope 'Global' -Enabled $True -Recipient 'VIPs@contoso.com'
```

Managing Journaling Traffic and Security

If you are using an internal mailbox as your journaling recipient, you should be aware that it may collect a large amount of traffic. Though you can use the same mailbox for all journal reports generated in your organization, you may need to create multiple mailboxes to control mailbox size and ensure that your backup windows can be maintained. If you are using the Unified Messaging role in your organization, you may not want to journal UM-generated messages, such as voicemail, because of the large amount of storage space it requires. (On the other hand, you may be required to preserve these types of messages as well as your regular email.)

Journal mailboxes should be kept very secure and safe from everyday access because they may one day be material evidence in the event that your business is sued or must prove compliance to auditors.

To guard against the loss of journaling reports in the event of trouble within your Exchange Server organization, you can designate an *alternative journal mailbox*. This mailbox will receive any nondelivery reports that are issued if your journaling recipient cannot receive deliveries.

Unfortunately, you can configure only a single alternative mailbox for your entire organization. Not only can this cause performance and mailbox size issues, but your local regulations may prevent you from mixing multiple types of journal information in one mailbox.

Using the Set-TransportConfig cmdlet, you can set the JournalReportNdrTo and the VoicemailJournalingEnabled parameters. Out of the box, an alternative journal mailbox (JournalingReportNdrTo) is not set and voicemail messages (VoicemailJournalingEnabled) are journaled, as shown in the following example:

```
Get-TransportConfig | fl *journal*
JournalingReportNdrTo         : <>
VoicemailJournalingEnabled    : True
```

Email messages that have an AD RMS template applied to them are protected using certificates from the AD RMS server. This could pose a problem when journaling is enabled in your organization. Luckily for us, Exchange Server 2016 can decrypt and journal an unencrypted version of a message. The decryption of journal reports is configurable using the Set-IRMConfiguration cmdlet. Using the Get-IRMConfiguration cmdlet, as shown here, will report the current value of the JournalReportDecryptionEnabled parameter:

```
Get-IRMConfiguration | fl *journal*
JournalReportDecryptionEnabled : True
```

INTEROPERABILITY WITH OFFICE 365

As mentioned earlier, journaling takes place when the message is passed through the transport pipeline. When your organization is in a hybrid configuration, some emails will not pass through the transport pipeline of your on-premises servers. For example, if an Office 365 user sent an email message to a recipient with a mailbox in Office 365, the message wouldn't pass through the transport pipeline of the on-premises servers; therefore, journaling wouldn't apply to that message. To combat this problem, create a mirror copy of the journaling rules in Office 365.

Another consideration to take into account is the placement of the journal mailbox while your organization is in a hybrid configuration. An Office 365 mailbox cannot be designated as a journal mailbox for an on-premises journaling rule. However, you can designate an on-premises mailbox as a journal mailbox in Office 365.

Reading Journal Reports

The journaling process creates a special Exchange Server message known as the *journal report*. This message is essentially a wrapper that contains a summary of the original message properties. It also contains a pristine copy of the original message that generated the report, neatly attached to the journal report.

The journal reports are designed to be human and machine readable, allowing you to automate the processing of journal reports via a third-party application and perform manual checks on the data.

The following are the fields that Exchange Server 2016 places in the journal report:

To   The SMTP address of a recipient in the To header or the SMTP envelope recipient. If the message was sent through a distribution list, this field contains the Expanded field. If the message was forwarded, this field contains the Forwarded field.

Cc   The SMTP address of a recipient in the Cc header or the SMTP envelope recipient. If the message was sent through a distribution list, this field contains the Expanded field. If the message was forwarded, this field contains the Forwarded field.

Bcc   The SMTP address of a recipient in the Bcc header or the SMTP envelope recipient. If the message was sent through a distribution list, this field contains the Expanded field. If the message was forwarded, this field contains the Forwarded field.

Recipient   The SMTP address of a recipient who is not a member of the Exchange Server 2016 organization, such as Internet recipients or recipients on legacy Exchange servers.

Sender   The sender's SMTP address, found in either the From or Sender header of the message.

On Behalf Of   The relevant SMTP address if the Send On Behalf Of feature was used.

Subject   The Subject header.

Message-ID   The internal Exchange Message-ID.

The Bottom Line

Create and manage message classifications to control message flow.   Message classifications provide a way to visibly tag selected messages and show that they require specific treatment. On their own, they're merely advisory; but combined with transport rules and mailbox rules, they can become powerful selection criteria for managing messages and ensuring policy compliance.

Master It   You need to use message classifications to manipulate messages by using Outlook. You verify that custom message classifications are available from Outlook on the web. From Outlook, you look around but cannot find any options that relate to the custom message classifications. What do you need to do first?

Control message flow and manipulate messages by using transport rules.   Transport rules give you a powerful, centralized method for creating automated policy enforcement in your environment.

Master It   You need to add a logo to an email disclaimer; you notice that you cannot include an image in the New Transport Rules Wizard. The availability of adding logos to a disclaimer was a major decision point of your Exchange Server 2016 implementation. What do you need to do to make the logo visible in the disclaimer?

Protect sensitive information by creating data loss prevention policies.   Using DLP policies you can enforce that all messages are subject to DLP rules, or you can allow users to bypass DLP rules by providing a business justification.

Master It   Your company's compliance officer requires that email messages containing U.S. bank routing numbers be redirected to the senders' manager for approval and that an incident report be generated and sent to the employees of the legal department. What do you need to do to make sure you meet the requirements of the compliance officer?

Part 5

Troubleshooting and Operating

Chapter 24

Troubleshooting Exchange Server 2016

Despite our care and attention, despite our best efforts to design the perfect Exchange server environment, something will inevitably go wrong at some point. Whether it's an unintended configuration setting, faulty hardware, a change to a dependency, or—gasp—a bug in the product, something invariably happens to cause problems for end users and ultimately for us, the administrators.

So what do you do when the lights go out on the Exchange server, figuratively speaking? The goal of this chapter is to outline tried-and-true strategies for recovering an Exchange server as quickly as possible.

IN THIS CHAPTER, YOU WILL LEARN TO:

◆ Narrow the scope of an Exchange server problem

◆ Use basic Exchange Server troubleshooting tools

◆ Troubleshoot Mailbox server problems

◆ Troubleshoot mail transport problems

Basic Troubleshooting Principles

We can't overemphasize this key point: to troubleshoot Exchange Server, you have to understand the architecture. Understanding which functions of Exchange Server are controlled by which server roles is absolutely critical, or else you could spend a lot of time troubleshooting the wrong server.

Troubleshooting Exchange Server 2016 often involves collecting and reviewing information from a series of servers, rather than focusing on one. For example, a user complains that he isn't receiving new email. There are a number of possible causes for this:

◆ The user's client isn't receiving notifications of new email.

◆ The user's client can't connect to the Mailbox server to retrieve new email.

◆ All copies of the relevant mailbox database are offline.

◆ The user's mailbox is full.

◆ Transport agents preclude delivery of email to this end user.

A closer look at this list shows an interesting breakdown. The first two issues could loosely be categorized as client-access issues, the next two as database issues, and the last as a transport issue. Unfortunately, this no longer corresponds nicely to the Exchange server roles because all those functions have now been rolled into only two roles. We'll cover troubleshooting in this chapter first by covering the general troubleshooting tools and then by troubleshooting client access, database storage, and then mail flow issues. However, before we dive right into the tools, let's take a moment to consider what troubleshooting involves.

When faced with a technical problem, your immediate impulse is often to jump right into the system and start clicking. While this can be successful, particularly when you're resolving a problem you've seen hundreds of times and know like the back of your own hand, it's not necessarily a reproducible strategy. What happens when you encounter a problem you haven't seen before? What do you do when you truly have no idea what the root cause could be?

The first step in troubleshooting a problem, any problem, is to define *what the problem is*. In many cases, this requires asking for more information. When an end user says she can't send email, does she mean that she can't open Outlook? That she can't generate a new email? That she clicks Send but the email never leaves the Drafts or Outbox folder? Or that she's sent messages that were never received? The end result is the same—the user can't send email—but the root causes are very different.

Once the problem has been defined, the next step is to determine the scope of the problem. This often helps clarify the direction of further troubleshooting. By determining how many users are affected—and more importantly, determining what those users have in common—you can rule out some possibilities and focus on things with a greater impact. For example, if one user can't send email, the root cause could be many things unique to that user, from Outlook configuration to network connectivity to a disabled user account.

However, if a second user has a similar issue, it's more likely to be something they have in common. Are they in the same network segment, perhaps? If 10 users on different floors all report Outlook problems, there might be a problem on an Exchange server. Are all 10 users in the same database, for example, or in the same Active Directory site?

There are a number of clarifying questions that are extremely useful in determining the scope of a particular problem:

- How many users are affected by the outage?

- Do all the affected users access Exchange Server through the same method, such as Outlook, Outlook on the web, or ActiveSync?

- What exactly are the users trying to do when they encounter the problem?

- Are other users able to perform the same task without problems?

- Are all of the users in the same database?

- Are all of the users in the same site?

- Does the problem occur all the time, only some of the time, or rarely?

The answers to these will often rule out possibilities right from the start. If one user can't log into Outlook successfully, but another in the same database can, you know immediately that the relevant database must be mounted and accessible, and you can then concentrate on other things.

Speaking of concentrating on other things, one of the most difficult things in troubleshooting is ignoring the unimportant distractions and focusing on what's causing the issue. It's often difficult to differentiate between what's important and what's not unless you know where to start (which is why defining the problem is so important).

Here's an example: an end user reports that he can't send email to a specific user, and during investigation you also discover that he can't access a particular public folder. Is the public folder problem directly related to the email problem? It might be—if the recipient's mailbox is on a server that also houses the only instance of that public folder and that server is inaccessible, that would explain both problems. But in many cases it might not—the mailbox database that contains the public folder mailboxes might be dismounted or the user might not have permissions. Although there's at least one explanation that covers both problems, many more exist that are unique to the secondary problem. The steps to troubleshoot internal mail flow are different from those required to troubleshoot public folder access, so if you're trying to resolve a problem with internal email, concentrate on that and leave the public folder issue for later. Essentially, isolate the issue and start investigating it. Divide and conquer.

General Server Troubleshooting Tools

During troubleshooting, some steps should be the same no matter what the symptoms are. Yes, you need to define the problem, as discussed earlier, and you also need to understand the scope of the issue. But once you've determined that the problem is indeed server-based rather than specific to a group of clients, what's next? This section will focus on the key tools you should use first.

Event Viewer (Diagnostic Logging)

Troubleshooting a server involves data collection and analysis, and the best ways to collect that data are the same regardless of server role. The Event Viewer includes detailed information about recent system and application errors, and this should always be an administrator's first move in the event of crisis.

Windows Server 2012 R2 servers have two categories of event logs: Windows logs and Applications and Services logs. The Windows logs contain the event logs available in previous versions of Windows: Application, Security, and System event logs, as well as two additional logs available only since Windows Server 2012 R2, the Setup log and the ForwardedEvents log.

Windows logs store events from legacy applications and events that apply to the entire system. Applications and Services logs store events from a single application, such as Exchange Server, or components, such as a specific service, rather than events that might have system-wide impact.

Once you've determined the scope of a problem, and you've positively identified the root cause as server related, your next step should be to check the event logs on the relevant system. Because Exchange Server has so many moving parts, so to speak, you'll often find a large number of events clustered together at the time of the reported issue. The default logging level for the majority of services and categories is Lowest, which means that only critical, error, and warnings of logging level 0 will be written to the event log.

If the events generated during the problem aren't quite enough, you might need to increase the logging level for a specific service and category—for example, MSExchange Transport\ Mail Submission—to Low, Medium, or High. There is another logging level, Expert, but this generates so many events that it should be used only for short periods, typically when working directly with Microsoft support.

As with nearly everything in Exchange Server 2016, you can configure diagnostic logging through either the Exchange Admin Center (EAC) or the Exchange Management Shell (EMS).

ENABLING DIAGNOSTIC LOGGING

In the initial release of Exchange Server 2007, diagnostic logging was removed from the Exchange Management Console (EMC), and the only way you could increase logging for a particular service was by using the Set-EventLogLevel cmdlet. Because PowerShell was still new at the time (Exchange Server 2007 was many administrators' first exposure to it), the change wasn't well received, and so Microsoft reintroduced diagnostic logging control to the console in Service Pack 2, and diagnostic logging control is still an administrator favorite in Exchange Server 2016.

If you run through the installation process of Exchange Server 2016, you will soon realize that logging is a major consideration from the outset. As discussed earlier, Exchange Server 2016 requires that you have 30 GB of available space on the drive where you install Exchange Server, and we recommend much more than that. The majority of this space will be filled by log files—not the database transaction log files that you have learned to love and respect but the diagnostic and performance log files you dread to dig through.

Figure 24.1 displays the default directory where all log files are found. Logging is enabled by default on all Exchange servers and cannot be disabled. Microsoft recommends that you open a call to product support should your entire installation drive become full and cause issues with your Exchange server.

The way to configure diagnostic logging in Exchange Server 2016 is through the Set-EventLogLevel cmdlet. This cmdlet does *not* take a server parameter. Instead, the server is specified as part of the identity string. There are quite a few logs for Exchange Server, with each log handling a very specific subset of Exchange Server. To see a complete list of all the logs and their current logging level, run the following command:

```
Get-EventLogLevel
```

The syntax you use to set the logging level for a log is relatively straightforward. You target the individual log names and specify the level of logging. For example, to set the SmtpReceive log to High, run the following command:

```
Set-EventLogLevel -Identity "NYC-EX1\MSExchangeTransport\SmtpReceive" -Level High
```

It's always a good idea to reset the logging back to Lowest (the lowest level available) when you're finished troubleshooting. Increased logging can add significantly to event log growth, and depending on your settings, it might fill up your event log quickly or overwrite events.

Once you've identified the target server and configured logging, you might not see relevant events right away. You may need to reproduce the issue (for example, by having the user send another email or attempt to force a connection for a mail queue) before Exchange Server logs anything of value. Exchange Server events themselves will always appear in the Application event log and in the logging directories shown in Figure 24.1.

FIGURE 24.1
The logging directory on the Exchange server

Diagnostic events include a wealth of information, but the most important pieces are the following:

Description   Although the field is unnamed in Windows Server 2012 R2, it's the equivalent of the legacy Description field from previous versions of Windows. This includes the text of the event and will in many cases include additional error codes or critical information. For example, the well-known and widely feared -1018 error isn't an event—it's a JET error code that appears within the description text of other ESE events, like ESE error 474. The description may also include a link to further information on the Microsoft support site.

Source   This tells you which component logged the event. Note that this will typically be the underlying service name rather than the "friendly" name.

Event ID   This is the specific event number. Along with the Source, this is the most important information for the event.

Level   This reflects the severity of the event and can range from Informational to Error.

Logged   This displays the date and time of the event *in local time*. This information is stored in the event in UTC (Coordinated Universal Time), and the Event Viewer displays the equivalent local time—if you're looking at a remote server, make sure you take this into account!

Task Category   This is the subcomponent of the service that logged the event. Not all services provide this additional information, but the majority of Exchange Server services do. This corresponds to the categories visible in the Manage Diagnostic Logging Properties Wizard or via `Set-EventLogLevel`.

Depending on the error, you should see information similar to the event shown in Figure 24.2.

FIGURE 24.2
Viewing an event
from the Exchange
Application logs

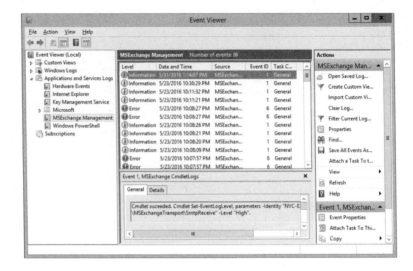

Many Exchange Server events include detailed diagnostic steps in the Description field, which is extremely convenient in times of trouble. Even if the event doesn't provide much information, you might be able to find more in the TechNet Library at https://technet.microsoft .com/library/mt170645%28v=exchg.160%29.aspx. If you can't find information on the specific event here, there's always the Microsoft Knowledge Base (http://support.microsoft .com/search/?adv=1) or your favorite search engine.

The *Test-** Cmdlets

PowerShell cmdlets control so much functionality in Exchange Server 2016 that it's not a surprise to see troubleshooting cmdlets as well. The Test-* cmdlets in Exchange Server are solid tools in the back pockets of Exchange Server administrators. My recommendation is to use them frequently because they use few resources on the servers and provide a wealth of useful information. For a complete list of all Test-* cmdlets, run the following command:

```
Get-Command Test-*
```

TEST-SERVICEHEALTH

Another extremely useful cmdlet is Test-ServiceHealth, which does what its name suggests: it checks the health of all required Exchange Server services on the server. Because the cmdlet recognizes roles as well, it doesn't check for every service; it only looks for the services the installed roles use. For example, if you're running the test on an Edge Transport server, it will not check for the MSExchangeMailSubmission service, which is available only on a Mailbox server.

This cmdlet also uses a very simple syntax; just type **Test-ServiceHealth**, press Enter, and peruse the results. The output from this cmdlet is preformatted into a table and simply reports on the status of the required services; an example of the output is shown in Figure 24.3.

FIGURE 24.3
Using the Test-
ServiceHealth
cmdlet

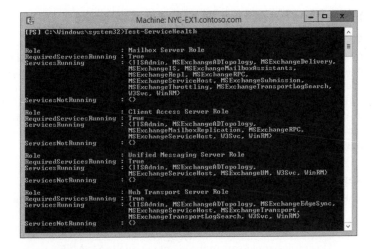

If you want to quickly check the status of a single server, this cmdlet can save a lot of time and effort. However, this cmdlet doesn't run against multiple servers at once. To check the configuration of a group of servers or even every server in the organization, you need to create a script for the Test-ServiceHealth cmdlet so that it loops through each server that you want to test.

REPLACING THE EXCHANGE BEST PRACTICE ANALYZER

If you've been using Exchange Server for the last few years, you're probably familiar with the Exchange Best Practice Analyzer (generally known as ExBPA). You'll be sad to hear, as we were, that the ExBPA has been retired as of Exchange Server 2013.

So one of the common questions that we get is, "How do you replace the functionalities provided by the ExBPA?" and the answer is not always a great one. First, in order to replace the ExBPA, you really need to be familiar with the Exchange Management Shell and its "troubleshooting" cmdlets. In fact, if you are new to managing Windows Server 2012 R2 servers, you'll find that the PowerShell and Test-* cmdlets are prevalent there as well.

In a recent attempt to solve several configuration problems at a client site, we were able to identify the root cause of connectivity and certificate errors by running only two cmdlets: Test-MapiConnectivity and Test-ActiveSyncConnectivity. (See the section "Using *Test-MapiConnectivity*" later in this chapter.) Sure, both of these cmdlets require a bit of experience with their syntax, but at the end of the day they helped resolve major configuration issues that would have required a full ExBPA test. This was in fact quicker and more efficient, though not as pretty and graphics-oriented.

Troubleshooting Mailbox Servers

With the shift of the client access services to the Mailbox server role in Exchange Server 2016, the Mailbox server's role essentially encompasses data storage, mail transport, client connectivity (covered in a dedicated section in this chapter), and Unified Messaging functionalities. The primary focus of troubleshooting Mailbox servers rests on three things: database replication health, server performance, and email delivery. These aren't the only things Mailbox servers do, of course, but they're probably the most common troubleshooting topics. But before we get into those, let's recap some of the standard troubleshooting techniques you should apply to a Mailbox server.

General Mailbox Server Health

When dealing with Mailbox server issues, you'll want to perform these basic checks:

◆ Are all required Exchange Server services able to start as necessary?

◆ Do you see any errors in the event log relating to MSExchangeDatabase, MSExchangeDatabase ➤ Instances, or MSExchangeSubmission Mailbox?

◆ Are there any Active Directory issues that might have a negative impact on Exchange Server?

Obviously, the Test-ServiceHealth cmdlet would be useful in detecting basic problems, such as a dismounted database or a stopped service. The Get-ServerHealth cmdlet is also useful in detecting health issues. You can run the following command to list the current health status of the Exchange components on a server named LON-EX1:

```
Get-ServerHealth –Identity LON-EX1 | FT Name, AlertValue
```

Test-ServiceHealth and Get-ServerHealth should always be the first two cmdlets you execute when troubleshooting a Mailbox server, simply because they check many areas of the environment at once.

Using *Test-MapiConnectivity*

Like its close cousin, Test-OutlookConnectivity, Test-MapiConnectivity will help you determine problems accessing a specific mailbox. It logs into a target mailbox (which you can specify with the –Identity parameter), the system mailbox in a specific database (which you can specify with –Database), or the system mailbox in every active database on a server (through –Server). The output for all three variants looks like the following:

```
Test-MAPIConnectivity -Server Server1
MailboxServer      Database          Result    Error
-------------      --------          ------    -----
Server1            MailboxDatabase... Success
Server1            MailBoxDatabase... Success
Test-MAPIConnectivity GTaylor
MailboxServer      Database          Result    Error
-------------      --------          ------    -----
Server1            MailBoxDatabase... Success
```

```
Test-MAPIConnectivity -Database MailboxDatabase-001
MailboxServer      Database            Result    Error
-------------      --------            ------    -----
Server1            MailBoxDatabase... Success
```

This is a useful (and quick) cmdlet for narrowing the possible scope of a problem; Test-MapiConnectivity essentially tests not only the Exchange Server Information Store but also ADAccess and RPCoverHTTP access, so a successful test against any mailbox on a server proves that those three components are at least functioning. If you can log into the system mailbox for a database but not into a user mailbox in that same database, the problem is clearly something unique to that user.

What is also very interesting about this cmdlet is that although it tests access to the mailbox database and essentially is a Mailbox server testing tool, it does *not* indirectly test the availability of the Client Access service. The Client Access service is the entry point of client requests to mailboxes, so if your Test-MapiConnectivity cmdlet retrieves a successful connection, that successful connection will be to the entry point on the Mailbox servers, not necessarily the one that users/Outlook/Outlook on the web and others will take to access the mailbox. We actually find that to be a positive aspect of this cmdlet, since it allows you to segment your troubleshooting results to pinpoint the source of a problem.

For end-to-end connectivity checks, use the Test-OutlookConnectivity cmdlet. This cmdlet tests both RPC over HTTP and MAPI over HTTP connection types. For example, to test the RPC connectivity, run the following command:

```
Test-OutlookConnectivity -ProbeIdentity "OutlookRpcSelfTestProbe"
```

Checking Poison Mailboxes

One feature that might lead to confusion for users (and more than a few administrators!) is poison mailbox detection. By default, Mailbox servers will tag any mailbox that causes a thread in the store.exe service to crash or that is connected to five or more "hung" threads. If a mailbox is tagged three times in two hours, Exchange Server 2016 will block access to that mailbox for up to six hours or until the administrator unblocks it, whichever comes first. If a user reports that she cannot connect to a mailbox, but other users have no difficulty, check to see if there are any quarantined mailboxes on the server. You can do this either through Performance Monitor (through the MSExchangeIS Mailbox\Quarantined Mailbox Count performance counter) or through the Get-MailboxStatistics cmdlet. For example, to find out if mailbox GillianK is quarantined, simply use this command:

```
Get-MailboxStatistics GillianK | Format-List DisplayName, IsQuarantined
```

Exchange Server 2016 will also write an event to the Application log when it quarantines a mailbox.

Do not confuse this feature with a poison message queue that is also stored on the Exchange Server Mailbox server. This queue contains messages that Exchange Server deems harmful to the environment while they are being transported in and out of an Exchange Server organization. These messages are not lost, since they will continue to exist in the poison message queue until an administrator deletes them manually.

Checking Database Replication Health

The introduction of continuous replication in Exchange Server 2007 dramatically changed the face of disaster recovery, because administrators could deploy two separate copies of a single database, each on a physically separate server. There were a few limitations, of course; end users still connected to the *server*, not just the database, so problems with the underlying cluster would render both database copies inaccessible. Standby continuous replication (introduced in Exchange Server 2007 Service Pack 1) provided another disaster-recovery option, but this had its limits as well—it was purely manual and, depending on the configuration, would require at least a setup "trick" (setup /recovercms) or even wholesale "rehoming" of users. A successful activation of a standby copy was also heavily dependent on replication of both DNS and Active Directory information, so users might still be unable to connect even after the issue was resolved.

Database availability groups (DAGs) in Exchange Server 2016 provide multiple copies of a single database on different servers, even in different datacenters, so a single server failure should have a significantly smaller impact on an Exchange Server deployment. Other architectural changes—namely Client Access namespaces—effectively hide the server object from the end user, so the actual location of the active database is immaterial from the end user's perspective.

Database replication health is, loosely speaking, how successful Exchange Server is at keeping database copies in sync. This depends on server configuration, network health, and a few other things. However, you can check the health of the replication infrastructure quite easily with two cmdlets. The first cmdlet, Test-ReplicationHealth, checks the health of the replication services and alerts you to any errors it finds. The output is extremely easy to read, as shown here:

```
Test-ReplicationHealth
Server          Check                        Result      Error
------          -----                        ------      -----

EX1      ReplayService                       Passed
EX1      ActiveManager                       Passed
EX1      TasksRpcListener                    Passed
EX1      DatabaseRedundancyCheck             Passed
EX1      DatabaseAvailabilityCheck           Passed
```

Once you've validated the replication services, you can check the replication status for the databases themselves with Get-MailboxDatabaseCopyStatus. You can focus on a particular database by using the –Identity parameter or check the status for all mailbox database copies on a specific server by using –MailboxServer. You could even check the status of one specific database on one specific server by including both parameters. Here is an example of using the Get-MailboxDatabaseCopyStatus cmdlet where the results are filtered to show only a subset of the data being reported:

```
Get-MailboxDatabaseCopyStatus | Format-List
Name,Status,LastInspectedLogTime,ContentIndexState
Name              Status     LastInspectedLogTime    ContentIndex
                                                     State

----              ------     --------------------    ----------
MDB001\EX1        Mounted    5/13/2016 8:44:03 AM    Healthy
```

```
MDB002\EX1      Mounted    5/15/2016 8:03:24 PM    Healthy
MDB003\EX1      Mounted    5/15/2016 8:12:56 PM    Healthy
```

There are many possible causes for replication errors, including the following:

◆ Transient network-connectivity issues

◆ Permissions issues

◆ Insufficient disk space on the target server

The general troubleshooting steps we covered in the beginning of this chapter will help you determine the exact cause of a replication problem.

With the reduction in functionality, Mailbox servers have become significantly easier to troubleshoot than in the past. There are a number of useful cmdlets for validating mailbox database availability and mailbox access, among them `Get-MailboxStatistics` and `Test-MapiConnectivity`. Two additional cmdlets, `Test-ReplicationHealth` and `Get-MailboxDatabaseCopyStatus`, provide insight into the replication of those databases across member servers in the organization.

Troubleshooting Mail Flow

Message delivery is arguably the most important piece of Exchange Server 2016, and it's only fitting that Microsoft has provided a formidable arsenal of troubleshooting weapons to deal with pesky delivery failures. You'll have your pick of tools, from self-serve choices, such as message tracking in the Exchange Admin Center, to several forms of tracing, to the inevitable cmdlets.

However, just because you have an array of choices doesn't mean you have to use them right away. Again, it's important to approach a message-delivery problem with clear eyes and ask probing questions about what you're facing. Remember the example earlier in the chapter, with the end user who couldn't send email? There were a number of plausible explanations for this, some of which didn't involve message delivery at all! So it's still important to gather the essential information:

◆ Can the user send any emails at all? Is nondelivery restricted to a subset of users?

◆ Does the user receive a delivery status notification? If so, what is the delivery code?

◆ Is the recipient in the same Exchange Server organization or in a different organization (presumably on the Internet)?

◆ How close do messages get to their destination?

◆ What is the messaging path between the end user and the recipient?

These questions, though relatively simple, conceal a bewildering list of possible root causes. Consider the impact on message delivery on the following:

DNS Failure   Mailbox servers can't locate A records and, therefore, can't reach next-hop servers.

Site Link Failure   No site link exists between sender and recipient.

Transport Failure Transport services on all of the Mailbox servers in the user's site are inaccessible.

Transport Agent A transport rule prevents this email from reaching the recipient (because of sender restrictions, content restrictions, or recipient issues).

Mailbox Limits The recipient's mailbox is full, but nondelivery reports do not reach the sender for whatever reason.

Messages Stuck in Queue A transient failure has temporarily stopped messages at a back-off location.

Back Pressure Transport services are temporarily throttling message delivery due to resource constraints.

This isn't even an exhaustive list, but it includes a wealth of possibilities. Now, there are few listed here that you would probably detect by performing the basic troubleshooting steps we covered earlier in this chapter (like DNS failure or transport failure). We'll begin with a simple cmdlet to check basic mail flow, which is typically the first step in locating undelivered messages, and then move on to message tracking and agent logging.

Using *Test-Mailflow*

Assuming you've done some of the basic checking (is the user's client connected to a database, are transport services available, and so on), you'll probably want to test that mail is flowing in the organization. There's an aptly named cmdlet for just this job: Test-Mailflow.

The cmdlet's basic function is simply to send and receive email from the system mailbox of the target server, but it can do so much more. The syntax is extremely simple: Test-Mailflow followed by the source server, then –TargetMailboxServer, -TargetDatabase, or –TargetEmailAddress. The different options mean that you can start with a Mailbox server, and if that test succeeds, focus on the user's database and then the user's email address. If you've deployed multiple databases in a DAG, you should skip the first step and start with –TargetDatabase.

```
Test-Mailflow
RunspaceId          : cae78d94-0032-4f1f-999f-3a2f3b8448ea
TestMailflowResult  : Success
MessageLatencyTime  : 00:00:03.9558691
IsRemoteTest        : False
Identity            :
IsValid             : True
ObjectState         : New
```

The output from Test-Mailflow doesn't need much interpretation. The most important piece is the TestMailflowResult property. If it reads Success, you know that you can reach that server, database, or email address, and you know that email is flowing, at least for some combination of user and database. The next property, MessageLatencyTime, lets you know the time it took for the message to reach the destination server. The IsRemoteTest property simply indicates whether the message left the server (this will also be True if you use the –TargetEmailAddress parameter).

However, if your test fails, the TestMailflowResult property reads *FAILURE*, and that's unfortunately the only indicator you receive—no messages about where the failure might have occurred or other useful information. That's when you need to start figuring out where the messages are stopped, and for that we need to move into different tools. We'll start with the Queue Viewer and then look into message tracking.

Utilizing the Queue Viewer

So, if you've been following along with this book, you've read plenty about the Exchange Admin Center (EAC) and how it is the primary graphical interface for managing Exchange Server 2016 servers. And that's true; we're not backing down from this one. However, rarely you'll use the trusted Microsoft Management Console (MMC) to manage certain aspects of Exchange Server. The Queue Viewer is one of those rare examples.

The Queue Viewer is a tool that is available through an MMC snap-in named Exchange Toolbox. The Exchange Toolbox provides a virtual toolbox in the MMC that contains the Queue Viewer, alongside a number of other useful tools (some of which we'll cover later in this section). A big believer in truth in advertising, the Queue Viewer allows you to, yes, view the contents of the various delivery queues. Obviously, you need to connect to a Mailbox server to use this tool, but you can open the Queue Viewer from anywhere and then connect to the appropriate Mailbox server. The interface for the Queue Viewer is shown in Figure 24.4.

FIGURE 24.4

Using the Queue Viewer interface

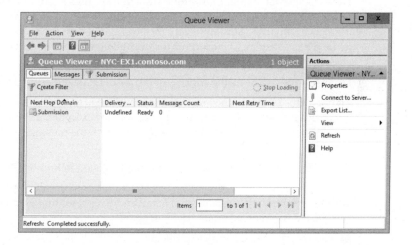

It's largely unchanged from Exchange Server 2013, but it didn't need any enhancements; it tells you the status of the queues, how many messages are pending delivery, and where the mail is heading, among other things. The list of queues is a bit thinner than in previous versions of Exchange Server (particularly when compared to the positively garrulous Exchange Server 2003), but if there's a problem with a particular queue, it'll be listed here.

Most of the columns in the Queues tab are relatively self-explanatory, but here's a brief rundown of what you'll see on this page:

Next-Hop Domain This is where the mail is heading next, whether a server in a different site, a server in the same site, or an Internet host.

Delivery Type This indicates where the messages are heading next in their journey to the recipient.

Status This simply indicates whether the queue state is Active (sending messages at the moment), Suspended (stopped through administrative action), Ready (able to send messages should any arrive), or Retry (unable to send messages). Queues in a Retry state are the most obvious candidates for additional review and analysis, but remember that queues can fail because of the sending server as well as the recipient.

Message Count This lets you know how many messages are stuck in this queue.

Next Retry Time This is applicable only to queues in a Retry state and lets you know the next time Exchange Server will attempt to "wake up" the queue for delivery.

You can perform a small number of tasks on the queues, including temporarily stopping them (Suspend), forcing them to connect if they've failed (Retry), or deleting all the messages (Remove messages with or without a nondelivery report). This can be useful for restarting mail flow after you've resolved a problem somewhere else in the environment or for deleting a quantity of undesired email. The Actions pane at the right of the MMC will display only valid actions for the queue you've selected.

The Messages tab has similar information to the Queues tab, and it's generally most useful when you've clicked a queue and then selected View Messages. You can click the Messages tab right away, but it'll show you every message queued on the server, which might take a little while for a busy system. The columns for the Messages tab are similar to those on the Queues tab:

From Address This is the address of the sender, taken directly from the SMTP envelope.

Status This indicates the message status, which is generally the same as the parent queue but is also influenced by administrator action (for example, if the administrator has tried to delete the message while it was being delivered, the message will appear as Pending Remove).

Size (KB) This is the size of the message, displayed in kilobytes.

SCL This is the spam confidence level (SCL) rating; the values range from –1 through 9, with –1 representing authenticated email and 9 representing email that is almost certainly unsolicited commercial email (UCE, or spam).

Queue ID This value indicates the queue in which the message appears. If you chose a specific queue and then selected View Messages, this should be the same for all messages and should reflect the queue you chose on the Queues tab.

Message Source Name This indicates the Exchange Server component that delivered the message to this particular queue. Depending on your architecture, this could be a Hub Transport server in another site, a Mailbox server in the same site, or possibly even an application or client submitting a message directly to the Hub Transport server via SMTP.

Subject   This is the subject of the email, taken from the SMTP envelope.

Last Error   This indicates the last error experienced when attempting delivery of this message. This typically appears only if the message is in a Suspended, Retry, or Pending state.

The Queue Viewer is useful for locating a message that hasn't been delivered, but the message-tracking feature is also useful for this in larger environments, and depending on the Last Error field for the queue or message in question, you may be able to figure out what your next move should be. However, the one drawback to the Queue Viewer is that unless you have a simple topology, you might not necessarily know exactly *how* a message reached that particular server. For that type of analysis, you need something a little more detailed (like message tracking, also known as Delivery Reports in Exchange Server 2013 and Exchange Server 2016, which we'll cover next).

Using Message Tracking

With end-user message tracking in the Exchange Control Panel, Exchange Server 2010 introduced a wrinkle into what used to be a purely administrative task. In a reversal, we now see the tool that was designed for end users make an appearance in the administrative management console, the Exchange Admin Center. The conscientious administrator now has three choices for tracking messages:

◆   Allow the end user to search for messages via the Exchange Admin Center

◆   Track messages via the Exchange Admin Center

◆   Track messages via the Exchange Management Shell

These options are listed in order of power and usability, so we'll start with the simplest first: end-user message tracking.

SELF-SERVICE MESSAGE TRACKING IN THE EXCHANGE ADMIN CENTER

Before Exchange Server 2010, the only way an end user could determine the delivery status of a message was by requesting delivery receipts, but there were two drawbacks: many companies would block delivery (and read) receipts from leaving the Exchange Server organization, and many users elected to never send them at all. This left a functionality gap that the Exchange Admin Center helps fill. EAC enables end users to gather information about their own messages (or other people's messages if they have the permissions). This can be incredibly useful for environments with lots of tech-savvy users but would require a little investment in training, documentation, and, above all, communication. The security conscious among us need not fear: the message-tracking function in the EAC adheres to the same role-based access control regime as all the other Exchange Server components, so users couldn't use this interface to just browse their way through random users' message histories.

To access the self-service message-tracking component, simply log into EAC, click Organize Email, and then click Delivery Reports in the right pane. This displays the message-tracking screen shown in Figure 24.5.

FIGURE 24.5

Viewing message tracking in EAC

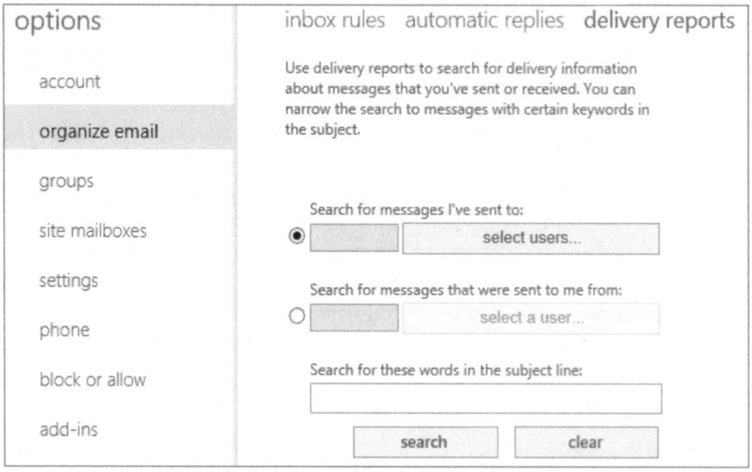

Although the title of the message-tracking pane seems to indicate that it's processing delivery reports, don't worry: Exchange Server hasn't been secretly appending delivery reports to every email your users have been sending! It's simply processing delivery information taken from the message-tracking logs (remember, message tracking is enabled by default in Exchange Server 2016).

Assuming the logs are still available, users should be able to determine information about their own messages, although as in medicine sometimes a little knowledge is a dangerous thing! Users might become so enamored of self-service message tracking that they check the status of all their messages, so any small delay could turn into *more* help desk calls, not fewer. You'll need to balance the needs of the community with the realistic expectations of delivery performance.

MESSAGE TRACKING VIA THE EXCHANGE ADMIN CENTER FOR ADMINISTRATORS

The message-tracking tool, also listed as Delivery Reports in Exchange Server 2016, is very different from the one you encountered in Exchange Server 2010 and earlier. Administrators can search for messages from any sender, to any recipient, with any subject line, using wildcards and filters as necessary to focus on the critical data.

To launch message tracking from within the Exchange Admin Center, select Mail Flow in the navigation pane at the left and then choose Delivery Reports in the display panel. This launches the web-based message-tracking tool, which is the same tool an end user would use but with a few additional options. The big difference is that as an administrator you will be able to track everyone's messages and not just your own, as shown in Figure 24.6.

Once you've launched the tool, you'll be presented with what might be a bewildering array of possibilities. You can track on any of a number of fields, including the mailbox to search, the sender, and keywords that appear in the subject line.

Once you've entered all the relevant criteria, click Search to begin searching for messages. Depending on your search criteria, this process could take a significant amount of time.

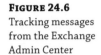

FIGURE 24.6
Tracking messages from the Exchange Admin Center

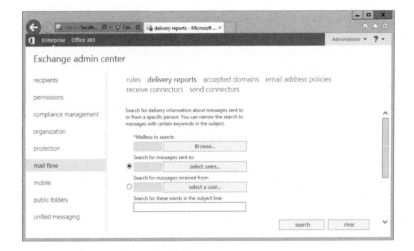

The Message Tracking Results page is a little confusing when you first encounter it, but it makes sense after you've visited it a few times. Because messages pass through different stages during the mail-transfer process, you should (hopefully) see multiple entries for every message. At a bare minimum, a message should be listed three times, for the original notification to a Hub Transport server in the local site (SUBMIT), the delivery to the database on the receiving Mailbox server (DELIVER), and the ultimate delivery to the recipient (RECEIVE). If the recipient is in a different site, you'll see the delivery (SEND) of the message from one Hub Transport to another, and if there are multiple recipients, you'll probably see TRANSFER, which indicates that a message was bifurcated en route.

The message-tracking tool in the console can be useful, but it's a lot slower than building your own queries with PowerShell. After you've tracked messages a few times with the Exchange Admin Center, you'll probably be comfortable enough to forgo the graphical user interface (GUI) and just use the shell.

MESSAGE TRACKING USING THE EXCHANGE MANAGEMENT SHELL

Because the message-tracking tool in the Exchange Admin Center portion of Outlook on the web uses the `Get-MessageTrackingLog` cmdlet, there's little to do here but show the actual output of the cmdlet, with no input:

```
Get-MessageTrackingLog | Format-table EventID,Source,Sender,MessageSubject
```

There are a few advantages to using the shell over the Exchange Admin Center. Essentially, you get much more flexibility and granularity in your searches. You can initiate searches based on `EventID`, source event, sender, recipient, subject, or even source server. Now, if you were around before Exchange Server 2013, you might remember that these search criteria were available in previous versions in the Exchange Management Console (the legacy administrative console), but to have this flexibility today, you must use the Exchange Management Shell.

Now that we've gone through message tracking, you should be well equipped to determine whether a message was delivered and if not, where it stalled.

Exploring Other Tools

If you've used all the tools and techniques we've outlined to troubleshoot a mail issue and your problem isn't solved, you might be facing more than a simple mail-flow issue. If you long for some of the tools you used in previous versions, force yourself to hone your shell technique. It's true: Microsoft has not yet updated the Routing Log Viewer or the Mail Flow Troubleshooter (both great transport troubleshooting tools from previous versions of Exchange Server), but you can still get by with the Exchange Management Shell and its powerful scripting ability.

There are myriad troubleshooting tools and techniques, so we don't have room to cover them all. But there are a few additional things we want to mention:

◆ **Telnet.** You can install the Telnet client feature and use it to test port connectivity (such as whether port 25 is responding) as well as connectors. For example, you can Telnet to port 25 and use commands in the Telnet session to send a test email. You can get valuable information back from the server if the test email isn't accepted.

◆ **Outlook's message header viewer.** In Outlook, you can view message headers to track the exact path that an email message took from the sender to your mailbox. To view the headers, open the email, and then click the diagonal down arrow in the bottom-right corner of the Tags section. The properties of the email will be shown with the headers at the bottom of the window.

◆ **Look through protocol logs.** SMTP is used throughout an Exchange environment and for Internet delivery of email. You can enable and view the SMTP protocol logs to gain insight into problems.

Lastly, if you've deployed transport agents in your environment, you may need to enable pipeline tracing, which essentially records every message to disk for later review. However, pipeline tracing is rather complex and is typically used only in conjunction with a Microsoft support case, so we won't cover it here—not to mention that it would deserve its own chapter! If you're curious about what pipeline tracing entails, what it offers, and (if you're brave enough) how to enable it, have a look at this page:

```
http://technet.microsoft.com/en-us/library/bb125018(v=exchg.150).aspx
```

TROUBLESHOOTING WHEN IPv6 IS INVOLVED

You may have noticed by now that Windows Server 2008 R2 and Windows Server 2012 R2 servers have IPv6 enabled for their network interfaces by default. In most cases, this is not of much concern to Exchange Server 2016 servers, except for some particular scenarios. The most common that we've come across recently is the lack of IPv6 DNS records. We've noticed that some ISPs allow IPv6 traffic on their networks, yet most network administrators may not be ready for the trouble this might cause.

Here are the specifics. In an effort to minimize the flood of spam received by their users, some large cloud-based email companies, such as Google and Yahoo, reject email messages sent by servers that do not have DNS records in the Reverse Lookup zones. Most organizations have created such DNS records for the IPv4 addresses, but have failed to do so for the IPv6 address. Most will not feel any symptoms, until the day the Exchange server starts to deliver email messages to @gmail.com addresses by using IPv6, and those emails are rejected.

To avoid the flood of users complaining about bounced email messages, do yourself a favor and create reverse DNS records for both IPv4 and IPv6 addresses used to deliver email messages to the Internet.

Troubleshooting Client Connectivity

Many of us subconsciously assume that "client" means Outlook (an overzealous business owner may ask you to "Please fix our Outlook server!"), but it's not the only client software (or device) capable of accessing Exchange Server 2016. Outlook is the most popular, but there are also Outlook on the web and ActiveSync-enabled devices like Google's Android and Apple's iPhone. Despite the obvious differences between these devices, they all rely on the same basic mechanisms to connect—locating the Mailbox server and connecting to the appropriate interface. Many architectural changes have been introduced to the Mailbox server role in this release of Exchange Server, but the basic premise still applies; identify your server's name, try to resolve its IP address, and attempt a connection to its required TCP/UDP ports.

Before troubleshooting the server components, it's a good idea to test the following:

♦ Verify that the client can successfully ping the Mailbox server by both IP and fully qualified domain name. If the forest includes multiple domains, ping the Mailbox server by short (NetBIOS) name as well, so that you can verify that NetBIOS names are being resolved correctly.

♦ For a mobile device, verify that the device can access Internet-based content by browsing to a known website.

♦ Verify the username-and-password combination for the mailbox you're attempting to access.

♦ Use Outlook on the web to see if the issue occurs there, too.

If these tests fail, the problem may not be unique to Exchange Server, or if it is, it may not be unique to the Mailbox server role.

Troubleshooting Autodiscover

The Autodiscover service is the most important initial consideration for Outlook client connectivity. As described in Chapter 6, "Understanding the Exchange Autodiscover Process," the Autodiscover service generates an XML file with all the appropriate user settings and sends it to Outlook, which then uses that information to connect the users to their mailboxes. But how does Outlook know where to find Autodiscover in the first place? Depending on the client's location (on the corporate network or the Internet), the client will either check Active Directory for an appropriate record or look for a specific URL. There are a few different ways to check this, all of them very useful.

INTERNAL CLIENTS

Internal clients connect to Active Directory and check for the service connection point records, which are automatically published as part of the setup process. One easy way to validate Autodiscover for internal clients is with the Outlook Test E-mail AutoConfiguration tool. This useful little feature was introduced in Outlook 2007 and simply goes through the steps for Autodiscover without making changes to the current configuration. To access this wizard, start Outlook, Ctrl+right-click the Outlook icon in the notification area (system tray), and then select Test E-mail AutoConfiguration from the context menu. You can see a sample of the Test E-mail AutoConfiguration tool in Figure 24.7.

FIGURE 24.7
Using the
Test E-mail
AutoConfiguration
tool

After providing appropriate user credentials and ensuring that only the check box for Use Autodiscover is selected, click Test to begin the configuration check. The AutoConfiguration test checks for much more than just Autodiscover: it also locates Availability Service, OOF, Offline Address Book, Unified Messaging, Outlook on the web, and Exchange Admin Center URLs, making this one of the most useful client-based configuration tools.

If the AutoConfiguration test fails, the tool will display an error message. The four most common error codes, along with the most common root causes, are listed here:

`0x80072EE7 - ERROR_INTERNET_NAME_NOT_RESOLVED`   A missing host record for the Autodiscover service in the domain naming service

`0X80072F17 - ERROR_INTERNET_SEC_CERT_ERRORS`   An incorrect certificate configuration on the Exchange Server computer that has the Mailbox server role installed

`0X80072EFD - ERROR_INTERNET_CANNOT_CONNECT`   Issues that are related to the domain naming service

`0X800C820A - E_AC_NO_SUPPORTED_SCHEMES`   Incorrect security settings in Outlook

Because Exchange Server 2016 requires Outlook Anywhere connectivity for both internal and external clients, the AutoConfiguration test checks the client configuration for Outlook Anywhere. When a client connectivity failure occurs, it's important to ensure that the names used to connect to Client Access services can be resolved both internally and externally.

EXTERNAL CLIENTS

If external clients can't connect to Exchange Server, you may need to ensure that you've configured your environment properly for remote access to the Exchange Server organization. Here are some of the configurations you would apply to an existing organization to configure access to Outlook with the name `outlook.konopizza.ca`. (In each case, you'll obviously need to substitute your own domain name space.)

♦ To configure the external Autodiscover name for Outlook Anywhere, the appropriate command is as follows:

```
Enable-OutlookAnywhere -Server CAS01 -ExternalHostname "OUTLOOK.KONOPIZZA.CA"
-ExternalAuthenticationMethod "Basic" -SSLOffloading:$False
```

♦ The equivalent command for Web Service clients is as follows:

```
Set-WebServicesVirtualDirectory -identity "CAS01\EWS (Default Web Site)"
-externalurl https://OUTLOOK.KONOPIZZA.CA/EWS/Exchange.asmx
-BasicAuthentication:$True
```

♦ Here's the equivalent command for ActiveSync clients:

```
Set-ActiveSyncVirtualDirectory -identity "CAS01\Microsoft-Server-ActiveSync
(Default Web Site)" -externalurl https://OUTLOOK.KONOPIZZA.CA/Microsoft-Server
-ActiveSync
```

♦ And here's the equivalent command for the Offline Address Book:

```
Set-OABVirtualDirectory -identity "CAS01\OAB (Default Web Site) " -OUTLOOK
.KONOPIZZA.CA/oab
```

If you are in the process of configuring your organization for remote access, there is a great solution for troubleshooting your configurations in Exchange Server 2016: the Microsoft Remote Connectivity Analyzer (RCA). In 2008 Microsoft quietly released the beta of this extremely useful tool, then called the Exchange Server Remote Connectivity Analyzer. It simulates a number of connectivity scenarios, including Autodiscover, Exchange ActiveSync, Outlook Anywhere, and incoming Internet SMTP email. To use the RCA, simply browse to `https://testconnectivity.microsoft.com` and select the appropriate option (see Figure 24.8).

Today, this tool provides assistance to administrators who have hybrid environments with Office 365 and even coexistence with other technologies such as Skype for Business.

FIGURE 24.8
The Remote
Connectivity
Analyzer

Select the test you want to run.

| Exchange Server | SfB / Lync | Office 365 | Client | Message Analyzer |

Microsoft Exchange ActiveSync Connectivity Tests
◉ Exchange ActiveSync
○ Exchange ActiveSync Autodiscover

Microsoft Exchange Web Services Connectivity Tests
○ Synchronization, Notification, Availability, and Automatic Replies
○ Service Account Access (Developers)

Microsoft Office Outlook Connectivity Tests
○ Outlook Connectivity
○ Outlook Autodiscover

Internet Email Tests
○ Inbound SMTP Email
○ Outbound SMTP Email
○ POP Email
○ IMAP Email

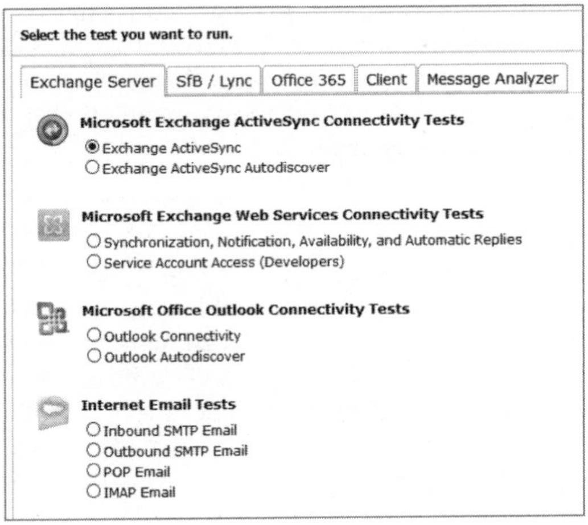

Using the *Test-* Connectivity* Cmdlets

Microsoft recommends that to ensure full redundancy you deploy at least two Mailbox servers in every site. This recommendation assumes that your site definitions correctly include all appropriate subnets, that your servers' IP addresses are correctly configured, and that all DNS records are properly registered in the appropriate zones.

If your client can access Autodiscover, you know that you can connect to at least one Client Access server, but it is possible to access one service on a Client Access system but not others. How can you tell if other necessary components on the Client Access server are functioning properly? Sometimes you can take a more surgical approach and focus on one protocol. For this, we'll use a series of cmdlets called `Test-*Connectivity` (where * is the protocol or client you're testing).

TROUBLESHOOTING USING CMDLETS

You've probably noticed that troubleshooting Exchange Server 2016 involves a lot of cmdlets, and you're right! The Exchange Server product group worked hard to ensure that administrators had easy-to-use, robust, focused troubleshooting tools right at their fingertips, and the resulting family of cmdlets serves as a testament to those efforts.

Depending on the client you're testing, you'll want to use one of the following cmdlets:

◆ `Test-ActiveSyncConnectivity`

◆ `Test-ImapConnectivity`

◆ `Test-OutlookConnectivity`

◆ `Test-PopConnectivity`

◆ `Test-WebServicesConnectivity`

These cmdlets are all pretty self-explanatory; they correspond to the most popular connectivity models (although it's important to note that the cmdlets to test POP3 and IMAP4 connectivity don't include the version numbers for the protocols—it's just POP and IMAP).

The suite of cmdlets listed here provides comprehensive coverage for connectivity issues. If you can run these successfully but still can't connect your client, there's a good chance that the problem isn't with Exchange Server at all.

The Bottom Line

Narrow the scope of an Exchange Server problem.   One of the most important troubleshooting skills that an Exchange Server administrator must possess is the ability to quickly and effectively narrow the scope of problem. Determining the commonalities in a problem can help you quickly locate and solve a problem.

Master It   Seven of your 400 users are reporting an error in Outlook that indicates that they cannot connect to the Exchange server. What are some things you would determine to narrow the scope of the problem?

Use basic Exchange Server troubleshooting tools.   A number of tools are available that will help you troubleshoot Exchange Server problems and possibly determine future issues. These include the Event Viewer, the Remote Connectivity Analyzer, Exchange Server diagnostics logging, and the `Test-ServiceHealth` cmdlet.

Master It   After installing a recent Cumulative Update, you have started noticing intermittent issues with your Exchange server. What tool or tools could you run to help you identify potential issues?

Troubleshoot Mailbox server problems.   The Mailbox server is at the core of your Exchange Server organization; all Exchange Server data is located and serviced via this Exchange server role. When the Exchange Mailbox server role is not functioning correctly, this will cause a fast-moving ripple effect through your organization that will affect more and more users. Tools such as the `Test-MapiConnectivity` cmdlet can help you determine whether a mailbox can be reached.

As companies look to find ways to keep their Exchange Server infrastructure up and running as much as possible, the Exchange Server 2016 database availability group high-availability feature is becoming increasingly prevalent in small businesses. The `Test-ReplicationHealth` and `Get-MailboxCopyStatus` cmdlets can help test the health of the DAG replication.

Master It   A user named Zoe is reporting that she cannot use Outlook to access her mailbox, yet she can access it via Outlook on the web. What tool could you use to determine whether the mailbox is accessible via Outlook?

Troubleshoot mail transport problems.   The Exchange Server 2016 Mailbox role plays the all-important part of delivering all messages that are processed via the Exchange Server 2016 infrastructure. This is true even if a message is sent from one user to another on the same mailbox database, and the transport services are invoked to act in delivering the message.

A number of useful tools are available to help you and your users determine where a problem may exist. These include the Exchange Server 2016 Queue Viewer, the `Test-MailFlow` cmdlet, and message tracking.

Master It   A user is reporting that they are sending email but that the recipient is never getting the message. The user is convinced your server is not delivering the message. You would like the user to determine whether the message is leaving your organization. What would you advise the user to do?

## Chapter 25

Backing Up and Restoring Exchange Server

Exchange Server 2013 and Exchange Server 2016 expand on the framework introduced in the previous versions for protecting and recovering server data. Refinements to the product's architecture in the areas of message transport, client access, and database availability groups continue to drive Exchange Server's resiliency to new levels. However, there are still situations where a hardware failure, human error, or even a natural disaster can require manual intervention to restore data and return the system to normal service conditions. Fortunately, Exchange Server 2016 offers the ability to back up and restore data directly from Windows Server Backup in Windows Server 2012 R2 and Windows Server 2012.

IN THIS CHAPTER, YOU WILL LEARN TO:

- ◆ Back up Exchange Server

- ◆ Prepare to recover the Exchange server

- ◆ Use Windows Server Backup to back up the server

- ◆ Use Windows Server Backup to recover the data

- ◆ Recover Exchange Server data using alternative methods

- ◆ Recover an entire Exchange server

Backing Up Exchange Server

Exchange Server gives your organization the ability to store very large amounts of data. In most cases, this data is considered mission-critical. Your users potentially send and receive hundreds of emails per day. Over time, this amount of email adds up. In some cases, the only copy of an email or company data will be in the end user's mailbox.

Before you can successfully perform any backups, you must define your backup strategy. Your organization's requirements will drive the strategy you need to deploy. Deploying a backup strategy without considering recovery scenarios or backup requirements will set you up for failure. Knowing the backup requirements will also help you define the correct tool for the job.

You must know why you are backing up the data. Once you understand this, you will be able to define your goals and requirements. By establishing your goals and requirements, you will also have gathered the necessary information for the backup schedule.

With Exchange Server 2016, Volume Shadow Copy Service (VSS) backups are the only option for performing backups. VSS technology allows you to take manual or automatic backup copies or snapshots of data, even if it has a lock, on a specific volume at a specific point in time over regular intervals. Make sure that your backup solution is certified to perform Exchange Server 2016 VSS backups.

In order to meet a company's business requirements for data recovery in the event of any type of failure, backup strategies should be well planned. Once the backup strategies and procedures are defined, performing the backup is not a difficult job. Restore procedures should be documented well and tested on a regular basis so that data restoration is performed correctly. Planning, documenting, and testing the restoration procedures helps a lot, keeping in mind how much pressure company employees and management put on administrators or backup operators during the restoration process—everyone wants their email data back, and nobody wants to wait for the restoration process to complete. Various VSS backup solutions are available for Exchange Server—including hardware-based VSS providers on a storage area network (SAN) and software-based VSS provider solutions. This chapter will focus on the solutions that Exchange Server provides out of the box.

IMPORTANT VSS-BACKUP TERMINOLOGY

The following are some VSS backup–related terms you'll see in this chapter:

Requestor   The application that requests the creation of a shadow copy. This is typically the backup application itself. Windows Server Backup, Microsoft System Center Data Protection Manager, and many third-party backup applications have built-in VSS requestors.

Provider   The interface that provides the functionality to make the shadow copy. Windows Server includes a VSS provider.

Writer   Application-specific software that acts to ensure that application data is ready for shadow copy creation and is consistent upon backup completion.

Having functional backups is an extremely important part of the IT administrator's job. The first reason to keep a functional backup is for data recovery; the second (and sometimes forgotten) reason for backups is to provide transaction-log truncation. Exchange Server has always protected itself in case the system was unable to be backed up. As you know, when the transaction log location fills up, the mailbox database dismounts. So, if you were unable to back up your server for several days, you risked having the server taken offline and, therefore, answering to the end users.

Windows Server 2012 R2 and Windows Server 2012 have kept up with the ever-changing backup technology by providing a plug-in that gives you the ability to make VSS backups of the Exchange Server data. VSS has enabled servers to be backed up in a fraction of the time of traditional tapes. What used to take hours now takes minutes.

When Windows Server backs up Exchange Server data, it also performs checks against that data. These checks make sure the files that have been backed up are in good shape and prepared for any recovery efforts. Once the snapshot has been taken of the Exchange Server data, verification is run against the data. If there are any issues with the snapshot, you will receive errors and be able to work on the data to figure out where the problem is. Once the issue has been located, you can make adjustments.

Determining Your Strategy

In the past, there were several reasons why you needed to back up your databases. Some of the popular reasons were as follows:

◆ Single-message recovery

◆ Mailbox recovery

◆ Database recovery

◆ Entire-server recovery

Just as there are times when you will want to perform backups, there also will be times when you may not need to restore a server database. For example, if you are utilizing database availability groups (DAGs) and the disk where the mailbox database was located failed, you may not need to restore the mailbox database from your backup. Instead, you may choose to replace the failed disk with a new one and then reseed a database copy on the new disk.

PRACTICING DATA RECOVERY

You are probably familiar with many scenarios in which you need to recover Exchange Server data. When such a scenario arises, you must know how to handle it. Some will be simple to handle, such as a deleted mailbox or deleted messages, while others will be more complicated and time-consuming, such as server or site recovery.

Regardless of the scenario, you need to have a well-documented recovery plan. Practicing recovery is just as important as having the recovery plan. We know that practicing is about as much fun as having your teeth pulled, but the wrong time to figure out how to perform the recovery is when the recovery becomes necessary. When you are in the middle of a disaster, you don't have time to stumble through figuring it out.

Think of the practice as insurance. You put a lot of money in your insurance in the hope that you will not need it. But when you need it, you are glad you have it. Don't get caught without insurance in your organization.

ESTABLISHING YOUR RECOVERABILITY GOALS

Once you understand why you want to perform backups, you can determine the goals for data recovery. Think about how you are maintaining your backups, how long you are keeping the backups, and how quickly you need to restore the data. These scenarios will help you determine what your backup architecture should look like. One example is to keep one copy of your backups onsite (in addition to storing them offsite) to meet your Recovery Time Objective (RTO).

Each scenario could have different recovery objectives. Table 25.1 shows how recoverability goals can differ based on the scenario.

TABLE 25.1:   Sample Scenarios with Recovery Goals

SCENARIO	DATA RETENTION GOAL	DATA RESTORATION GOAL
Corrupted database	Restored database must not be older than 1 day.	Must have empty mailboxes with basic send and receive capabilities up within 1 hour, and the database must be restored within 8 hours.
Mailbox deletion	Restored data must be less than 30 days old.	Mailbox must be restored within 1 hour.
Recover a message that was deleted more than 30 days ago	Must be able to restore messages for up to 60 days.	Message must be restored within 1 business day.

The key is to determine the minimum and maximum lengths of time that backed-up data must be kept and to select a backup methodology that allows you to restore the data within your target restoration goal.

SETTING A BACKUP SCHEDULE

Knowing what you are backing up is just as important as the other factors. To determine your backup schedule, you must know how much data you are going to back up and what the backup rate is for your specific environment. Look at the databases you are backing up, where you will place the data once it is backed up, and how the data will get there. All of these concerns factor into the design of your backup window. Once you put numbers to this information, you can do the simple math to figure out your backup window. Not only will you be able to determine your window, but you will also understand what your backup schedule will look like.

Your backup schedule will take into account the backup strategy you have identified, the recoverability goals, and the organizational requirements for the backups. You may also hear terms like Recovery Point Object (RPO) and Recovery Time Objective (RTO).

The RPO is the maximum acceptable amount of data loss after an unscheduled outage, defined as a measurement of time. This is generally the point in time before the event at which the data could be successfully recovered. The RPO varies from organization to organization. Some businesses might only need a backup since the most recent close of business, while other businesses may require a backup from the point of failure.

The RTO is the maximum acceptable length of time that Exchange Server can be down after a failure or disaster. It is a function of the extent to which the interruption disrupts normal operations. The RTO is measured in seconds, minutes, hours, or days and is an important consideration in disaster-recovery planning. Next, you need to determine a schedule that will map to your requirements.

If you have to back up 2.5 TB of Exchange Server data and you can back up and restore 500 GB per hour, then you are looking at 5 hours for the process to complete. (These numbers are completely random and are just used as examples.) If you need to restore your data in 4 hours, you are not going to make it. In this case, you would have to decrease the amount of Exchange Server data. You can do that by adjusting the settings for deleted-item retention or adding another Exchange server to the environment. By adding an additional server, you will be able to move some of the mailboxes, level out the amount of data per server, and fit your backup into your backup window.

Let's look at the example from Table 25.1. You see that the restored databases must be less than one day old, which tells you that the Exchange Server databases must be backed up daily. You also will note that you should be able to recover messages for a maximum of 60 days, which tells you that you must keep the database backups for 60 days. That means that no matter what solution you decide to implement, you must have enough tapes or disk space to hold the 60 backups that you will be keeping.

Alternatively, you could enable a feature that we will discuss more in this chapter—single-item recovery. However, enabling this for all mailboxes has the potential to increase the amount of disk space consumed by each mailbox, so that needs to be factored in as well. There may be more than one way to achieve an objective, and each solution may offer different advantages and disadvantages. It is important to explore all of your options to determine which solution is right for your organization.

Keep in mind that database backups should not be the primary recovery mechanism. The recommended solution would be to implement database copies. Having multiple copies online is much quicker to implement. You also don't have to worry about corruption during a restore of the database(s).

Backup Alternatives with Exchange Server

So far we have talked about the need for a successful backup of your data. Now let's look at another possibility. With Exchange Server 2010, Microsoft introduced an alternative to the standard backup methodology. Think about an environment in which you don't perform backups and you don't have to store backups. Microsoft chose this solution, known as Native Data Protection (NDP), for their internal deployment of Exchange Server 2010 and continues to use it within the Exchange Server 2013 and Exchange Server 2016–based Office 365 Exchange Online service. NDP works by relying on multiple technologies—such as log shipping and data replication, single item recovery, mailbox deletion, and deleted item retention—to ensure that multiple copies of every database exist to provide redundancy within the datacenter and between datacenters. If ever there is a failure, causing an active database copy to become unavailable, another copy is activated automatically. By doing this, Microsoft has been able to minimize backup and maintenance costs.

This may be a lifestyle change for most IT shops. Imagine the conversation you will have with the CIO when you tell him that you are not going to back up his Exchange Server mailbox. Naturally, this will not be the most welcoming topic. We have all run across situations that we wanted to change but can't because things have always been done a certain way. Backups are just the next topic in that conversation. Even after you have had the discussion, you still may not be the most popular person in the room. As you know, Exchange Server 2016 brings technical capabilities that will help fill in the gap. Here are some of the most common issues and their solutions:

Individual Message Recovery Within Retention Time   By default, Exchange Server is set to keep deleted items for 14 days. This *deleted-item retention policy* is an adjustable setting that can be specified based on the organization's requirements.

Individual Message Recovery After Retention Time Expires   No more need for a third-party solution. Exchange Server gives you the ability to recover an individual item—just enable and configure. This is known as *single-item recovery*.

Logical Corruption on Mailbox Database   If you know when the logical corruption occurred, you can use the transaction log replay lag on the DAG to recover the database minus the log that caused the corruption in the original database. This is known as using a *lagged mailbox database copy*.

Mailbox Recovery   By default, Exchange Server is set to keep deleted mailboxes for 30 days. This *deleted-mailbox retention policy* is an adjustable setting that can be specified based on the organization requirements.

Hard-Drive Failure   Multiple copies of the database placed in the DAG help protect against drive failures.

Complete Server Failure   Because no single server can host more than one copy of a given database, distributing the database copies across multiple servers in a DAG replicates data and provides redundancy for the server.

Site Failure   Stretch the DAG across to a remote datacenter instead of performing offsite backups.

Microsoft recommends that you have a minimum of three non-lagged copies in your DAG before you implement this backup alternative. Non-lagged database copies may be located on RAID-less, JBOD disks. However, a lagged database copy should be placed on a RAID array because in the event of a logical corruption, the lagged copy will be the only healthy database copy in the DAG. How many times have you been told not to use circular logging unless you are performing a migration or are in a situation where recovery is not a high priority? Well, here is one of those situations. Since you are not performing a standard backup, you will not allow Exchange Server to truncate the logs. Because of this, circular logging is a must. If you don't enable circular logging, you will most certainly fill up the transaction logs and bring down the databases.

Native data protection uses a kind of circular logging. Unlike traditional circular logging on stand-alone databases, which is controlled by the Microsoft Exchange Information Store service, circular logging on mailbox database copies is controlled by the Microsoft Exchange Replication service. The two services communicate and work together to ensure that a given log file has been successfully replicated and replayed into all copies of the database, and is no longer needed, before it is discarded and reused. This form of circular logging is referred to as continuous-replication circular logging.

For more information on the Microsoft preferred architecture for Exchange Server 2016, visit following link: https://blogs.technet.microsoft.com/exchange/2015/10/12 /the-exchange-2016-preferred-architecture/.

Preparing to Back Up and Recover the Exchange Server

Preparing the server and the environment is the first step to making sure that you are able to recover the server in case the worst happens. It is also one of the easiest things you will do. Making sure that you have protected your servers and have a documented recovery plan will help you when the need arises for a recovery. It is not a matter of *if* you will need it but *when* you will need it.

Before you can perform a supported backup of your Exchange servers, you must prepare the operating system. Windows Server 2012 R2 and Windows Server 2012 come with the features to back up Exchange Server, filesystems, and other applications. These features are not installed during the normal setup of the server; you must manually install them. You can perform the installation from within Windows PowerShell or from Server Manager. The easiest way to do this is to open Windows PowerShell and type the following two commands:

```
Import-Module ServerManager
Add-WindowsFeature Windows-Server-Backup
```

When the command has completed, you should receive the following:

```
Success Restart Needed Exit Code Feature Result
------- -------------- --------- --------------
True    No             Success   {Windows Server Backup}
```

Your server is now configured to allow you to back up your Exchange Server data.

Using Windows Server Backup to Back Up the Exchange Server

To back up the Exchange server from within Windows, you don't just hit a few buttons and walk away. You need to select the correct settings for the backup to work, so that it can be restored and so that it's supported by Microsoft.

Since you have chosen to use the Windows 2012 R2 or Windows Server 2012 to perform the backups for your Exchange Server environment, we need to look at what the requirements are and what will make your backups and restores successful. Before you start configuring your backups, let's see what is required before and during the backup process.

All backups must be performed on the Windows Server 2012 R2 or Windows Server 2012 servers locally. You are not able to back up a remote server. For example, you are not able to install the backup features on a Windows 2012 domain controller named DC01 and then back up the Exchange Server mailbox server named EX-MBX01. In this scenario, the backup must be run from the server EX-MBX01.

Your account must also be delegated rights to either the local Backup Operators group or the local Administrator group. You cannot pick and choose the information you want to back up.

Your only option is to back up an entire volume. All of the Exchange Server data must be on the same dataset so you can restore the Exchange Server data.

You can either run a onetime backup or use the Task Scheduler to perform a recurring backup. Your backup strategy will help you determine which is best for your environment. Either way, the same basic information is needed. Remember, to truncate the transaction logs you must perform a full backup.

Most of the Exchange servers in your organization will have multiple databases. One thing to keep in mind is that if your databases are located on the same logical drive, you cannot restore a single database by using the Windows Server backups. All databases in the backup set will be restored. Keep this in mind because you will need enough space to perform the restorations, and you don't want to be fooled into believing that you can piece a restoration together. On the other side, Microsoft recommends that you locate multiple databases on the same logical drive for better performance, easier management, and faster reseed times. If you decide to follow Microsoft best practices and recommendations for database locations, it will be much more effi-cient when you perform the backup by using another product, such as Microsoft System Center Data Protection Manager or a third-party backup solution that is supported for Exchange Server 2016. Keep in mind that you cannot necessarily back up Exchange Server 2016 with the same backup software that you used to back up Exchange Server 2010 or Exchange Server 2013. One exception to this statement is Windows Server Backup, which is included in Windows Server 2012 R2 and Windows Server 2012.

Exchange Server provides the option to back up a passive copy of the database(s). However, this option is not available to you if you are using the Windows Server 2012 R2 and Windows Server 2012 backup features. Since the Windows Server Backup VSS requestor is communicat-ing with the Exchange Server 2016 VSS writer, the system knows if the database is not the active copy. You are only able to perform backups on the active copy of the database.

Backup copies of the Exchange Server database can be stored either locally on the server or on a separate storage device. You can use drive letters or a UNC path as the destination for the backup. You will have the opportunity to specify the location as you move through the Backup Wizard.

Performing the Backup

As you know, you can perform a onetime backup or schedule the backups. We are going to look at everything involved with both options and then perform the backups.

VERIFYING THAT THE BACKUP FEATURES ARE INSTALLED

Make sure that you have installed the backup features on the server. You can run a command from within Windows PowerShell to verify. The following command will give you the informa-tion. (Just because you see the application icon for Windows Server Backup does not mean that you have installed the feature.)

```
Get-WindowsFeature
```

After this command runs, you will see a long list of features and roles for the server. The items with an empty set of brackets [ ] beside them have not been installed; the items with [X] beside them have been installed. Look for the line that pertains to Windows Server Backup and confirm that it has the [X], indicating that the feature is installed.

If you are not a fan of PowerShell, you can follow these steps:

1. From the taskbar, click Server Manager.

2. Choose Tools.

3. Select Windows Server Backup.

4. If you have already installed the Windows Server Backup feature, you will see the window shown in Figure 25.1, and you are all set to continue. If you have not installed the Windows Server Backup feature, you'll receive the message "Windows Server Backup is not installed on this computer," and you'll need to install it before you move on.

FIGURE 25.1

Windows Server Backup has been installed

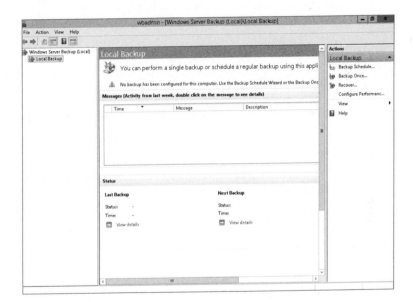

ONETIME BACKUP

With Windows Server Backup installed, it is time to perform the onetime backup of the data volume.

1. From the taskbar, select Server Manager ➤ Tools ➤ Windows Server Backup.

2. In the Actions pane, click Backup Once. The Backup Once Wizard appears.

3. On the Backup Options screen, select Different Options and click Next.

4. On the Select Backup Configuration screen, select Custom (so that you can select only the volumes that contain the Exchange Server data) and click Next.

5. On the Select Backup Items screen, click Add Items.

This screen lets you decide which volumes to back up. Make sure you have selected the correct volumes for the location of the Exchange Server data, and click OK.

6. Click Advanced Settings. On the VSS Settings tab, select the VSS Full Backup radio button and click OK. Remember, only a full backup will truncate the logs if you are backing up a stand-alone database without circular logging enabled. Click Next.

7. On the Specify Destination Type screen, select the proper location for your backup. For this scenario, we are backing up to a local drive. Click Next.

8. On the Select Backup Destination screen, select the correct location from the Backup Destination drop-down list and click Next.

9. At the Confirmation screen, select Backup.

AUTOMATED BACKUPS

If you are going to be using the Windows Server 2012 R2 or Windows Server 2012 backup mechanism, you can automate the process. Follow these steps:

1. On the taskbar, select Server Manager ➤ Tools ➤ Windows Server Backup.

2. In the Actions pane, click Backup Schedule. The Backup Schedule Wizard appears. Click Next.

3. On the Select Backup Configuration screen, select Custom (so that you can select only the volumes that contain the Exchange Server data) and click Next.

4. On the Select Items For Backup screen, click Add Items and select the volumes containing the Exchange Server databases and transaction logs that you want to back up. Click OK.

5. Select Advanced Settings ➤ VSS Settings, and click VSS Full Backup. Click OK, and then click Next.

6. On the Specify Backup Time screen, select Once A Day, specify the time that you want to perform the backup, and click Next.

7. On the Select Backup Destination Type screen, select the appropriate radio button to choose where you want to store your backups. It is recommended to use a hard disk that is dedicated to only storing backups. Click Next.

8. On the Select Destination Disk screen, click Show All Available Disks.

9. Place a check mark in the box beside the drive you are backing up to, and then click OK (see Figure 25.2).

10. You are now back to the Select Destination Disk screen. Notice that the Next button is unavailable; that's because you must place a check mark in the box beside the volume that you will be using, just as you did in the previous step.

    Place a check mark in the box, and click Next.

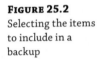

FIGURE 25.2
Selecting the items
to include in a
backup

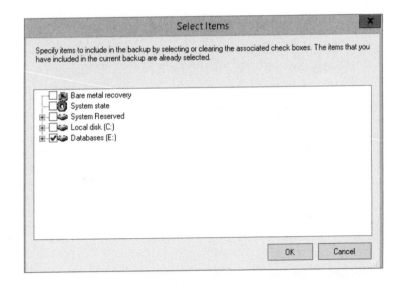

11. You will see a warning dialog reminding you that Windows Server Backup will be formatting the disk. Click Yes after verifying there is no data on the volume you will be using.

12. Click Finish on the Confirmation screen.

13. Once the processing has completed, the Summary screen appears; click Close.

Your server is now backing up your Exchange Server data. At this point you can use the onetime method or the recurring method. Windows Server Backup will allow you to write to internal or external disks. You can also have a mixture of disks. You may choose to have your daily backups sent to an external storage device, while the onetime backups are backed up to a local disk for quick and easy recovery. Just make sure you have enough space on the destination drive, no matter where you write the backup.

The length of time the backup will take depends on several factors, such as the size of the Exchange Server databases and transaction logs that are being backed up. Another factor is the location of the data being copied and the location to which it is being written. If you choose to back up to a remote location, you need to think about the network bandwidth and latency from the server and the storage. Different types of storage make a difference as well. If you are using a SAN, your server may have a 4 Gbps connection to the storage. If you are using an iSCSI device, you may have only a 1 Gbps connection to the network and then to the storage. No matter what storage you are writing to, consider the type and speed of the drives that are writing the data. As you know, there is a big difference in performance between 15 K RPM drives in a SAN compared to 7,200 RPM SATA drives.

Using Windows Server Backup to Recover the Data

Now that you have backed up your Exchange Server data, let's restore that data. There are several ways to recover the data for the users and the organization.

USERS CAN RECOVER EMAIL

Although the ability has been around for several generations of Exchange Server, many users don't realize they can recover their own email. The easiest way for users to recover deleted email is to use the Recover Deleted Items option in Outlook or Outlook on the web. We know this seems simple, but don't let that fool you. Educating the help desk and, in turn, the end users will go a long way. Once you train users to recover their own messages within the allotted time, you will hopefully decrease the number of calls you get.

Recovering the Database

Just because you backed up the entire volume during the backup sequence does not mean you need to restore the entire volume to recover your Exchange Server data. You have the ability to recover only the Exchange Server application data. At this point, you also have the opportunity to decide where you want the data restored. Do you want it restored to its original location or to an alternative location?

One of the key things to remember is that you cannot pick and choose the database(s) you want to recover. When you use Windows Server Backup to restore the database, all the databases in the backup set will be restored. Think about this before you give the command to restore the backup and overwrite all your data when you only needed a portion of the data.

RECOVERING TO THE ORIGINAL LOCATION

By restoring the data to the same location, you are recovering the data and overwriting the current Exchange Server data. You might need to do this in case of database corruption. However, restoring the data to the same location is only needed in organizations that have only one Exchange server or if a database that needs to be restored doesn't have other copies on the DAG members. Databases that have multiple copies in the DAG may be restored by the reseeding process from a healthy database copy. If you have only one copy of the database, you should restore the data to the original location only if you truly don't need the existing data. If you overwrite the data, you will not be able to recover it. Since it is the only copy of your database, it is recommended that you perform an offline backup on the corrupted database before you replace it with the backup, in case you need to retrieve data from it later. When you are restoring to the original location, you can leave the database in a *dirty shutdown*. The recovery will perform the proper steps to get the database healthy. There are occasions where the database cannot be cleaned up without help. You can either perform more in-depth troubleshooting and maintenance with the eseutil.exe command, or you can pick a different backup to restore. You can make that call as you move through your restoration.

To restore from a specific volume, follow these steps:

In Exchange Amin Center:

1. On the left Navigation pane, click servers, and on the tabs, click databases.

2. Select the database you want to restore and then click the Edit button.

3. In the Mailbox database window, on the left Navigation pane, click Maintenance; and in the Details pane, click "This database can be overwritten by a restore."

In Window Server Backup:

1. Open Windows Server Backup.

2. In the Actions pane on the right, select Recover.

3. On the Getting Started screen, select This Server (*ServerName*) and then click Next.

4. On the Select Backup Date screen, select the date from which you want to restore data. If there are multiple backups for that date, select the time of the backup that you want to use. Click Next when you have selected the backup date and time you want.

5. On the Select Recovery Type screen, select Applications and then click Next.

6. On the Select Application screen, make sure Exchange is highlighted and click Next (see Figure 25.3).

   By default, if you are recovering the last backup, Exchange Server will replay the log files for the backup. You must tell the backup application if you do not want to perform the log replay; select the "Do not perform a roll-forward recovery of the application databases" check box.

7. On the Specify Recovery Options screen, the option Recover To Original Location should be selected; if it's not, select it and click Next.

8. The Confirmation screen gives you a recap of the recovery you are getting ready to perform. Click Recover.

9. Once the recovery is complete, click Close.

The recovery application will now start performing the recovery. You will be able to see the status throughout the recovery. When you have restored the Exchange Server database and logs, log into the account and look at the contents. You should see the information that was there before the backup. If there is any discrepancy, check the event log for any errors and then run the complete test again. If you kept the default settings and let the recovery play the transaction logs, your Exchange server will be restored and up to date.

FIGURE 25.3
Selecting the application to recover

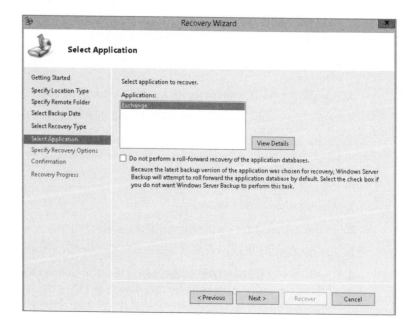

RECOVERING TO AN ALTERNATIVE LOCATION

When you recover to an alternative location, you can extract data from the restored data. Before you can perform any work on the restored database, you need to put it in a clean state. You will use the eseutil.exe command to accomplish this task.

1. Perform steps 1 through 6 from the procedure in the "Recovering to the Original Location" section.

2. On the Specify Recovery Options screen, select the option Recover To Another Location. Click Browse and browse to the location where you want to place the recovered files; click Next.

3. The Confirmation screen gives you a recap of the recovery you are about to perform. Click Recover.

4. Once the recovery is complete, click Close.

5. Open a command prompt and change the working directory to the location of the restore.

6. Run the eseutil.exe command against the database with the base name (also known as log prefix) of the database.

   The base name is the first three characters of the log files for the restored database. If your log file is named E0500000004.log, your base name will be E05. Your command will look like this:

   ```
   Eseutil /r BaseName /L<path to logs>.
   ```

You may receive the following error message:

```
Operation terminated with error -1216 (JET_errAttachedDatabaseMismatch.
An outstanding database attachment has been detected at the start or end
of recovery, but database is missing or does not match attachment info)
after xx seconds.
```

If you receive this message, run the command with the /i switch so that it will ignore any inconsistencies in the database:

```
Eseutil.exe /r E05 /i
```

7. Now your database should be in a consistent state. You can redirect the original database and use the restored database. Run the Move-DatabasePath cmdlet from the Exchange Management Shell. You will also need to use the ConfigurationOnly parameter. Your command should look like this:

```
Move-DatabasePath -Identity DB05 -EdbFilePath
C:\RestoredExchange\DB05.edb
-LogFolderPath C:\RestoredExchange -ConfigurationOnly
```

Your Exchange Server database is not ready yet because you must mount the database. You can mount the database via EMS or EAC; but before you do, be sure to designate the database as eligible for being overwritten by a restore. Otherwise, you will receive an error when you attempt to mount the database.

8. To designate the database as eligible to be overwritten by a restore, run the following command:

```
Set-MailboxDatabase -Identity DB05 -AllowFileRestore $true
```

9. After you have successfully mounted the database, be sure to revert this setting by running the following:

```
Set-MailboxDatabase -Identity DB05 -AllowFileRestore $false
```

USING BACKUPS FOR TESTING

You can test your backup by performing a recovery of the data to an alternative location. You use real Exchange Server data for testing. You may be testing mailbox recovery or single-item recovery scenarios.

Restoring to an alternative location gives you a perfect situation to test the recovery to verify that all the data is accessible. A successful backup does not mean that the successful recovery will give you good, usable data. By restoring the database(s) to an alternative location, you can run through a number of recovery options to verify that the data is there and that your staff is well equipped to handle restores when the pressure is on. By running through the recovery process when times are good, you and your staff will become familiar with the recovery steps and options needed to restore any of the server roles, configuration, and data. This will help you notice something that may be out of the ordinary if you are performing the emergency restoration.

Recover Exchange Server Data Using Alternative Methods

An Exchange Server administrator could find himself in a recovery situation where the restoration of a production database may not be desirable. Perhaps a user or administrator error has led to a situation that only impacts a single user. Or, as the Exchange Server product evolves and we start to see solutions designed with much larger databases and the use of NDP, administrators may need to rely on other methods besides database restoration for their data recovery needs.

Working with Disconnected Mailboxes

A mailbox becomes disconnected when it is no longer associated with an account in Active Directory. By default, all of the disconnected mailboxes are kept for 30 days before they are purged from the system. During this time, the disconnected mailbox can be reconnected to a valid Active Directory account by using the `Connect-Mailbox` cmdlet or the Connect Mailbox Wizard from the EAC. This allows you to clean up from an accidental user deletion. Since the disconnected mailbox is not associated with any Active Directory account, you must have a way to identify the mailbox. There are three ways to do so:

- Display name of the mailbox
- Legacy distinguished name (LegacyDN)
- Globally unique identifier (GUID)

The following command shows you the list of disconnected mailboxes. You can see that we have also included a date command. This should help narrow your search for the specific mailbox.

```
Get-MailboxStatistics -Server CONTOSO-EX01 | where
{$_.DisconnectDate -ne $null} | fl DisplayName, MailboxGUID, LegacyDN,
DisconnectDate
```

 Real World Scenario

MISSING DISCONNECTED MAILBOXES

Exchange Server administrators are sometimes surprised when a mailbox that was recently disabled in EAC is not immediately reflected as disconnected within the Exchange Information Store. This could occur for a number of reasons, such as a delay in Active Directory replication or possibly the database where the mailbox was homed was dismounted at the time the user was disabled. That was the case for an organization that recently had an urgent need to reconnect a high-profile mailbox that had been mistakenly disabled. However, the disconnected mailbox was not showing up in the EAC or when running the `Get-MailboxStatistics` command discussed previously. The company's Exchange Server administrator tried to run the `Clean-MailboxDatabase` cmdlet but discovered it is no longer available in Exchange Server 2016. A quick explanation of the `Update-StoreMailboxState` cmdlet and how it can be used in Exchange Server 2016 to synchronize the mailbox state between Active Directory and the Exchange Information Store soon put the customer back on track, and they were then able to see the disconnected mailbox and reconnect it.

Once you have the mailbox identifier, you can reconnect the mailbox to an account with the following command:

```
Connect-Mailbox MailboxID -Database DatabaseName -User UserToConnectTo
  -Alias MailboxAlias
```

At any time, you have the ability to permanently delete the disconnected mailbox. The Remove-Mailbox cmdlet from the EMS will delete the mailbox. You must set the Permanent parameter to $True when you use this command.

By using the StoreMailboxIdentity parameter with the Remove-Mailbox cmdlet, you can permanently delete the data within the mailbox database of a disconnected mailbox. Use the Get-MailboxStatistics cmdlet with the StoreMailboxIdentity parameter to determine the values you need to supply for this cmdlet.

You can also adjust the number of days that you must keep the mailboxes. This setting will affect all the mailboxes in the database. However, it will affect only the database that is specified in the cmdlet. To change the retention time to 60 days, you would run this command:

```
Set-MailboxDatabase DB05 -MailboxRetention 60.00:00:00
```

You can also configure this setting using the EAC:

1. Select Servers from the Feature pane.

2. Click the Databases tab.

3. Select the database you want to adjust, and click the pencil icon from the toolbar to modify the database's properties.

4. In the Database Properties dialog, select Limits.

5. In the Keep Deleted Mailboxes For (Days) field, enter the number of days that you want to keep deleted mailboxes.

6. Click Save to save the changes and close the Properties dialog.

Using a Recovery Database

You may already be familiar with what was the Recovery Storage Group feature in earlier versions of Exchange Server, which became known as the recovery database in Exchange Server 2010. The basic concept is the same in Exchange Server 2013 and in Exchange Server 2016 in that you can mount a database and extract data from it. The recovery database allows you to mount a restored database and extract mailbox data from it via the New-MailboxRestoreRequest cmdlet. After the data has been removed, it can be exported or merged into an existing mailbox.

You can restore an existing database to a recovery database in one of two ways. If you already have a recovery database, Exchange Server can dismount the active database, restore it on the recovery database and log files, and then mount the database. You can also restore the database to an alternative location. Once Exchange Server has brought the database up to date, you can configure the recovery database to point to the recovered database.

Either method allows you to mount the database and perform a recovery and extraction of the target data. You can use databases only from Exchange Server 2016, not from previous versions of Exchange Server. If you need to extract data from previous versions of Exchange Server, you will have to use the recovery database on an Exchange Server 2010 server or Exchange

Server 2013. The target mailbox you will be using must be located in the same Active Directory forest as the database that will be mounted in the recovery database.

When you use the recovery database, the folder access control lists are not preserved. Due to the nature of the recovery database, there is no need to preserve any access control list information.

MAILBOX AND RECOVERY DATABASE DIFFERENCES

The recovery database is not the same as the standard mailbox database; here are the differences:

♦ Recovery databases are created in the EMS.

♦ Mail cannot be sent or received from a mailbox in the recovery database.

♦ The recovery database cannot be used to insert information into the Exchange Server environment.

♦ No client access is available to the recovery database through any protocols.

♦ No system or mailbox policy settings are applied.

♦ A single recovery database can be mounted at a time and does not count against the limit of 5 databases in Exchange Standard Edition or the limit of 100 databases in Exchange Enterprise Edition.

♦ You cannot perform a backup against the recovery database.

♦ Any mailboxes that are in the recovery database are not connected to the original mailboxes in any way.

There are several situations where a recovery database would be the proper selection for the restore:

♦ Dial-tone recovery (same server)

♦ Dial-tone recovery (alternative server)

♦ Mailbox recovery

♦ Individual item recovery

There are instances when a recovery database should not be used. If you have to rebuild your Active Directory topology, thereby restoring multiple Exchange Server databases, or you need to restore the entire server, you would not choose to use a recovery database.

WHAT IS A DIAL TONE RECOVERY?

A *dial tone recovery* refers to providing users with basic send and receive capabilities from their mailbox soon after an outage has occurred. Depending on the specifics of the environment and the outage, performing a full restore of the mailbox database(s) from tape can be a very time-consuming process, lasting hours or even days. This is especially true if the database size(s) is hundreds of gigabytes or even terabytes. Rather than having users remain completely nonoperational for that period of time, an alternative is to create brand-new empty mailbox database and "move" the users to it by using the `Set-Mailbox` cmdlet with the `-Database` parameter.

Although the users will not have access to any historical data from prior to the outage, they can at least send and receive new messages. Once the original database is restored, it can be swapped with the dial tone database, and any changes made to the mailbox during the outage can be exported from the dial tone database and imported back into the restored database.

Recovering Single Messages

Exchange Server 2016 uses Dumpster 2.0 to handle the messages throughout the various phases of the deletion process. When a user removes an email item using the Recover Deleted Items feature, it is moved to a Purges folder that lives in the Recoverable Items folder. This feature is available only if single-item recovery has been enabled, because single-item recovery is disabled by default. Neither the Purges folder nor the messages within the folder can be seen by the end user. Any administrators who have been delegated the right to perform discovery searches can search the Purges folder and recover the email item for the end user. By doing this, your standard administration staff can help the end user without needing the permission to restore and mount the user's database. Because the database does not need to be restored, the process is much easier.

The only individuals who can perform discovery searches are those who have been granted the Discovery Management RBAC role.

Here is a breakdown of what happens to an email message:

1. The email is delivered to the user's Inbox, where it remains unless it is moved to another folder by the user or a mailbox rule.

2. The user deletes the email.

3. The email is moved from the Deleted Items folder to the Deletions folder in Dumpster 2.0 automatically.

4. The email is purged by the user and moved to the Purges folder in Dumpster 2.0, where the user can no longer access it, but it is still accessible to the administrator.

5. The Versions folder is used to preserve items that are modified prior to their expiration by performing a copy-on-write.

6. If no action is taken to recover the email within the defined deleted-item retention windows (14 days by default), then it is permanently removed from the Exchange Server database.

All items in the Recoverable Items folder will be indexed and can be searched using the discovery cmdlets. The Recoverable Items folder is located in the NON_IPM_Subtree of the user's mailbox, which means that if the mailbox is moved, the dumpster moves with it. Prior to Dumpster 2.0, a mailbox move meant that the user would lose access to items that had been deleted from the mailbox. There are three subfolders in the Recoverable Items folder:

Deletions All soft-deleted items from the Deleted Items folder within the mailbox end up here. The user can see these items when they access the Recover Deleted Items feature in Outlook or Outlook on the web.

Versions The original item and any modifications of the item are placed here, when either a litigation hold (covered in Chapter 18, "Managing Archiving and Compliance") or single-item recovery is enabled. This folder is not visible to the end user.

Purges All hard-deleted items end up here, when either legal hold or single-item recovery is enabled. This folder is not visible to the end user.

Recoverable items are not counted against the user's quota. These messages are instead counted against the recoverable items size limits. There is a 20 GB soft limit for the recoverable items. At the 20 GB point, administrators are notified of the size by an event in the event log and by an Operations Manager alert if Operations Manager is deployed in the environment. The alert fires as soon as the 20 GB limit is reached and once a day until it has been addressed. There is a hard limit of 30 GB on the recoverable items. You can run two EMS commands to set the warning level and the quota sizes:

```
Set-Mailbox -Identity MailboxName -RecoverableItemsWarningQuota 12GB
Set-Mailbox -Identity MailboxName -RecoverableItemsQuota 15GB
```

Earlier, we said email is removed from Exchange Server at the 14-day mark. This is the default setting for Exchange Server. If you have installed Exchange Server 2016 and have not made any changes, then your system is set up for the 14 days. You can change the amount of time that the messages will stay in the dumpster before they are removed. There are good and bad points to making this change. If you make the change to keep the messages for 30 days, you can recover a user's mail for the extra 16 days; that is the good part. The not-so-good part is that now you have increased your storage requirements. Depending on the size of your organization and the amount of email that is sent and received, this may not be a huge problem. But if you have a large organization and your users send and receive a lot of email, this may end up being a large problem. Each organization is different—just be sure that before you make a change to the default settings you fully understand the impact on the environment.

Another thing to consider is the number of times that you have to perform these single-item restores of messages that are older than the default settings. If you find that your organization is not performing this type of restore often or that the data is within the 14 days, then there is no reason to change the defaults. This information will help you decide if changing the defaults is the right way to go. If you are performing the restores past the 14 days but only a few times a year, what is the impact? Changing the defaults would fix the problem, but at what cost? Would it have been just as easy to perform a restore of the database for those few cases? That is something you will need to research. Table 25.2 shows the breakout for the single-item recovery features. It will help you see what the settings will provide you in the end.

TABLE 25.2:   Single-Item Recovery Features

FEATURE STATE	SOFT-DELETED ITEMS KEPT IN DUMPSTER	MODIFIED AND HARD-DELETED ITEMS KEPT IN DUMPSTER	USER CAN PURGE ITEMS FROM DUMPSTER	MRM AUTOMATICALLY PURGES ITEMS FROM DUMPSTER
Single Item recovery disabled	Yes	No	Yes	Yes, 14 days by default and 120 days for calendar items
Single-item recovery enabled	Yes	Yes	No	Yes, 14 days by default and 120 days for calendar items
Litigation hold enabled	Yes	Yes	No	No

CONFIGURING FOR SINGLE-ITEM RECOVERY

Since you know you can change the default number of days from 14 to a new number, let's look at how to do it. For this example, we will change the limit to 30 days. A simple command from the EMS enables single-item recovery for a specific mailbox.

ENABLING SINGLE-ITEM RECOVERY

The following command will enable single-item recovery on a specific user's mailbox:

```
Set-Mailbox MailboxName -SingleItemRecoveryEnabled $True
```

Once you have enabled single-item recovery, you must specify the amount of time for which the items will be recoverable, which will override the database retention settings for that user:

```
Set-Mailbox MailboxName -RetainDeletedItemsFor NumberofDays
```

You can combine these commands into a single one. To enable all the mailboxes on the same database and set the number of days to 30, type the following command:

```
Get-Mailbox -Database DatabaseName | Set-Mailbox
-SingleItemRecoveryEnabled $True -RetainDeletedItemsFor 30
```

You can also set all mailboxes on a single server by changing the -Database switch to the -Server switch, as in the following command: (You must enable single-item recovery first.)

```
Get-Mailbox -Server ServerName | Set-Mailbox
-SingleItemRecoveryEnabled $True -RetainDeletedItemsFor 30
```

You have enabled the mailboxes for single-item recovery; now perform the recovery. There are two ways to search mailboxes for deleted items: by using the Search-Mailbox cmdlet in EMS, also known as Discovery Search, and by conducting an In-Place eDiscovery search in the EAC. However, only the Search-Mailbox cmdlet will allow you to search exclusively for items that have been purged. An In-Place eDiscovery search will search through the mailbox for deleted and nondeleted items, and present both in the results.

Next, you will use the EAC and an In-Place eDiscovery Search tool to locate the message that needs to be recovered. Once you have located the message, you will export it from the Discovery Search Mailbox into the user's mailbox.

You must know what item you are looking for in the Discovery Search Mailbox. You can use date ranges, keywords, sender or recipient address, or message type. First, you need to create the Discovery Search.

1. Open a web browser and navigate to the EAC URL on one of your Mailbox servers (for example, https://mail.contoso.net/ecp).

2. If you get a certificate error, you may be using a nontrusted self-signed certificate. Click the option Continue To This Website.

3. Log in to the web interface with an account that has access to create and execute Discovery Searches. Any member of the Discovery Management Exchange security group will have the necessary permissions.

4. Select Compliance Management from the Feature pane. If you don't see Compliance Management in the Feature pane, you don't have permissions to perform Discovery Searches.

5. Select In-Place eDiscovery & Hold.

6. Click the + (Add) sign to create a new search. The New In-Place eDiscovery & Hold dialog will open.

7. Type a name for the search, and enter a description, if desired. It may be a good idea to put information, such as a help desk case number or details about the items being recovered, here. Other individuals with search permissions will be able to view your search, so make sure that you use a descriptive name (see Figure 25.4). Click Next.

8. Select the option Specify Mailboxes To Search, and click the + (Add) sign to select the mailbox from which you want to recover items.

9. Select the correct mailbox, click + (Add) and then click OK. Click Next.

10. On the Search Query page, you can specify characteristics of the message you are trying to recover that will help filter it from other messages. The more details you can obtain from the end user about the message you are trying to recover, the more targeted the

results of your search will be. Enter the information to build the search query, and click Next (see Figure 25.5).

11. On the In-Place Hold Settings page, just click Finish.

new in-place eDiscovery & hold

Create a search across mailboxes by specifying a filter. You can also place the search results on hold. You can then view statistics, preview, copy, or export the search results.

Name and description

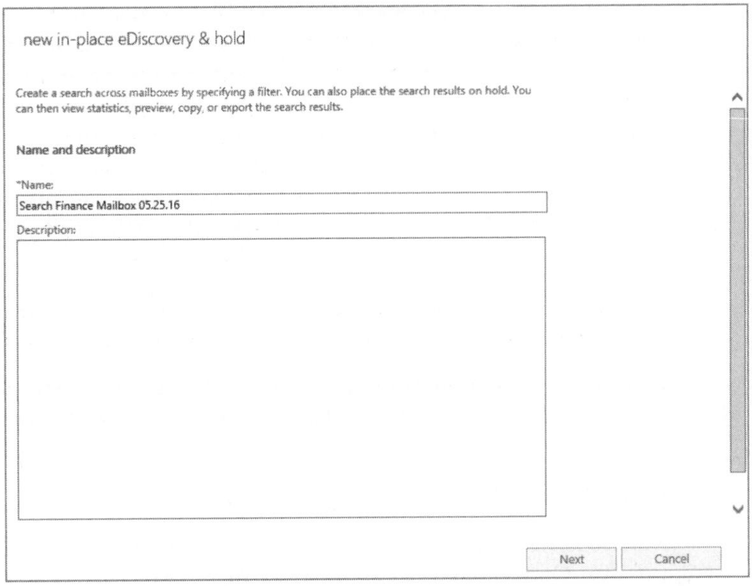

*Name:

Search Finance Mailbox 05.25.16

Description:

Next   Cancel

new in-place eDiscovery & hold

Mailboxes

○ Search all mailboxes
○ Don't search any mailboxes
◉ Specify mailboxes to search

+ −

Public folders

☐ Search all public folders

ⓘ In-Place Hold is a premium feature that requires an Enterprise Client Access License (CAL). Learn more

Back   Next   Cancel

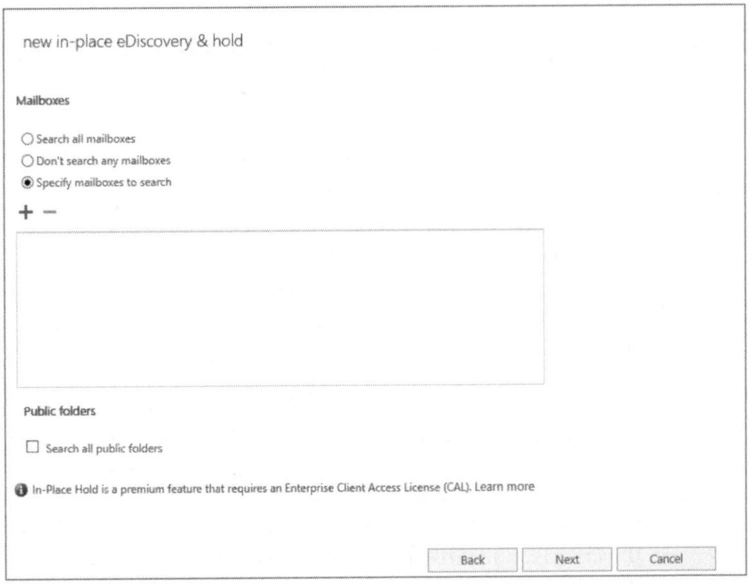

THE NEW IN-PLACE EDISCOVERY & HOLD WIZARD

As its name suggests, the new In-Place eDiscovery & Hold Wizard can be used for multiple purposes. In addition to recovering deleted items for a single user, it can be used to search across multiple mailboxes simultaneously and consolidate results into one report or place the results on hold so that they are protected from permanent deletion. Be aware that using the tool for this purpose requires that each mailbox being searched be licensed with an Enterprise Client Access License (eCAL).

At this point, you should see your Discovery Search in the EAC, along with any other Discovery Searches that exist. By clicking on the Discovery Search that you created, you can see the current status in the Details pane, which will include the number of items found and the total size of the results. Next, you can preview the search results or export them to a Discovery Search Mailbox. To export the items, follow these steps:

1. On the In-Place eDiscovery & Hold tab in EAC, select the drop-down menu next to the magnifying glass in the toolbar, and select Copy Search Results.

2. Select any additional options you want by checking the respective check box, and then click Browse to select the Discovery Search Mailbox to which the results should be copied.

3. Click Copy.

Now you can open the Discovery Search Mailbox and view the results for the search (see Figure 25.6). Once you have located the message(s), you can create a directory in which to place these items. All you need to do is drag the messages from the Recoverable Items folder to the folder you just created.

FIGURE 25.6
Search results
in the Discovery
Search Mailbox

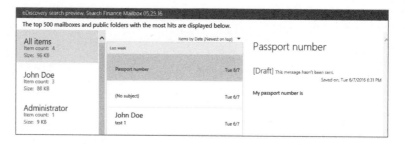

The Discovery Search Mailbox is a resource mailbox. As such, it does not have an owner. You will only be able to view the Discovery Search Mailbox if you have permission to do so. When you ran the Discovery Search, all the email that fit the criteria was copied to this mailbox. To view the results of the search, click the Open link in the Properties pane on the right. The Discovery Search Mailbox will open via Outlook on the web and you will see the results. The results will be under a folder with the same name as the search you created. If you searched multiple mailboxes, you will see separate folders for each mailbox containing messages that meet the criteria. You will notice the Primary Mailbox folder and the Recoverable Items folder.

The Primary Mailbox folder contains the undeleted mail items. The Recoverable Items folder contains the mail items that the user had deleted and that are still within the retention window.

Now that the data has been recovered to the Discovery Search Mailbox, there are two options to get it back to the user. Both options involve EMS, and neither can be completed from the EAC. You can either use the `Search-Mailbox` cmdlet to simultaneously restore the data to the user's mailbox and delete it from the Discovery Search Mailbox, or you can use the `New-MailboxExportRequest` cmdlet to export the data to a `.pst` file. Regardless of the method used, the user running the command should be assigned the Discovery Management RBAC role. The following example command will export the mail items from the Discovery Search Mailbox to the Recovered Mail folder inside Johnn's mailbox:

```
Search-Mailbox "Discovery Search Mailbox" -SearchQuery "Seattle"
-TargetMailbox John -TargetFolder "Recovered Mail"
```

John's mail items have been recovered to the Recovered Mail folder in his active Exchange Server mailbox. At this point he is able to do anything that he needs to do with these mail items.

Recovering Public Folders

Exchange Server 2013 introduced modern public folders stored in public folder mailboxes in a mailbox database, and Exchange Server 2016 follows that architecture as well. Therefore, the procedure for restoring databases where public folder mailboxes are located is similar to the procedure described for restoring any Exchange Server 2016 databases. A user can restore a Public Folder item from Outlook within the retention period, because Public Folder data, similar to email items, has a retention period. There are some recovery scenarios for recovering public folder data that are specific to public folders mailboxes:

♦ When you need to recover deleted public folders within the retention period, if you are recovering the public folder, you should have assigned owner permissions at that public folder level.

♦ If the folder is a root folder, you should have assigned owner permissions for the root folder.

♦ If the folder is a child folder, you should have assigned owner permissions for the parent public folder.

♦ When recovering public folders by using a recovery database, you must create target folders in the target public-folder mailbox, because the restoration procedure does not create the folder structure. Once you create the folder structure manually, you should use the `New-MailboxRestoreRequest` cmdlet to merge recovered data with the mailbox database where the public folder data are located.

♦ If you need to recover both primary and secondary public-folder mailboxes and a new public folder mailbox is created, public folders on the secondary public-folder mailbox are considered orphaned and might be located by running the `Get-PublicFolder-LostAndFound` cmdlet. The procedure for restoring the public folder structure includes setting the appropriate path to the public folder data in the primary public-folder mailbox. The command needed to perform this step is the `Get-PublicFolder-LostAndFound` cmdlet where the output should be piped to the `Set-PublicFolder` cmdlet.

Recovering the Entire Exchange Server

Sometimes (hopefully, not many times!) you will need to restore an entire server. We say not many because you should have engineered a good Exchange Server solution that includes proactive monitoring, good supporting resources for the services (people), and a well-thought-out and tested disaster-recovery plan. These pieces will not ensure that you will never need to recover any of your Exchange servers, but they will place you in a better position to deal with such a situation.

Recovering an Exchange server is a relatively straightforward task. Since almost all the configuration settings for the Exchange servers are kept in Active Directory, you will use the setup /m:RecoverServer command to install and recover an Exchange Server. However, you cannot use this command for a Mailbox server that was part of a DAG without satisfying some prerequisites:

◆ The server on which recovery is being performed must be running the same operating system as the lost server. You cannot recover an Exchange Server 2016 computer that was running Windows Server 2012 on a server running Windows Server 2012 R2, or vice versa.

◆ The server on which recovery is being performed should have the same performance characteristics and hardware configuration as the lost server.

◆ The recovery steps must be run from an Exchange Server 2016 computer that has the Mailbox role installed.

Mailbox Server Role

It is likely that you have deployed multiple Mailbox servers as DAG members in your organization, so losing one of the servers should not result in a service outage to the user community. Because of the multiple servers, combined with the proper load balancing you have in place, all of your users will still be able to access their email using any method they choose: Outlook on the web, ActiveSync, or Outlook Anywhere. You will also be able to send and receive email since the Hub Transport server component now resides within the Mailbox server role and offers resiliency through its Shadow Redundancy and Safety Net functionality. First, you will need to reset the computer account of the server you are recovering in Active Directory. This will enable you later to use the same name for the new computer and to join that computer to the domain. Then you should install the OS, and configure the new Windows server with exactly the same name, domain, and network settings as the computer that has failed. At the end, you will use the setup /m:RecoverServer command to restore the server. Don't forget that your servers need to be at the same code level for the OS before you run this command. You must have the correct Cumulative Update (CU) and hotfixes that were in use on the server before proceeding. After Exchange Server has been installed via the setup /m:RecoverServer command, update Exchange Server to the latest CU to include any hotfixes or updates that have been approved by your organization.

Since you have the ability to configure Outlook on the web pages, be sure to back up any customizations. When you perform a restore with the /m:RecoverServer switch, the server will have only the configuration pieces that are stored in Active Directory. Make sure that you have a method for backing up your certificates and any other IIS customizations that you have performed.

Before you can begin to recover the Exchange server, make sure you have the correct permissions. To successfully perform the restore, you will need the Server Management permission. Here are the steps for performing the recovery:

1. Reset the computer account for the lost server through Active Directory Users and Computers.

2. Reinstall the operating system. The operating system and NetBIOS name must be the same as for the server you are replacing. If the name is not the same, the recovery will fail.

3. Join the server to the same domain as the lost server.

4. Install the necessary prerequisites and operating system component.

5. Log on to the server being recovered and open a command prompt.

6. Navigate to the Exchange Server 2016 installation files and run the following command:

   ```
   setup /m:RecoverServer /IAcceptExchangeServerLicenseTerms
   ```

The `/m:RecoverServer` parameter operates under the same assumptions as in previous versions of Exchange Server, which is that the replacement server will be running the same OS and should have the same performance characteristics as the server you are recovering. The NetBIOS name and the IP address must be the same as well.

When you run a setup function with the `/m:RecoverServer` parameter, the Setup program will ask Active Directory for the relevant configuration information. This information will be pulled from Active Directory and used during the reinstallation of the server.

You can also use the `Export-TransportRuleCollection` cmdlet to export the transport rules from the Mailbox server. This data can be used to help document your environment in case you need to rebuild this information from scratch in a greenfield scenario.

When restoring Exchange Server with the `setup/m: RecoverServer` parameter, some data, such as certificates and custom audio prompts if unified messaging is deployed, is not restored and must be restored manually.

Database Availability Group Members

Mailbox servers that are members of a DAG require special consideration before a lost server can be recovered using the `/m:RecoverServer` switch:

1. If any of the database copies on the server are lagged copies, document the replay lag and truncation lag settings by running the following command:

   ```
   Get-MailboxDatabase DB05 | FL *lag*
   ```

2. Remove all database copies that exist on the server by running the following command one time for each mailbox database copy:

   ```
   Remove-MailboxDatabaseCopy DB05\EX-MBX01
   ```

3. Remove the failed server from the DAG's configuration in Active Directory by using the following command. Note that if the server is offline and not reachable via network communications, the `-ConfigurationOnly` parameter must be included.

   ```
   Remove-DatabaseAvailabilityGroupServer –Identity DAG01
   –MailboxServer EX-MBX01 -ConfigurationOnly
   ```

4. Reset the Mailbox server's computer account in Active Directory.

5. Run `Setup /m:RecoverServer /IAcceptExchangeServerLicenseTerms`.

6. Once Setup is complete and all required post-installation patches have been installed, add the recovered Mailbox server back to the DAG by executing the following:

```
Add-DatabaseAvailabilityGroupServer -Identity DAG01 -MailboxServer EX-MBX01
```

7. After the Mailbox server has been added back to the DAG, reconfigure the mailbox database copies by running the following command one time for each database:

```
Add-MailboxDatabaseCopy -Identity DB05 -MailboxServer EX-MBX01
```

If the mailbox database copy being added back is a lagged copy, you can compensate for this using the information gathered in step 1, in combination with the command you just ran. For example, if the `ReplayLagTime` and `TruncationLagTime` for the database copy is 14 days, this could be configured using the following:

```
Add-MailboxDatabaseCopy -Identity DB05 -MailboxServer EX-MBX01
-ReplayLagTime 14.00:00:00 -TruncationLagTime 14.00:00:00
```

The Bottom Line

Back up Exchange Server. Performing backups is the somewhat easy part of the equation. The more difficult part is defining the requirements for the backup.

Master It Document the goals for your backup solution.

Prepare to backup the Exchange server. Before you can perform any backups from Windows Server 2012 R2, you must install the backup features.

Master It What do you need to do to install the backup features on Windows 2012 R2?

Use Windows Server Backup to back up the server. There is always a need to back up your servers. Since you have the requirements, you need to perform the backup.

Master It Perform a recurring backup utilizing the Windows Server 2012 R2 backup features.

Use Windows Server Backup to recover the data with the Recovery Database. You may need to restore your Exchange Server data for several reasons. One of the reasons is that you need to give a user email items that had been deleted but that are still recoverable.

Master It Perform restore of email for a user by using the Recovery Database where restored mailbox items will be located in a target folder named RecoveryFolder.

Recover an entire Exchange server. There may be occasions when you need to reinstall the entire Exchange server.

Master It How do you recover the Mailbox server?

Appendix

The Bottom Line

Each of "The Bottom Line" sections in the chapters suggests exercises to deepen your skills and understanding. Sometimes there is only one possible solution, but often you are encouraged to use your skills and creativity to create something that builds on what you know and lets you explore one of many possible solutions.

Chapter 1

Understand email fundamentals. To gain the best advantage from Exchange Server 2016, you should have a good grounding in general email applications and principles.

Master It What two application models have email programs traditionally used? Which one does Exchange Server use? Can you name an example of the other model?

Solution The two models are shared files, in which a central shared filesystem is used to store messages and each client has access to those files, and client/server, where the central email server and clients communicate using a distinct protocol. The client/server model allows the system to provide stronger safeguards and permissions, better performance, and greater integrity for the data. Exchange Server has always used a client/server model. Its predecessor, Microsoft Mail, was a shared filesystem.

Identify email-administration duties. Installing an Exchange Server system is just the first part of the job. Once it's in place, it needs to be maintained. Be familiar with the various duties and concerns that will be involved with the care and feeding of Exchange Server.

Master It What are the various types of duties that a typical Exchange Server administrator will expect to perform?

Solution Some of the routine administrative duties are creating new mailboxes, troubleshooting email delivery problems, configuring clients to connect to Exchange Server, and reading log files and event logs.

Chapter 2

Understand the key changes in Exchange Server 2016. Significant updates were made to the Exchange Server 2016 architecture to continue the improvement to the scalability, security, and stability. The Mailbox role handles mailboxes, public folders, transport, and client connectivity. Compliances features, such as compliance search and eDiscovery, are greatly enhanced and simplified. The disk I/O requirements continue to be reduced, enabling organizations to run their Exchange servers on lower-performing storage.

Master It You are planning your email data storage strategy, especially for long-term storage. You want to minimize or eliminate the use of .pst files. Which technology should you use to maintain email data indefinitely?

Solution You can use archive mailboxes to eliminate the use of .pst files. Archive mailboxes can be stored on lower-performing storage to reduce the costs associated with storing email indefinitely.

Understand the Mailbox role's expanded duties. Over the last couple of versions of Exchange Server, the Exchange server roles have been updated. In each version, a server role was consolidated, enabling organizations to reduce their server footprint and simplify their environments.

Master It You are planning a training session for your junior administrators to prepare them in their SMTP connectivity troubleshooting tasks. Which server role should you recommend they inspect when attempting to troubleshoot email delivery problems?

Solution If Edge Transport servers are in the environment and the email is coming from the Internet or going to the Internet, you should look at the Edge Transport servers. If the email is staying internal, you should look at the Mailbox servers.

Chapter 3

Distinguish between availability, backup and recovery, and disaster recovery. When it comes to keeping your Exchange Server 2016 deployment healthy, you have a lot of options provided out of the box. Knowing which problems they solve is critical to deploying them correctly.

Master It You have been asked to select a backup type that will back up all data once per week but on a daily basis will ensure that the server does not run out of transaction log disk space.

Solution You can opt for a full backup once a week and incremental backups daily. In both cases, purge transaction logs after completion.

Determine the best option for disaster recovery. When creating your disaster-recovery plans for Exchange Server 2016, you have a variety of options to choose from. Exchange Server 2016 further enhances the built-in capabilities to provide disaster recovery.

Master It What are the different types of disaster recovery?

Solution The two models are shared files, in which a central shared filesystem is used to store messages and each client has access to those files, and client/server, where the central email server and clients communicate using a distinct protocol. The client/server model allows the system to provide stronger safeguards and permissions, better performance, and greater integrity for the data. Exchange Server has always used a client/server model. Its predecessor, Microsoft Mail, was a shared filesystem.

Distinguish between the different types of availability meant by the term *high availability*. The term *high availability* means different things to different people. When you design and deploy your Exchange Server 2016 solution, you need to be confident that everyone is designing for the same goals.

Master It   What four types of availability are there?

Solution   Service availability, network availability, data availability, and storage availability.

Implement the four pillars of compliance and governance activities.   Ensuring that your Exchange Server 2016 organization meets your regular operational needs means thinking about the topics of compliance and governance within your organization.

Master It   What are the four pillars of compliance and governance as applied to a messaging system?

Solution   Discovery (finding email data), Compliance (meeting legal, regulatory, government requirements), Archival (keeping email for a specified period of time or indefinitely), and Retention (deciding when to remove data from Exchange Server).

Chapter 4

Evaluate the possible virtualization impacts.   Knowing the impacts that virtualization can have will help you make the virtualization a success. Conversely, failure to realize how virtualization will impact your environment can end up making virtualization a poor choice.

Master It   What kind of impact would virtualizing Exchange have in your environment?

Solution   Virtualization will reduce power and cooling costs, will reduce your total server count, and will speed up the time it takes to deploy new servers.

Evaluate the existing Exchange environment.   Before you can determine the feasibility of a virtualized Exchange environment, you must know how your current systems are performing.

Master It   Are your Exchange servers good candidates for virtualization?

Solution   Yes, if you have an existing and healthy virtualization environment with ample power and connectivity.

Determine when physical servers are the right choice.   There will be times when virtualization of Exchange Server isn't appropriate for an organization.

Master It   What are some common reasons to stick with physical servers for Exchange Server?

Solution   You might stick with physical servers if your Exchange Server hardware requirements exceed the capacity of your virtual infrastructure. You also might stick with physical servers if your virtualization hosts are underpowered. Also, in some cases, you might want a physical Exchange server in a remote branch office where you do not have virtualization.

Chapter 5

Use PowerShell command syntax.   The PowerShell is an easy-to-use command-line interface that allows you to manipulate many aspects of the Windows operating system, Registry, and filesystem. The Exchange Management Shell extensions allow you to manage all aspects of an Exchange Server organization and many Active Directory objects.

PowerShell cmdlets consist of a verb (such as Get, Set, New, or Mount) that indicates what is being done and a noun (such as Mailbox, Group, ExchangeServer) that indicates on which object the cmdlet is acting. Cmdlet options such as -Debug, -Whatif, and -ValidateOnly are common to most cmdlets and can be used to test or debug problems with a cmdlet.

Master It You need to use the Exchange Management Shell cmdlet Set-User to change the city to Irvine for all members of the IT distribution list. But you want to first confirm that the command will do what you want to do without actually making the change. Which command should you use?

Solution Run the Get-DistributionGroupMember 'IT' | Set-User -City 'Irvine' -WhatIf command. This command will show you which users are being targeted by the command while also showing you that the user object is being configured. The -WhatIf parameter is helpful to validate actions and targets of actions, especially before you run a potentially destructive command.

Understand object-oriented use of PowerShell. Output of a cmdlet is not simple text but rather objects. These objects have properties that can be examined and manipulated.

Master It You are using the Set-User cmdlet to set properties of a user's Active Directory account. You need to determine the properties that are available to use with the Set-User cmdlet. What can you do to view the available properties?

Solution Run the Get-Help Set-User -Detailed command. This will show you all of the available properties of the Set-User cmdlet along with other details and example commands.

Get help with using PowerShell. Many options are available when you are trying to figure out how to use a PowerShell cmdlet, including online help and the Exchange Server documentation. PowerShell and the EMS make it easy to "discover" the cmdlets you need to do your job.

Master It How would you locate all the cmdlets available to manipulate a mailbox? You are trying to figure out how to use the Set-User cmdlet and would like to see an example. How can you view examples for this cmdlet?

Solution Run the Get-Help Set-User -Examples command.

Chapter 6

Work with Autodiscover. Autodiscover is a key service in Exchange Server 2016, both for ensuring hassle-free client configuration and for keeping the Exchange servers in your organization working together smoothly. Autodiscover can be used by Outlook 2010, Outlook 2013, Outlook 2016, Entourage, Outlook for Mac 2016, Windows Mobile/Windows Phone, and other mobile devices like Android, iOS, and even Windows RT devices.

Master It You are configuring Outlook 2016 to connect to Exchange Server and you want to diagnose a problem that you are having when connecting. Which tool can you use?

Solution You can go to https://testconnectivity.microsoft.com/ and run connectivity tests to troubleshoot the problem.

Troubleshoot Autodiscover.   In a large organization with multiple Active Directory sites or multiple namespaces, it is essential to track the Autodiscover traffic and understand where client queries will be directed.

Master It   If you have multiple Active Directory sites, what should you do to control the client flow of requests for Autodiscover information?

Solution   You should use site affinity to ensure that clients get Autodiscover information from their closest Active Directory site.

Manage Exchange Server certificates.   Exchange Server 2016 servers rely on functional X.509v3 digital certificates to ensure proper TLS security.

Master It   Which tools will you need to create and manage Exchange Server certificates?

Solution   Exchange Admin Center (EAC) and Exchange Management Shell (EMS) are two tools that you can use to create and manage certificates.

Chapter 7

Quickly size a typical server.   Using a properly equipped server for testing can yield a much more positive experience than using a poorly equipped one. Taking the time to obtain the right hardware will avoid problems later.

Master It   What parameters must be kept in mind when sizing a lab/test server?

Solution

- X64 Intel or AMD64 CPU, with a minimum of two cores

- Windows Server Standard Edition 2012 R2 or Windows Server Standard Edition 2012

- A minimum of 8 GB of RAM

- A page file size of RAM+ 10 MB

- 30 GB of disk space available on the installation drive for binaries

- At least 200 MB available on the system drive

- 500 MB available for the transport queue, by default, on the installation drive

- Space for mailbox databases and transaction logs.

- A system drive formatted with NTFS

- A drive where Exchange binaries are located, formatted with NTFS

- The Resilient File System (ReFS) feature in Windows Server 2012 for volumes that host mailbox databases and transaction logs, where the integrity feature in ReFS is disabled

- One network adapter with a minimum bandwidth of 1 Gbps

- A physical or virtual machine

- If running as virtual machine, Windows Server 2012 R2 Hyper-V, Windows Server 2012 Hyper-V, Hyper-V 2012 R2, or Hyper-V 2012

Install the necessary Windows Server 2012 or Windows Server 2012 R2 prerequisites. Certain settings must be configured before Exchange Server 2016 is installed.

Master It What is involved in installing and configuring the prerequisites?

Solution The server has a static IP address and is joined to an Active Directory domain. The server is not a domain controller.

- The Active Directory forest and domain functional level are at a minimum of Windows Server 2008 R2.

- You have an administrative account that is a member of the Schema Admins, Domain Admins, and Enterprise Admins security groups.

- There is a domain controller in the same Active Directory site in which the Exchange server will reside.

- In an administrative instance of PowerShell, run the following command:

  ```
  Install-WindowsFeature AS-HTTP-Activation, Desktop-Experience, NET-
  Framework-45-Features, RPC-over-HTTP-proxy, RSAT-Clustering, RSAT-
  Clustering-CmdInterface, RSAT-Clustering-Mgmt, RSAT-Clustering-PowerShell,
  Web-Mgmt-Console, WAS-Process-Model, Web-Asp-Net45, Web-Basic-Auth, Web-
  Client-Auth, Web-Digest-Auth, Web-Dir-Browsing, Web-Dyn-Compression,
  Web-Http-Errors, Web-Http-Logging, Web-Http-Redirect, Web-Http-Tracing,
  Web-ISAPI-Ext, Web-ISAPI-Filter, Web-Lgcy-Mgmt-Console, Web-Metabase,
  Web-Mgmt-Console, Web-Mgmt-Service, Web-Net-Ext45, Web-Request-Monitor,
  Web-Server, Web-Stat-Compression, Web-Static-Content, Web-Windows-Auth,
  Web-WMI, Windows-Identity-Foundation
  ```

- In an administrative instance of PowerShell, run the following command:

  ```
  Install-WindowsFeature RSAT-ADDS
  ```

- Download and install the following components:

  - Microsoft .NET Framework 4.5.2

  - Microsoft Unified Communications Managed API 4.0, Core Runtime 64-bit

Install an Exchange Server 2016 server. You should provide a basic, bare-bones server for testing and evaluation.

Master It What installation methods can be used to install Exchange Server 2016?

Solution Once Exchange Server 2016 prerequisites are met, you can choose from two installation methods:

- **GUI setup:** From the installation media folder, double-click `setup.exe` and follow the installation steps.

- **Command line, unattended setup:** Run the following command:

  ```
  setup.exe /mode:install /role:Mailbox
  ```

Configure Exchange to send and receive email. Your new Exchange server should interact with other email systems.

Master It What are the configuration requirements for sending and receiving email?

Solution In order to send and receive email, Exchange Server should have the following components configured:

- **Send Connector:** You need to create the Send connector because it is not created by default during the Exchange setup.

- **Receive Connector:** The Default Front End Receive connector on each Exchange server is configured to receive email from the Internet from anonymous senders. Additionally, you need to configure appropriate MX records in DNS in order to be able to receive email from Internet.

- **Accepted domain:** If your Active Directory domain isn't the same as your SMTP domain, you have to create the accepted domain.

- **Email address policy:** The email address policy defines the email address format, which by default is `alias@ActiveDirectorydomain`. If you want a different email address format, you need to modify the default email address policy.

Configure recipients, contacts, and distribution groups. Add mailbox-enabled users, mail-enabled contacts, and distribution groups to Exchange.

Master It How are recipients created, and what's the difference between them?

Solution Exchange Server 2016 includes various types of recipients that can be created and managed by using both Exchange Admin Center and Exchange Management Shell. The Exchange recipients that are most commonly used include:

- **User Mailboxes.** Active Directory accounts that have a mailbox located in Exchange.

- **Mail users.** Active Directory accounts that do not have a mailbox located in Exchange and have an external email address.

- **Distribution groups.** Active Directory objects that have an email address but not a mailbox. Distribution groups contain Exchange recipients, such as user mailboxes, mail-enabled users, mail-enabled contacts, or other distribution groups.

- **Contacts.** Mail-enabled contacts are objects that represent external recipients, such as vendors or clients.

Chapter 8

Understand the Exchange Server 2016 server roles. Exchange Server 2016 supports two unique server roles. The features of the roles in Exchange Server 2007, 2010, and 2013 have been moved to the Mailbox server role in Exchange Server 2016. The Mailbox server handles much more in Exchange Server 2016 than just the Exchange Server database engine. The Mailbox role now handles Unified Messaging, Client Access, and Transport services.

The Client Access server role functionalities in Exchange Server 2013 are now part of the Mailbox server role. Client access services in Exchange 2016 hold a lot of key responsibilities.

Client access services in Exchange 2016 are still the end point for most of the protocols in the organization, such as SMTP, HTTP, and RTP. The main functions of the client access services are to authenticate an incoming request, locate the next hop for the request, and proxy or redirect the request to the next hop.

Master It   Which Exchange server role provides access to the mailbox database for Outlook on the web and Outlook clients?

Solution   The Mailbox server role

Explore possible server role configurations.   Server role number and placement can be designed to meet most organizational and configuration requirements.

For small organizations that do not need high availability, one server that hosts the Mailbox role will suffice provided it has sufficient hardware even if it needs to support 500 or more mailboxes. Companies that need high availability will deploy at least two mailbox server roles in DAG. Companies that need high availability but for any reason (such as budget constraints) are not able to provide high availability might choose to migrate to Office 365.

We do not recommend installing Exchange Server 2016 on a domain controller.

All server roles can be virtualized. Depending on the client load, Mailbox servers may also be virtualized as long as you remain within Microsoft's support boundaries. It is important to size out your Exchange Server 2016 deployment before committing to a virtual or physical server deployment.

Master It   Your company has approximately 400 mailboxes. Your users require only basic email services (email, shared calendars, Outlook, and Outlook on the web). You already have two servers that function as domain controllers/global catalog servers. What would you recommend to support the 400 mailboxes?

Solution   If the company does not need high availability, one server that has sufficient hardware will be deployed with the Mailbox server role installed. If the company needs high availability, it will deploy two mailbox server roles in DAG.

Chapter 9

Use the right hardware for your organization.   There are several tools provided online to help you properly size the amount of RAM, as well as the hard disk configuration for your deployment. One other resource that you should not overlook is your hardware vendor. Very often vendors have created custom tools to help you properly size your environment relative to your organizational needs.

If you want to get a fair idea as to what you should plan, use the tables in this chapter, based on both mailbox size and message volume. Remember, you should try both sizing methods and select the option that projects the most RAM and the largest storage volume. You can never have enough RAM or storage space.

Ensure that the processor core number of Mailbox servers is adequate to keep up with the load clients will place on these servers.

Start with the Exchange Server 2016 Server Role Requirements Calculator and try different combinations of options. It can serve as a solid guideline for deployments, from small- to medium-size companies, as well as large multinational organizations.

If you are missing a component, you will receive feedback from Exchange Server 2016 when you attempt to install the application. The components are going to differ from server operating system to server operating system and from role combination to role combination.

If you find it necessary to integrate Exchange Server 2016 with either Exchange Server 2010 or Exchange Server 2013, you will want to make sure you have installed the latest Service Packs and updates for the host operating systems and the server applications.

Master It   What is the primary tool you can use to ascertain the appropriate configuration of an Exchange Server 2016 deployment based on the number of users and message volume?

Solution   The tool is the Exchange Server 2016 Server Role Requirements Calculator. You can download it from the following URL:

```
http://blogs.technet.com/b/exchange/archive/2015/10/15/exchange-server-role-
requirements-calculator-update.aspx
```

Configure Windows Server 2012 R2 and Windows Server 2012 to support Exchange Server 2016.   Make sure you have all of the prerequisite features and modules. Using PowerShell is the most efficient method for quickly and completely installing all of the necessary components.

Master It   You need to verify that all of prerequisites are met. How can you accomplish this from PowerShell?

Solution   For the Exchange Server 2016 Mailbox server role, complete the following steps:

1. In Windows PowerShell, run the following command:

```
Install-WindowsFeature AS-HTTP-Activation, Desktop-Experience, NET-
Framework-45-Features, RPC-over-HTTP-proxy, RSAT-Clustering, RSAT-
Clustering-CmdInterface, RSAT-Clustering-Mgmt, RSAT-Clustering-PowerShell,
Web-Mgmt-Console, WAS-Process-Model, Web-Asp-Net45, Web-Basic-Auth, Web-
Client-Auth, Web-Digest-Auth, Web-Dir-Browsing, Web-Dyn-Compression,
Web-Http-Errors, Web-Http-Logging, Web-Http-Redirect, Web-Http-Tracing,
Web-ISAPI-Ext, Web-ISAPI-Filter, Web-Lgcy-Mgmt-Console, Web-Metabase,
Web-Mgmt-Console, Web-Mgmt-Service, Web-Net-Ext45, Web-Request-Monitor,
Web-Server, Web-Stat-Compression, Web-Static-Content, Web-Windows-Auth,
Web-WMI, Windows-Identity-Foundation, RSAT-ADDS
```

2. Install .NET Framework 4.5.

3. Install Microsoft Unified Communications Managed API 4.0, Core Runtime 64-bit.

For the Exchange Server 2016 Edge Transport server role, complete the following steps:

1. In Windows PowerShell, run the following command:

```
Install-WindowsFeature ADLDS
```

2. Install .NET Framework 4.5.2.

Confirm that Active Directory is ready. Make sure that you have set your Active Directory domain and forest functional levels to Windows Server 2008 at a minimum. You should not encounter any problems if you set your domain and forest functional levels to Windows Server 2012 or Windows Server 2012 R2.

Avoid frustration during installation or potential problems in the future that may result from domain controllers or global catalog servers running older versions of the software.

Master It   You must verify that your Active Directory meets the minimum requirements to support Exchange Server 2016. What should you check?

Solution   You should verify that your Active Directory domain functional level and forest functional level are at least Windows Server 2008 or newer.

Verify that previous versions of Exchange Server can interoperate with Exchange Server 2016.   Exchange Server 2016 will interoperate only with specific previous versions of Exchange Server.

Master It   You must verify that the existing legacy Exchange servers in your organization are running the minimum versions of Exchange Server required to interoperate with Exchange Server 2016. What should you check?

Solution   You can have Exchange Server 2016 installed in coexistence with Exchange Server 2010, Exchange Server 2013, or both Exchange Server 2010 and 2013.

Chapter 10

Implement important steps before installing Exchange Server 2016.   One of the things that slow down an Exchange Server installation is finding out you are missing some specific Windows component, feature, or role. Reviewing the necessary software and configuration components will keep your installation moving along smoothly.

The minimum requirements for the Mailbox server role are at least 30 GB of free space and 8 GB of RAM. However, you need to calculate the proper hardware requirements for your implementation. Ensure that you are using Windows Server 2012 or Windows Server 2012 R2 with the most recent updates. Install the Windows Server roles and features necessary for the Exchange Server's role requirements.

Master It   You are working with your Active Directory team to ensure that the Active Directory is ready to support Exchange Server 2016. What are the minimum prerequisites that your Active Directory must meet in order to support Exchange Server 2016?

Solution   All domain controllers must be running Windows Server 2008 or later. The Active Directory forest must be at the Windows Server 2008 functional level or higher.

Prepare the Active Directory forest for Exchange Server 2016 without actually installing Exchange Server.   In some organizations, the Exchange administrator or installer may not have the necessary Active Directory rights to prepare the Active Directory schema, the forest, or a child domain. Here is a breakdown of the steps involved and the associated group membership requirements to complete each:

◆   Running the Exchange Server 2016 setup.exe program from the command line with the /PrepareSchema option allows the schema to be prepared without installing Exchange. A user account that is a member of the Schema Admins group is necessary to extend the Active Directory schema.

◆ Running the Exchange Server 2016 `setup.exe` program from the command line with the `/PrepareAD` option allows the forest root domain and the Active Directory configuration partition to be prepared without installing Exchange. A user account that is a member of the Enterprise Admins group is necessary to make all the changes and updates necessary in the forest root. When preparing a child domain, a member of the Enterprise Admins group or the child domain's Domain Admins group may be used.

Master It You have provided the Exchange 2016 installation binaries to your Active Directory team so that the forest administrator can extend the Active Directory schema. She wants to know what she must do in order to extend only the schema to support Exchange Server 2016. What must she do?

Solution From the command line and in the same folder as the Exchange Server 2016 `setup.exe` file, run this command:

```
Setup.exe /PrepareSchema /IAcceptExchangeServerLicenseTerms
```

Employ the graphical user interface to install Exchange Server 2016. The graphical user interface can be used for most Exchange Server installations that do not require specialized prestaging or nonstandard options. The GUI will provide all the necessary configuration steps, including Active Directory preparation.

The GUI allows you to install the Mailbox or Edge Transport roles on a server.

Master It You are implementing Exchange Server 2016 for a large organization with strict security requirements. You want to implement the Active Directory split-permissions security model to ensure that Exchange administrators and Active Directory administrators have separate sets of permissions. When you use the GUI to install Exchange Server 2016, this option is not available. Why is this option not available?

Solution The option to implement the Active Directory split-permissions security model is presented on the Organizational Name screen during installation. This screen is available only if an Exchange organization does not already exist. This screen is not displayed if a previous version of Exchange Server has already been deployed or if Active Directory has already been prepared for Exchange Server 2016

Determine the command-line options available when installing Exchange. The Exchange 2016 command-line installation program has a robust set of features that allow all installation options to be chosen from the command line exactly as if you were installing Exchange Server 2016 using the graphical user interface.

Master It You are attempting to use the command line to install an Exchange Server 2016 Mailbox server role. What is the proper command-line syntax to install this role?

Solution To install the Mailbox server role, use the following command:

```
Setup.exe /mode:install /role:mailbox /IAcceptExchangeServerLicenseTerms
```

Chapter 11

Choose between an upgrade and a migration. The migration path that you take will depend on a number of factors, including the amount of disruption you can put your users through and the current version of your messaging system.

Master It Your company is currently running Exchange Server 2010 and is supporting 3,000 users. You have a single Active Directory forest. You have purchased new hardware to support Exchange Server 2016. Management has asked that the migration path you choose have minimal disruption on your user community. Which type of migration should you use? What high-level events should occur?

Solution   You should pick a normal upgrade to Exchange Server 2016. The following high-level events should occur:

1.   Evaluate and meet the requirements.

2.   Install the Exchange Server 2016 servers.

3.   Move email transport, messaging, and client access services to the new servers.

4.   Remove the old servers from service.

Choose between on-premises deployment and Office 365.   A common choice today is deciding whether to move your mailbox data into the cloud. Office 365 is Microsoft's cloud solution, of which Exchange Online is a part.

Master It   You work at a university using Exchange Server 2010 on-premises for 10,000 students. You want to offer the functionality present in Exchange Server 2016 to your students, but you have budgetary constraints and cannot replace all of the required servers. What is your best course of action?

Solution   Microsoft offers Office 365 for Education, a basic-level subscription, at no cost to colleges and universities. Very little local hardware is required to have a fully hybrid solution that synchronizes the on-site Active Directory to Office 365.

Note that Office 365 is not the right solution for all organizations. Every organization needs to carefully evaluate their requirements and ensure that Office 365 meets those requirements. It is worth noting that low-cost and free options are also available for nonprofit organizations.

Determine the factors you need to consider before upgrading.   Organizations frequently are delayed in their expected deployments due to things they overlooked when preparing for their upgrade.

Master It   You are planning your Exchange Server 2016 upgrade from an earlier version. What are some key factors that you must consider when planning the upgrade?

Solution   You must consider the following factors:

◆   Confirm that all domain controllers are Windows Server 2008 or newer.

◆   Ensure that there are no Exchange Server 2007 or older servers.

◆   Review all third-party products currently in use and that interoperate with your messaging system. Confirm that you have versions that will work with Exchange Server 2016.

◆   Examine your current backup procedures, backup storage, and processes. Ensure that the existing system will work with Exchange Server 2016 or identify what changes will be required.

Understand coexistence with legacy Exchange servers. Coexistence with earlier versions of Exchange Server is a necessary evil unless you are able to move all your Exchange Server data and functionality at one time. Coexistence means that you must keep your old Exchange servers running for one of a number of functions, including message transfer, email storage, public folder storage, or mailbox access. One of the primary goals of any upgrade should be to move your messaging services (and mailboxes) over to new servers as soon as possible.

Master It You are performing a normal upgrade from Exchange Server 2013 to Exchange Server 2016. Your desktop clients are a mix of Outlook 2010 and Outlook 2013. You quickly moved all your mailbox data to Exchange Server 2016. Why should you leave your Exchange Server 2013 servers online for a few weeks after the mailbox moves have completed?

Solution Even though all of the mailboxes have been migrated, it is possible that there are still applications or devices, such as scanners, configured to use the Exchange 2013 servers. Leaving Exchange Server 2013 servers up for a few weeks gives you time to monitor SMTP protocol logs and verify that the servers are not being used by applications or devices.

However, at some point, you need to remove Exchange Server 2013 and resolve to fix any problems that may occur. Some applications might only be used every few months. It is not reasonable to wait for an extended period of time to identify all infrequently used applications that are using the old Exchange servers.

Perform a cross-forest migration. Cross-forest migrations are by far the most difficult and disruptive migrations. These migrations move mailboxes as well as other messaging functions between two separate mail systems. User accounts and mailboxes usually have to be created for the new organization; user attributes, such as email addresses, phone numbers, and so forth must be transferred to the new organization. Metadata such as "reply-ability" of existing messages as well as folder rules and mailbox permissions must also be transferred.

Although simple tools are provided to move mailboxes from one Exchange Server organization to another, large or complex migrations may require third-party migration tools.

Master It You have a business subsidiary that has an Exchange Server 2010 organization with approximately 2,000 mailboxes; this Exchange Server organization is not part of the corporate Active Directory forest. The users all use Outlook 2013. You must move these mailboxes to Exchange Server 2016 in the corporate Active Directory forest. What four options are available to you to move email to the new organization?

Solution To move mailboxes between Exchange organizations, you have the following options:

◆ Use third-party migration tools.

◆ Use the Exchange Server 2016 `New-MoveRequest` cmdlet.

◆ Use the Exchange Server 2016 `New-MigrationBatch` cmdlet.

◆ Export the mailboxes in the source organization to a PST file and then import it using the `New-MailboxImportRequest` cmdlet.

Chapter 12

Determine what built-in roles and role groups provide you with the permissions you need. Exchange Server 2016 includes a vast number of built-in management roles out of the box. Many of these roles are already assigned to role groups that are ready for you to use. To use these built-in roles, figure out which roles contain the permissions you need. Ideally, determine which role groups you can use to gain access to these roles.

> **Master It** As part of your recent email compliance and retention initiative, your company hired a consultant to advise you on what you can do to make your Exchange implementation more compliant. The consultant claims that he needs escalated privileges to your existing journal rules so he can examine them. Because you tightly control who can make changes to your Exchange organization, you don't want to give the consultant the ability to modify your journal rules, though you don't mind if he is able to view the configuration details of Exchange. What EMS command can you run to find out what role the consultant can be assigned to view your journal rules but not have permissions to modify them or create new ones? What role do you want to assign to the consultant?
>
> **Solution** To determine which role has permissions to run the Get-JournalRule cmdlet, run the following command:
>
> ```
> Get-ManagementRoleEntry "*\Get-JournalRule"
> ```
>
> The three roles discovered with this command are Journaling, View-Only Configuration, and O365SupportviewConfig. To avoid giving him any more permissions than necessary, you can assign the View-Only Configuration role to the consultant.

Assign permissions to administrators using roles and role groups. When assigning permissions to administrators, the preferred method is to assign management roles to role groups and then add the administrators account to the appropriate role group. However, Exchange allows you to assign management roles directly to the administrator's account if you want.

> **Master It** Earlier in the day, you determined that you need to assign a certain role to your email compliance consultant. You've created a role group called Email Compliance Evaluation and you need to add your consultant to this role group. What command would you use in the EMS to add your consultant, Sam, to this role group?
>
> **Solution** Since you've already created the group, you could use Active Directory management tools to add Sam to the group. If you prefer, you can use the following command in the EMS:
>
> ```
> Add-RoleGroupMember "Email Compliance Evaluation" -Member Sam
> ```

Grant permissions to end users for updating their address list information. RBAC doesn't apply only to Exchange administrators. You can also use RBAC to assign roles to end-user accounts so users can have permissions to update their personal information, Exchange settings, and their distribution groups.

> **Master It** You've decided that you want to give your users the ability to modify their contact information in the global address list. You want to make this change as quickly as possible and have it apply to all existing users and new users coming into your Exchange

organization immediately. You determine that using the EAC would be the easiest way to make this change. What would you modify in the EAC to make this change?

Solution If you want to give all users the ability to modify their own information, you need to use a role assignment policy. Assuming that you have not modified the default configuration, all of the users are configured with the Default Role Assignment Policy. You can edit the policy to allow users to change their own information.

By default, users already have the ability to edit MyAddressInformation, MyMobileInformation, and MyPersonal Information. The only other item you can add is MyProfileInformation, which includes MyDisplayName and MyName.

Create custom administration roles and assign them to administrators. If you can't find an existing role that meets your needs, don't worry! You can create a custom role in Exchange Server 2016 and assign the permissions you need to the custom role.

Master It Your company has asked you to allow administrators in the Baltimore office to manage mailbox settings for all users in the Baltimore OU. Your company does not want the administrators in the Baltimore office to be able to change the mailbox storage limits for individual mailboxes. What would you implement to ensure that administrators in the Baltimore office can only manage mailboxes in the Baltimore OU and are not able to change the mailbox storage limits?

Solution There are two elements to this solution. First, you need to create a custom role that has only the necessary permissions. Secondly, you need to create a scope that limits access to the Baltimore OU.

1. Determine which parent role you should use for your custom role.

2. Create the custom role with the appropriate parent.

3. Remove the unnecessary management role entries to leave only the permissions that you want it to have.

4. If desired, create a custom role group to which the custom role will have a role assignment.

5. Create a role assignment to assign the custom role and scope to a role group.

6. Add your administrators in the Baltimore office to the role group that has the custom role assigned to it.

Audit RBAC changes using the Exchange Management Shell and built-in reports in the Exchange Administration Center. Assigning RBAC permissions is the easy part, determining who has been assigned what permissions can be a bit tricky. Luckily EMS can be used to determine the roles assigned to users.

Master It Your company has purchased a partner company, which has an administrator named Dave. You have been tasked with providing Dave with the same level of RBAC permissions in your Exchange Server 2016 organization that he has in his Exchange Server 2016 organization. What command would you run in your partner's organization to determine the roles assigned to Dave?

Solution The Get-ManagementRoleAssignment cmdlet with the GetEffectiveUsers parameter will display the roles to which Dave has access. In the following example, the Role column shows the management role that has been assigned and the RoleAssigneeName shows any role groups in which Dave is a member.

```
Get-ManagementRoleAssignment -GetEffectiveUsers |
Where EffectiveUserName -eq "Dave" | ft Name,Role,RoleAssigneeName
```

In most cases, you'll be able to identify the standard role groups that Dave is a member of and add him to the same role groups in your Exchange organization. If you identify any custom role groups, you'll need to evaluate whether you need to re-create them or provide similar access with the role groups that already exist in your Exchange organization.

Chapter 13

Identify the various types of recipients. Most recipient types in Exchange Server 2016 have been around since the early days of Exchange. Each serves a specific purpose and has objects that reside in Active Directory.

Master It Your company has multiple Active Directory domains that exist in a single forest. You must make sure that the following needs for your company are met:

♦ Group managers cannot, by mistake, assign permissions to a user by adding someone to a group.

♦ Temporary consultants for your company must not be able to access any internal resources.

Solution You should provision distribution groups instead of mail-enabled security groups. Distribution groups cannot be used to apply permission to a resource.

Use the Exchange Administration Center to manage recipients. Historically, Exchange administrators mainly used a combination of Active Directory tools and Exchange-native tools to manage Exchange servers and objects. That has all changed with Exchange Server 2016, mainly with the advent of the remote PowerShell implementation of the Exchange Management Shell, but also with the browser-based version of the Exchange Administration Center.

Master It You are responsible for managing multiple Exchange organizations, and you need to apply identical configurations to servers in all organizations. If you are just starting out with Exchange Server 2016 and you are not yet familiar with Remote PowerShell and Exchange Management Shell, you need some guidance regarding the commands that must be used. What should you do?

Solution Watch some of the Exchange Courses, particularly for management, which are available from Microsoft Virtual Academy (https://mva.microsoft.com /product-training/exchange#!index=2&lang=1033).

Configure accepted domains and define email address policies. Accepted domains and email address policies, once a single concept, have been broken up since Exchange Server

2007, and that it is still the case in Exchange Server 2016. This gives you more flexibility in managing email address suffixes and SMTP domains that will be accepted by your Exchange servers.

Master It You plan to accept mail for multiple companies inside your organization. Once accepted, the mail will be rerouted to the SMTP servers responsible for each of those companies. What do you need to create in your organization?

Solution You need to create an accepted domain for each of the domains you plan to accept and relay email. Each of these accepted domains should be configured as an external relay domain, since you will not be hosting any mailboxes for these organizations. If you deployed an Edge Transport server in your environment, you will need to also configure one or more Send connectors with the appropriate namespace on the Edge Transport server.

Chapter 14

Create and delete user mailboxes. Exchange Server 2016 supports the same types of mail-enabled users as previous versions of Exchange Server. These are mailbox-enabled users who have a mailbox on your Exchange server and the mail-enabled user account. The mail-enabled user account is a security principal within your organization (and would appear in your global address list), but its email is delivered to an external email system.

There are four different types of mailbox-enabled user accounts: a User mailbox, a Room Resource mailbox, an Equipment Resource mailbox, and a Linked mailbox. You can perform mailbox management tasks via either the Exchange Administration Center or the Exchange Management Shell.

Master It Your Active Directory forest has a trust relationship to another Active Directory forest that is part of your corporate IT infrastructure. The administrator in the other forest wants you to host their email. What type of mailboxes should you create for the users in this other forest?

Solution You should provision linked mailboxes, which are mailboxes associated with accounts in another trusted forest.

Master It You must modify user Marie Jewel's office name with Honolulu. You want to do this using the Exchange Management Shell. What command would perform this task?

Solution You should use the Set-User cmdlet with the Office parameter to update the office name.

Master It You need to increase the maximum number of senders that can be included in the safe senders list for Pierce Jewel's mailbox from 1,024 to 4,096. You want to make this change using the Exchange Management Shell. What command would you use?

Solution You should use the Set-Mailbox cmdlet with the MaxSafeSenders parameter to update the maximum number of senders in the safe senders list.

Manage mailbox permissions. A newly created mailbox allows only the owner of the mailbox to access the folders within that mailbox. An end user can assign someone else permissions to access individual folders within their mailbox or to send mail on their behalf using the Outlook client. The administrator can assign permissions to the entire mailbox for other users. Further, the administrator can assign a user the Send As permission to a mailbox.

Master It   All executives within your organization share a single administrative assistant whose username is Cheyenne Pike; all of the executives belong to a mail distribution group called Executives. All of the executives want you to grant user Cheyenne Pike access to all of the folders within their mailboxes. Name two ways you can accomplish this.

Solution   The first method (most common) to grant the user access to all of the folders within the executives' mailboxes would include using the Get-DistributionGroupMember cmdlet to retrieve the members of the Executives group and then assigning permission to the mailbox using the Add-MailboxPermission cmdlet. The second option (less common) would also include using the Get-DistributionGroupMember cmdlet to retrieve the members of the Executives group. However, this latter option includes using the Add-MailboxFolderPermission cmdlet to assign Owner rights to each folder within the mailboxes. For simpler automation, you would need to use the Get-MailboxFolderStatistics cmdlet to retrieve the name of all the folders within each mailbox before assigning the appropriate permission.

Move mailboxes to another database.   Exchange Server 2016 implements a way to move mailbox content from one mailbox database to another. Although you initiate the move using the administrative tools (i.e., the EAC and the EMS cmdlet New-MoveRequest), the Microsoft Exchange Server Mailbox Replication service (MRS) that runs on each Mailbox server manages the moves and migrates the data.

Master It   You want to use the EMS to move the mailbox for Treyden Jewel from mailbox database MBX-001 to MBX-002. The move should ignore up to three bad messages before it fails. What command should you use?

Solution   You should use the EMS cmdlet New-MoveRequest with the value of MBX-002 for the parameter TargetDatabase and the value of 3 for the parameter BadItemLimit.

Master It   You have submitted a move request for user Treyden Jewel. You want to check the status and statistics of the move request to see if it has completed; you want to use the Exchange Management Shell to do this. What command would you type?

Solution   You can use the EMS cmdlet Get-MoveRequest to view the status of a mailbox move or use the EMS cmdlet Get-MoveRequestStatistics to view detailed information of a mailbox move.

Perform bulk manipulation of mailbox properties.   By taking advantage of piping and the EMS, you can perform bulk manipulation of users and mailboxes in a single command that previously might have taken hundreds of lines of scripting code.

Master It   You want to move all of your executives to a single mailbox database called MBX-004. All of your executives belong to a mail distribution group called Executives. How could you accomplish this task with a single command?

Solution   To move all of your executives to a different mailbox database, you can use the EMS cmdlet Get-DistributionGroupMember to retrieve the membership of the distribution list and pipe the output to the EMS cmdlet New-MoveRequest.

Use Messaging Records Management to manage mailbox content. Messaging Records Management provides you with control over the content of a user's mailbox. Basic MRM features allow you to automatically purge old content, such as deleted items or junk email. You can create new managed folders within the user's mailbox as well as move content to these folders.

> **Master It** You are managing an Exchange Server organization that was transitioned from Exchange Server 2010. You have found that many of your users are not emptying the contents of their Deleted Items and Junk E-mail folders. You want to automatically purge any content in these folders after 14 days. What are the steps you should take to do this?

> **Solution** Create two RPTs that apply to a default folder—one for the Deleted Items folder and the other for the Junk Email folder—with the retention action of Delete and Allow Recovery and with a retention period of 14 days.

Chapter 15

Create and mail-enable contact objects. In some cases, you should not create a mail user but instead choose an object with fewer privileges—a mail contact. Mail contacts can be used to provide easy access to external email contacts by using your internal address lists. Mail users can be used to provide convenient access to internal resources for workers who require an externally hosted email account.

> **Master It** You periodically update the email addresses for your Active Directory contacts. However, some users report that they are not seeing the updated contact address in the address list and that they receive nondelivery reports (NDRs) when sending email to some contacts. What should you do?

> **Solution** The most likely cause is that you didn't properly mail-enable some of the contacts in Active Directory, which would explain why the contacts are not visible in the address list. Contacts that are properly mail-enabled will have the attribute `targetAddress` populated with their external email address.

Manage mail-enabled contacts and mail-enabled users in a messaging environment. All Exchange Server–related attributes for mail users and mail contacts are unavailable from Active Directory Users and Computers. To manage all Exchange Server–related attributes, you must use the Exchange Admin Center or the EMS tools.

> **Master It** Whether you want to manage users in bulk, need to create multiple users in your domain or multiple mail contacts in your organization, or simply want to change the delivery restrictions for 5,000 recipients, which tool should you use?

> **Solution** The EMS is the most efficient tool for managing recipient objects in bulk and is the tool you can use to manage most of the Exchange Server-related objects and configuration.

Choose the appropriate type and scope of mail-enabled groups. Although you can modify your group scope or group type at any time after the group has been created, it's always a best practice to create all groups as universal groups in an environment that hosts Exchange servers.

Master It   Your company needs to ensure that if an administrator adds a user to a distribution list, that user will not get any unnecessary access to resources on the network. How should you ensure that this type of administrative mistake does not impact the security of your networking environment?

Solution   You can accomplish this requirement using a couple of options. With the first, less common, solution, you can require that no security groups be configured with a universal scope. Since mail-enabled security groups require a universal scope, this would ensure administrators don't mistakenly grant unnecessary access to resources when adding a user to a distribution group. However, this solution prevents you from using these types of groups for other, legitimate purposes and requires that you maintain this setup in your environment. The other, more common, solution is to configure each mail-enabled security group with a manager of the group. In this scenario, if the administrators are not defined as the manager of the group, they will receive a warning that they lack sufficient permission when adding a user to a distribution group. However, with the appropriate permission, they can use a parameter to bypass the security restriction to add a user to the distribution group.

Create and manage mail-enabled groups.   Creating and managing distribution groups can mostly be done from the Exchange Admin Center, with only limited options that require the Exchange Management Shell.

Master It   You want to simplify the management of groups in your organization. You recently reviewed the functionalities of dynamic distribution groups and decided that this technology can provide the desired results. You need to identify the tools that should be used to manage dynamic distribution groups. What tools should you choose?

Solution   Although you can use the EMC and the EMS to manage dynamic distribution groups, only the EMS allows you to change the properties of a dynamic distribution group that aren't available in the EAC and to change properties for multiple groups.

Explore the moderation features of Exchange Server 2016.   Moderation and moderated groups are one of the self-service features of Exchange Server 2016 that allow a user to review messages sent to an email address on your server.

Master It   You need to enable moderation of email messages sent to particular recipients in your organization. You recently reviewed the multiple methods to enable moderation of distribution groups and other recipients in Exchange Server 2016. Which moderation method should you use based on each option's advantages and limitations?

Solution   In Exchange Server 2016, you can enable moderation of email messages using one of two options: configure a distribution group for moderation or configure a mail flow rule. You should consider creating a moderated distribution group when all the messages to the group must be approved. On the other hand, you should consider a mail flow rule if you require approval for messages that match specific criteria or that are sent to a specific person.

Chapter 16

Understand how resource mailboxes differ from regular mailboxes.   Resource mailboxes serve a different purpose in Exchange Server 2016 than user mailboxes and, therefore, have different features and capabilities. Understanding how resource mailboxes are different, including what added features are provided, can help improve the end-user experience and increase adoption rate.

> **Master It**   You are planning to create resource mailboxes to support conference rooms and other resource scheduling. Identify how the resource mailboxes are different from user mailboxes.

> **Solution**   Resource mailboxes are very similar to user mailboxes but are typically assigned either to a physical location, such as a conference room, a training room, or an auditorium, or to a piece of equipment, such as a laptop or company pool vehicle. Meeting organizers can reserve resource mailboxes by including them in meeting requests as resources. A key difference with resource mailboxes is that you can configure them to automatically accept or decline meeting requests sent from meeting organizers. In addition, the properties of a resource mailbox can include information about the location and seating capacity as well as information about resources associated with the mailbox, such as whiteboards and video teleconferencing tools.

Create resource mailboxes.   Creating resource mailboxes is easy with the tools in Exchange Server. Users need resource mailboxes for conference rooms and equipment to allow for easier, more informative scheduling.

> **Master It**   What tools are available to create resource mailboxes and to define additional schema properties for resource mailboxes?

> **Solution**   You can use the Exchange Admin Center or the Exchange Management Shell to create and manage the properties of resource mailboxes.

Configure resource mailbox booking and scheduling policies.   Properly configured resource mailboxes help users find the correct resource and determine whether it is available when needed. When the resource mailbox is properly configured, users can quickly and easily find conference rooms that have the proper capacity and features needed to hold a meeting.

> **Master It**   You need to configure a resource mailbox to handle automatic scheduling. What tools can you use?

> **Solution**   You can use the Exchange Admin Center or the Exchange Management Shell to automate scheduling of resource mailboxes. However, the EMS provides more options that you can configure for resource scheduling.

Convert resource mailboxes.   Converting mailboxes from one type to another allows your organization to be flexible. As business requirements change, you can ensure that the right types of resource mailboxes are available.

> **Master It**   After provisioning a shared mailbox for a team within your organization, you have received clarification that they only require a calendar resource with automated booking. You need to convert this mailbox to an Exchange Server 2016 resource mailbox. What steps should you take?

> **Solution**   You can use the EMS cmdlet `Set-Mailbox` with the value of `Room` for the parameter type to convert a mailbox to a resource mailbox.

Chapter 17

Understand the architectural changes made to public folders.   If you're coming new to Exchange Server 2016 or don't have a lot of investment in public folders in your current Exchange Server organization, you will need to learn the modern public folder architecture. Thorough understanding on how modern public folders work will allow you to design an efficient collaboration solution for your organization.

Master It   You are the administrator of a distributed messaging environment that runs Exchange Server 2016. You plan to deploy a collaboration solution, and you are currently evaluating public folders as well as site mailboxes and shared mailboxes. You need to identify the potential strengths of this approach and present recommendations to your company's executives. What information should you present?

Solution   The public folder architecture, also known as "modern public folders," enables organizations implementing Exchange Server 2016 to easily support and scale the infrastructure. In Exchange Server 2016, public folders are stored in a special type of mailbox called a *public folder mailbox*, but in essence those public folder mailboxes are normal mailboxes and Exchange Server treats them as it does users' mailboxes.

The database availability group (DAG) replicates public folder mailboxes and their contents as it does any other mailboxes in the organization. Therefore, there is no need to manage and troubleshoot public folders separately, and there are no different procedures to use in troubleshooting public folder replication.

End users do not see any difference; they use public folders as they were using them in the previous versions of Exchange Server.

The primary hierarchy holds the public-folder tree hierarchy and folder structure, which helps identify permissions on the folders and the parents and children of that folder.

From a high-availability point of view, public folder mailboxes are treated as normal mailboxes; they are replicated via the database continuous replication that runs on Exchange servers that are members of the DAG.

Manage public folders.   You are managing a large distributed Exchange Server infrastructure, and you want to create a hierarchy of public folders to reflect the organizational structure of your enterprise environment. How can you do it in Exchange Server 2016?

Master It   Start with the public folder mailbox, and then define the various departments within your folder structure. You can add various nested folders underneath the Departments parent folder, manage the folder structure underneath, and modify the permission structure to reflect the needs of the organization.

Solution   All of this can be managed through the EAC, but often you can get more feedback from the Exchange Management Shell:

```
New-Mailbox -PublicFolder
```

Chapter 18

Understand the basic principles of email archiving.   An archiving solution not only provides a way to ease the pain of storage problems on Exchange Server whether they are with the databases or with PST files but also assists in helping organizations become compliant and make discovery of email easier.

Master It   How can government organizations actively comply with regulations and open-records laws?

Solution   The Freedom of Information Act allows for the full or partial disclosure of previously unreleased information and documents controlled by the U.S. government. Enabling In-Place Archive mailboxes for users can help toward this end.

Ensure your company complies with regulations.   It is extremely important that your messaging system be configured in such a way that email data is managed according to laws and regulations.

Master It   Which laws and regulations are in effect in your business, and what does it mean for your organization?

Solution   Work with your legal and HR departments to determine which laws and regulations you need to comply with. Once you have these policies, use Exchange Server retention management policies to configure email retention and manage content as defined by the regulations.

Enable Exchange Server 2016 in-place archiving.   Exchange Server 2016 allows for efficient management of the user's primary mailbox by enabling the mailbox for archiving and using policies to move the content between the mailbox and the archive.

Master It   How does archiving allow older email content to be moved automatically from the primary mailbox to the In-Place Archive?

Solution   You can archive-enable a mailbox from the EAC Feature pane by selecting Recipients ➤ Mailboxes tab ➤ *the specific mailbox* ➤ the toolbar Edit button ➤ Mailbox Features ➤ Archiving ➤ Enable and specifying the database where you would like the archive mailbox to reside.

You can also use PowerShell to enable it, like this:

```
Enable-Mailbox "John Doe" -Archive
```

Use Exchange Server 2016 retention policies.   Retention policies define how long data must be retained before it is automatically removed when the time setting has been met.

Master It   You can create as many policies as you need; however, in many organizations, retention policies will be created per department (for instance, finance).

Solution   You can assign a retention policy to a mailbox by using the following PowerShell command:

```
Set-Mailbox "John Doe" -RetentionPolicy "Finance"
```

Use Exchange Server 2016 In-Place eDiscovery and Hold.   In certain situations, you may need to prevent emails from being deleted for a period of time while an end user is away and unable to attend to their mailbox.

Master It   Without retention hold, and depending on the policies that may be active and applied to the user, messages may have been moved from the primary mailbox to the archive or even deleted. What is the cmdlet to put a mailbox on retention hold?

Solution   You can put a mailbox on hold by using the following PowerShell command:

```
Set-Mailbox JohnDoe@contoso.com -LitigationHoldEnabled $True
```

Chapter 19

Identify the core components of Exchange Server database storage. The ability to identify the components of your Exchange servers that provide storage functionality will allow you to properly plan and troubleshoot storage.

Master It When you plan the storage configuration for your server, you need to accurately identify the messaging requirements and patterns of your users. After you have done so, how do you identify an acceptable storage solution?

Solution The messaging requirements and patterns of your users can be used to calculate the disk activity created by those users. More active users generate a higher level of disk activity that is measured in IOPS.

Although it is possible to manually calculate the IOPS per mailbox based on usage patterns, most attempts to directly measure IOPS per user end up being inaccurate. Instead, you should use the Exchange Server Role Requirements Calculator. You can enter the messaging requirements of your users into this spreadsheet and the number of IOPS required is returned. You can also select various storage configurations to see whether they meet the requirements for your scenario.

Plan for disk storage requirements for Exchange Server databases. A major paradigm shift has occurred in the Exchange Server messaging world. Up to now, administrators have been focused on their IOPS and the capacity of their disks to handle the client requests. Today, administrators have to rethink the way they plan for server storage, though they still need to think about IOPS and capacity, storage capabilities, and limits.

Master It When planning for storage requirements for Exchange, you must take many factors into consideration. Many of them have to do with storage type, capacity, load, and redundancy. However, many administrators don't always plan for the number of databases that need be created and opt for a reactionary approach to mailbox database creation. What are the considerations for determining the number of mailbox databases to create?

Solution Exchange Server 2016 Standard edition is limited to five mailbox databases, while Exchange Server 2016 Enterprise edition can have up to 100 mailbox databases. However, these hard limits should not be what determines the number of mailbox databases in your organization.

The number of mailbox databases in your organization is determined by the size of the databases and the performance for recovery. When mailbox databases are not replicated, you need to be able to restore the database in a reasonable period of time for disaster recovery. Microsoft recommends 200 GB as a maximum, but it depends on your recovery requirements.

Replicated databases can be larger because it is assumed that they will not be restored from a backup. However, even with replicated databases, you need to consider the time to reseed.

Manage Mailbox Databases. You can use either the EAC or EMS to create and manage mailbox databases. Some of the more advanced options are available only in EMS by using Windows PowerShell cmdlets.

Master It One of the options you can configure for a mailbox database is circular logging. Circular logging purges mailbox database transaction logs after they are committed to the database. When should circular logging be used and not be used?

Solution Circular logging should be used only for replicated databases. When circular logging is enabled for replicated databases, the transaction logs are purged only after they have been replicated to all databases copied.

You should not use circular logging for nonreplicated databases. The transaction logs are part of the recovery solution. After restoring a mailbox database, you can replay the transaction logs to bring the database up to the point in time where the database failed. For this scenario to be successful, you should store transaction logs and mailbox databases on separate physical drives.

Chapter 20

Understand database replication. Mailbox databases can be replicated between Mailbox servers in different AD sites. Replicating databases between AD sites ensures mailbox services could be online and available if the Mailbox server in the primary site were to fail.

Master It Your company has a DAG that is stretched across two datacenters. All databases should be mounted in the primary datacenter where the end users are located. Last week, a server had a hardware failure, causing all the databases on that Mailbox server to fail over. After the failover, you noticed that some of the databases were mounted on Mailbox servers in the secondary datacenter. What solution should be put in place to prevent mailbox databases from being activated in the secondary datacenter?

Solution The first thing to check is the Activation Preference that has been assigned to each of the database copies. Ensure that the database copies in the primary datacenter have the lowest activation preference. However, depending on the situation, this is not enough.

To ensure that databases are not automatically mounted in the second datacenter, you need to block automatic activation. You can do this per mailbox database copy or per Mailbox server. In this scenario, the secondary datacenter is used only for disaster recovery. So, you can use the `Set-MailboxServer` cmdlet with the `-DatabaseCopyAutoActivation Blocked` parameter to prevent any mailbox databases from being automatically activated on the Mailbox server in the secondary datacenter.

Manage a database availability group. Lagged database copies maintain an older database state by suppressing when transaction logs are written to the mailbox database. A lagged database can be used to restore mailbox content that has been removed or manipulated.

Master It A user has reported that email messages are missing from her Inbox today that were present yesterday. After checking the client and the Recoverable Items folder, the messages are still missing. Unfortunately, single-item recovery is not enabled. The user's mailbox is on a mailbox database that has a passive lagged copy that delays committing logs for seven days. What steps should you perform to restore the lagged database copy?

Solution   Here are the steps you should perform:

1. To preserve the state of the lagged copy, suspend replication.

2. Copy the database and transaction logs to a different directory. You might also want to take a snapshot of the database and logs.

3. Resume replication to the lagged database copy.

4. From the copy of the lagged database, remove the checkpoint file.

5. If you are recovering only to a specific point in time, remove the log files after that point in time.

6. Create a recovery database using the copy of the lagged database and mount it.

7. Recover the data you require from the recovery database.

Before mounting the recovery database in step 6, you may need to use `eseutil.exe` to place the database in a clean state.

Understand site resiliency for Exchange Server 2016.   When you are designing a DAG, Service Level Agreement (SLA), Recovery Time Objective (RTO), Recovery Point Objective (RPO), business requirements, and technical requirements should be used to model how the DAG is implemented.

Master It   Your company has three datacenters spread across the continental United States. Each datacenter has a low-latency, high-throughput WAN connection to the other datacenters. Users are located in two of the three datacenters. Management requires that mailbox services must be online if the power fails in one of the datacenters. Due to budget restrictions, the solution must use the minimum number of servers. How would you design a DAG solution to meet management's requirements?

Solution   This scenario is well suited to implementing the Exchange Server 2016 preferred architecture. Implement Exchange servers in the two sites with users and a witness server at the third site without users. If a power outage occurs at any of the three datacenters, the remaining two datacenters will continue to function and service clients.

At the cost of increasing complexity, you could attempt to optimize placement of the active database copies to be where the users are located. To do this, you will need to place users for each site in separate databases and then set the database copies in the local site with a lower Activation Preference. This will not guarantee that the closest database copy is active, but it increases the likelihood.

Chapter 21

Understand namespaces.   A namespace is the FQDN that is used to access Exchange services. The internal URLs for various services are configured to use the local hostname after installation. This means that each server is assigned its own namespace.

Master It   Your colleague has configured several Exchange Server 2016 deployments with a single server. In these deployments, he left the namespace at the default value and everything worked properly. You are both working on a project with four Exchange servers in the first site. How does the namespace need to be configured differently with multiple servers?

Solution   Within a single site, all Exchange servers need to share the same namespace. To implement this, you need to select a namespace that is not the name of any server, such as `mail.contoso.com`. Then the URLs for all Exchange services on all servers are configured to use the shared namespace.

After the services are configured, you need to implement a load balancing solution for the namespace. You can use a hardware-based load balancer or DNS round robin.

Understand certificates.   Certificates are installed on Exchange server to secure communication with clients. The names in the certificate are also used to verify the identity of the server. If a client accesses a namespace that is not included in the certificate, an error is displayed to the client.

Master It   You have installed a new server running Exchange Server 2016. You selected the namespace `mail.contoso.com` and have configured all of the virtual directories to use this namespace by using the Exchange Admin Center. You have also obtained a SAN certificate from a public CA that is trusted by all of your clients. The SAN certificate has been assigned to the SMTP and IIS servers. When you test connectivity to the server by using Outlook on a domain-joined computer, you are getting certificate errors. What is the most likely cause of these errors?

Solution   Not all of the necessary URLs for connectivity to Exchange services can be configured in the Exchange Admin Center. To configure the internal URL for Autodiscover, you need to use the `Set-ClientAccessService` cmdlet with the `-AutodiscoverInternalURI` parameter. To set the internal and external URLs for MAPI over HTTP, you need to use the `Set-MapiVirtualDirectory` cmdlet.

Understand calendar sharing.   Exchange Server 2010 includes several ways to share calendar information. You can implement organization relationships and sharing policies to control the information that is shared.

Master It   Your company has recently purchased a competitor. Your company is using Exchange Server 2016 and the recently purchased company is using Exchange Server 2013. It will be an extended period of time before the email systems are merged. In the meantime, you need to configure both systems to allow free/busy information sharing. What steps are required to do this?

Solution   Both Exchange Server 2016 and Exchange Server 2013 can perform federated sharing. Federated sharing with an organization policy can be used to provide sharing between the two organizations. When an organization relationship is used, there is no need for users to manually share their calendars.

The following steps must be performed in each organization:

1. Create a federation trust.

2. Create a security group with membership corresponding to the users that will be sharing calendar information over the organization relationship.

3. Create an organization relationship for the other organization that identifies the correct security group and the proper permissions for viewing calendar information.

4. Test the ability to view free/busy information in the other organization.

Chapter 22

Create and manage Send connectors and Receive connectors. All messages delivered by an Exchange server are routed through Exchange connectors. The source servers of Send connectors are always Mailbox servers.

Master It You've been called in to deploy Exchange Server 2016 in a "greenfield" deployment, where no messaging system is present. Installing Exchange Server is pretty easy, even for the least experienced IT consultants.

But... surprise! After your successful installation, you notice that emails cannot be sent to the Internet. You need to connect this new organization to the Internet. What configuration will allow your customer to book his golf games by email?

Solution In order to be able to send messages to the Internet, you must create a Send connector.

Master It You need to plan for the deployment of an Exchange Server 2016 organization. You quickly notice that the organization is concerned about reducing the number of physical servers. Of course, virtualized installation of Exchange Server is always possible, but this customer has very little expertise in virtualization technologies.

They ask you a very important question: do they really need an Edge Transport server on their network?

Solution One reason the customer needs an Edge Transport server is for the antispam and anti-malware protection. If they don't want to deploy an Edge Transport server, they might subscribe to Exchange Online Protection. Furthermore, they might purchase a third-party antispam and anti-malware solution.

Chapter 23

Create and manage message classifications to control message flow. Message classifications provide a way to visibly tag selected messages and show that they require specific treatment. On their own, they're merely advisory; but combined with transport rules and mailbox rules, they can become powerful selection criteria for managing messages and ensuring policy compliance.

Master It You need to use message classifications to manipulate messages by using Outlook. You verify that custom message classifications are available from Outlook on the web. From Outlook, you look around but cannot find any options that relate to the custom message classifications. What do you need to do first?

Solution The default message classifications are not published to Outlook on the web or Outlook by default. Additional configuration is needed on the Outlook client and the

Exchange servers for the clients to see the default message classifications. Outlook on the web supports the display and manual selection of message classifications. To use them in Outlook 2016, you must manually deploy them. No GUI exists for creating and managing classifications; you must use the Exchange Management Shell (EMS). However, once the classifications are created, you can use the EAC to apply them using transport rules.

Control message flow and manipulate messages by using transport rules. Transport rules give you a powerful, centralized method for creating automated policy enforcement in your environment.

Master It You need to add a logo to an email disclaimer; you notice that you cannot include an image in the New Transport Rules Wizard. The availability of adding logos to a disclaimer was a major decision point of your Exchange Server 2016 implementation. What do you need to do to make the logo visible in the disclaimer?

Solution In Exchange Server 2016, an administrator can create HTML disclaimers as a transport rule action. Exchange Server 2016 HTML disclaimer text can include HTML tags. This allows you to create messages with the rich functionality available in HTML code. More importantly, in Exchange Server 2016 you can add images to an HTML disclaimer by using IMG tags. You have to place the image files on a publicly accessible web server. Once you have verified that the image is available by using a URL, you can add the path to the disclaimer action in the transport rule, as in this example:

```
<IMG src="http://Server.adatum.com/images/logo.gif"
```

Protect sensitive information by creating data loss prevention policies. Using DLP policies you can enforce that all messages are subject to DLP rules, or you can allow users to bypass DLP rules by providing a business justification.

Master It Your company's compliance officer requires that email messages containing U.S. bank routing numbers be redirected to the senders' manager for approval and that an incident report be generated and sent to the employees of the legal department. What do you need to do to make sure you meet the requirements of the compliance officer?

Solution Data Loss Prevention in Exchange Server 2016 is designed to analyze, monitor, report, and prevent sensitive information from being exposed to unwanted parties. The classification of sensitive information varies for each company and region. DLP has been designed with the understanding that sensitive information is unique to each organization.

You will create a transport rule that will use DLP policy that can detect emails containing U.S. bank routing numbers and redirect them to the senders' manager for approval. Furthermore, you will configure a transport rule action to generate an incident report and send it to the legal department.

Chapter 24

Narrow the scope of an Exchange Server problem. One of the most important troubleshooting skills that an Exchange Server administrator must possess is the ability to quickly and effectively narrow the scope of problem. Determining the commonalities in a problem can help you quickly locate and solve a problem.

Master It   Seven of your 400 users are reporting an error in Outlook that indicates that they cannot connect to the Exchange server. What are some things you would determine to narrow the scope of the problem?

Solution   In a situation where a large number of users are reporting the same problem, you should figure out if they are all in the same location, on the same network, or connected to the same server or DAG. With so many users having the same problem, it is likely that the root cause is on the server side or the network side. You can find out if they can get to their mailbox by using Outlook on the web. This tells you whether their mailboxes (and, therefore, mailbox database) are accessible. If so, you might want to look toward the network or firewalls. You also want to find out if every person at the site where the 400 users are also has the same issue (and if not, find out what's different, such as the subnet, server, or DAG).

Use basic Exchange Server troubleshooting tools.   A number of tools are available that will help you troubleshoot Exchange Server problems and possibly determine future issues. These include the Event Viewer, the Remote Connectivity Analyzer, Exchange Server diagnostics logging, and the Test-ServiceHealth cmdlet.

Master It   After installing a recent Cumulative Update, you have started noticing intermittent issues with your Exchange server. What tool or tools could you run to help you identify potential issues?

Solution   If you are having connectivity issues from clients, you should start with the Remote Connectivity Analyzer. If issues are not related to connectivity, you should start with testing the service health (Test-ServiceHealth). From there, you should go through the Windows event logs and gather information at a client if a client is having trouble. On the nontechnical side, you should immediately search the Internet to find out if other people are reporting problems with the cumulative update. This specific step is a key step that you should not ignore. We recommend doing that within a few minutes of troubleshooting. It is also a good idea to open a case with Microsoft Support; if there are known issues with the Cumulative Update, a workaround might be available.

Troubleshoot Mailbox server problems.   The Mailbox server is at the core of your Exchange Server organization; all Exchange Server data is located and serviced via this Exchange server role. When the Exchange Mailbox server role is not functioning correctly, this will cause a fast-moving ripple effect through your organization that will affect more and more users. Tools such as the Test-MapiConnectivity cmdlet can help you determine whether a mailbox can be reached.

As companies look to find ways to keep their Exchange Server infrastructure up and running as much as possible, the Exchange Server 2016 database availability group high-availability feature is becoming increasingly prevalent in small businesses. The Test-ReplicationHealth and Get-MailboxCopyStatus cmdlets can help test the health of the DAG replication.

Master It   A user named Zoe is reporting that she cannot use Outlook to access her mailbox, yet she can access it via Outlook on the web. What tool could you use to determine whether the mailbox is accessible via Outlook?

Solution   You should use the Test-OutlookConnectivity cmdlet to start the troubleshooting process. You can target a server or an individual mailbox.

Troubleshoot mail transport problems. The Exchange Server 2016 Mailbox role plays the all-important part of delivering all messages that are processed via the Exchange Server 2016 infrastructure. This is true even if a message is sent from one user to another on the same mailbox database, and the transport services are invoked to act in delivering the message.

A number of useful tools are available to help you and your users determine where a problem may exist. These include the Exchange Server 2016 Queue Viewer, the `Test-MailFlow` cmdlet, and message tracking.

Master It A user is reporting that they are sending email but that the recipient is never getting the message. The user is convinced your server is not delivering the message. You would like the user to determine whether the message is leaving your organization. What would you advise the user to do?

Solution The user can use the Exchange Admin Center to track the message and figure out whether it is leaving the organization.

Chapter 25

Back up Exchange Server. Performing backups is the somewhat easy part of the equation. The more difficult part is defining the requirements for the backup.

Master It Document the goals for your backup solution.

Solution The organization should perform risk analysis and answer the following questions:

◆ What data might be lost and needs to be backed up?

◆ How fast is the backup process?

◆ How long does the backup data need to be kept?

◆ How fast is the recovery process?

The IT Department should work with the business decision makers to determine the backup and restore strategy for the organization.

Prepare to recover the Exchange server. Before you can perform any backups from Windows Server 2012 R2, you must install the backup features.

Master It What do you need to do to install the backup features on Windows 2012 R2?

Solution You can use Server Manager or Windows PowerShell to install Windows Server backup features in Windows Server 2012 R2 or Windows Server 2012.

If you use Server Manager, you can follow these steps:

1. From the taskbar, click Server Manager.

2. Choose Tools.

3. Select Windows Server Backup.

You can also open Windows PowerShell and type the following two commands:

```
Import-Module ServerManager
Add-WindowsFeature Windows-Server-Backup
```

Use Windows Server Backup to back up the server. There is always a need to back up your servers. Since you have the requirements, you need to perform the backup.

Master It Perform a recurring backup utilizing the Windows Server 2012 R2 backup features.

Solution Follow these steps to perform a daily Exchange Server backup:

1. On the taskbar, select Server Manager ➤ Tools ➤ Windows Server Backup.

2. In the Actions pane, click Backup Schedule. The Backup Schedule Wizard appears. Click Next.

3. On the Select Backup Configuration screen, select Custom (so that you can select only the volumes that contain the Exchange Server data) and click Next.

4. On the Select Items For Backup screen, click Add Items and select the volumes containing the Exchange Server databases and transaction logs that you want to back up. Click OK.

5. Select Advanced Settings ➤ VSS Settings, and select VSS Full Backup. Click OK and then click Next.

6. On the Specify Backup Time screen, select Once A Day, specify the time that you want to perform the backup, and click Next.

7. On the Select Backup Destination Type screen, select the appropriate radio button to choose where you want to store your backups. It is recommended to use a hard disk that is dedicated to only storing backups. Click Next.

8. On the Select Destination Disk screen, click Show All Available Disks.

9. Place a check mark in the box beside the drive you are backing up to, and then click OK.

10. You are now back to the Select Destination Disk screen. Notice that the Next button is unavailable; that's because you must place a check mark in the box beside the volume that you will be using, just as you did in the previous step. Place a check mark in the box, and click Next.

11. You will see a warning dialog reminding you that Windows Server Backup will be formatting the disk. Click Yes after verifying there is no data on the volume you will be using.

12. Click Finish on the Confirmation screen.

13. Once the processing has completed, the Summary screen appears; click Close.

Use Windows Server Backup to recover the data with the Recovery Database. You may need to restore your Exchange Server data for several reasons. One of the reasons is that you need to give a user email items that had been deleted but that are still recoverable.

Master It Perform restore of email for a user by using the Recovery Database where restored mailbox items will be located in a target folder named RecoveryFolder.

Solution   Follow these steps to perform a restore by using the Exchange Server Recovery Database:

1. Open Windows Server Backup.

2. In the Actions pane on the right, select Recover.

3. On the Getting Started screen, select This Server (*ServerName*), and then click Next.

4. On the Select Backup Date screen, select the date and time, and click Next.

5. On the Select Recovery Type screen, select Applications and click Next.

6. On the Select Application screen, make sure Exchange is highlighted and click Next. By default, if you are recovering the last backup, Exchange Server will replay the log files for the backup. You must tell the backup application if you do not want to perform the log replay; select the "Do not perform a roll-forward recovery of the application databases" check box.

7. On the Specify Recovery Options screen, select the option Recover To Another Location. Click Browse and browse to the location where you want to place the recovered files; click Next.

8. The Confirmation screen gives you a recap of the recovery you are about to perform. Click Recover.

9. Once the recovery is complete, click Close.

10. Create a recovery database by using following command:

    ```
    New-MailbosDaatabase -Recovery -Name RDB -Edbfilepath "Folder where you
    restored the database" -logfolderpath "Folder you restored the transaction
    log files"
    ```

11. Open a command prompt and change the working directory to the location of the restore.

12. Run the eseutil.exe command with the following parameters:

    ```
    Eseutil /r "log prefix" /d
    ```

13. Mount the recovery database by typing:

    ```
    Mount-Database RecoveryDB
    ```

14. Type following command to restore a missing email:

    ```
    New-MaiboxRestoreRequest -SourceDatabase RDB -SourceStoreMailbox "The name
    of the user's mailbox" -TargetRootFolder "RecoveryFolder"
    ```

Recover an entire Exchange server.   There may be occasions when you need to reinstall the entire Exchange server.

Master It   How do you recover the Mailbox server?

Solution   The steps for recovering the mailbox server that is not a DAG member include:

1. Reset the computer account for the lost server through Active Directory Users and Computers.

2. Reinstall the operating system. The operating system and NetBIOS name must be the same as for the server you are replacing. If the name is not the same, the recovery will fail.

3. Join the server to the same domain as the lost server.

4. Install the necessary prerequisites and operating-system component.

5. Log on to the server being recovered and open a command prompt.

6. Navigate to the Exchange Server 2016 installation files and run the following command:

   ```
   setup /m:RecoverServer /IAcceptExchangeServerLicenseTerms
   ```

7. Restore the databases by using the backup software. If the server is a DAG member, reseed the databases from the healthy server according to the instructions in this chapter.

The steps for performing the recovery of the mailbox server that is a DAG member include:

1. Remove all database copies that exist on the server by running the following command one time for each mailbox database copy. For example:

   ```
   Remove-MailboxDatabaseCopy DB05\EX-MBX01
   ```

2. Remove the failed server from the DAG's configuration in Active Directory by using the following command. Note that if the server is offline and not reachable via network communications, then the -ConfigurationOnly parameter must be included. For example:

   ```
   Remove-DatabaseAvailabilityGroupServer -Identity DAG01
   -MailboxServer EX-MBX01 -ConfigurationOnly
   ```

3. Reset the Mailbox server's computer account in Active Directory.

4. Run Setup /m:RecoverServer /IAcceptExchangeServerLicenseTerms.

5. Once Setup is complete and all required post-installation patches have been installed, add the recovered Mailbox server back to the DAG by executing the following:

   ```
   Add-DatabaseAvailabilityGroupServer -Identity DAG01 -MailboxServer EX-MBX01
   ```

6. After the Mailbox server has been added back to the DAG, reconfigure the mailbox database copies by running the following command one time for each database:

   ```
   Add-MailboxDatabaseCopy -Identity DB05 -MailboxServer EX-MBX01
   ```

Index

Note to the reader: Throughout this index **boldfaced** page numbers indicate primary discussions of a topic. *Italicized* page numbers indicate illustrations.